THIRD EDITION

The Ancient World

READINGS IN SOCIAL AND CULTURAL HISTORY

Edited by

D. BRENDAN NAGLE
University of Southern California

STANLEY M. BURSTEIN
California State University, Los Angeles

D1247367

UPPER SADDLE RIVER, NEW JERSEY 07458

Library of Congress Cataloging-in-Publication Data

Stanley M. Burstein.—3 ed.
   p. cm.
Includes bibliographical references.
ISBN 0-13-193040-0
   1. History, Ancient—Sources.   I. Nagle, D. Brendan,   II. Burstein, Stanley Mayer.
D52.A43   2006
930—dc22   2004063814

Editorial Director: *Charlyce Jones-Owen*
Executive Editor: *Charles Cavaliere*
Associate Editor: *Emsal Hasan*
Editorial Assistant: *Shannon Corliss*
Managing Editor: *Joanne Riker*
Production Liaison: *Joanne Hakim*
Executive Marketing Manager: *Heather Shelstad*
Marketing Assistant: *Cherron Gardner*
Manufacturing Buyer: *Benjamin Smith*
Cover Art Director: *Jayne Conte*
Cover Design: *Bruce Kenselaar*
Cover Illustration/Photo: *Hisham F. Ibrahim/Photodisc Green/Getty Images, Inc.*
Manager, Cover Visual Research & Permissions: *Karen Sanatar*
Composition/Full-Service Project Management: *Rosaria Cassinese/Prepare Inc.*
Printer/Binder: *The Courier Companies*

For Pat and Dorothy

Credits and acknowledgments borrowed from other sources and reproduced, with permission, in this textbook appear on appropriate page within text.

Pearson Education LTD., London
Pearson Education Singapore, Pte. Ltd
Pearson Education, Canada, Ltd
Pearson Education–Japan
Pearson Education Australia PTY, Limited

Pearson Education North Asia Ltd
Pearson Educación de Mexico, S.A. de C.V.
Pearson Education Malaysia, Pte. Ltd
Pearson Education, Upper Saddle River, New Jersey

10 9 8 7 6 5 4 3

ISBN 0-13-193040-0

Contents

Preface

Our aim in this reader is to provide students in ancient history and civilization courses with a selection of texts illustrating the social and cultural life of the peoples of Western Asia, Europe, and the Mediterranean in antiquity.

At times we were overwhelmed by the richness of available material, but more often, time and chance had already limited our selection to a handful of texts. In recognition of developing scholarly understanding of the nature of Late Antiquity, we have extended our coverage in this third edition to include Northern Europe, Byzantium, and early Islam. We have also made additions in the area of gender relations.

In making our choices of readings we had the assistance of a large number of colleagues and friends, who helped us at various stages in the preparation of the textbook. Our thanks go to Winthrop Lindsay Adams, Steve Chrissanthos, John K. Evans, P. C. Finney, Allen Horstman, Lee Reams, Brigette Russell, Dave Smith, Carol Thomas, and Mehmet Yavuz, all of whom either contributed suggestions, read parts of the manuscript, or both. We are especially grateful to JoAnn Scurlock and Richard E. Averbeck for generously supplying us with their translations of Assyrian and Sumerian inscriptions. Our daughters, Eliza and Miriam, did a careful job of editing the text, for which we are grateful. Prentice Hall's reviewers made many helpful suggestions: Blake Beattie, University of Louisville; Rachel Stocking, Southern Illinois University at Carbondale; Rebecca Peterson, Graceland University.

This reader is a joint, not parallel, product. Our interests dictated that Egypt and Greece should fall to Stanley Burstein, while D. Brendan Nagle was responsible for Mesopotamia, Israel, Rome, and the overall structure of the work. Unless otherwise noted, the translations are our own.

D. Brendan Nagle
Stanley M. Burstein

Chapter 1

▼▼▼

Temples and Priests

Temples had a central place in the life of the early Mesopotamian city-state. Individual gods were believed to own particular cities, together with their contents, and to live in their temples. Inevitably, the priests who ran the temples had a great deal to do with organizing and running city affairs. Apart from maintaining the all-important home of the god, priests had to look after such temple property as its storage facilities, its houses, land, schools, and the huge herds of animals required for sacrifices. At Ur, at one point, 350,000 sheep and goats were owned by just one of the temples! Directly or indirectly, thousands of people, among them the best educated and most highly skilled, depended on the temple for their livelihood.

In Egypt, life also revolved around local temples, but in a different way, and not nearly to the degree it did in Mesopotamia. This was so because temples in Mesopotamia were integral parts of their individual city-states, whereas in Egypt there were no independent cities. Temples, instead, served local populations as parts of a gigantic, integrated religious pyramid, the top of which was occupied by pharaoh, the god-king of Egypt. Egypt is best thought of as a kind of huge temple-state with the pharaoh as its chief priest and king, whose main responsibility was the maintenance of *Ma'at*, justice and order, throughout the land.

The religious experience of the megastates, Egypt and Mesopotamia, however, did not have the same lasting effect on world history as did that of the ministate, Israel. Israel's religious experience derived from two distinct sources. Yahwism, the religion of seminomadic peoples in the deserts east of the Nile delta, represents one. The second was the product of the grafting of temple and palace to Yahwism after the conquest of Canaan made clear that a centralized government of some kind was needed if surrounding hostile peoples were to be resisted. Subsequently, temple and palace—priest and king—played counterpoint to the earlier belief that claimed authority directly from personal religious experience. Long before the institutionalization of Israelite religion in Canaan, this tradition of religion derived from personal experience was well established. At the beginning, Abraham obeyed the god that told him to abandon his homeland for a land that would be given him; Moses listened to the voice in the burning bush. Even after the building of temple and palace the voice of God still spoke to individuals in apparently haphazard fashion, to peasants like Amos or Micah, or to aristocrats like Isaiah. Some of the most dramatic scenes in Israel's history (and indeed in all history) derive from confrontation between prophet and priest or king.

At the purely personal level, the religious experiences of all three traditions, Mesopotamian, Egyptian, and Israelite, seem at times to be almost interchangeable. The anguish of Job in biblical literature has its counterpart in the Babylonian Ludlul bel Nemeqi. Some of the psalms, and the wisdom literature in general (Proverbs, Ecclesiastes, and Sirach, for example), share a common outlook, content, and sometimes even verbal similarities with the religious literature of the other traditions. The flood stories of Mesopotamia and Genesis (first reading) show how closely, and yet with what different emphasis, the cultures of the region interacted with each other. The presence in the Bible of a love lyric, the Song of Songs, reveals the extraordinarily diverse religious background of which the Bible is itself a diverse reflection. The monotheism (or henotheism) of the pharaoh Akh-en-aten seems to have been a form of personal religion that he tried (unsuccessfully) to extend to all of Egypt, whereas that of Israel was the product of the historical experience of the nation as a whole.

1.1   Flood Stories

Several stories of a great flood that destroyed practically the whole human race are to be found in the mythologies and legends of the Near East and Greece. One of the most complete is contained in the great Mesopotamian poem, The Epic of Gilgamesh. *The poem tells the adventures of Gilgamesh, the king of ancient Uruk (modern Warka), who, with his companion Enkidu, performs great deeds and wins an immortal name for himself. When Enkidu dies, however, Gilgamesh is inconsolable and struggles with the futility of life. He insists that there must be meaning in his friend's death and begins a quest for immortality. This brings him to Utnapishtim, the sole survivor of a great flood that destroyed the human race in earlier times. For his piety and obedience to the god Ea, Utnapishtim was made immortal. He tells Gilgamesh that there is no permanence on earth, "that houses do not stand forever; contracts are made only for a time; and in death there is no difference between slave and master." Gilgamesh replies that as far as appearances go, Utnapishtim looks like an ordinary human being. How, therefore, did he achieve immortality? Utnapishtim responds with the story of the flood (first reading).*

The earliest written fragments of The Epic of Gilgamesh *date to at least 2150 B.C., but there is clear indication that the story itself is much older. The written form of the poem was kept alive from generation to generation in the scribal schools of Mesopotamia, where it was worked and reworked for centuries. Fragments of the* Epic *have been found at various sites across the Middle East in Sumerian (the language in which the poem was first composed), Akkadian (the language of the ancient Babylonians and Assyrians), as well as in Hurrian and Hittite. According to Mesopotamian tradition, the most complete version of the* Epic *was assembled around 1300 B.C. by a priest named Sin-leqe-unnini of Uruk. A large portion of this version of the* Epic *was found by archaeologists in the nineteenth century in the palace library of the Assyrian king, Ashurbanipal (668–627 B.C.).[1]*

Although apparent similarities with the biblical story of Noah abound, the differences between the two tales are profound. The Sumerian flood story reflects the Mesopotamian cultural view of the limitations of humans and gods, the precariousness of life, and the always present possibility of the return of the world to chaos. By contrast, the account of Noah is part of the larger biblical story of the saving acts of God in history which begins with the creation of the world. In this account, Noah is the bringer of a new

---

[1]*The Epic of Gilgamesh*, 3rd ed., trans. N. K. Sandars (Harmondsworth and Baltimore, MD: Penguin Classics, 1972), pp. 108–113. Copyright © N. K. Sandars, 1960, 1964, 1972. Reproduced by permission of Penguin Books Ltd.

age who rescues humans from the return to chaos in the deluge. Noah becomes a second father of the human race after all the other descendants of Adam have perished. When the deluge subsides, God promises never to destroy the human race again and forms a covenant with Noah, symbolized by the rainbow. In the biblical version there is never any suggestion that the forces of chaos will return or that creation itself is in jeopardy. The God of Noah, unlike the gods of Mesopotamia, is firmly in control of both the material world and of the process of history itself.[2]

1.1.1   The Flood in *The Epic of Gilgamesh*

'You know the city Shurrupak, it stands on the banks of Euphrates? That city grew old and the gods that were in it were old. There was Anu, lord of the firmament, their father, and warrior Enlil their counselor, Ninurta the helper, and Ennugi watcher over canals; and with them also was Ea. In those days the world teemed, the people multiplied, the world bellowed like a wild bull, and the great god was aroused by the clamor. Enlil heard the clamor and he said to the gods in council, "The uproar of mankind is intolerable and sleep is no longer possible by reason of the babel." So the gods agreed to exterminate mankind. Enlil did this, but Ea because of his oath warned me in a dream. He whispered their words to my house of reeds, "Reed-house, reed-house! Wall, O wall, hearken reed-house, wall reflect; O man of Shurrupak, son of Ubara-Tutu; tear down your house and build a boat, abandon possessions and look for life, despise worldly goods and save your soul alive. Tear down your house, I say, and build a boat. These are the measurements of the barque as you shall build her: let her beam equal her length, let her deck be roofed like the vault that covers the abyss; then take up into the boat the seed of all living creatures."

'When I had understood I said to my lord, "Behold, what you have commanded I will honor and perform, but how shall I answer the people, the city, the elders?" Then Ea opened his mouth and said to me, his servant, "Tell them this: I have learnt that Enlil is wrathful against me, I dare no longer walk in his land nor live in his city; I will go down to the Gulf to dwell with Ea my lord. But on you he will rain down abundance, rare fish and shy wild-fowl, a rich harvest-tide. In the evening the rider of the storm will bring you wheat in torrents."

Utnapishtim builds the boat.

'In the first light of dawn all my household gathered round me, the children brought pitch and the men whatever was necessary. On the fifth day I laid the keel and the ribs, then I made fast the planking. The ground-space was one acre, each side of the deck measured one hundred and twenty cubits, making a square. I built six decks below, seven in all, I divided them into nine sections with bulkheads between. I drove in wedges where needed, I saw to the punt-poles, and laid in supplies. The carriers brought oil in baskets, I poured pitch into the furnace and asphalt and oil; more oil was consumed in caulking, and more again the master of the boat took into his stores. I slaughtered bullocks for the people and every day I killed sheep. I gave the shipwrights wine to drink as though it were river water, raw wine and red wine and oil and white wine. There was feasting then as there is at the time of the New Year's festival; I myself anointed my head. On the seventh day the boat was complete.

---

[2]Genesis 6:9–9:15. New International Version (NIV). Copyright © 1973, 1978, 1984 by International Bible Society. Used by permission.

'Then was the launching full of difficulty; there was shifting of ballast above and below till two thirds was submerged. I loaded into her all that I had of gold and of living things, my family, my kin, the beast of the field both wild and tame, and all the craftsmen. I sent them on board, for the time that Shamash had ordained was already fulfilled when he said, "In the evening, when the rider of the storm sends down the destroying rain, enter the boat and batten her down." The time was fulfilled, the evening came, the rider of the storm sent down the rain. I looked out at the weather and it was terrible, so I too boarded the boat and battened her down. All was now complete, the battening and the caulking; so I handed the tiller to Puzur-Amurri the steersman, with the navigation and the care of the whole boat.

The flood begins.

'With the first light of dawn a black cloud came from the horizon; it thundered within where Adad, lord of the storm was riding. In front over hill and plain Shullat and Hanish, heralds of the storm, led on. Then the gods of the abyss rose up; Nergal pulled out the dams of the nether waters, Ninurta the war-lord threw down the dykes, and the seven judges of hell, the Annunaki, raised their torches, lighting the land with their livid flame. A stupor of despair went up to heaven when the god of the storm turned daylight to darkness, when he smashed the land like a cup. One whole day the tempest raged, gathering fury as it went, it poured over the people like the tides of battle; a man could not see his brother nor the people be seen from heaven. Even the gods were terrified at the flood, they fled to the highest heaven, the firmament of Anu; they crouched against the walls, cowering like curs. Then Ishtar the sweet-voiced Queen of Heaven cried out like a woman in travail: "Alas the days of old are turned to dust because I commanded evil; why did I command this evil in the council of all the gods? I commanded wars to destroy the people, but are they not my people, for I brought them forth? Now like the spawn of fish they float in the ocean."

'The great gods of heaven and of hell wept, they covered their mouths. 'For six days and six nights the winds blew, torrent and tempest and flood overwhelmed the world, tempest and flood raged together like warring hosts. When the seventh day dawned the storm from the south subsided, the sea grew calm, the flood was stilled; I looked at the face of the world and there was silence, all mankind was turned to clay. The surface of the sea stretched as flat as a roof top; I opened a hatch and the light fell on my face. Then I bowed low, I sat down and I wept, the tears streamed down my face, for on every side was the waste of water.

The flood subsides.

'I looked for land in vain, but fourteen leagues distant there appeared a mountain, and there the boat grounded; on the mountain of Nisir the boat held fast, she held fast and did not budge. One day she held, and a second day on the mountain of Nisir she held fast and did not budge. A third day, and a fourth day she held fast on the mountain and did not budge; a fifth day and a sixth day she held fast on the mountain. When the seventh day dawned I loosed a dove and let her go. She flew away, but finding no resting-place she returned. Then I loosed a swallow, and she flew away but finding no resting-place she returned. I loosed a raven, she saw that the waters had retreated, she ate, she flew around, she cawed, and she did not come back. Then I threw everything open to the four winds, I made a sacrifice and poured out a libation on the mountain-top. Seven and again seven cauldrons I set up on their stands, I heaped up wood and cane and cedar and myrtle. When the gods smelled the sweet savour, they gathered like flies over the sacrifice. Then, at last, Ishtar also came, she lifted her necklace with the jewels of heaven that once Anu had made to please her. "O you gods here present, by the lapis lazuli round my neck I shall remember these days as I remember the jewels of my throat; these last days I shall not forget. Let all the gods gather round the sacrifice, except Enlil. He shall not approach this offering, for without reflection he brought the flood; he consigned my people to destruction."

'When Enlil had come, when he saw the boat, he was wroth and swelled with anger at the gods, the host of heaven, "Has any of these mortals escaped? Not one was to have survived the destruction." Then the god of the wells and canals Ninurta opened his mouth and said to the warrior Enlil, "Who is there of the gods that can devise without Ea? It is Ea alone who knows all things." Then Ea opened his mouth and spoke to warrior Enlil, "Wisest of gods, hero Enlil, how could you so senselessly bring down the flood?"

> *"Lay upon the sinner his sin,*
> *Lay upon the transgressor his transgression,*
> *Punish him a little when he breaks loose,*
> *Do not drive him too hard or he perishes;*
> *Would that a lion had ravaged mankind*
> *Rather than the flood,*
> *Would that a wolf had ravaged mankind*
> *Rather than the flood,*
> *Would that famine had wasted the world*
> *Rather than the flood,*
> *Would that pestilence had wasted mankind*
> *Rather than the flood."*

' "It was not I that revealed the secret of the gods; the wise man learned it in a dream. Now take your counsel what shall be done with him." Then Enlil went up into the boat, he took me by the hand and my wife and made us enter the boat and kneel down on either side, he standing between us. He touched our foreheads to bless us, saying, "In time past Utnapishtim was a mortal man; henceforth he and his wife shall live in the distance at the mouth of the rivers." Thus it was that the gods took me and placed me here to live in the distance, at the mouth of the rivers.'

1.1.2   The Flood in Genesis

Noah was a righteous man, blameless among the people of his time, and he walked with God. Noah had three sons: Shem, Ham, and Japheth. Now the earth was corrupt in God's sight, and full of violence. . . . So God said to Noah, "I am going to put an end to all people, for the earth is filled with violence because of them. So make yourself an ark of cypress wood; make rooms in it and coat it with pitch inside and out . . . I am going to bring floodwaters on the earth to destroy all life under the heavens, every creature that has breath of life in it. Everything on earth will perish. But I will establish my covenant with you, and you will enter the ark—you and your sons and your wife and your sons' wives. . . .

The Lord then said to Noah, "Go into the ark, you and your whole family, because I have found you righteous in this generation. Take with you seven of every kind of clean animal, a male and its mate, and two of every kind of unclean animal, a male and its mate, and also seven of every kind of bird, male and female, to keep their various kinds alive throughout the earth. And Noah did all that the Lord commanded him. And Noah and his sons and his wife and his sons' wives entered the ark to escape the waters of the flood. . . .

In the six hundredth year of Noah's life, on the seventeenth day of the second month—on that day all the springs of the great deep burst forth, and the flood gates of the heavens were opened. And rain fell on the earth forty days and forty nights. . . . For forty days the flood kept coming on the earth, and as the waters increased they lifted the ark high above the earth. The waters rose and increased greatly on the earth, and the ark floated on the surface of the water. They rose greatly on the earth and all the high mountains under the entire heavens were covered. . . . Every living thing that moved on the earth perished. . . .

The waters flooded the earth for a hundred and fifty days. But God remembered Noah and all the wild animals and the livestock that were with him in the ark, and he sent a wind over the earth and the waters receded. Now the springs of the deep and the floodgates of the heavens had been closed, and the rain had stopped falling from the sky. The water receded steadily from the earth. At the end of the hundred and fifty days the water had gone down, and on the seventeenth day of the seventh month the ark came to rest on the mountains of Ararat. . . .

After forty days Noah opened the window he had made in the ark and sent out a raven, and it kept flying back and forth until the water had dried up from the earth. Then he sent out a dove to see if the water had receded from the surface of the ground. But the dove could find no place to set its feet because there was water over all the surface of the earth; so it returned to Noah in the ark. He reached out his hand and took the dove and brought it back to himself in the ark.

After several more tries the dove finally fails to return, having found a place to set down, proving that the earth had finally dried.

Then God said to Noah, "Come out of the ark. . . . Bring out every kind of living creature that is with you . . . so they can multiply on the earth and be fruitful and increase in number upon it." So Noah came out, together with his sons and his wife and his sons' wives. All the animals and all the creatures that move along the ground and all the birds—everything that moves on the earth—came out of the ark, one kind after another. . . .

Then God said to Noah and to his sons with him, "I now establish my covenant with you and your descendants after you and with every living creature that was with you—the birds, the livestock and all the wild animals, all those that came out of the ark with you—every living creature on earth. I establish my covenant with you: Never again will all life be cut off by the waters of a flood; never again will there be a flood to destroy the earth." And God said, "This is the sign of the covenant I am making between me and you and every living creature with you, a covenant for all generations to come: I have set my rainbow in the clouds, and it will be the sign of the covenant between me and the earth. . . . Whenever I bring clouds over the earth and the rainbow appears in the clouds, I will remember my covenant between me and you and all living creatures of every kind. Never again will the waters become a flood to destroy all life."

1.2   Divinity and Its Limitations

The core of Egyptian ideology was that a god, Horus, was incarnate in the person of the pharaoh and ruled Egypt on behalf of his fellow gods. This view was summed up in the designation of the Egyptian people as the "Cattle of the Gods." The pharaoh's word was law, and all appointments were made by the king, aided only by his fellow gods. The official view is clearly illustrated in the following biographical inscription, The Induction of Nebwennef, in which Ramses II (1290–1224 B.C.) appoints the nobleman Nebwennef High Priest of Amon at Thebes, one of the most important positions in Egypt. Despite his own divinity and the assistance of the other gods, Ramses still uses ordinary political horse sense. Instead of appointing a High Priest from within the ranks of the temple elite at Thebes, he chooses an outsider who, presumably, will be more responsive to his own, not the temple priesthood's, interests. Ramses also leaves intact Nebwennef's old power base at Denderah to ensure a counterweight to the power of the priests of Amon at Thebes.[3]

Then was introduced into His Majesty's presence the First Prophet of Amun, Nebwennef . . . [*who*], at that time was still only First Prophet of Anhur and of Hathor, mistress at Denderah, and overseer of the priests of all the gods, southward to Hraihiamun and northward to Thinis.

Then His Majesty said to him: "You are [*to be*] the First Prophet of Amun. His treasury and his granaries are under your seal; you are commander of his house, and all his provisions are under your charge. The temple of Hathor, mistress of Denderah, is under your charge as well, just as are the offices of your ancestors and the post wherein you functioned formerly. As surely as Re lives for me and loves me, and my father Amun favors me!

I mentioned to Amun the names of every last courtier and even the commander of infantry, and then proceeded to repeat for him (Amun) the names of the priests and princes of his house who stand in his presence; but he was not satisfied with any one of them until I pronounced your name to him. Perform well for him, as he has desired you. I know that you are competent. May he establish you before his house, grant you old age within it, and effect your burial in the city."

The pharaohs ruled Egypt with a multitude of officials and presided over a large, often faction-ridden court. Two kings, Amenemhet I (1991–1962 B.C.) and Ramses III (1182–1151 B.C.), died as a result of palace conspiracies, and other kings had to cope with rebellions by disaffected nobles. To succeed, a king required formidable political skills, as can be seen in the remarkable document known as the Instruction to Merikare, *which purports to be a record of the advice given the young king Merikare (ca. 2100 B.C.) by his aged father and predecessor. It reveals clearly what kind of person the pharaoh should be and how he should conduct himself.*[4] *. . .*

If you encounter a townsman whose deed is a transgression against you, lay a suit against him before the court; crush him, for he is an enemy. An orator is the scum of the city. Curb the rabble and force the heat out of them without getting unduly angry with them. As for the enemy who is poor, he spreads hostility, the pauper it is that causes trouble. The army which proves unruly (?) let them end up eating (?) . . . when the rabble grows angry, let them into the storehouse. . . . Be just in the sight of god. . . .

Get skill in words so that you may be strong . . . words are stouter than any weapon, and the trained mind cannot be taken advantage of. . . .

Emulate your fathers, your ancestors . . . behold, their words abide in writing; open and read that you may attain to knowledge. The skilled man develops only through having been

---

[3]From A. Kirk Grayson and Donald B. Redford, *Papyrus and Tablet* (Upper Saddle River, NJ: Prentice Hall, 1973), p. 6. By permission.
[4]Grayson and Redford, *Papyrus and Tablet*, pp. 12–14.

taught. Do not be evil, kindness is best; make your monuments endure through love of you . . . thanks is given for rewards, and they will pray for your health first and foremost.

Respect your officers, prosper your people; make fast your frontiers and boundaries, for it is a good thing to act for the future. Respect the lively, alert person, but the dull-witted is a miserable fellow. . . .

Exalt your officers that they may perform your laws. One who is rich in his own house does not show partiality, an owner of property is one who lacks not. But the pauper does not speak what he knows is true, and he who says 'Oh that I had . . . !' is not straightforward. He shows partiality to him whom he loves, and leans towards him who has bribes. Great is a great man whose great ones are great, and strong the king who has courtiers, and wealthy the man rich in great men. You should speak the truth in your house, that the great men who are in the land may fear you. Things go normally for the straightforward lord; it is the front of the house (i.e., the master's quarters) that instills fear in the back (i.e., the servants' quarters).

Act justly that you may endure on earth. Quiet the weeper, oppress not the widow, do not deprive a man of his paternal property, do no harm to officials on their own land. Beware of punishing wrongfully, do not kill—it is of no advantage to you. Punish rather with flogging and imprisonment, and thus will the land be stabilized. Judge the enemy whose plottings have been found out; God knows the refractory and God condemns him to a bloody end (?). . . . Do not kill a man whose ability you know, one with whom long ago you recited the writings (i.e., a schoolmate). . . .

Levy your draftees that the Residence may love you, increase your adherents from the present generation. See! Your cities are filled with new recruits. Twenty years it is that the youth are at ease in pursuit of their desire; then a new generation comes forth on the heels of its predecessor (?). . . . Enrich your officials, promote your fighting men, increase the numbers of the levies of your retainers; let them be provided with various things, endowed with fields and presented with cattle.

Do not distinguish between a gentleman's son and a commoner; take a man unto yourself because of his ability, that all tasks of skill may be performed. . . . Protect your frontier, raise up your monuments: a work-gang is useful to him who possesses it. Make monuments for God: the result is to perpetuate the name of him who does it. A man ought to do what is beneficial to his *bai*: monthly service as a priest, wearing white sandals, going to the temple, discretion (?) regarding the mysteries, entering the shrine, eating bread in the temple. . . .

He-of-the-Two-Banks (the king) is a wise man, the king who possesses courtiers cannot be foolish. He was intelligent (even) when he emerged from the womb, and God has elevated him over millions of men.

Kingship is a fine office. It has no son or brother to be perpetuated upon its monuments, but one carries on from another; a man acts on his predecessor's behalf, in order that what he has done may be carried on by another who comes after him. . . .

1.3   The Gods in Their Temples: A Sacred Marriage Drama

In Sumerian theology there was a close connection between temples, rituals, morality, and economic prosperity. Stability and prosperity was guaranteed by the gods who owned the cities of Sumer and dwelt in their temples. According to Mesopotamian mythological thinking, the gods had created mankind to relieve them of the chore of work and it was the job of their human servants to work to keep them fed, clothed, and entertained and to provide suitable dwelling places for them. Around 2130 B.C., Gudea, ruler or ensi of the city of Lagash, had a dream in which he was told to build and equip a temple for Ningirsu and his wife Baba, the protective deities of the city. The text is an extraordinarily elaborate document found inscribed on two large clay cylinders and, in abbreviated form, on some of Gudea's statue bases. It describes in dramatic and idealized fashion a series of events beginning with Gudea's dream and ending with the actual occupation of the temple by the gods and the performance of the Sacred Marriage whose enactment guaranteed abundance at harvest time.[5]

Gudea the ruler made (everything) pleasant in the city. He humbled (all) in the land. He silenced all the assemblies, turned back conflicts, (and) removed filth from the path. In the city beside the mother of the sick man, blessed water was placed. The herds of animals, the creatures of the plain, laid down next to each other (?). Among the lions and leopards (?), the dragons of the plain, sweet rest was established. At (the time of) dawn petition, when the prayer (ending) the night (was pronounced), when the moon of the dawn appeared (?) its [*i.e., the temple's*] king was ready to alight. The warrior, Ningirsu, proceeded to enter into the temple: Yes, its king went into the temple. He is (like) an eagle gazing at a wild bull. The warrior is entering into his temple, being a storm calling to battle. . . . Baba, her going to her cella [*her room in the temple*] was (like) a righteous woman who cares for her house. Her entering beside her bed was (like) the Tigris at the flood stage. Her sitting down beside her (?) is (like) the lady, the daughter of holy An raising fruit (to her mouth) in a beautiful garden. Light was coming forth. The destiny was determined. (With) Baba entering into her cella (and) the Lagash province (providing) abundance, day dawned (yea) Utu [*the sun god*] lifted the head high over Lagash in the land (of Sumer). . . . Their bed standing in (their) bed chamber is like a mother cow lying in its stall. On the holy bed spread strewn with bright herbs, Mother Baba with lord Ningirsu take pleasure in their lying together.

Having completed his great temple, Gudea celebrates a feast and proclaims the connection between the worship of the gods, morality, and economic prosperity.

Gudea had built the Eninnu. He had perfected the *mes* [*i.e., the offices and functions of the temple*]. Into its house of fat and cream, fat and cream did enter. In its Ekuanka [*sacred storage room*], food was placed. He relaxed (?) and washed his hands. When his king entered into the temple, for seven days the slave girl was indeed equal with her mistress; the slave indeed stood beside (his) master . . . the tongue which spoke wickedness he removed, (and) he removed (all) evil things from the temple. To the laws of Nanshe and Ningirsu he paid close attention. The wealthy man did not bring (grief) to the orphan, (and) the powerful man did not bring (grief) to the widow. In the house which had no heir he installed its daughter as its heir. When he [*Gudea*] caused majestic justice to go forth for him [*Utu*], on the complaining ones he put his foot. . . . For the upright steward of mother Nanshe [*i.e., for Gudea*] without cessation the temple brought forth abundance. The territory made the (pile of) spotted barley increase for him. Lagash stretched out the hand in abundance with the ruler.

[5]From Richard E. Averbeck, *A Preliminary Study of Ritual and Structure in the Cylinders of Gudea*, Vol. II (Ph.D. dissertation, Dropsie College, 1987), pp. 609–708, passim. By permission.

1.4   Sacred Prostitution

Sacred prostitution, both male and female, was practiced widely throughout the ancient world. The rationale behind it seems to have been the belief that having intercourse with prostitutes dedicated to the gods at their temples encouraged the gods to ensure the fertility of families, fields, and flocks. Herodotus describes the practice in Babylon.[6]

The Babylonians have one most shameful custom. Every woman born in the country must once in her life go and sit down in the precinct of Aphrodite [*goddess of love and fertility*] and there have intercourse with a stranger. Many of the richer women, who are too proud to mix with the rest, drive in covered carriages to the precinct followed by a large number of their attendants, and there take up their station. Most, however, seat themselves within the holy enclosure with wreaths of string around their heads, and here there is always a great crowd, some coming and others going. The lines of cord mark out paths in all directions among the women, and the strangers pass along them to make their choice. A woman who has once taken her seat is not allowed to return home until one of the strangers throws a silver coin into her lap and takes her outside to lie with him. . . . The woman goes with the first man who throws her money, and rejects no one. When she has had intercourse with the man, and so satisfied the goddess, she returns home.

Sacred prostitution was also practiced in Canaan and constituted a serious problem for the guardians of the worship of Yahweh. At times, sacred prostitution even became part of the worship of Yahweh at his temple in Jerusalem. The reforming king Josiah of Judah (640–609 B.C.) made an effort to curb the practice and "destroyed the houses of the male cult prostitutes which were in the house of the Lord" (2 Kings 23:7). To demonstrate Yahweh's fidelity and to protest Israel's infidelity the prophet Hosea married a prostitute, who may well have been a sacred prostitute. Another prophet, Ezekiel, metaphorically describes Israel as a cult prostitute who sets herself up in Yahweh's temple waiting for her lovers: "You bathed yourself for them, painted your eyes and put on your jewelry. You sat on an elegant couch, with a table spread before it on which you had placed the incense and oil that belonged to Yahweh."[7] The apocryphal Letter of Jeremiah (ca. 200 B.C. or later) denounces pagan practices, including sacred prostitution.

Women serve meals for gods of silver and gold and wood. . . . And the women, with cords about them sit along the passageways, burning bran for incense; and when one of them is led off by one of the passers-by and is lain with, she derides the woman next to her, because she was not as attractive as herself and her cord was not broken. Everything to do with these idols is a sham. Why then must any one think that they are gods, or call them gods?[8]

1.5   Covenant and Consequences

The demands of a personal relationship with the divinity underlie all Israelite religion. Abraham responded to the call of his personal god to leave his homeland for a "land I will give you" and for the promise of being the father of many nations. The relationship was sealed by the shedding of the blood of sacrificed

---

[6]Herodotus 1.199, Rawlinson translation modified.
[7]Ezekiel 23:36–44. NIV.
[8]Letter of Jeremiah 6:30, 43. *The Oxford Annotated Apocrypha.* © Copyright 1965 by Oxford University Press. By Permission.

animals, signifying the existence of a binding commitment on Abraham's part. The Patriarch took this relationship so seriously that he was willing to sacrifice his only son, Isaac, at his god's command. Similarly, the covenant between Yahweh and the whole people of Israel at Sinai involved commitment. Like the covenant with Abraham, it was sealed in sacrificial blood. However, how exactly the terms of the covenant were to be observed was not easily resolved. One approach was to regard living up to the covenant as a matter of obeying specific, well-known rules. The first text below, the "Shema" (Hear!), the declaration of God's unity, reflects this viewpoint.[9] The Shema *is the basic theological statement of the religion of Israel, and later of Judaism. Its recitation was part of the Temple service and was continued after its destruction in the synagogue. The* Shema *was to be recited twice daily, in the evening and the morning.*

1.5.1   Hear O Israel! The *Shema*

Hear, O Israel: The Lord our God, the Lord is one. Love the Lord your God with all your heart and with all your soul and with all your strength. These commandments that I give you today are to be upon your hearts. Impress them on your children. Talk about them when you sit at home and when you walk along the road, when you lie down and when you get up. Tie them as symbols on your hands and bind them on your foreheads. Write them on the doorframes of your houses and on your gates.

The Lord said to Moses, "Speak to the Israelites and say to them: 'Throughout the generations to come you are to make tassels on the corners of your garments with a blue cord on each tassel. You will have these tassels to look at and so you will remember all the commands of the Lord, that you may obey them and not prostitute yourselves by going after the lusts of your hearts and eyes. Then you will remember to obey all my commands and will be consecrated to your God. I am the Lord your God, who brought you out of Egypt to be your God. I am the Lord your God.'"

1.5.2   The Covenant as a Marriage Contract: *Hosea*

Another, equally traditional view of the covenant comes from the prophet Hosea. The prophet does not see the covenant as a set of detailed ordinances dictating specific behavior, but rather as a personal relationship, a general commitment, from which flow responses rather than obligations. For Hosea the relationship between Yahweh and Israel formed during the Exodus and at Sinai is like a marriage contract: exclusive, binding, loving, but not limited to specific do's-and-don'ts. But Israel proved to be unfaithful, her love "like a morning cloud, like the dew that goes early away." She has become a prostitute with many lovers, and many children by them. Nevertheless, like a devoted husband who refuses to give up, Yahweh continues to pursue his errant bride.[10]

> "Rebuke your mother, rebuke her,
>   for she is not my wife,
>   and I am not her husband.
> Let her remove the adulterous look from her face
>   and the unfaithfulness from between her breasts.

---

[9]Deuteronomy 6:4–9; Numbers 15:37–41. NIV.
[10]Hosea 2:2–7; 14–20. NIV.

Otherwise I will strip her naked
  and make her as bare as on the day she was born;
I will make her like a desert,
   turn her into a parched land,
   and slay her with thirst.
I will not show my love to her children,
   because they are the children of adultery.
Their mother has been unfaithful
   and conceived them in disgrace.
She said, 'I will go after my lovers,
   who give me my food and my water,
   my wool and my linen, my oil and my drink.'
Therefore I will block her path with thorn bushes;
   I will wall her in so that she cannot
   find her way.
She will chase after her lovers but not catch them;
   she will look for them but not find them.
Then she will say,
   'I will go back to my husband as at first,
   for then I was better off than now.'. . .
"Therefore I am now going to allure her;
   I will lead her into the desert
   and speak tenderly to her.
There I will give her back her vineyards
   and make the Valley of Achor [*Valley of Trouble*]
   a door of hope.
There she will sing as in the days of her youth,
   as in the day she came out of Egypt.
"In that day," declares the Lord,
   "you will call me 'my husband';
   you will no longer call me 'my master.'[11]

I will remove the names of the Baals from her lips;
   no longer will their names be invoked.
In that day I will make a covenant for them
   with the beasts of the field and the
   birds of the air
   and the creatures that move along the ground.
Bow and sword and battle
   I will abolish from the land,
   so that all may lie down in safety.
   I will betroth you to me forever;
I will betroth you in righteousness
   and justice, in love and compassion.

---

[11]There is a play on words here. The word *Baal* means "master." The idols that Israel has been pursuing are the Baals of Canaan.

I will betroth you in faithfulness,
   and you will acknowledge the Lord. . . .

"I will plant her for myself in the land;
   I will show my love to the one I
   called 'Not my loved one.'
I will say to those called 'Not my
   people,' 'You are my people';
   and they will say, 'You are my God.'"

Another prophet, Micah, a contemporary of Isaiah (ca. 700 B.C.), summed up the covenant as follows:[12]

With what shall I come before the Lord,
   and bow down before the exalted God?
Shall I come before him with burnt offerings,
   with calves a year old?
Will the Lord be pleased with thousands of rams,
   with ten thousand rivers of oil?
Shall I give my first-born for my transgression,
   the fruit of my body for the sin of my soul?
He has showed you, O man, what is good.
   And what does the Lord require of you?
To act justly and to love mercy
   and to walk humbly with your God.

1.6   The Call of the Prophet

Prophets as diviners and providers of oracles were a characteristic feature of all ancient Middle Eastern religions. They provided the necessary oracles for war or any major national policy and thus had an established place alongside priests in the cultic system. In such a position they also had a place in established Israelite religion. However, Israel was unique in the ancient world in producing another type of prophet, one independent of the state, capable of criticizing people or priest, king or general.

The call to the prophet Samuel came to him while he was still a youngster serving at the shrine of Yahweh at Shiloh before the establishment of the monarchy and before the Ark of the Covenant had been moved by David to Jerusalem. There were more dramatic calls, perhaps, such as those of Elisha, Isaiah, and Ezekiel, but the story of Samuel has a special charm and reveals the very personal aspect of the prophetic call.[13]

The boy Samuel ministered before the Lord under Eli. In those days the word of the Lord was rare; there were not many visions. One night Eli, whose eyes were becoming so weak that he could barely see, was lying down in his usual place. The lamp of God had not yet gone out, and Samuel was lying down in the temple of the Lord where the ark of God was. Then the Lord called Samuel. Samuel answered, "Here I am." And he ran to Eli and said,

---

[12]Micah 6:6–8. NIV.
[13]1 Samuel 3:1–17. NIV.

"Here I am; you called me." But Eli said, "I did not call; go back and lie down." So he went and lay down.

Again the Lord called, "Samuel!" And Samuel got up and went to Eli and said, "Here I am; you called me." "My son," Eli said, "I did not call; go back and lie down." Now Samuel did not yet know the Lord: The word of the Lord had not yet been revealed to him. The Lord called Samuel a third time, and Samuel got up and went to Eli and said, "Here I am; you called me." Then Eli realized that the Lord was calling the boy. So Eli told Samuel, "Go and lie down, and if he calls you, say, 'Speak, Lord, for your servant is listening.' " So Samuel went and lay down in his place.

Then the Lord came and stood there, calling as at the other times, "Samuel, Samuel!" Then Samuel said, "Speak, for your servant is listening." And the Lord said to Samuel, "See, I am about to do something in Israel that will make the ears of everyone who hears of it tingle. At that time I will carry out against Eli everything I spoke against his family—from beginning to end. For I told him that I would judge his family forever because of the sin he knew about; his sons made themselves contemptible, and he failed to restrain them. Therefore, I swore to the house of Eli, 'The guilt of Eli's house will never be atoned for by sacrifice or offering.' " Samuel lay down until morning and then opened the doors of the house of the Lord. He was afraid to tell Eli the vision, but Eli called him and said, "Samuel, my son." Samuel answered, "Here I am." "What was it he said to you?" Eli asked. "Do not hide it from me. May God deal with you, be it ever so severely, if you hide from me anything he told you." So Samuel told him everything, hiding nothing from him. Then Eli said, "He is the Lord; let him do what is good in his eyes."

1.7   Prophets and Palaces: Jeremiah Confronts the King

A dramatic example of a prophet in action is found in the following story about Jeremiah, whose ministry spans the critical years leading up to the destruction of Jerusalem by the Babylonians in 587 B.C. (see Chapter 2). The diplomatic situation was complex. The Assyrian Empire had just collapsed, and for a while the kingdom of Judah came under Egyptian control; then the Babylonians intervened and forced Jerusalem into their alliance. Located on the critically important frontier between two of the great powers of the region, Judah was in an impossible situation. It is not difficult to appreciate the dilemma of King Jehoiakim, Jeremiah's opponent, who found his policies being undermined by the prophet. Forbidden to speak publicly, Jeremiah circumvented the king's order by having his secretary, Baruch, step in for him. The source of the story is Baruch himself.[14] (Another confrontation of palace and prophet can be found in Chapter 2, between Ahab, Jezebel, and Elijah.)

In the fourth year of Jehoiakim, son of Josiah king of Judah, this word came to Jeremiah from the Lord: "Take a scroll and write on it all the words I have spoken to you concerning Israel, Judah, and all the other nations from the time I began speaking to you in the reign of Josiah till now. Perhaps when the people of Judah hear about every disaster I plan to inflict on them, each of them will turn from his wicked way; then I will forgive their wickedness and their sin."

---

[14]Jeremiah 36. NIV.

So Jeremiah called Baruch son of Neriah, and while Jeremiah dictated all the words the Lord had spoken to him, Baruch wrote them on the scroll. Then Jeremiah told Baruch, "I am restricted; I cannot go to the Lord's temple. So you go to the house of the Lord on a day of fasting and read to the people from the scroll the words of the Lord that you wrote as I dictated. Read them to all the people of Judah who come in from their towns. Perhaps they will bring their petition before the Lord, and each will turn from his wicked ways, for the anger and wrath pronounced against this people by the Lord are great."

Baruch son of Neriah did everything Jeremiah the prophet told him to do; at the Lord's temple he read the words of the Lord from the scroll. In the ninth month of the fifth year of Jehoiakim son of Josiah king of Judah, a time of fasting before the Lord was proclaimed for all the people in Jerusalem and those who had come from the towns of Judah. From the room of Gemariah son of Shaphan the secretary, which was in the upper courtyard at the entrance of the New Gate of the Temple, Baruch read to all the people at the Lord's Temple the words of Jeremiah from the scroll.

When Micaiah son of Gemariah, the son of Shaphan, heard all the words of the Lord from the scroll, he went down to the secretary's room in the royal palace, where all the officials were sitting: Elishama the secretary, Delaiah son of Shemaiah, Elnathan son of Acbor, Gemariah son of Shaphan, Zedekiah son of Hananiah, and all the other officials. After Micaiah told them everything he had heard, Baruch read to the people from the scroll, all the officials sent Jehudi son of Nethaniah, the son of Shelemiah, the son of Cushi, to say to Baruch, "Bring the scroll from which you have read to the people and come." So Baruch son of Neriah went to them with the scroll in his hand. They said to him, "Sit down, please, and read it to us."

So Baruch read it to them. When they heard all these words, they looked at each other in fear and said to Baruch, "We must report all these words to the king." Then they asked Baruch, "Tell us, how did you come to write all this? Did Jeremiah dictate it?"

"Yes," Baruch replied, "he dictated all these words to me, and I wrote them in ink on the scroll."

Then the officials said to Baruch, "You and Jeremiah, go and hide. Don't let anyone know where you are."

After they put the scroll in the room of Elishama the secretary, they went to the king in the courtyard and reported everything to him. The king sent Jehudi to get the scroll, and Jehudi brought it from the room of Elishama the secretary and read it to the king and all the officials standing beside him. It was the ninth month and the king was sitting in the winter apartment, with a fire burning in the firepot in front of him. Whenever Jehudi had read three or four columns of the scroll, the king cut them off with a scribe's knife and threw them into the firepot, until the entire scroll was burned in the fire. The king and all his attendants who heard all these words showed no fear, nor did they tear their clothes. Even though Elnathan, Delaiah, and Gemariah urged the king not to burn the scroll, he would not listen to them. Instead, the king commanded Jerahmeel, a son of the king, Seraiah son of Azriel, and Shelemiah son of Abdeel to arrest Baruch the scribe and Jeremiah the prophet. But the Lord had hidden them.

After the king burned the scroll containing the words that Baruch had written at Jeremiah's dictation, the word of the Lord came to Jeremiah: "Take another scroll and write on it all the words that were on the first scroll, which Jehoiakim king of Judah burned up. Also tell Jehoiakim king of Judah, 'This is what the Lord says: You burned that scroll and said, "Why did you write on it that the king of Babylon would certainly come and destroy this land and cut off both men and animals from it?" Therefore, this is what the Lord says about Jehoiakim king of Judah: 'He will have no one to sit on the throne of David; his body will be thrown out and exposed to the heat by day and the frost by night. I will punish him and his children and his attendants for their wickedness; I will bring on them and those living in Jerusalem and the people of Judah every disaster I pronounced against them, because they have not listened.'"

So Jeremiah took another scroll and gave it to the scribe Baruch son of Neriah, and as Jeremiah dictated, Baruch wrote on it all the words of the scroll that Jehoiakim king of Judah had burned in the fire. And many similar words were added to them.

1.8   "I Will Be with Him in Trouble": Personal Religion and Piety

Personal religious attitudes evolved alongside public rituals, though never completely separate from them. In Psalm 130 (the "De Profundis"—that is, "Out of the Depths") the poet reflects on the omniscience of God, who knows all our sins yet offers "unfailing love . . . and full redemption." The poet borrows from Mesopotamian mythology the image of the scribe of the underworld who keeps daily records of human behavior. The well-known Psalm 91 talks of confidence in God.[15]

Psalm 130

Out of the depths I cry to you, O Lord;
   O Lord, hear my voice.
Let your ears be attentive to my cry for mercy.

If you, O Lord, kept a record of sins,
   O Lord, who could stand?
But with you there is forgiveness;
   therefore you are feared.

I wait for the Lord, my soul waits, and in his word I put my hope.
   My soul waits for the Lord
more than watchmen wait for the morning,
more than watchmen wait for the morning.

O Israel, put your hope in the Lord,
   for with the Lord is unfailing love
   and with him is full redemption.
He himself will redeem Israel
   from all their sins.

Psalm 91

He who dwells in the shelter of the Most High
   will rest in the shadow of the Almighty.
I will say of the Lord, "He is my refuge and my fortress,
   my God in whom I trust."

---

[15]Psalms 130 and 91. NIV.

Surely he will save you from the fowler's snare
> and from the deadly pestilence.
He will cover you with his feathers,
> and under his wings you will find refuge;
> his faithfulness will be your shield and rampart.
You will not fear the terror of night
> nor the arrow that flies by day
> nor the pestilence that stalks in the darkness,
> nor the plague that destroys at midday.
A thousand may fall at your side,
> ten thousand at your right hand,
> but it will not come near you.

You will only observe with your eyes
> and see the punishment of the wicked.
If you make the Most High your dwelling—
> even the Lord, who is my refuge—
> then no harm will befall you,
> no disaster will come near your tent.
For he will commend his angels concerning you
> to guard you in all your ways;
> they will lift you up in their hands,
> so that you will not strike your foot against a stone.
You will tread upon the lion and the cobra;
> you will trample the great lion and the serpent.
"Because he loves me," says the Lord, "I will rescue him;
> I will protect him, for he acknowledges my name.
He will call upon me, and I will answer him;
> I will be with him in trouble,
> I will deliver him and honor him.
With long life will I satisfy him
> and show him my salvation."

1.9   Empire, Exile, and Monotheism

Egyptian gods were viewed as the creators and rulers of creation, but creation was believed to be originally limited to Egypt. Only Egypt truly existed, and only Egyptians were truly human. The acquisition of an empire extending from the central Sudan to southern Syria in the New Kingdom period (ca. 1570–1090 B.C.), however, expanded the concept of creation ruled by the gods to include the world outside Egypt. The clearest exposition of this new view of the gods as rulers of the whole world is contained in the great hymn to Aten by Akh-en-aten (ca. 1367–1350 B.C.) in which the king proclaims Aten, the physical sun itself, as the sole god, creator, and ruler of the world.[16] Similar ideas, expressed at times in almost identical language, are to be found in Psalm 104 in the Bible.

---

[16]Adapted from the translation of J. H. Breasted, *Development of Religion and Thought in Ancient Egypt* (New York: Charles Scribner's Sons, 1912), pp. 324–328.

1.9.1   The Great Hymn to the Aten

Universal Splendor and Power of Aten

Your dawning is beautiful in the horizon of the sky,
O living Aten, Beginning of life!
When you rise in the eastern horizon,
You fill every land with your beauty.
You are beautiful, great, glittering, high above every land,
Your rays, they encompass the lands, even all that you have made.
You are Re, and you carry them all away captive;
You bind them by your love.
Though you are far away, your rays are upon earth;
Though you are on high, your [footprints are the day].

Night

When you set in the western horizon of the sky,
The earth is in darkness like the dead;
They sleep in their chambers,
Their heads are wrapped up,
Their nostrils are stopped,
And none sees the other,
While all their things are stolen
Which are under their heads,
And they know it not.
Every lion comes forth from his den,
All Serpents, they sting.
Darkness . . .
The world is in silence,
He that made them rests in his horizon.

Day and Humanity

Bright is the earth when you rise in the horizon.
When you shine as Aten by day
You drive away the darkness.
When you send forth your rays,
The Two Lands [*Egypt*] are in daily festivity,
Awake and standing upon their feet
When you have raised them up.
Their limbs bathed, they take their clothing,
Their arms uplifted in adoration to your dawning.
(Then) in all the world they do their work.

Day and the Animals and Plants

All cattle rest upon their pasturage,
The trees and the plants flourish,

The birds flutter in their marshes,
Their wings uplifted in adoration to you.
All the sheep dance upon their feet,
All winged things fly,
They live when you have shone upon them.

Day and the Waters

The barques sail up-stream and down-stream alike.
Every highway is open because you dawn.
The fish in the rivers leap up before you.
Your rays are in the midst of the great green sea.

Creation of Humanity

Creator of the germ in woman,
Maker of seed in man,
Giving life to the son in the body of his mother,
Soothing him that he may not weep,
Nurse (even) in the womb,
Giver of breath to animate every one that he makes!
When he comes forth from the body . . . on the day of his birth,
You open his mouth in speech,
You supply his necessities.

Creation of Animals

When the fledgling in the egg chirps in the shell,
You give him breath therein to preserve him alive.
When you have [brought him together],
To (the point of) bursting it in the egg,
He comes forth from the egg
To chirp [with all his might].
He goes about upon his two feet
When he has come forth therefrom.

The Whole Creation

How manifold are your works!
They are hidden from before (us),
O sole God, whose power no other possesses.
You did create the earth according to your heart
While you were alone.
Men, all cattle large and small,
All that are upon earth,
That go about upon their feet;
[All] that are on high,
That fly with their wings.
The foreign countries, Syria and Kush,

The land of Egypt;
You set every man into his place,
You supply their necessities.
Every one has his possessions,
And his days are reckoned,
The tongues are divers in speech,
Their forms likewise and their skins are distinguished.
(For) you make different the strangers.

Watering the Earth in Egypt and Abroad

You make the Nile in the Nether World,
You bring it as you desire,
To preserve alive the people.
For you have made them for yourself,
The lord of them all, resting among them;
You lord of every land, who rises for them.
You Sun of day, great in majesty.
All the distant countries,
You make (also) their life,
You have set a Nile in the sky;
When it falls for them,
It makes waves upon the mountains,
Like the great green sea,
Watering their fields in their towns.
How excellent are your designs, O lord of eternity!
There is a Nile in the sky for the strangers
And for the cattle of every country that go upon their feet.
(But) the Nile, it comes from the Nether World for Egypt.

The Seasons

Your rays nourish every garden;
When you rise they live,
They grow by you.
You make the seasons
In order to create all your work:
Winter to bring coolness,
And heat that [they may taste] you.
You did make the distant sky to rise therein,
In order to behold all that you have made,
You alone, shining in your form as living Aten,
Dawning, glittering, going afar and returning.
You make millions of forms
Through yourself alone;
Cities, towns, and tribes, highways and rivers.
All eyes see you before them,
For you are Aten of the day over the earth.

Revelation to the King

You are in my heart,
There is no other that knows you
Save your son Akh-en-Aten.
You have made him wise
In your designs and in your might.
The world is in your hand,
Even as you have made them.
When you have risen they live,
When you set, they die;
For you are length of life of yourself,
Men live through you,
While (their) eyes are upon your beauty
Until you set.
All labor is put away
When you set in the west.
You did establish the world,
And raise them up for your son,
who came forth from your limbs,
The king of Upper and Lower Egypt,
Living in Truth, Lord of the Two Lands,
Nefer-khepru-Re, the Sole one of Re,
Son of Re, living in Truth, lord of Diadems
Akh-en-Aten, whose life is long;
(And for) the chief royal wife, his beloved,
Mistress of the Two Lands, Nefer-nefru-Aten, Nefertiti,
Living and flourishing for ever and ever.

1.9.2 Yahweh: The Lord of History

The destruction of Solomon's temple in Jerusalem and the deportation to Babylon of many Judaeans led to a crisis in the religion of Israel. With the Temple destroyed, and the priests and people scattered, the only way to withstand absorption and disappearance was to find alternate forms of worship. Emphasis began to be laid on prayer and study and on the spiritual and abstract side of Israel's religious tradition. With this shift came also an emphasis on the universality of Yahweh. Writing during the exile, the author of the last part of Isaiah has God say that if he has the heavens as his throne and the earth as his footstool, then what kind of house could humans possibly build for him? (Isaiah 66.1) But if Yahweh is thus the creator of the universe with no need of temples, he is also the Lord of all peoples, not just of Israel. The God of Isaiah is not an abstract, philosophical deity, but Yahweh, the Lord of History, who is directing all things to a final, predetermined end.[17]

For the Lord of Hosts has a day in store
    for all the proud and lofty,

---

[17]Isaiah 2:12–22. NIV.

for all that is exalted
(and they will be humbled),
for all the cedars of Lebanon, tall and lofty,
and all the oaks of Bashan,
for all the towering mountains
and all the high hills,
for every lofty tower
and every fortified wall,
for every trading ship and every stately vessel.
The arrogance of man will be brought low
and the pride of man humbled;
the Lord alone will be exalted in that day,
and the idols will totally disappear.
Men will flee to caves in the rocks
and to holes in the ground
from the dread of the Lord
and the splendor of his majesty,
when he rises to shake the earth.

1.10   Tombs and Immortality

Throughout the entire history of ancient Egypt, the preparation of a tomb was a central concern of Egyptians, from the mighty Pharaoh to the lowliest subject, and for a good reason. Essential to the attainment of an afterlife was a secure place for the mummified body of the dead person, and a clearly identified place at which could be made the prayers and food offerings believed necessary for the continued well-being of the dead. For both functions a tomb seemed ideally suited, but was it? The anonymous New Kingdom text given below, Papyrus Chester Beatty 4, argues that historical experience in the form of innumerable tomb robberies and repeated failures of relatives to make the required food offerings suggest otherwise. The author's solution to this problem was a radically new conception of immortality in which a person survived death not in the material sense of traditional Egyptian thought, but metaphorically as a memory in the minds of future generations. This new form of immortality could be obtained only by a new form of tomb, namely, a book, which would preserve the name of its author by its continuing to be read after the author's death. By reading between the lines, we can get a clear picture of the other strategies the Egyptians used to achieve immortality.[18]

1.10.1   Book Writing: A New Form of Immortality

If you but do this, you are versed in writings.
As to those learned scribes,
Of the time that came after the gods,
They who foretold the future,

---

[18]From Miriam Lichtheim, *Ancient Egyptian Literature:* Vol. II: *The New Kingdom* (Berkeley and Los Angeles: University of California Press, 1976), pp. 176–177.

Their names have become everlasting,
While they departed, having finished their lives,
And all their kin are forgotten.

They did not make for themselves tombs of copper,
With stelae of metal from heaven.
They knew not how to leave heirs,
Children [of theirs] to pronounce their names;
They made heirs for themselves of books,
Of Instructions they had composed.

They gave themselves [the scroll as lector]-priest,
The writing board as loving son.
Instructions are their tombs,
The reed pen is their child,
The stone-surface their wife.
People great and small
Are given them as children,
For the scribe, he is their leader.

Their portals and mansions have crumbled,
Their *ka*-servants are [gone];
Their tombstones are covered with soil,
Their graves are forgotten.
Their name is pronounced over their books,
Which they made while they had being;
Good is the memory of their makers,
It is for ever and all time!

Be a scribe, take it to heart,
That your name become as theirs.
Better is a book than a graven stela,
Than a solid [tomb-enclosure].
They act as chapels and tombs
In the heart of him who speaks their name;
Surely useful in the graveyard
Is a name in people's mouth!

Man decays, his corpse is dust,
All his kin have perished;
But a book makes him remembered
Through the mouth of its reciter.
Better is a book than a well-built house,
Than tomb-chapels in the west;
Better than a solid mansion,
Than a stela in the temple!

Is there one here like Hardedef?
Is there another like Imhotep?
None of our kin is like Neferti,

Or Khety, the foremost among them.
I give you the name of Ptah-emdjehuty,
Of Khakheperre-sonb.
Is there another like Ptahhotep,
Or the equal of Kaires?
Those sages who foretold the future,
What came from their mouth occurred;
It is found as (their) pronouncement,
It is written in their books.
The children of others are given to them
To be heirs as their own children.
They hid their magic from the masses,
It is read in their Instructions.
Death made their names forgotten
But books made them remembered!

1.10.2   Caught in the Act: Ancient Egyptian Tomb Robbers

Bearing out the opinion of the author of the Beatty Papyrus is the following account of tomb robberies in the royal necropolis. In times of disorder any worthwhile tomb was likely to be looted. Not even the pharaohs could guarantee themselves immortality through the physical preservation of their remains. Sometime during the reign of Ramses IX (ca. 1191 B.C.) an inspection of the royal necropolis at Thebes, initiated by Pewero, chief of police, revealed a number of instances of looting. Eight of the thieves were caught and their confession recorded by a careful scribe. Not to be overlooked is the fact that only the actual looters were tried, although the robberies could not have occurred without the collusion of the high officials in charge of the cemeteries. There was some hope in that thieves had been unable to force their way into some of the inspected tombs.[19]

[There were sent] the inspectors of the great and august necropolis, the scribe of the vizier and the scribe of the overseer of the White House of Pharaoh . . . [in order to inspect] the sepulchers of former kings, the tombs and resting places of the nobles, [located on] the west of the city. [The inspectors were]: (1) The governor of the city and vizier, Khamwese; (2) the king's butler, Nesuamon, the scribe of the Pharaoh; (3) the major-domo of the house of the Divine Votress of Amon Re . . . Neferkere-em-Per-Amon. [This was done because of the] thieves on the west of the city, concerning whom the mayor, the chief of police of the great and holy necropolis of Pharaoh on the west of Thebes, Pewero, had reported to the vizier, the nobles, and butlers of Pharaoh.

There follows a list of the tombs inspected. Two examples are given, one of an unlooted tomb, the other of a tomb where the robbers were successful.

The pyramid of King Sekhemre-Upmat, Son of Re, Intef. It was found in the course of being tunneled into by the thieves, at the place where the stela of its pyramid was set up. Inspected on this day; it was found uninjured; the thieves had been unable to enter it.

---

[19]*Papyrus Abbot* Pl. 1, 2; *Papyrus Amherst* Col. 2, *Ancient Records of Egypt*, Vol. 4, trans. James Henry Breasted (Chicago: University of Chicago Press, 1906), pp. 253, 255, 265–266.

The pyramid of King Sekhemre-Shedtowe, Son of Re, Sebekemsaf. . . . It was found that the thieves had broken into it by mining work through the base of the pyramid, from the outer chamber of the tomb of the overseer of the granary of King Menkheperre [*Thutmose III*] Nebamon. The burial place of the king was found void of its lord, as well as the burial place of the great king's wife, Nubkhas . . . the thieves having laid their hand upon them.

Now follows the confession of the tomb-robbers.

"We penetrated [all the burial places], we found her resting likewise. We opened their coffins and their coverings in which they were. We found this august mummy of this king. . . . There was a numerous list of amulets and ornaments of gold at its throat; its head had a mask of gold upon it; the august mummy of the king was overlaid with gold throughout. Its coverings were wrought with gold and silver, within and without; inlaid with every splendid costly stone.

"We stripped off the gold, which we found on the august mummy of this god, and its amulets and ornaments which were at its throat, and the coverings wherein it rested. We found the King's wife likewise; we stripped off all that we found on her likewise. We set fire to their coverings. We stole their furniture, which we found with them, being vases of gold, silver, and bronze. We divided, and made the gold which we found on these two gods, on their mummies, and the amulets, ornaments, and coverings into eight parts."

List of thieves: [*The first three names are missing*]

—The stonecutter of the "House-of-Amon-Re-King-of-God," Hapi, under charge of the High Priest of Amon.
—The artisan of the "House-of Amon-Re-King-of-Gods," Iramon, under charge of the master of the hunt, Nesuamon [*one of the inspectors!*].
—The peasant, Amenemhab, of the house of Emenopet, who administers in the district of Amenopet, under the charge of the High Priest of Amon.
—The water carrier, Kemwese, of the shrine of King Menkheprure [*Thutmose IV*]. . . .
—Ehenefer, son of Nakhtemmut, formerly in the hand of Telamon, the black slave of the High Priest of Amon.

Total of the people who were in the pyramid of this great god: eight men.

Chapter 2

▾▾▾

Palaces and Kings

In early times the temple was the predominant institution in Mesopotamia, but the palace soon grew to be of equal or even greater significance. Duplicating the bureaucracy of the temple, the palace gave Mesopotamian kings a high degree of control over the resources necessary for maintaining order at home and defending their cities in time of war—the twin responsibilities of all rulers. Now for the first time in history, leaders possessed efficient means of marshalling, disciplining, and supplying large bodies of soldiers.

Citizenship, the great by-product of urbanization, made Mesopotamian warfare particularly destructive since it had the potential to involve whole populations in war, and not just the upper classes or professionals. The archives of Sumerian cities are full of the records of endless wars among individual cities. Lagash defeated and was in turn defeated by Umma, which then went on to conquer the rest of Sumer. At another time, Uruk (biblical Erech) topped the list of city-states; then it was Ur, and later Isin and Larsa. Conversely, however, citizenship and the growth of monarchy contributed to another development: the quest for a just society and a written code of laws.

The objective of expanding an individual city-state's power over others tantalized many ambitious rulers. Sargon of Akkad (2334–2279 B.C.) succeeded in unifying all of Mesopotamia under his rule, creating the world's first known empire. Ur-Nammu laid the foundation for Ur's dominance (the so-called Ur III Dynasty, 2111–2004 B.C.). In the next millennium Shamshi-Adad of Assyria (1813–1781 B.C.) and Hammurapi of Babylon (1792–1750 B.C.) each founded empires, neither of which long outlived the deaths of their founders.

In the tenth century a revitalized Assyria in the northern part of Mesopotamia took the war-making potential of urban society a step beyond that of the individual city-state. Guided by a competent dynasty and utilizing the resources of a whole region, the Assyrians succeeded in extending their influence over most of the Middle East. Instituting desperate defensive measures against the invaders, the Assyrians first built up a formidable military establishment but soon learned the techniques of imperial control. In the end, the task of uniting so huge and diverse a region exhausted Assyria, and its empire fell to a coalition of Babylonians and Medes. Between 615 B.C. and 612 B.C. the Assyrian capitals of Nineveh, Kalah, Assur, and Dur-Sharrukin were annihilated, and Babylonians and Medes divided Assyria's empire. But the Medes were soon absorbed by the Persians (in 550 B.C.), who then went on to swallow up Babylon (539 B.C.) and all of Mesopotamia. Henceforth, Mesopotamia was reduced to the level of a province in a gigantic cosmopolitan empire reaching from Greece to India. The glory of the region faded along with its independence.

At an early date, portions of Egypt also achieved the capacity to wage war on as large a scale as Mesopotamia. By around 3100 B.C. national unification at a level of solidity and permanence not dreamed of in Mesopotamia had been achieved by the pharaohs, the god-kings of Egypt. Unity, once achieved, lasted for extraordinarily long periods of time. Protected by its isolated geographical position, united by the Nile and a powerful centralized government, Egypt rarely suffered the fragmentation of Mesopotamia and for the most part escaped the invasions and migrations experienced by that region. Whether the pharaohs were as successful in the administration of justice as were the rulers of Mesopotamia is an interesting but insoluble question. They were certainly more effective maintainers of order, and the ideology of justice, or *Ma'at*, was given great prominence in their proclamations. However, since the pharaonic system put all power in the hands of the pharaoh, responsibility for justice devolved in practice on his delegates. In the final analysis, justice in Egypt depended on the quality of the pharaoh's administrators and how seriously they accepted the official ideology.

Left out in all of this discussion is the fate of innumerable small states wedged between, or on the fringes of, the great powers. They are represented in the readings that deal with Israel, and their fate may be inferred accordingly. Samaria, the capital of the northern kingdom of Israel, fell to the Assyrians in 721 B.C. Jerusalem, capital of Judah (or Judaea), the southern kingdom, was taken and destroyed by the Babylonians in 587 B.C. Caught in the same wars and suffering many of the same experiences were the cities and alliances of Phoenicia, Philistia, and Syria. All ended up, along with Egypt and Mesopotamia, as subjects of the Persian Empire.

2.1   Loyalty to the King: The Egyptian Theory of Government

The central truth of Egyptian culture was that Egypt was the creation of the gods and that its continued existence and welfare were the responsibility of the pharaoh, who was the incarnation on earth of the sky god Horus. The well-being of all Egyptians was dependent on the king's success in his endless struggle to maintain the cosmic order. To assist him in that effort was the primary duty of his subjects. Such is the message of the following text from the Middle Kingdom (ca. 2050–1800 B.C.). Known as the "Loyalist Instruction," it teaches the overriding importance of loyalty to the king, whose ability to guarantee prosperity for his subjects is indicated by his identification with various powerful deities such as the sun god Re; the creator god Khnum; the cat-headed goddess Bastet; and the lion-headed warrior goddess Sakhmet, the goddess of pestilence.[1]

> Adore the king, Nymaatre [*Amenemhet II (1842–1797)*] living forever. . . . Place his majesty in friendly fashion in your thoughts.
>
> He is Perception, which is in all hearts, and his eyes pierce through every being.
>
> He is Re, by whose rays one sees, for he is the one who illumines the Two Lands [*i.e., Upper and Lower Egypt*] more than the sun disk.

---

[1]From William Kelly Simpson, R. O. Wente, and E. F. Wente, Jr., *The Literature of Ancient Egypt*, 2nd ed. (New Haven, CT: Yale University Press, 1978), pp. 198–200.

He is the one who makes the land green, even more than a high inundation: he has filled the Two Lands with victory and life. . . .
His utterance is Abundance. . . .
He is Khnum for all limbs, The Begetter of the begotten.
He is Bastet, who protects the Two Lands.
The one who praises him will be protected by his arm.
He is Sakhmet against those who disobey his orders, and the one with whom he disagrees will be laden with sorrows.
The one whom the king loves shall be a well-provided spirit;
there is no tomb for anyone who rebels against His Majesty, and his corpse shall be cast to the waters.

2.2   But if Pharaoh Fails . . . ?

In Egyptian thought the principal result of creation was the establishment of order in Egypt. The world outside the Nile Valley belonged to the forces of chaos and evil, and the chief obligation of the king was to defend Egypt against the continuous efforts of the forces of chaos to disrupt the orderly existence of Egypt. For the king to fail in this struggle threatened not just order in Egypt but also creation itself. This concept can be seen in the text known as the Prophecy of Neferty in the vivid pictures of disorder in the social and natural world that are claimed to be the result of the intrusion of Asian nomads into the eastern Delta at the end of the Old Kingdom (ca. 2200 B.C.). The reality was something different: Weakened central government at the end of the Old Kingdom allowed the frontier defenses to decay and encouraged nomads to penetrate into the Delta itself. Still the shock of the collapse of central authority left a great impression on later generations and needed to be explained.[2]

See now, there are no more officials in the present state of the land. What was accomplished is as that which was never accomplished, as it were at the outset of Re's creation. The land has completely gone to ruin without exception. . . . This land is destroyed, and nobody thinks of it, nobody speaks of it, nobody weeps for it.

What is the land like? The sun disk is clouded over and does not shine that mankind may see. People cannot live if the storm clouds come over. . . . The river of Egypt is empty, and the water is crossed on foot. Water will have to be looked for the ships to sail on, for its normal course has become a sand-bank, while the normal sand-banks have become water: the fluid turns into the solid. The southwind shall oppose the northwind, the heaven has no single breeze. . . . Destroyed indeed is that beneficence of the fish-pools, and those who bore the fish knives, laden down with fish and fowl.

All good things are gone, and the land cast down in distress because of the food-needs of the barbarians who are everywhere in the land. Enemies appear on the east, the Asiatics will descend into Egypt. A fort will be breached even though another is nearby, for its garrison will not listen. The siege ladder will be run up in the night, the fort will be entered, the ramparts scaled, while everyone sleeps and he who reclines says, "I am on watch."

---

[2]From A. Kirk Grayson and Donald B. Redford, *Papyrus and Tablet* (Upper Saddle River, NJ: Prentice Hall, 1973), pp. 18–19. By permission.

2.3   Women in Power

Occasionally women came to power directly themselves, but more often they exercised influence indirectly through their status as mothers, sisters, wives, or daughters. In very early Sumer, at Kish, Ku Baba was given a dynasty all to herself. Enheduanna, daughter of Sargon of Akkad (2334–2279 B.C.), was influential in sustaining her father's power in Sumer through her role as chief priestess at Ur and Uruk. Mer-Neith was possibly pharaoh in her own right, but in any case a very influential figure in the shadowy, critical years of unification at the beginning of Egyptian history. During the New Kingdom period Hatshepsut (1490–1469 B.C.) was an important pharaoh. One of the best known queens of the ancient world was Semiramis, the Assyrian Queen Sammu-ramat, wife of Shamshi-Adad V (824–811 B.C.) and regent after his death during the minority of their son Adad-Nirari III. One of the most interesting examples of women in power is that of Queen Jezebel, consort of Ahab, King of Israel (869–850 B.C.). Part of her significance for us is that she speaks for many of the queens in the small nations who made up an important part of the ancient Middle East.

2.3.1   Ku Baba[3]

In Kish, Ku Baba, a barmaid, she who made firm the foundation of Kish, became king and ruled one hundred years.

2.3.2   Zakutu, Wife of Sennacherib

Zakutu was the wife of the Assyrian King Sennacherib (704–681 B.C.). After the assassination of her husband by one of his elder sons, her own son Esarhaddon succeeded to the throne, though only after a bloody struggle with his brothers. Undoubtedly she played some role in this process. Certainly, during Esarhaddon's reign she exercised considerable power, as the following report suggests.[4]

> To the mother of the king my lord! The words of your servant Naid Marduk: Greetings to the mother of the king my lord! May the gods Ashur, Shamash, and Marduk keep the king my lord in health. May they decree well-being for the mother of the king my lord. After the Elamites came against us and seized the bridge, I wrote to the mother of the king my lord to report their coming. Now they have ripped up the bridge, tied up the bridge pontoons somewhere, and will not release them. We do not know if they will come again or not. If they should come, I shall report to the mother of the king my lord. Then may my lord order troops for us.

2.3.3   Jezebel

Jezebel was a Phoenician princess, the daughter of the King of Sidon, and the wife of King Ahab of Israel (869–850 B.C.). She was the mother of Ahab's two successors, and her daughter Athaliah was the wife of Jehoram, King of Judah, and the mother of Ahaziah, his successor. When Ahaziah was murdered, Athaliah became queen and ruled for seven years until her own assassination. By any count Jezebel was an important figure in the history of Israel, but she had the misfortune to have her biography (actually only a partial biography) written by her enemies. To appreciate her side of the story, we must try to read

---

[3]Grayson and Redford, *Papyrus and Tablet*, p. 130
[4]Grayson and Redford, *Papyrus and Tablet*, p. 134.

between the lines of an extremely hostile tradition. As was the custom of most foreign queens in a strange country, Jezebel continued to worship the gods of her homeland. Her husband followed suit and joined her in the worship of Baal, the Canaanite sky god. The strong-willed queen, however, was opposed by the equally formidable prophet Elijah, and the story of the confrontation between her priests and the prophet on Mount Carmel is told in detail in 1 Kings 17–19. Elijah won this round but was nevertheless forced to flee for his life, and for the moment he drops out of the story. Jezebel, still supreme in the palace, continued to advise her husband, Ahab.[5]

Some time later there was an incident involving a vineyard belonging to Naboth the Jezreelite. The vineyard was in Jezreel, close to the palace of Ahab king of Samaria. Ahab said to Naboth, "Let me have your vineyard to use for my vegetable garden, since it is close to my palace. In exchange I will give you a better vineyard or, if you prefer, I will pay you whatever it is worth." But Naboth replied, "The Lord forbid that I should give you the inheritance of my fathers."

So Ahab went home, sullen and angry. . . . He lay on his bed sulking and refused to eat. His wife Jezebel came in and asked him, "Why are you so sullen? Why won't you eat?" He answered her, "Because I said to Naboth the Jezreelite, 'Sell me your vineyard; or if you prefer, I will give you another vineyard in its place.' But he said, 'I will not give you my vineyard.'" Jezebel his wife said, "Is this how you act as king over Israel? Get up and eat! Cheer up. I'll get you the vineyard of Naboth the Jezreelite."

Jezebel arranged for false charges of blasphemy to be brought against Naboth, and he was stoned to death.

As soon as Jezebel heard that Naboth had been stoned to death, she said to Ahab, "Get up and take possession of the vineyard of Naboth the Jezreelite that he refused to sell you. He is no longer alive, but dead." When Ahab heard that Naboth was dead, he got up and went down to take possession of Naboth's vineyard.

Then the word of the Lord came to Elijah the Tishbite: "Go down to meet Ahab King of Israel, who rules in Samaria. He is now in Naboth's vineyard, where he has gone to take possession of it. Say to him, 'This is what the Lord says: Have you not murdered a man and seized his property?' Then say to him, 'This is what the Lord says: In the place where dogs licked up Naboth's blood, dogs will lick up your blood—yes, yours!'"

Ahab said to Elijah, "So you have found me, my enemy?" "I have found you," he answered, "because you have sold yourself to do evil in the eyes of the Lord. I am going to bring disaster on you. I will consume your descendants and cut off from Ahab every last male in Israel—slave or free. . . . And also concerning Jezebel the Lord says: 'Dogs will devour Jezebel by the wall of Jezreel.'"

The prediction of Elijah in due course proves true, though the ultimate lesson was not quite what the author of the story hoped it would be. In battle with the Aramaeans (Syrians), Ahab was seriously wounded, but in order not to discourage his troops, he heroically ordered that he be propped up in his chariot facing the enemy.

---

[5] 1 Kings 21—22; 2 Kings 9. New International Version (NIV). Copyright © 1973, 1978, 1984 by International Bible Society. Used by permission.

All day long the battle raged, and the king was propped up in his chariot facing the Aramaeans. The blood from his wound ran onto the floor of the chariot, and that evening he died. As the sun was setting, a cry spread through the army: "Every man to his town; everyone to his land!" So the king died and was brought to Samaria, and they buried him there. They washed the chariot at a pool in Samaria and the dogs licked up his blood. . . .

Some years after Ahab's death, Jezebel's son Jehoram, now the ruling king of Israel, was murdered in a revolt stirred up by the prophet Elisha. The author of the story notes with satisfaction that Jehoram was killed in the property of Naboth the Jezreelite. The revolt was led by an adventurer named Jehu, who went on to massacre 70 of Ahab's descendants. Their heads were piled, Assyrian fashion, in two heaps at the entry of Samaria; the temple of Baal was turned into a latrine. Cornered, finally, the aging Jezebel prepared for her end and dramatically confronted her enemies with courage and style— and sarcasm.

Then Jehu went to Jezreel. When Jezebel heard about it, she painted her eyes, arranged her hair, and looked out of a window. As Jehu entered the gate, she asked, "Have you come in peace, Zimri [*an assassin who had disposed of the ruling family before Ahab*], you murderer of your master? He looked up at the window and called out, "Who is on my side? Who?" Two or three eunuchs looked down at him. "Throw her down!" Jehu said. So they threw her down, and some of her blood spattered the wall and the horses as they trampled her underfoot. Jehu went in and ate and drank. "Take care of that cursed woman," he said, "and bury her, for she is a king's daughter." But when they went out to bury her, they found nothing except her skull, her feet, and her hands. They went back and told Jehu, who said, "This is the word of the Lord that he spoke through his servant Elijah the Tishbite: On the plot of ground at Jezreel dogs will devour Jezebel's flesh. Jezebel's body will be like refuse on the ground in the plot at Jezreel, so that no one will be able to say, 'This is Jezebel.'"

2.3.4 Athaliah

Although Jezebel perished at the hands of Jehu, her influence continued through her daughter, Athaliah. Raised in Samaria, the capital of the Northern Kingdom (Israel), Athaliah became a zealous devotee of Baal Melkart, the Phoenician god to whom her mother was dedicated. She was married to King Jehoram of the Southern Kingdom, Judah, and wielded considerable influence over him as well as over her son Ahaziah when he became king briefly in 842 B.C. Ahaziah had the misfortune to be visiting his uncle, King Joram of Israel, at the time of Jehu's coup (see previous reading) and was murdered along with him. Athaliah then determined to rule alone in her own right. The reading offers one of the few inside accounts of a palace coup.[6]

When Athaliah, the mother of Ahaziah, saw that her son was dead, she proceeded to destroy the whole royal family. But Jehosheba, the daughter of King Jehoram and sister of Ahaziah, took Joash son of Ahaziah and stole him away from among the royal princes, who were about to be murdered. She put him and his nurse in a bedroom to hide him from Athaliah; so he was not killed. He remained hidden with his nurse at the temple of the Lord for six years while Athaliah ruled the land.

---

[6]2 Kings 11:1–16. NIV.

In the seventh year Jehoiada sent for the commands of units of a hundred, the Carites, and the guards, and had them brought into the temple of the Lord. He made a covenant with them and put them under oath. Then he showed the king's son. He commanded them, saying, "This is what you are to do: You who are in the three companies that are going on duty on the Sabbath—a third of you guarding the royal palace, a third the Sur Gate, and a third at the gate behind the guard, who take turns guarding the temple—and you who are in the other two companies that normally go off Sabbath duty are all to guard the temple for the king. Station yourselves around the king, each man with his weapon in his hand. Anyone who approaches your ranks must be put to death. Stay close to the king wherever he goes.

The commanders did just as Jehoiada the priest ordered. . . . Jehoiada brought out the king's son and put the crown on him; he presented him with a copy of the covenant and proclaimed him king. They anointed him, and the people clapped their hands shouted, "Long live the king!" When Athaliah heard the noise made by the guards and the people, she went to the people at the temple of the Lord. She looked and there was the king standing by the pillar as the custom was. The officers and the trumpeters were beside the king, and all the people of the land were rejoicing and blowing trumpets. Then Athaliah tore her robes and called out, "Treason! Treason!" Jehoiada the priest ordered the commanders, "Bring her out between the ranks and put to the sword anyone who follows her." For the priest had said, "She must not be put to death in the temple of the Lord." So they seized her as she reached the place where the horses enter the palace grounds, and there she was put to death.

2.4   A Critique of Kingship: The Negative View of Samuel

Kingship was clearly central to both Mesopotamia and Egypt, but only secondarily so to Israel. David and Solomon are remembered as ideal kings in the Bible, but most of their successors are summed up in the formula "He did what was evil in the sight of the Lord," repeated throughout the Books of Kings as a kind of summary of the reign of the individual ruler. The monarchy was a late and ambiguous institution in Israel, and only with difficulty inserted into the older, less structured political tradition of the nation. The acceptance of a king, the prophet Samuel warned, would have the effect of making the Israelites just like all the other people around them. It would be interesting to know how widely Samuel's view of monarchy was shared throughout southwest Asia.[7]

Samuel told all the words of the Lord to the people who were asking him for a king. He said, "This is what the king who will reign over you will do: He will take your sons and make them serve with his chariots and horses, and they will run in front of his chariots. Some he will assign to commanders of thousands and commanders of fifties, and others to plow his ground and reap his harvest, and still others to make his weapons of war and equipment for his chariots.

"He will take your daughters to be perfumers and cooks and bakers. He will take the best of your fields and vineyards and olive groves and give them to his attendants. He will take a tenth of your grain and of your vintage and give it to his officials and attendants. Your menservants and maidservants and the best of your cattle and donkeys he will take for his own use.

---

[7]1 Samuel 8:10–21. NIV.

He will take a tenth of your flocks, and you yourselves will become his slaves. When that day comes you will cry out for relief from the king you have chosen, and the Lord will not answer you in that day."

But the people refused to listen to Samuel. "No!" they said. "We want a king over us. Then we will be like all the other nations, with a king to lead us and to go out before us and fight our battles."

2.5   War and Warfare

2.5.1   Sumerian Intercity Wars: Umma versus Lagash

Lagash was one of the great historical city-states of Sumer in southern Mesopotamia. Its rulers were dedicated builders of temples and irrigation canals and promoters of their city's interests. The following text, found in the form of an inscription on two clay cylinders, gives the Lagashite version of one of the endless rounds of disputes with nearby Umma (only 18 miles away). The date is around 2500 B.C., thus centuries before the building activities of Gudea mentioned in Chapter 1. The episode will serve to illustrate a problem inherent in all of Sumerian history: the issue of access to water. Entemena is on the throne, having succeeded his uncle Eannatum, in whose reign began this particular dispute over water rights and over a district known as Guedin. A settlement had been brokered by the ruler of Kish, a certain Mesilim, but it was apparently unsatisfactory to Umma. Here two generations of the dispute are briefly recounted, but it went on for many more.

The translation is extremely literal and follows the word order of the original Sumerian inscription. Ningirsu and Shara are the chief gods of Lagash and Umma, respectively; Enlil is the head of the Sumerian pantheon. Eannatum and Enannatum are brothers and successive rulers of Lagash. Entemena is son of Enannatum. Note the method of destruction—flooding—used by Ili of Umma (see Phase 3). Nearly 1,800 years later the same technique would be used by Sennacherib in his vendetta against Babylon (see later in this chapter).[8]

Phase 1

Enlil, king of the lands, father of the gods—by his immutable word Ningirsu and Shara delimited their lands. Mesilim, King of Kish, at the command of his deity Kadi concerning the plantation of that field set up a stele [*boundary marker*] in that place.

Ush, ruler of Umma, a plan to seize it formed. That stele he broke in pieces, into the plain of Lagash he advanced. Ningirsu, the hero of Enlil, by his just command, upon Umma made war. At the command of Enlil his great net ensnared them. Their burial mound on the plain in that place he erected.

Phase 2

Eannatum, ruler of Lagash, brother of the father of Entemena [*who put up this inscription*] . . . for Enakalli, ruler of Umma, the land delimited. That canal from the great river to Guedin he carried. The field of Ningirsu 210 spans its boundary to the power of Umma he

---

[8]George A. Barton, "Inscriptions of Entemena #7," *The Royal Inscriptions of Sumer and Akkad* (New Haven, CT: Yale University Press, 1929), pp. 61, 63, 65.

opened. The royal field not to seize he ordered. At the canal a stele he inscribed. The stele of Mesilim to its place he returned. On the plain of Mesilim he did not encroach. At the boundary line of Ningirsu, as a protecting structure, the sanctuary of Enlil, the sanctuary of Ninkhursag . . . he built. The grain of Nina [*goddess of Oracles*], the grain of Ningirsu, one storehouse-full the men of Umma by harvesting had eaten; a penalty he caused them to bear. 144,000 *gur*, a great storehouse full they brought. The taking of this grain was not to be repeated in the future.

Urlumma, ruler of Umma, the boundary canal of Ningirsu, the boundary canal of Nina drained; those steles into the fire threw, he broke in pieces; the sanctuaries, the dwellings of the gods, the protecting shrines, the buildings that had been made, he destroyed. As the mountains he was puffed up; over the boundary canal of Ningirsu he crossed. Enannatum, ruler of Lagash, in the field of Ugigga, the irrigated field of Ningirsu, into battle passed. Entemena, the beloved son of Enannatum, completely overthrew him. Urlumma fled. In the midst of Umma he killed him. Of his force, 60 soldiers on the bank of the canal "Meadow-recognized-as-holy-from-the-great-dagger" he left behind. These men—their bones on the plain he left. Mounds for them in five places he heaped up. Then Ili, Priest of Ininni of Esh in Girsu, over Umma as a vassal ruler he established.

Phase 3

Ili, the ruler of Umma, took it into his hand. The boundary canal of Ningirsu, unto the bank of the Tigris above from the banks of Girsu, a great protecting structure of Ningirsu, he drained. The grain of Lagash, a storehouse of 3,600 *gur* he took. Entemena, ruler of Lagash, declared hostilities on Ili, whom for a vassal he had set up. Ili, ruler of Umma, the dyked and irrigated field wickedly flooded; the boundary canal of Ningirsu, the boundary canal of Nina he commanded to ruin. . . . Enlil and Ninkhursag did not permit. Entemena, ruler of Lagash, whose name was spoken by Ningirsu, according to the righteous word of Enlil, according to the righteous word of Nina, their canal from the river Tigris to the great river had constructed, the protecting structure, its foundation he had made of stone . . . its place restored.

2.5.2 Sargon of Akkad: The Idea of Empire

Sargon of Akkad (2334–2279 B.C.) was the first Mesopotamian king to unify successfully all the city-states of Sumer. He boasted that his kingdom stretched from the Persian Gulf to the Mediterranean. The city of Ebla referred to in the inscription has been recently discovered and is in the process of excavation.[9]

For a more systematic (and lyrical) exposition of the ideology of empire, see "To Fill the Vast Land . . ." in a later section of this chapter, the inscription of Sargon II of Assyria.

The god Enlil gave to Sargon the Upper and Lower Sea [*Mediterranean and Persian Gulf*]. Sargon the king bowed down to the god Dagan in Tuttul and prayed. Dagan gave to him the Upper Land [*Syria*]: Mari, Yarmuti, Ebla, as far as the cedar forest and the mountains of shining metal [*Taurus Mountains*]. In his eleventh year Sargon conquered the entire western land. He brought it under one authority. He erected his statues in the west. He brought across the western booty by raft.

---

[9]Grayson and Redford, *Papyrus and Tablet*, p. 94.

2.5.3   Egyptian Imperialism and Terror

In imperial Egypt of the New Kingdom (ca. 1570–1090 B.C.) the king's obligation to defend Egypt against the forces of disorder was transformed into a duty to extend the borders of Egypt and subject foreign lands and their inhabitants to the rule of the god-king of Egypt. This reinterpretation of the relationship between Egypt and its neighbors is expressed in the inscription on the victory stele of Thutmose I (ca. 1511 B.C.) from Tombos in the Sudan. Especially noteworthy are the negative stereotypes of non-Egyptians in this text and the emphasis on gore that anticipates the royal Assyrian inscriptions.[10]

Regnal year 2, 2nd month of Inundation, day 15, under the Majesty of . . . the king of Upper and Lower Egypt 'Akheperkare, given life, the son of Re, Thutmose. . . , being the second year after he was inducted and rose to power as overlord of the Two Lands, to rule what the sun-disc encircles, viz. the Southland and the Northland, from the limits of the "Portions" of the Two Lands; when, at the Union of the Two Lands, he sat upon the throne of Geb, and the crowns and the mighty double diadem were elevated.

Now His Majesty had taken his inheritance and had seated himself upon the dais of Horus in order to extend the frontiers of Thebes, the property of She-who-Faces-Her-Lord, to enslave the dirty ones, the foreigners, and those whom the god detests, the Hau-nebu. . . . The southerners come north and the northerners come south, and all lands together bear their tribute to the Good God, the primordial king, 'Akheperkare, may he live eternally.'

Victorious is Horus, Lord of the Two Lands! He has tied up the. . . (?), their towns are his in utter subservience; the skin-clad (?) people tramp on foot to His Majesty and bow low to Her-that-is-in-his-forehead. He has felled the chief of the Nubians, and the negro withers and chokes in his grasp, for he has taken over the boundaries of his two sides. There was no escape for the recalcitrant ones who had contravened his protection, not one of them was spared; the Nubian bowmen fell to his slaughter and were laid prostrate throughout their lands; their gore inundated their valleys, the mouths of which were worn smooth (?) as with a cloudburst of driving rain. The carrions were overhead, a host of birds, picking and carrying away, and the crocodile fastened himself to the fugitive who had hidden himself from the stout-armed Horus . . . fortress of his entire army, who turns facing the Nine Bows together, like a young panther in a herd at rest. The power of His Majesty blinded them, he who had attained the limits of the earth in its breadth, who had trod its extremities in his victorious might seeking battle, but finding no one who would face him; he who had broken into valleys which the ancestors had not known, and the former wearers of the "Two Ladies" had not seen. His southern boundary is at the forefront of this land [*i.e., Nubia*], his northern at that encircling stream in which the current flows southward [*i.e., the Euphrates*]. Nothing like this happened to former kings! His name has reached the circumference of the sky . . . the oath is taken in his name in all lands, so great is his power! It has not been seen in the annals of past kings since the Followers of Horus.

Breath is granted by him to the one who follows him, his largess goes to him that adheres to his path. Lo, His Majesty is Horus who has seized upon his kingship of millions of years, the islands of the Ocean are subservient to him, and the entire earth is under his feet. . . !

----

[10]Grayson and Redford, *Papyrus and Tablet*, pp. 24–25.

2.5.4   Assyrian Use of Terror

Like other rulers, Assyrian monarchs practiced terror as a matter of state policy (for use of terror in Israel, see "Jezebel" above; for Egypt, the preceding "Egyptian Imperialism and Terror"). The Assyrian approach was, however, more purposeful and systematic. In the first reading we have Sargon II's report of how he put down the revolt of the Northern Kingdom of Israel (721 B.C.) and sacked its capital, Samaria. He casually remarks that he deported 27,280 people but goes on to say he replaced them with new inhabitants, made the city larger, incorporated it into the Assyrian Empire, and restored trade with Egypt. (See "To Fill the Vast Land. . ." for a statement of this monarch's imperial ideals.)

    Babylon, always a thorn in the Assyrian side, was destroyed by Sennacherib (704–681 B.C.) but restored by his successor.

Samaria[11]

The man from Samaria [*King Hosea*], who had conspired with another king hostile to me in order to serve no longer as a tributary king and in order to pay tribute no longer to me, went to war against me. However, thanks to the power of the great gods, my lords, when I fought with them, I carried off 27,280 people along with their chariots and gods, in which they had trusted. I included 200 chariots as part of my royal army. The remainder of them I settled within Assyria. I restored Samaria and made it bigger than before. I settled there people whom I had captured [*in another campaign*]. A eunuch of mine I established as governor over them. I counted them with the Assyrians. . . . I opened the closed trading ports with Egypt and brought together the people of Ashur and Egypt so that they could trade with one another.

Babylon[12]

I swiftly marched to Babylon, which I was intent upon conquering. I blew like the onrush of a hurricane and enveloped the city like a fog. I completely surrounded it and captured it by breaching and scaling the walls. . . I did not spare his mighty warriors, young or old, but filled the city square with their corpses. Shuzubu, king of Babylon, together with his family and officers, I captured alive and took them to my country. I turned over to my men to keep the property of that city, silver, gold, gems—all movable goods. My men took hold of the statues of the gods in the city and smashed them. They took possession of the property of the gods.

    The statues of Adad and Shala, gods of the city Ekallati that Marduk-nadin-ahe, king of Babylonia, had taken to Babylon at the time of Tiglath-pileser I, king of Assyria, I brought out of Babylon after four hundred and eighteen years. I returned them to the city of Ekallati.

    The city and houses I completely destroyed from foundations to roof and set fire to them. I tore down both inner and outer city walls, temples, temple-towers made of brick and clay—as many as there were—and threw everything into the Arahtu canal. I dug a ditch inside the city and thereby levelled off the earth on its site with water. I destroyed even the outline of its foundations. I flattened it more than any flood could have done. In order that the site of that city and its temples would never be remembered, I devastated it with water so that it became a mere meadow.

---

[11]*Prism of Sargon II of Assyria from Nimrud, iv* pp. 24–49, trans. J. Scurlock. By permission.
[12]Grayson and Redford, *Papyrus and Tablet*, p. 110.

2.5.5 The Fall of Jerusalem

Judaea survived the depredations of the Assyrians only to fall victim to their successors, the Babylonians. In 587 B.C. the city was captured and destroyed by Nebuchadnezzar II (604–562 B.C.). Large numbers of its population were transported to Babylon. Unfortunately, we do not have the Babylonian account of this particular event, but we do have the story of the capture of Jerusalem on a previous campaign, in 597 B.C., also by Nebuchadnezzar.[13]

The seventh year (598–597 B.C.): In the month Kislev [*December/January*] the king of Babylonia called up his army, marched to the west, and laid siege to the city of Judah [*i.e., Jerusalem*]. On the second day of the month Adar [*March 16, 597 B.C.*] he took the city. He captured the king [*Jehoiachin*], and a king of his own choice [*Zedekiah*] he appointed in the city. He brought vast tribute to Babylon.

The fate of Jerusalem and of Zedekiah at the end of the second siege is told in the Second Book of Kings.[14]

Now Zedekiah rebelled against the king of Babylon.

So in the ninth year of Zedekiah's reign, on the tenth day of the tenth month, Nebuchadnezzar, king of Babylon, marched against Jerusalem with his whole army. He encamped outside the city and built siege works all around it. The city was kept under siege until the eleventh year of King Zedekiah. By the ninth day of the fourth month the famine in the city had become so severe that there was no food for the people to eat. Then the city wall was broken through, and the whole army fled at night through the gate between the two walls near the king's garden, though the Babylonians were surrounding the city. They fled toward the Arabah, but the Babylonian army pursued the king and overtook him in the plains of Jericho. All his soldiers were separated from him and scattered, and he was captured. He was taken to the king of Babylon at Riblah, where sentence was pronounced on him. They killed the sons of Zedekiah before his eyes. Then they put out his eyes, bound him with bronze shackles and took him to Babylon.

On the seventh day of the fifth month, in the nineteenth year of Nebuchadnezzar, king of Babylon, Nebuzaradan, commander of the imperial guard, an official of the king of Babylon, came to Jerusalem. He set fire to the temple of the Lord, the royal palace and all the houses of Jerusalem. Every important building he burned down. The whole Babylonian army, under the commander of the imperial guard, broke down the walls around Jerusalem. Nebuzaradan, the commander of the guard, carried into exile the people who remained in the city, along with the rest of the populace and those who had gone over to the king of Babylon. But the commander left behind some of the poorest people of the land to work the vineyards and fields.

The Babylonians broke up the bronze pillars, the movable stands and the bronze Sea that were at the temple of the Lord and they carried the bronze to Babylon. They also took away the pots, shovels, wick trimmers, dishes, and all the bronze articles used in the temple service. The commander of the imperial guard took away the censers and sprinkling bowls—all that were made of pure gold or silver.

---

[13]Grayson and Redford, *Papyrus and Tablet*, p. 104.
[14]2 Kings 25. NIV.

The bronze from the two pillars, the Sea and the movable stands, which Solomon had made for the temple of the Lord, was more than could be weighed. Each pillar was twenty-seven feet high. The bronze capital on top of one pillar was four and a half feet high and was decorated with a network and pomegranates of bronze all around. The other pillar, with its network, was similar.

The commander of the guard took as prisoners Seraiah, the chief priest, Zephaniah, the priest next in rank and the three doorkeepers. Of those still in the city, he took the officer in charge of the fighting men and five royal advisers. He also took the secretary who was chief officer in charge of conscripting the people of the land and sixty of his men who were found in the city. Nebuzaradan, the commander, took them all and brought them to the king of Babylon at Riblah. There at Riblah, in the land of Hamath, the king had them executed.

So Judah went into captivity, away from her land.

2.5.6   The Horrors of Siege

When Samaria, capital of Israel, was besieged by Benhadad, king of Syria (ca. 850 B.C., exact date unknown), a woman complained to the Israelite king (not identified) that she had been fooled into making a deal with a neighbor.[15]

As the king of Israel was passing by on the wall, a woman cried to him, "Help me, my Lord, O king!" The king replied, "If the Lord does not help you, where can I get help for you? from the threshing floor? from the wine-press?" Then he asked her, "What's the matter?" She replied, "This woman said to me, 'Give up your son, so that we may eat him today, and tomorrow we'll eat my son.' So we cooked my son, and ate him. The next day I said to her, 'Give up your son, so that we may eat him,' but she had hidden him." When the king heard the woman's words, he tore his robes. . . .

A less drastic alternative was used at Nippur in Sumer when it was under siege by the Assyrians ca. 620 B.C. The following document is a bill of sale dating from that event.[16]

In the third year of Sin-sharra-ishkun, king of Assyria, Nippur was besieged and exit through the gate was impossible. With one shekel of silver one could buy a mere seah of barley [*ten times the normal price*]. . . . People sold their children for silver. Gugalla said to Ninurta-uballit, son of Bel-usatu: "Take my young daughter Rindu and keep her alive. She shall be your maid. Give me six shekels of silver so that I can eat." Ninurta-uballit agreed . . . and took Rindu for six shekels of silver.

2.5.7   POWs and MIAs

Lots of complications attend war. What happens, for instance to a prisoner-of-war's or MIA's wife, children, and property? Some of the following suggest the possibilities in Mesopotamia ca. 1800 B.C., in the time of Hammurapi, king of Babylon. They were sufficiently commonplace to deserve inclusion in that king's great collection of laws. As is usually the case, the drafters of these laws try to think of every eventuality.[17]

---

[15]2 Kings 6. NIV.
[16]Grayson and Redford, *Papyrus and Tablet*, p. 113.
[17]Based on *The Code of Hammurabi, King of Babylon*, trans. Robert Francis Harper (Chicago: University of Chicago Press, 1904), pp. 19–20, 47.

27. If an officer or a constable who is in a garrison of the king is captured, and afterward his field and garden is given to another, and he conducts his business—if the former owner returns and arrives in his city, his field and garden shall be restored to him, and he himself shall conduct his business.

28. If an officer or a constable who is in a fortress of the king is captured and his son is able to conduct the business, the field and the garden shall be given to him and he shall conduct the business of his father.

29. If his son is too young and is not able to conduct the business of his father, they shall give one-third of the field and of the garden to his mother, and his mother shall rear him.

30. If an officer or a constable from the beginning neglects his field, his garden and his house and leaves them uncared for, and another after him takes his field, his garden and his house, and conducts his business for three years; if the former owner returns and desires his field, his garden and his house, they shall not give them to him; he who has taken them and conducted the business shall continue to do so.

134. If a man is captured and there is insufficient maintenance for his wife in his house she may go to another house; that woman has no blame.

135. If a man is captured and there is insufficient maintenance for his wife in his house, and she openly goes to another house and bears children; if later her husband returns and comes back to his city, that woman shall return to her husband and the children shall go to their father.

2.6 "A Palace of Cedar, Cypress, Juniper . . . and Tamarisk": Builders as Well as Destroyers

Despite the emphasis on destruction, we should not forget that the kings were also great builders. To Assyrians, the Assyrian monarchs portrayed themselves as benevolent rulers, shepherds, and fathers of their people, great builders, engineers, and bringers of prosperity. Sennacherib, the destroyer of Babylon, describes himself as "The great king, the mighty king . . . who digs canals, opens wells, runs irrigation ditches, who brings plenty and abundance to the wide acres of Assyria." In the following reading, Ashurnasirpal II (883–859 B.C.), one of the pioneers of Assyrian policies of terror, rebuilds the city of Calah.[18] *See also the inscription of Sargon II, later in this chapter in "To Fill the Vast Land. . . ."*

The former city of Calah [*modern Nimrud*], which Shalmaneser of Assyria, a prince who preceded me, had built—that city had fallen into decay and lay in ruins; it was turned into a mound and ruin heap. That city I built anew, peoples whom my hand had conquered, from the lands which I had subdued, from the land of Suhi, from the land of Laqe, in its entirety, from the city of Sirku on the other side of the Euphrates, from the land of Zamua to its farthest border, from Bit-Adini and the land of Hatte, and of Liburna of the land of Hattini, I took and I settled therein.

I dug a canal from the Upper Zab, and I named it Pati-hegalli. I laid orchards round about it; fruit and wine I offered to Assur, my lord. . . . The ancient mound I removed, I dug down

---

[18]From Daniel David Luckenbill, *The Ancient Records of Assyria and Babylonia*, Vol. 1 (Chicago: University of Chicago Press, 1926), pp. 171–173.

to the water level, 120 courses of bricks I descended into the depth. I built the wall thereof; from its foundation unto its top I built and completed it. . . .

A palace of cedar, cypress, juniper, boxwood, mulberry, pistachio-wood, and tamarisk, for my royal dwelling and for my lordly pleasure for all time I founded therein. Beasts of the mountains and of the seas I fashioned in white limestone, and set them up in its gates. I adorned it; I made it glorious, and put copper nails all around it. Door-leaves of cedar, cypress, juniper, and mulberry I hung in the gates thereof; and silver, gold, lead, copper, and iron, the spoil of my hand from the lands which I had brought under my sway, in great quantities I took and I placed therein.

2.7   An Imperial Coup d'Etat: The Behistun Inscription of Darius I

Inscribed in three languages—Old Persian, Babylonian, and Elamite—on the orders of Darius I (521–486 B.C.) three hundred feet above the ground on the face of a cliff in northern Iran, the Behistun inscription is one of the most important of all ancient documents. Not only did it provide the key to deciphering cuneiform and make possible the recovery of the history of the ancient Near East, but it also is the principal source for understanding the ideology of the Persian Empire, the last and greatest of the ancient Near Eastern empires. Darius I recounts in it how Ahurimazda, the Zoroastrian god of light and truth, entrusted to him rule over an enormous empire that stretched from the coast of Turkey (Ionia) in the west to the borders of India in the east (Gandara), and from Egypt in the south to the Russian steppes in the north (Saca), and enabled him to suppress the forces of evil and the "lie" represented by the false king Gomates, a story known also from the Greek historian Herodotus. Ironically, most historians now believe that despite Darius's repeated professions of "truthfulness," the Behistun inscription actually represents propaganda on the part of Darius and his allies justifying their rebellion against the family of Cyrus I.[19]

1. I am Darius, the great king, the king of kings, the king of Persia, the king of the provinces, the son of Hystaspes, the grandson of Arsames, the Achaemenian.

2. Says Darius the king—My father was Hystaspes; the father of Hystaspes was Arsames; the father of Arsames was Ariaramnes; the father of Ariaramnes was Teispes; the father of Teispes was Achaemenes.

3. Says Darius the king—On that account we have been called Achaemenians; from antiquity we have descended; from antiquity our family have been kings.

4. Says Darius the king—There are eight of my race who have been kings before me; I am the ninth; nine of us have been kings in succession.

5. Says Darius the king—By the grace of Ahurimazda I am King; Ahurimazda has granted me the empire.

6. Says Darius the king—These are the countries which have come to me; by the grace of Ahurirmazda I have become king of them: Persia, Susiana, Babylonia, Assyria, Arabia, Egypt, those which are of the sea, Sparda, Ionia, Media, Armenia, Cappadocia, Parthia, Zarangia, Aria, Chorasmia, Bactria, Sogdiana, Gandara, Saca, Thatagush, Arachosia, and Maka; in all twenty-three provinces.

---

[19]"The Behistun Inscription of Darius I" Column 1, 1–14, based on the translation of Henry Rawlinson. From Francis R. B. Godolphin, *The Greek Historians*, Vol. 2 (New York: Random House, 1942) pp. 623–625.

7. Says Darius the king—These are the provinces which have come to me; by the grace of Ahurimazda they have become subject to me; they have brought tribute to me. That which has been said to them by me, both by night and by day, it has been done by them.

8. Says Darius the king—Within these countries, the man who was good, him I have right well cherished. Whoever was evil, him have I utterly rooted out. By the grace of Ahurimazda, these are the countries by whom my laws have been observed. As it has been said to them by me, so by them it has been done.

9. Says Darius the king—Ahurimazda granted me the empire. Ahurimazda brought help to me, so that I gained this empire. By the grace of Ahurimazda I hold this empire.

10. Says Darius the king—This is what was done by me after that I became king. A man named Cambyses, son of Cyrus, of our race, he was here king before me. Of that Cambyses there was a brother, Bardes was his name; of the same mother, and of the same father with Cambyses. Afterwards Cambyses slew that Bardes. When Cambyses had slain Bardes, it was not known to the people that Bardes had been slain. Afterwards Cambyses proceeded to Egypt. When Cambyses had proceeded to Egypt, then the state became wicked. Then the lie became abounding in the land, both in Persia, and in Media, and in the other provinces.

11. Says Darius the king—Afterwards there was a certain man, a Magian, named Gomates. He arose from Pissiachada, the mountain named Aracadres, from thence. On the fourteenth day of the month Vayakhna, then it was that he arose. He thus lied to the state, "I am Bardes, the son of Cyrus, the brother of Cambyses." Then the whole state became rebellious. From Cambyses it went over to him, both Persia, and Media, and the other provinces. He seized the empire. On the ninth day of the month Garmapada, then it was he so seized the empire. Afterwards Cambyses, unable to endure, died.

12. Says Darius the king—The empire of which Gomates, the Magian, dispossessed Cambyses, that empire from the olden time had been in our family. After Gomates the Magian had dispossessed Cambyses both of Persia and Media and the dependent provinces, he did according to his desire: he became king.

13. Says Darius the king—There was not a man, neither Persian, nor Median, nor any one of our family, who would dispossess that Gomates, the Magian, of the crown. The state feared him exceedingly. He slew many people who had known the old Bardes; for that reason he slew them. "Lest they should recognize me that I am not Bardes, the son of Cyrus." No one dared to say anything concerning Gomates, the Magian, until I arrived. Then I prayed to Ahurimazda; Ahurimazda brought help to me. On the tenth day of the month Bagayadish, then it was, with my faithful men, I slew that Gomates, the Magian, and those who were his chief followers. The fort named Sictachotes in the district of Media called Nisaea, there I slew him. I dispossessed him of the empire. By the grace of Ahurimazda I became king: Ahurimazda granted me the scepter.

14. Says Darius the king—The empire which had been taken away from our family, that I recovered. I established it in its place. As it was before, so I made it. The temples which Gomates, the Magian, had destroyed, I rebuilt. The sacred offices of the state, both the religious chants and the worship, I restored to the people, which Gomates, the Magian, had deprived them of. I established the state in its place, both Persia, and Media, and the other provinces. As it was before, so I restored what had been taken away. By the grace of Ahurimazda I did this. I arranged so that I established our family in its place. As it was before, so I arranged it, by the grace of Ahurimazda, so that Gomates, the Magian, should not supersede our family.

2.8   "That the Strong Might not Oppress the Weak, and that they Should Give Justice to Orphans and Widows"

The primary function of pharaohs and kings alike was, at a minimum, to defend their country and, if possible, enrich it. A second role, or perhaps better, a concomitant role for the king, was that of bringer or maintainer of order and justice. In the Sumerian formula, kings were supposed to be the sustainers of Misharum *and* Kittum. *The former term meant "justice" or "law", while* Kittum *was broader, something like "law and order" (similar to Egyptian* Ma'at*). In a sense this dual function was the king's basic domestic policy. Hammurapi of Babylon published a collection (not a code) of laws during his reign, of which parts of the prologue and epilogue are given below. His collection, although more systematic than any known prior one, is by no means the first publication of laws for Mesopotamia. For centuries, the city-states of Mesopotamia had developed their own collection of laws, mostly actually precedents and some royal decrees, and there grew up a common customary law throughout the region. It was from this general source that Hammurapi drew his collection. The tradition that kings were supposed to sustain justice was a constant in Mesopotamia history.*[20]

2.8.1   Hammurapi's Justice

Prologue

At that time Anu and Bel called me, Hammurapi . . . to cause justice to prevail in the land, to destroy the wicked and evil, to prevent the strong from oppressing the weak, to go forth like the Sun over the Black-Headed Race [*traditional name for the Sumerians*], to enlighten the land. . . . When Marduk [*chief god of Babylon*] sent me to give justice to the people and let them have good rule, I established truth and justice [*Kittum* and *Misharum*] in the land and promoted the welfare of the people. . . .

Epilogue

The great gods called me and I am indeed the shepherd who brings peace, whose scepter is just and whose beneficent protection is spread over my city. In my bosom I carried the people of the land of Sumer and Akkad; under my protection I brought their brethren into security; in my wisdom I hid them.

That the strong might not oppress the weak, and that they should give justice to the orphan and the widow I have inscribed my words upon my monument and established them in the presence of my statue, "King of Justice," in Babylon. . . .

These are the just laws which Hammurapi, the wise king, established and by which he gave the land stable support and good government. . . . Let any oppressed man who has a case come before my image, "King of Justice." Let him read the inscription on my monument! Let him give heed to my weighty words! And may my monument enlighten him as to his case and may he understand his case! May he set his heart at ease! And let him exclaim: "Hammurapi indeed is a ruler who is like a real father to his people." . . . Let him read my words and pray with a full heart before Marduk, my Lord, and Zarpanit, my Lady, and may the protecting deities, the gods who enter Esagila [*the great temple of Marduk at Babylon*], daily in the midst of Esagila, look with favor on his wishes. . . .

---

[20]Based on *The Code of Hammurabi*, trans. Harper, pp. 3–9, 99–103.

In the days that are yet to come, for all future time, may the king who is in the land observe the words of justice which I have written upon my monument! May he not alter the judgments of the land which I have pronounced, or the decisions of the country that I have rendered. May he not efface my statutes! If that man have wisdom, if he wish to give his land government, let him give attention to the words which I have written upon my monument! And may this monument enlighten him as to procedure and administration, the judgments which I have pronounced, and the decisions which I have rendered for the land! Let him justly rule the Black-Headed people. Let him pronounce judgments for them and render for them decisions! Let him root out the wicked and the evildoer from the land! Let him promote the welfare of his people!

In this reading, dating from over a thousand years later, Sargon II of Assyria (721–705 B.C.) expresses himself lyrically on the role of kings as builders and maintainers of justice.[21]

2.8.2 "To Fill the Vast Land with a Plenitude of Food and Lasting Happiness: The Characteristics of a Perfect Kingship"

Sargon, governor for Enlil, ruler for the god Ashur, chosen by Anu and Dagan, the great king, the mighty king . . . king of Assyria, king of the four quarters . . . , who established an exemption from taxes and military service for Sippar, Nippur and Babylon [*cities of Babylonia*] and protected them in their weakness, made good their damages, who reinstituted the interrupted privileges of the city of Ashur [*former capital of Assyria*], abolished the work duties of Der [*an Assyrian fortress between Babylonia and Elam*] and brought relief to its inhabitants; the ablest among all the kings, who extended his protection over Harran [*a city in northern Syria*] . . . the mighty man, clad in splendor, whose armies when sent out cause the enemy's downfall, who appoints his own eunuchs as governors over them and who imposes taxes on them just as for the Assyrians. . . .

[T]he very able king, full of good thoughts, who was concerned with repopulating abandoned regions, cultivating abandoned land, planting orchards on steep mountains where no crop had ever sprouted; he thought of having these grow and produce a crop. He also conceived the idea of drawing furrows in the wasteland and letting the harvesters sing the work song, of opening up springs into catchment basins in the meadows and of letting the abundance of water irrigate above and below . . . to fill the vast land of Assyria [*thanks to wells*] with a plenitude of food and lasting happiness, the characteristics of a perfect kingship, to save all mankind from hunger and starvation, so that not even the poor would be employed in carrying the grape-harvest, so as not to interrupt the gifts for the sick, so as to keep oil, . . . the only means for making tired muscles relax, cheap, so as to have linseed as cheap as barley in the market. . . .

[*I planned the construction of a new city, Dur-Sharruken*] . . . As befitting the meaning of my name, which the great gods have bestowed upon me [*Sargon means "just king"*], that is, in order to protect righteousness and justice, to guide well the disabled, and not to oppress the weak—I reimbursed the owners of the fields [*confiscated to build the town*] with silver or bronze according to the value shown in their deeds of sale, and in order not to create bad feeling in those who did not want to take silver, I gave these people fields corresponding to their former fields, wherever they wanted to have them.

---

[21]From the Barrell Cylinder of Sargon II from Khorsabad, trans. J. Scurlock. By permission.

2.8.3   The Justice of the Pharaoh

Few legal documents have survived in Egypt. The ideology of the divine king precluded the existence of law codes such as those known from Mesopotamia, since the king's word itself was law, and the fragility of papyrus, the chief writing material used by the Egyptians, inevitably limited the survival of documents of all types. Nevertheless, the maintenance of Ma'at, *justice, in Egypt was one of the chief duties of the king, as is clear from the speech of instruction addressed to the vizier, the chief legal officer of Egypt, upon his taking office.*[22]

Then said His Majesty to him: "Watch over the office of vizier and be vigilant concerning everything that is done in it. Lo, it is the king-pin of the entire land. Lo, as for the vizierate, it is not at all pleasant, but bitter. . . . It is the bronze in a wall of gold to the house of its master. Lo, he is one who should not show favoritism to officials or councilors, nor make chattels of any people. . . . So you must yourself see to it that everything is done in accordance with what is in the law and that everything is done exactly so. . . . Lo, as for the official who is in the public eye, water and wind report on all that he does, and lo, what he does is not unknown. Indeed, if a wrong comes about which he perpetrated upon another official for his wrong, that he should not induct him on the word of a functionary, it will become known at the publication of his decision through his saying it in the presence of the functionary in question. . . . What he does cannot be ignored. Lo, the refuge of the official is the performance of things in accordance with instructions. . . . Now this is teaching, and may you act accordingly. Regard the man whom you know the same way as the man whom you do not know, the one who has access to you like the one who lives far from your house. Lo, as for the official who acts like this, he flourishes here in this place. Do not pass over a petitioner before you have given his plea a hearing. If there be a petitioner who petitions you, do not mete out punishment simply on what he has to say; but punish him only when you have informed him about what you are punishing him for. . . . Do not get angry with a man over nothing, but get angry over the thing which should provoke anger. Display your fear-inspiring qualities and you will be feared. The real official is the official who is feared. Lo, the dignity of the official is the performance of *ma'at*. Lo, even if a man displays his fear-inspiring qualities a millionfold, and there be in him an element of injustice that people know about, then they do not say of him "he is a gentleman!" . . . Lo, may you strive to perform your office, and to perform it justly. Lo, what is wanted in the conduct of a vizier is the performance of *ma'at*."

2.8.4   "They Carry the Sheaves, but Still Go Hungry; They Tread the Winepresses, yet Suffer Thirst"

The proclamations of the pharaohs and kings are impressive as declarations of what they would like to happen, but for a pessimistic picture of life we turn to the well-known but difficult Book of Job *in the Bible. A classic of Hebrew thought and poetry, it contains one of the best descriptions from western Asia of the kinds of injustice that were undoubtedly commonplace from the Persian Gulf to Egypt—and beyond. The description of the homeless is timeless, as are the words used to describe the malnourished and exploited: "They carry the sheaves, but still go hungry; they tread the winepresses, yet suffer thirst."* Job

---

[22]Grayson and Redford, *Tablet and Papyrus*, p. 7.

also deals (unsympathetically and unsentimentally) with the criminal class: those who operate only at night, for whom "deep darkness is their morning."[23]

> Why does the Almighty not set times for judgment?
>   Why must those who know him look in vain for such days?
> Men move boundary stones;
>   they pasture flocks they have stolen.
> They drive away the orphan's donkey
>   and take the widow's ox in pledge.
> They thrust the needy from the path
>   and force all the poor of the land into hiding.
> Like wild donkeys in the desert,
>   the poor go about their labor of foraging food;
>   the wasteland provides food for their children.
> They gather fodder in the fields
>   and glean in the vineyards of the wicked.
> Lacking clothes, they spend the night naked;
>   they have nothing to cover themselves in the cold.
> They are drenched by mountain rains
>   and hug the rocks for lack of shelter.
> The fatherless child is snatched from the breast;
>   the infant of the poor is seized for a debt.
> Lacking clothes, they go about naked;
>   they carry the sheaves, but still go hungry.
> They crush olives among the terraces;
>   they tread the winepresses, yet suffer thirst.
> The groans of the dying rise from the city,
>   and the souls of the wounded cry out for help.
>   But God charges no one with wrongdoing.
>
> There are those who rebel against the light,
>   who do not know its ways or do not stay in its paths.
> When daylight is gone, the murderer rises up
>   and kills the poor and needy;
>   in the night he steals forth like a thief.
> The eye of the adulterer watches for the dusk;
>   he thinks, "No eye will see me,"
>   and he keeps his face concealed.
> In the dark, men break into houses,
>   but by day they shut themselves in;
>   they want nothing to do with the light.
> For all of them, deep darkness is their morning;
>   they make friends with the terrors of darkness.

---

[23]Job 24:1–17. NIV.

2.8.5   A Model Persian Governor: Cyrus the Younger (Ca. 400 B.C.)

The Persian Empire was ruled by an aristocracy educated, according to the Greek historian Herodotus, to do three things: ride, draw a bow, and tell the truth. These values are clearly visible in the eulogy by the Greek historian Xenophon of Cyrus the Younger, who governed western Asian Minor in the last decade of the fifth century B.C. before unsuccessfully rebelling against his brother Artaxerxes II (405–359 B.C.). Xenophon also clearly illustrates the use by the Persians of public spectacle, whether in the form of rewards or punishment, to convey social and political messages and influence behavior.[24]

So died Cyrus, a man the kingliest and most worthy to rule all the Persians who have lived since the elder Cyrus, according to the concurrent testimony of all who are reputed to have known him intimately. To begin from the beginning, when he was still a boy, and while being brought up with his brother and the other lads, his unrivalled excellence was recognized. For the sons of the noblest Persians, it must be known, are brought up, one and all, at the king's court. Here lessons of sobriety and self-control may be learned, while there is nothing base to see or hear. There is the daily spectacle ever before the boy of some receiving honor from the king, and again of others receiving dishonor; and the tale of all this is in their ears, so that from earliest boyhood they learn how to rule and to be ruled.

In this training, Cyrus was held to be first a paragon of modesty among his fellows, rendering an obedience to his elders which exceeded that of many of his own inferiors; and next he bore away the palm for skill in horsemanship and for love of the animal itself. Likewise in matters of war, in the use of the bow and the javelin, he was held by men in general to be at once the aptest of learners and the most eager practitioner. As soon as his age permitted, the same pre-eminence showed itself in his fondness for the chase. He did not lack a certain appetite for perilous adventure in facing the wild beasts themselves. Once a bear made a furious rush at him, and without wincing, he grappled with her. He was pulled from his horse, receiving wounds, the scars of which were visible through life; but in the end he slew the creature, nor did he forget him who first came to his aid, but made him enviable in the eyes of many.

After he had been sent down by his father to be satrap of Lydia and Great Phrygia and Cappadocia, and had been appointed general of the forces, whose business it is to muster in the plain of the Castolus, nothing was more noticeable in his conduct than the importance which he attached to the faithful fulfillment of every treaty or compact or undertaking entered into with others. He would tell lies to no one. This was doubtless why he won the confidence alike of individuals and of the communities entrusted to his care. In case of hostility, a treaty made with Cyrus was a guarantee sufficient to the combatant that he would suffer nothing contrary to its terms. Therefore, in the war with Tissaphernes, all the states of their own accord chose Cyrus rather than Tissaphernes, except only the men of Miletus, and these were only alienated through fear of him, because he refused to abandon their exiled citizens. His deeds and words bore emphatic witness to his principle. Even if they were weakened in number or in fortune, he would never abandon those who had once become his friends.

He made no secret of his endeavor to outdo his friends and his foes alike in reciprocity of conduct. The prayer has been attributed to him, "God grant I may live long enough to recompense my friends and requite my foes with a strong arm." However this may be, no one, at

---

[24]Xenophon, Anabasis 1.99, Trans. by Henry G. Dakyns from Francis R. B. Godolphin, *The Greek Historians* (New York: Random House, 1942), Vol. 2, pp. 244–245.

least in our days, ever drew together so ardent a following of friends, eager to lay at his feet their money, their cities, their own lives and persons. It is not to be inferred from this that he suffered the malefactor and the wrongdoer to laugh him to scorn; on the contrary, these he punished most unflinchingly. It was no rare sight to see on the well-trodden highways, men who had forfeited hand or foot or eye. The result was that throughout the satrapy of Cyrus any one, Greek or barbarian, provided he were innocent, might fearlessly travel wherever he pleased, and take with him whatever he wished. However, as all allowed, it was for the brave in war that he reserved especial honor. To take the first instance to hand, he had a war with the Pisidians and Mysians. Being himself at the head of an expedition into those territories, he could observe those who voluntarily encountered risk. He made these men rulers of the territory, which he subjected, and afterwards honored them with other gifts. So that, if the good and brave were set on a pinnacle of fortune, cowards were recognized as their natural slaves; and so it happened that Cyrus never had lack of volunteers in any service of danger, whenever it was expected that his eye would be upon them.

Chapter 3

⋎⋎⋎

Daily Life

One of the most accessible sources for information on daily life in Mesopotamia is the law codes. In particular the collection of laws know as the *Code of Hammurapi* provides a good deal of understanding of Mesopotamian society. *Papyrus Lansing*, a document praising the life of the government bureaucrat, offers insight into the daily life of Egypt, but from a different perspective. The story of Ruth from the Hebrew Scriptures is one of the few nonlegal, noncommercial documents from ancient times that shows what life at the level of village society was like.

Babylonian society of Hammurapi's day (ca. 1800 B.C.) was divided by status: There were those who possessed full citizenship; those who were in some way dependent on some institution, such as the temple or the palace; and slaves. Punishment for offences varied with one's status, though even slaves had rights and received some protection under the law. The laws covered a great variety of subjects. Consumers were protected against faulty products and workmanship (#233); tavern life was regulated, watering of beer being specifically mentioned (#108,109). Crime could be punished severely if the recommendations of the laws were actually followed. Take, for example, the crime of burglary. A burglar could easily break into a house by breaking through the mudbrick walls between houses, but a burglar caught in the act was to be killed on the spot, thrown into the hole he had made, and walled up (#21)! Medical practice was hazardous for both patient and practitioner: If a physician opens an abcess in a man's eye and blinds the man, his fingers shall be cut off (#218). What could happen in bad economic times is hinted at: Wives and children could be sold off to pay debts (#117).

Women, especially married women, received a lot of attention, as did children, especially where property was involved. Under what circumstances was it possible to disinherit one's children (#168, 191)? How were widows to be protected against their predatory children (#150)? Great complications could arise because of the toleration of mistresses (#117, 137, 170, 171). Naturally, many of the pronouncements of the code have to do with agricultural life, the economic foundation of all ancient societies. There are, for instance, regulations regarding animals, tenancies, rent, and irrigation (#53, 54).

Overall, Mesopotamian law aimed at a kind of general fairness combined with toughness. It was one thing, for instance, to steal an item from a temple precinct; the punishment for this was savage, since the crime involved sacrilege and therefore danger to the community. It was another thing, however, to steal property that belonged to the temple but was not *in* the temple itself, although the penalty was still stiff: thirtyfold restitution.

From an entirely different perspective, the praise of bureaucrats in *Papyrus Lansing* offers insight into Egyptian daily life. With tongue wedged firmly in cheek, the author checks off and dismisses all occupations except those of the professional bureaucrat, whose job "is worth more than an inheritance" and is more "pleasing than wine." Occupations involving manual labor such as farming make easy targets. The satire on the military is interesting in that it suggests the essentially unmilitary character of Egyptian culture. Another message that comes through with equal clarity from the same satire is the smug, isolationist, xenophobic attitude of Egypt's ruling classes.

3.1   Marriage and Property

From the viewpoint of ancient society, marriage served the essential purposes of producing and identifying legitimate children (and potential heirs), and making possible the orderly transmission of property from one generation to the next, not to mention the not always certain perpetuation of the society itself. Another aspect of marriage was political: Marriages were used as a way of creating useful alliances between families for mutual assistance. In a world where governmental protection of the individual was minimal, it was essential to have the support of as strong a family as possible. Self-help was a necessity in all ancient societies; hence, the more children, especially male, the better. This view is expressed well in the Bible: "Like arrows in the hands of a warrior are sons born in one's youth. Blessed is the man whose quiver is full of them. They will not be put to shame when they contend with their enemies in the gate."[1] *These unsentimental views of children and marriage predominate in the ancient law codes and seem at odds with modern models of affectionate, compassionate marriage. It should be pointed out that the law emphasized the interests of society rather than of the individual, and the codes should not be interpreted to mean loving marriages did not exist.*[2] *For a more romantic view of marriage and daily life, see the Book of Ruth from the Hebrew Scriptures at the end of this chapter.*

159. If a man who has brought a betrothal present to the house of his father-in-law and has paid the marriage settlement falls in love with another woman and says to his father-in-law, "I will not take your daughter," the father of the daughter shall keep for himself whatever present was brought to him.

160. If a man brings a betrothal present to the house of his father-in-law and has paid the marriage settlement, and the father of the daughter says, "I will not give you my daughter," he [*the father-in-law*] must double the amount which was brought to him and return it.

162. If a man takes a wife and she bears him children and then dies, her father may not claim her dowry. Her dowry belongs to her children.

163. If a man takes a wife and she does not present him with children and dies, then if his father-in-law returns to him the marriage settlement which he brought to the house of his

---

[1]Psalm 127:3–5. New International Version (NIV). Copyright © 1973, 1978, 1984 by International Bible Society. Used by permission.
[2]From *The Code of Hammurabi, King of Babylon*, trans. Robert Francis Harper, (Chicago: University of Chicago Press), 1904, pp. 11–97, passim.

father-in-law, he [*the widower*] may not claim the dowry of that woman. Her dowry belongs to the house of her father.

164. If the man's father-in-law does not return to him the marriage settlement, he [*the widower*] may deduct from his wife's dowry the amount of the marriage settlement and return the rest of her dowry to the house of her father.

165. If a man gives a field, garden, or house to his favorite son and has drawn it up in the form of a sealed deed, then, after the father dies, when the brothers divide property, he [*the favorite son*] shall keep the present the father gave him, but otherwise they shall divide the goods of their father's house equally.

166. If a man takes wives for his sons but does not take a wife for his youngest son, after the father dies, when the brothers divide the property, they shall give from the goods of the father's house to their youngest brother, who has not taken a wife, money for a marriage settlement in addition to his portion, and thus enabling him to take a wife.

167. If a man takes a wife and she bears him children and she then dies, and after her death he takes another wife, and she bears him children and later the father dies, the children of the mothers shall not divide the estate. They shall receive the dowries of their respective mothers and they shall divide equally the goods of the house of the father.

168. If a man decides to disinherit his son and says to the judges, "I will disinherit my son," the judges shall inquire into the facts of the case, and if the son has not committed a crime sufficiently grave to be disinherited, the father may not disinherit him.

191. If a man who has taken a young child as his son and reared him, but after establishing his own house and acquiring children, then plans to cut off the adopted son, that son shall not go away destitute. The father who reared him shall give him one third of his inheritance when he leaves; but he shall not give him part of a field, garden, or house.

3.2   Marriage and Children

Most ancient societies took the view that families were immortal entities, fixed and essential units of the states to which they belonged. Their perpetuation was therefore a matter of public business, not the purely private affair it seems to be in modern societies. For example, there was a great deal of public pressure on individuals, especially heirs, to see that family names were perpetuated and the family property protected. When a marriage was barren, divorce was one possibility, but when the heirs or husbands died, then other steps had to be taken to ensure that the family continued (see the story of Ruth in this chapter). There was also the problem of identifying legitimate heirs, a special complication in a society where slavery was common. Poverty or war could create other kinds of problems (see Chapter 2, "POWs and MIAs").

137. If a man decides to divorce a concubine [*a mistress*] who has borne him children, or a wife who has presented him with children, he must return to that woman her dowry and give her the income of field, garden, and goods and she shall bring up her children; from the time that her children are grown up, from whatever is given to her children they shall give to her a portion corresponding to that of a son, and the man of her choice may marry her.

138. If a man would divorce his wife who has not borne him children, he shall give her money to the amount of her marriage settlement and he shall make good to her the dowry which she brought from her father's house; then he may divorce her.

142. If a woman hates her husband and says, "You shalt not have me," they shall inquire into her case for her defects; and if she has been a careful household manager and is without reproach, while her husband has been going about disparaging her, that woman is without blame. She shall receive her dowry and shall go to her father's house.

143. If she has not been a careful household manager, but has gadded about, neglected her house, and disparaged her husband, they shall throw that woman into the water.

170. If a man's wife bears him children and his female slave bears him children, and the father during his lifetime says to the children which the slave woman bore him, "You are my children," and reckon them with the children of his wife, after the father dies the children of the wife and the children of the slave woman shall divide the goods of the father's house equally. The child of the wife shall have the right of choice at the division.

171. But if the father during his lifetime has not said to the children which the female slave bore him, "You are my children," after the father dies, the children of the slave woman shall not share in the goods of the father's house with the children of the wife. The slave woman and her children shall be given their freedom. The children of the wife may not lay claim to the children of the slave woman for service [*i.e., turn them into slaves*]. The wife shall receive her dowry and the settlement which her husband made for her and deeded to her in writing on a tablet, and she may dwell in the house of her husband and enjoy the property as long as she lives. She cannot sell it, however, for after her death it belongs to her children.

172. If her husband shall not have made a settlement on her, they shall make good her dowry and she shall receive from the goods of her husband's house a portion corresponding to that of a son. If her children scheme to drive her out of the house, the judges shall inquire into the facts of the case and if the children be in the wrong, she shall not go out from her husband's house. If the woman wishes to leave, she shall leave to her children the settlement which her husband made for her; she shall receive the dowry of her father's house, and the husband of her choice may marry her.

150. If a man gives to his wife field, garden, house or goods and has executed this arrangement in writing, after the death of her husband her children cannot make claims against her. The mother after her death may will the estate to her children whom she loves, but she may not deed it to a stranger.

3.3   Laws Regarding Sex

Status was always a key question in the ancient world when it came to legitimate sex. Were the parties involved free, dependent, or slave; married or unmarried? Generally, sex with or among full citizens was more carefully regulated than sex between free and unfree people. Property and its proper transmission lurked in the background as a complicating issue.

129. If the wife of a man has been caught in bed with another man, they shall bind them both and throw them into the water. If the husband of the woman wishes to spare his wife, then the king may save his servant.

130. If a man force himself on the betrothed wife of another who has not known a male and is living in her father's house, and he lie in her bosom, and they catch him, that man shall be put to death and the woman shall go free.

131. If a man accuse his wife and she has not been caught lying with another man, she shall take an oath in the name of god and shall return to her house.

153. If a woman brings about the death of her husband for the sake of another man, they shall impale her.

154. If a man has intercourse with his daughter, they shall expel that man from the city.

155. If a man have betrothed a bride to his son and his son has intercourse with her, and if he [*the father*] afterward lie in her bosom and they catch him, they shall bind that man and throw him into the water.

157. If a man lie in the bosom of his mother after the death of his father, they shall burn both of them.

3.4   Disputes, Litigation, Punishment

3.4.1   Runaway Slaves

15. If a man aids a male or female slave of the palace, or a male or female slave of a freedman to escape from the city gate, he shall be put to death.

16. If a man harbors in his house a male or female slave who has fled from the palace or from a freeman, and does not bring out the slave at the demand of the police, the owner of the house shall be put to death.

17. If a man seize a fugitive male or female slave in the field and bring that slave back to his owner, the owner of the slave shall pay him two shekels of silver.

18. If the fugitive slave will not identify his owner, he [*the man who caught him*] shall bring him to the palace and they shall inquire into his case and they shall return him to his owner.

226. If a brander, without the consent of the owner of the slave, brand a slave with the sign that he cannot be sold, they shall cut off the fingers of that brander.

3.4.2   Crime and Punishment

21. If a man make a breach in a house [*i.e., has broken through the mudbrick wall*], they shall put him to death in front of that breach and wall him up.

22. If a man commits robbery and is caught, that man shall be put to death.

23. If the robber is not captured, the man who has been robbed shall, in the presence of god, make an itemized statement of his loss, and the city and the governor in whose province and jurisdiction the robbery was committed shall compensate him for whatever was lost.

25. If a fire break out in a man's house and a man who goes to extinguish it cast his eye on the furniture of the owner of the house, and takes the furniture of the owner of the house, that man shall be thrown into that fire.

3.4.3   Conducting Business

104. If a merchant gives an agent grain, wool, oil, or goods of any kind with which to trade, the agent shall record the money obtained for them and reimburse the merchant. The agent shall take a sealed receipt for the money which he gives to the merchant.

105. If the agent is careless and does not take a receipt for the money which he has given to the merchant, the money not recorded shall not be credited to his account.

108. If a wine seller refuses grain as the price of drink but accepts money instead, or if she makes the measure for drink smaller than the measure for grain, they shall convict her and throw her in the water.

109. If outlaws gather in the house of a wine seller, and she does not arrest them and bring them to the palace, she shall be put to death.

120. If a man stores his grain in bins in the house of another and an accident happens to the granary, or the owner of the house opens a bin and takes grain, or he raises a dispute about the grain, or denies the amount which was stored in his house, the owner of the grain shall declare his grain in the presence of god, and the owner of the house shall double the amount of grain which he took and restore it to the owner of the grain.

64. If a man gives his orchard to a gardener to manage, the gardener shall give to the owner of the orchard two-thirds of the produce of the orchard, as long as he is in possession of the orchard; he himself shall take one-third.

65. If the gardener does not properly manage the orchard and he diminishes the produce, the gardener shall measure out the produce of the orchard on the basis of the adjacent orchards.

3.4.4   Negligence

53. If a man neglects to strengthen his dyke and does not strengthen it, and a break occurs in his dyke and the water damages the farmland, the man in whose dyke the break has been made shall restore the grain which he has damaged.

54. If he is not able to restore the grain, they shall sell him and his goods, and the farmers whose grain the water has carried away shall share the results of the sale.

218. If a physician operates on a man for a severe wound with a bronze lancet and causes the man's death; or opens an abscess in the eye of a man with a bronze lancet and destroys the man's eye, they shall cut off his [*the physician's*] fingers.

233. If a builder builds a house for a man and its construction does not meet the requirements, and a wall cracks, that builder shall strengthen that wall at his own expense.

235. If a man hires his boat to a boatman and the boatman is careless and sinks or wrecks the boat, the boatman shall replace the boat to the owner of the boat.

237. If a man hires a boatman and a boat and loads it with grain, wool, oil, dates, or any other kind of freight, and that boatman is careless and sinks the boat or wrecks its cargo, the boatman shall replace the boat which he sank and whatever portion of the cargo he wrecked.

3.4.5   Debt

117. If a man is in debt and sells his wife, son, or daughter, or binds them over to service, they shall work for three years in the house of their purchaser or master; the fourth year they shall be given their freedom.

119. If a man is in debt and he sells his female slave who has borne him children, the owner of the female slave [*i.e., the man in debt*] shall repay the money which the merchant paid him, and he shall ransom his maid servant.

3.5   Papyrus Lansing: A Bureaucrat's View of Life[3]

Title

[Beginning of the instruction in letter-writing made by the royal scribe and chief overseer of the cattle of Amen-Re, King of Gods, Nebmare-nakht] for his apprentice, the scribe Wenemdiamun.

Praise of the Scribe's Profession

[The royal scribe] and chief overseer of the cattle of Amen-[Re, King of Gods. Nebmare-nakht speaks to the scribe Wenemdiamun]. [Apply yourself to this] noble profession. . . . You will find it useful. . . . You will be advanced by your superiors. You will be sent on a mission. . . . Love writing, shun dancing; then you become a worthy official. Do not long for the marsh thicket. Turn your back on throw stick and chase. By day write with your fingers; recite by night. Befriend the scroll, the palette. It pleases more than wine. Writing for him who knows it is better than all other professions. It pleases more than bread and beer, more than clothing and ointment. It is worth more than an inheritance in Egypt, than a tomb in the west.

Advice to the Unwilling Pupil

Young fellow, how conceited you are! You do not listen when I speak. Your heart is denser than a great obelisk, a hundred cubits high, ten cubits thick. When it is finished and ready for loading, many work gangs draw it. It hears the words of men; it is loaded on a barge. Departing from Yebu it is conveyed, until it comes to rest on its place in Thebes.

So also a cow is bought this year, and it plows the following year. It learns to listen to the herdsman; it only lacks words. Horses brought from the field, they forget their mothers. Yoked they go up and down on all his majesty's errands. They become like those that bore them, that stand in the stable. They do their utmost for fear of a beating.

But though I beat you with every kind of stick, you do not listen. If I knew another way of doing it, I would do it for you, that you might listen. You are a person fit for writing, though you have not yet known a woman. Your heart discerns, your fingers are skilled, your mouth is apt for reciting.

Writing is more enjoyable than enjoying a basket of . . . and beans; more enjoyable than a mother's giving birth, when her heart knows no distaste. She is constant in nursing her son; her breast is in his mouth every day. Happy is the heart [of] him who writes; he is young each day.

All Occupations Are Bad Except That of the Scribe

See for yourself with your own eye. The occupations lie before you.

The washerman's day is going up, going down. All his limbs are weak, [from] whitening his neighbors' clothes every day, from washing their linen.

The maker of pots is smeared with soil, like one whose relations have died. His hands, his feet are full of clay, he is like one who lives in the bog.

---

[3]From Miriam Lichtheim, *Ancient Egyptian Literature:* Vol. II: *The New Kingdom* (Berkeley University of California Press, 1976), pp. 168–172. Used by permission.

The cobbler mingles with vats. His odor is penetrating. His hands are red with madder, like one who is smeared with blood. He looks behind him for the kite, like one whose flesh is exposed.

The watchman prepares garlands and polishes vase stands. He spends a night of toil just as one on whom the sun shines.

The merchants travel downstream and upstream. They are as busy as can be, carrying goods from one town to another. They supply him who has wants. But the tax collectors carry off the gold, that most precious of metals.

The ships' crews from every house (of commerce), they receive their loads. They depart from Egypt for Syria, and each man's god is with him. (But) not one of them says: "We shall see Egypt again!"

The carpenter who is in the shipyard carries the timber and stacks it. If he gives today the output of yesterday, woe to his limbs! The shipwright stands behind him to tell him evil things.

His outworker who is in the fields, his is the toughest of all the jobs. He spends the day loaded with his tools, tied to his toolbox. When he returns home at night, he is loaded with the tool box and the timbers, his drinking mug, and his whetstones.

The scribe, he alone, records the output of all of them. Take note of it!

The Misfortunes of the Peasant

Let me also expound to you the situation of the peasant, that other tough occupation. [Comes] the inundation and soaks him. . . , he attends to his equipment. By day he cuts his farming tools; by night he twists rope. Even his midday hour he spends on farm labor. He equips himself to go to the field as if he were a warrior. The dried field lies before him; he goes out to get his team. When he has been after the herdsman for many days, he gets his team and comes back with it. He makes for it a place in the field. Comes dawn, he goes to make a start and does not find it in its place. He spends three days searching for it; he finds it in the bog. He finds no hides on them; the jackals have chewed them. He comes out, his garment in his hand, to beg for himself a team.

When he reaches his field he finds [it] broken up. He spends time cultivating, and the snake is after him. It finishes off the seed as it is cast to the ground. He does not see a green blade. He does three plowings with borrowed grain. His wife has gone down to the merchants and found nothing for barter. Now the scribe lands on the shore. He surveys the harvest. Attendants are behind him with staffs, Nubians with clubs. One says (to him), "Give grain." "There is none." He is beaten savagely. He is bound, thrown in the well, submerged head down. His wife is bound in his presence. His children are in fetters. His neighbors abandon them and flee. When it's over, there's no grain.

If you have any sense, be a scribe. If you have learned about the peasant, you will not be able to be one. Take note of it! . . .

The Scribe Does Not Suffer Like the Soldier

Furthermore. Look, I instruct you to make you sound; to make you hold the palette freely. To make you become one whom the king trusts; to make you gain entrance to treasury and granary. To make you receive the shipload at the gate of the granary. To make you issue the offerings on feast days. You are dressed in fine clothes; you own horses. Your boat is on the river;

you are supplied with attendants. You stride about inspecting. A mansion is built in your town. You have a powerful office, given you by the king. Male and female slaves are about you. Those who are in the fields grasp your hand, on plots that you have made. Look, I make you into a staff of life! Put the writings in your heart, and you will be protected from all kinds of toil. You will become a worthy official.

Do you not recall the (fate of) the unskilled man? His name is not known. He is ever burdened [like an ass carrying] in front of the scribe who knows what he is about.

Come, [let me tell] you the woes of the soldier, and how many are his superiors: the general, the troop-commander, the officer who leads, the standard-bearer, the lieutenant, the scribe, the commander of fifty, and the garrison-captain. They go in and out in the halls of the palace, saying: "Get laborers!" He is awakened at any hour. One is after him as (after) a donkey. He toils until the Aten (*sun*) sets in his darkness of night. He is hungry, his belly hurts; he is dead while yet alive. When he receives the grain-ration, having been released from duty, it is not good for grinding.

He is called up for Syria. He may not rest. There are no clothes, no sandals. The weapons of war are assembled at the fortress of Sile. His march is uphill through mountains. He drinks water every third day: it is smelly and tastes of salt. His body is ravaged by illness. The enemy comes, surrounds him with missiles, and life recedes from him. He is told: "Quick, forward, valiant soldier! Win for yourself a good name!" He does not know what he is about. His body is weak, his legs fail him. When victory is won, the captives are handed over to his majesty, to be taken to Egypt. The foreign woman faints on the march; she hangs herself [on] the soldier's neck. His knapsack drops, another grabs it while he is burdened with the woman. His wife and children are in their village; he dies and does not reach it. If he comes out alive, he is worn out from marching. Be he at large, be he detained, the soldier suffers. If he leaps and joins the deserters, all his people are imprisoned. He dies on the edge of the desert, and there is none to perpetuate his name. He suffers in death as in life. A big sack is brought for him; he does not know his resting place.

Be a scribe, and be spared from soldiering! You call and one says, "Here I am." You are safe from torments. Every man seeks to raise himself up. Take note of it!

3.6   "Wash and Perfume Yourself and Put on Your Best Clothes"

The tale of Ruth and her mother-in-law Naomi is a charming and apparently naive tale of ordinary people. Why it was significant for the authorities who allowed it to become part of the Bible is not certain. The fact that Ruth was the grandmother of the great king David has to be significant, but since she was a foreigner from Moab, a land particularly hated by the Israelites, it might be expected that this point would be covered up. Since it was not, some interpreters have thought that the story was intended to counteract narrow nationalistic views and emphasize the universal concern of Yahweh for all peoples. Whatever the reasons that motivated the story's recording, composition, and inclusion in the Bible, much of its interest derives from the fact that its concerns are timeless. It tells of the affection between two women of two different generations and two nationalities under very difficult circumstances. It emphasizes the importance of the continuity of the family, a value of overriding importance in premodern societies. Simple common sense and human psychology come to the fore, as when Naomi tells Ruth not to approach Boaz (the potential husband) until he has eaten dinner and had enough to drink so that "his heart is merry."

Apart from these themes, the story of Ruth provides a lot of information about daily life in ancient villages and the way law was practiced there. According to the law of the Levirate, when an Israelite husband died without an heir, the next of kin had an obligation to marry the widow and raise up children to inherit the family name and property. If the next-of-kin did not live up to his obligations, a widow could go to the town's gates, where the clan elders spent their time waiting for cases, and make a petition so that her husband's name might "not be blotted out of Israel" (Deuteronomy 25:6). In part, this is the way the story of Ruth works out, though Ruth did not have to make a scene with the city fathers to achieve her goal. Instead, Boaz, the targeted relative who, it turns out, was not the one with the primary responsibility to marry Ruth, goes to the city gates and maneuvers the relative who did have that obligation into giving up his claim. It is interesting that it is not until this point that we learn that, in addition to the matter of the survival of the family, there is also family property involved. Naomi's shrewdness is as much a part of this story as is the affection of the two women for each other.[4]

Naomi and Ruth

In the days when the judges ruled, there was a famine in the land, and a man from Bethlehem in Judah, together with his wife and two sons, went to live for a while in the country of Moab. The man's name was Elimelech, his wife's name Naomi, and the names of his two sons were Mahlon and Kilion. They were Ephrathites from Bethlehem, Judah. And they went to Moab and lived there.

Now Elimelech, Naomi's husband, died, and she was left with her two sons. They married Moabite women, one named Orpah and the other Ruth. After they had lived there about ten years, both Mahlon and Kilion also died, and Naomi was left without her two sons and her husband.

When she heard in Moab that the Lord had come to the aid of his people by providing food for them, Naomi and her daughters-in-law prepared to return home from there. With her two daughters-in-law she left the place where she had been living and set out on the road that would take them back to the land of Judah.

Then Naomi said to her two daughters-in-law, "Go back, each of you, to your mother's home. May the Lord show kindness to you, as you have shown to your dead and to me. May the Lord grant that each of you will find rest in the home of another husband."

Then she kissed them and they wept aloud and said to her, "We will go back with you to your people."

But Naomi said, "Return home, my daughters. Why would you come with me? Am I going to have any more sons, who could become your husbands? Return home, my daughters; I am too old to have another husband. Even if I thought there was still hope for me—even if I had a husband tonight and then gave birth to sons—would you wait until they grew up? Would you remain unmarried for them? No, my daughters. It is more bitter for me than for you, because the Lord's hand has gone out against me!"

At this they wept again. Then Orpah kissed her mother-in-law good-bye, but Ruth clung to her.

"Look," said Naomi, "your sister-in-law is going back to her people and her gods. Go back with her."

---

[4]The Book of Ruth. NIV. Used by permission.

But Ruth replied, "Don't urge me to leave you or to turn back from you. Where you go I will go, and where you stay I will stay. Your people will be my people and your God my God. Where you die I will die, and there I will be buried. May the Lord deal with me, be it ever so severely, if anything but death separates you and me." When Naomi realized that Ruth was determined to go with her, she stopped urging her.

So the two women went on until they came to Bethlehem. When they arrived in Bethlehem, the whole town was stirred because of them, and the women exclaimed, "Can this be Naomi?"

"Don't call me Naomi," she told them. "Call me Mara,[5] because the Almighty has made my life very bitter. I went away full, but the Lord has brought me back empty. Why call me Naomi? The Lord has afflicted me; the Almighty has brought misfortune upon me."

So Naomi returned from Moab accompanied by Ruth the Moabitess, her daughter-in-law, arriving in Bethlehem as the barley harvest was beginning.

Ruth Meets Boaz

Now Naomi had a relative on her husband's side, from the clan of Elimelech, a man of standing, whose name was Boaz.

And Ruth the Moabitess said to Naomi, "Let me go to the fields and pick up the leftover grain behind anyone in whose eyes I find favor."

Naomi said to her, "Go ahead, my daughter." So she went out and began to glean in the fields behind the harvesters. As it turned out, she found herself working in a field belonging to Boaz, who was from the clan of Elimelech.

Just then Boaz arrived from Bethlehem and greeted the harvesters, "The Lord be with you!"

"The Lord bless you!" they called back.

Boaz asked the foreman of his harvesters, "Whose young woman is that?" The foreman replied, "She is the Moabitess who came back from Moab with Naomi. She said, 'Please let me glean and gather among the sheaves behind the harvesters.' She went into the field and has worked steadily from morning till now, except for a short rest in the shelter."

So Boaz said to Ruth, "My daughter, listen to me. Don't go and glean in another field and don't go away from here. Stay here with my servant girls. Watch the field where the men are harvesting, and follow along after the girls. I have told the men not to touch you. And whenever you are thirsty, go and get a drink from the water jars the men have filled."

At this, she bowed down with her face to the ground. She exclaimed, "Why have I found such favor in your eyes that you notice me—a foreigner?"

Boaz replied, "I've been told all about what you have done for your mother-in-law since the death of your husband—how you left your father and mother and your homeland and came to live with a people you did not know before. May the Lord repay you for what you have done. May you be richly rewarded by the Lord, the God of Israel, under whose wings you have come to take refuge."

"May I continue to find favor in your eyes, my lord," she said. "You have given me comfort and have spoken kindly to your servant though I do not have the standing of one of your servant girls."

At mealtime Boaz said to her, "Come over here. Have some bread and dip it in the wine vinegar."

---

[5]There is a play on words here. Naomi means "pleasant," while Mara means "bitter."

When she sat down with the harvesters, he offered her some roasted grain. She ate all she wanted and had some left over. As she got up to glean, Boaz gave orders to his men, "Even if she gathers among the sheaves, don't embarrass her. Rather, pull out some stalks for her from the bundles and leave them for her to pick up, and don't rebuke her."

So Ruth gleaned in the field until evening. Then she threshed the barley she had gathered, and it amounted to about an ephah. She carried it back to town, and her mother-in-law saw how much she had gathered. Ruth also brought out and gave her what she had left over after she had eaten enough.

Her mother-in-law asked her, "Where did you glean today? Where did you work? Blessed be the man who took notice of you!"

Then Ruth told her mother-in-law about the one at whose place she had been working. "The name of the man I worked with today is Boaz," she said.

"The Lord bless him!" Naomi said to her daughter-in-law. "He has not stopped showing his kindness to the living and the dead." She added, "That man is our close relative; he is one of our kinsman-redeemers."

Then Ruth the Moabitess said, "He even said to me, 'Stay with my workers until they finish harvesting all my grain.'"

Naomi said to Ruth her daughter-in-law, "It will be good for you, my daughter, to go with his girls, because in someone else's field you might be harmed."

So Ruth stayed close to the servant girls of Boaz to glean until the barley and wheat harvests were finished. And she lived with her mother-in-law.

Ruth and Boaz at the Threshing Floor

One day Naomi, her mother-in-law, said to her, "My daughter, should I not try to find a home for you, where you will be well provided for? Is not Boaz, with whose servant girls you have been, a kinsman of ours? Tonight he will be winnowing barley on the threshing floor. Wash and perfume yourself, and put on your best clothes. Then go down to the threshing floor, but don't let him know you are there until he has finished eating and drinking. When he lies down, note the place where he is lying. Then go and uncover his feet and lie down. He will tell you what to do."

"I will do whatever you say," Ruth answered. So she went down to the threshing floor and did everything her mother-in-law told her to do.

When Boaz had finished eating and drinking and was in good spirits, he went over to lie down at the far end of the grain pile. Ruth approached quietly, uncovered his feet and lay down. In the middle of the night something startled the man, and he turned and discovered a woman lying at his feet.

"Who are you?" he asked.

"I am your servant Ruth," she said. "Spread the corner of your garment over me, since you are a kinsman-redeemer."

"The Lord bless you, my daughter," he replied. "This kindness is greater than that which you showed earlier: You have not run after the younger men, whether rich or poor. And now, my daughter, don't be afraid. I will do for you all you ask. All my fellow townsmen know that you are a woman of noble character. Although it is true that I am near of kin, there is a kinsman-redeemer nearer than I. Stay here for the night, and in the morning if he wants to redeem, good; let him redeem. But if he is not willing, as surely as the Lord lives I will do it. Lie here until morning."

So she lay at his feet until morning, but got up before anyone could be recognized; and he said, "Don't let it be known that a woman came to the threshing floor."

He also said, "Bring me the shawl you are wearing and hold it out." When she did so, he poured into it six measures of barley and put it on her. Then he went back to town.

When Ruth came to her mother-in-law, Naomi asked, "How did it go, my daughter?"

Then Ruth told her everything Boaz had done for her and added, "He gave me these six measures of barley, saying, 'Don't go back to your mother-in-law empty-handed.'"

Then Naomi said, "Wait, my daughter, until you find out what happens. For the man will not rest until the matter is settled today."

Boaz Marries Ruth

Meanwhile Boaz went up to the town gate and sat there. When the kinsman-redeemer he had mentioned came along, Boaz said, "Come over here, my friend, and sit down." So he went over and sat down.

Boaz took ten of the elders of the town and said, "Sit here," and they did so. Then he said to the kinsman-redeemer, "Naomi, who has come back from Moab, is selling the piece of land that belonged to our brother Elimelech. I thought I should bring the matter to your attention and suggest that you buy it in the presence of these seated here and in the presence of the elders of my people. If you will redeem it, do so. But if you will not, tell me, so I will know. For no one has the right to do it except you, and I am next in line."

"I will redeem it," he said.

Then Boaz said, "On the day you buy the land from Naomi and from Ruth the Moabitess, you acquire the dead man's widow, in order to maintain the name of the dead with his property."

At this, the kinsman-redeemer said, "Then I cannot redeem it because I might endanger my own estate. You redeem it yourself. I cannot do it."

(Now in earlier times in Israel, for the redemption and transfer of property to become final, one party took off his sandal and gave it to the other. This was the method of legalizing transactions in Israel.)

So the kinsman-redeemer said to Boaz, "Buy it yourself." And he removed his sandal.

Then Boaz announced to the elders and all the people, "Today you are witnesses that I have bought from Naomi all the property of Elimelech, Kilion, and Mahlon. I have also acquired Ruth the Moabitess, Mahlon's widow, as my wife, in order to maintain the name of the dead with his property, so that his name will not disappear from among his family or from the town records. Today you are witnesses!"

Then the elders and all those at the gate said, "We are witnesses. May the Lord make the woman who is coming into your home like Rachel and Leah, who together built up the house of Israel. May you have standing in Ephrathah and be famous in Bethlehem. Through the offspring the Lord gives you by this young woman, may your family be like that of Perez, whom Tamar bore to Judah."

The Genealogy of David

So Boaz took Ruth and she became his wife. Then he went to her, and the Lord enabled her to conceive, and she gave birth to a son. The women said to Naomi, "Praise be to the Lord, who this day has not left you without an heir. May he become famous throughout Israel! He will renew your life and sustain you in your old age. For your daughter-in-law, who loves you and who is better to you than seven sons, has given him birth."

Then Naomi took the child, laid him in her lap and cared for him. The women living there said, "Naomi has a grandson." And they named him Obed. He was the father of Jesse, the father of David.

This, then, is the family line of Perez:

Perez was the father of Hezron,
Hezron the father of Ram,
Ram the father of Amminadab,
Amminadab the father of Nahshon,
Nahshon the father of Salmon,
Salmon the father of Boaz,
Boaz the father of Obed,
Obed the father of Jesse,
and Jesse the father of David.

Chapter 4

▼▼▼

The Origin and Spread of the *Polis* System

Aristotle once observed that "Man is a political animal." This famous quotation is usually invoked as evidence of Aristotle's prescience in recognizing the universality of government in human society—an interpretation he would have indignantly repudiated. A more accurate translation would be "Man is a *polis* animal," a translation that reflects the absolute centrality of the *polis* (pl. poleis) to the ancient Greek experience. In the Greek view the *polis* set them apart from all other peoples. Unfortunately, it could also foster prejudice, as exemplified by Aristotle's notorious theory that all barbarians were slaves by nature; this theory played a prominent role in sixteenth-century A.D. discussions of the place of Native Americans in the European empires in the New World. But what is a *polis*?

The conventional translation of *polis* is "city-state." That term captures well one of the central features of the *polis* system—namely, that every *polis* is or ought to be independent and sovereign—but it is seriously misleading in two ways. First, the word "city" conjures up an image of large, socioeconomically diverse urban centers with imposing architecture. An unusual *polis* such as fifth-century B.C. Athens might fulfill such expectations, but the vast majority of the more than a thousand *poleis* scattered throughout the Greek world rarely had territories exceeding a hundred square miles and had citizen bodies of a few thousand or less, little in the way of significant public buildings, and overwhelmingly agricultural economies. Second, the word "state" suggests a formal governmental structure responsible for the maintenance of internal order and the conduct of foreign relations, but *poleis* normally had few permanent political institutions. Rather, *poleis* had *politai*, "citizens," who in Aristotle's phrase, "govern and are governed in turn." A *polis*, therefore, was not so much a state in the modern sense of that term as it was a community of self-governing citizens. For reasons that will become clear in Chapter 5, this meant in practice that the core of a *polis* was composed of adult males whose citizenship was validated by fictitious claims of descent, usually father to son, from common ancestors. Theirs and theirs alone were the right both to own land and to participate in all aspects of public affairs and the obligation to defend the *polis* and its interests, as is well illustrated by the fact that Greek documents regularly identify as the agency responsible for political activity not the *polis* but its citizens, not Athens or Sparta but the Athenians or the Spartans.

Less clear is the origin of the *polis* system. Historians often claim that its origin is to be found in the rugged geography of Greece, with its limited water sources, scattered patches of farmland, and difficult communications, all of which, it is said, encouraged the political fragmentation characteristic of classical Greece. Geography, however, is not destiny. More than a century of productive archaeological activity, beginning with Heinrich Schliemann's dramatic discoveries at Troy and Mycenae in the 1870s, has demonstrated that the political landscape of second-millennium B.C. Greece was dominated by a small number of kingdoms ruled from fortified palaces. The few surviving records of these kingdoms, which are written in an early form of Greek called Linear B, reveal that, unlike the later *poleis*, these kingdoms had complex class structures and were governed by scribal bureaucracies similar to those of the states of the Ancient Near East. The Mycenaean Age and its kingdoms ended violently about 1100 B.C. Then ensued a period of severe economic and cultural retrenchment and population decline that historians call the Dark Ages. During the almost 350 years of the Dark Ages the basic unit of Greek life was the self-sufficient farming village, and it was from groups of such villages that the new *poleis* emerged in the eighth century B.C. The lack of significant foreign enemies during the critical early centuries of its existence allowed the *polis* system to take root and spread from its Aegean home throughout much of the Mediterranean and Black Sea basins. The result was that until the great crisis of the ancient Western world in the third century A.D., almost a millennium later, the Greeks were, as Aristotle said, "*polis* animals."

4.1   A Greek Definition of the *Polis*

The Politics *of Aristotle (384–322 B.C.) is the fullest and most important surviving ancient analysis of the* polis *system. The central feature of all of Aristotle's works is the attempt to base theoretical analysis on an extensive body of empirical data, and especially so in the* Politics. *The content of the* Politics *was derived from data collected for a survey of political behavior unequaled in scope and scale before modern times: the description of the constitutions of 158 Greek and selected non-Greek states. Although not a perfectly finished work—the* Politics *seems, in fact, to be composed of the syllabi of several courses Aristotle gave at his school in Athens sometime between 335 and his death in 322 B.C.—the work contains a comprehensive account of the* polis *system, including a description of the full variety of known* polis *constitutions (both real and imaginary) and the strengths and weaknesses of their institutions. This selection from the* Politics *provides a theoretical definition of the* polis *as a natural association of rational human beings, and an analysis and evaluation of the relationships between the various categories of individuals that compose the citizen body.*[1]

He who thus considers things in their first growth and origin, whether a state or anything else, will obtain the clearest view of them. In the first place (1) there must be a union of those who cannot exist without each other; for example, of male and female, that

---

[1]Aristotle, *Politics* 1.1.2. From *The Politics of Aristotle*, Vol. 1, trans. Benjamin Jowett (Oxford: Clarendon Press, 1885), pp. 2–4.

the race may continue; and this is a union which is formed, not of deliberate purpose, but because, in common with other animals and with plants, mankind have a natural desire to leave behind them an image of themselves. And (2) there must be a union of natural ruler and subject, that both may be preserved. For he who can foresee with his mind is by nature intended to be lord and master, and he who can work with his body is a subject, and by nature a slave; hence master and slave have the same interest. Nature, however, has distinguished between the female and the slave. For she is not niggardly, like the smith who fashions the Delphian knife for many uses; she makes each thing for a single use, and every instrument is best made when intended for one and not for many uses. But among barbarians no distinction is made between women and slaves, because there is no natural ruler among them: they are a community of slaves, male and female. Wherefore the poets say,

It is proper that Greeks should rule over barbarians;

as if they thought that the barbarian and the slave were by nature one.

Out of these two relationships between man and woman, master and slave, the family first arises, and Hesiod is right when he says,

First house and wife and an ox for the plough, . . .

The family is the association established by nature for the supply of men's everyday wants, and the members of it are called by Charondas "companions of the cupboard" and by Epimenides the Cretan, "companions of the manger." But when several families are united, and the association aims at something more than the supply of daily needs, then comes into existence the village. And the most natural form of the village appears to be that of a colony from the family, composed of the children and grandchildren, who are said to be "suckled with the same milk." And this is the reason why Greek states were originally governed by kings; because the Greeks were under royal rule before they came together, as the barbarians still are. Every family is ruled by the eldest, and therefore in the colonies of the family the kingly form of government prevailed because they were of the same blood. As Homer says [of the Cyclopes]:

Each one gives law to his children and to his wives.

For they lived dispersedly, as was the manner in ancient times. Wherefore men say that the Gods have a king, because they themselves either are or were in ancient times under the rule of a king. For they imagine, not only the forms of the Gods, but their ways of life to be like their own.

When several villages are united in a single community, perfect and large enough to be nearly or quite self-sufficing, the state comes into existence, originating in the bare needs of life, and continuing in existence for the sake of a good life. And therefore, if the earlier forms of society are natural, so is the state, for it is the end of them, and the [completed] nature is the end. For what each thing is when fully developed, we call its nature, whether we are speaking of a man, a horse, or a family. Besides, the final cause and end of a thing is the best, and to be self-sufficing is the end and the best.

Hence it is evident that the state is a creation of nature, and that man is by nature a political animal. And he who by nature and not by mere accident is without a state, is either above humanity, or below it; he is the

Tribeless, lawless, heartless one,

whom Homer denounces—the outcast who is a lover of war; he may be compared to a bird which flies alone.

4.2   Greek Life in the Eighth Century B.C. I: "The Shield of Achilles"

The clearest idea of Greek life at the time the polis *system originated is found in the* Iliad. *The* Iliad *and the* Odyssey *are the central texts of Greek culture, the two books familiar to all educated Greeks. Allusions to them abound in Greek literature and art from the seventh century B.C. to the end of antiquity. Two centuries of scholarship have demonstrated that these two remarkable poems are the final products of a tradition of oral poetry stretching back to the second millennium B.C. Like all such poetry—and fortunately for the historian—the Homeric epics are characterized by anachronism. While they claim to tell the story of an event of the late second millennium B.C., the Trojan War, the social and economic background against which that story unfolds is that of the poet's own time. In the case of the* Iliad, *that time is the late eighth century B.C., the period in which the basic elements of classical Greek civilization can first clearly be distinguished. It was also the period in which archaeologists find the first clear evidence of renewed urbanization in the Greek world after the collapse of Mycenaean civilization in the late second millennium B.C. A vivid picture of Greek life in war and peace at the end of the Dark Ages is found in Book 18 of the* Iliad, *in the description of the shield created for the poem's hero, Achilles, by the god Hephaestus.*[2]

When he had so said he left her and went to his bellows, turning them towards the fire and bidding them do their office. Twenty bellows blew upon the melting-pots, and they blew blasts of every kind, some fierce to help him when he had need of them, and others less strong as Hephaestus willed it in the course of his work. He threw tough copper into the fire, and tin, with silver and gold; he set his great anvil on its block, and with one hand grasped his mighty hammer while he took the tongs in the other.

First he shaped the shield so great and strong, adorning it all over and binding it round with a gleaming circuit in three layers; and the baldric was made of silver. He made the shield in five thicknesses, and with many a wonder did his cunning hand enrich it.

He wrought the earth, the heavens, and the sea; the moon also at her full and the untiring sun, with all the signs that glorify the face of heaven—the Pleiads, the Hyads, huge Orion, and the Bear, which men also call the Wain and which turns round ever in one place, facing Orion, and alone never dips into the stream of Oceanus.

He wrought also two cities, fair to see and busy with the hum of men. In the one were weddings and wedding-feasts, and they were going about the city with brides whom they were escorting by torchlight from their chambers. Loud rose the cry of Hymen, and the youths danced to the music of flute and lyre, while the women stood each at her house door to see them.

---

[2]Homer, *Iliad* 18, lines 468–608. From *The Iliad of Homer*, trans. Samuel Butler (London: A. C. Fifield, 1914), pp. 314–317.

Meanwhile the people were gathered in assembly, for there was a quarrel, and two men were wrangling about the blood-money for a man who had been killed, the one saying before the people that he had paid damages in full, and the other that he had not been paid. Each was trying to make his own case good, and the people took sides, each man backing the side that he had taken; but the heralds kept them back, and the elders sat on their seats of stone in a solemn circle, holding the staves which the heralds had put into their hands. Then they rose and each in his turn gave judgement, and there were two talents laid down, to be given to him whose judgement should be deemed the fairest.

About the other city there lay encamped two hosts in gleaming armor, and they were divided whether to sack it, or to spare it and accept the half of what it contained. But the men of the city would not yet consent, and armed themselves for a surprise; their wives and little children kept guard upon the walls, and with them were the men who were past fighting through age; but the others sallied forth with Ares and Pallas Athena at their head—both of them wrought in gold and clad in golden raiment, great and fair with their armor as befitting gods, while they that followed were smaller. When they reached the place where they would lay their ambush, it was on a river-bed to which live stock of all kinds would come from far and near to water; here, then, they lay concealed, clad in full armor. Some way off them there were two scouts who were on the look-out for the coming of sheep or cattle, which presently came, followed by two shepherds who were playing on their pipes, and had not so much as a thought of danger. When those who were in ambush saw this, they cut off the flocks and herds and killed the shepherds. Meanwhile the besiegers, when they heard much noise among the cattle as they sat in council, sprang to their horses, and made with all speed towards them; when they reached them they set battle in array by the banks of the river, and the hosts aimed their bronze-shod spears at one another. With them were Strife and Riot, and fell Fate who was dragging three men after her, one with a fresh wound, and the other unwounded, while the third was dead, and she was dragging him along by his heel: and her robe was bedrabbled in men's blood. They went in and out with one another and fought as though they were living people hauling away one another's dead.

He wrought also a fair fallow field, large and thrice ploughed already. Many men were working at the plough within it, turning their oxen to and fro, furrow after furrow. Each time that they turned on reaching the headland a man would come up to them and give them a cup of wine, and they would go back to their furrows looking forward to the time when they should again reach the headland. The part that they had ploughed was dark behind them, so that the field, though it was of gold, still looked as if it were being ploughed—very curious to behold.

He wrought also a field of harvest wheat, and the reapers were reaping with sharp sickles in their hands. Swathe after swathe fell to the ground in a straight line behind them, and the binders bound them in bands of twisted straw. There were three binders, and behind them there were boys who gathered the cut corn in armfuls and kept on bringing them to be bound: among them all the owner of the land stood by in silence and was glad. The servants were getting a meal ready under an oak, for they had sacrificed a great ox, and were busy cutting him up, while the women were making a porridge of much white barley for the laborers' dinner.

He wrought also a vineyard, golden and fair to see, and the vines were loaded with grapes. The bunches overhead were black, but the vines were trained on poles of silver. He ran a ditch of dark metal all round it, and fenced it with a fence of tin; there was only one path to it, and by this the vintagers went when they would gather the vintage. Youths and maidens all blithe and full of glee, carried the luscious fruit in plaited baskets; and with them there went a boy who made sweet music with his lyre, and sang the Linus-song with his clear boyish voice.

He wrought also a herd of horned cattle. He made the cows of gold and tin, and they lowed as they came full speed out of the yards to go and feed among the waving reeds that grow by the banks of the river. Along with the cattle there went four shepherds, all of them in gold, and their nine fleet dogs went with them. Two terrible lions had fastened on a bellowing bull that was with the foremost cows, and bellow as he might they haled him, while the dogs and men gave chase: the lions tore through the bull's thick hide and were gorging on his blood and bowels, but the herdsmen were afraid to do anything, and only hounded on their dogs; the dogs dared not fasten on the lions but stood by barking and keeping out of harm's way.

The god wrought also a pasture in a fair mountain dell, and a large flock of sheep, with a homestead and huts, and sheltered sheepfolds.

Furthermore he wrought a green, like that which Daedalus once made in Cnossus for lovely Ariadne. Hereon there danced youths and maidens whom all would woo, with their hands on one another's wrists. The maidens wore robes of light linen, and the youths well-woven shirts that were slightly oiled. The girls were crowned with garlands, while the young men had daggers of gold that hung by silver baldrics; sometimes they would dance deftly in a ring with merry twinkling feet, as it were a potter sitting at his work and making trial of his wheel to see whether it will run, and sometimes they would go all in line with one another, and much people was gathered joyously about the green. There was a bard also to sing to them and play his lyre, while two tumblers went about performing in the midst of them when the man struck up with his tune.

All round the outermost rim of the shield he set the mighty stream of the river Oceanus.

4.3   Greek Life in the Eighth Century B.C. 2: Hesiod's *Works and Days*

In "The Shield of Achilles," Homer portrays life at the end of the Dark Ages bathed in a bright light. A different and harsher vision is provided by Homer's Boeotian contemporary, the poet Hesiod. Hesiod uses the occasion of a suit between himself and his brother over the division of their father's property to describe in a manner reminiscent of the contemporary Jewish prophets life in a world in which the gods have ordained that man can prosper only through endless toil in competition with his neighbors.[3]

(ll. 1–10) Muses of Pieria who give glory through song, come hither, tell of Zeus your father and chant his praise. Through him mortal men are famed or unfamed, sung or unsung alike, as great Zeus wills. For easily he makes strong, and easily he brings the strong man low; easily he humbles the proud and raises the obscure, and easily he straightens the crooked and blasts the proud,—Zeus who thunders aloft and has his dwelling most high. Attend thou with eye and ear, and make judgments straight with righteousness. And I, Perses, would tell of true things.

Hesiod urges his brother to understand that there is no shortcut to prosperity. Life is competition and the only way to succeed is to work more successfully than others.

So, after all, there was not one kind of Strife alone, but all over the earth there are two. As for the one, a man would praise her when he came to understand her; but the other is blameworthy: and they are wholly different in nature. For one fosters evil war and battle, being

---

[3]Hesiod, *Works and Days* (selections) from *Hesiod, The Homeric Hymns, and Homerica*, trans. H. G. Evelyn–White (Cambridge, MA: Harvard University Press, 1914).

cruel: her no man loves; but perforce, through the will of the deathless gods, men pay harsh Strife her honor due. But the other is the elder daughter of dark Night, and the son of Cronos who sits above and dwells in the aether, set her in the roots of the earth: and she is far kinder to men. She stirs up even the shiftless to toil; for a man grows eager to work when he considers his neighbor, a rich man who hastens to plough and plant and put his house in good order; and neighbor vies with his neighbor as he hurries after wealth. This Strife is wholesome for men. And potter is angry with potter, and craftsman with craftsman, and beggar is jealous of beggar, and minstrel of minstrel.

Perses, lay up these things in your heart, and do not let that Strife who delights in mischief hold your heart back from work, while you peep and peer and listen to the wrangles of the court house. Little concern has he with quarrels and courts who has not a year's victuals laid up betimes, even that which the earth bears, Demeter's grain. When you have got plenty of that, you can raise disputes and strive to get another's goods. But you shall have no second chance to deal so again: nay, let us settle our dispute here with true judgement divided our inheritance, but you seized the greater share and carried it off, greatly swelling the glory of our bribe-swallowing lords who love to judge such a cause as this. Fools! They know not how much more the half is than the whole, nor what great advantage there is in mallow and asphodel.

For the gods keep hidden from men the means of life. Else you would easily do work enough in a day to supply you for a full year even without working; soon would you put away your rudder over the smoke, and the fields worked by ox and sturdy mule would run to waste. But Zeus in the anger of his heart hid it, because Prometheus the crafty deceived him; therefore he planned sorrow and mischief against men. He hid fire; but that the noble son of Iapetus stole again for men from Zeus the counselor in a hollow fennel-stalk, so that Zeus who delights in thunder did not see it. But afterwards Zeus who gathers the clouds said to him in anger:

"Son of Iapetus, surpassing all in cunning, you are glad that you have outwitted me and stolen fire—a great plague to you yourself and to men that shall be. But I will give men as the price for fire an evil thing in which they may all be glad of heart while they embrace their own destruction."

For ere this the tribes of men lived on earth remote and free from ills and hard toil and heavy sickness which bring the Fates upon men; for in misery men grow old quickly. Or if you will, I will sum you up another tale well and skillfully—and do you lay it up in your heart,—how the gods and mortal men sprang from one source.

Although Zeus did not deprive humanity of the fire stolen by Prometheus, he and the other gods took away the possibility of a life free from suffering. In this section Hesiod describes the "fall of man" from the blessed life of the Golden Age to the harsh conditions of the Iron Age—the late Dark Ages—in which Hesiod lives.

First of all, the deathless gods who dwell on Olympus made a golden race of mortal men who lived in the time of Cronos when he was reigning in heaven. And they lived like gods without sorrow of heart, remote and free from toil and grief: miserable age rested not on them; but with legs and arms never failing they made merry with feasting beyond the reach of all evils. When they died, it was as though they were overcome with sleep, and they had all good things; for the fruitful earth unforced bare them fruit abundantly and without stint. They dwelt in ease and peace upon their lands with many good things, rich in flocks and loved by the blessed gods.

But after earth had covered this generation—they are called pure spirits dwelling on the earth, and are kindly, delivering from harm, and guardians of mortal men; for they roam everywhere over the earth, clothed in mist and keep watch on judgements and cruel deeds, givers of wealth; for this royal right also they received;—then they who dwell on Olympus made a second generation which was of silver and less noble by far. It was like the golden race neither in body nor in spirit. A child was brought up at his good mother's side an hundred years, an utter simpleton, playing childishly in his own home. But when they were full grown and were come to the full measure of their prime, they lived only a little time in sorrow because of their foolishness, for they could not keep from sinning and from wronging one another, nor would they serve the immortals, nor sacrifice on the holy altars of the blessed ones as it is right for men to do wherever they dwell. Then Zeus the son of Cronos was angry and put them away, because they would not give honor to the blessed gods who live on Olympus.

But when earth had covered this generation also—they are called blessed spirits of the underworld by men, and, though they are of second order, yet honor attends them also—Zeus the Father made a third generation of mortal men, a brazen race, sprung from ash trees; and it was in no way equal to the silver age, but was terrible and strong. They loved the lamentable works of Ares and deeds of violence; they ate no bread, but were hard of heart like adamant, fearful men. Great was their strength and unconquerable the arms which grew from their shoulders on their strong limbs. Their armor was of bronze, and their houses of bronze, and of bronze were their implements: there was no black iron. These were destroyed by their own hands and passed to the dank house of chill Hades, and left no name: terrible though they were, black Death seized them, and they left the bright light of the sun.

But when earth had covered this generation also, Zeus the son of Cronos made yet another, the fourth, upon the fruitful earth, which was nobler and more righteous, a godlike race of hero-men who are called demigods, the race before our own, throughout the boundless earth. Grim war and dread battle destroyed a part of them, some in the land of Cadmus at seven-gated Thebes when they fought for the flocks of Oedipus, and some, when it had brought them in ships over the great sea gulf to Troy for rich-haired Helen's sake: there death's end enshrouded a part of them. But to the others, father Zeus the son of Cronos gave a living and an abode apart from men, and made them dwell at the ends of earth. And they live untouched by sorrow in the islands of the blessed along the shore of deep swirling Ocean, happy heroes for whom the grain-giving earth bears honey-sweet fruit flourishing thrice a year, far from the deathless gods, and Cronos rules over them (5); for the father of men and gods released *him* from his bonds. And these last equally have honor and glory.

And again far-seeing Zeus made yet another generation, the fifth, of men who are upon the bounteous earth. Thereafter, would that I were not among the men of the fifth generation, but either had died before or been born afterwards. For now truly is a race of iron, and men never rest from labor and sorrow by day, and from perishing by night; and the gods shall lay sore trouble upon them. But, notwithstanding, even these shall have some good mingled with their evils. And Zeus will destroy this race of mortal men also when they come to have gray hair on the temples at their birth (6). The father will not agree with his children, nor the children with their father, nor guest with his host, nor comrade with comrade; nor will brother be dear to brother as aforetime. Men will dishonor their parents as they grow quickly old, and will carp at them, chiding them with bitter words, hard-hearted they, not knowing the fear of the gods. They will not repay their aged parents the cost of their nurture, for might shall be their right: and one man will sack another's city. There will be no favor for the man who keeps his oath or for the just or for the good; but rather men will praise the evil-doer and his violent dealing. Strength will be right and reverence will cease to be; and the wicked will hurt the worthy man, speaking false words against him, and will swear an oath upon them. Envy, foul-mouthed, delighting in evil, with scowling face, will go along with wretched men one and all. And then Aidos [*i.e. Shame*] and Nemesis {*i.e. Retribution*], with their sweet forms wrapped in white robes, will go from the wide-pathed earth and forsake mankind to join the company of the deathless gods: and bitter sorrows will be left for mortal men, and there will be no help against evil.

Hesiod emphasizes that above all man should pursue justice through honest toil and not violence.

And now I will tell a fable for princes who themselves understand. Thus said the hawk to the nightingale with speckled neck, while he carried her high up among the clouds, gripped fast in his talons, and she, pierced by his crooked talons, cried pitifully. To her he spoke disdainfully: "Miserable thing, why do you cry out? One far stronger than you now holds you fast, and you must go wherever I take you, songstress as you are. And if I please I will make my meal of you, or let you go. He is a fool who tries to withstand the stronger, for he does not get the mastery and suffers pain besides his shame." So said the swiftly flying hawk, the long-winged bird.

But you, Perses, listen to right and do not foster violence; for violence is bad for a poor man. Even the prosperous cannot easily bear its burden, but is weighed down under it when he has fallen into delusion. The better path is to go by on the other side towards justice; for Justice beats Outrage when she comes at length to the end of the race. But only when he has suffered does the fool learn this. For Oath keeps pace with wrong judgments. There is a noise when Justice is being dragged in the way where those who devour bribes and give sentence with crooked judgements, take her. And she, wrapped in mist, follows to the city and haunts of the people, weeping, and bringing mischief to men, even to such as have driven her forth in that they did not deal straightly with her. But they who give straight judgements to strangers and to the men of the land, and go not aside from what is just, their city flourishes, and the people prosper in it: Peace, the nurse of children, is abroad in their land, and all-seeing Zeus never decrees cruel war against them. Neither famine nor disaster ever haunt men who do true justice; but lightheartedly they tend the fields which are all their care. The earth bears them victual in plenty, and on the mountains the oak bears acorns upon the top and bees in the midst. Their woolly sheep are laden with fleeces; their women bear children like their parents. They flourish continually with good things, and do not travel on ships, for the grain-giving earth bears them fruit. But for those who practice violence and cruel deeds far-seeing Zeus, the son of Cronos, ordains a punishment. Often even a whole city suffers for a bad man who sins and devises presumptuous deeds, and the son of Cronos lays great trouble upon the people, famine and plague together, so that the men perish away, and their women do not bear children, and their houses become few, through the contriving of Olympian Zeus. And again, at another time, the son of Cronos either destroys their wide army, or their walls, or else makes an end of their ships on the sea. . . . That man is altogether best who considers all things himself and marks what will be better afterwards and at the end; and he, again, is good who listens to a good adviser; but whoever neither thinks for himself nor keeps in mind what another tells him, he is an unprofitable man. But do you at any rate, always remembering my charge, work, high-born Perses, that Hunger may hate you, and venerable Demeter richly crowned may love you and fill your barn with food; for Hunger is altogether a meet comrade for the sluggard. Both gods and men are angry with a man who lives idle, for in nature he is like the stingless drones who waste the labor of the bees, eating without working; but let it be your care to order your work properly, that in the right season your barns may be full of victual. Through work men grow rich in flocks and substance, and working they are much better loved by the immortals. Work is no disgrace: it is idleness which is a disgrace. But if you work, the idle will soon envy you as you grow rich, for fame and renown attend on wealth. And whatever be your lot, work is best for you, if you turn your misguided mind away from other men's property to your work and attend to your livelihood as I bid you. An evil shame is the needy man's companion, shame which both greatly harms and prospers men: shame is with poverty, but confidence with wealth. . . .

Call your friend to a feast; but leave your enemy alone; and especially call him who lives near you: for if any mischief happen in the place, neighbors come ungirt, but kinsmen stay to gird themselves. A bad neighbor is as great a plague as a good one is a great blessing; he who enjoys a good neighbor has a precious possession. Not even an ox would die but for a bad neighbor. Take fair measure from your neighbor and pay him back fairly with the same measure, or better, if you can; so that if you are in need afterwards, you may find him sure.

Do not get base gain: base gain is as bad as ruin. Be friends with the friendly, and visit him who visits you. Give to one who gives, but do not give to one who does not give. A man gives to the free-handed, but no one gives to the close-fisted. Give is a good girl, but Take is bad and she brings death. For the man who gives willingly, even though he gives a great thing, rejoices in his gift and is glad in heart; but whoever gives way to shamelessness and takes something himself, even though it be a small thing, it freezes his heart. He who adds to what he has, will keep off bright-eyed hunger; for it you add only a little to a little and do this often, soon that little will become great. What a man has by him at home does not trouble him: it is better to have your stuff at home, for whatever is abroad may mean loss. It is a good thing to draw on what you have; but it grieves your heart to need something and not to have it, and I bid you mark this. Take your fill when the cask is first opened and when it is nearly spent, but midways be sparing: it is poor saving when you come to the lees.

Hesiod emphasizes that hard work, prudence, and planning are the keys to prosperity and the good life for humanity.

Let the wage promised to a friend be fixed; even with your brother smile—and get a witness; for trust and mistrust alike ruin men. Do not let a flaunting woman coax and cozen and deceive you: She is after your barn. The man who trusts womankind trusts deceivers. There should be an only son, to feed his father's house, for so wealth will increase in the home; but if you leave a second son you should die old. Yet Zeus can easily give great wealth to a greater number. More hands mean more work and more increase. If your heart within you desires wealth, do these things and work with work upon work. . . . First of all, get a house, and a woman and an ox for the plough—a slave woman and not a wife, to follow the oxen as well—and make everything ready at home, so that you may not have to ask of another, and he refuses you, and so, because you are in lack, the season pass by and your work come to nothing. Do not put your work off till tomorrow and the day after; for a sluggish worker does not fill his barn, nor one who puts off his work: industry makes work go well, but a man who puts off work is always at hand-grips with ruin. . . . Get two oxen, bulls of nine years; for their strength is unspent and they are in the prime of their age: they are best for work. They will not fight in the furrow and break the plough and then leave the work undone. Let a brisk fellow of forty years follow them, with a loaf of four quarters and eight slices for his dinner, one who will attend to his work and drive a straight furrow and is past the age for gaping after his fellows, but will keep his mind on his work. No younger man will be better than he at scattering the seed and avoiding double-sowing; for a man less staid gets disturbed, hankering after his fellows. . . . Pass by the smithy and its crowded lounge in winter time when the cold keeps men from field work,—for then an industrious man can greatly prosper his house—lest bitter winter catch you helpless and poor and you chafe a swollen foot with a shrunk hand. The idle man who waits on empty hope, lacking a livelihood, lays to heart mischief-making; it is not an wholesome hope that accompanies a needy man who lolls at ease while he has no sure livelihood.

Farming is the surest way to prosperity, but if a person desires to supplement his income by trade, he must plan carefully to avoid the dangers of seafaring.

But if desire for uncomfortable seafaring seize you; when the Pleiades plunge into the misty sea to escape Orion's rude strength, then truly gales of all kinds rage. Then keep ships no longer on the sparkling sea, but bethink you to till the land as I bid you. Haul up your ship upon the land and pack it closely with stones all round to keep off the power of the winds which blow damply, and draw out the bilge-plug so that the rain of heaven may not rot it. Put away all the tackle and fittings in your house, and stow the wings of the sea-going ship neatly, and hang up the well-shaped rudder over the smoke. You yourself wait until the season for sailing is come, and then haul your swift ship down to the sea and stow a convenient cargo in it, so that you may bring home profit, even as your father and mine, foolish Perses, used to sail on shipboard because he lacked sufficient livelihood. And one day he came to this very place crossing over a great stretch of sea; he left Aeolian Cyme and fled, not from riches and substance, but from wretched poverty which Zeus lays upon men, and he settled near Helicon in a miserable hamlet, Ascra, which is bad in winter, sultry in summer, and good at no time. But you, Perses, remember all works in their season but sailing especially. Admire a small ship, but put your freight in a large one; for the greater the lading, the greater will be your piled gain, if only the winds will keep back their harmful gales. If ever you turn your misguided heart to trading and wish to escape from debt and joyless hunger, I will show you the measures of the loud-roaring sea, though I have no skill in seafaring nor in ships; for never yet have I sailed by ship over the wide sea, but only to Euboea from Aulis where the Achaeans once stayed through much storm when they had gathered a great host from divine Hellas for Troy, the land of fair women. Then I crossed over to Chalcis, to the games of wise Amphidamas where the sons of the great-hearted hero proclaimed and appointed prizes. And there I boast that I gained the victory with a song and carried off an handled tripod which I dedicated to the Muses of Helicon, in the place where they first set me in the way of clear song. Such is all my experience of many-pegged ships; nevertheless I will tell you the will of Zeus who holds the aegis; for the Muses have taught me to sing in marvelous song. . . . Another time for men to go sailing is in spring when a man first sees leaves on the topmost shoot of a fig-tree as large as the foot-print that a cow makes; then the sea is passable, and this is the spring sailing time. For my part I do not praise it, for my heart does not like it. Such a sailing is snatched, and you will hardly avoid mischief. Yet in their ignorance men do even this, for wealth means life to poor mortals; but it is fearful to die among the waves. But I bid you consider all these things in your heart as I say. Do not put all your goods in hallow ships; leave the greater part behind, and put the lesser part on board; for it is a bad business to meet with disaster among the waves of the sea, as it is bad if you put too great a load on your wagon and break the axle, and your goods are spoiled. Observe due measure: and proportion is best in all things.

A person should think of marriage and establishing a household only when his prosperity is secure. Even then prudence in the selection of a wife is essential to success.

Bring home a wife to your house when you are of the right age, while you are not far short of thirty years nor much above; this is the right age for marriage. Let your wife have been grown up four years, and marry her in the fifth. Marry a maiden, so that you can teach her careful ways, and especially marry one who lives near you, but look well about you and see that your marriage will not be a joke to your neighbors. For a man wins nothing better than a good wife, and, again, nothing worse than a bad one, a greedy soul who roasts her man without fire, strong though he may be, and brings him to a raw old age.

4.4 Colonization and the Expansion of the *Polis* System: The Case of Cyrene

Between the mid eighth century B.C. *and the late sixth century* B.C., *Greeks founded hundreds of new* poleis *in the Mediterranean and Black Sea basins. Founding a colony was a difficult and dangerous process with a high risk of failure, and failure could mean death for the colonists. Only strong incentives could induce people to take such risks. Dreams of wealth from trade with non-Greeks such as the iron-rich Etruscans of Italy may have attracted some potential colonists, but for most, colonization represented hope for land and a new start—an escape from the socioeconomic and political tensions of archaic Greece. The hopes and fears of those first Greek explorers and colonists are evident in the* Odyssey: *their fears in the fantastic tales of Odysseus' encounters with savage monsters in his wanderings, and their hopes in Homer's account of Phaeacia, the perfect* polis *founded in a land of plenty at the ends of the earth. For a concrete idea of the circumstances that resulted in the foundation of a colony, historians turn to the fifth-century* B.C. *historian Herodotus' account of the founding of the city of Cyrene in modern Libya, and to a remarkable fourth-century* B.C. *Cyrenaean inscription that preserves the original terms under which the colony was organized.*[4]

4.4.1 Herodotus' Account

150. Thus far the history is delivered without variation both by the Theraeans and the Lacedaemonians; but from this point we have only the Theraean narrative. Grinus (they say), the son of Aesanius, a descendant of Theras, and king of the island of Thera, went to Delphi to offer a hecatomb on behalf of his native city. He was accompanied by a large number of the citizens, and among the rest by Battus, the son of Polymnestus, who belonged to the Minyan family of the Euphemidae. On Grinus consulting the oracle about other matters, the priestess gave him for answer that he should found a city in Libya. Grinus

---

[4]Herodotus, *The History of the Persian Wars* 4.150–159 (selections). From *The History of Herodotus*, Vol. 3, trans. George Rawlinson (New York: D. Appleton & Co., 1859–1860), pp. 102–109.

replied to this, "I, O lord, am too far advanced in years, and too inactive, for such a work. Bid one of these youngsters undertake it." As he spoke, he pointed towards Battus; and thus the matter rested for that time. When the embassy returned to Thera, small account was taken of the oracle by the Theraeans, as they were quite ignorant where Libya was, and were not so venturesome as to send out a colony in the dark.

151. Seven years passed from the utterance of the oracle, and not a drop of rain fell in Thera: All the trees in the island, except one, were killed with the drought. The Theraeans upon this sent to Delphi, and were reminded reproachfully, that they had never colonised Libya. So, as there was no help for it, they sent messengers to Crete, to inquire whether any of the Cretans, or of the strangers sojourning among them, had ever travelled as far as Libya: and these messengers of theirs, in their wanderings about the island, among other places visited Itanus, where they fell in with a man, whose name was Corobius, a dealer in purple. In answer to their inquiries, he told them that contrary winds had once carried him to Libya, where he had gone ashore on a certain island which was named Platea. So they hired this man's services, and took him back with them to Thera. A few persons then sailed from Thera to reconnoitre. Guided by Corobius to the island of Platea, they left him there with provisions for a certain number of months, and returned home with all speed to give their countrymen an account of the island.

152. During their absence, which was prolonged beyond the time that had been agreed upon, Corobius' provisions failed him. He was relieved, however, after a while, by a Samian vessel, under the command of a man named Colaeus, which, on its way to Egypt, was forced to put in at Platea. The crew, informed by Corobius of all the circumstances, left him sufficient food for a year. . . .

153. The Theraeans who had left Corobius at Platea, when they reached Thera, told their countrymen that they had colonised an island on the coast of Libya. They of Thera, upon this, resolved that men should be sent to join the colony from each of their seven districts, and that the brothers in every family should draw lots to determine who were to go. Battus was chosen to be king and leader of the colony. So these men departed for Platea on board of two fifty-oared ships. . . .

157. In this place they continued two years, but at the end of that time, as their ill luck still followed them, they left the island to the care of one of their number, and went in a body to Delphi, where they made complaint at the shrine, to the effect that, notwithstanding they had colonised Libya, they prospered as poorly as before. Hereon the priestess made them the following answer:

> Knowest thou better than I, fair Libya abounding in fleeces? Better the stranger than he who has trod it? O clever Theraeans!

Battus and his friends, when they heard this, sailed back to Platea: it was plain the god would not hold them acquitted of the colony till they were absolutely in Libya. So, taking with them the man whom they had left upon the island, they made a settlement on the mainland directly opposite Platea, fixing themselves at a place called Aziris, which is closed in on both sides by the most beautiful hills, and on one side is washed by a river.

158. Here they remained six years, at the end of which time the Libyans induced them to move, promising that they would lead them to a better situation. So the Greeks left Aziris,

and were conducted by the Libyans towards the west, their journey being so arranged, by the calculations of their guides, that they passed in the night the most beautiful district of that whole country, which is the region called Irasa. The Libyans brought them to a spring, which goes by the name of Apollo's fountain, and told them, "Here, Grecians, is the proper place for you to settle; for here the sky has a hole in it."

159. During the lifetime of Battus, the founder of the colony, who reigned forty years, and during that of his son Arcesilaus, who reigned sixteen, the Cyrenaeans continued at the same level, neither more nor fewer in number than they were at the first. But in the reign of the third king, Battus, surnamed the Happy, the advice of the Pythian priestess brought Greeks from every quarter into Libya, to join the settlement. The Cyrenaeans had offered to all comers a share in their lands; and the oracle had spoken as follows:

> He that is backward to share in the pleasant Libyan acres, sooner or later, I warn him, will feel regret at his folly.

Thus a great multitude were collected together to Cyrene, and the Libyans of the neighborhood found themselves stripped of large portions of their lands.

4.4.2   Oath of the Colonists[5]

Resolved by the Assembly. Since Apollo spontaneously told Battus and the Theraeans to found a colony in Cyrene, the Theraeans decided to dispatch Battus as the founder of the colony and king. The Theraeans shall sail as his comrades. They shall sail on equal terms; and one son shall be enrolled from each family. Those who sail shall be adults, and any free man from the Theraeans who wishes, may also sail.

If the colonists secure the settlement, any colonist who sails later to Libya shall have a share in the citizenship and honors. He also shall receive a lot from the unassigned land. But if they do not make the settlement secure, and the Theraeans cannot come to their aid and they suffer troubles for five years, the colonists may return without fear to Thera. They may return to their own property and become citizens of Thera.

If anyone is unwilling to sail when sent by the city, let him be subject to the death penalty and let his property be confiscated. Whoever receives or protects such a person—whether a father his son or a brother his brother—shall suffer the same punishment as the person who refused to sail. On these terms oaths were sworn by those remaining at Thera and those sailing to found the colony. They also cursed those who transgressed these conditions and did not abide by them, both those settling in Libya and those staying here.

They formed wax images and burned them while they uttered these curses, all of them together, men and women, boys and girls. The person who does not abide by these oaths, but transgresses, shall melt and flow away just as these images, he and his descendants and his property. But may there be many things and those good ones to those who abide by these oaths, both those sailing to Libya and those remaining in Thera, to themselves and their descendants.

---

[5]*Supplementum Epigraphicum Graecorum* 9.3. From Sarah B. Pomeroy et al., *Ancient Greece: A Political, Social, and Cultural History* (New York: Oxford University Press, 1999), p. 92. Used by permission.

4.5   Greeks and Non-Greeks in the Greek Colonies: The Foundation of Lampsacus

Colonization always involves encounters between peoples, and Greek colonization was no exception. Polyphemus, the cannibalistic Cyclops whose people "had no council places and laws" in the Odyssey, *was every colonist's nightmare, but few actually met such savages. Greek settlers sought land to farm and opportunities for trade, and that search brought them into areas already inhabited by settled populations. The results of such encounters varied. Sometimes they were mutually beneficial, as in central Italy or southern France, where the appearance of Greek luxury goods in native settlements attests to profitable trade. More often, unfortunately, the meeting was marked by suspicion and even violence, as is briefly noted at the end of Herodotus' account of the foundation of Cyrene, and as is clearly illustrated in this "cuckoo-in-the-nest" story taken by Plutarch from the history of the city of Lampsacus on the Turkish coast of the Hellespont by the fifth-century B.C. historian, Charon of Lampsacus.[6]*

There were twin brothers named Phobus and Blepsus from Phocaea, members of the family of the Codridae. One of these brothers, Phobus, was the first to throw himself into the sea from the Leucadian rocks, as Charon, the Lampsacenian, records. Possessing royal power and influence, he sailed along the coast to Parium on personal business. Becoming a friend and guest of Mandron, the ruler of the Pityoessenian Bebrycians, he came to their aid and fought as the ally of this people which was being harassed by its neighbors.

Mandron gave many other signs of friendliness to Phobus when he sailed away and promised to give him a portion of the land and city if he should wish to come to Pityoessa together with colonists from Phocaea. Phobus, therefore, persuaded his fellow citizens and dispatched his brother, who brought colonists with him. The colonists received from Mandron what they expected. Growing rich from spoils and loot seized from neighboring barbarians, they became first sources of envy and then fear to the Bebrycians. Desiring, therefore, to rid themselves of the settlers, they failed to persuade Mandron, who was a good and just man with regard to the Greeks. When Mandron was away, however, they prepared a plot to kill the Phocaeans.

Lampsace, the daughter of Mandron, an unmarried young woman, who had foreknowledge of the plot, at first tried to deter her friends and relatives and convince them that they were setting their hands to a terrible and unholy deed in killing men who had been benefactors and allies and now were fellow citizens. But as she did not persuade them, she told the Greeks in secret what was being done and urged them to be on their guard. They prepared a sacrifice and feast and invited the Pityoessenians to come outside the city to it. Then they divided themselves into two groups, and one seized the walls and the other slaughtered the Pityoessenians.

After gaining control of the city in this way, they sent after Mandron and urged him to rule jointly with men chosen from themselves. Lampsace, who had died from an illness, they buried in great state in the city and named it Lampsacus after her. And when Mandron begged off living with them in order to escape the suspicion of treachery and asked that he be allowed to take with him the children and wives of the dead, they sent them away gladly without doing them any harm. To Lampsace they first gave heroic honors and later they voted to offer sacrifice to her as a goddess; and they continue doing so.

---

[6]Plutarch, *Virtues of Women* 18.

4.6   Greeks and Scythians in the Black Sea: Coexistence and Interaction

Not all encounters between Greek colonists and non-Greeks ended in the sort of definitive Greek victory celebrated in the story of Lampsace. On the north coast of the Black Sea, Greek settlers came in contact with the Scythians, Iranian-speaking nomads who dominated the steppelands of Ukraine. Greek cities such as Olbia, a Milesian colony located on the lower Bug River in western Ukraine, had to find accommodations with the Scythians to survive. The resulting interaction was beneficial for both peoples. The Greek colonies provided trade goods and artisans, who created spectacular art works for the Scythian elite in exchange for the products of their territory such as skins, slaves, and grain. The terms of such accommodation were always precarious and required constant negotiation, as is clearly illustrated by Herodotus' vivid account of the unfortunate fate of the Scythian king Scylas, who tried to live in both worlds.[7]

76.   The Scythians have an extreme hatred of all foreign customs, particularly of those in use among the Greeks. . . .

78.   Ariapeithes, the Scythian king, had several sons, among them, this Scylas, who was the child, not of a native Scyth, but of a woman of Istria. Brought up by her, Scylas gained an acquaintance with the Greek language and letters. Some time afterwards, Ariapeithes was treacherously slain by Spargapeithes, king of the Agathyrsi; whereupon Scylas succeeded to the throne, and married one of his father's wives, a woman named Opoea. This Opoea was a Scythian by birth, and had brought Ariapeithes a son called Oricus. Now when Scylas found himself king of Scythia, as he disliked the Scythic mode of life, and was attached, by his upbringing to the manners of the Greeks, he made it his usual practice, whenever he came with his army to the town of the Borysthenites, who, according to their own account, are colonists of the Milesians. He made it his practice, I say, to leave the army before the city, and having entered within the walls by himself, and carefully closed the gates, to exchange his Scythian dress for Grecian garments, and in this attire to walk about the market-place, without guards or retinue. The Borysthenites kept watch at the gates, so that no Scythian might see the king dressed this way. Scylas, meanwhile, lived exactly as the Greeks, and even offered sacrifices to the gods according to the Grecian rites. In this way he would pass a month, or more, with the Borysthenites, after which he would clothe himself again in his Scythian dress, and so take his departure. This he did repeatedly, and even built himself a house in Borysthenes, and married a wife there who was a native of the place.

79.   But when the time came, that was ordained to bring him woe, the occasion of his ruin was the following. He wanted to he initiated in the rites of the Bacchic Dionysus, and was on the point of obtaining admission to the rites, when a most strange prodigy occurred to him. The house, which he possessed, as I mentioned a short time back, in the city of the Borysthenites, a building of great extent and erected at a vast cost, round which there stood a number of sphinxes and griffins carved in white marble, was struck by lightning from on high and burnt to the ground. Scylas, nevertheless, went on, and received the initiation. Now the Scythians generally reproach the Greeks with their Bacchanal rage, and to say that it is not reasonable to imagine there is a god who impels men to madness. No sooner, therefore, was Scylas

---

[7]*The History of Herodotus*, trans. George Rawlinson. From Francis R. B. Godolphin, *The Greek Historians*, Vol. 1 (New York: Random House, 1942), pp. 252–255.

initiated in the Bacchic mysteries than one of the Borysthenites went and carried the news to the Scythians. "You Scyths laugh at us," he said, "because we rave when the god seizes us. But now our god has seized upon your king, who raves like us, and is maddened by the influence. If you think I do not tell you true, come with me, and I will show him to you." The chiefs of the Scythians went with the man accordingly, and the Borysthenite, conducting them into the city, placed them secretly on one of the towers. Presently Scylas passed by with the band of revelers, raving like the rest, and was seen by the watchers. Regarding the matter as a very great misfortune, they instantly departed, and came and told the army what they had witnessed.

80. When, therefore, Scylas, after leaving Borysthenes, was about returning home, the Scythians broke out into revolt. They put at their head Octamasadas, grandson (on the mother's side) of Teres. Then Scylas, when he learned the danger with which he was threatened, and the reason of the disturbance, made his escape to Thrace. Octamasadas, discovering whither he had fled, marched after him, and had reached the Ister [*i.e., the Danube*], when he was met by the forces of the Thracians. The two armies were about to engage, but before they joined battle, Sitalces sent a message to Octamasadas to this effect, "Why should there be trial of arms between us? You are my own sister's son, and you have in your keeping my brother. Surrender him into my hands, and I will give Scylas back to you. So neither you nor I will risk our armies." Sitalces sent this message to Octamasadas by a herald, and Octamasadas, with whom a brother of Sitalces had formerly taken refuge, accepted the terms. He surrendered his own uncle to Sitalces, and obtained in exchange his brother Scylas. Sitalces took his brother with him and withdrew; hut Octamasadas beheaded Scylas upon the spot. Thus rigidly do the Scythians maintain their own customs, and thus severely do they punish those who adopt foreign usages.

Chapter 5

▼▼▼

Warfare and the *Polis*

Greek-speaking peoples inhabited the southern portion of the Balkan peninsula from at least the first half of the second millennium B.C. From the earliest days of Greek settlement in Greece until the Roman conquest in the second century B.C. permanently ended ancient Greek independence, the ancient sources allow no doubt that the central fact of the history of Greece in antiquity was war. Greek literature began with Homer's *Illiad*, a celebration of war, and war was the great theme of Greek historiography. Indeed, the normality of war was so taken for granted that Greek thinkers felt no need to examine seriously the causes of war. Greek diplomacy lacked even the concept of peace before the fourth century B.C. What historians call peace treaties were in actuality only armistices that specified the length of time before hostilities could legitimately resume. Not surprisingly, throughout Greek history the primary male social role was that of a warrior.

The primacy of the warrior role is already evident in the Homeric epics, but there its exercise is limited to the members of the small warrior elite Homer calls "heroes and kings." This situation changed with the spread of the *polis* and the almost simultaneous adoption of hoplite warfare in the seventh century B.C. Reduced to its essentials, hoplite warfare involved the collision, in a brief but fierce battle, of two armies composed of large numbers of similarly equipped armored infantry fighting in close formations called "phalanxes." Victory belonged to the *polis* whose army could best maintain its discipline and cohesion in conflicts whose horror is vividly evoked by the Spartan poet Tyrtaeus.

Since the *polis* was essentially a community of citizens, the introduction of hoplite warfare inevitably meant that the citizen body became a community of warriors whose chief obligation was to serve in the city's phalanx. A young man's admission to the privileges and responsibilities of citizenship was marked by the bestowal of his first set of arms and armor in public ceremonies such as the Athenian Apatouria. Death in battle while defending one's city brought honor and regard from one's fellow citizens. The twin obligations of serving in the phalanx for the whole of one's adult life, roughly from age 18 to 60, and of providing one's own arms and armor meant that a *polis's* citizen body was in essence an unusually tightly knit "men's club" of propertied farmers held together by fictive ties of kinship and the shared experience of battle.

The intimate linkage between service as a warrior and citizenship was common to all *poleis*, but it was clearest at the south Peloponnesian city of Sparta. There the need to maintain control of a large and restive slave population resulted in the formation of a unique society whose institutions were intended to ensure that every citizen could and did perform the role of a warrior. From antiquity almost to the present, the apparent success of Sparta in producing a citizen body embued with a common civic ideal that placed the welfare of the community above that of the individual has inspired reform-minded philosophers and political theorists of all political persuasions to hold up Sparta as a mirror to their own societies in the form of speculative fictions such as Thomas More's *Utopia* and Jean Jacques Rousseau's *Social Contract*.

Closely connected to the spread of the hoplite style of fighting was a dramatic change in the place of athletics in Greek public life and the value placed on athletic achievements in Greek popular culture. The reason for this seemingly surprising development is clear. Warrior, citizen, and athlete were the three principal aristocratic public male roles in ancient Greece, a fact well illustrated by the use of the image of the young male athlete to represent both the good warrior and the good citizen in Greek art. Understandably, therefore, Greek aristocrats, who, because of phalanx tactics, were denied the opportunity to win personal glory and political and social influence in their *poleis* through individual success in battle, turned increasingly to the other competitive sphere available to them, athletics, to achieve the same goals.

The results were twofold. First, the five major athletic festivals—the Olympian, Panathenaic, Ithmian, Nemean, and Pythian games—became some of the few truly Panhellenic institutions as their popularity soared, and they attracted athletes from the whole Greek world. Second, athletic victors became celebrities. Their feats were celebrated by leading artists and poets, and their cities rewarded them by supplementing the prizes they had already won at the games with valuable gifts, special privileges, and, most important, leadership positions in public life.

Although the close connection between athletic success and political and social prominence was denounced as early as the sixth century B.C. by intellectuals such as Xenophanes, who claimed that philosophy was a sounder preparation for public life, their views had little influence on Greek public opinion. Athlete-politicians, such as the Diagorids, who dominated politics at Rhodes for over two generations in the fifth and early fourth centuries B.C. remained a central feature of *polis* life throughout the archaic and classical periods of Greek history. Only the emergence in the Hellenistic period of career athletes, who devoted their life to training and competing in the games in the circuit, severed the tie between athletic victory and public influence.

5.1   The Aristocratic Warrior

The close connection between political privilege and military service is evident at the very beginning of classical Greek history and literature in the Iliad. *In this work, Homer depicts the societies of both the Greeks and the Trojans as dominated by a warrior elite of great landowners he calls "heroes" and "kings." These aristocratic warriors claimed to be descendants of the gods, and, because of their central role in battle, they alone had the right to take an active role in the governance of their communities. This relationship between military function and socioeconomic and political position is placed in a positive light in this speech, assigned the Lycian hero Sarpedon.*[1]

---

[1]Homer, *Iliad* 12, lines 290–328. From *The Iliad of Homer*, trans. Samuel Butler (London: A. C. Fifield, 1914), pp. 195–196.

5.1.1   The Warrior Ideal

Still the Trojans and brave Hector would not yet have broken down the gates and the great bar, had not Zeus turned his son Sarpedon against the Argives as a lion against a herd of horned cattle. Before him he held his shield of hammered bronze, that the smith had beaten so fair and round, and had lined with ox hides which he had made fast with rivets of gold all round the shield; this he held in front of him, and brandishing his two spears came on like some lion of the wilderness, who has been long famished for want of meat and will dare break even into a well-fenced homestead to try and get at the sheep. He may find the shepherds keeping watch over their flocks with dogs and spears, but he is in no mind to be driven from the fold till he has had a try for it; he will either spring on a sheep and carry it off, or be hit by a spear from some strong hand—even so was Sarpedon fain to attack the wall and break down its battlements. Then he said to Glaucus son of Hippolochus, "Glaucus, why in Lycia do we receive especial honor as regards our place at table? Why are the choicest portions served us and our cups kept brimming, and why do men look up to us as though we were gods? Moreover we hold a large estate by the banks of the river Xanthus, fair with orchard lawns and wheat-growing land; it becomes us, therefore, to take our stand at the head of all the Lycians and bear the brunt of the fight, that one may say to another, 'Our princes in Lycia eat the fat of the land and drink the best of wine, but they are fine fellows; they fight well and are ever at the front in battle.' My good friend, if, when we were once out of this fight, we could escape old age and death thenceforward and for ever, I should neither press forward myself nor bid you do so, but death in ten thousand shapes hangs ever over our heads, and no man can elude him: therefore let us go forward and either win glory for ourselves, or yield it to another."

The real (and sometimes arbitrary) power that the archaic warrior aristocrats could exercise over the rest of their society by virtue of their military preeminence is vividly expressed in the scolion, or drinking song, ascribed to a Cretan warrior named Hybrias.[2]

5.1.2   The Warrior and Society: The Drinking Song of Hybrias

My great wealth is my spear and sword and fine animal hide shield, the defense of my flesh. For it is with this that I sow, with this that I reap, with this that I tread out the sweet wine from the grape. Because of this I am called lord of slaves. As for those who do not dare to bear spear and sword and fine animal hide shield, the defense of flesh, they all bend their knee in fear and do me reverence, addressing me as lord and great king.

5.2   The Hoplite Revolution and the Citizen Soldier

The link between community leadership and the achievement of personal glory in battle evident in Sarpedon's speech was severed in the seventh century B.C. with the adoption of the phalanx tactics typical of hoplite warfare by the poleis of the Greek mainland. Composed of anonymous masses of similarly armed soldiers, the phalanx was the ideal military expression of the communal ideal of the polis.

---

[2]Athenaeus, *Deipnosophists* 15.695–696.

The earliest literary evidence for the redefinition of the relationship between the military and the community is provided by the poem of the mid-seventeenth-century B.C. Spartan poet Tyrtaeus. In this poem, Tyrtaeus clearly states for the first time the idea that the willingness to endure the horrid reality of hoplite battle was the primary obligation of a citizen. Tyrtaeus expresses this idea in negative terms by highlighting the scorn of the community for a coward.[3]

5.2.1   The Reality of Battle

It is a fine thing for a good man to fall in the front line fighting on behalf of his country; but it is a grievous fate for a man to leave his city and rich fields and wander begging with his dear mother, aged father, small children, and wedded wife. For he will be met with hostility by those to whom he comes, humbled by need and awful poverty. He shames his family and ruins his noble beauty, and every form of disgrace and evil follows him. If, therefore, there is no concern or respect or regard or pity for a wandering man, let us fight with all our heart for this land and let us die for our children without ever a thought for our lives. Make the heart in your chests great with courage and do not hesitate to fight with the enemy.

O Young men, stand beside each other and fight. Do not begin shameful flight or fear. Do not leave behind, fallen to the ground, the old men whose knees are no longer agile, for this, indeed, is disgraceful, that an old man, already white haired and gray of beard, lie fallen in the front line, breathing out his brave soul in the dust while holding his bloody genitals in his dear hands. It is a disgraceful sight and one foul to see: his naked flesh. But for a young man all is in order while he has the beautiful bloom of beloved youth. While he is alive, he is admired by men and desired by women and beautiful when he falls in the front line. So let each man set his feet firmly on the earth and wait, biting his lip with his teeth.

The positive side of the hoplite ideal is illustrated in this selection, where the Athenian statesman Solon offers the Lydian king Croesus the case of the Athenian Tellus as the exemplar of the idea that a happy life is one that ends well: Tellus died in battle defending Athens, received from his fellow citizens the honor of a civic funeral, and was survived by sons who would fill his place in the citizen body.[4]

5.2.2   A Good Citizen: Tellus of Athens

28. Croesus afterwards, in the course of many years, brought under his sway almost all the nations to the west of the Halys. The Lycians and Cilicians alone continued free; all the other tribes he reduced and held in subjection. They were the following: the Lydians, Phrygians, Mysians, Mariandynians, Chalybians, Paphlagonians, Thynians, and Bithynian Thracians, Carians, Ionians, Dorians, Aeolians, and Pamphylians.

---

[3]Tyrtaeus Fragment 10. From *Elegy and Iambus*, Vol. 1, ed. J. M. Edmonds (Cambridge, MA: Harvard University Press, 1931), pp. 69–71.
[4]Herodotus, *The History of the Persian Wars* 1.28–31 (selections). From *The History of Herodotus*, Vol. 1, trans. George Rawlinson (New York: D. Appleton & Co., 1859–1860), pp. 133–135.

29. When all these conquests had been added to the Lydian empire, and the prosperity of Sardis was now at its height, there came thither, one after another, all the sages of Greece living at the time, and among them Solon, the Athenian. He was on his travels, having left Athens to be absent ten years, under the pretence of wishing to see the world, but really to avoid being forced to repeal any of the laws which, at the request of the Athenians, he had made for them. Without his sanction the Athenians could not repeal them, as they had bound themselves under a heavy curse to be governed for ten years by the laws which should be imposed on them by Solon.

30. On this account, as well as to see the world, Solon set out upon his travels, in the course of which he went to Egypt to the court of Amasis, and also came on a visit to Croesus at Sardis. Croesus received him as his guest, and lodged him in the royal palace. On the third or fourth day after, he bade his servants conduct Solon over his treasuries, and show him all their greatness and magnificence. When he had seen them all, and, so far as time allowed, inspected them, Croesus addressed this question to him, "Stranger of Athens, we have heard much of your wisdom and of your travels through many lands, from love of knowledge and a wish to see the world. I am curious therefore to inquire of you, whom, of all the men that you have seen, you consider the most happy?" This he asked because he thought himself the happiest of mortals; but Solon answered him without flattery, according to his true sentiments, "Tellus of Athens, sire." Full of astonishment at what he heard, Croesus demanded sharply, "And wherefore do you deem Tellus happiest?" To which the other replied, "First, because his country was flourishing in his days, and he himself had sons both beautiful and good and he lived to see children born to each of them, and these children all grew up; and further because, after a life spent in what our people look upon as comfort, his end was surpassingly glorious. In a battle between the Athenians and their neighbors near Eleusis, he came to the assistance of his countrymen, routed the foe, and died upon the field most gallantly. The Athenians gave him a public funeral on the spot where he fell, and paid him the highest honors."

31. Thus did Solon admonish Croesus by the example of Tellus, enumerating the manifold particulars of his happiness. . . .

32. . . . Croesus broke in angrily, "What, stranger of Athens, is my happiness then, valued so little by you, that you do not even put me on a level with private men?"

"Croesus," replied the other, "you asked a question concerning the condition of man, of one who knows that the power above us is full of jealousy, and fond of troubling our lot. A long life gives one to witness much, and experience much oneself, that one would not choose. . . . For yourself, Croesus, I see that you are wonderfully rich, and the lord of many nations; but with respect to your question, I have no answer to give, until I hear that you have closed your life happily. For assuredly he who possesses great store of riches is no nearer happiness than he who has what suffices for his daily needs, unless luck attend upon him, and so he continue in the enjoyment of all his good things to the end of life."

On the other hand, a man's inability to fulfill the warrior role was always considered grounds for potentially excluding him from the ranks of the full citizens, as can be seen in this selection, where the fourth-century B.C. Athenian historian and essayist Xenophon claims that, unlike farmers, tradesmen cannot be good citizens because the conditions of their work render them unfit for hoplite service.

5.2.3   Only Farmers Can Be Good Citizens[5]

v.—All this I relate to you (continued Socrates) to show you that quite high and mighty people find it hard to hold aloof from agriculture, devotion to which art would seem to be thrice blest, combining as it does a certain sense of luxury with the satisfaction of an improved estate, and such a training of physical energies as shall fit a man to play a free man's part. Earth, in the first place, freely offers to those that labor all things necessary to the life of man; and, as if that were not enough, makes further contribution of a thousand luxuries. It is she supplies with sweetest scent and fairest show all things wherewith to adorn the altars and statues of the gods, or deck man's person. It is to her we owe our many delicacies of flesh or fowl or vegetable growth; since with the tillage of the soil is closely linked the art of breeding sheep and cattle, whereby we mortals may offer sacrifices well pleasing to the gods, and satisfy our personal needs withal.

Earth, too, adds stimulus in wartime to earth's tillers; she pricks them on to aid the country under arms, and this she does by fostering her fruits in open field, the prize of valor for the mightiest. For this also is the art athletic, this of husbandry; as thereby men are fitted to run, and hurl the spear, and leap with the best.

For myself, I marvel greatly if it has ever fallen to the lot of freeborn man to own a choicer possession, or to discover an occupation more seductive, or of wider usefulness in life than this.

But, furthermore, earth of her own will gives lessons in justice and uprightness to all who can understand her meaning, since the nobler the service of devotion rendered, the ampler the riches of her recompense. One day, perchance, these pupils of hers, whose conversation in past times was in husbandry, shall, by reason of the multitude of invading armies, be ousted from their labors. The work of their hands may indeed be snatched from them, but they were brought up in stout and manly fashion. They stand, each one of them, in body and soul equipped; and, save God himself shall hinder them, they will march into the territory of those their human hinderers, and take from them the wherewithal to support their lives. Since often enough in war it is surer and safer to quest for food with sword and buckler than with all the instruments of husbandry.

But there is yet another lesson to be learnt in the public school of husbandry—the lesson of mutual assistance.

"Shoulder to shoulder" must we march to meet the invader; "shoulder to shoulder" stand to compass the tillage of the soil. Therefore it is that the husbandman, who means to win in his avocation, must see that he creates enthusiasm in his workpeople and a spirit of ready obedience; which is just what a general attacking an enemy will scheme to bring about, when he deals out gifts to the brave and castigation to those who are disorderly.

Nor will there be lacking seasons of exhortation, the general haranguing his troops and the husbandman his laborers; nor because they are slaves do they less than free men need the lure of hope and happy expectation, that they may willingly stand to their posts.

It was an excellent saying of his who named husbandry "the mother and nurse of all the arts," for while agriculture prospers all other arts alike are vigorous and strong, but where the land is forced to remain desert, the spring that feeds the other arts is dried up; they dwindle, I had almost said, one and all, by land and sea.

---

[5]Xenophon, *Oeconomicus* 5–6.10 (selections). From *The Works of Xenophon*, Vol. 3, trans. H. G. Dakyns (London: Macmillan & Co., 1890), pp. 218–224.

Soc. Well, then, we agreed that economy was the proper title of a branch of knowledge, and this branch of knowledge appeared to be that whereby men are enabled to enhance the value of their houses or estates; and by this word "house or estate" we understood the whole of a man's possessions; and "possessions" again we defined to include those things which the possessor should find advantageous for the purposes of his life; and things advantageous finally were discovered to mean all that a man knows how to use and turn to good account. Further, for a man to learn all branches of knowledge not only seemed to us an impossibility, but we thought we might well follow the example of civil communities in rejecting the base mechanic arts so called, on the ground that they destroy the bodies of the artisans, as far as we can see, and crush their spirits.

The clearest proof of this, we said, could be discovered if, on the occasion of a hostile in-road, one were to seat the husbandman and the artisans apart in two divisions, and then proceed to put this question to each group in turn: "Do you think it better to defend our country districts or to retire from the fields and guard the walls?" And we anticipated that those concerned with the soil would vote to defend the soil; while the artisans would vote not to fight, but, in docile obedience to their training, to sit with folded hands, neither expending toil nor venturing their lives.

5.3   The Hoplite *Polis:* Sparta

Hoplite warfare eventually became the norm for all Greek poleis. The city where the social implications of this form of warfare were most fully realized, however, was Sparta. The masses of enslaved fellow Greeks, called Helots, who were the source of the city's prosperity, also posed an ever-present threat of rebellion. Faced with this danger, the Spartans sought security by remolding their city's institutions to enable every Spartan to serve in the hoplite phalanx. The result was a unique society in which every male Spartan passed through a strictly regimented educational system that was intended to transform him into a hoplite ready to face the rigors of battle described above by Tyrtaeus. Paradoxically, this "boot camp" polis was probably also the earliest Greek democracy, since it was first in Sparta that every male was able to fulfill the citizen's primary obligation of serving his city as a warrior and thereby gained the right to attend the assembly and hold at least some elective offices. For almost three centuries, from the mid seventh century B.C. until 371 B.C. when the city was massively defeated by Thebes and impoverished as a result of the loss of most of her Helots, the Spartan army seemed invincible. Xenophon's Constitution of the Spartans gives a vivid picture of Sparta just before her defeat by Thebes, one that is all the more valuable because the author was one of the few Greek authors to write about Sparta from personal experience, having lived there during his exile from Athens in the early fourth century B.C.[6]

1. I recall the astonishment with which I first noted the unique population of Sparta among the states of Hellas, the relatively sparse population, and at the same time the extraordinary power and prestige of the community. I was puzzled to account for the fact. It was only when I came to consider the peculiar institutions of the Spartans that my wonderment ceased. Or rather, it is transferred to the legislator who gave them those laws, obedience to which has been the secret of their prosperity. This legislator, Lycurgus, I

---

[6]Xenophon, *The Constitution of the Spartans* (selections). From *The Works of Xenophon*, Vol. 2, trans. Dakyns, pp. 295–323.

admire, and hold him to have been one of the wisest of mankind. Certainly he was no servile imitator of other states. It was by a stroke of invention rather, and on a pattern much in opposition to the commonly accepted one, that he brought his fatherland to this pinnacle of prosperity.

Marriage and the Rearing of Children

Take for example—and it is well to begin at the beginning—the whole topic of the begetting and rearing of children. Throughout the rest of the world the young girl, who will one day become a mother (and I speak of those who may be held to be well brought up), is nurtured on the plainest food attainable, with the scantiest addition of meat or other condiments; while as to wine they train them either to total abstinence or to take it highly diluted with water. And in imitation, as it were, of the handicraft type, since the majority of artificers are sedentary, we, the rest of the Hellenes, are content that our girls should sit quietly and work wools. That is all we demand of them. But how are we to expect that women nurtured in this fashion should produce a splendid offspring?

Lycurgus pursued a different path. Clothes were things, he held, the furnishing of which might well enough be left to female slaves. And, believing that the highest function of a free woman was the bearing of children, in the first place he insisted on the training of the body as incumbent no less on the female than the male; and in pursuit of the same idea instituted rival contests in running and feats of strength for women as for men. His belief was that where both parents were strong their progeny would be found to be more vigorous.

And so again after marriage. In view of the fact that immoderate intercourse is elsewhere permitted during the earlier period of matrimony, he adopted a principle directly opposite. He laid it down as an ordinance that a man should be ashamed to be seen visiting the chamber of his wife, whether going in or coming out. When they did meet under such restraint the mutual longing of these lovers could not but be increased, and the fruit which might spring from such intercourse would tend to be more robust than theirs whose affections are cloyed by satiety. By a farther step in the same direction he refused to allow marriages to be contracted at any period of life according to the fancy of the parties concerned. Marriage, as he ordained it, must only take place in the prime of bodily vigor, this too being, as he believed, a condition conducive to the production of healthy offspring. Or again, to meet the case which might occur of an old man wedded to a young wife. Considering the jealous watch which such husbands are apt to keep over their wives, he introduced a directly opposite custom; that is to say, he made it incumbent on the aged husband to introduce some one whose qualities, physical and moral, he admired, to beget him children. Or again, in the case of a man who might not desire to live with a wife permanently, but yet might still be anxious to have children of his own worthy the name, the lawgiver laid down a law in his behalf. Such a one might select some woman, the wife of some man, well born herself and blest with fair offspring, and, the sanction and consent of her husband first obtained, raise up children for himself through her.

The Education of a Boy

2. I wish now to explain the systems of education in fashion here and elsewhere. Throughout the rest of Hellas the custom on the part of those who claim to educate their sons in the best way is as follows. As soon as the children are of an age to understand what is said to them they are immediately placed under the charge of Paidagogoi (or tutors), who are also attendants,

and sent off to the school of some teacher to be taught grammar, music, and the concerns of the palaestra [*gymnasium*].

But when we turn to Lycurgus, instead of leaving it to each member of the state privately to appoint a slave to be his son's tutor, he set over the young Spartans a public guardian, the Paidonomos, to give him his proper title, with complete authority over them. This guardian was selected from those who filled the highest magistracies. He had authority to hold musters of the boys, and as their overseer, in case of any misbehavior, to chastise severely. The legislator further provided the pastor with a body of youths in the prime of life, and bearing whips, to inflict punishment when necessary, with this happy result that in Sparta modesty and obedience ever go hand in hand, nor is there lack of either.

3. Coming to the critical period at which a boy ceases to be a boy and becomes a youth, we find that it is just then that the rest of the world proceed to emancipate their children from the private tutor and the schoolmaster, and, without substituting any further ruler, are content to launch them into absolute independence.

Here, again, Lycurgus took an entirely opposite view of the matter. This, if observation might be trusted, was the season when the tide of animal spirits flows fast, and the froth of insolence rises to the surface; when, too, the most violent appetites for pleasures invade the mind. This, then, was the right moment at which to impose constant labors upon the growing youth, and to devise for him a subtle system of absorbing occupation. And by a crowning enactment, which said that he who shrank from the duties imposed on him would forfeit henceforth all claim to the glorious honors of the state, he caused, not only the public authorities, but those personally interested in the youths to take serious pains so that no single individual of them should by an act of cowardice find himself utterly despised within the body politic.

Furthermore, in his desire firmly to implant modesty in them he imposed a special rule. In the streets they were to keep their hands within the folds of the cloak; they were to walk in silence and without turning their heads to gaze, but rather to keep their eyes fixed upon the ground before them. And hereby it would seem to be proved conclusively that, even in the matter of quiet bearing and sobriety, the masculine type may claim greater strength than that which we attribute to the nature of women. At any rate, you might sooner expect a stone image to find voice than one of those Spartan youths; to divert the eyes of some bronze statue were less difficult. And as to quiet bearing, no bride ever stepped in bridal bower with more natural modesty. Note them when they have reached the public table. The plainest answer to the question asked, that is all you need expect to hear from their lips.

Daily Life in Sparta

With regard to those who have already passed the vigor of early manhood, and on whom the highest magistracies henceforth devolve, there is a like contrast. In Greece generally we find that at this age the need of further attention to physical strength is removed, although the imposition of military service continues. But Lycurgus made it customary for that section of his citizens to regard hunting as the highest honor suited to their age; but not to the exclusion of any public duty. And his aim was that they might be equally able to undergo the fatigues of war with those in the prime of early manhood.

5. The above is a fairly exhaustive statement of the institutions traceable to the legislation of Lycurgus in connection with the successive stages of a citizen's life. It remains that I should endeavor to describe the style of living which he established for the whole body, irrespective of age. It will be understood that, when Lycurgus first came to deal with the question,

the Spartans, like the rest of the Greeks, used to mess privately at home. Tracing more than half the current misdemeanors to this custom, he was determined to drag his people out into the daylight, and so he invented the public mess-rooms. Whereby he expected at any rate to minimise the transgression of orders. . . .

This too must be borne in mind, that in other states equals in age, for the most part, associate together, and such an atmosphere is little conducive to modesty. Whereas in Sparta Lycurgus was careful so to blend the ages that the younger men must benefit largely by the experience of the elder—an education in itself, and the more so since by custom of the country, conversation at the common meal has reference to the honorable acts which this man or that man may have performed in relation to the state. The scene, in fact, but little lends itself to the intrusion of violence or drunken riot; ugly speech and ugly deeds alike are out of place. Among other good results obtained through this out-door system of meals may be mentioned these: There is the necessity of walking home when the meal is over, and a consequent anxiety not to be caught tripping under the influence of wine, since they all know of course that the supper-table must be presently abandoned, and that they must move as freely in the dark as in the day, even the help of a torch to guide the steps being forbidden to all on active service. . . .

6. There are other points in which this legislator's views run counter to those commonly accepted. Thus: in other states the individual citizen is master over his own children, servants and belongings generally; but Lycurgus, whose aim was to secure to all the citizens a considerable share in one another's goods without mutual injury, enacted that each one should have an equal power over his neighbor's children as over his own. The principle is this. When a man knows that this, that, and the other person are fathers of children subject to his own authority, he must perforce deal by them even as he desires his own children to be dealt by. And, if a boy chance to have received a whipping, not from his own father but some other, and goes and complains to his own father, it would be thought wrong on the part of that father if he did not inflict a second whipping on his son. A striking proof, in its way, how completely they trust each other not to impose dishonorable commands upon their children.

7. There are yet other customs in Sparta which Lycurgus instituted in opposition to those of the rest of Greece, and the following among them. We all know that in the generality of states every one devotes his full energy to the business of making money: one man as a tiller of the soil, another as a mariner, a third as a merchant, whilst others depend on various arts to earn a living. But at Sparta Lycurgus forbade his freeborn citizens to have anything whatsoever to do with the concerns of money-making. As freemen, he enjoined upon them to regard as their concern exclusively those activities upon which the foundations of civic liberty are based.

8. But to proceed. We are all aware that there is no state in the world in which greater obedience is shown to magistrates, and to the laws themselves, than Sparta. But, for my part, I am disposed to think that Lycurgus could never have attempted to establish this healthy condition, until he had first secured the unanimity of the most powerful members of the state. I infer this for the following reasons. In other states the leaders in rank and influence do not even desire to be thought to fear the magistrates. Such a thing they would regard as in itself a symbol of servility. In Sparta, on the contrary, the stronger a man is the more readily does he bow before constituted authority. And indeed, they pride themselves on their humility, and on a prompt obedience, running, or at any rate not crawling with laggard step, at the word of

command. Such an example of eager discipline, they are persuaded, set by themselves, will not fail to be followed by the rest. And this is precisely what has taken place. It is reasonable to suppose that it was these same noblest members of the state who combined to lay the foundation of the ephorate, after they had come to the conclusion themselves that of all the blessings which a state, or an army, or a household can enjoy, obedience is the greatest. Since, as they could not but reason, the greater the power with which men fence about authority, the greater the fascination it will exercise upon the mind of the citizen, to the enforcement of obedience.

Accordingly the ephors are competent to punish whomsoever they choose: they have power to exact fines on the spur of the moment; they have power to depose magistrates in mid career, nay, actually to imprison and bring them to trial on the capital charge. Entrusted with these vast powers, they do not, as do the rest of states, allow the magistrates elected to exercise authority as they like, right through the year of office; but, in the style rather of despotic monarchs, or presidents of the games, at the first symptom of an offence against the law they inflict chastisement without warning and without hesitation.

But of all the many beautiful contrivances invented by Lycurgus to kindle a willing obedience to the laws in the hearts of the citizens, none, to my mind, was happier or more excellent than his unwillingness to deliver his code to the people at large, until, attended by the most powerful members of the state, he had betaken himself to Delphi, and there made inquiry of the god whether it were better for Sparta, and conducive to her interests, to obey the laws which he had framed. And not until the divine answer came, "Better will it be in every way," did he deliver them, laying it down as a last ordinance that to refuse obedience to a code which had the sanction of the Pythian god himself was a thing not illegal only, but impious.

9. The following too may well excite our admiration for Lycurgus. I speak of the consummate skill with which he induced the whole state of Sparta to regard an honorable death as preferable to an ignoble life. And indeed if any one will investigate the matter, he will find that by comparison with those who make it a principle to retreat in face of danger, actually fewer of these Spartans die in battle, since, to speak truth, salvation, it would seem, attends on virtue far more frequently than on cowardice—virtue, which is at once easier and sweeter, richer in resource and stronger of arm, than her opposite. And that virtue has another familiar attendant—to wit, glory—needs no showing, since all wish to ally themselves somehow with the good.

Yet the actual means by which he gave currency to these principles is a point which it were well not to overlook. It is clear that the lawgiver set himself deliberately to provide all the blessings of heaven for the good man, and a sorry and ill-starred existence for the coward.

In other states the man who shows himself base and cowardly wins to himself an evil reputation and the nickname of a coward, but that is all. For the rest he buys and sells in the same market-place with the good man; he sits beside him at the play; he exercises with him in the same gymnasium, and all as suits his humor. But at Lacedaemon there is not one man who would not feel ashamed to welcome the coward at the common mess-table, or to try conclusions with such an antagonist in a wrestling bout. Consider the day's round of his existence. The sides are being picked for a game of ball, but he is left out as the odd man: there is no place for him. During the choric dance he is driven away into ignominious quarters. Nay, in the very streets it is he who must step aside for others to pass, or, being seated, he must rise and make room, even for a younger man. At home he will have his maiden relatives to support in their isolation (and they will hold him to blame for their unwedded lives). A hearth with no wife to bless it—that is a condition he must face, and yet he will have to pay damages for incurring it. Let him not roam abroad with a smiling countenance; let him not imitate men whose fame is irreproachable, or he shall feel on his back the blows of his superiors. Such being the weight of infamy which is laid upon all cowards, I, for my part, am not surprised if in Sparta they deem death preferable to a life so steeped in dishonor and reproach.

The Spartan Way of War

11. The above form a common stock of blessings, open to every Spartan to enjoy, alike in peace and in war. But if any one desires to be informed in what way the legislator improved upon the ordinary machinery of warfare and in reference to an army in the field, it is easy to satisfy his curiosity.

In the first instance, the ephors announce by proclamation the limit of age to which the service applies for cavalry and heavy infantry; and in the next place, for the various handicraftsman. So that, even on active service, the Lacedaemonians are well supplied with all the conveniences enjoyed by people living as citizens at home. All implements and instruments whatsoever, which an army may need in common, are ordered to be in readiness, some on wagons and others on baggage animals. In this way anything omitted can hardly escape detection.

For the actual encounter under arms, the following inventions are attributed to him. The soldier has a crimson-coloured uniform and a heavy shield of bronze; his theory being that such an equipment has no sort of feminine association, and is altogether most warrior-like. It is most quickly burnished, it is least readily tarnished.

He further permitted those who were above the age of early manhood to wear their hair long. For so, he conceived, they would appear of larger stature, more free and indomitable, and of a more terrible aspect.

So furnished and accoutred, he divided his citizen soldiers into six *morae* (regimental divisions) of cavalry and heavy infantry. Each of these citizen regiments has one polemarch (colonel), four captains of companies, eight lieutenants, each in command of a half company, and sixteen commanders of sections. At the word of command any such regimental division can be formed readily either into single file or into three files abreast, or into six files abreast.

The Decline of Sparta and the Spartan Ideal

14. Now, if the question be put to me whether the laws of Lycurgus remain still to this day unchanged, that indeed is an assertion which I should no longer venture to maintain; knowing, as I do, that in former times the Lacedaemonians preferred to live at home on moderate means, content to associate exclusively with themselves rather than to play the part of governor-general in foreign states and to be corrupted by flattery; knowing further, as I do, that formerly they dreaded to be detected in the possession of gold, whereas nowadays there are not a few who make it their glory and their boast to be possessed of it. I am very well aware that in former days alien acts were put in force for this very object. To live abroad was not allowed. And why? Simply in order that the citizens of Sparta might not take the infection of dishonesty and light-living from foreigners; whereas now I am very well aware that those who are reputed to be leading citizens have but one ambition, and that is to live to the end of their days as governors-general on a foreign soil. The days were when their sole anxiety was to fit themselves to lead the rest of Greece. But nowadays they concern themselves much more to wield command than to be fit themselves to rule. And so it has come to pass that whereas in old days

the states of Hellas flocked to Lacedaemon seeking her leadership against the supposed wrong-doer, now numbers are inviting one another to prevent the Lacedaemonians again recovering their empire. Yet, if they have incurred all these reproaches, we need not wonder, seeing that they are so plainly disobedient to the god himself and to the laws of their own lawgiver Lycurgus.

5.4   Heroic Athletics: The Chariot Race at Patroclus's Funeral Games

According to a famous American sportsman, "Winning isn't everything, it's the only thing." The Greeks would have agreed, as can be seen from Homer's vivid description of a chariot race, the earliest account of an athletic event in Western literature. Homer's account brilliantly evokes the excitement of the race itself. Equally important, it clearly illustrates the importance the Greeks ascribed not only to winning but also to avoiding the public humiliation that was the inevitable result of defeat.[7]

When they had thus raised a mound they were going away, but Achilles stayed the people and made them sit in assembly. He brought prizes from the ships—cauldrons, tripods, horses and mules, noble oxen, women with fair girdles, and dark iron.

The first prize he offered was for the chariot races—a woman skilled in all useful arts, and a three-legged cauldron that had ears for handles, and would hold twenty-two measures. This was for the man who came in first. For the second there was a six-year-old mare, unbroken, and in foal to a he-ass; the third was to have a goodly cauldron that had never yet been on the fire; it was still bright as when it left the maker, and would hold four measures. The fourth prize was two talents of gold, and the fifth a two-handled urn as yet unsoiled by smoke. Then he stood up and spoke among the Argives saying,

"Son of Atreus, and all other Achaeans, these are the prizes that lie waiting the winners of the chariot races. At any other time I should carry off the first prize and take it to my own tent; you know how far my steeds excel all others—for they are immortal; Poseidon gave them to my father Peleus, who in his turn gave them to myself; but I shall hold aloof, I and my steeds that have lost their brave and kind driver, who many a time has washed them in clear water and anointed their manes with oil. See how they stand weeping here, with their manes trailing on the ground in the extremity of their sorrow. But do you others set yourselves in order through-out the host, whosoever has confidence in his horses and in the strength of his chariot."

Thus spoke the son of Peleus and the drivers of chariots bestirred themselves. First among them all uprose Eumelus, king of men, son of Admetus, a man excellent in horsemanship. Next to him rose mighty Diomed son of Tydeus; he yoked the Trojan horses which he had taken from Æneas, when Apollo bore him out of the fight. Next to him, yellow-haired Menelaus son of Atreus rose and yoked his fleet horses, Agamemnon's mare Æthe, and his own horse Podargus. The mare had been given to Agamemnon by Echepolus son of Anchises, that he might not have to follow him to Ilius, but might stay at home and take his ease; for Zeus had endowed him with great wealth and he lived in spacious Sicyon. This mare, all eager for the race, did Menelaus put under the yoke.

Fourth in order Antilochus, son to noble Nestor son of Neleus, made ready his horses, and fifth in order Meriones got ready his horses. They then all mounted their chariots and cast

---

[7]Homer, *Iliad* 23, lines 262–595 (selections). From *The Iliad of Homer*, trans. Butler, pp. 383–391.

lots. Achilles shook the helmet, and the lot of Antilochus son of Nestor fell out first; next came that of King Eumelus, and after his, those of Menelaus son of Atreus and of Meriones. The last place fell to the lot of Diomed son of Tydeus, who was the best man of them all. They took their places in line; Achilles showed them the doubling-post round which they were to turn, some way off upon the plain; here he stationed his father's follower Phoenix as umpire, to note the running, and report truly. . . .

At the same instant they all of them lashed their horses, struck them with the reins, and shouted at them with all their might. They flew full speed over the plain away from the ships, the dust rose from under them as it were a cloud or whirlwind, and their manes were all flying in the wind. At one moment the chariots seemed to touch the ground, and then again they bounded into the air; the drivers stood erect, and their hearts beat fast and furious in their lust of victory. Each kept calling on his horses, and the horses scoured the plain amid the clouds of dust that they raised.

It was when they were doing the last part of the course on their way back towards the sea that their pace was strained to the utmost and it was seen what each could do. The horses of the descendant of Pheres now took the lead, and close behind them came the Trojan stallions of Diomed. They seemed as if about to mount Eumelus's chariot, and he could feel their warm breath on his back and on his broad shoulders, for their heads were close to him as they flew over the course. Diomed would have now passed him, or there would have been a dead heat, but Phoebus Apollo to spite him made him drop his whip. Tears of anger fell from his eyes as he saw the mares going on faster than ever, while his own horses lost ground through his having no whip. Athena saw the trick which Apollo had played the son of Tydeus, so she brought him his whip and put spirit into his horses; moreover she went after the son of Admetus in a rage and broke his yoke for him; the mares went one to one side the course, and the other to the other, and the pole was broken against the ground. Eumelus was thrown from his chariot close to the wheel; his elbows, mouth, and nostrils were all torn, and his forehead was bruised above his eyebrows; his eyes filled with tears and he could find no utterance. But the son of Tydeus turned his horses aside and shot far ahead, for Athena put fresh strength into them and covered Diomed himself with glory.

Menelaus son of Atreus came next behind him, but Antilochus called to his father's horses. "On with you both," he cried, "and do your very utmost. I do not bid you try to beat the steeds of the son of Tydeus, for Athena has put running into them, and has covered Diomed with glory; but you must overtake the horses of the son of Atreus and not be left behind, or Æthe who is so fleet will taunt you. Why, my good fellows, are you lagging? I tell you, and it shall surely be—Nestor will keep neither of you, but will put both of you to the sword, if we win any the worse a prize through your carelessness. Hie after them at your utmost speed: I will hit on a plan for passing them in a narrow part of the way, and it shall not fail me."

They feared the rebuke of their master, and for a short space went quicker. Presently Antilochus saw a narrow place where the road had sunk. The ground was broken, for the winter's rain had gathered and had worn the road so that the whole place was deepened. Menelaus was making towards it so as to get there first, for fear of a foul, but Antilochus turned his horses out of the way, and followed him a little on one side. The son of Atreus was afraid and shouted out, "Antilochus, you are driving recklessly; rein in your horses; the road is too narrow here, it will be wider soon, and you can pass me then; if you foul my chariot you may bring both of us to a mischief."

But Antilochus plied his whip, and drove faster, as though he had not heard him. They went side by side for about as far as a young man can hurl a disc from his shoulder when he is trying his strength, and then Menelaus's mares drew behind, for he left off driving for fear the horses should foul one another and upset the chariots; thus, while pressing on in quest of victory, they might both come headlong to the ground. Menelaus then upbraided Antilochus and said, "There is no greater trickster living than you are; go, and bad luck go with you: the Achæans say not well that you have understanding, and come what may you shall not bear away the prize without sworn protest on my part."

Then he called on his horses and said to them, "Keep your pace, and slacken not; the limbs of the other horses will weary sooner than yours, for they are neither of them young."

The horses feared the rebuke of their master, and went faster, so that they were soon nearly up with the others.

Meanwhile the Achæans from their seats were watching how the horses went, as they scoured the plain amid clouds of their own dust. Idomeneus captain of the Cretans was first to make out the running, for he was not in the thick of the crowd, but stood on the most commanding part of the ground. The driver was a long way off, but Idomeneus could hear him shouting, and could see the foremost horse quite plainly—a chestnut with a round white star, like the moon, on its forehead. He stood up and said among the Argives, "My friends, princes and counsellors of the Argives, can you see the running as well as I can? There seems to be another pair in front now, and another driver; those that led off at the start must have been disabled out on the plain. I saw them at first making their way round the doubling-post, but now, though I search the plain of Troy, I cannot find them. Perhaps the reins fell from the driver's hand so that he lost command of his horses at the doubling-post, and could not turn it. I suppose he must have been thrown out there, and broken his chariot, while his mares have left the course and gone off wildly in a panic. Come up and see for yourselves, I cannot make out for certain, but the driver seems an Ætolian by descent, ruler over the Argives, brave Diomed the son of Tydeus."

As he was speaking, the son of Tydeus came driving in, plying his whip lustily from his shoulder, and his horses stepping high as they flew over the course. The sand and grit rained thick on the driver, and the chariot inlaid with gold and tin ran close behind his fleet horses. There was little trace of wheelmarks in the fine dust, and the horses came flying in at their utmost speed. Diomed stayed them in the middle of the crowd, and the sweat from their manes and chests fell in streams on to the ground. Forthwith he sprang from his goodly chariot, and leaned his whip against his horses' yoke; brave Sthenelus now lost no time, but at once brought on the prize, and gave the woman and the ear-handled cauldron to his comrades to take away. Then he unyoked the horses.

Next after him came in Antilochus of the race of Neleus, who had passed Menelaus by a trick and not by the fleetness of his horses; but even so Menelaus came in as close behind him as the wheel is to the horse that draws both the chariot and its master. The end hairs of a horse's tail touch the tire of the wheel, and there is never much space between wheel and horse when the chariot is going; Menelaus was no further than this behind Antilochus, though at first he had been a full disc's throw behind him. He had soon caught him up again, for Agamemnon's mare Æthe kept pulling stronger and stronger, so that if the course had been longer he would have passed him, and there would not even have been a dead heat. Idomeneus's brave squire Meriones was about a spear's cast behind Menelaus. His horses were slowest of all, and he was the worst driver. Last of them all came the son of Admetus, dragging his chariot and driving his horses on in front. When Achilles saw him he was sorry, and stood up among the Argives saying, "The best man is coming in last. Let us give him a prize for it is reasonable. He shall have the second, but the first must go to the son of Tydeus."

Thus did he speak and the others all of them applauded his saying, and were for doing as he had said, but Nestor's son Antilochus stood up and claimed his rights from the son of Peleus. "Achilles," said he, "I shall take it much amiss if you do this thing; you would rob me of my prize, because you think Eumelus's chariot and horses were thrown out, and himself too, good man that he is. He should have prayed duly to the immortals; he would not have come in last if he had done so. If you are sorry for him and so choose, you have much gold in your tents, with bronze, sheep, cattle and horses. Take something from this store if you would have the Achaeans speak well of you, and give him a better prize even than that which you have now offered; but I will not give up the mare, and he that will fight me for her, let him come on."

Achilles smiled as he heard this, and was pleased with Antilochus, who was one of his dearest comrades. So he said,

"Antilochus, if you would have me find Eumelus another prize, I will give him the bronze breastplate with a rim of tin running all round it which I took from Asteropæus. It will be worth much money to him."

He bade his comrade Automedon bring the breastplate from his tent, and he did so. Achilles then gave it over to Eumelus, who received it gladly.

But Menelaus got up in a rage, furiously angry with Antilochus. An attendant placed his staff in his hands and bade the Argives keep silence: the hero then addressed them. "Antilochus," said he, "what is this—from you who have been so far blameless? You have made me cut a poor figure and baulked my horses by flinging your own in front of them, though yours are much worse than mine are; therefore, O princes and counsellors of the Argives, judge between us and show no favour, lest one of the Achæans say, 'Menelaus has got the mare through lying and corruption; his horses were far inferior to Antilochus's, but he has greater weight and influence.' Nay, I will determine the matter myself, and no man will blame me, for I shall do what is just. Come here, Antilochus, and stand, as our custom is, whip in hand before your chariot and horses; lay your hand on your steeds, and swear by earth-encircling Poseidon that you did not purposely and guilefully get in the way of my horses."

And Antilochus answered, "Forgive me; I am much younger, King Menelaus, than you are; you stand higher than I do and are the better man of the two; you know how easily young men are betrayed into indiscretion; their tempers are more hasty and they have less judgment; make due allowances therefore, and bear with me; I will of my own accord give up the mare that I have won, and if you claim any further chattel from my own possessions, I would rather yield it to you, at once, than fall from your good graces henceforth, and do wrong in the sight of heaven."

5.5 An Athletic Dynasty: the Diagorids of Rhodes

In the publicly oriented ethics of the Greeks an athletic victory was not complete if it was not made known to the widest possible audience. One popular way to do so with important implications for the development of Greek art was for the victor to set up a statue of himself in the sanctuary where he won his victory. The result was that the sites of the Panhellenic athletic festivals became virtual outdoor museums of the best of Greek sculpture. Pausanias, the second-century A.D. *author of a still extant guidebook to ancient Greece, denoted particular attention to recording these monuments of athletic achievement. The selection translated below describes the monuments commemorating the achievements of the most famous of all Greek athletic families, that of Diagoras of Rhodes and his descendants. The story that one of Diagoras's daughters accompanied her son to the Olympics disguised as a man reflects the fact that it was a capital offense for a married woman to attend the Olympic games.*[8]

After viewing these statues, you will come to the statues of the Rhodian athletes Diagoras and his family. They are set up next to each other in the following order. Acusilaus, who took the crown in the men's boxing, and Dorieus, the youngest of the family, who was victorious in all-in-fighting in three straight Olympics. Even before Dorieus, however, Damagetus also defeated those entering the all-in-fighting event. These men were brothers and sons of Diagoras. Next to them is set up the statue of Diagoras, who gained the victory in men's boxing. A Megarian sculptor, Callicles, the son of Theocosmus, who also made the statue of Zeus at Megara, sculpted the statue of Diagoras.

The sons of Diagoras's daughters were also boxers and won Olympic victories: Eucles, the son of Callianax and Callipateira, the daughter of Diagoras, in the men's class and Peisirodus in the boys' class. The mother of Peisirodus disguised herself in the clothes of a male trainer and brought her son to the games. The statue of this Peisirodus is also set up on the Altis beside that of his mother's father. People say that Diagoras came to Olympia together with his sons Acusilaus and Damagetus. The young men, after they had won victories in their events, carried him through the throne while he was showered with flowers and called blessed by the Greeks because of his sons.

The family of Diagoras was by origin Messenian in the female line and descended from a daughter of Aristomenes. Dorieus, the son of Diagoras, in addition to his Olympic victories, was victor eight times in the Isthmian games and seven in the Nemean games. He is also said to have won an uncontested victory at the Pythian games. He and Peisirodus were announced as Thurians, since they had been driven out from Rhodes by their political opponents and found refuge at Thurii in Italy. Later, however, Dorieus returned to Rhodes. He was a man who manifested the closest support for Sparta. He even fought a sea battle against the Athenians with his own ships. He was captured by Athenian triremes and brought to Athens as a prisoner. The Athenians, before Dorieus arrived at Athens, had been furious with him and made threats. But when they came together in the assembly and the Athenians saw a man who was so tall and who had achieved such fame in the position of a prisoner of war, they changed their opinion and let him go, although they could have justly punished him. The death of Dorieus is recorded in Androtion's history of Athens. Androtion says that when the Persian king's fleet and his admiral Conon were at Caunus and the Rhodians had been persuaded by Conon to revolt from the Spartans and join the king and the Athenian alliance, Dorieus, who happened to be away from Rhodes in the interior of the Peloponnesus at that time, was arrested by the Spartans. He was brought to Sparta, convicted of doing harm to Sparta, and sentenced to death.

---

[8]Pausanias, *Guide to Greece* 6.7.

5.6   Athletics and the *Polis:* a Philosophical Critique

The prominent position of athletics in Greek life was not without its critics. The earliest was Xenophanes (ca. 580–478 B.C.) a philosopher-poet from the Greek city of Colophon on the coast of western Turkey. Unwilling to live under Persian rule, in about the mid sixth century B.C. he went into voluntary exile in Sicily, where he spent the rest of his life. Xenophanes was not so much an original thinker as a popularizer, who used the new ideas of the early philosophers to criticize traditional Greek attitudes. A good example is the iconoclastic treatment of athletics in the poem translated below.[9]

If one should win a victory thanks to the swiftness of his feet or when competing in the pentathlon there in the sanctuary of Zeus by the streams of Pisa at Olympia, or if one should gain the prize in wrestling or painful boxing, or in that fearful contest people call all-in-fighting, to his fellow citizens he would be thought more glorious to look on than ever, and he would win the right to a prominent front row seat at the games and he would gain from his *polis* the right to meals at public expense and a gift which would be his personal treasure. And if his victory were won with horses, he would also gain all these things, even though he is not as worthy as I. For our wisdom is better than the strength of men or horses.

But this custom is completely wrong, nor is it right to prefer strength to good wisdom. For even if there were a good boxer among the citizens or one skilled in the pentathlon or wrestling, or, indeed, even if there were a great sprinter, which holds the front rank among the athletic achievements of men, the *polis* would still not be better governed because of this. A *polis* would gain little joy if someone should win in competition by the banks of the Pisa; for that victory would not fill its storehouses.

---

[9]Xenophanes Fragment 2. From *Elegy and Iambus*, Vol. 1, ed. Edmonds, pp. 192–194.

Chapter 6

▼▼▼

The Crisis of the
Archaic *Polis*

Great changes occurred in every aspect of Greek life during the seventh and sixth centuries B.C. Population increased and new *poleis* appeared throughout the Mediterranean and Black Sea basins. At the same time, vigorous economic growth occurred on a scale unequaled since the second millennium B.C., as can be seen from the proliferation of conspicuous expenditures by the new *polis* governments and their richer citizens: stone temples, city walls, fountain houses, and stone and metal statuary. Finally, the invention and spread of coinage toward the end of the period began to alter the very nature of wealth and economic activity.

These two centuries were also the golden age of the Greek aristocracies. The weak rulers of the Dark Ages were replaced by hereditary aristocracies, who were enriched by the economic opportunities of the Archaic Period. Typical features of the later Greek aristocratic lifestyle were the great athletic festivals and the drinking party, or *symposium*. The demands of newly rich Greek aristocrats also stimulated the expansion of luxury crafts and new artistic forms such as lyric poetry, sculpture, and the production of fine ceramic and metal tableware and jewelry. The impact on Greek culture of the new aristocratic ideal, with its emphasis on refinement and elegance, can be seen at its best in the celebration of male and female beauty in archaic Greek poetry and the statues of beautiful young men and women that fill the museums of the Western world.

Paradoxically, these two centuries were also the period in which aristocratic domination of Greek social and political life was seriously challenged for the first time. A frequent refrain in the literature of the period is that "Wealth is the man/ no poor man is good or honored." At the same time that the widespread adoption of hoplite warfare undermined aristocratic military primacy, economic growth fostered the appearance of nonaristocratic rich, for whom Greek society offered no status commensurate with their wealth. Whatever the source of their wealth, the attempts of the new rich to penetrate the closed circle of the aristocracies of the Greek cities provoked ridicule, and even fear when they found supporters among ambitious but disaffected aristocrats. Thus in Section 6.2 the aristocratic Megarian poet Theognis views with foreboding the willingness of some aristocrats in sixth-century B.C. Megara to arrange marriages for their sons with the daughters of men distinguished only by their wealth.

The aspirations of the new rich were an affront to the pride of Greek aristocrats. The sharpening of the division between the rich and the poor during the seventh and sixth centuries B.C., however, directly threatened aristocratic domination of the Greek cities. The causes of the problems are obscure, but the demands for cancellation of debts and redivision of land typical of Greek revolutionary movements suggest that the growing population of the archaic *poleis* led to land shortages, the effects of which could only be aggravated by the Greek laws of debt, which often threatened defaulting debtors with slavery. Sometimes tensions could be eased by colonization, which offered the disaffected hope of land and a fresh start elsewhere. Occasionally, reforms imposed by lawgivers such as the Athenian Solon succeeded in defusing problems before they reached crisis levels. All too often, however, efforts at reform were only partially successful or failed entirely, and the result was revolution, the establishment of tyranny—the Greek term for a military dictatorship—and the violent end of aristocratic rule. Many Greek cities experienced such crises during these two centuries, but the best documented cases are those of Corinth and Athens.

6.1   Aspects of Aristocratic Life at Its Peak

The four poems in this section illuminate different aspects of Greek aristocratic life from the seventh century B.C. to the end of the sixth century B.C.

6.1.1   A Fine *Symposium*: Xenophanes

From the seventh century B.C. onward, the heart of aristocratic culture was the symposium. *A male-only drinking party, the* symposium *offered aristocratic males a rich mixture of music, dance, poetry, games, and sex. New forms of poetry called* lyric, *because they were sung to accompaniment of the lyre, were created for* symposia. *Potters and metal workers produced a variety of fine drinking and mixing vessels for* symposia *while even house design was adapted to the needs of the* symposium. *In this poem, the sixth-century B.C. philosopher-poet Xenophanes of Colophon offers an idealized picture of a fine* symposium.

For now the floor is clean and the hands of everyone and the drinking cups also. A slave boy crowns the guests with woven wreathes. Another boy offers them sweet smelling myrrh in a bowl. The mixing bowl stands ready in the center, full of good cheer. Other wine, which declares that it will never fail, is ready in the jug, smooth and with a fine bouquet. In the middle, frankincense releases its holy odor; and the water is cool and sweet and pure. Yellow loaves of bread and a splendid table loaded with cheese and thick honey stands before us. The altar between us has been decked all round with flowers. The house is full of singing and dancing and feasting.

Merry men must first praise the god with pious stories and pure words. When they have offered libations and prayed that they be able to do what is just—for these are the preliminaries—it is not arrogance to drink as much as would allow a man who is not sunk in old age to come home without a servant to guide him. And that man must also be praised who, while drinking, reveals himself noble with a good memory and striving for excellence. He should not recount the battles of the Titans and the Giants, nor anything about the Centaurs, inventions of our ancestors, or bitter political disputes—there is nothing beneficial in these things—but it is always good to have reverence for the gods.

6.1.2   The Life of an Aristocrat: Alcaeus

Athletics, war, and politics were the main themes of aristocratic life. In this poem the seventh-century B.C. *Lesbian poet Alcaeus recalls from exile the splendid array of weapons he had kept in his home.*[1]

The great house is all agleam with bronze. War has bedecked the whole roof with bright helmets, from which hang waving horse-hair plumes to make adornment for the heads of men; the pegs are hidden with bright brazen greaves to ward off the strong arrow, corselets of new linen cloth and hollow shields are piled upon the floor, and beside them swords of Chalcidian steel, and many a doublet, many a kilt. These we cannot forget, so soon as we undertake this task.

6.1.3   When You Are "Repulsive to Boys and a Laughingstock to Women": Mimnermus on Old Age

As Greek art and literature abundantly demonstrate, aristocratic culture was in many ways a youth culture, valuing above all physical beauty, bravery, athletic achievement, and sensuality. In this poem the elegiac poet Mimnermus of Smyrna eloquently voices the despair that comes with old age, which robs men of all those things.

What is life and what is pleasure without Golden Aphrodite? May I die when secret love, pleasing gifts, and bed no longer concern me. Such are the flowers of youth that are dear to men and women. But when grim old age approaches, and makes a man completely disgusting and evil, and foul cares always fill his thoughts, and looking on the rays of the sun does not please him, then he is repulsive to boys and a laughing stock to women. So painful has god made old age.

6.1.4   A Woman's View of Aristocratic Life: Sappho's "To Anactoria"

Much less is known about the social life and values of aristocratic Greek women than of men. Such evidence as there is, however, indicates that their culture, like that of their male counterparts, also emphasized music, poetry, and eroticism. In this poem by Alcaeus's contemporary, the poetess Sappho deftly asserts the superiority of female beauty to the military virtues dear to aristocratic males.[2]

The fairest thing in all the world some say is a host of foot, and some again a navy of ships, but to some it is the heart's beloved. And it is easy to make this understood by any. Helen, who far surpassed all mankind in beauty, chose for the best of men the destroyer of all the honor of Troy, and thought not so much either of child or parent dear, but was led

---

[1]Adapted from *Lyra Graeca*, ed. and trans. J. M. Edmonds (Cambridge, MA: Harvard University Press, 1928), Vol. 1, pp. 333–335.
[2]Adapted from *Lyra Graeca*, p. 209.

astray by Love to bestow her heart afar, for woman is ever easy to be bent when she thinks lightly of what is near and dear. See to it then that you remember us Anactoria, now that we are parted from one of whom I would rather hear the sweet sound of her footfall and see the brightness of her beaming face than all the chariots and armored footmen of Lydia. I know that in this world man cannot have the best; yet to wish that one had share [in what was once shared is better than to forget it].

6.2   The Crisis of the Aristocracy 1: The Laments of Theognis

Theognis is the author of two books of short poems. The few facts that are known concerning his life suggest that he was an aristocrat from the city of Megara, just west of Athens, and that he wrote during the sixth century B.C. The main theme of his poetry is one common to aristocratic literature worldwide: the transmission of wisdom acquired by an experienced adult during his life to a young male protege. The topics of his poetry are varied, but one that recurs frequently is the disruption of aristocratic social and political life by new wealth. The translation of the poems has been kept as literal as possible so as to highlight the simple moral oppositions characteristic of aristocratic morality, in which nobles are "good" and commoners are "bad," and any advancement by the latter is viewed as a threat to a just social order.[3]

Dangerous Times for Megara

Cyrnus, this city is pregnant, and I fear that it will bring forth a man (= tyrant) who will be the chastiser of our evil arrogance. For the citizens are sensible but their leaders have turned straight toward complete evil.

Greed and the Origins of Social Strife

Never, Cyrnus, have good men (= nobility) destroyed a city; but whenever it pleases bad men (= non-nobles) to act arrogantly and corrupt the people and render judgments in favor of unjust men for their own gain and power, then do not expect that this city will remain unshaken for long, not even if it now lies in great peace, not when these things have become dear to bad men: the gains that accompany public ill. For from these come divisions and communal slaughters and rulers. May such things never please this city.

The End of the Aristocratic Monopoly of Government

Cyrnus, this city is the same city, but its people are different. Those who previously knew neither judgments nor laws, but wore goatskins about their flanks, and grazed like deer outside this city, now even these are good men, O Son of Polypaus. And they who formerly were nobles are now of no account. Who can endure observing these things? Laughing, they deceive each other, these men who know the stamp of neither bad nor good.

Wealth and the Decline of the Aristocracy

We seek rams and asses, Cyrnus, and horses that are well-bred, and one wishes to breed them from good stock. But to wed the bad daughter of a bad man does not shame a noble

---

[3]Theognis, *Elegies* 1, lines 39–42, 43–52, 53–60, and 183–192.

man, if one gives him much wealth; nor does a woman refuse to be the bedmate of a rich man, but she wishes a rich man instead of a good man. For they honor riches; and a noble man weds the offspring of a bad man and a bad man that of a noble man. Wealth confuses the stock. So do not wonder, O Son of Polypaus, that the stock of the citizens is obscured. For noble things are mixed with bad things.

6.3   Portrait of a Vulgar Upstart: Anacreon

The core of Theognis's complaint is that social status is no longer determined by birth but by wealth. What disturbed him is well illustrated by the sixth-century B.C. poet Anacreon's vivid portrait of the upstart Artemon who went from slave to rich man.[4]

Once he went about in the pointed hat of a Cimmerian, with wooden knuckle bones in his ears, and about his ribs a hairy oxhide that had been the unwashed cover of a wretched shield—the scoundrel Artemon, who made a fraudulent living by consorting with bread-wenches and whores-for-choice, with his neck often bound to the whipping-stock or else to the wheel, and his back often scarred with the leather scourge and his hair and beard plucked out; but now he goes in a coach, wearing earrings of gold like a mix-with-all, and carries an ivory sunshade as though he were a woman.

6.4   The Crisis of the Aristocracy 2: Corinth

Situations such as those alluded to by Theognis occurred in many Greek cities. The earliest and best-known example is that of Corinth. Under the rule of a single extended family known as the Bacchiads and blessed with an economically advantageous location on the Isthmus of Corinth, Corinth prospered during the Archaic Period, founding colonies in Sicily, the Adriatic Sea, and northern Greece and becoming an important commercial center. Their monopoly of power and social isolation rendered the Bacchiads vulnerable, and their rule was overthrown in a rebellion led by Cypselus, a member of their family, who founded a tyranny that ruled Corinth for almost a century before being suppressed by Sparta in 587 B.C. Herodotus's account of the rise of the Cypselid tyranny occurs in a speech critical of Spartan support of the overthrown Athenian tyrant Hippias ca. 500 B.C. that highlights the aristocratic view of tyranny as the negation of a just social and political order.[5]

92. Such was the address of the Spartans (sc. *recommending the reestablishment of the Athenian tyranny*). The greater number of the allies listened without being persuaded. None however broke silence, but Sosicles the Corinthian, who exclaimed:

"Surely the heaven will soon be below, and the earth above, and men will henceforth live in the sea, and fish take their place upon the dry land, since you, Lacedaemonians, propose to put down free governments in the cities of Greece, and to set up tyrannies in their stead. There

---

[4]Adapted from *Lyra Graeca*, Vol. 2, pp. 189–191.
[5]*The History of Herodotus*, trans. by George Rawlinson. From Francis R. B. Godolphin, *The Greek Historians*, Vol. 1 (New York: Random House, 1942), pp. 252–255.

is nothing in the whole world so unjust, nothing so bloody, as a tyranny. If, however, it seems to you a desirable thing to have the cities under despotic rule, begin by putting a tyrant over yourselves, and then establish despots in the other states. While you continue yourselves, as you have always been, unacquainted with tyranny, and take such excellent care that Sparta may not suffer from it, to act as you are now doing is to treat your allies unworthily. If you knew what tyranny was as well as ourselves, you would be better advised than you now are in regard to it. The government at Corinth was once an oligarchy—a single clan, called the Bacchiads, who intermarried only among themselves, held the management of affairs. Now it happened that Amphion, one of these, had a daughter, named Labda, who was lame, and whom therefore none of the Bacchiads would consent to marry; so she was taken to wife by Aetion, son of Echecrates, a man of the township of Petra, who was, however, by descent of the race of the Lapithae, and of the house of Caeneus. Aetion, as he had no child either by this wife, or by any other, went to Delphi to consult the oracle concerning the matter. Scarcely had he entered the temple when the priestess saluted him in these words:

> No one honors you now, Aetion, worthy of honor;
> Labda shall soon be a mother—her offspring a rock, that will
>   one day
> Fall on the kingly race, and right the city of Corinth.

By some chance this address of the oracle to Aetion came to the ears of the Bacchiads, who until then had been unable to perceive the meaning of another earlier prophecy which likewise bore upon Corinth, and pointed to the same event as Aetion's prediction. It was the following:

> When mid the rocks an eagle shall bear a carnivorous lion,
> Mighty and fierce, he shall loosen the limbs of many beneath
>   them.
> Brood well upon this, all you Corinthian people,
> You who dwell by fair Peirene, and beetling Corinth.

The Bacchiads had possessed this oracle for some time, but they were quite at a loss to know what it meant until they heard the response given to Aetion; then, however, they at once perceived its meaning, since the two agreed so well together. Nevertheless, though the bearing of the first prophecy was now clear to them, they remained quiet, intending to put to death the child, which Aetion was expecting. As soon therefore, as his wife was delivered, they sent ten of their number to the township where Aetion lived, with orders to make away with the baby. So the men came to Petra, and went into Aetion's house, and there asked, if they might see the child. Labda, who knew nothing of their purpose, but thought their inquiries arose from a kindly feeling towards her husband, brought the child, and laid him in the arms of one of them. Now they had agreed during their journey that whoever first got hold of the child should dash it against the ground. It happened, however, by a providential chance, that the baby, just as Labda put him into the man's arms, smiled in his face. The man saw the smile, and was touched with pity, so that he could not kill it. He therefore passed it on to his neighbor, who gave it to a third; and so it went through all the ten without any one choosing to be the murderer.

The mother received her child back, and the men went out of the house and stood near the door, and there blamed and reproached one another, especially accusing the man who had first had the child in his arms, because he had not done as had been agreed upon. At last, after spending much time this way, they resolved to go into the house again and all take part in the murder. But it was fated that evil should come upon Corinth from the progeny of Aetion. So it happened that Labda, as she stood near the door, heard all that the men said to one another. Fearful of their changing their mind, and returning to destroy her baby, she carried him off and hid him in what seemed to her the most unlikely place to be suspected, a cypsel or grain-bin. She knew that when they came back to look for the child, they would search all her house, and so indeed they did. Not finding the child after looking everywhere, they decided to go away and report to those by whom they had been sent that they had done their bidding. And thus they reported on their return home. Aetion's son grew up and in commemoration of the danger from which he had escaped, was named Cypselus after the grain-bin.

When he had grown up, he went to Delphi, and on consulting the oracle, received a response which was two-sided. It was the following:

See there comes to my dwelling a fortunate man,
Cypselus, son of Aetion, and king of the glorious Corinth,
He and his children too, but not his children's children.

Such was the oracle; and Cypselus (ca. 657–627 B.C.) put so much faith in it that he immediately made his attempt, and thereby became master of Corinth. Having thus got the tyranny, he showed himself a harsh ruler—many of the Corinthians he drove into banishment, many he deprived of their fortunes, and a still greater number of their lives. His reign lasted thirty years, was prosperous to its end; insomuch that he left the government to Periander (ca. 627–587 B.C.), his son.

This prince at the beginning of his reign was of a milder temper than his father; but after he corresponded by means of messengers with Thrasybulus, tyrant of Miletus, he became even more savage. On one occasion he sent a herald to ask Thrasybulus what kind of government it was safest to set up in order to rule with honor. Thrasybulus led the messenger without the city, and took him into a field of wheat, through which he began to walk, while he asked him again and again concerning his trip from Corinth, while breaking off as he walked and throwing away all such ears of wheat as were higher than the rest. In this way he went through the whole field, and destroyed all the best and richest part of the crop. Then, without a word, he sent the messenger back. On the return of the man to Corinth, Periander was eager to know what Thrasybulus had advised. The messenger reported, however, that he had said nothing; and he wondered that Periander had sent him to so strange a man, who seemed to have lost his senses, since he did nothing but destroy his own property. And upon this he told how Thrasybulus had behaved at the interview. Periander, perceiving what the action meant, and knowing that Thrasybulus advised the destruction of all the leading citizens, treated his subjects from this time forward with the very greatest cruelty. Where Cypselus had spared any, and had neither put them to death nor banished them, Periander completed what his father had left unfinished. One day he stripped all the women of Corinth stark naked, for the sake of his own wife Melissa. He had sent messengers into Thesprotia to consult the oracle of the dead upon the Acheron concerning a pledge, which had been given into his charge by a stranger, and Melissa appeared, but refused to speak or tell where the pledge was. "She was cold," she said, "having no clothes; the garments buried with her were of no manner of use, since they had not been burnt. And this should be her token to Periander, that what she said was true—the oven was cold when he baked his loaves in it." When this message was brought him, Periander knew the token for he had had intercourse with the dead body of Melissa. Wherefore he immediately issued a proclamation that all the wives of the Corinthians should go to the temple of Hera. So the women dressed themselves in their best clothes, and went out, as if to a festival. Then, with the help of his guards, whom he had placed for the purpose, he stripped them one and all, making no difference between the free women and the slaves; and, taking their clothes to a pit, he called on the name of Melissa, and burnt the whole heap. When this was done, he sent a second time to the oracle, and Melissa's ghost told him where he would find the stranger's pledge. Such, Lacedaemonians, is tyranny and such are the deeds, which spring from it.

In another passage, Herodotus gives further examples of Periander's legendary cruelty, describing the family chaos that followed the death of his wife, and incidentally illustrating the emergence of Corinth as a major Aegean power, establishing diplomatic ties with states such as Lydia and exercising direct rule over some of its colonies such as Corcyra.

48.   The Corinthians likewise right willingly lent a helping hand towards the expedition against Samos; for a generation earlier, about the time of the seizure of the wine-bowl, they too had suffered insult at the hands of the Samians. It happened that Periander, son of Cypselus, had taken 300 boys, children of the chief nobles among the Corcyraeans, and sent them to Alyattes for eunuchs; the men who had them in charge touched at Samos on their way to Sardis; whereupon the Samians, having found out what was to become of the boys when they reached that city, first prompted them to take sanctuary at the temple of Artemis; and after this, when the Corinthians, as they were forbidden to tear the suppliants from the holy place, sought to cut off from them all supplies of food, invented a festival in their behalf, which they celebrate to this day with the self-same rites, Each evening, as night closed in, during the whole time that the boys continued there, choirs of youths and virgins were placed about the temple, carrying in their hands cakes made of sesame and honey, in order that the Corcyraean boys might snatch the cakes, and so get enough to live upon.

49.   And this went on for so long, that at last the Corinthians who had charge of the boys gave them up, and took their departure, upon which the Samians conveyed them back to Corcyra. If, now, after the death of Periander, the Corinthians and Corcyraeans had been good friends, it is not to be imagined that the former would ever have taken part in the expedition against Samos for such a reason as this; but as, in fact, the two people have always, ever since the first settlement of the island, been enemies to one another, this outrage was remembered, and the Corinthians bore the Samians a grudge for it. Periander had chosen the youths from among the first families in Corcyra, and sent them to Sardis for castration, to revenge a wrong which he had received. For it was the Corcyracans, who began the quarrel and injured Periander by an outrage of a horrid nature.

50.   After Periander had put to death his wife Melissa, it chanced that on this first affliction a second followed of a different kind. His wife had borne him two sons, and one of them had now reached the age of seventeen, the other of eighteen years, when their mother's father, Procles, tyrant of Epidaurus, asked them to his court. They went, and Procles treated them with much kindness, as was natural, considering they were his own daughter's children. At length,

when the time for parting came, Procles, as he was sending them on their way, said "Know you now, my children, who it was that caused your mother's death?" The elder son took no account of this speech, but the younger, whose name was Lycophron, was sorely troubled at it—so much so that when he got back to Corinth, looking upon his father as his mother's murderer, he would neither speak to him, nor answer when spoken to, nor utter a word in reply to all his questionings. So Periander at last growing furious at such behavior, banished him from his house.

51. The younger son gone, he turned to the elder and asked him what it was that their grandfather had said to them. Then he related how kind and friendly a fashion he had received them; but, not having taken any notice of the speech, which Procles had uttered at parting, he quite forgot to mention it. Periander insisted that it was not possible this should be all— their grandfather must have given them some hint or other—and he went on pressing him, till at last the lad remembered that parting speech and told it. Periander, after he had turned the whole matter over in his thoughts, and felt unwilling to give way at all, sent a messenger to the persons who had opened their houses to his outcast son and forbade them to harbor him. Then the boy, when he was chased from one friend, sought refuge with another, but was driven from shelter to shelter by the threats of his father, who menaced all those that took him in, and commanded them to shut their doors against him, Still as fast as he was forced to leave one house he went to another, and was received by the inmates; for his acquaintance, although in no small alarm, yet gave him shelter, as he was Periander's son.

52. At last Periander made proclamation that whoever harbored his son or even spoke to him, should forfeit a certain sum of money to Apollo. On hearing this no one any longer liked to take him in, or even to converse with him, and he himself did not think it right to seek to do what was forbidden. So, abiding by his resolve, he made his lodging in the public porticos. When four days had passed in this way, Periander seeing how wretched his son was, that he neither washed nor took any food, felt moved with compassion towards him. Wherefore, foregoing his anger, he approached him, and said, "Which is better, my son, to fare as now you fare, or to receive my crown and all the good things that I possess, on the one condition of submitting to your father? See, now, though my own child, and lord of this wealthy Corinth, you have brought yourself to a beggar's life, because you resist and treat with anger him whom you should least oppose. If there has been a calamity, and you bear me ill will on that account, think that I too feel it, and am the greatest sufferer, in as much as it was by me that the deed was done. For yourself, now that you know how much better a thing it is to be envied than pitied, and how dangerous it is to indulge anger against parents and superiors, come back with me to your home." With such words as these did Periander chide his son; but the son made no reply except to remind his father that he owed the god the penalty for coming and talking with him. Then Periander knew that there was no cure for the youth's malady, nor means of overcoming it; so he prepared a ship and sent him away out of his sight to Corcyra, which island at that time belonged to him. As for Procles, Periander, regarding him as the true author of all his present troubles, went to war with him as soon as his son was gone, and not only made himself master of his kingdom Epidaurus, but also took Procles himself, and carried him into captivity.

53. As time went on, and Periander came to be old, he found himself no longer equal to the oversight and management of affairs. Seeing, therefore, in his eldest son no manner of ability, but knowing him to be dull and blockish, he sent him to Corcyra and recalled Lycophron

to take the kingdom. Lycophron, however, did not even ask the bearer of this message a question. But Periander's heart was set upon the youth, so he sent again to him, this time by his own daughter, the sister of Lycophron, who would, he thought, have more power to persuade him than any other person. Then she, when she reached Corcyra, spoke thus with her brother, "Do you wish the kingdom, brother, to pass into strange hands, and our father's wealth to be made a prey, rather than yourself return to enjoy it? Come back home with me, and cease to punish yourself. It is scant gain, this obstinacy. Why seek to cure evil by evil? Mercy, remember, is by many set above justice. Many, also, while pushing their mother's claims have forfeited their father's fortune. Power is a slippery thing—it has many suitors; and he is old and stricken in years let not your inheritance go to another." Thus did the sister, who had been tutored by Periander what to say, urge all the arguments most likely to have weight with her brother. He however answered that so long as he knew his father to be still alive, he would never go back to Corinth. When the sister brought Periander this reply, he sent to his son a third time by a herald, and said he would come himself to Corcyra, and let his son take his place at Corinth as heir to his kingdom. To these terms Lycophron agreed and Periander was making ready to pass into Corcyra and his to return to Corinth, when the Corcyraeans, being informed of what was taking place, to keep Periander away, put the young man to death. For this reason it was that Periander took vengeance on the Corcyraeans.

6.5   The Crisis of the Aristocracy 3: Athens

Crises did not always end with the establishment of a tyrant. Instead, a lawgiver might be appointed, who was empowered to impose necessary reforms and incorporate them into a written law code—one of the earliest public uses of literacy in Greece—that would become authoritative upon the end of his term of office. The best documented example of the appointment of a lawgiver is that of Athens, where a severe crisis that had brought the city to the verge of civil war was resolved by a series of reforms carried out in 594 B.C. by the aristocratic poet and lawgiver Solon. The principal source of information for the Athenian crisis was Solon's own poetry; extensive quotations from it are preserved in Aristotle's famous Constitution of Athens, *a work long thought lost until an ancient papyrus copy was discovered in Egypt in 1889. There is much scholarly dispute about the origins and course of the crisis, but two facts are clear. First, Solon defused the immediate problem by ending a system of sharecropping called* Hectemorage *and outlawing at Athens the practice of enslaving debtors who failed to repay their loans. Second, although Solon himself cannot be described as a democrat, he made an essential contribution to the development of the later Athenian democracy by substituting wealth for noble birth as the criterion for holding political office.[6]*

2. After this event there was contention for a long time between the upper classes and the populace. Not only was the constitution at this time oligarchical in every respect, but the poorer classes, men, women, and children, were the serfs of the rich. They were known as Pelatae and also as Hectemores, because they cultivated the lands of the rich at the rent thus

---

[6]Aristotle, *The Constitution of Athens* 2.5–12 (selections), trans. Frederick G. Kenyon. From Francis R. B. Godolphin, *The Greek Historians*, Vol. 2 (New York: Random House, 1942), pp. 679–685.

indicated. The whole country was in the hands of a few persons, and if the tenants failed to pay their rent they were liable to be haled into slavery, and their children with them. All loans were secured upon the debtor's person, a custom which prevailed until the time of Solon, who was the first to appear as the champion of the people. But the hardest and bitterest part of the constitution in the eyes of the masses was their state of serfdom. Not but what they were also discontented with every other feature of their lot; for, to speak generally, they had no part nor share in anything.

5. (Since) . . . the many were in slavery to the few, the people rose against the upper class. The strife was keen, and for a long time the two parties were ranged in hostile camps against one another, till at last, by common consent, they appointed Solon to be mediator and Archon, and committed the whole constitution to his hands. . . . By birth and reputation Solon was one of the foremost men of the day, but in wealth and position he was of the middle class, as is generally agreed, and is, indeed, established by his own evidence in these poems, where he exhorts the wealthy not to be grasping.

6. As soon as he was at the head of affairs, Solon liberated the people once and for all, by prohibiting all loans on the security of the debtor's person; and in addition he made laws by which he cancelled all debts, public and private. This measure is commonly called the *Seisachtheia* (removal of burdens), since thereby the people had their loads removed from them.

7. Next Solon drew up a constitution and enacted new laws; and the ordinances of Draco ceased to be used, with the exception of those relating to murder. The laws were inscribed on the wooden stands, and set up in the King's Porch, and all swore to obey them; and the nine Archons made oath upon the stone, declaring that they would dedicate a golden statue if they should transgress any of them. This is the origin of the oath to that effect which they take to the present day. Solon ratified his laws for a hundred years; and the following was the fashion in which he organised the constitution. He divided the population according to property into four classes, just as it had been divided before, namely, *Pentacosiomedimni*, Knights, *Zeugitae*, and *Thetes*. The various magistracies, namely, the nine Archons, the Treasurers, the Commissioners for Public Contracts, the Eleven, and the Fiscal Clerks, he assigned to the *Pentacosiomedimni*, the Knights, and the *Zeugitae*, giving offices to each class in proportion to the value of their rateable property. To those who ranked among the *Thetes* he gave nothing but a place in the Assembly and in the juries. A man had to rank as a Pentacosiomedimnus if he made, from his own land, 500 measures, whether liquid or solid. Those ranked as Knights who made 300 measures, or, as some say, those who were able to maintain a horse. In support of the latter definition they adduce the name of the class, which may be supposed to be derived from this fact, and also some votive offerings of early times; for in the Acropolis there is a votive offering, a statue of Diphilus, bearing this inscription:

> Anthemion, the son of Diphilos, made this dedication to the gods, when he exchanged the status of a Thete for that of a Knight (*Hippeis*).

And a horse stands in evidence beside the man, implying that this was what was meant by belonging to the rank of Knight. At the same time it seems reasonable to suppose that this class, like the *Pentacosiomedimni*, was defined by the possession of an income of a certain number of measures. Those ranked as *Zeugitae* who made 200 measures, liquid or solid; and the rest ranked as *Thetes*, and were not eligible for any office. Hence it is that even at the present day, when a candidate for any office is asked to what class he belongs, no one would think of saying that he belonged to the *Thetes*.

9. Such, then, was his legislation concerning the magistracies. There are three points in the constitution of Solon which appear to be its most democratic features: first and most important, the prohibition of loans on the security of the debtor's person; secondly, the right of every person who so willed to claim redress on behalf of any one to whom wrong was being done; thirdly, the institution of the appeal to the jury-courts; and it is to this last, they say, that the masses have owed their strength most of all, since, when the democracy is master of the voting-power, it is master of the constitution. Moreover, since the laws were not drawn up in simple and explicit terms (but like the one concerning inheritances and wards of state), disputes inevitably occurred, and the courts had to decide in every matter, whether public or private. Some persons in fact believe that Solon deliberately made the laws indefinite, in order that the final decision might be in the hands of the people. This, however, is not probable, and the reason no doubt was that it is impossible to attain ideal perfection when framing a law in general terms; for we must judge of his intentions, not from the actual results in the present day, but from the general tenor of the rest of his legislation.

11. When he had completed his organization of the constitution in the manner that has been described, he found himself beset by people coming to him and harassing him concerning his laws, criticising here and questioning there, till, as he wished neither to alter what he had decided on nor yet to be an object of ill will to every one by remaining in Athens, he set off on a journey to Egypt, with the combined objects of trade and travel, giving out that he should not return for ten years. He considered that there was no call for him to expound the laws personally, but that every one should obey them just as they were written. Moreover, his position at this time was unpleasant. Many members of the upper class had been estranged from him on account of his abolition of debts, and both parties were alienated through their disappointment at the condition of things which he had created. The mass of the people had expected him to make a complete redistribution of all property, and the upper class hoped he would restore everything to its former position, or, at any rate, make but a small change. Solon, however, had resisted both classes. He might have made himself a despot by attaching himself to whichever party he chose, but he preferred, though at the cost of incurring the enmity of both, to be the saviour of his country and the ideal lawgiver.

12. The truth of this view of Solon's policy is established alike by common consent, and by the mention he has himself made of the matter in his poems. Thus:

> To the people I gave as much privilege as was proper, neither taking away from nor adding to their honor. As for those who had power and were pre-eminent in wealth, I took care that nothing shameful should happen to them. I stood firm, protecting both with my strong shield, and I allowed neither to be unjustly victorious.

Once more he speaks of the abolition of debts and of those who before were in servitude, but were released owing to the Seisachtheia:

> Which of those tasks for which I collected together the people did I give up before completing. In the judgement of time let my best witness to these matters be black earth, great mother of the Olympian deities. I pulled up from her the boundary markers

that had been planted in her everywhere. The earth that was formerly enslaved is now free. Many Athenians, who had been sold—some unjustly, some justly—I brought back to their divinely founded fatherland. Men who had fled into exile under the compulsion of debt and no longer spoke the Attic tongue because of their many wanderings, and men who endured bitter slavery here, trembling in fear at their master's whims, these men I made free. I used my power to do these things, uniting force and justice, and I accomplished what I had promised. I wrote laws equally for the bad and the good, accommodating straight justice to each. Had someone else, an evil-minded and ambitious man, taken up the goad as I did, he would not have held the people back. For if I had then done what they desired for their enemies, or what their opponents planned for them, this city would have been bereft of many men. For this reason I set up a firm defense on all sides, turning like a wolf in the midst of a pack of dogs.

Chapter 7

❦

Husbands, Wives, and Slaves

The Domestic Foundations of the *Polis*

Once established, the *polis* remained at the center of Greek life until the early centuries of the Christian Era. As was pointed out in Chapter 4, the politically active portion of a *polis* was its male citizens, its *politai*. A socioeconomic definition of the *polis* is less simple. At its simplest, a *polis* was a small-scale agricultural community whose citizens were economically self-sufficient. The ultimate building blocks of a *polis* were, therefore, the economic units to which the citizens belonged and which supported them, their *oikoi*, or "households." Economically, an *oikos* consisted of a house plot and one or more blocks of arable land "belonging to it." Socially, an *oikos* was composed of the adult male citizen, who was its head, his wife, and their children, who represented the future of the household, its slaves and other unrelated dependents, and its livestock. Ideally, a *polis* consisted of a fixed number of such households; laws in some cities, especially colonial cities, tried to maintain constant the number of *oikoi* by, for example, forbidding the sale of a household's original agricultural land plot.

The core of an *oikos* was a married couple. According to the *Oeconomicus*, Xenophon's fourth-century B.C. treatise on household management, marriage was viewed as a partnership of man and woman for the purpose of managing an *oikos*. Responsibilities were clearly divided. The woman's sphere was the house and all that went on within it, while the man was responsible for all relations between the household and the outside world. It was, however, an uneasy and an unequal partnership.

The Greek economic ideal was autarchy, self-sufficiency, for both *polis* and *oikos*, in an environment of scarcity. Women were viewed both as critical to the survival of the household and as a potential threat to its welfare. A woman brought to an *oikos* her managerial skills, wealth in the form of her dowry, and, most important, the potential for its continued survival in her sexuality. At the same time, she was viewed not as a producer of wealth but as a consumer, whose demands could easily bring ruin to a household by wasting its limited resources. Likewise, the same sexuality that was the promise of the *oikos*' survival could, if allowed to function unchecked, also confound the purity of the patrilineal descent lines that linked the *polis* and its constituent households to both their past and their future. The most explicit statement of this view of women as a source of both hope and danger to the *oikos* is to be found in the catalog of negative stereotypes of women in *On Women* by sixth-century B.C. poet Simonides of Amorgos, but similar remarks are common in early Greek literature.

The inequality in the relationship between husband and wife was in part the result of the significant age difference at marriage of males and females during the Archaic and Classical Periods: Women married in their early or middle teens and men in their late twenties or thirties. Equally important were the serious legal disabilities imposed on Greek women. The extent of these disabilities varied throughout the Greek world (women could own land in fifth-century B.C. Gortyn in Crete but not in contemporary Athens), but common to most Greek law codes was the principle that a woman remained a legal minor throughout her whole life and therefore required a male guardian, be it her father or her husband or even her son, for all but the most insignificant transactions. Not surprisingly, therefore, epitaphs for Greek citizen women, such as that for Sokratea translated in Section 7.2, single out for commemoration their performance in the three roles assigned women in Greek society: dutiful daughter, loyal wife, and mother of citizens.

Although Greek law and custom fostered significant inequalities between husband and wife in most areas of social and economic life, in one area, however, they were equals—namely, in their authority over the unfree members of their household, its slaves.

Slavery was one of the central features of Greek life. The exact size of the slave population in Greece is one of the most hotly contested issues in ancient historiography, but on one point all scholars agree. Although few Greeks relied entirely on slave labor for their support, ownership of slaves was widespread throughout the society. Free Greeks and slaves worked side by side in all occupations from the most menial to the most skilled, and slaves lived on the most intimate terms with their masters in their *oikoi*. Not surprisingly, as the *Oeconomicus* reveals, management of the household slaves was one of the chief concerns of Greek husbands and wives. The daily reality of slaves' lives is harder to grasp. Greek law afforded slaves few protections against their masters. Corporal punishment of and free sexual access to their slaves were both permitted to masters, and the testimony of slaves was admissible in court only if extracted under torture. Some slaves, such as the enterprising Neaera and her daughters, might be manumitted and prosper, but for many the pitiful fate of the anonymous concubine in Antiphon's speech *Against a Stepmother* must have been an ever-present possibility.

Modern scholars are understandably embarrassed by the seemingly obvious contradiction between the Greek ideal of freedom and the pervasiveness of slavery in Greek life. Few Greek thinkers shared that embarrassment, but their complacency should not be surprising, since slavery was a prominent feature of all the civilizations known to the Greeks. Indeed, Xenophon and other reformers even professed to see social and economic benefits in the expansion of slavery. Other Greek thinkers, such as Plato, however, did increasingly come to believe for both ideological and practical reasons that Greeks should not enslave Greeks, but even his view remained a utopian dream. Throughout Greek history the reality remained that anyone, Greek or barbarian, might, as a prisoner of war, as a victim of kidnapping, or, outside Athens, as a defaulting debtor, find himself swept up into the slave trade, a trade whose horrors Herodotus dramatically illustrates in the tale of the eunuch's revenge.

7.1   The Education of a Wife

Reflecting the central place occupied by the oikos *in Greek life, the various extant classical treatises on* oikonomia *are concerned not with the* "economy" *in the modern sense, but with the successful management of a household in all of its aspects. In this passage from the earliest surviving example of such a work, the* Oeconomicus *of Xenophon, a follower of Socrates who wrote in the early fourth century B.C., an Athenian landowner named Ischomachus is depicted as describing to Socrates how he explained to his young bride the separate but complementary roles of husband and wife in the running of a household.*[1]

Socrates (he proceeded), I certainly do not spend my days indoors, if for no other reason, because my wife is quite capable of managing our domestic affairs without my aid.

Ah! (said I), Ischomachus, that is just what I should like particularly to learn from you. Did you yourself educate your wife to be all that a wife should be, or when you received her from her father and mother was she already proficient and well skilled to discharge the duties appropriate to a wife?

Well skilled! (he replied). What proficiency was she likely to bring with her, when she was not quite fifteen at the time she wedded me, and during the whole prior period of her life had been most carefully brought up to see and hear as little as possible, and to ask the fewest questions? Or do you not think one should be satisfied, if at marriage her whole experience consisted in knowing how to take the wool and make a dress, and seeing how her mother's handmaidens had their daily spinning-tasks assigned them? For (he added), as regards control of appetite and self-indulgence, she had received the soundest education, and that I take to be the most important matter in the bringing-up of man or woman.

The Reasons for Marriage

Soc. Pray narrate to me, Ischomachus, I beg of you, what you first essayed to teach her. To hear that story would please me more than any description of the most splendid gymnastic contest or horse-race you could give me.

Why, Socrates (he answered), when after a time she had become accustomed to my hand, that is, was tamed sufficiently to play her part in a discussion, I put to her this question: "Did it ever strike you to consider, dear wife, what led me to choose you as my wife among all women, and your parents to entrust you to me of all men? It was certainly not from any difficulty that might beset either of us to find another bedfellow. That I am sure is evident to you. No! It was with deliberate intent to discover, I for myself and your parents in behalf of you, the best partner of house and children we could find, that I sought you out, and your parents, acting to the best of their ability, made choice of me. If at some future time God grant us to

---

[1]Xenophon, *Oeconomicus* 7.3–6 (selections). From *The Works of Xenophon*, Vol. 3, trans. H. G. Dakyns (London: Macmillan & Co., 1890), pp. 225–247.

have children born to us, we will take counsel together how best to bring them up, for that too will be a common interest, and a common blessing if happily they shall live to fight our battles and we find in them hereafter support and succor when we ourselves are old. But at present there is our house here, which belongs alike to both. It is common property, for all that I possess goes by my will into the common fund, and in the same way all that you deposited was placed by you in the common fund. We need not stop to calculate in figures which of us contributed most, but rather let us lay to heart this fact, that whichever of us proves the better partner, he or she at once contributes what is most worth having."

Thus I addressed her, Socrates, and thus my wife made answer: "But how can I assist you? What is my ability? Nay, everything depends on you. My business, my mother told me, was to be sober-minded!"

The Unique Talents of Men and Women

"But what is there that I can do," my wife inquired, "which will help to increase our joint estate?"

"Assuredly," I answered, "you may strive to do as well as possible what Heaven has given you a natural gift for and which the law approves."

"And what may these things be?" she asked.

"To my mind they are not the things of least importance," I replied, "unless the things which the queen bee in her hive presides over are of slight importance to the bee community; for the gods" (so Ischomachus assured me, he continued), "the gods, my wife, would seem to have exercised much care and judgment in compacting that twin-system which goes by the name of male and female, so as to secure the greatest possible advantage to the pair. Since no doubt the underlying principle of the bond is first and foremost to perpetuate through procreation the races of living creatures; and next, as the outcome of this bond, for human beings at any rate, a provision is made by which they may have sons and daughters to support them in old age.

"But whereas both of these, the indoor and the outdoor occupations alike, demand new toil and new attention, to meet the case," I added, "God made provision from the first by shaping, as it seems to me, the woman's nature for indoor and the man's for outdoor occupations. Man's body and soul He furnished with a greater capacity for enduring heat and cold, wayfaring and military marches; or, to repeat, He laid upon his shoulders the outdoor works.

"While in creating the body of woman with less capacity for these things," I continued, "God would seem to have imposed on her the indoor works; and knowing that He had implanted in the woman and imposed upon her the nurture of new-born babes, He endowed her with a larger share of affection for the new-born child than He bestowed upon man. And since He had imposed on woman the guardianship of the things imported from without, God, in His wisdom, perceiving that a fearful spirit was no detriment to guardianship, endowed the woman with a larger measure of timidity than He bestowed on man. Knowing further that he to whom the outdoor works belonged would need to defend them against malign attack, He endowed the man in turn with a larger share of courage."

The Duties of Men and Women

"Now, being well aware of this, my wife," I added, "and knowing well what things are laid upon the two us by God Himself, must we not strive to perform, each in the best way possible, our respective duties? Law, too, gives her consent—law and the usage of mankind, by sanctioning the wedlock of man and wife; and just as God ordained them to be partners in their children, so the law establishes their common ownership of house and estate. Custom, moreover, proclaims as beautiful those excellences of man and woman with which God gifted them at birth. Thus for a woman to bide tranquilly at home rather than roam abroad is no dishonor; but for a man to remain indoors, instead of devoting himself to outdoor pursuits, is a thing discreditable. But if a man does things contrary to the nature given him by God, the chances are, such insubordination escapes not the eye of Heaven: he pays the penalty, whether of neglecting his own works, or of performing those appropriate to woman." . . .

"Yes," I answered, "you will need in the same way to stay indoors, despatching to their toils without those of your domestics whose work lies there. Over those whose appointed tasks are wrought indoors, it will be your duty to preside; yours to receive the stuffs brought in; yours to apportion part for daily use, and yours to make provision for the rest, to guard and garner it so that the outgoings destined for a year may not be expended in a month. It will be your duty, when the wools are introduced, to see that clothing is made for those who need; your duty also to see that the dried wheat is rendered fit and serviceable for food. . . .

"But there are other cares, you know, and occupations," I answered, "which are yours by right, and these you will find agreeable. This, for instance: to take some maiden who knows naught of carding wool and to make her proficient in the art, doubling her usefulness; or to receive another quite ignorant of housekeeping or of service, and to render her skilful, loyal, serviceable, till she is worth her weight in gold; or again, when occasion serves, you have it in your power to requite by kindness the well-behaved whose presence is a blessing to your house; or maybe to chasten the bad character, should such a one appear. But the greatest joy of all will be to prove yourself my better; to make me your faithful follower; knowing no dread lest as the years advance you should decline in honor in your household, but rather trusting that, though your hair turn gray, yet, in proportion as you come to be a better helpmate to myself and to the children, a better guardian of our home, so will your honor increase throughout the household as mistress, wife, and mother, daily more dearly prized. Since," I added, "it is not through excellence of outward form, but by reason of the luster of virtues shed forth upon the life of man, that increase is given to things beautiful and good."

That, Socrates, or something like that, as far as I may trust my memory, records the earliest conversation which I held with her.

7.2   The Short Sad Life of a Good Woman: The Epitaph of Sokratea of Paros

Although in her second-century B.C. epitaph, Sokratea seems to speak in her own voice to passersby, it, like the rest of the burial equipment, would have been commissioned by her husband and, therefore, reflects his assessment of his wife's character and life.[2]

Nikander was my father, Paros my fatherland, and Sokratea was my name. Parmenion, husband, laid me in my tomb and granted this favor to me to serve as a memorial also to future generations of a life lived in good repute. The irresistable Erinys of childbirth

---

[2]*Inscriptiones Graecae* 12, 5, 310, lines 3–10.

separated unhappy me from my pleasant life through a hemorrhage. I could not even succeed in bringing my child into the light through my labors, but he lies in my womb among the dead.

7.3   If Only we Could Reproduce Without Women. . .!

"Two days are sweetest for a woman, the day a man marries her and the day he carries her out dead." So wrote the sixth-century B.C. *poet Hipponax. From Homer to the end of antiquity, Greek writers celebrated marriage as a partnership of a man and woman for the successful management of a household and the continuation of a family. However, there is also, almost as continuous and strong a strain of misogynism in Greek thought, characterized by the idea that good women, whose prudence and self-control would help an* oikos *to flourish, are few and far between. The clearest expression of this aspect of Greek thought is the catalog of female stereotypes contained in the poem* On Women *by the sixth-century* B.C. *satirist Semonides of Amorgos.*[3]

> From the beginning the god made the mind of woman
> A thing apart. One he made from the long-haired sow;
> While she wallows in the mud and rolls about on the ground,
> Everything at home lies in a mess.
> And she doesn't take baths but sits about
> In the shit in dirty clothes and gets fatter and fatter.
> The god made another one from the evil fox,
> A woman crafty in all matters—she doesn't miss a thing,
> Bad or good. The things she says are sometimes good
> And just as often bad. Her mood is constantly shifting.
> The next one was made from a dog, nimble, a bitch like its mother,
> And she wants to be in on everything that's said or done.
> Scampering about and nosing into everything,
> She yaps it out even if there's no one to listen.
> Her husband can't stop her with threats,
> Not if he flies into a rage and knocks her teeth out with a rock,
> Not if he speaks to her sweetly when they happen to be sitting among friends.
> No, she stubbornly maintains her unmanageable ways.
> Another one the Olympian gods fashioned from the dust of the earth,
> And gave her to man: the simple-minded type. This kind of woman
> Can't distinguish between good and bad. The only thing she understands how
>   to do
> Is eat. Not even if the gods have sent a bitter winter storm
> Does she have the sense (though she's freezing) to drag a chair close to the
>   fire.
> Another is from the sea, and she has two kinds of dispositions;

---

[3]Trans. Marylin Arthur in Sarah B. Pomeroy, *Goddesses, Whores, Wives, and Slaves: Women in Classical Antiquity* (New York: Schocken Books, 1975), pp. 49–52. Used by permission.

One day she's full of laughter and good spirits,
And a friend who came to visit would remark of her:
"There's not a better or a fairer woman than this
In the whole of the human race!"
Another day she's completely unbearable—you can't even look at her
Or come near her, but at such times she rages terribly,
Snarling like a bitch over her pups;
Unfriendly and out of temper with everyone,
No less with her friends than with her enemies.
Just as the sea itself is often smooth and calm
And safe—a great delight to sailors
In the summer season; but it often rages
And swells up with deeply resounding waves.
It's this that such a kind of woman is most like
In her temperament; for the sea's nature is changeable.
Another woman is from the stumbling and obstinate donkey,
Who only with difficulty and with the use of threats
Is compelled to agree to the perfectly acceptable things
She had resisted. Otherwise in a corner of the house
She sits munching away all night long, and all day long she sits munching at
    the hearth.
Even so she'll welcome any male friend
Who comes around with sex on his mind.
Another kind of woman is the wretched, miserable tribe that comes from the
    weasel.
As far as she is concerned, there is nothing lovely or pleasant
Or delightful or desirable in her.
She's wild over love-making in bed,
But her husband wants to vomit when he comes near her.
She's always stealing and making trouble for the neighbors,
And she often filches the sacrificial offerings from the altars.
Another woman is born of the delicate, long-maned mare,
Who maneuvers her way around the slavish and troublesome housework,
And wouldn't put a finger to the mill, or so much as lift
The sieve, or sweep the dirt out of the house
Or go into the kitchen, for fear she'll get dirty.
She introduces her husband to the pinch of poverty.
Every day she takes a bath at least twice,
Sometimes three times, and anoints herself with fragrant oil.
She always wears her hair long and flowing,
Its deep richness highlighted with flowers.
And so such a woman is a thing of beauty for others to look upon,
But she's only a burden to her husband
Unless he happens to be a tyrant or a prince,
The kind whose heart is delighted by such things.

Another one is from the monkey. In this case Zeus has outdone himself
In giving husbands the worst kind of evil.
She has the ugliest face imaginable; and such a woman
Is the laughingstock throughout the town for everyone.
Her body moves awkwardly all the way up to its short neck;
She hardly has an ass and her legs are skinny. What a poor wretch is
    the husband
Who has to put his arms around such a mess!
Like a monkey she knows all kinds of tricks
And routines, and she doesn't mind being laughed at.
Not that there's anything that she can do well—no, it's this
That concerns and occupies her all day long:
How can she accomplish the greatest amount of harm.
Another woman is from the bee; the man who gets her is fortunate.
To her alone no blame is attached,
But life flourishes and prospers under her care.
She grows old cherishing a husband who cherishes her,
After she has borne to him a lovely and distinguished group of children.
Among all women her excellence shines forth,
And a godlike grace is shed about her.
She does not take pleasure in sitting among the women
When they are discussing sex.
Such women are granted to husbands as a special favor from Zeus,
For they are the best of all and exceptionally wise.
These are all the various tribes of women that exist now
And remain among men by the devising of Zeus.
For Zeus designed this as the greatest of all evils:
Women. Even if in some way they seem to be a help;
To their husbands especially they are a source of evil.
For there is no one who manages to spend a whole day
In contentment if he has a wife,
Nor will he find himself able to speedily thrust famine out of the house,
Who is a hateful, malicious god to have as a houseguest.
But whenever a man seems to be especially content at home.
Thanks either to good fortune from the gods or to his good relations with
    the rest
Of mankind, she'll find fault somewhere and stir up a dispute.
For whosoever wife she is, she won't receive graciously
Into the house a friend who comes to visit.
And you know, the very one who appears to be most moderate and prudent
Actually turns out to be most outrageous and shameful.
And when her husband is still in shock from finding out about her, the
Neighbors are having a good laugh because even he made a mistake in
    his choice.
For each man likes to regale others with stories of praise about his own wife,

While at the same time finding fault with any other man's wife.
We don't realize that we all share the same fate.
For Zeus designed this as the greatest of all evils
And bound us to it in unbreakable fetters.
Therefore Hades welcomes into his realm
Men who have fought together for the sake of a woman.

7.4   Slaves: The Best and Most Necessary of Possessions

Homer said that slavery destroys half a man's manhood. The Greeks viewed slaves as essential to the successful functioning of a household, but they did not indulge in the illusion that slaves were happy in their lot. Greek literature once included a significant number of works devoted to advising owners how to manage this important but dangerous form of property. None of these works survive, but a good idea of their content is provided by the discussion of slavery in the Oeconomica, *a late-fourth-century* B.C. *treatise on household management written by an unknown member of Aristotle's school.*[4]

Of possessions the first in importance, the most necessary, the best, and the most relevant to the subject of household management is man. For this reason, it is necessary that slaves be trained to be reliable.

There are two types of slaves: overseers and workers. Since we see that education creates young people with characters of various sorts, it is necessary that one rear carefully those slaves to whom tasks similar to those of freemen are to be assigned.

A master's conduct toward his slaves should be such as to not encourage either insolence or slackness. He should grant a large share of respect to the more responsible slaves and an abundance of food to the workers. Since wine makes even freemen insolent and many nations withhold it even from free men, as the Carthaginians do during a military campaign, it is clear that slaves should be given no wine or very little.

The life of a slave has three aspects: work, punishment, and food. For a slave to not be punished nor made to work but to be fed makes him insolent. But for a slave to work and experience punishment but not to receive food is outrageous and makes a slave weak. What remains, therefore, is to furnish both work and food in sufficient amounts. For it is not possible to govern people who are not paid, and for slaves their pay is their food. The same thing occurs in the case of slaves as happens with regard to other kinds of persons: whenever things do not get better for those who improve and there is no prize for excellence and penalty for badness, they become worse. For this reason, it is necessary to exercise careful supervision, allocating food, clothing, leisure, and punishment to or witholding them from each slave according to his merit in word and deed. Acting this way, masters will follow the example of doctors in the matter of medicine, noting only that food is not medicine because it is always present.

The best kind of slaves for work are those that are neither extremely timid nor extremely brave, for both types cause problems. Those who are too timid do not endure, and those who are very spirited are not easy to manage.

---

[4]Ps. Aristotle, *Oeconomica* 1.5.

A limit should be set to everything. For it is right and advantageous that freedom be set as a reward. Slaves will willingly work whenever they are offered a reward and the period of their enslavement is specified. Masters should look on the bearing of children as a source of hostages for the good behavior of their slaves.

An owner ought not to have many slaves of the same ethnic background in a household, a rule that also holds true for cities. One should offer sacrifices and provide sources of pleasure more on account of slaves than of freemen, because the reasons such things exist concern them more than they do freemen.

7.5   "We Have Mistresses for Our Pleasure": Sex and Slavery in the *Oikos*

A fourth-century B.C. *orator observed,* "We have mistresses for our pleasure, concubines to serve our person, and wives to bear us legitimate children." *Freedom of sexual access by masters to their slaves is one of the basic characteristics of all slave systems. The tension created in the* oikos *by this situation and the insecurity of the life of even the most privileged slave are both illustrated in the fifth-century* B.C. *Athenian orator Antiphon's vivid account of how a scheming woman exploited the anxieties of a slave girl to bring about the death of her husband.*[5]

There was in our house an upper room, which Philoneos used to occupy whenever he had business in town. This Philoneos was an honest, respectable man, a friend of my father's. He had a concubine, whom he was intending to dispose of to a brothel. My stepmother, having heard of this, made a friend of the woman; and when she got to know of the injury Philoneos was proposing to do her, she sent for her. When the woman came, my stepmother told her that she herself also was being wrongly treated, by my father; and that if the woman would do as she said, she was clever enough to restore the love of Philoneos for his concubine, and my father's love for herself. As she expressed it, hers was the creative part, the other woman's part was that of obeying orders. She asked her therefore if she was willing to act as her assistant; and the woman promised to do so—very readily, I imagine.

Later, it happened that Philoneos had to go down to the Peiraeus (*the port of Athens*) in connection with a religious ceremony to Zeus, Guardian of Property; and at the same time my father was preparing for a voyage to Naxos. It seemed to Philoneos an excellent idea, therefore, that he should make the same trip serve a double purpose: that he should accompany my father, his friend, down to the harbour, and at the same time perform his religious duty and entertain him to a feast. Philoneos's concubine went with them, to help with the sacrifice and the banquet.

When they arrived at the port, they of course performed the sacrifice. When the religious ceremony was over, the woman began to deliberate with herself as to how and when she should administer the drug, whether before dinner or after dinner. The result of her deliberation was

---

[5]Reprinted from Antiphon, "Against a Step-Mother, On a Charge of Poisoning," in Kathleen Freeman, *The Murder of Herodes and Other Trials from the Athenian Law Courts* (New York: W. W. Norton, 1963; rpt., Indianapolis: Hackett Publishing Company, Inc.), pp. 89–90.

that she decided to do so after dinner, thus carrying out the instructions of this Clytaemnestra, my stepmother.

The whole story of the dinner would be too long for me to tell or you to hear; but I shall try to narrate the rest to you in the fewest possible words—that is, how the actual administration of the poison was accomplished.

When they had finished dinner, they naturally—as one of them was sacrificing to Zeus and entertaining a guest, and the other was about to set off on a voyage and was dining with his friend—they naturally were proceeding to pour libations, and accompany them with an offering of incense. Philoneos's concubine, as she was serving them with the wine for the libation—a libation that was to accompany prayers destined, alas! gentlemen, not to be fulfilled—poured in the poison. And in the belief that she was doing something clever, she gave the bigger dose to Philoneos, thinking that perhaps the more she gave him, the more he would love her. She still did not know that she had been deceived by my stepmother, and did not find out until she was already involved in disaster. She poured in a smaller dose for my father.

The two men poured out their libation; and then, taking in hand that which was their own destroyer, they drained their last draught.

Philoneos dropped dead instantly. My father was seized with an illness from which he died in three weeks. For this, the woman who had acted under orders has paid the penalty for her offence, in which she was an innocent accomplice: She was handed over to the public executioner after being broken on the wheel. But the woman who was the real cause, who thought out and engineered the deed—she will pay the penalty now, if you and Heaven so decree.

7.6   Freedom and Its Problems: The Life of Neaera

Although slavery was legally a status that could extend over a slave's whole life and was inherited by his or her children, Greek theorists strongly recommended that slaves be offered the opportunity of earning their freedom as an incentive to good behavior and high productivity. Unlike the situation at Rome, however, where freedom brought with it automatic citizenship, freedom for a slave in Greece was hedged about with severe restrictions. A freed slave had no political rights, could not marry a citizen, and had only limited property rights. Nevertheless, as the numerous grave monuments of freed slaves indicate, freedom was eagerly sought despite the second-class legal and social status that accompanied it. A rare insight into the social world of freed slaves in Greece is provided by the following account of the early life of a freedwoman named Neaera.[6]

She was one of seven little girls bought when small children by Nicaretê, a freedwoman who had been the slave of Charisius of Elis, and the wife of Charisius's cook Hippias. Nicaretê was a clever judge of beauty in little girls, and moreover she understood the art of rearing and training them skilfully, having made this her profession from which she drew her livelihood. She used to address them as daughters, so that she might exact the largest fee from those who wished to have dealings with them, on the ground that they were freeborn girls; but after she

---

[6]Reprinted from Ps. Demosthenes, "An Illegal Union: Against Neaera," in Kathleen Freeman, *The Murder of Herodes and Other Trials from the Athenian Law Courts* (New York: W. W. Norton, 1963; rpt., Indianapolis: Hackett Publishing Company, Inc.), pp. 197–205. All rights reserved by Hackett Publishing Company, Inc.

had reaped her profit from the youth of each of them, one by one, she then sold the whole lot of them together, seven in all: Anteia, Stratola, Aristocleia, Metaneira, Phila, Isthmias, and the defendant Neaera. . . .

Lysias the professor of rhetoric was the lover of Metaneira. He decided that in addition to the other expenses he had incurred for her, he would like to get her initiated. He thought that the rest of his expenditure went to her owner, but whatever he spent on her over the festival and the initiation ceremony would be a present for the girl herself. He therefore asked Nicaretê to come to the Mysteries and bring Metaneira so that she could be initiated, and he promised to instruct her himself in the Mysteries.

When they arrived, Lysias did not admit them to his house, out of respect for his own wife, who was the daughter of Brachyllus and his own niece, and for his mother, who was somewhat advanced in years and lived in the same house. Instead, he lodged them—that is, Metaneira and Nicaretê—with Philostratus of Colonus, who was still a bachelor and also a friend of his. The women were accompanied by the defendant Neaera, who was already working as a prostitute, though she was not yet of the proper age. . . .

After that, she worked openly at Corinth as a prostitute, and became famous. Among her lovers were Xenocleides the poet and Hipparchus the actor, who had her on hire. . . .

After that, she acquired two lovers, Timanoridas of Corinth and Eucrates of Leucas. These men found Nicaretê's charges excessive, as she expected them to pay all the daily expenses of her household; so they paid down to Nicaretê 30 minas as the purchase-price of Neaera, and bought her outright from her mistress, according to the law of that city, to be their slave. They kept her and made use of her for as long as they wished. Then, being about to get married, they informed her that they did not wish to see the woman who had been their own mistress plying her trade in Corinth nor kept in a brothel: They would be glad to receive less money for her than they had paid, and to see her also reaping some benefit. They therefore offered to allow her, towards the price of her freedom, 1,000 drachmas, that is, 500 each; as for the 20 minas remaining, they told her to find this sum herself and repay it to them.

Neaera, on hearing these propositions from Timanoridas and Eucrates, sent messages to a number of her former lovers, asking them to come to Corinth. Among these was Phrynion, an Athenian from Paeania, the son of Demon, and the brother of Demochares, a man who was living a dissolute and extravagant life, as the older of you [*jurors*] remember. When Phrynion arrived, she told him of the proposition made to her by Eucrates and Timanoridas, and handed him the money which she had collected from her other lovers as a contribution towards the purchase of her freedom, together with her own savings, asking him to make up the amount to the 20 minas, and pay it to Eucrates and Timanoridas, so that she should be free.

Phrynion was delighted to hear this proposition of hers. He took the money which had been contributed by her other lovers, made up the deficit himself, and paid the 20 minas to Eucrates and Timanoridas as the price of her freedom and on condition that she would not practise her profession in Corinth. . . .

When they arrived here at Athens, he kept her and lived with her in a most dissolute and reckless way. He took her out to dinner with him wherever he went, where there was drinking; and whenever he made an after-dinner excursion, she always went too. He made love to her openly, anywhere and everywhere he chose, to excite the jealousy of the onlookers at his privilege. . . .

However, finding herself treated with the most outrageous brutality by Phrynion, instead of being loved as she had expected, or having attention paid to her wishes, she packed up the goods in his house, including all the clothes and jewellery which he had provided for her personal adornment, and taking with her two servants, Thratta and Coccalina, ran away to Megara.

This happened when Asteius was Chief Magistrate at Athens (373–372 B.C., *thirty years or more before the present trial*), during your second war against Sparta. Neaera spent two years in Megara; but her profession did not produce sufficient income to run her house, as she was extravagant, and the Megarians are mean and stingy, and there was no great foreign colony there because it was war-time, and the Megarians favoured the Spartan side, but you [*Athenians*] were in command of the seas. She could not go back to Corinth because the terms of her release by Eucrates and Timanoridas were that she should not practise her profession there.

However, peace came under the Magistracy of Phrasicleides (371–370 B.C.), after the battle of Leuctra between Sparta and Thebes (July, 371 B.C.). It was then that our opponent Stephanus visited Megara. He put up at her house, as that of a prostitute, and became her lover. She told him her whole life story and of her ill-treatment at the hands of Phrynion, and gave him the things she had taken with her when she left Phrynion. She longed to live in Athens, but was afraid of Phrynion, because she had done him wrong and he was furious with her. She knew the violence and arrogance of his character. She therefore made the defendant Stephanus her protector, and while they were still in Megara, he talked encouragingly and filled her with hope, saying that Phrynion would be sorry for it if he laid hands on her, as he himself would take her as his wife, and would introduce the sons she already had to his clansmen as being his own, and would make citizens of them. No one on earth, he said, should do her any harm.

And so he arrived here at Athens from Megara with her and her three children, Proxenus, Ariston, and a daughter, who now bears the name of Phano. He took her and the children to the little house which he owned, alongside the Whispering Hermes, between the house of Dorotheus the Eleusinian and the house of Cleinomachus, which now Spintharus has bought from him for 7 minas. Thus, this place was the whole of Stephanus's property at that time—he had nothing else.

He had two reasons for bringing her here: first, that he would have a handsome mistress without expense; second, that her profession would provide him with the necessaries of life and keep the household, for he had no other source of income, except what he picked up by occasional blackmail.

When Phrynion heard that she was in Athens and living with the defendant, he took some young men with him and went to Stephanus's house to get her. Stephanus asserted her freedom, according to law, and Phrynion thereupon summoned her before the Polemarch, under surety. In proof of this I will bring before you the Polemarch of that year. . . .

When she had thus been bailed out by Stephanus and was living with him, she carried on the same profession no less than before, but she exacted a larger fee from those who wished to consort with her, as having now a certain position to keep up and as being a married woman. Stephanus helped her by blackmail: If he caught any rich unknown stranger making love to her, he used to lock him up in the house as an adulterer caught with his wife, and extract a large sum of money from him—naturally, because neither Stephanus nor Neaera had anything, not even enough to meet their daily expenses, but their establishment was large. There were himself and herself to keep, and three small children—the ones she had brought with her to him—and two maids and a manservant; and above all, she had acquired the habit of good living, as formerly it had been others who had provided her with all necessaries. And Stephanus here was not making anything worth mentioning out of politics: He was not yet a public speaker, but just a political hireling, one of those who stand by the platform and shout, who bring indictments and lay information against people for money, who lend their names to be inscribed on other men's proposals.

That was before he came under the patronage of Callistratus of Aphidna. I will later explain to you how that happened and for what reason, when I have finished with the defendant Neaera, and have shown you that she is an alien, and has committed great offences against you and has sinned against religion. I want you to realize that he himself deserves no less a punishment than Neaera, but actually a much greater, in so far as he declares himself to be an Athenian citizen and yet has shown such a deep contempt for the laws, and for yourselves, and for religion, that he has not enough restraint even to keep quiet for shame at his misdeeds, but has brought a trumped-up charge against, among others, myself, and has caused my relative here to bring him and Neaera to trial in such a way that her true status should be examined, and his criminal character should be revealed.

To continue: Phrynion began his lawsuit against Stephanus, on the grounds that Stephanus had robbed him of the defendant Neaera and made a free woman of her, and that Stephanus had received the goods of which Neaera had robbed him when she left. However, their friends brought them together and persuaded them to submit the dispute to arbitration. The arbitrator who sat on Phrynion's behalf was Satyrus of Alôpecê, the brother of Lacedaemonius, and on Stephanus's behalf, Saurias of Lampra, They chose as umpire Diogeiton of Acharnae. These three met in the temple, and after hearing the facts from both the litigants and also from the woman herself, they gave their judgment, which was accepted by the litigants: namely, that the woman should be free and her own mistress, but that the goods which Neaera had taken from Phrynion when she left should all be returned to Phrynion, except the clothes and jewellery and maid-servants which had been bought for Neaera herself; further, that she should spend the same number of days with each of them; but that if they agreed to any other arrangement, this same arrangement should hold good; that the woman's upkeep should be provided by the person with whom she was living at the time; and that for the future the litigants should be friends and should bear no malice. Such was the settlement brought about by the decision of arbitrators in the case of Phrynion and Stephanus, concerning the defendant Neaera. . . .

When the business was over, the friends of each party, those who had assisted them at the arbitration and the rest, did as I believe is usual in such cases, especially when a mistress is in dispute: they went to dine with each of them at the times when he had Neaera with him, and she dined and drank with them as mistresses do. . . .

I have now outlined the facts about Neaera, and have supported my statements with evidence: that she was originally a slave, was twice sold, and practiced the profession of a prostitute; that she ran away from Phrynion to Megara, and on her return to Athens was summoned before the Polemarch under surety.

7.7   How to Become a Slave: Be in the Wrong Place at the Wrong Time

Greek slave law emphasized the potentially hereditary nature of slavery. The reality, however, was that most slaves had not been born into that status but became slaves through some accident: capture in war, kidnapping, sale to satisfy a debt, and so on. Nevertheless, despite its importance to Greek social and economic life, little evidence survives concerning the ancient slave trade. A rare insight into this aspect of Greek life is provided by the fourth-century B.C. orator Demosthenes, who recounts how the Athenian farmer Nicostratus was kidnapped by a warship from the neighboring city of Aegina and enslaved while pursuing several of his own slaves, who had run away.[7]

4. I have known this man Nicostratus, jurors, who is my neighbor and my contemporary, for a long time. When my father died and I began to live in the country, where I still live, we had many dealings with each other, because we are neighbors and contemporaries. As time passed, we developed very good feelings for each other, and I was so well inclined toward him, that he never failed to receive from me whatever he needed. He likewise was helpful to me in watching over and managing my affairs, and whenever I happened to be away either on public service as a trierarch (= commander of a trireme) or for some personal business, I left him in charge of all matters concerning my farm.

5. While I was serving as trierarch near the Peloponnesus, I had to transport from there to Sicily the ambassadors, whom the people had chosen. The voyage was on short notice. I wrote to him, accordingly, that I was leaving and would not be able to come home lest I delay the ambassadors. I also instructed him to watch over and manage my affairs at home just as in previous times.

6. During my absence three slaves ran away from his farm. Two of them I had given him and one he had bought. While he was pursuing them, he was captured by a trireme, brought to Aegina, and sold there. When I returned—I was still in command of my trireme—Deinon, his brother, came to me, and told me of Nicostratus's misfortune. He also told me that, although Nicostratus had written letters to him, he himself had not gone after him because of the lack of travel money. And he told me at the same time that he had heard that Nicostratus was in very bad circumstances.

7. When I had heard these things, I was moved by his misfortune, and I gave his brother Deinon 300 drachmas for travel money and immediately sent him to Nicostratus. After he returned home, Nicostratus came to me first thing, and greeted me and praised me because I had provided his brother with travel money. He also bewailed his misfortune and, condemning his relatives, he asked me for help, just as before I had been a true friend to him. In tears he said that he had been ransomed for twenty-six minas and he urged me to contribute to the ransom.

8. When I heard these things, I pitied him, seeing at the same time that he was in a bad state. He also showed me the sores on his limbs from the fetters, of which he still has the scars, but if you order him to show them, he will be unwilling. I answered him that, just as I was a true friend to him before, so also now I would help him in his misfortune. I would forgive the

---

[7]Demosthenes, *Against Nicostratus* 53.4–11.

three hundred drachmas, which I had given to his brother as travel money so that he could go to him; and I would advance him a thousand drachmas toward the ransom as a loan.

9. And I did not merely promise him this in word and not do it in fact; but, although I was not prosperous because of my dispute with Phormion and the loss to him of the property, which my father had left me, I brought to Theocles, who had then had a bank, cups, and a gold crown, which I still had from my inheritance, and I told him to give Nicostratus a thousand drachmas, and I gave this money to him as a gift, and I admit that I gave it to him.

10. A few days later, however, he approached me in tears and said that the strangers, who had lent him the ransom, were demanding payment from him; and that according to the contract he had thirty days to pay it back or he would owe double the amount. Moreover, no one wished to buy his farm, which was next to mine, or give him a loan on it. For his brother, Arethousius, whose slaves were mentioned earlier, would not allow anyone to buy it or make a loan on it, on the ground that the money was owed to him.

11. "You, therefore," he said, "provide me with the balance of the money before the thirty days are up in order that the thousand drachmas which I have paid not be lost and I become liable to seizure. And," he said, "After I pay off the strangers, I will obtain a loan from my friends, and pay you back what you lent me. And you know," he said, "that the laws order that a person who has been ransomed from enemies shall belong to the ransomer, if he does not repay the ransom."

7.8   The Slave Trade: A Eunuch's Revenge

Further evidence concerning the operation of the ancient slave trade is provided by Herodotus' capsule biography of Hermotimus, a eunuch of the Persian King Xerxes, and the revenge he took on the man responsible for his enslavement.[8]

104. Xerxes likewise sent away at this time one of the principal of his eunuchs, a man named Hermotimus, a Pedasian, who was bidden to take charge of his sons. Now the Pedasians inhabit the region above Halicarnassus, and it is related of them that in their country the following circumstance happens. When a mischance is about to befall any of their neighbors within a certain time, the priestess of Athena in their city grows a long beard. This has already taken place on two occasions.

105. The Hermotimus of whom I spoke above was, as I said, a Pedasian, and he, of all men whom we know, took the most cruel vengeance on the person who had done him an injury. He had been made a prisoner of war, and when his captors sold him, he was bought by a certain Panionius, a native of Chios, who made his living by a most nefarious traffic. Whenever he could get any boys of unusual beauty, he castrated them and, carrying them to Sardis or Ephesus, sold them for large sums of money, for the barbarians value eunuchs more than others since they regard them as more trustworthy. Many were the slaves that Panionius, who made his living by the practice, had thus treated, and among them was this Hermotimus of whom I have here made mention. However, he was not without his share of good fortune, for after a while he was

[8]Herodotus, *The History of the Persian Wars* 8.104–106. From *The History of Herodotus*, Vol. 4, trans. George Rawlinson (New York: D. Appleton & Co., 1859–1860), pp. 288–290.

sent from Sardis, together with other gifts, as a present to the king. Nor was it long before he came to be esteemed by Xerxes more highly than all his eunuchs.

106. When the king was on his way to Athens with the Persian army and abode for a time at Sardis, Hermotimus happened to make a journey upon business into Mysia; and there, in a district that is called Atarneus but that belongs to Chios, he chanced to fall in with Panionius. Recognizing him at once, he entered into a long and friendly talk with him wherein he counted up the numerous blessings he enjoyed through his means, promised him all manner of favors in return, if he would bring his household to Sardis and live there. Panionius was overjoyed and, accepting the offer made him, came presently and brought with him his wife and children. Then Hermotimus, when he had got Panionius and all his family into his power, addressed him in these words: "You, who make a living by viler deeds than anyone else in the whole world, what wrong to you or yours had I or any of mine done, that you should have made me nothing and no longer a man? Surely you thought that the gods took no note of your crimes. But they in their justice have delivered you, the doer of unrighteousness, into my hands; and now you cannot complain of the vengeance which I am resolved to take on you."

After these reproaches, Hermotimus commanded the four sons of Panionius to be brought and forced the father to castrate them with his own hand. Unable to resist, he did as Hermotimus required; and then his sons were made to treat him in the self-same way. So in this way there came to Panionius requital at the hands of Hermotimus.

Chapter 8

Chapter 8

Empire and Democracy: The Classical *Polis*

The Greek city-states (*poleis*) developed in an environment uniquely free of external threat, thanks to the absence of a single dominant imperial power in the eastern Mediterranean for much of the first half of the first millennium B.C.[1] That security ended with the sudden appearance in the mid sixth century B.C. of the Persian Empire. Its first three rulers, Cyrus I (559–530 B.C.), Cambyses (530–522 B.C.), and Darius I (522–486 B.C.), created the greatest of all ancient Near Eastern empires, one that stretched from the Aegean to what is now Pakistan. Attempts to extend Persian rule to mainland Greece in 490 and 480–479 B.C. failed. Athens bore the brunt of the Persian assault in both invasions: In 490 B.C. Athens faced the invaders virtually alone at Marathon. A decade later, Athens was captured and sacked by the Persians. But together with Sparta and her allies, Athens's fleet won the key naval victory at Salamis, and a year later the Greek alliance decisively defeated the Persians on land at Plataea and ended the threat of Persian conquest.

Athens emerged from the shadow of the Persian threat at the head of an alliance of island and East Greek *poleis*, the so-called Delian League, and intent on vengeance and the liberation of Persia's remaining Greek subjects. During the next half century, the Delian League grew to almost 200 members, but as the Persian threat receded the Delian League gradually changed from an association of free allies into an Athenian empire. Along with the growth of Athens's imperial power, there was increased tension between Athens and Sparta, her chief rival for preeminence in Greece, until war broke out in 431 B.C. The 27 years of the Peloponnesian War (431–404 B.C.) did more than result in the defeat of Athens and the dissolution of her empire. It devastated Greece and brought hard times that challenged the most basic Greek ideas about appropriate social roles for free men, as the selection from the historian Xenophon (at the end of this chapter) makes clear. Equally important, fourth-century B.C. Greece found itself once again vulnerable to foreign threat, this time not from Persia in the east but from a newly

---

[1]Printed with the permission of the National Center for History in Schools and the Regents of the University of California. Adapted from *The Golden Age of Greece: Imperial Democracy* (1991), pp. xiii–xvi.

unified and invigorated kingdom of Macedon in the north. During the half century of imperial glory between the Persian and Peloponnesian Wars, however, a prosperous and confident Athens was the political and cultural center of the Greek world and her democracy a spur to revolution and reflection.

All Greek *poleis* were democratic in that sovereignty rested with the citizenry that elected its own officials and could meet in assembly to decide issues of concern to the community. What differentiated *poleis* was the identity of the citizens and the extent to which the assembly could take the political initiative. Reduced to its essential element, citizenship implied the ability to serve the *polis* as a warrior. In practice, this meant that in most *poleis* the assembly's powers were limited. Full citizenship, and, therefore, the right to attend the assembly, was restricted to those wealthy enough to equip themselves as hoplites. Sparta overcame these limitations and created her unique military democracy by using her Helots to provide all Spartans with a minimum income sufficient to allow them to serve in the hoplite phalanx. But the powers of even Sparta's assembly were limited to approving or rejecting questions preselected for it by a council dominated by the Spartan rich. Athens took a different road to democracy.

The Athenian democracy of the fifth century B.C. was the product of two distinct but convergent series of events. The first was the transformation of Athenian political structure, through a series of reforms initiated by Solon in the early sixth century B.C. and continued by Cleisthenes at the end of the century, so as to concentrate decision-making power in the Athenian assembly. These reforms encouraged participation by a broad spectrum of the Athenian male population in political activity at all levels. The second was the enhancement of the military value, and, therefore, the political value, of even the poorest Athenians who rowed the city's triremes. This happened as a result of the essential contribution made by the Athenian navy to the Greek victory over Persia in 480 B.C. and to the acquisition and maintenance of the Athenian empire in the following decades.

The linkage of democracy and empire is evident in every area of fifth-century B.C. Athenian life. The tribute of the allies financed the great building program on the Athenian Acropolis, one of the enduring glories of Athenian culture, and helped subsidize the participation of the citizen body in the political life of the democracy. In a prosperous Athens could be found luxuries of all kinds from all of the world known to the Greeks. Also to be found in fifth-century B.C. Athens was a new analytical approach to the study of politics. The selections from *The History of the Peloponnesian War* by the Athenian historian Thucydides explore the impact of an increasingly brutal war on morality and civic values, and the unknown essayist whom historians call "The Old Oligarch" uses the principle of self-interest to explain the paradoxical success of the Athenian democracy, a form of government that violated traditional Greek norms of good government.

8.1   The Golden Age: A Greek View

The idea that the unexpected Greek victory over the Persians in 480–479 B.C. not only saved Greece from slavery but also ushered in a cultural "Golden Age" under the leadership of Athens is not just a modern view. It was also how the Greeks interpreted the history of this period, as is illustrated by this selection from the universal history of the first-century B.C. *historian Diodorus. Particularly noteworthy is how Diodorus intensified the picture of the fifth century as a period of extraordinary cultural achievement by anachronistically including in it such fourth-century* B.C. *luminaries as the philosophers Plato and Aristotle and the rhetorician Isocrates.*[2]

A person would rightly feel perplexed who considered the inconsistency of human life. For none of the agreed-on goods are found to be given to men in perfect form nor are any of the ills absolutely free of some advantage. This can be shown by considering past events, especially the greatest. For the campaign of Xerxes, the king of the Persians, caused the greatest fear among the Greeks because of the huge size of his army, since the stake for which they were about to fight was their enslavement. They all assumed that they would suffer a similar fate as the Greek cities of Asia which had been enslaved previously. But when the war, contrary to expectation, came to an unanticipated conclusion, not only did the inhabitants of Greece escape from danger, but they gained great fame, and every Greek city was filled with such abundance that all were astounded at their reversal of fortune. For the next fifty years, Greece experienced a great surge of prosperity. In this period the arts flourished because of the abundance, and the greatest artists known to posterity existed then, among whom was the sculptor Pheidias. Education also advanced greatly, and philosophy and rhetoric were highly esteemed by all the Greeks, but especially by the Athenians. The philosophers included Socrates, Plato, and Aristotle; the orators, Pericles and Isocrates together with the students of Isocrates. There were also famous generals: Miltiades, Themistocles, Aristides, Cimon, Myronides, and many others. . . . The Athenians especially advanced in repute and vigor and became renowned throughout the world. For they increased their power to such a degree that without the Spartans and the Peloponnesians they defeated, on their own, great Persian forces on both land and sea and so humbled the famed Persian Empire that they compelled the Persians to sign a treaty freeing all the cities in Asia.

8.2   The Persian Empire and the Greek Worldview

The role of the Persian Empire in Greek history was not, however, just that of the Greek's principal enemy. It also linked for the first time the inhabited world from eastern Europe to western India, facilitating trade and the exchange of ideas throughout this vast region. The effects of this exchange are illustrated by these two passages from the historian Herodotus. In the first, Herodotus describes how the late-sixth-century B.C. *mythographer and geographer Hecataeus of Miletus had his genealogical claims to divine descent deflated by the immensely long historical memory of the Egyptians; while in the second, Herodotus uses the example of the mad Persian king Cambyses (530–522 B.C.), who desecrated Egyptian temples and tombs, to argue for the relativity of all cultural values, including those of the Greeks.*[3]

---

[2]Diodorus 12.1–2.
[3]The History of Necodotus, Trans. by George Rawlinson, 2.143–146,3.38 (adapted). From Francis R. B. Godolphin, *The Greek Historians*, Vol. 1 (New York: Random House, 1942), pp. 149–151, 181.

8.2.1   Greeks are Newcomers Compared to the Egyptians

143. When Hecataeus the prose writer was at Thebes, and, discoursing of his genealogy, traced his descent to a god in the person of his sixteenth ancestor, the priests of Zeus did to him exactly as they afterwards did to me, though I made no boast of my family. They led me into the inner sanctuary, which is a spacious chamber, and showed me a multitude of colossal statues, in wood, which they counted up, and found to amount to the exact number they had said; the custom being for every high priest during his lifetime to set up his statue in the temple. As they showed me the figures and reckoned them up, they assured me that each was the son of the one preceding him; and this they repeated throughout the whole line, beginning with the representation of the priest last deceased, and continuing till they had completed the series. When Hecataeus, in giving his genealogy, mentioned a god as his sixteenth ancestor, the priests opposed their genealogy to his, going through this list, and refusing to allow that any man was ever born of a god. Their colossal figures were each, they said, a Piromis, born of a Piromis, and the number of them was 345; through the whole series Piromis followed Piromis, and the line did not run up either to a god or a hero. The word *Piromis* may be rendered "gentleman."

144. Of such a nature were, they said, the beings represented by these images—they were very far indeed from being gods. However, in the times anterior to them it was otherwise; then Egypt had gods for its rulers, who dwelt upon the earth with men, one being always supreme above the rest. The last of these was Horus, the son of Osiris, called by the Greeks Apollo. He deposed Typhon, and ruled over Egypt as its last god-king. Osiris is named Dionysus by the Greeks.

145. The Greeks regard Heracles, Dionysus, and Pan as the youngest of the gods. With the Egyptians, contrariwise, Pan is exceedingly ancient, and belongs to those whom they call "the eight gods," who existed before the rest. Heracles is one of the gods of the second order, who are known as "the twelve"; and Dionysus belongs to the gods of the third order, whom the twelve produced. I have already mentioned how many years intervened according to the Egyptians between the birth of Heracles and the reign of Amasis [sc. 17,000 years]. From Pan to this period they count a still longer time; and even from Dionysus, who is the youngest of the three, they reckoned 15,000 years to the reign of that king. In these matters they say they cannot be mistaken, as they have always kept count of the years, and noted them in their registers. But from the present day to the time of Dionysus, the reputed son of Semele, daughter of Cadmus, is a period of not more than 1,600 years; to that of Heracles, son of Alcmena, is about 900; while to the time of Pan, son of Penelope (Pan, according to the Greeks, was her child by Hermes), is a shorter space than to the Trojan war, 800 years or thereabout.

146. It is open to all to receive whichever he may prefer of these two traditions; my own opinion about them has been already declared. If indeed these gods had been publicly known, and had grown old in Greece, as was the case with Heracles, son of Amphytrion, Dionysus, son of Semele, and Pan, son of Penelope, it might have been said that the last-mentioned personages were men who bore the names of certain previously existing gods. But Dionysus, according to the Greek tradition, was no sooner born than he was sewn up in Zeus's thigh, and carried off to Nysa, above Egypt, in Ethiopia; and as to Pan, they do not even profess to

know what happened to him after his birth. To me, therefore, it is quite manifest that the names of these gods became known to the Greeks after those of their other deities, and that they count their birth from the time when they first acquired a knowledge of them. Thus far my narrative rests on the accounts given by the Egyptians.

8.2.2   All Customs Are Relative

38. Thus it appears certain to me, by a great variety of proofs, that Cambyses was raving mad; he would not else have set himself to make a mock of holy rites and long-established usages. For if one were to offer men to choose out of all the customs in the world such as seemed to them the best, they would examine the whole number, and end by preferring their own; so convinced are they that their own usages far surpass those of all others. Unless, therefore, a man was mad, it is not likely that he would make sport of such matters. That people have this feeling about their laws may be seen by very many proofs: among others, by the following. Darius, after he had got the kingdom, called into his presence certain Greeks who were at hand, and asked them what he should pay them to eat the bodies of their fathers when they died, to which they answered that there was no sum that would tempt them to do such a thing. He then sent for certain Indians, of the race called Callatians. These men eat their fathers, and he asked them, while the Greeks stood by (they understood with the help of an interpreter all that was said), "What he should give them to burn the bodies of their fathers at their decease?" The Indians exclaimed aloud, and bade him forbear such language. Such is men's wont herein; and Pindar was right, in my judgment, when he said, "Custom is the king over all."

8.3   The Athenian Empire: Origins and Structure

Later Greeks, such as Diodorus, viewed the development of the Athenian Empire through rose-tinted glasses as a glorious episode in the Greek struggle for freedom. Aristotle, in the following selection from his Constitution of Athens, *provides a brief but realistic analysis of the events that resulted in the establishment of the Delian League in 476 B.C. and the extensive involvement of Athenian citizens in the affairs of Athens' empire.*[4]

23. So far, then, had the city progressed by this time, growing gradually with the growth of the democracy; but after the Persian wars the Council of Areopagus once more developed strength and assumed the control of the state. It did not acquire this supremacy by virtue of any formal decree, but because it had been the cause of the battle of Salamis being fought. When the generals were utterly at a loss how to meet the crisis and made proclamation that every one should see to his own safety, the Areopagus provided a donation of money, distributing eight drachmas to each member of the ships' crews, and so prevailed on them to go on board. On these grounds people bowed to its

---

[4]Aristotle, *The Constitution of Athens* 23–24, trans. Frederick G. Kenyon. From Francis R. B. Godolphin, *The Greek Historians*, Vol. 2 (New York: Random House, 1942), pp. 695–696.

prestige; and during this period, Athens was well administered. At this time they devoted themselves to the prosecution of the war and were in high repute among the Greeks, so that the command by sea was conferred upon them, in spite of the opposition of the Lacedaemonians. The leaders of the people during this period were Aristides, son of Lysimachus, and Themistocles, son of Neocles, of whom the latter appeared to devote himself to the conduct of war, while the former had the reputation of being a clever statesman and the most upright man of his time. Accordingly the one was usually employed as general, the other as political adviser. The rebuilding of the fortifications they conducted in combination, although they were political opponents; but it was Aristides who, seizing the opportunity afforded by the discredit brought upon the Lacedaemonians by Pausanias, guided the public policy in the matter of the defection of the Ionian states from the alliance with Sparta. It follows that it was he who made the first assessment of tribute from the various allied states, two years after the battle of Salamis, in the archonship of Timosthenes; and it was he who took the oath of offensive and defensive alliance with the Ionians, on which occasion they cast the masses of iron into the sea.

24. After this, seeing the state growing in confidence and much wealth accumulated, he advised the people to lay hold of the leadership of the league, and to quit the country districts and settle in the city. He pointed out to them that all would be able to gain a living there, some by service in the army, others in the garrisons, others by taking a part in public affairs; and in this way they would secure the leadership. This advice was taken; and when the people had assumed the supreme control they proceeded to treat their allies in a more imperious fashion, with the exception of the Chians, Lesbians, and Samians. These they maintained to protect their empire, leaving their constitutions untouched, and allowing them to retain whatever dominion they then possessed. They also secured an ample maintenance for the mass of the population in the way which Aristides had pointed out to them. Out of the proceeds of the tributes and the taxes and the contributions of the allies more than 20,000 persons were maintained. There were 6,000 jurymen, 1,600 bowmen, 1,200 Knights, 500 members of the Council, 500 guards of the dockyards, besides fifty guards in the Acropolis. There were some 700 magistrates at home, and some 700 abroad. Further, when they subsequently went to war, there were in addition 2,500 heavy-armed troops, twenty guard-ships, and other ships which collected the tributes, with crews amounting to 2,000 men, selected by lot; and besides these there were the persons maintained at the Prytaneum, and orphans, and jailers, since all these were supported by the state.

8.4   Imperial Democracy: A Critical View

"The Old Oligarch" *is the name given by scholars to an anonymous author who, in the 430s or 420s* B.C., *wrote a short essay that attempted to explain to Greek conservatives the reasons for the paradoxical success of the Athenian democracy. Eschewing the moralizing approach characteristic of traditional Greek political thought, the author used the principle of "enlightened self-interest" to demonstrate that the Athenian poor, the backbone of the Athenian navy, supported the "bad" democracy*

*because a "good" government would deprive them of a share in government and the benefits it provided.
In developing his argument, "The Old Oligarch" provides a vivid picture of the prosperous, cosmopolitan
society of mid-fifth-century* B.C. *Athens.*[5]

Democracy and the Poor

1. Now, as for the constitution of the Athenians, and the type or manner of constitution
which they have chosen, I praise it not, insofar as the very choice involves the welfare of the
baser folk as opposed to that of the better class. I repeat, I withhold my praise so far; but, given
the fact that this is the type agreed upon, I propose to show that they set about its preservation in the right way; and that those other transactions in connection with it, which are
looked upon as blunders by the rest of the Hellenic world, are the reverse.

In the first place, I maintain, it is only just that the poorer classes and the common
people of Athens should be better off than the men of birth and wealth, seeing that it is the
people who man the fleet, and have brought the city her power. The steersman, the boatswain,
the lieutenant, the look out man at the prow, the shipwright—these are the people who supply the city with power far more than her heavy infantry and men of birth and quality. This
being the case, it seems only just that offices of state should be thrown open to every one both
in the ballot and the show of hands, and that the right of speech should belong to any one
who likes, without restriction. For, observe, there are many of these offices which, according
as they are in good or in bad hands, are a source of safety or of danger to the People, and in
these the People prudently abstains from sharing; as, for instance, it does not think it incumbent on itself to share in the functions of the general or of the commander of cavalry.
The commons recognizes the fact that in forgoing the personal exercise of these offices, and
leaving them to the control of the more powerful citizens, it secures the balance of advantage
to itself. It is only those departments of government which bring pay and assist the private
estate that the People cares to keep in its own hands.

In the next place, in regard to what some people are puzzled to explain—the fact that
everywhere greater consideration is shown to the base, to poor people and to common folk,
than to persons of good quality—so far from being a matter of surprise, this, as can be
shown, is the keystone of the preservation of the democracy. It is these poor people, this
common folk, this worse element, whose prosperity, combined with the growth of their
numbers, enhances the democracy. Whereas, a shifting of fortune to the advantage of the
wealthy and the better classes implies the establishment on the part of the commons of a
strong power in opposition to itself. In fact, all the world over, the cream of society is in opposition to the democracy. Naturally, since the smallest amount of intemperance and injustice, together with the highest scrupulousness in the pursuit of excellence, is to be found in
the ranks of the better class, while within the ranks of the People will be found the greatest amount of ignorance, disorderliness, rascality since poverty acts as a stronger incentive
to base conduct, not to speak of lack of education and ignorance, traceable to the lack of means
which afflicts the average of mankind.

---

[5]From *The Constitution of the Athenians* by "The Old Oligarch," trans. H. G. Dakyns, in Godolphin, *The Greek Historians*, Vol.
2, pp. 633–643.

The Plight of the Rich in the Democracy

Another point is the extraordinary amount of license granted to slaves and resident aliens at Athens, where a blow is illegal, and a slave will not step aside to let you pass him in the street. I will explain the reason of this peculiar custom. Supposing it were legal for a slave to be beaten by a free citizen, or for a resident alien or freedman to be beaten by a citizen, it would frequently happen that an Athenian might be mistaken for a slave or an alien and receive a beating; since the Athenian People is not better clothed than the slave or alien, nor in personal appearance is there any superiority. Or if the fact itself that slaves in Athens are allowed to indulge in luxury, and indeed in some cases to live magnificently, be found astonishing, this too, it can be shown, is done of set purpose. Where you have a naval power dependent upon wealth we must perforce be slaves to our slaves, in order that we may get in our slave-rents, and let the real slave go free. Where you have wealthy slaves it ceases to be advantageous that my slave should stand in awe of you. In Lacedaemon my slave stands in awe of you. But if your slave is in awe of me there will be a risk of his giving away his own moneys to avoid running a risk in his own person. It is for this reason then that we have established an equality between our slaves and free men; and again between our resident aliens and full citizens, because the city stands in need of her resident aliens to meet the requirements of such a multiplicity of arts and for the purposes of her navy. That is, I repeat, the justification of the equality conferred upon our resident aliens.

The common people put a stop to citizens devoting their time to athletics and to the cultivation of music, disbelieving in the beauty of such training, and recognizing the fact that these are things the cultivation of which is beyond its power. On the same principle, in the case of the choregia, the management of athletics, and the command of ships, the fact is recognized that it is the rich man who trains the chorus, and the People for whom the chorus is trained; it is the rich man who is naval commander or superintendent of athletics, and the People that profits by their labors. In fact, what the People looks upon as its right is to pocket the money. To sing and run and dance and man the vessels is well enough, but only in order that the People may be the gainer, while the rich are made poorer. And so in the courts of justice, justice is not more an object of concern to the jurymen than what touches personal advantage.

The Advantages of Empire

To speak next of the allies, and in reference to the point that emissaries from Athens come out, and, according to common opinion, calumniate and vent their hatred upon the better sort of people, this is done on the principle that the ruler cannot help being hated by those whom he rules; but that if wealth and respectability are to wield power in the subject cities the empire of the Athenian People has but a short lease of existence. This explains why the better people are punished with infamy, robbed of their money, driven from their homes, and put to death, while the baser sort are promoted to honor. On the other hand, the better Athenians protect the better class in the allied cities. And why? Because they recognize that it is to the interest of their own class at all times to protect the best element in the cities. It may be urged that if it comes to strength and power the real strength of Athens lies in the capacity of her allies to contribute their money quota. But to the democratic mind it appears a higher advantage still for the individual Athenian to get hold of the wealth of the allies, leaving them only enough to live upon and to cultivate their estates, but powerless to harbour treacherous designs.

Again, it is looked upon as a mistaken policy on the part of the Athenian democracy to compel her allies to voyage to Athens in order to have their cases tried. On the other hand, it is easy to reckon up what a number of advantages the Athenian People derives from the practice impugned. In the first place, there is the steady receipt of salaries throughout the year derived from the court fees. Next, it enables them to manage the affairs of the allied states while seated at home without the expense of naval expeditions. Thirdly, they thus preserve the partisans of the democracy, and ruin her opponents in the law courts. Whereas, supposing the several allied states tried their cases at home, being inspired by hostility to Athens, they would destroy those of their own citizens whose friendship to the Athenian People was most marked. But besides all this the democracy derives the following advantages from hearing the cases of her allies in Athens. In the first place, the one per cent tax levied in Peiraeus is increased to the profit of the state; again, the owner of a lodging house does better, and so, too, the owner of a pair of beasts, or of slaves to be let out on hire; again, heralds and criers are a class of people who fare better owing to the sojourn of foreigners at Athens. Further still, supposing the allies had not to resort to Athens for the hearing of cases, only the official representative of the imperial state would be held in honor, such as the general, or trierarch, or ambassador. Whereas now every single individual among the allies is forced to pay flattery to the People of Athens because he knows that he must betake himself to Athens and win or lose his case at the bar, not of any stray set of judges, but of the sovereign People itself, such being the law and custom at Athens. He is compelled to behave as a suppliant in the courts of justice, and when some juryman comes into court, to grasp his hand. For this reason, therefore, the allies find themselves more and more in the position of slaves to the people of Athens.

2. As to the heavy infantry, an arm the deficiency of which at Athens is well recognized, this is how the matter stands. They recognize the fact that, in reference to the hostile power, they are themselves inferior, and must be, even if their heavy infantry were more numerous. But relatively to the allies, who bring in the tribute, their strength even on land is enormous. And they are persuaded that their heavy infantry is sufficient for all purposes, provided they retain this superiority. Apart from all else, to a certain extent fortune must be held responsible for the actual condition. The subjects of a power which is dominant by land have it open to them to form contingents from several small states and to muster in force for battle. But with the subjects of a naval power it is different. As far as they are groups of islanders it is impossible for their states to meet together for united action, for the sea lies between them, and the dominant power is master of the sea. And even if it were possible for them to assemble in some single island unobserved, they would only do so to perish by famine. And as to the states subject to Athens which are not islanders, but situated on the continent, the larger are held in check by need and the small ones absolutely by fear, since there is no state in existence which does not depend upon imports and exports, and these she will forfeit if she does not lend a willing ear to those who are masters by sea. In the next place, a power dominant by sea can do certain things which a land power is debarred from doing; as, for instance, ravage the territory of a superior, since it is always possible to coast along to some point, where either there is no hostile force to deal with or merely a small body; and in case of an advance in force on the part of the enemy they can take to their ships and sail away. Such a performance

is attended with less difficulty than that experienced by the relieving force on land. Again, it is open to a power so dominating by sea to leave its own territory and sail off on as long a voyage as you please. Whereas the land power cannot place more than a few days' journey between itself and its own territory, for marches are slow affairs; and it is not possible for an army on the march to have food supplies to last for any great length of time. Such an army must either march through friendly territory or it must force a way by victory in battle. The voyager meanwhile has it in his power to disembark at any point where he finds himself in superior force, or, at the worst, to coast by until he reaches either a friendly district or an enemy too weak to resist. Again, those diseases to which the fruits of the earth are liable as visitations from heaven fall severely on a land power, but are scarcely felt by the naval power, for such sicknesses do not visit the whole earth everywhere at once. So that the ruler of the sea can get in supplies from a thriving district. And if one may descend to more trifling particulars, it is to this same lordship of the sea that the Athenians owe the discovery, in the first place, of many of the luxuries of life through intercourse with other countries. So that the choice things of Sicily and Italy, of Cyprus and Egypt and Lydia, of Pontus or Peloponnese, or wheresoever else it be, are all swept, as it were, into one center, and all owing, as I say, to their maritime empire. And again, in process of listening to every form of speech, they have selected this from one place and that from another—for themselves. So much so that while the rest of the Greeks employ each pretty much their own peculiar mode of speech, habit of life, and style of dress, the Athenians have adopted a composite type, to which all sections of Hellas, and the foreigner alike, have contributed.

As regards sacrifices and temples and festivals and sacred enclosures, the People sees that it is not possible for every poor citizen to do sacrifice and hold festival, or to set up temples and to inhabit a large and beautiful city. But it has hit upon a means of meeting the difficulty. They sacrifice—that is, the whole state sacrifices—at the public cost a large number of victims; but it is the People that keeps holiday and distributes the victims by lot among its members. Rich men have in some cases private gymnasia and baths with dressing rooms, but the People takes care to have built at the public cost a number of palaestras, dressing rooms, and bathing establishments for its own special use, and the mob gets the benefit of the majority of these, rather than the select few or the well-to-do.

As to wealth, the Athenians are exceptionally placed with regard to Greek and foreign communities alike, in their ability to hold it. For, given that some state or other is rich in timber for shipbuilding, where is it to find a market for the product except by persuading the ruler of the sea? Or, suppose the wealth of some state or other to consist of iron, or may be of bronze, or of linen yarn, where will it find a market except by permission of the supreme maritime power? Yet these are the very things, you see, which I need for my ships. Timber I must have from one, and from another iron, from a third bronze, from a fourth linen yarn, from a fifth wax. Besides which they will not suffer their antagonists in those parts, to carry these products elsewhere, or they will cease to use the sea. Accordingly I, without one stroke of labor, extract from the land and possess all these good things, thanks to my supremacy on the sea; while not a single other state possesses the two of them. Not timber, for instance, and yarn together, the same city. But where yarn is abundant, the soil will be light and devoid of timber. And in the same way bronze and iron will not be products of the same city. And so for the rest, never two, or at best three, in one state, but one thing here and another thing there. Moreover, above and beyond what has been said, the coastline of every mainland presents, either some jutting promontory, or adjacent island, or narrow strait of some sort, so that those who are masters of the sea can come to moorings at one of these points and wreak vengeance on the inhabitants of the mainland.

The Economic Advantages of Democracy

3. I repeat that my position concerning the constitution of the Athenians is this: the type of constitution is not to my taste, but given that a democratic form of government has been agreed upon, they do seem to me to go the right way to preserve the democracy by the adoption of the particular type which I have set forth.

But there are other objections brought, as I am aware, against the Athenians, by certain people, and to this effect. It not seldom happens, they tell us, that a man is unable to transact a piece of business with the council or the People, even if he sit waiting a whole year. Now this does happen at Athens, and for no other reason save that, owing to the immense mass of affairs, they are unable to work off all the business on hand and dismiss the applicants. And how in the world should they be able, considering in the first place that they, the Athenians, have more festivals to celebrate than any other state throughout the length and breadth of Greece? [*During these festivals, of course, the transaction of any sort of affairs of state is still more out of the question.*] In the next place, only consider the number of cases they have to decide, what with private suits and public causes and scrutinies of accounts, more than the whole of the rest of mankind put together; while the senate has multifarious points to advise upon concerning peace and war, concerning ways and means, concerning the framing and passing of laws, and concerning the matters affecting the state perpetually occurring, and endless questions touching the allies; besides the receipt of the tribute, the superintendence of dockyards and temples. Can, I ask again, anyone find it at all surprising that, with all these affairs on their hands, they are unequal to doing business with all the world?

But some people tell us that if the applicant will only address himself to the senate or the People with a bribe in his hand he will do a good stroke of business. And for my part I am free to confess to these gain-sayers that a good many things may be done at Athens by dint of money; and I will add, that a good many more still might be done, if the money flowed still more freely and from more pockets. One thing, however, I know full well, that as to transacting with every one of these applicants all he wants, the state could not do it, not even if all the gold and silver in the world were the inducement offered.

Here are some of the cases which have to be decided on. Someone fails to fit out a ship: Judgment must be given. Another puts up a building on a piece of public land: Again judgment must be given. Or, to take another class of cases: Adjudication has to be made between the patrons of choruses for the Dionysia, the Thargelia, the Panathenaea, the Prometheia, and the Hephaestia, year after year. Also as between the trierarchs, 400 of whom are appointed each year, of these, too, any who choose must have their cases adjudicated on, year after year. But that is not all. There are various magistrates to examine and approve and decide between; there are orphans whose status must be examined; and guardians of prisoners to appoint. These, be it borne in mind, are all matters of yearly occurrence; while at intervals there are exemptions and abstentions from military service which call for adjudication, or in connection with some other extraordinary misdemeanor, some case of outrage and violence of an exceptional character, or some charge of impiety. A whole string of others I simply omit; I am content to have named the most important part with the exception of the assessments of tribute which occur, as a rule, at intervals of four years.

There is another point in which it is sometimes felt that the Athenians are ill advised, in their adoption, namely, of the less respectable party, in a state divided by faction. But if so, they do it advisedly. If they chose the more respectable, they would be adopting those whose views and interests differ from their own, for there is no state in which the best element is friendly to the people. It is the worst element which in every state favors the democracy—on the principle that like favors like. It is simple enough then. The Athenians choose what is most akin to themselves. Also on every occasion on which they have attempted to side with the better classes, it has not fared well with them, but within a short interval the democratic party has been enslaved, as for instance in Boeotia; or, as when they chose the aristocrats of the Milesians, and within a short time these revolted and cut the people to pieces; or, as when they chose the Lacedaemonians as against the Messenians, and within a short time the Lacedaemonians subjugated the Messenians and went to war against Athens.

I seem to overhear a retort, "No one, of course, is deprived of his civil rights at Athens unjustly." My answer is, that there are some who are unjustly deprived of their civil rights, though the cases are certainly rare. But it will take more than a few to attack the democracy at Athens, since you may take it as an established fact, it is not the man who has lost his civil rights justly that takes the matter to heart, but the victims, if any, of injustice. But how in the world can anyone imagine that many are in a state of civil disability at Athens, where the People and the holders of office are one and the same? It is from iniquitous exercise of office, from iniquity exhibited either in speech or action, and the like circumstances, that citizens are punished with deprivation of civil rights in Athens. Due reflection on these matters will serve to dispel the notion that there is any danger at Athens from persons visited with disfranchisement.

8.5   Athens and Her Subjects: The Case of Erythrae

Aristotle and "The Old Oligarch" clearly illustrate the intimate involvement of Athenians of all social classes in the ongoing management of the Athenian Empire. A rare insight into the situation of Athens's allies is provided by the so-called Erythrae Decree. Erythrae, a Greek city on the west coast of modern Turkey, overthrew its Persian-supported tyrant in the mid 450s B.C. and joined the Delian League. The Athenian decree translated below is essentially the "constitution" of the new Erythraean democracy. Particularly noteworthy is the clearly subordinate status of Erythrae implied by the obligation of its citizens to provide sacrificial victims for the Great Panathenaea and to swear an oath of allegiance to Athens and by the direct involvement of Athenian officials in the organization and operation of the Erythraean government.[6]

. . . [*So and so*] made the motion. The Erythraeans are to bring sacrificial victims to the Great Panathenaea. The victims are to be worth not less than three minas and the sacrificers are to allocate to each of the Erythraeans who may be present a portion of the meat worth one drachma. If the sacrificial victims that are brought are not worth three minas as has been prescribed, the sacrificers are to buy sacrificial victims and the costs are to be assigned to the Erythraean people. As for the meat, anyone who wishes may take some.

---

[6]*Inscriptiones Graecae* 1^2.10.

The Council of the Erythraeans, which is to be chosen by the lot, shall number 120 men. Each person who is designated by lot shall undergo scrutiny in the Council of the Erythraeans. No one may be a councilor who is less than 30 years of age, nor may a foreigner be a councilor. Convicted violators shall be liable to prosecution. No one may be a councilor more than once every four years. The [*Athenian*] Overseers and garrison commander shall now conduct the allocation and establish the Council, but in the future the Council and the garrison commander shall do it. Before entering office, each of those who are to serve as councilors for the Erythraeans shall swear an oath by Zeus, Apollo, and Demeter, invoking destruction on himself if he swears falsely and on his children, and he shall swear the oath over burning victims. Each councilor shall serve according to the established law. If he does not, he shall pay a fine of one thousand drachmas and pay not less to the Erythraean people. The Erythraean Council shall swear the following oath:

> I will be the best and most just councilor that I can for the Erythraean people and the Athenians and the allies, and I will not revolt from the Athenian people or from the allies of the Athenians, neither on my own initiative nor persuaded by another. Nor will I defect on my own initiative or persuaded by anyone else, nor will I welcome back on my own initiative or persuaded by anyone else any of those who fled into exile to the Persians without the approval of the Athenians and the people, nor will I drive into exile any of those who remain in Erythrae without the approval of the Athenians and the people.
>
> If any Erythraean kills another Erythraean, let him die if he is convicted. But if he goes into exile, let him be exiled from the whole Athenian alliance, and let his property be confiscated by the Erythraean people. And if anyone is convicted of seeking to betray Erythrae to the tyrants, let him and his children be killed with impunity. But if his children are supporters of the Erythraean people and the Athenians, they shall be acquitted, and, after having forfeited all of the property of their condemned father, let them regain half of that property and let the other half become public property.

8.6   Imperial Democracy: A Favorable View—Pericles' Funeral Oration (Selections)

No systematic defense of the Athenian democracy comparable to the critique of "The Old Oligarch" *survives. However, on one occasion—namely, the public funeral for those who had died fighting for the city— it was traditional for leading Athenian politicians to praise Athens and her achievements. The most famous such speech was that delivered in 431 B.C. by Pericles, one of the chief architects of the Athenian empire, in honor of those killed during the first year of the Peloponnesian War. The only extant record of this speech is that contained in Thucydides'* History of the Peloponnesian War. *Although scholars dispute the faithfulness of Thucydides' version to what Pericles actually said, it does provide a vivid image of Athens and her democratic ideals at the peak of her imperial power.*[7]

---

[7]From Thucydides, *The History of the Peloponnesian War* 2.35–46. From Benjamin Jowett, *Thucydides Translated into English*, Vol. 1 (Oxford: Clarendon Press, 1900), pp. 126–135.

Athens and Her Dead

35. "Most of those who have spoken here before me have commended the lawgiver who added this oration to our other funeral customs; it seemed to them a worthy thing that such an honor should be given at their burial to the dead who have fallen on the field of battle. But I should have preferred that, when men's deeds have been brave, they should be honored in deed only, and with such an honor as this public funeral, which you are now witnessing. Then the reputation of many would not have been imperiled on the eloquence or want of eloquence of one, and their virtues believed or not as he spoke well or ill. For it is difficult to say neither too little nor too much; and even moderation is apt not to give the impression of truthfulness. The friend of the dead who knows the facts is likely to think that the words of the speaker fall short of his knowledge and of his wishes; another who is not so well informed, when he hears of anything which surpasses his own powers, will be envious and will suspect exaggeration. Mankind is tolerant of the praises of others so long as each hearer thinks that he can do as well or nearly as well himself, but, when the deed is beyond him, jealousy is aroused and he begins to be incredulous. However, since our ancestors have set the seal of their approval upon the practice, I must obey, and to the utmost of my power shall endeavor to satisfy the wishes and beliefs of all who hear me.

36. "I will speak first of our ancestors, for it is right and becoming that now, when we are lamenting the dead, a tribute should be paid to their memory. There has never been a time when they did not inhabit this land, which by their valor they have handed down from generation to generation, and we have received from them a free state. But if they were worthy of praise, still more were our fathers, who added to their inheritance, and after many a struggle transmitted to us their sons this great empire. And we ourselves assembled here today, who are still most of us in the vigor of life, have chiefly done the work of improvement, and have richly endowed our city with all things, so that she is sufficient for herself both in peace and war. Of the military exploits by which our various possessions were acquired, or of the energy with which we or our fathers drove back the tide of war, Greek or barbarian, I will not speak; for the tale would be long and is familiar to you. But before I praise the dead, I should like to point out by what principles of action we rose to power, and under what institutions and through what manner of life our empire became great. For I conceive that such thoughts are not unsuited to the occasion, and that this numerous assembly of citizens and strangers may profitably listen to them.

Athenian Democracy

37. "Our form of government does not enter into rivalry with the institutions of others. We do not copy our neighbors, but are an example to them. It is true that we are called a democracy, for the administration is in the hands of the many and not of the few. But while the law secures equal justice to all alike in their private disputes, the claim of excellence is also recognized; and when a citizen is in any way distinguished, he is preferred to the public service, not as a matter of privilege, but as the reward of merit. Neither is poverty a bar, but a man may benefit his country whatever be the obscurity of his condition. There is no exclusiveness in our public life, and in our private intercourse we are not suspicious of one another, nor angry with our neighbor if he does what he likes; we do not put

on sour looks at him which, though harmless, are not pleasant. While we are thus unconstrained in our private intercourse, a spirit of reverence pervades our public acts; we are prevented from doing wrong by respect for authority and for the laws, having an especial regard to those which are ordained for the protection of the injured as well as to those unwritten laws which bring upon the transgressor of them the reprobation of the general sentiment.

38. "And we have not forgotten to provide for our weary spirits many relaxations from toil; we have regular games and sacrifices throughout the year; at home the style of our life is refined; and the delight which we daily feel in all these things helps to banish melancholy. Because of the greatness of our city the fruits of the whole earth flow in upon us; so that we enjoy the goods of other countries as freely as of our own.

40. "For we are lovers of the beautiful, yet with economy, and we cultivate the mind without loss of manliness. Wealth we employ, not for talk and ostentation, but when there is a real use for it. To avow poverty with us is no disgrace; the true disgrace is in doing nothing to avoid it. An Athenian citizen does not neglect the state because he takes care of his own household; and even those of us who are engaged in business have a very fair idea of politics. We alone regard a man who takes no interest in public affairs, not as a harmless, but as a useless character; and if few of us are originators, we are all sound judges of a policy. The great impediment to action is, in our opinion, not discussion, but the want of that knowledge which is gained by discussion preparatory to action. For we have a peculiar power of thinking before we act and of acting too, whereas other men are courageous from ignorance but hesitate upon reflection. And they are surely to be esteemed the bravest spirits who, having the clearest sense both of the pains and pleasures of life, do not on that account shrink from danger. In doing good, again, we are unlike others; we make our friends by conferring, not by receiving favors. Now he who confers a favor is the firmer friend, because he would fain by kindness keep alive the memory of an obligation; but the recipient is colder in his feelings, because he knows that in requiting another's generosity he will not be winning gratitude but only paying a debt. We alone do good to our neighbors not upon a calculation of interest, but in the confidence of freedom and in a frank and fearless spirit.

41. "To sum up: I say that Athens is the school of Greece, and that the individual Athenian in his own person seems to have the power of adapting himself to the most varied forms of action with the utmost versatility and grace. This is no passing and idle word, but truth and fact; and the assertion is verified by the position to which these qualities have raised the state. For in the hour of trial Athens alone among her contemporaries is superior to the report of her. No enemy who comes against her is indignant at the reverses which he sustains at the hands of such a city; no subject complains that his masters are unworthy of him. And we shall assuredly not be without witnesses: there are mighty monuments of our power which will make us the wonder of this and of succeeding ages; we shall not need the praises of Homer or of any other panegyrist whose poetry may please for the moment, although his representation of the facts will not bear the light of day. For we have compelled every land and every sea to open a path for our valor, and have everywhere planted eternal memorials of our friendship and of our enmity. Such is the city for whose sake these men nobly fought and died; they could not bear the thought that she might be taken from them; and every one of us who survive should gladly toil on her behalf.

Advice to the Living

44. "Wherefore I do not now commiserate the parents of the dead who stand here; I would rather comfort them. You know that your life has been passed amid manifold vicissitudes; and that they may be deemed fortunate who have gained most honor, whether an honorable death like theirs, or an honorable sorrow like yours, and whose days have been so ordered that the term of their happiness is likewise the term of their life. I know how hard it is to make you feel this, when the good fortune of others will too often remind you of the gladness which once lightened your hearts. And sorrow is felt at the want of those blessings, not which a man never knew, but which were a part of his life before they were taken from him. Some of you are of an age at which they may hope to have other children, and they ought to bear their sorrow better; not only will the children who may hereafter be born make them forget their own lost ones, but the city will be doubly a gainer. She will not be left desolate, and she will be safer. For a man's counsel cannot have equal weight or worth, when he alone has no children to risk in the general danger. To those of you who have passed their prime, I say, 'Congratulate yourselves that you have been happy during the greater part of your days; remember that your life of sorrow will not last long, and be comforted by the glory of those who are gone. For the love of honor alone is ever young, and not riches, as some say, but honor is the delight of men when they are old and useless.'

45. "To you who are the sons and brothers of the departed, I see that the struggle to emulate them will be an arduous one. For all men praise the dead, and, however preeminent your virtue may be, hardly will you be thought, I do not say to equal, but even to approach them. The living have their rivals and detractors, but when a man is out of the way, the honor and good will which he receives is unalloyed. And if I am to speak of womanly virtues to those of you who will henceforth be widows, let me sum them up in one short admonition: To a woman not to show more weakness than is natural to her sex is a great glory, and not to be talked about for good or for evil among men.

46. "I have paid the required tribute, in obedience to the law, making use of such fitting words as I had. The tribute of deeds has been paid in part; for the dead have been honorably interred, and it remains only that their children should be maintained at the public charge until they are grown up: this is the solid prize with which, as with a garland, Athens crowns her sons living and dead, after a struggle like theirs. For where the rewards of virtue are greatest, there the noblest citizens are enlisted in the service of the state. And now, when you have duly lamented, every one his own dead, you may depart."

8.7   The Plague at Athens (430–429 B.C.)

In the second year of the Peloponnesian War, Athens experienced an unprecedented catastrophe: A major epidemic struck the city. Although the exact nature of the disease is unknown—suggestions include typhus, bubonic plague, and smallpox—perhaps as many as one-third of the population of Athens including Pericles died before it ended. Thucydides' account of the demoralization of the Athenians during the plague is a masterpiece of sociological analysis. With its careful description of the typical symptoms and course of the disease and suspicion of supernatural explanations, it also is an excellent example of early Greek scientific medical analysis.[8]

---

[8]Thucydides, *The History of the Peloponnesian War* 2.47—54. From Jowett, *Thucydides Translated*, Vol. 1, pp. 135–140.

47. Such was the order of the funeral celebrated in this winter, with the end of which ended the first year of the Peloponnesian War. As soon as summer returned, the Peloponnesian army, comprising as before two-thirds of the force of each confederate state, under the command of the Lacedaemonian king Archidamus, the son of Zeuxidamus, invaded Attica, where they established themselves and ravaged the country. They had not been there many days when the plague broke out at Athens for the first time. A similar disorder is said to have previously smitten many places, particularly Lemnos, but there is no record of a pestilence occurring elsewhere, or of so great a destruction of human life. For a while physicians, in ignorance of the nature of the disease, sought to apply remedies; but it was in vain, and they themselves were among the first victims, because they oftenest came into contact with it. No human art was of any avail, and as to supplications in temples, inquiries of oracles, and the like, they were utterly useless, and at last men were overpowered by the calamity and gave them all up.

48. The disease is said to have begun south of Egypt in Aethiopia; it descended into Egypt and Libya, and after spreading over the greater part of the Persian empire, suddenly fell upon Athens. It first attacked the inhabitants of the Piraeus, and it was supposed that the Peloponnesians had poisoned the cisterns, no conduits having as yet been made there. It afterwards reached the upper city, and then the mortality became far greater. As to its probable origin or the causes which might or could have produced such a disturbance of nature, every man, whether a physician or not, will give his own opinion. But I shall describe its actual course, and the symptoms by which any one who knows them beforehand may recognize the disorder should it ever reappear. For I was myself attacked, and witnessed the sufferings of others.

49. The season was admitted to have been remarkably free from ordinary sickness; and if anybody was already ill of any other disease it was absorbed in this. Many who were in perfect health, all in a moment, and without any apparent reason, were seized with violent heats in the head and with redness and inflammation of the eyes. Internally the throat and the tongue were quickly suffused with blood, and the breath became unnatural and fetid. There followed sneezing and hoarseness; in a short time the disorder, accompanied by a violent cough reached the chest; then fastening lower down, it would move the stomach and bring on all the vomits of bile to which physicians have ever given names; and they were very distressing. An ineffectual retching producing violent convulsions attacked most of the sufferers; some as soon as the previous symptoms had abated, others not until long afterwards. The body externally was not so very hot to the touch, nor yet pale; it was of a livid color inclining to red, and breaking out in pustules and ulcers. But the internal fever was intense; the sufferers could not bear to have on them even the finest linen garment; they insisted on being naked, and there was nothing, which they longed for more eagerly than to throw themselves into cold water. And many of those who had no one to look after them actually plunged into the cisterns, for they were tormented by unceasing thirst, which was not in the least assuaged whether they drank little or much. They could not sleep; a restlessness, which was intolerable, never left them. While the disease was at its height, the body, instead of wasting away, held out amid these sufferings in a marvelous manner. Either they died on the seventh or ninth day, not of weakness—for their strength was not exhausted—but of internal fever, which was the end of most. If they survived, then the disease descended into the bowels and there produced violent ulceration; severe diarrhea at the same time set in and at a later stage caused exhaustion, which finally with few exceptions carried them off. For the disorder, which had originally settled in the head, passed gradually through the whole body. If a person got over the worst,

it would often seize the extremities and leave its mark, attacking the genitals and the fingers and the toes; and some escaped with the loss of these, some with the loss of their eyes. Some again had no sooner recovered than they were seized with a forgetfulness of all things and knew neither themselves nor their friends.

50. The malady took a form not to be described, and the fury with which it fastened upon each sufferer was too much for human nature to endure. There was one circumstance, in particular, which distinguished it from ordinary diseases. The birds and animals, which feed on human flesh, although so many bodies were lying unburied, either never came near them, or died if they touched them. This was proved by a remarkable disappearance of the birds of prey, who were not to be seen either about the bodies or anywhere else; while in the case of the dogs the fact was even more obvious, because they live with man.

51. Such was the general nature of the disease: I omit many strange peculiarities, which characterized individual cases. None of the ordinary sicknesses attacked any one while it lasted, or, if they did, they ended in the plague. Some of the sufferers died from want of care, others equally who were receiving the greatest attention. No single remedy could be deemed a specific; for that which did good to one did harm to another. No constitution was of itself strong enough to resist or weak enough to escape the attacks; the disease carried off all alike and defied every mode of treatment. Most appalling was the despondency which seized upon any one who felt himself sickening; for he instantly abandoned his mind to despair and, instead of holding out, absolutely threw away his chance of life. Appalling too was the rapidity with which men caught the infection; dying like sheep if they attended on one another; and this was the principal cause of mortality. When they were afraid to visit one another, the sufferers died in their solitude, so that many houses were empty because there had been no one left to take care of the sick; or if they ventured they perished, especially those who aspired to heroism. For they went to see their friends without thought of themselves and were ashamed to leave them, even at a time when the very relations of the dying were at last growing weary and ceased to make lamentations, overwhelmed by the vastness of the calamity. But whatever instances there may have been of such devotion, more often the sick and the dying were tended by the pitying care of those who had recovered, because they knew the course of the disease and were themselves free from apprehension. For no one was ever attacked a second time, or not with a fatal result. All men congratulated them, and they themselves, in the excess of their joy at the moment, had an innocent fancy that they could not die of any other sickness.

52. The crowding of the people out of the country into the city aggravated the misery; and the newly arrived suffered most. For, having no houses of their own, but inhabiting in the height of summer stifling huts, the mortality among them was dreadful, and they perished in wild disorder. The dead lay as they had died, one upon another, while others hardly alive wallowed in the streets and crawled about every fountain craving for water. The temples in which they lodged were full of the corpses of those who died in them; for the violence of the calamity was such that men, not knowing where to turn, grew reckless of all law, human and divine. The customs, which had hitherto been observed at funerals, were universally violated, and they buried their dead each one as best he could. Many, having no proper appliances because the deaths in their household had been so frequent, made no scruple of using the burial place of others. When one man had raised a funeral pyre, others would come, and throwing on their dead first, set fire to it; or when some other corpse was already burning, before they could be stopped would throw their own dead upon it and depart.

53. There were other and worse forms of lawlessness, which the plague introduced at Athens. Men who had hitherto concealed their indulgence in pleasure now grew bolder. For, seeing the sudden change, how the rich died in a moment, and those who had nothing immediately inherited their property, they reflected that life and riches were alike transitory, and they resolved to enjoy themselves while they could, and to think only of pleasure. Who would be willing to sacrifice himself to the law of honor when he knew not whether he would live to be held in honor? The pleasure of the moment and any sort of thing, which conduced to it, took the place both of honor and of expediency. No fear of God or law of man deterred a criminal. Those, who saw all perishing alike, thought that the worship or neglect of gods made no difference. For offences against human law no punishment was to be feared; no one would live long enough to be called to account. Already a far heavier sentence had been passed and was hanging over a man's head; before that fell, why should he not take a little pleasure?

54. Such was the grievous calamity which now afflicted the Athenians; within the walls their people were dying, and without, their country was being ravaged. In their troubles they naturally called to mind a verse which the elder men among them declared to have been current long ago:

A Dorian war will come and a plague with it.

There was a dispute about the precise expression; some saying *limos*, a famine, and not *loimos*, a plague, was the original word. Nevertheless, as might have been expected, for men's memories reflected their sufferings, the argument in favor of *loimos* prevailed at the time. If ever in future years another Dorian war arises which happens to be accompanied by a famine, they will probably repeat the verse in the other form. The answer of the oracle to the Lacedaemonians, when the god was asked whether they should go to war or not, and he replied that if they fought with all their might, they would conquer, and that he himself would take their part, was not forgotten by those who heard of it, and they quite imagined that they were witnessing the fulfillment of his words. The disease certainly did set in immediately after the invasion of the Peloponnesians, and did not spread into Peloponnesus in any degree worth speaking of, while Athens felt its ravages most severely, and next to Athens the places which were most populous. Such was the history of the plague.

8.8   War and Politics: The Case of Corcyra

As was pointed out by "The Old Oligarch" and illustrated by the Erythrae Decree, support of democratic factions was a characteristic feature of Athenian policy during the decades prior to the outbreak of the Peloponnesian War in 431 B.C. The inevitable result was the identification of democracy with subjection to Athenian rule and the internationalizing of polis *politics as Athens and Sparta increasingly intervened in the internal affairs of various Greek cities to ensure the political ascendancy of their partisans. In this passage, the historian Thucydides gives a dramatic account of how in 427 B.C., this aspect of the rivalry between imperial Athens and Sparta led to the total disruption of normal social and political relations in the city of Corcyra on the island of Corfu in the Adriatic Sea.[9]*

---

[9]Thucydides, *The History of the Peloponnesian War* 3.79–83, 85. From Jowett, *Thucydides Translated*, Vol. 1, pp. 239–246.

79. The Corcyraeans, who were afraid that the victorious enemy would sail to the city and have recourse to some decisive measure, such as taking on board the prisoners in the island, conveyed them back to the temple of Hera and guarded the city. But the Peloponnesians, although they had won the battle, did not venture to attack the city, but returned to their station on the mainland with thirteen Corcyraean ships which they had taken. On the next day they still hesitated, although there was great panic and confusion among the inhabitants. It is said that Brasidas advised Alcidas to make the attempt, but he had not an equal vote with him. So they only disembarked at the promontory of Leucimne and ravaged the country.

80. Meanwhile the people of Corcyra, dreading that the fleet of the Peloponnesians would attack them, held a parley with the other faction, especially with the suppliants, in the hope of saving the city; they even persuaded some of them to go on board the fleet; for the Corcyraeans still contrived to man 30 ships. But the Peloponnesians, after devastating the land till about midday, retired. And at nightfall the approach of 60 Athenian vessels was signaled to them from Leucas. These had been sent by the Athenians under the command of Eurymedon, the son of Thucles, when they heard of the revolution and of the intended expedition of Alcidas to Corcyra.

81. The Peloponnesians set out that very night on their way home, keeping close to the land and transporting the ships over the Leucadian isthmus, that they might not be seen sailing round. When the Corcyraeans perceived that the Athenian fleet was approaching while that of the enemy had disappeared, they took the Messenian troops, who had hitherto been outside the walls, into the city and ordered the ships which they had manned to sail round into the Hyllaic harbour. These proceeded on their way. Meanwhile they killed any of their enemies whom they caught in the city. On the arrival of the ships, they disembarked those whom they had induced to go on board and despatched them; they also went to the temple of Hera and, persuading about 50 of the suppliants to stand their trial, condemned them all to death. The majority would not come out, and, when they saw what was going on, destroyed one another in the enclosure of the temple where they were, except a few who hung themselves on trees or put an end to their own lives in any other way that they could. And during the seven days which Eurymedon after his arrival remained with his 60 ships, the Corcyraeans continued slaughtering those of their fellow citizens whom they deemed their enemies; they professed to punish them for their designs against the democracy, but in fact some were killed from motives of personal enmity, and some, because money was owing to them, by the hands of their debtors. Every form of death was to be seen; and everything, and more than everything, that commonly happens in revolutions, happened then. The father slew the son, and the suppliants were torn from the temples and slain near them; some of them were even walled up in the temple of Dionysus, and there perished. To such extremes of cruelty did revolution go; and this seemed to be the worst of revolutions, because it was the first.

82. For not long afterwards nearly the whole Greek world was in commotion; in every city the Greek chiefs of the democracy and of the oligarchy were struggling, the one to bring in the Athenians, the other the Lacedaemonians. Now in time of peace, men would have had no excuse for introducing either, and no desire to do so; but, when they were at war, the introduction of a foreign alliance on one side or the other to the hurt of their enemies and the advantage of themselves was easily effected by the dissatisfied party. And revolution brought

upon the cities of Greece many terrible calamities, such as have been and always will be while human nature remains the same, but which are more or less aggravated and differ in character with every new combination of circumstances. In peace and prosperity both states and individuals are actuated by higher motives, because they do not fall under the dominion of imperious necessities; but war, which takes away the comfortable provision of daily life, is a hard master and tends to assimilate men's characters to their conditions.

When troubles had once begun in the cities, those who followed carried the revolutionary spirit further and further and determined to outdo the report of all who had preceded them by the ingenuity of their enterprises and the atrocity of their revenges. The meaning of words had no longer the same relation to things but was changed by them as they thought proper. Reckless daring was held to be loyal courage; prudent delay was the excuse of a coward; moderation was the disguise of unmanly weakness; to know everything was to do nothing. Frantic energy was the true quality of a man. A conspirator who wanted to be safe was a recreant in disguise. The lover of violence was always trusted, and his opponent suspected. He who succeeded in a plot was deemed knowing, but a still greater master in craft was he who detected one. On the other hand, he who plotted from the first to have nothing to do with plots was a breaker up of parties and a poltroon who was afraid of the enemy. In a word, he who could outstrip another in a bad action was applauded, and so was he who encouraged to evil one who had no idea of it. The tie of party was stronger than the tie of blood, because a partisan was more ready to dare without asking why. (For party associations are not based upon any established law, nor do they seek the public good; they are formed in defiance of the laws and from self-interest.) The seal of good faith was not divine law, but fellowship in crime. If an enemy when he was in the ascendant offered fair words, the opposite party received them, not in a generous spirit, but by a jealous watchfulness of his actions. Revenge was dearer than self-preservation. Any agreements sworn to by either party, when they could do nothing else, were binding as long as both were powerless. But he who on a favorable opportunity first took courage, and struck at his enemy when he saw him off his guard, had greater pleasure in a perfidious than he would have had in an open act of revenge; he congratulated himself that he had taken the safer course, and also that he had overreached his enemy and gained the prize of superior ability. In general the dishonest more easily gain credit for cleverness than the simple for goodness; men take a pride in the one but are ashamed of the other.

The cause of all these evils was the love of power, originating in avarice and ambition, and the party-spirit which is engendered by them when men are fairly embarked in a contest. For the leaders on either side used specious names, the one party professing to uphold the constitutional equality of the many, the other the wisdom of an aristocracy, while they made the public interests, to which in name they were devoted, in reality their prize. Striving in every way to overcome each other, they committed the most monstrous crimes; yet even these were surpassed by the magnitude of their revenges which they pursued to the very utmost, neither party observing any definite limits of either justice or public expediency, but both alike making the caprice of the moment their law. Either by the help of an unrighteous sentence, or grasping power with the strong hand, they were eager to satiate the impatience of party-spirit. Neither faction cared for religion; but any fair pretence which succeeded in effecting some odious purpose was greatly lauded. And the citizens who were of neither party fell a prey to both; either they were disliked because they held aloof, or men were jealous of their surviving.

83. Thus revolution gave birth to every form of wickedness in Hellas. The simplicity which is so large an element in a noble nature was laughed to scorn and disappeared. An attitude of perfidious antagonism everywhere prevailed; for there was no word binding enough, nor oath terrible enough to reconcile enemies. Each man was strong only in the conviction that nothing was secure; he must look to his own safety and could not afford to trust others. Inferior intellects generally succeeded best. For, aware of their own deficiencies, and fearing the capacity of their opponents, for whom they were no match in powers of speech, and whose subtle wits were likely to anticipate them in contriving evil, they struck boldly and at once. But the cleverer sort, presuming in their arrogance that they would be aware in time, and disdaining to act when they could think, were taken off their guard and easily destroyed.

85. Such were the passions which the citizens of Corcyra, first of all Greeks, displayed towards one another. After the departure of Eurymedon and the Athenian fleet the surviving oligarchs, who to the number of 500 had escaped, seized certain forts on the mainland and thus became masters of the territory on the opposite coast which belonged to Corcyra. Thence issuing forth, they plundered the Corcyraeans in the island and did much harm, so that there was a great famine in the city. They also sent ambassadors to Lacedaemon and Corinth, begging that they might be restored, but, failing of their object, they procured boats and auxiliaries, and passed over to Corcyra, about 600 in all; then, burning their boats that they might have no hope but in the conquest of the island, they went into Mount Istone, and building a fort there, became masters of the country to the ruin of the inhabitants of the city.

8.9   "War is a Hard Master": The Melian Dialogue

In 416 B.C., Athens attacked the island of Melos, a colony of Sparta that, according to Thucydides, had been neutral in the Peloponnesian War. After a brief siege, the Athenians captured the city, executed its male population, sold the rest of the Melians into slavery, and resettled the island with their own citizens. A hundred years later the fate of Melos was still cited as a prime example of the excesses of Athenian imperialism. In the following selection, Thucydides uses the negotiations between the Athenians and the Melians as the occasion to analyze the nature and application of imperial power. Although it is doubtful that either the Athenians or Melians used the exact arguments ascribed to them by Thucydides, the "Melian Dialogue," with its scorn for arguments based on religious tradition and its invocation of the "Laws of Nature," is a remarkable example of fifth-century B.C. rationalism applied to the analysis of political action.[10]

84. In the ensuing summer, Alcibiades sailed to Argos with twenty ships and seized any of the Argives who were still suspected to be of the Lacedaemonian faction, 300 in number; and the Athenians deposited them in the subject islands near at hand. The Athenians next made an expedition against the island of Melos with 30 ships of their own, six Chian, and two Lesbian, 1,200 hoplites and 300 archers besides 20 mounted archers of their own, and about 1,500 hoplites furnished by their allies in the islands. The Melians are

---

[10]Thucydides, *The History of the Peloponnesian War* 5.84–116. From Jowet, *Thucydides Translated*, Vol. 2, pp. 167–177.

colonists of the Lacedaemonians who would not submit to Athens like the other islanders. At first they were neutral and took no part. But when the Athenians tried to coerce them by ravaging their lands, they were driven into open hostilities. The generals, Cleomedes the son of Lycomedes and Tisias the son of Tisimachus, encamped with the Athenian forces on the island. But before they did the country any harm, they sent envoys to negotiate with the Melians. Instead of bringing these envoys before the people, the Melians desired them to explain their errand to the magistrates and to the chief men. They spoke as follows:

85. "Since we are not allowed to speak to the people, lest, forsooth, they should be deceived by seductive and unanswerable arguments which they would hear set forth in a single uninterrupted oration (for we are perfectly aware that this is what you mean in bringing us before a select few), you who are sitting here may as well make assurance yet surer. Let us have no set speeches at all, but do you reply to each several statement of which you disapprove, and criticize it at once. Say first of all how you like this mode of proceeding."

86. The Melian representatives answered: "The quiet interchange of explanations is a reasonable thing, and we do not object to that. But your warlike movements, which are present not only to our fears but to our eyes, seem to belie your words. We see that, although you may reason with us, you mean to be our judges, and that at the end of the discussion, if the justice of our cause prevail and we therefore refuse to yield, we may expect war; if we are convinced by you, slavery."

87. *Athenians*: Nay, but if you are only going to argue from fancies about the future, or if you meet us with any other purpose than that of looking your circumstances in the face and saving your city, we have done; but if this is your intention, we will proceed.

88. *Melians*: It is an excusable and natural thing that men in our position should have much to say and should indulge in many fancies. But we admit that this conference has met to consider the question of our preservation; and therefore let the argument proceed in the manner which you propose.

89. *Athenians*: Well, then, we Athenians will use no fine words; we will not go out of our way to prove at length that we have a right to rule because we overthrew the Persians, or that we attack you now because we are suffering any injury at your hands. We should not convince you if we did; nor must you expect to convince us by arguing that, although a colony of the Lacedaemonians, you have taken no part in their expeditions, or that you have never done us any wrong. But you and we should say what we really think, and aim only at what is possible, for we both alike know that into the discussion of human affairs the question of justice enters only where the pressure of necessity is equal, and that the powerful exact what they can and the weak grant what they must.

90. *Melians*: Well, then, since you set aside justice and invite us to speak of expediency, in our judgment it is certainly expedient that you should respect a principle which is for the common good; and that to every man when in peril a reasonable claim should be accounted a claim of right, and any plea which he is disposed to urge, even if failing of the point a little, should help his cause. Your interest in this principle is quite as great as ours, inasmuch as you, if you fall, will incur the heaviest vengeance and will be the most terrible example to mankind.

91. *Athenians*: The fall of our empire, if it should fall, is not an event to which we look forward with dismay; for ruling states such as Lacedaemon are not cruel to their vanquished enemies. And we are fighting not so much against the Lacedaemonians as against our own subjects who may some day rise up and overcome their former masters. But this is a danger

which you may leave to us. And we will now endeavor to show that we have come in the interests of our empire, and that in what we are about to say we are seeking only the preservation of your city. For we want to make you ours with the least trouble to ourselves, and it is for the interests of us both that you should not be destroyed.

92. *Melians*: It may be your interest to be our masters, but how can it be ours to be your slaves?

93. *Athenians*: To you the gain will be that by submission you will avert the worst; and we shall be all the richer for your preservation.

94. *Melians*: But must we be your enemies? Will you not receive us as friends if we are neutral and remain at peace with you?

95. *Athenians*: No, your enmity is not half so mischievous to us as your friendship; for the one is in the eyes of our subjects an argument of our power, the other of our weakness.

96. *Melians*: But are your subjects really unable to distinguish between states in which you have no concern and those that are chiefly your own colonies and in some cases have revolted and been subdued by you?

97. *Athenians*: Why, they do not doubt that both of them have a good deal to say for themselves on the score of justice, but they think that states like yours are left free because they are able to defend themselves, and that we do not attack them because we dare not. So that your subjection will give us an increase of security as well as an extension of empire. For we are masters of the sea, and you who are islanders, and insignificant islanders too, must not be allowed to escape us.

98. *Melians*: But do you not recognize another danger? For, once more, since you drive us from the plea of justice and press upon us your doctrine of expediency, we must show you what is for our interest, and, if it be for yours also, may hope to convince you: Will you not be making enemies of all who are now neutrals? When they see how you are treating us, they will expect you some day to turn against them; and if so, are you not strengthening the enemies whom you already have and bringing upon you others who, if they could help, would never dream of being your enemies at all?

99. *Athenians*: We do not consider our really dangerous enemies to be any of the peoples inhabiting the mainland, who, secure in their freedom, may defer indefinitely any measures of precaution which they take against us, but islanders who, like you, happen to be under no control, and all who may be already irritated by the necessity of submission to our empire—these are our real enemies, for they are the most reckless and most likely to bring themselves as well as us into a danger which they cannot but foresee.

100. *Melians*: Surely then, if you and your subjects will brave all this risk, you to preserve your empire and they to be quit of it, how base and cowardly would it be in us, who retain our freedom, not to do and suffer anything rather than be your slaves.

101. *Athenians*: Not so, if you calmly reflect: for you are not fighting against equals to whom you cannot yield without disgrace, but you are taking counsel whether or not you shall resist an overwhelming force. The question is not one of honor but of prudence.

102. *Melians*: But we know that the fortune of war is sometimes impartial, and not always on the side of numbers. If we yield now, all is over; but if we fight, there is yet a hope that we may stand upright.

103. *Athenians*: Hope is a good comforter in the hour of danger, and when men have something else to depend upon, although hurtful, she is not ruinous. But when her spendthrift

nature has induced them to stake their all, they see her as she is in the moment of their fall, and not till then. While the knowledge of her might enable them to beware of her, she never fails. You are weak and a single turn of the scale might be your ruin. Do not you be thus deluded; avoid the error of which so many are guilty, who, although they might still be saved if they would take the natural means, when visible grounds of confidence forsake them, have recourse to the invisible, to prophecies and oracles and the like, which ruin men by the hopes which they inspire in them.

104. *Melians*: We know only too well how hard the struggle must be against your power, and against fortune, if she does not mean to be impartial. Nevertheless we do not despair of fortune; for we hope to stand as high as you in the favor of heaven, because we are righteous, and you against whom we contend are unrighteous; and we are satisfied that our deficiency in power will be compensated by the aid of our allies the Lacedaemonians; they cannot refuse to help us, if only because we are their kinsmen, and for the sake of their own honor. And therefore our confidence is not so utterly blind as you suppose.

105. *Athenians*: As for the gods, we expect to have quite as much of their favor as you: for we are not doing or claiming anything which goes beyond common opinion about divine or men's desires about human things. Of the gods we believe, and of men we know, that by a law of their nature wherever they can rule they will. This law was not made by us, and we are not the first who have acted upon it; we did but inherit it, and shall bequeath it to all time, and we know that you and all mankind, if you were as strong as we are, would do as we do. So much for the gods; we have told you why we expect to stand as high in their good opinion as you. And then as to the Lacedaemonians—when you imagine that out of very shame they will assist you, we admire the simplicity of your idea but we do not envy you the folly of it. The Lacedaemonians are exceedingly virtuous among themselves and according to their national standard of morality. But, in respect of their dealings with others, although many things might be said, a word is enough to describe them; of all men whom we know they are the most notorious for identifying what is pleasant with what is honorable, and what is expedient with what is just. But how inconsistent is such a character with your present blind hope of deliverance!

106. *Melians*: That is the very reason why we trust them; they will look to their interest and therefore will not be willing to betray the Melians, who are their own colonists, lest they should be distrusted by their friends in Hellas and play into the hands of their enemies.

107. *Athenians*: But do you not see that the path of expediency is safe, whereas justice and honor involve danger in practice, and such dangers the Lacedaemonians seldom care to face?

108. *Melians*: On the other hand, we think that whatever perils there may be, they will be ready to face them for our sakes and will consider danger less dangerous where we are concerned. For if they need to act we are close at hand, and they can better trust our loyal feeling because we are their kinsmen.

109. *Athenians*: Yes, but what encourages men who are invited to join in a conflict is clearly not the good-will of those who summon them to their side, but a decided superiority in real power. To this no men look more keenly than the Lacedaemonians; so little confidence have they in their own resources that they attack their neighbors only when they have numerous allies, and therefore they are not likely to find their way by themselves to an island when we are masters of the sea.

110. *Melians*: But they may send their allies: the Cretan sea is a large place; and the masters of the sea will have more difficulty in overtaking vessels which want to escape than the

pursued in escaping. If the attempt should fail they may invade Attica itself, and find their way to allies of yours whom Brasidas did not reach: and then you will have to fight, not for the conquest of a land in which you have no concern, but nearer home, for the preservation of your confederacy and of your own territory.

111. *Athenians*: Help may come from Lacedaemon to you as it has come to others, and should you ever have actual experience of it, then you will know that never once have the Athenians retired from a siege through fear of a foe elsewhere. You told us that the safety of your city would be your first care, but we remark that, in this long discussion, not a word has been uttered by you which would give a reasonable man expectation of deliverance. Your strongest grounds are hopes deferred, and what power you have is not to be compared with that which is already arrayed against you. Unless after we have withdrawn, you mean to come, as even now you may, to a wiser conclusion, you are showing a great want of sense. For surely you cannot dream of flying to that false sense of honor which has been the ruin of so many when danger and dishonor were staring them in the face. Many men with their eyes still open to the consequences have found the word honor too much for them and have suffered a mere name to lure them on, until it has drawn down upon them real and irretrievable calamities; through their own folly they have incurred a worse dishonor than fortune would have inflicted upon them. If you are wise, you will not run this risk; you ought to see that there can be no disgrace in yielding to a great city which invites you to become her ally on reasonable terms, keeping your own land and merely paying tribute; and that you will certainly gain no honor if, having to choose between two alternatives, safety and war, you obstinately prefer the worse. To maintain our rights against equals, to be politic with superiors, and to be moderate towards inferiors is the path of safety. Reflect once more when we have withdrawn, and say to yourselves over and over again that you are deliberating about your one and only country, which may be saved or may be destroyed by a single decision.

112. The Athenians left the conference: the Melians, after consulting among themselves, resolved to persevere in their refusal and answered as follows, "Men of Athens, our resolution is unchanged, and we will not in a moment surrender that liberty which our city, founded 700 years ago, still enjoys; we will trust to the good-fortune which, by the favor of the gods, has hitherto preserved us, and for human help to the Lacedaemonians, and endeavor to save ourselves. We are ready however to be your friends, and the enemies neither of you nor of the Lacedaemonians, and we ask you to leave our country when you have made such a peace as may appear to be in the interest of both parties."

113. Such was the answer of the Melians; the Athenians, as they quitted the conference, spoke as follows, "Well, we must say, judging from the decision at which you have arrived, that you are the only men who deem the future to be more certain than the present, and regard things unseen as already realised in your fond anticipation, and that the more you cast yourselves upon the Lacedaemonians and fortune, and hope, and trust them, the more complete will be your ruin."

114. The Athenian envoys returned to the army, and the generals, when they found that the Melians would not yield, immediately commenced hostilities. They surrounded the town of Melos with a wall, dividing the work among the several contingents. They then left troops of their own and of their allies to keep guard both by land and by sea, and retired with the greater part of their army; the remainder carried on the blockade.

115.　About the same time the Argives made an inroad into Phliasia and lost nearly 80 men, who were caught in an ambuscade by the Phliasians and the Argive exiles. The Athenian garrison in Pylos took much spoil from the Lacedaemonians; nevertheless the latter did not renounce the peace and go to war, but only notified by a proclamation that if any one of their own people had a mind to make reprisals on the Athenians he might. The Corinthians next declared war upon the Athenians on some private grounds, but the rest of the Peloponnesians did not join them. The Melians took that part of the Athenian wall which looked towards the agora by a night assault, killed a few men, and brought in as much grain and other necessaries as they could; they then retreated and remained inactive. After this the Athenians set a better watch. So the summer ended.

116.　In the following winter the Lacedaemonians had intended to make an expedition into the Argive territory, but finding that the sacrifices which they offered at the frontier were unfavourable, they returned home. The Argives, suspecting that the threatened invasion was instigated by citizens of their own, apprehended some of them; others, however, escaped. About the same time the Melians took another part of the Athenian wall, for the fortifications were insufficiently guarded. Whereupon the Athenians sent fresh troops, under the command of Philocrates the son of Demeas. The place was now closely invested, and there was treachery among the citizens themselves. So the Melians were induced to surrender at discretion. The Athenians thereupon put to death all who were of military age and made slaves of the women and children. They then colonised the island, sending thither 500 settlers of their own.

8.10　Religion in the Classical *Polis*: The Affair of the Herms

The overt rationalism of works such as "The Old Oligarch's" essay on the Athenian constitution and the Melian dialogue can easily lead to the belief that religion was of little significance in fifth-century Greek culture. The same impression is conveyed by the seeming materialism of many Greek religious documents. Thus, a fourth-century B.C. *Athenian decree concerning the proper conduct of sacrifices at the Panathenaea is devoted mostly to regulating the distribution of the meat from the sacrifices, specifying that*

> five portions of meat are to be allocated to the Prytanes, three to the nine Archons and the Treasurer of Athena, one to the Sacrificers, and three to the Generals and the Taxiarchs; the usual portions are to be given to those Athenians participating in the procession and to the girls who are basket-bearers, and the rest of the meat is to be distributed to the Athenians.[11]

A very different assessment of the religious feelings of the Athenian populace is suggested, however, by Thucydides' account of the hysteria that gripped Athens in 415 B.C., *on the eve of the Athenian invasion of Sicily, as a result of the mutilation of the Herms—the vandalizing of the fetishlike pillars with a human head and an erect male genital organ that stood in front of most Athenian homes and were believed to promote fertility.*[12]

---

[11]*Inscriptions Graecae* 2^2.334.
[12]Thucydides, *The History of the Peloponnesian War* 5.27–28, 53, 60. From Jowett, *Thucydides Translated*, Vol. 2, pp. 199–200, 219, 224–225.

28. Certain metics and servants gave information, not indeed about the Hermae, but about the mutilation of other statues which had shortly before been perpetrated by some young men in a drunken frolic; they also said that the mysteries were repeatedly profaned by the celebration of them in private houses, and of this impiety they accused, among others, Alcibiades. A party who were jealous of his influence over the people, which interfered with the permanent establishment of their own, thinking that if they could get rid of him they would be supreme, took up and exaggerated the charges against him, clamorously insisting that both the mutilation of the Hermae and the profanation of the mysteries were part of a conspiracy against the democracy, and that he was at the bottom of the whole affair. In proof they alleged the excesses of his ordinary life, which were unbecoming in the citizen of a free state.

The hysteria reached its peak a year later in 414 B.C., when the Athenians, suspecting that the mutilation of the Herms was the work of plotters against the democracy, authorized the mass arrest and detention of the suspects.

53. There they found that the vessel Salaminia had come from Athens to fetch Alcibiades, who had been put upon his trial by the state and was ordered home to defend himself. With him were summoned certain of his soldiers, who were accused, some of profaning the mysteries, others of mutilation of the Hermae. For after the departure of the expedition the Athenians prosecuted both enquiries as keenly as ever. They did not investigate the character of the informers, but in their suspicious mood listened to all manner of statements and seized and imprisoned some of the most respectable citizens on the evidence of wretches; they thought it better to sift the matter and discover the truth, and they would not allow even a man of good character against whom an accusation was brought to escape without a thorough investigation, merely because the informer was a rogue. For the people, who had heard by tradition that the tyranny of Pisistratus and his sons ended in great oppression, and knew moreover that their power was overthrown, not by Harmodius or any efforts of their own, but by the Lacedaemonians, were in a state of incessant fear and suspicion.

60. The Athenian people, recalling these and other traditions of the tyrants which had sunk deep into their minds, were suspicious and savage against the supposed profaners of the mysteries; the whole affair seemed to them to indicate some conspiracy aiming at oligarchy or tyranny. Inflamed by these suspicions, they had already imprisoned many men of high character. There was no sign of returning quiet, but day by day the movement became more furious and the number of arrests increased. At last, one of the prisoners, who was believed to be deeply implicated, was induced by a fellow prisoner to make a confession—whether true or false I cannot say; opinions are divided, and no one knew at the time, or to this day knows, who the offenders were. His companion argued that even if he were not guilty he ought to confess and claim a pardon; he would thus save his own life and at the same time deliver Athens from the prevailing state of suspicion. His chance of escaping would be better if he confessed his guilt in the hope of a pardon than if he denied it and stood his trial. So he gave evidence against both himself and others in the matter of the Hermae. The Athenians were delighted at finding out what they supposed to be the truth: They had been in despair at the thought that the conspirators against the democracy would never be known, and they immediately liberated the informer and all whom he had not denounced. The accused they brought to trial, and executed

such of them as could be found. Those who had fled they condemned to death, and promised a reward to anyone who would kill them. No one could say whether the sufferers were justly punished, but the beneficial effect on the city at the time was undeniable.

8.11   The Demos Must be Pure: Athenian Law on Teachers and Their Students

The affair of the Herms revealed not only the demos' deep religiosity, but also its suspicion of the Athenian aristocracy. Another area where the values of the demos and the aristocracy came into conflict was pederasty, the ritualized homoerotic relationship between an older male and an adolescent boy, which was a central feature of Greek aristocratic life. Although even Solon, the founding father of the democracy, celebrated pederasty in a famous couplet—"until he loves a boy in the lovely bloom of youth, desiring his thighs and sweet mouth"—Athenian laws, such as that concerning teachers, reveal an equally strong unease with this aspect of aristocratic culture, viewing it as a potential threat to the purity and health of the demos itself.[13]

Consider how much attention that ancient lawgiver, Solon, gave to morality, as did Draco and the other lawgivers of those days. First, you recall, they laid down laws to protect the morals of our children, and they expressly prescribed what were to be the habits of the freeborn boy, and how he was to be brought up; then they legislated for the adolescents, and next for the other age groups in succession, including in the provision not only private citizens, but also the public men. And when they had inscribed these laws, they gave them to you in trust, and made you their guardians. . . .

In the first place, consider the case of the teachers. Although the very livelihood of these men, to whom we necessarily entrust our own children, depends on their good character, while the opposite conduct on their part would mean poverty, yet it is plain that the lawgiver distrusts them; for he expressly prescribes, first, at what time of day the freeborn boy is to go to the schoolroom; next, how many other boys may go there with him, and when he is to go home. He forbids the teacher to open the schoolroom, or the gymnastic trainer the wrestling school, before sunrise, and he commands them to close the doors before sunset; for he is exceedingly suspicious of their being alone with a boy, or in the dark with him. He prescribes what children are to be admitted as pupils, and their age at admission. He provides for a public official who shall superintend them, and for the oversight of slave-attendants of school boys. He regulates the festivals of the muses in the schoolrooms, and of Hermes in the wrestling schools. Finally, he regulates the companionships that the boys may form at school, and their cyclic dances. He prescribes, namely, that the *choragus*, a man who is going to spend his own money for your entertainment, shall be a man of more than forty years of age when he performs this service, in order that he may have reached the most temperate time of his life before he comes into contact with your children.

---

[13] Aeschines, *Against Timarchus* 6–7, 9–20. From: *The Speeches of Aeschines*, trans. by Charles Darwin Adams (Cambridge, MA: Harvard University Press, 1919).

These laws, then, shall be read to you, to prove that the lawgiver believed that it is the boy who has been well brought up that will be a useful citizen when he becomes a man. But when a boy's natural disposition is subjected at the very outset to vicious training, the product of such wrong nurture will be, as he believed, a citizen like this man Timarchus. . . .

Now after this, fellow citizens, he lays down laws regarding crimes which, great as they undoubtedly are, do actually occur, I believe, in the city. For the very fact that certain unbecoming things were being done was the reason for the enactment of these laws by the men of old. At any rate, the law says explicitly: If any boy is let out for hire as a prostitute, whether it be by father or brother or uncle or guardian or by anyone else who has control of him, prosecution is not to lie against the boy himself, but against the man who let him out for hire, and against the other, it says, because he hired him. And the law has made the penalties for both offenders the same. Moreover, the law frees a son, when he has become a man, from all obligation to support or to furnish a home to a father by whom he has been hired out for prostitution; but when the father is dead, the son is to bury him and perform the other customary rites. . . .

But what other law has been laid down for the protection of our children? The law against panders. For the lawgiver imposes the heaviest penalties if any person act as pander in the case of a freeborn child or a freeborn woman.

And what other law? The law against outrage, which includes all such conduct in one summary statement, wherein it stands expressly written: if any one outrage a child . . . or a man or woman, or anyone, free or slave, or if he commit any unlawful act against any one of these. Here the law provides prosecution for outrage, and it prescribes what bodily penalty he shall suffer, or what fine he shall pay. . . .

Now perhaps someone, on first hearing this law, may wonder for what possible reason this word "slaves" was added in the law against outrage. But if you reflect on the matter, fellow citizens, you will find this to be the best provision of all. For it was not for the slaves that the lawgiver was concerned, but he wished to accustom you to keep a long distance away from the crime of outraging freemen, and so he added the prohibition against even the outraging of slaves. In a word, he was convinced that in a democracy that man is unfit for citizenship who outrages any person whatsoever. And I beg you, fellow citizens, to remember this also, that here the lawgiver is not yet addressing the person of the boy himself but those who are near him—father, brother, guardian, teachers—and in general those who have control of him. But as soon as the young man has been registered in the list of citizens, and knows the laws of the state, and is now able to distinguish between right and wrong, the lawgiver no longer addresses another, Timarchus, but now the man himself. And what does he say? "If any Athenian," he says, "shall have prostituted his person, he shall not be permitted to become one of the nine archons," because, no doubt, that official wears the wreath; "nor to discharge the office of priest," as being not even clean of body; "nor shall he act as an advocate for the state," he says, "nor shall he ever hold any office whatsoever, at home or abroad, whether filled by lot or by election; nor shall he be a herald or an ambassador"—nor shall he prosecute men who have served as ambassadors, nor shall he be a hired accuser—"nor ever address council or assembly," not even though he be the most eloquent orator in Athens. And if any one act contrary to these prohibitions, the lawgiver has provided for criminal process on the charge of prostitution, and prescribed the heaviest penalties therefore.

8.12　Defeat and Hard Times: Athens after the Peloponnesian War

The Peloponnesian War ended in 404 B.C. with the defeat of Athens by Sparta, the loss of Athens's empire, and the replacement of the democracy by a narrow oligarchy supported by Sparta, the so-called "Thirty." The brutal regime of the "Thirty," which the philosopher Plato said made the democracy seem a "Golden Age," lasted less than a year. The social and economic dislocations that resulted from the devastation of the war and forced repatriation of Athenians, who had been settled on land in the empire that had been seized from rebellious allies and subjects, lasted into the early fourth century B.C. The straitened circumstances of late fifth-century Athens challenged traditional Greek ideas concerning the proper roles of men and women and the nature of work. In this selection from his Memorable Statements of Socrates, *Xenophon shows Socrates offering practical advice to formerly prosperous Athenians who were having difficulty adjusting to the harsh realities of post–Peloponnesian War Athens.*[14]

Soc: You seem to have some trouble on your mind, Aristarchus; if so, you should share it with your friends. Perhaps together we might lighten the weight of it a little.

Aristarchus answered: Yes, Socrates, I am in sore straits indeed. Ever since the party strife declared itself in the city, what with the rush of people to Peiraeus, and the wholesale banishments, I have been fairly at the mercy of my poor deserted female relatives. Sisters, nieces, cousins, they have all come flocking to me for protection. I have fourteen freeborn souls, I tell you, under my single roof, and how are we to live? We can get nothing out of the soil—that is in the hands of the enemy; nothing from my house property, for there is scarcely a living soul left in the city; my furniture? no one will buy it; money? there is none to be borrowed—you would have a better chance to find it by looking for it on the road than to borrow it from a banker. Yes, Socrates, to stand by and see one's relatives die of hunger is hard indeed, and yet to feed so many at such a pinch impossible.

After he had listened to the story, Socrates asked: How comes it that Ceramon, with so many mouths to feed, contrives not only to furnish himself and them with the necessaries of life, but to realise a handsome surplus, whilst you being in like plight are afraid you will one and all perish of starvation for want of the necessaries of life?

Ar: Why, bless your soul, do you not see he has only slaves and I have freeborn souls to feed?

Soc: And which should you say were the better human beings, the freeborn members of your household or Ceramon's slaves?

Ar: The free souls under my roof without a doubt.

Soc: Is it not a shame, then, that he with his baser folk to back him should be in easy circumstances, while you and your far superior household are in difficulties?

Ar: To be sure it is, when he has only a set of handicraftsmen to feed, and I my liberally educated household.

Soc: What is a handicraftsman? Does not the term apply to all who can make any sort of useful product or commodity?

Ar: Certainly.

---

[14]Xenophon, *Memorabilia* 2.7–8. From *The Works of Xenophon*, Vol. 3, trans. H. G. Dakyns (London: Macmillan & Co., 1890), pp. 70–76.

Soc: Barley meal is a useful product, is it not?

Ar: Preeminently so.

Soc: And loaves of bread?

Ar: No less.

Soc: Well, and what do you say to cloaks for men and for women—tunics, mantles, vests?

Ar: Yes, they are all highly useful commodities.

Soc: Then your household do not know how to make any of these?

Ar: On the contrary, I believe they can make them all.

Soc: Then you are not aware that by means of the manufacture of one of these alone—his barley meal store—Nausicydes not only maintains himself and his domestics, but many pigs and cattle besides, and realises such large profits that he frequently contributes to the state benevolences; while there is Cyrêbus, again, who, out of a bread factory, more than maintains the whole of his establishment and lives in the lap of luxury; and Dêmeas of Collytus gets a livelihood out of a cloak business, and Menon as a mantle-maker, and so, again, more than half the Megarians by the making of vests.

Ar: Bless me, yes! They have got a set of barbarian fellows, whom they purchase and keep, to manufacture by forced labor whatever takes their fancy. My kinswomen, I need not tell you, are freeborn ladies.

Soc: Then, on the ground that they are freeborn and your kinswomen, you think that they ought to do nothing but eat and sleep? Or is it your opinion that people who live in this way—I speak of freeborn people in general—lead happier lives, and are more to be congratulated, than those who give their time and attention to such useful arts of life as they are skilled in? Is this what you see in the world, that for the purpose of learning what it is well to know, and of recollecting the lessons taught, or with a view to health and strength of body, or for the sake of acquiring and preserving all that gives life its charm, idleness and inattention are found to be helpful, whilst work and study are simply a dead loss? Pray, when those relatives of yours were taught what you tell me they know, did they learn it as barren information which they would never turn to practical account, or, on the contrary, as something with which they were to be seriously concerned some day, and from which they were to reap solid advantage? Do human beings in general attain to well-tempered manhood by a course of idling, or by carefully attending to what will be of use? Which will help a man the more to grow in justice and uprightness, to be up and doing, or to sit with folded hands revolving the ways and means of existence? As things now stand, if I am not mistaken, there is no love lost between you. You cannot help feeling that they are costly to you, and they must see that you find them a burden? This is a perilous state of affairs, in which hatred and bitterness have every prospect of increasing, whilst the preexisting bond of affection is likely to be snapped.

But now, if only you allow them free scope for their energies, when you come to see how useful they can be, you will grow quite fond of them, and they, when they perceive that they can please you, will cling to their benefactor warmly. Thus, with the memory of former kindnesses made sweeter, you will increase the grace which flows from kindnesses tenfold; you will in consequence be knit in closer bonds of love and domesticity. If, indeed, they were called upon to do any shameful work, let them choose death rather than that; but now they know, it would seem, the very arts and accomplishments which are regarded as the loveliest and the most suitable for women; and the things which we know, any of us, are just those which we can best perform, that is to say, with ease and expedition; it is a joy to do them, and the result is beautiful. Do not hesitate, then, to initiate your friends in what will bring advantage to them and you alike; probably they will gladly respond to your summons.

Well, upon my word (Aristarchus answered), I like so well what you say, Socrates, that though hitherto I have not been disposed to borrow, knowing that when I had spent what I got I should not be in a condition to repay, I think I can now bring myself to do so in order to raise a fund for these works.

Thereupon a capital was provided; wools were purchased; the goodman's relatives set to work, and even whilst they breakfasted they worked, and on and on till work was ended and they supped. Smiles took the place of frowns: They no longer looked askance with suspicion, but full into each other's eyes with happiness. They loved their kinsman for his kindness to them. He became attached to them as helpmates; and the end of it all was, he came to Socrates and told him with delight how matters fared; "and now," he added, "they tax me with being the only drone in the house, who sits and eats the bread of idleness." . . .

VIII.—At another time chancing upon an old friend whom he had not seen for a long while, he greeted him thus:

Ar: What quarter of the world do you hail from, Euthërus?

The other answered: From abroad, just before the close of the war; but at present from the city itself. You see, since we have been denuded of our possessions across the frontier, and my father left me nothing in Attica, I must needs bide at home, and provide myself with the necessaries of life by means of bodily toil, which seems preferable to begging from another, especially as I have no security on which to raise a loan.

Soc: And how long do you expect your body to be equal to providing the necessaries of life for hire?

Euth: Goodness knows, Socrates—not for long.

Soc: And when you find yourself an old man, expenses will not diminish, and yet no one will care to pay you for the labor of your hands.

Euth: That is true.

Soc: Would it not be better then to apply yourself at once to such work as will stand you in good stead when you are old—that is, address yourself to some large proprietor who needs an assistant in managing his estate? By superintending his works, helping to get in his crops, and guarding his property in general, you will be a benefit to the estate and be benefited in return.

Euth: I could not endure the yoke of slavery, Socrates! (he exclaimed).

Soc: And yet the heads of departments in a state are not regarded as adopting the badge of slavery because they manage the public property, but as having attained a higher dignity of freedom rather.

Euth: In a word, Socrates, the idea of being held to account to another is not at all to my taste.

Soc: And yet, Euthërus, it would be hard to find a work which did not involve some liability to account; in fact it is difficult to do anything without some mistake or other, and no less difficult, if you should succeed in doing it immaculately, to escape all unfriendly criticism. I wonder now whether you find it easy to get through your present occupations entirely without reproach. No? Let me tell you what you should do. You should avoid censorious persons and attach yourself to the considerate and kindhearted, and in all your affairs accept with a good grace what you can and decline what you feel you cannot do. Whatever it be, do it heart and soul, and make it your finest work. There lies the method at once to silence fault-finders and to minister help to your own difficulties. Life will flow smoothly, risks will be diminished, provision against old age secured.

8.13   Personal Religion in Classical Greece: The Case of Xenophon

Because of his lack of sympathy for the restored Athenian democracy, Xenophon left Athens shortly after the Peloponnesian War, becoming one of the mercenary soldiers, who were a prominent feature of fourth-century B.C. Greece. After participating in Cyrus the Younger's unsuccessful revolt against his brother Artaxerxes II in 401 B.C., and then fighting on the Spartan side against Athens in the 390s B.C., for which he was exiled from his homeland, Xenophon retired to a country estate near Sparta. In this passage he recounts his devotion to the goddess Artemis and the intimate connection between her and his life in exile.[15]

At this time and place, they divided the money accruing from the sale of the captives (sc. captured by Cyrus the Younger's Greek mercenaries); and a tithe selected for Apollo and Artemis of the Ephesians was divided between the generals, each of whom took a portion to guard for the gods, Neon the Asinaean taking on behalf of Cheirisophus. Out of the portion, which fell to Xenophon, he caused a dedication offering to Apollo to be made and dedicated among the treasures of the Athenians at Delphi. It was inscribed with his own name, and that of Proxenus, his friend, who was killed with Clearchus. The gift for Artemis of the Ephesians was, in the first instance, left behind by him in Asia at the time when he left that part of the world himself with Agesilaus on the march into Boeotia. He left it behind in charge of Megabyzus, the sacristan of the goddess, thinking that the voyage on which he was starting was likely to be dangerous. In the event of his coming out of it alive, he charged Megabyzus to restore to him the deposit; but should any evil happen to him, then he was to cause to be made and dedicate on his behalf to Artemis, whatsoever thing he thought would pleasing to the goddess.

In the days of his banishment, when Xenophon was now established by the Lacedaemonians as a colonist in Scillus, a place which lies on the main road to Olympia, Megabyzus arrived on his way to Olympia as a spectator to attend the games, and restored to him the deposit. Xenophon took the money and bought for the goddess a plot of ground at a point indicated to him by the oracle. The plot, it so happened, had its own Selinus river flowing through it, just as at Ephesus the river Selinus flows past the temple of Artemis, and in both streams fish and mussels are to be found. On the estate at Scillus there is hunting and shooting of all sorts of beasts of the chase.

Here with the sacred money he built an altar and a temple, and ever after, year by year, tithed the fruits of the land in their season and sacrificed to the goddess, while all the citizens and neighbors, men and women, shared in the festival. The goddess herself provided for the banqueters meat and loaves and wine and sweetmeats, with portions of the victims sacrificed from the sacred pasture, as also of those which were slain in the chase. For Xenophon's own sons, with the sons of the other citizens, always made a hunting excursion against the festival day,

---

[15]Xenophon, *Anabasis* 5.4, trans. H. G. Dakyns, in Goodolphin, *The Greek Historians,* Vol. 2, pp. 324–325.

in which any grown men who liked might join. The game was captured partly from the sacred district itself, partly from Pholoe, pigs and gazelles and stags. The place lies on the direct road from Lacedaemon to Olympia, about two and one-half miles from the temple of Zeus in Olympia, and within the sacred enclosure there is meadow-land and wood-covered hills, suited to the breeding of pigs and goats and cattle and horses, so that even the pack-animals of the people passing to the feast fare sumptuously. The shrine is girdled by a grove of cultivated trees, yielding dessert fruits in their season. The temple itself is a facsimile on a small scale of the great temple at Ephesus, and the image of the goddess is like the golden statue at Ephesus, save only that it is made not of gold, but of cypress wood. Beside the temple stands a column bearing this inscription:

> The place is sacred to Artemis. He who holds it and enjoys the fruits of it is bound to sacrifice yearly a tithe of the produce. And from the residue thereof to keep in repair the shrine. If any man fail in any of this, the goddess herself will look to the matter.

Chapter 9

The Hellenistic Age

A remarkable new era opened with the thirteen-year reign of Alexander the Great (336–323 B.C.). By his conquest of the Persian Empire, Alexander destroyed a state system that had regulated affairs in western Asia for over two centuries. His premature death at the age of 33 deprived Alexander of the opportunity to implement whatever plans he had for the organization of his empire. His chief generals warred more than forty years before a new political system emerged in Asia. That new political system represented a major change from the recent past: The territory of the old Persian Empire was divided into several large kingdoms—most important were those of the Ptolemies in Egypt and the Seleucids in Asia—in which Greeks played a prominent role.

Until recently, historians have taken a "melting pot" approach to understanding the Hellenistic Period (336–330 B.C.), viewing it as a time in which Greek and non-Greek cultures interacted to produce a new cosmopolitan civilization. Contemporary scholars hold a much less benign view of the nature of Hellenistic society. Far from blending to form a new culture, Greek and native societies tended to coexist with only limited contact between them in the new Macedonian-ruled kingdoms that were formed out of the wreckage of Alexander's empire. In other words, the Macedonian kingdoms in Egypt and Asia were essentially colonial regimes in which ethnicity was the principal determinant of social and political position. Whether or not Alexander intended his empire to be governed by a mixed elite of Macedonians, Greeks, and natives, in Ptolemaic Egypt and Seleucid Asia only Macedonians and Greeks belonged to the governing elites. The results of this situation were various and are explored in the readings, but one of the most important was that the Hellenistic Period was a time of unprecedented opportunity for Greeks, who immigrated in substantial numbers in the third century B.C. to populate the new cities Alexander and his successors founded in Egypt and Asia and to staff the new bureaucratic governments that governed their kingdoms.

Although Greeks and Macedonians made up less than 10 percent of the total population of the Hellenistic kingdoms, they monopolized the higher levels of political and economic life in Egypt and Asia. Not surprisingly, the Greeks prospered in their new homes, some mightily, but most modestly, as is illustrated by the charming picture of middle-class life in Alexandria drawn by the third-century B.C. poet Theocritus in the selection entitled "Middle Class Life in Hellenistic Alexandria." Entry into this privileged world required certification as a Greek, and, as apartheid was not characteristic of ancient Greek culture, over time many of the citizen bodies of the Hellenistic cities came to include a significant number of individuals whose Greekness was not so much a matter of birth as of culture, that is, of education. All other inhabitants of the Hellenistic kingdoms, whatever the status of their ancestors, had rights that were significantly inferior to those of the Greeks and Macedonians and were subject to harsher laws and higher taxes. It is not surprising, therefore, that social conflict during this period tended to take the form of fierce revolts by the peoples who wanted to restore native rule to the various Macedonian kingdoms; some, like the Maccabees in Judaea, were even successful.

Still, whatever their shortcomings, and they were many, for almost three centuries, until their remnants were absorbed into the expanding Roman Empire, the Macedonian kingdoms provided the framework for a vibrant and complex social and cultural life. Their cities—Greek, Egyptian, and Asiatic—were not only centers in which art, literature, philosophy, and science flourished but also places in which a wide variety of new social and economic roles developed for both men and women.

9.1 Alexander the Great: Two Contrasting Views

Not surprisingly in view of the momentous events of his reign, widely discrepant assessments of Alexander the Great and his achievements were current already in antiquity. His Greek contemporaries were generally hostile, but later Greek writers were more positive. Thus the early-second-century A.D. biographer and moralist Plutarch argues, in the selection from his On the Fortune of Alexander, *that Alexander's efforts on behalf of the spread of Greek culture in Asia were of greater benefit to mankind than those of philosophers. Much harder to determine are the views of the non-Greek subjects of Alexander and his successors, but the selection from the third book of the* Sibylline Oracles—*poetic commentaries on contemporary history written by Hellenistic Jews but falsely ascribed to various pagan Sibyls, that is, prophetesses—suggests that they were much less favorable.*

9.1.1 An Idealistic View[1]

2. And I think that he would speak in this way to Fortune, when she takes credit for his successes. "Do not slander my excellence, nor detract from my fame by diversion. Darius was your creation, whom you made master of the Persians from a servant and king's courier; and you also placed the royal diadem on Sardanapallus. As a result of my victory at Arbela, I went up to Susa. Cilicia opened to me broad Egypt; and the Granicus likewise Cilicia, which I reached by trampling under foot the corpses of Mithridates and Spithridates. Adorn yourself, and boast of kings, who never felt a wound or shed blood. They were fortunate, your Ochuses and Artaxerxes, who immediately after birth were placed on the throne of Cyrus by you. But my body carries many marks of Fortune, who fought against me as an enemy instead of being my ally. First, among the Illyrians I was wounded in the head with a stone, and received a blow in the neck with a club. Near

---

[1]Plutarch, *De Aex. Magni Fortuna aut Virtuta Oratio* 1, 2–6. Based on *Plutarch's Essays and Miscellanies,* Vol. 1, trans. several scholars, corrected and revised by William W. Goodwin (Boston: Little, Brown and Company, 1909), pp. 475–482.

Granicus I was wounded in the head with a barbarian scimitar; and at Issus in the thigh with a sword. At Gaza I was shot in the ankle with an arrow; and I was whirled around and dislocated my shoulder. In the land of the Maracandani my leg was split with an arrow. There remain the wounds I received in India and the sufferings of famine. Among the Assacani I was shot through the shoulder with an arrow and among the Gandridae in the leg. Among the Malli I was wounded by a missile from a bow that pierced my breast and drove in its iron head. I was also struck a blow in my neck, when the scaling-ladders broke that had been placed against the walls, and Fortune closed me in alone, offering so great a deed not to a renowned enemy, but to worthless barbarians. If Ptolemy had not covered me with his shield, and Limnaeus had not fallen before me, struck by innumerable missiles; or if the Macedonians had not courageously and forcefully overthrown the wall, that barbarian and nameless village would have become Alexander's tomb.

3. As for the troubles of the whole expedition, there were storms and parching droughts, deep rivers, peaks not even birds could reach, amazing sights of wild beasts, harsh living, and revolts and betrayals of rulers. And as for what happened before the expedition, Greece lay prostrate from the effects of the Philip's wars. But then the Thebans, rising from the defeat, shook from their arms the dust of Chaeronea; and Athens extended its hands to them and joined with them. All Macedon was secretly hostile, looking toward Amyntas and the sons of Aeropus. The Illyrians broke out into open war; and the Scythians were threatening their neighbors, who were in disorder; Persian gold, liberally scattered among the popular leaders of every city, was putting all Peloponnesus into commotion. King Philip's treasuries were empty of money, and there was, in addition, a debt, as Onesicritus records, of two hundred talents. In the midst of so much need and such menacing troubles, a youth, who was hardly past the age of childhood, dared hope for the conquest of Babylon and Susa, and, even to think of rule over all mankind; and all this, trusting only in his force of 30,000 infantry and 4,000 cavalry. For so many were his forces, according to Aristoboulus. Ptolemy, however, says that there were 30,000 infantry and 5,000 cavalry; and Anaximenes 43,000 infantry, and 5,500 cavalry. Now the glorious and magnificent campaign fund which Fortune had provided him was seventy talents, according to Aristobulus; or, as Duris reckons it, enough for only thirty days' provision.

4. Was Alexander, therefore, too ill advised and rash to set out upon so vast an undertaking with such limited resources? By no means. For whoever set out with greater or finer means than he: magnanimity, understanding, self-control, and courage, with which Philosophy supplied him for his expedition? Yes, he invaded Persia with greater assistance from Aristotle than from his father Philip. As for those who write how Alexander said that the *Iliad* and *Odyssey* accompanied him in his wars as his supplies, we believe them in honor to Homer. Should we object, however, if someone says that the *Iliad* and *Odyssey* accompanied him as relief from toil and a way of spending his leisure time; but that philosophical learning and works concerning fearlessness, courage, and, moreover, self-control and nobility of spirit, were his true equipment for the campaign? For, certainly, he never wrote about syllogisms or axioms; nor did he participate in walks in the Lyceum, or discuss theories in the Academy. For it is by such things that people define philosophy, who think it is a matter of talk, not of action. Yet Pythagoras, Socrates, Arcesilaus, and Carneades wrote nothing, although they were the most famous of the philosophers. Nor did they busy themselves in such great wars, civilize barbarian kings, found Greek cities among savage peoples, or teach laws to

and establish peace among lawless and ignorant people. They, however, lived at ease, and surrendered the business of writing to the Sophists. On what basis, therefore, were they believed to be philosophers? It was either from their sayings, or from the lives they led, or from the precepts, which they taught. Upon these grounds, therefore, let Alexander also be judged; and he will be seen from what he said, what he did, and what he taught to have been a philosopher.

5. And first, if you wish, consider the most paradoxical matter, and compare the students of Alexander with those of Plato and Socrates. They taught people who were naturally intelligent and spoke the same tongue, understanding, if nothing else, the Greek language; and even then they didn't persuade many. Indeed, men like Critias, Alcibiades, and Cleitophon spit out their teaching like a bit, and turned aside to another path. If you examine the instruction imparted by Alexander, however, he taught the Hyrcanians to marry, instructed the Arachosians how to farm, persuaded the Sogdians to support and not to kill their parents, and the Persians to honor and not to marry their mothers. O amazing philosophy, which induced the Indians to worship the Greek gods, and the Scythians to bury instead of eat their dead. We admire the power of Carneades, if, indeed, it made the Carthaginian Clitomacus, who was formerly called Hasdrubal, to follow a Greek way of life. We admire the character of Zeno, if, indeed, it persuaded the Babylonian Diogenes to become a philosopher. After Alexander civilized Asia, however, Homer was read, and the children of Persians, Susians, and Gedrosians chanted the tragedies of Euripides and Sophocles. Socrates lost his case to his Athenian accusers, who alleged that he introduced foreign deities, but because of Alexander, Bactria and Caucasus began to worship the Greek gods. Plato, moreover, although he proposed one constitution, could not persuade any people to use it because of its harshness. Alexander, however, overcame uncivilized and savage ways of life by building more than seventy cities among barbarian nations, and sowing Asia with Greek offices. A few of us study *The Laws* of Plato, but innumerable people have made and still make use of those of Alexander. The peoples Alexander vanquished were more blessed than they who escaped his conquests. For no one stopped them from living wretchedly, but those he conquered, he compelled to live happily. True, therefore, is the statement of Themistocles, when he became an exile, and he received great gifts from the king, and he acquired three tributary cities, one to supply him with bread, a second with wine, a third with relish: "O young men," he said, "we would have been undone, if we had not been undone." This, however, might even be more justly said of the peoples subdued by Alexander. Egypt would not have her Alexandria, nor Mesopotamia her Selcucia, nor Sogdiana her Propthasia, nor India her Bucephalia, nor Caucasus a Greek city nearby. For by founding these cities, savagery was extinguished and the worse changed to the better through habit. If philosophers take greatest pride in taming and making harmonious harsh and foolish customs, then Alexander, who changed innumerable peoples and savage natures, should be thought to have been a very great philosopher.

6. And, indeed, the much admired *Republic* of Zeno, the founder of the Stoic sect, focuses on one central point: that we all should not live divided into cities or into villages with their own laws. We should consider, instead, all peoples to be our fellow demes-men and citizens, and there should be one way of life and order as is true of a herd that feeds together and lives in a common pasture. Zeno wrote this, as though he were giving shape to a dream or image of an orderly philosophy or constitution, but Alexander realized the idea.

For he did not, as Aristotle advised him, rule the Greeks as a leader and the barbarians as supreme ruler, caring for the former as friends and kinsmen, and dealing with the latter as wild beasts or plants. If he had done so, he would have filled his empire with numerous wars and festering divisions. But thinking that he had come from god himself as the common moderator and arbiter of all peoples, he subdued by force those whom he could not unite by reason. He brought together from everywhere peoples, mixing together as in a loving cup their lives, customs, marriages and life styles. He ordered everyone to consider the inhabited world as their fatherland, the camp of his army as their stronghold and fortress, and good men as kin and evil men as foreigners. He would not have Hellenism and barbarism distinguished by Greek cloaks, shields, scimitars, or Median robes; but Hellenism was to be characterized by excellence and barbarism by evil. People were to consider their clothing and food and marriages and lifestyles common, having been mixed together through blood and offspring.

9.1.2 A Jaundiced View of Alexander's Conquests and Their Results[2]

But Macedonia will give birth to a grievous calamity for Asia, and the line of Zeus, a family of bastards and slaves, will be the source of severe pain for Europe. She will master the strong city of Babylon. Once called mistress of all the land the sun looks upon, she will be destroyed by an evil fate and be famed among her far wandering posterity.

Some day there will also come to the prosperous soil of Asia a faithless man—wild, lawless, fiery—wearing a purple mantle on his shoulders; for previously he, a man, was raised up by a thunderbolt. All Asia will bear an evil yoke, and the earth will drink up a mighty storm of slaughter. But, nevertheless, Hades will attend him in everything though he is unaware of it. Indeed, from those whose race he wishes to destroy will come they who will destroy his stock.

9.2   Alexandria and the Colonial World of Hellenistic Egypt

Cultural and political life in the new Hellenistic kingdoms centered in the new cities established by Alexander and his successors. The first and greatest of these cities was Alexandria, which Alexander had founded during his stay in Egypt in 331 B.C. In the first selection below, the first-century B.C. geographer Strabo clearly indicates the factors—superb location and lavish royal patronage—that made Alexandria the principal commercial and cultural center of the Hellenistic world. Next, Theocritus, court poet of Ptolemy II (282–246 B.C.), gives a vivid picture of Alexandria's cosmopolitan cultural life and the multi-ethnic character of its population. In the last analysis, the prosperity of Alexandria and its Greek citizens depended on the efficient exploitation of the agricultural wealth of Egypt. The third selection, excerpts from a memorandum of instructions from a Ptolemaic financial official to one of his subordinates, illustrates the ideal of benevolent but firm administration that was the official policy of the Ptolemaic rulers of Egypt. That the reality was, unfortunately, different is clear from the excerpts in the next selection from a general amnesty decree issued in 118 B.C. that reveals the Ptolemaic government to have been corrupt and extortionate in its treatment of its Egyptian subjects.

---

[2]*Sibylline Oracles* 3, lines 381–395.

9.2.1   A Hellenistic Metropolis: Alexandria in Egypt[3]

7. The site of Alexandria is advantageous for many reasons. For the city is bounded by two seas, on the north by the so-called Egyptian sea and on the south by Lake Mareia, which is also called Mareotis. The Nile fills Lake Mareia through many canals from both the south and the sides. Through these canals many more goods are brought to Alexandria than arrive from the sea, so that the lakeside harbor is richer than that on the sea, and by it more goods are exported from Alexandria than are imported into the city. . . .

8. The ground plan of the city is shaped like a military cloak. The long sides, which are both bounded by water, are thirty stades across. The short sides are formed by the isthmuses, which are each seven or eight stades in breadth and are hemmed in by the sea on one side and the lake on the other. The whole city is cut up by streets suitable for the riding of horses and the driving of chariots. Two, which are especially broad—being more than a plethron wide—meet at right angles and bisect each other.

Alexandria has many fine public precincts and palaces, which occupy a fourth or even a third of the city's whole perimeter; for just as each of the kings added some adornment to its public monuments, so each added his own residence to those already existing so that, in the words of Homer, "one was on top of another." All the palaces are connected to each other and to the harbor, including those outside the harbor. The Museum forms one portion of the palaces. It has a walkway, an arcade with benches, and a large building in which is located the dining hall of the scholars who belong to the Museum. The faculty has both property in common and a priest, who is in charge of the Museum and was formerly appointed by the kings and is now by Caesar [*Augustus*]. Also part of the palace complex is the building called the Sema, which is a circular structure in which are the tombs of the kings and that of Alexander. Ptolemy, the son of Lagus, because of greed and the desire to seize control of Egypt, anticipated Perdiccas by stealing the body of Alexander when he was bringing it back from Babylon and was turning toward this country. . . . Having brought the body of Alexander to Egypt, Ptolemy buried it in Alexandria, where it now still lies, but not, however, in the same sarcophagus; for the present one is of glass, but Ptolemy buried it in one of gold.

9.2.2   Middle-Class Life in Hellenistic Alexandria[4]

Gorgo: (*with her maid Eutychis at the door, as the maid Eunoa opens it*) Praxinoa at home?

Praxinoa: (*running forward*) Dear Gorgo! At last! She is at home. I quite thought you'd forgotten me.

(*to the maid*) Here, Eunoa, a chair for the lady, and a cushion in it.

Gorgo: (*refusing the cushion*) No, thank you, really.

Praxinoa: Do sit down.

Gorgo: (*sitting*) O how helpless I am. What with the crowds and the horses, Praxinoa, I barely got here alive. It's all big boots and people in uniform. And the street was never-ending, and you can't think how far your house is along it.

---

[3]Strabo, *Geography* 17.7–8 (selections).
[4]Theocritus, *Idyll* 15. Based on the translation of J. M. Edmonds in J. M. Edmonds, *The Greek Bucolic Poets* (London: William Heineman, 1912), pp. 177–195.

Praxinoa: That's my madman. Came and took one at the end of the world, and more an animal's den, too, than a fit place for a human being to live in. Just to prevent you and me being neighbors, out of sheer spite, the jealous old fool! He's always the same.

Gorgo: My dear, don't call your husband Dinon such things in front of the child. See how he's staring at you. (*to the child*) It's all right Zopyrion, my dear. She's not talking about daddy.

Praxinoa: By the Goddess, the child understands.

Gorgo: Nice Daddy.

Praxinoa: And yet that daddy of his the other day—the other day, now, I told him, "Daddy get mother some soap and rouge from the shop," and would you believe it? He came back with salt, the big fool!

Gorgo: Mine's just the same. Diocleidas is a perfect spendthrift. Yesterday he gave seven drachmas apiece for mere bits of dog's hair, mere pluckings of old bags, five of them, all filth, all work to be done over again. But come, my dear, get your cloak and gown. Let's go to the palace of wealthy King Ptolemy to see the Adonis. I hear the Queen has put together something marvelous this year.

Praxinoa: (*hesitating*) Fine folks, fine ways.

Gorgo: Yes. But sightseers make good gossips, you know, if you've been and other people haven't. It's time we were on the move.

Praxinoa: (*still hesitating*) It's always holidays with people who've nothing to do. (*suddenly making up her mind*) Here, Eunoa, you scratch-face, take up the spinning and put it away with the rest. Cats always will lie soft. Come, wake up. Quick, some water! (*to Gorgo*) Water's wanted first, and she brings the soap. (*to Eunoa*) Never mind; give it to me. (*Eunoa pours out the soap*) Not all that, you wicked waste! Pour out the water. (*Eunoa washes her mistress's hands and face*) Oh, you wretch! What do you mean by wetting my bodice like that? That's enough. (*to Gorgo*) I've got myself washed somehow, thank goodness. (*to Eunoa*) Now where's the key of the big cupboard? Bring it here. (*takes out and puts on a gown*)

Gorgo: (*referring to the style of the gown*) Praxinoa, that full gathering suits you really well. Do tell me what you paid for the material.

Praxinoa: Don't speak of it, Gorgo; it was more than two silver minas, and I can tell you I put my very soul into making it up.

Gorgo: Well, all I can say is, it's most successful.

Praxinoa: It's very good of you to say so. (*to Eunoa*) Come, put on my cloak and hat for me, and mind you, do it properly. (*Eunoa puts on her cloak and hat. She takes up the child*) No; I'm not going to take you, Baby. The bogey-horse bites little boys. (*the child cries*) You may cry as much as you like; I'm not going to have you lamed for life. (*to Gorgo, giving the child to the nurse*) Come along. Take Baby and amuse him, Phrygia, and call the dog indoors and lock the front door.

(*in the street*) Heavens, what a crowd! How we are to get through this mob and how long it's going to take us, I can't imagine. Talk of an antheap! I must say, you've done us many a good turn, Ptolemy, since your father went to heaven. Now no thief creeps up to mug us in the Egyptian way. They don't play those awful games now. They are all alike, all scum.

Gorgo dearest, what shall we do? The royal cavalry. Don't run me down, my good man. That bay's rearing. Look, what temper! Stand back, Eunoa, you reckless girl! He'll kill the man leading him. Thank goodness, my child remained at home.

Gorgo: It's all right, Praxinoa. We've got well beyond them, you see. They're all where they ought to be now.

Praxinoa: (*recovering*) And fortunately I can say the same of my poor wits. Ever since I was a girl, two things have frightened me more than anything else, a horrid slimy snake and a horse. Let's get on. Here's ever such a crowd pouring after us.

Gorgo: (*to an old woman*) Have you come from the palace, mother?

Old Woman: Yes, my dears.

Gorgo: Then we can get there all right, can't we?

Old Woman: Trying took Troy, my pretty ones; don't they say where there's a will there's a way?

Gorgo: That old lady gave us some oracles, didn't she?

Praxinoa: My dear, women know everything. They even know all about Zeus marrying Hera.

Gorgo: Look, Praxinoa, what a crowd there is at the door!

Praxinoa: Marvelous. Give me your arm, Gorgo; and you take hold of Eutychis's arm, Eunoa; and you hold on tight, Eutychis, or you'll be separated. We'll all go in together. Mind you, keep hold of me, Eunoa. Oh dear, oh dear, Gorgo! My summer cloak is torn right in two. (*to a stranger*) For Heaven's sake, as you wish to be saved, mind my cloak, sir.

First Stranger: I really can't help what happens; but I'll do my best.

Praxinoa: The crowd is simply enormous; they're pushing like a drove of pigs.

First Stranger: Don't be alarmed, madam; we're all right.

Praxinoa: You deserve to be all right to the end of your days, my dear sir, for the care you've been taking of us. (*to Gorgo*) What a kind considerate man! Poor Eunoa is getting crushed. (*to Eunoa*) Push, you coward, can't you? (*they pass in*)

That's all right. All inside, as the bridegroom said when he shut the door.

Gorgo: (*referring, as they move forward toward the dais, to the draperies which hang between the pillars*) Praxinoa, come here. Before you do anything else, I insist that you look at the embroideries. How delicate they are and how beautiful! Clothes worthy of the Gods!

Praxinoa: Mistress Athena! The weavers that made that material and the embroiderers who did that close detailed work are simply marvels. How realistically the things all stand and move about in it! They're living! It is wonderful what people can do. And the young man, how wonderful he looks lying on his silver couch with the down of manhood just showing on his cheeks. Thrice beloved Adonis, who is beloved even in Acheron.

Second Stranger: Ladies, stop that eternal cooing. Doves. They'll wear me out with their drawl.

Praxinoa: My word! Where does that man come from? What business is it of yours if we coo? Buy your slaves before you order them about. You're giving orders to Syracusans. If you must know, we're Corinthians by descent, like Belerophon himself. We talk Peloponnesian. I suppose Dorians may speak Doric! Persephone! Let's have no more masters than the one we have. I shall do just as I like, so don't waste your breath.

Gorgo: Be quiet, Praxinoa. She's about to begin to sing the Adonis, the Argive person's daughter—the skilled singer, who sang the dirge last year. You may be sure she'll give us something good. She's beginning now.

(*The Song*)

Mistress, you who love Golgi, Idalion, and high Eryx, Goldenfaced Aphrodite, a year has passed and the Hours, who are not to be rushed, are bringing back to you Adonis from ever-flowing Acheron, dear Hours, longed-for Hours, tardiest of the immortals, who always come bearing gifts to all mortals. Cypris, daughter of Dione, you who, they say, made Bernice an immortal from a mortal, pouring ambrosia into her woman's breast. Blessed lady, goddess of many names and temples, Bernice's daughter, Arsinoe, who is like Helen, shows her affection for Adonis with all good things. . . . Beloved Adonis, dear Adonis, be gracious for another year. Joyous has been your coming this year and it will be joyous when you come again.

Gorgo: O Praxinoa, how clever we women are! I do envy her knowing all that, and still more her having such a lovely voice. But I must be getting back. It's Diocleidas's dinner time, and that man is all pepper. I wouldn't advise anyone to come near him even when he's kept waiting for his food. Good-bye Adonis darling; and I trust only that you may find us all thriving when you come next year.

9.2.3   "Take Particular Care That No Fraud Occur": The Ideal of Honest and Efficient Administration[5]

During your tours of inspection, try, while making your rounds, to encourage each individual and to make them bolder. Do this not only by word but also, if some of them lay a complaint against the village scribes or headmen concerning some matter pertaining to farming, look into it and, so far as you can, put an end to such situations. And when the sowing has been completed, it would not be a bad idea if you made a careful inspection; for, thus, you will accurately observe the sprouting, and you will easily identify the fields that have been improperly sown or not sown at all; and you will learn from this those who were careless and you will know if some have employed the seeds for other purposes. In addition, the sowing of the nome in accordance with the plan for planting is to be one of your prime concerns. And if some are suffering because of their rents or even have been completely ruined, do not allow this to be unexamined. Also, make a list of the oxen involved in farming, both royal and private, and exercise due care that the calves of the royal cattle, when they are ready to eat hay, are sent to the calf-rearing barns.

It is your responsibility also that the designated provisions are transported to Alexandria—of these we are sending you a list—on schedule, and not only in the proper amount, but also tested and suitable for consumption. Go also to the weaving sheds in which the linen is woven and take special care that as many as possible of the looms are in operation and that the weavers are completing the amount of fabric specified in the plan. If some are behind in their assigned work, let them be fined for each category the scheduled price. Moreover, to the end that the linen be usable and have the number of threads specified in the regulation, pay careful attention. As for looms that are not in operation, have all of them transported to the nome metropolis and stored in the storerooms under seal. Conduct an audit also of the revenues, if it is possible, village by village, and this seems to be not impossible if you zealously apply yourself to the task; but if not, then toparchy by toparchy, accepting in the audit with regard to money taxes only what has been deposited at the bank; and with regard to the grain taxes and oil produce what has been measured and received by the sitologoi. If there is any deficiency in these, compel the toparchs and the tax farmers to pay to the banks for arrears in the grain tax the price specified in the schedule and for arrears in the oil produce by wet measure according to each category. . . .

---

[5]*P. Tebtunis* 703 (selections). From Stanley M. Burstein, *The Hellenistic Age from the Battle of Ipsos to the Death of Kleopatra VII* (Cambridge: Cambridge University Press, 1985), pp. 128–129. Used by permission.

As the revenue from the pasture dues is among the most significant, it will be particularly increased if you conduct the census in the best way. The most suitable time for it is around the month of Mesore, for, at this time, because the whole land is covered by the flood waters, the herdsmen send their herds to the highest places, as they are unable to disperse them to other places. You should also take care that goods are not sold for more than the specified prices. As for those goods without set prices and for which the vendors may charge what they wish, examine this carefully and, having determined a moderate profit for the merchandise being sold, compel the [—] make the disposition. . . .

Make a list also of the royal houses and of the gardens associated with them and who is supposed to care for each, and inform us. Further, it should be your concern also that affairs regarding the machimoi be handled in accordance with the memorandum which we drafted concerning persons who had absconded from their tasks and [—] sailors in order that to [—] the prisoners be confined until their transportation to Alexandria. Take particular care that no fraud occur or any other wrongful act, for it ought to be clearly understood by everyone living in the countryside and believed that all such matters have been corrected and that they are free from the former evil conditions, since no one has the power to do what he wishes but everything is being managed in the best way. Thus you will create security in the countryside and (increase) the revenues significantly. . . .

The reasons I sent you to the nome, I told you, but I thought it would be good also to send you a written copy of them in this memorandum. Afterwards, you should behave well and be upright in your duties, not become involved with bad company, avoid any involvement in corruption, believe that if you are not accused of such things, you will merit promotion, have this memorandum at hand and write concerning each matter as required.

9.2.4 Administrative Oppression in Ptolemaic Egypt: The Amnesty of 118 B.C.[6]

Col. I

King Ptolemaios and Queen Kleopatra, the sister, and Queen Kleopatra, the Wife, pardon those subject to their rule, all of them, for errors, wrongful acts, accusations, condemnations, charges of all sorts up to the 9th of Pharmouthi of the 52nd year except those guilty of willful murder and sacrilege. They have given orders also that those who have fled because of being accused of theft and other charges shall return to their own homes and resume their former occupations, and that they shall recover whatever of their property still remains unsold from that which had been seized as security because of these matters.

Col. II

They have given orders also that all those having land allotments and all those in possession of sacred land and other released land, who have intruded into royal land and others who possess more land than is proper, having withdrawn from all excess they possess and having declared themselves and paid a year's rent in kind, shall be forgiven for the period up to year 51—and they shall have full possession.

---

[6]*P. Tebtunis* 5 (selections). From Burstein, *The Hellenistic Age from the Battle of Ipsos to the Death of Kleopatra VII*, pp. 139–140. Used by permission.

Col. III

No one is to take away anything consecrated to the gods by force nor to apply forceful persuasion to the managers of the sacred revenues, whether villages or land or other sacred revenues, nor are taxes on associations or crowns or grain-taxes to be collected by anyone from property consecrated to the gods nor are the sacred lands to be placed under patronage on any pretext, but they are to allow them to be managed by the priests themselves.

Col. IV

They have given orders that the costs for the burial of Apis and Mnevis are to be sought from the royal treasury as also in the case of those who have been deified. Likewise, also the costs of the other sacred animals.

Col. VIII

They have given orders that strategoi and other officials are not to seize any of those living in the countryside for their private purposes nor are their animals to be requisitioned for any of their personal needs nor are their cattle to be seized nor are they to be forced to raise sacred animals or geese or birds or pigs or to furnish grain at a low price or in return for renewals of their leases nor to compel tasks to be performed by them as a gift on any pretext.

Col. IX

They have given orders also concerning suits of Egyptians against Greeks and concerning suits of Greeks against Egyptians or of Egyptians against Greeks of all categories except those of persons farming royal land and of those bound to government tasks and of others connected with the revenues, that those Egyptians who have made contracts in the Greek manner with Greeks shall be sued and sue before the *chrematistai*.[7] All Greeks who make contracts in the Egyptian manner shall be sued before the *laokritai*[8] in accordance with the laws of the country. The cases of Egyptians against Egyptians are not to be usurped by the chrematistai, but they are to allow them to be settled before the *laokritai* in accordance with the laws of the country.

9.3   Culture Contact, Culture Clash: Religion and Society in the Hellenistic World

Although a culturally and ethnically mixed civilization did not emerge in the Hellenistic Period, some interaction between Greek and non-Greek culture did occur in the various Hellenistic kingdoms, particularly in the area of religion. Being polytheists, Greeks, who settled in the new cities of Egypt and Asia, recognized and worshiped the gods of their new homes, as was only prudent. Egyptian and Asian

---

[7]*Chremitistai* are judges who administer Greek law in Greek.
[8]*Laokritai* are judges who administer Egyptian law in Egyptian.

deities attracted Greek followings, however, only when they were stripped of those aspects of their traditional cult that conflicted with Greek religious ideas. Thus in the first selection below, the early-second-century A.D. *Roman historian Tacitus tells how, during the reign of Ptolemy I, Greek and Egyptian theologians collaborated to create Sarapis, a Hellenized version of a Memphite form of the ancient Egyptian funerary god Osiris, who became the patron deity of Alexandria and whose cult was one of the most important rivals of early Christianity. Sarapis was not an isolated case. The Greek hymn in praise of Isis illustrates how the goddess Isis, traditionally the wife of Osiris and the divine mother of the Pharaonic rulers of Egypt, was worshiped by Hellenistic Greeks as a great mother goddess and the creator of civilization everywhere. The principal but not the only adherents of these new cults were Greeks. The next selection tells the story of three generations of an Egyptian priestly family who were responsible for bringing the cult of Sarapis to the Greek island of Delos in the central Aegean. Worshiping these Hellenized deities was one way ambitious non-Greeks could attempt to bridge the gap between themselves and their Greek and Macedonian overlords, but it was a way that could also alienate them from the more traditional elements of their own society, as can be seen in the final selection of this section, which recounts the ill-fated attempt in the late 170s and early 160s* B.C. *by a faction of the Hellenistic Jewish elite to introduce the worship of a Hellenized form of Yahweh as part of a plan to convert Jerusalem into a Greek city.*

9.3.1   The Origin of Sarapis[9]

83. The origin of this god Sarapis has not hitherto been made generally known by our writers. The Egyptian priests give this account. While Ptolemy, the first Macedonian king who consolidated the power of Egypt, was setting up in the newly built city of Alexandria fortifications, temples, and rites of worship, there appeared to him in his sleep a youth of singular beauty and more than human stature, who counselled the monarch to send his most trusty friends to Pontus, and fetch his effigy from that country. This, he said, would bring prosperity to the realm, and great and illustrious would be the city which gave it a reception. At the same moment he saw the youth ascend to heaven in a blaze of fire. Roused by so significant and strange an appearance, Ptolemy disclosed the vision of the night to the Egyptian priests, whose business it is to understand such matters. As they knew but little of Pontus or of foreign countries, he enquired of Timotheus, an Athenian, one of the family of the Eumolpids, whom he had invited from Eleusis to preside over the sacred rites, what this worship was, and who was the deity. Timotheus, questioning persons who had found their way to Pontus, learned that there was there a city Sinope, and near it a temple, which, according to an old tradition of the neighborhood, was sacred to the infernal Jupiter, for there also stood close at hand a female figure, to which many gave the name of Proserpine. Ptolemy, however, with the true disposition of a despot, though prone to alarm, was, when the feeling of security returned, more intent on pleasures than on religious matters; and he began by degrees to neglect the affair, and to turn his thoughts to other concerns, till at length the same apparition, but now more terrible and peremptory, denounced ruin against the king and his realm, unless his bidding were performed. Ptolemy then gave directions that an embassy should be despatched with presents to king Scydrothemis, who at that time

---

[9]Tacitus, *Histories* 4.83–48, trans. John Church and William Jackson Brodribb. From *The Complete Works of Tacitus* (New York: Random House, 1942), pp. 653–655.

ruled the people of Sinope, and instructed them, when they were on the point of sailing, to consult the Pythian Apollo. Their voyage was prosperous, and the response of the oracle was clear. The god bade them go and carry back with them the image of his father, but leave that of his sister behind.

84. On their arrival at Sinope, they delivered to Scydrothemis the presents from their king, with his request and message. He wavered in purpose, dreading at one moment the anger of the God, terrified at another by the threats and opposition of the people. Often he was wrought upon by the gifts and promises of the ambassadors. And so three years passed away, while Ptolemy did not cease to urge his zealous solicitations. He continued to increase the dignity of his embassies, the number of his ships, and the weight of his gold. A terrible vision then appeared to Scydrothemis, warning him to thwart no longer the purposes of the God. As he yet hesitated, various disasters, pestilence, and the unmistakeable anger of heaven, which grew heavier from day to day, continued to harass him. He summoned an assembly, and explained to them the bidding of the God, the visions of Ptolemy and himself, and the miseries that were gathering about them. The people turned away angrily from their king, were jealous of Egypt, and, fearing for themselves, thronged around the temple. The story becomes at this point more marvellous, and relates that the God of his own will conveyed himself on board the fleet, which had been brought close to shore, and, wonderful to say, vast as was the extent of sea that they traversed, they arrived at Alexandria on the third day. A temple, proportioned to the grandeur of the city, was erected in a place called Rhacotis, where there had stood a chapel consecrated in old times to Sarapis and Isis. Such is the most popular account of the origin and introduction of the God Sarapis. I am aware indeed that there are some who say that he was brought from Seleucia, a city of Syria, in the reign of Ptolemy III, while others assert that it was the act of the same king, but that the place from which he was brought was Memphis, once a famous city and the strength of ancient Egypt. The God himself, because he heals the sick, many identified with Aesculapius; others with Osiris, the deity of the highest antiquity among these nations; not a few with Jupiter, as being supreme ruler of all things; but most people with Pluto, arguing from the emblems which may be seen on his statues, or from conjectures of their own.

9.3.2   The Praises of Isis, Mistress of the Universe and Creator of Civilization[10]

Demetrios, the son of Artemidoros, who is also called Thraseas, a Magnesian from Magnesia on the Maeander, an offering in fulfillment of a vow to Isis. He transcribed the following from the stele in Memphis which stands by the temple of Hephaistos:

I am Isis, the tyrant of every land; and I was educated by Hermes, and together with Hermes I invented letters, both the hieroglyphic and the demotic, in order that the same script should not be used to write everything. I imposed laws on men, and the laws which I laid down no one may change. I am the eldest daughter of Kronos. I am the wife and sister of King Osiris. I am she who discovered the cultivation of grain for men. I am the mother

---

[10]*Inscriptiones Graecae* 12.14. From Burstein, *The Hellenistic Age from the Battle of Ipsos to the Death of Kleopatra VII*, p. 147. Used by permission.

of King Horos. I am she who rises in the Dog Star. I am she who is called goddess by women. By me the city of Bubastis was built. I separated earth from sky. I designated the paths of the stars. The sun and the moon's course I laid out. I invented navigation. I caused the just to be strong. Woman and man I brought together. For woman I determined that in the tenth month she shall deliver a baby into the light. I ordained that parents be cherished by their children. For parents who are cruelly treated I imposed retribution. Together with my brother Osiris I stopped cannibalism. I revealed initiations to men. I taught men to honor the images of the gods. I established precincts for the gods. The governments of tyrants I suppressed. I stopped murders. I compelled women to be loved by men. I caused the just to be stronger than gold and silver. I ordained that the true be considered beautiful. I invented marriage contracts. Languages I assigned to Greeks and barbarians. I caused the honorable and the shameful to be distinguished by Nature. I caused nothing to be more fearful than an oath. He who unjustly plotted against others I gave into the hands of his victim. On those who commit unjust acts I imposed retribution. I ordained that suppliants be pitied. I honor those who justly defend themselves. With me the just prevails. Of rivers and winds and the sea am I mistress. No one becomes famous without my knowledge. I am the mistress of war. Of the thunderbolt am I mistress. I calm and stir up the sea. I am in the rays of the sun. I sit beside the course of the sun. Whatever I decide, this also is accomplished. For me everything is right. I free those who are in bonds. I am the mistress of sailing. The navigable I make unnavigable whenever I choose. I established the boundaries of cities. I am she who is called Lawgiver. The island from the depths I brought up into the light. I conquer Fate. Fate heeds me. Hail Egypt who reared me.

9.3.3   How Sarapis Came to Delos: The Family of Apollonios, Priest of Sarapis[11]

The priest Apollonios recorded this in accordance with the command of Sarapis.

Apollonios, our grandfather, an Egyptian and a priest, came from Egypt with the god and continued serving him as was traditional. He is thought to have lived ninety-seven years. Demetrios, my father, succeeded him and also served the gods, and he was honored for his piety by the god with a bronze statue, which is set up in the temple of the god. He lived sixty-one years. After I took over the rites and attended scrupulously to the services, the god informed me in a dream that a Sarapieion of his own must be dedicated to him, and that it should not be in leased quarters as before. The god also told me that he would himself find the place where it was to be built and that he would indicate the place, and this happened. This place was full of dung. It was listed for sale on a little notice on the path through the market place; and as the god wished, the sale took place and the temple was built quickly in six months. Some men, however, conspired against us and the god and brought a public charge against the temple and myself about what penalty should be suffered or what fine should be paid. But the god promised me in a dream that we would win; and when the trial had been completed and we had won in a manner worthy of the god, we gave praise to the gods and rendered proper thanks.

---

[11]*Sylloge Inscriptionum Graecarum*³ 663. From Burstein, *The Hellenistic Age from the Battle of Ipsos to the Death of Kleopatra VII*, pp. 130–131. Used by permission.

9.3.4   Culture Clash: Jewish Resistance to Hellenism and the Origins of Hanukkah[12]

Jerusalem Transformed into a *Polis* (ca. 175 B.C.)

But when Seleucus died, and Antiochus, who was called Epiphanes, succeeded to the kingdom, Jason the brother of Onias supplanted his brother in the high priesthood, promising in a petition to the king 300 and threescore talents of silver, besides 80 talents from another fund, in addition to which he undertook to pay 150 more, if he was commissioned to set up a gymnasium and ephebeum and to register the Jerusalemites as citizens of Antioch. And when the king had given his assent, Jason at once exercised his influence in order to bring over his fellow-countrymen to Greek ways of life. Setting aside the royal ordinances of special favor to the Jews, obtained by John the father of Eupolemus who had gone as envoy to the Romans to secure their friendship and alliance, and seeking to overthrow the lawful modes of life, he introduced new customs forbidden by the law: He deliberately established a gymnasium under the citadel itself and made the noblest of the young men wear the Macedonian hat. And to such a height did the passion for Greek fashions rise, and the influx of foreign customs, thanks to the surpassing impiety of that godless Jason—no high priest he!—that the priests were no longer interested in the services of the altar, but despising the sanctuary, and neglecting the sacrifices, they hurried to take part in the unlawful displays held in the palaestra after the discus throwing had been announced—thus setting at naught what their fathers honored and esteeming the glories of the Greeks above all else. Hence, sore distress befell them; the very men for whose customs they were so keen and whom they desired to be like in every detail became their foes and punished them. For it is no light matter to act impiously against the laws of God; time will show that.

Now games, held every five years, were being celebrated at Tyre, in the presence of the king, and the vile Jason sent sacred envoys who were citizens of Antioch to represent Jerusalem, with 300 drachmas of silver for the sacrifice of Heracles. The very bearers, however, judged that the money ought not to be spent on a sacrifice but devoted to some other purpose, and, thanks to them, it went to fit out the triremes.

Abolition of Jewish Law (167 B.C.)

Antiochus, then, carried off from the temple 1,800 talents and hurried away to Antioch, thinking in his arrogance to make the land navigable and the sea passable by foot—so uplifted was he in heart. He also left governors behind him to ill-treat the Jewish people: at Jerusalem, Philip, a Phrygian by race, whose disposition was more barbarous than that of his master; at Gerizim, Andronicus; and, besides these, Menelaus, who lorded it worst of them all over the citizens. And in malice against the Jews he sent the Mysian commander Apollonius with an army of 22,000 under orders to slay all those that were of full age and to sell the women and the younger men. This fellow, on reaching Jerusalem, played the role of a man of peace, waiting till the holy day of the Sabbath; then, finding the Jews at rest from work, he commanded his men to parade in arms, put to the sword all who came to see what was going on, and rushing into the city with the armed men killed great numbers. Judas Maccabaeus, however, with

---

[12]Second Maccabees 4:7–21, 5:21–6.11, 8:1–7, 9–10:8, trans. James Moffatt. From *The Apocrypha and Pseudepigrapha of the Old Testament in English*, Vol. 1, ed. R. H. Charles (Oxford: Clarendon Press, 1913), pp. 136–137, 139–140, 142–145.

about nine others got away and kept himself and his companions alive in the mountains, as wild beasts do, feeding on herbs, in order that they might not be polluted like the rest.

6. Shortly after this the king sent an old Athenian to compel the Jews to depart from the laws of their fathers and to cease living by the laws of God; further, the sanctuary in Jerusalem was to be polluted and called after Zeus Olympius, while the sanctuary at Gerizim was also to be called after Zeus Xenius, in keeping with the hospitable character of the inhabitants. Now this proved a sore and altogether crushing visitation of evil. For the heathen filled the temple with riot and reveling, dallying with harlots and lying with women inside the sacred precincts, besides bringing in what was forbidden, while the altar was filled with abominable sacrifices which the law prohibited. And a man could neither keep the Sabbath, nor celebrate the feasts of the fathers, nor so much as confess himself to be a Jew. On the king's birthday every month they were taken—bitter was the necessity—to share in the sacrifice, and when the festival of the Dionysia came round they were compelled to wear ivy wreaths for the procession in honor of Dionysus. On the suggestion of Ptolemy, an edict was also issued to the neighboring Greek cities ordering them to treat the Jews in the same way and force them to share in the sacrifices, slaying any who refused to adopt Greek ways. Thus anyone could see the distressful state of affairs. Two women, for example, were brought up for having circumcised their children; they were paraded round the city, with their babies hanging at their breasts, and then flung from the top of the wall. Some others, who had taken refuge in the adjoining caves in order to keep the seventh day secretly, were betrayed to Philip and all burnt together, since they scrupled to defend themselves, out of regard to the honor of that most solemn day.

Armed Jewish Resistance Begins (167 B.C.)

8. But Judas, who is also called Maccabaeus, together with his companions, went round the villages by stealth, summoning their kinsfolk and mustering those who had adhered to Judaism, till they collected as many as 6,000. And they invoked the Lord to look upon the people whom all men oppressed, to have compassion on the sanctuary which the godless had profaned, and also to pity the ruined city which was on the point of being levelled with the ground, to hearken to the blood that cried to him, to remember the impious massacre of the innocent babes and the blasphemies committed against his name, and to manifest his hatred of evil. Now as soon as Maccabaeus had got his company together, the heathen found him irresistible, for the Lord's anger was now turned into mercy. He would surprise and burn both towns and villages, gaining possession of strategic positions and routing large numbers of the enemy. He took special advantage of the night for such attacks. And the whole country echoed with the fame of his valour.

The Purification of the Temple and the Restoration of Jewish Law (165 B.C.)

9. Now about that time it happened that Antiochus had to beat a disorderly retreat from the region of Persia. He had entered the city called Persepolis and tried to rob temples and get hold of the city; whereupon the people flew to arms and routed him, with the result that Antiochus was put to flight by the people of the country and broke up his camp in disgrace. And while he was at Ecbatana, news reached him of what had happened to Nicanor and the forces of Timotheus. So, in a transport of rage, he determined to wreak vengeance on the Jews for the defeat which he had suffered at the hands of those who had forced him to fly, and ordered his charioteer to drive on without halting till the journey was ended. Verily the

judgment of heaven upon him was imminent! For thus he spoke in his arrogance: When I reach Jerusalem, I will make it a common sepulchre of Jews. But the all-seeing Lord, the God of Israel, smote him with a fatal and unseen stroke; the words were no sooner out of his mouth than he was seized with an incurable pain in the bowels, and his internal organs gave him cruel torture—a right proper punishment for one who had tortured the bowels of other people with many an exquisite pang. He did not cease from his wild insolence, however, but waxed more arrogant than ever, breathing fire and fury against the Jews, and giving orders to hurry on with the journey. And it came to pass that he dropped from his chariot as it whirled along, so that the bad fall racked every limb of his body. Thus he who in his overweening haughtiness had supposed the waves of the sea were at his bidding and imagined he could weigh the high mountains in his scales, was now prostrate, carried along in a litter—a manifest token to all men of the power of God. Worms actually swarmed from the impious creature's body; his flesh fell off, while he was still alive in pain and anguish; and the stench of his corruption turned the whole army from him with loathing. A man who shortly before had thought he could touch the stars of heaven, none could now endure to carry, such was his intolerable stench. Then it was that, broken in spirit, he began to abate his arrogance, for the most part, and to arrive at some knowledge of the truth. For, as he suffered more and more anguish under the scourge of God, unable even to bear his own stench, he said: Right is it that mortal man should be subject to God and not deem himself God's equal. The vile wretch also made a vow to the Lord (who would not now have pity on him), promising that he would proclaim the holy city free—the city which he was hurrying to lay level with the ground and to make a common sepulchre—that he would make all the Jews equal to citizens of Athens—the Jews whom he had determined to throw out with their children to the beasts, for the birds to devour, as unworthy even to be buried—that he would adorn with magnificent offerings the holy sanctuary which he had formerly rifled, restoring all the sacred vessels many times over, and defraying from his own revenue the expense of the sacrifices; furthermore, that he would even become a Jew and travel over the inhabited world to publish abroad the might of God. But when his sufferings did not cease by any means (for God's judgment had justly come upon him), he gave up all hope of himself and wrote the following letter, with its humble supplication, to the Jews:

To his citizens, the loyal Jews, Antiochus their king and general wisheth great joy and health and prosperity. If you and your children fare well and your affairs are to your mind, I give thanks to God, as my hope is in heaven. As for myself, I am sick. Your esteem and goodwill I bear in loving memory. On my way back from Persia I have fallen seriously ill, and I think it needful to take into consideration the common safety of all my subjects—not that I despair of myself (for, on the contrary, I have good hopes of recovery), but in view of the fact that when my father marched into the upper country, he appointed his successor, in order that, in the event of anything unexpected occurring or any unwelcome news arriving, the residents at home might know whom the State had been entrusted to, and so be spared any disturbance. Besides these considerations, as I have noticed how the princes on the borders and the neighbors of my kingdom are on the alert for any opportunity and anticipate the coming event, I have appointed my son Antiochus to be king. I have often committed and commended him to most of you, when I hurried to the upper provinces. I have also written to him what I have written below. I therefore exhort and implore you to remember the public and private benefits you have received and to preserve, each of you, your present goodwill toward me and my son. For I am convinced that with mildness and kindness he will adhere to my policy and continue on good terms with you.

So this murderer and blasphemer, after terrible suffering such as he had inflicted on other people, ended his life most miserably among the mountains in a foreign land. His bosom-friend Philip brought the corpse home; and then, fearing the son of Antiochus, he betook himself to Ptolemy Philometor in Egypt.

10. Now Maccabaeus and his followers, under the leadership of the Lord, recaptured the Temple and the city and pulled down the altars erected by the aliens in the marketplace, as well as the sacred inclosures. After cleansing the sanctuary, they erected another altar of sacrifice, and striking fire out of flints they offered sacrifices after a lapse of two years, with incense, lamps, and the presentation of the shew-bread. This done, they fell prostrate before the Lord with entreaties that they might never again incur such disasters, but that, if ever they should sin, he would chasten them with forbearance, instead of handing them over to blasphemous and barbarous pagans. Now it so happened that the cleansing of the sanctuary took place on the very day on which it had been profaned by aliens, on the twenty-fifth day of the same month, which is Chislev. And they celebrated it for eight days with gladness like a feast of tabernacles, remembering how, not long before, during the feast of tabernacles they had been wandering like wild beasts in the mountains and the caves. So, bearing wands wreathed with leaves and fair boughs and palms, they offered hymns of praise to him who had prospered the cleansing of his own place, and also passed a public order and decree that all the Jewish nation should keep these ten days every year.

9.4   Jewish Life in the Diaspora: The Synagogue

Increasingly, Jews lived outside of Judea during the Hellenistic Period. Since the center of Jewish cult and worship remained the Temple at Jerusalem, diaspora Jews had to create a new focus for Jewish religious and communal life in the various non-Jewish cities in which they lived. Their solution was the synagogue, a meeting house where members of the Jewish community could meet for worship, education, and other communal functions. The following two passages illustrate the role of the synagogue in diaspora life. In the first passage the Talmud describes the main synagogue in Alexandria, which contained the largest and most influential diaspora Jewish community in the eastern Mediterranean. In the second, the Alexandrian Jewish philosopher Philo claims legitimacy for the Sabbath ritual as celebrated in the first century A.D. by ascribing its origin to Moses.

9.4.1   The Synagogue of Alexandria[13]

It has been taught, R. Judah stated, he who has not seen the double colonnade of Alexandria in Egypt has never seen the glory of Israel. It was said that it was like a huge basilica, one colonnade within the other, and it sometimes held twice the number of people that went forth from Egypt. There were in it seventy-one cathedra [sc. thrones] of gold, corresponding to the seventy-one members of the Great Sanhedrin, not one of them containing less than twenty-one

[13]*Tractate Sukkah*, trans. Rev. Dr. Israel W. Slotki. From *The Babylonian Talmud: Seder Mo'ed in Four Volumes*, Vol. 3 (London: The Soncino Press, 1938), pp. 244–245.

talents of gold, and a wooden platform in the middle upon which the attendant of the Synagogue stood with a scarf in his hand. When it was time to answer Amen [sc. after the reader
had finished a prayer], he waived his scarf and all the congregation duly responded. They
moreover did not occupy their seats promiscuously, but goldsmiths sat separately, metalworkers
separately, and weavers separately, so that when a poor man entered the place he recognized the
members of his craft and on applying to that quarter obtained a livelihood for himself and for
the members of his family.

9.4.2   Moses Ordains the Sabbath Ritual[14]

He [sc. Moses] required them to assemble at the same place on these seventh days, and sitting
together in a respectful and orderly manner, hear the laws read so that none should be ignorant of them. And indeed they always assemble and sit together, most of them in silence except when it is the practice to add something to signify their approval of what is read. But some
priest who is present or one of the elders reads the holy laws to them and expounds them point
by point until about the late afternoon, when they depart, having gained expert knowledge of
the holy laws and considerable advance in piety.

9.5   "Ptolemy is a Good Paymaster": Opportunities and Social Roles in the Hellenistic Period

*Contemporary historians are increasingly aware that the life of the vast majority of people—both Greek
and non-Greek—changed little in the Hellenistic Period. The low level of productivity of the ancient
economy meant that the vast bulk of the population continued to live in rural areas as subsistence farmers.
Nevertheless, for the urban minority the Hellenistic Period saw a significant increase in economic opportunity
and in the variety of available social roles, particularly in the new cities of Egypt and the Near East.
Not surprisingly, opportunities were greatest for the elite. The first selection below describes the career of
an important Greek official of Ptolemy I and Ptolemy II during the 280s and 270s B.C. and illustrates
how such individuals served as spokesmen for their home cities at the courts of their royal masters. The
opportunities available to most immigrants, however, were less glamorous. A selection from Menander
vividly depicts the hopes as well as the risks that confronted those who joined the armies of the Macedonian monarchs in the hope of gaining quick wealth in the east, while the next selection provides an insight
into the more mundane world of the Hellenistic bureaucracies with their multitude of minor but potentially
lucrative jobs and the means by which they were obtained.*

 *New opportunities also appeared for women during the Hellenistic Period. Opportunities were clear-
ly greatest for wealthy women, as can be seen from a selection illustrating the willingness of impoverished
cities such as Priene in western Anatolia even to allow women who would use their wealth for public purposes to hold political office (Phyle, wife of Thessalos). Education also created opportunities for some
women, not only upper-class intellectual women such as the Cynic philosopher Hipparchia, whose story is
told in this section, but also women from less distinguished backgrounds, such as the Athenian midwife
Phanostrate, whose epitaph is translated here, and the professional harpist Polygnota of Thebes, whose*

---

[14]Philo in Eusebius, *Evangelical Preparation* 8.7. Reprinted from F. E. Peters, *Judaism, Christianity, and Islam: The Classical
Texts*, Vol. 3 (Princeton, NJ: Princeton University Press, 1990), p. 37.

generosity to Apollo of Delphi is recorded. There were also significant changes in the roles of men and women within the institution of marriage during the Hellenistic Period. Traditionally, Greeks viewed marriage as a partnership of a man and a woman for the purpose of producing legitimate children to ensure the survival of the oikos *and* polis. *Although that view continued, Hellenistic thinkers increasingly emphasized the importance of the affective aspects of marriage, as can be seen from the observation of Stoic philosopher Antipater of Tarsus that* "the man who has had no experience of a married woman and children has not tasted true and noble happiness," *and from the popularity of stories of romantic love, such as that of Antiochus and Stratonice, translated here. More important, the provision in the marriage contract of a wife's right to seek a divorce because of her husband's sexual misbehavior is clear evidence that such ideals found practical expression in the recognition of greater equality in relations between husband and wife than had been accepted in archaic and classical Greece.*

9.5.1   An Athenian Boy Makes Good: The Life of Kallias, Ptolemaic Governor of Halicarnassus (Athens, 270–269 B.C.)[15]

The People (praises) Kallias, son of Thymochares, from Sphettos. In the archonship of Sosistratos (270/69), in the prytany of Pandionis which is the sixth, in which Athenodoros, son of Gorgippos, from Acharnai, was secretary, on the eighteenth day of Poseideon,[16] twenty-first day of the prytany; main assembly; of the proedroi the motion was put to the vote by the chairman, Epichares, son of Pheidostratos, from Erchia, and by his fellow proedroi. Resolved by the Boule[17] and the People; Euchares, son of Euchares, from Konthyle, introduced the motion. Kallias, when the People rose against those occupying the city, and it expelled the soldiers from the city, but the fort on the Museion hill was still occupied and the countryside was engaged in war by the soldiers from Peiraeus and Demetrios was marching from the Peloponnesos with an army against the city, Kallias, learning of the danger facing the city and having selected a thousand soldiers from those stationed with him on Andros and having distributed their salary to them and furnished their provisions, came quickly to the city to help the People, acting in accordance with the benevolent attitude of King Ptolemaios (I) toward the People. Marching out the soldiers who were with him into the countryside, he provided protection for the harvesting of the wheat, making every effort that as much wheat as possible into the city might be brought. And when Demetrios arrived, invested the city and laid siege to it, Kallias, fighting on behalf of the People and making sallies with his soldiers and being wounded, shrank from no risk on any occasion for the sake of saving the People. And King Ptolemaios, having sent Sostratos to accomplish what was advantageous for the city, and Sostratos inviting an embassy to meet him at Piraeus with which he would arrange terms of peace on behalf of the city with Demetrios, Kallias yielded in this to the strategoi and the Boule, undertook the embassy on behalf of the city and did everything that was advantageous for the city; and he remained in the city with the soldiers until the peace was completed. Then, having sailed to King Ptolemaios with the embassies sent by the People, he co-operated in every way and worked for the advantage of

---

[15]*Supplementum Epigraphicum Graecum* 28 (1978) 60. From Burstein, *The Hellenistic Age from the Battle of Ipsos to the Death of Kleopatra VII,* pp. 74–76. Used by permission.
[16]Poseidon, the sixth month of the Athenian calendar, equals December.
[17]The Boule or Council of 500 was responsible for preparing the agenda for the Athenian assembly.

the city. After the succession to the throne of Ptolemaios (II), the younger king, Kallias, having visited the city and the strategoi having summoned him and informed him of the state in which the city's affairs were and urged him to hasten on behalf of the city to King Ptolemaios in order that as soon as possible there might be some help for the city in the form of grain and money, at his own expense Kallias sailed to Kypros and, by there making a strong appeal to the king on behalf of the city, he obtained for the people fifty talents of silver and a gift of 20,000 medimnoi of wheat, which was measured out at Delos to those sent by the People. When the king held for the first time the Ptolemaeia, the sacrifice and the games in honor of his father, the People, having voted to send a sacred embassy and having requested Kallias to agree to be the chief envoy and to lead on behalf of the People the [*sacred embassy*], K[al]lias agreed to this request with enthusiasm; and, having refused the fifty minas that had been voted to him by the People for the (expenses) of the office of chief envoy and having contributed them to the *People*, he led [*the sacred embassy*] at his own expense well and (in a manner) [*worthy*] of the People, and he took care of the sacrifice on behalf of the city and all the other things, which were appropriate, in association with the sacred ambassadors. At the time the People was first about to hold the Panathenaia in honor of the Foundress after the city had been recovered, Kallias, having spoken with the king about the tackle that had to be prepared for the peplos and the king having donated it to the city, took care that it be prepared as well as possible for the goddess; and the sacred ambassadors who with him had been elected immediately brought the tackle back here. And now, having been stationed in Halikarnassos by King Ptolemaios, Kallias continues zealously aiding both the embassies and the sacred embassies sent by the People to King Ptolemaios, and he privately on behalf of each citizen coming to him exerts every effort as well as for the soldiers there stationed with him, considering as most important [the advantage] and, in general, the well-being of the city; [—] with regard to the fatherland [—] Kallias not ever having endured [—] when the people had been suppressed, but his own property he allowed to be given as a contribution during the oligarchy so that he did nothing against either the laws or the democracy, which is that of all the Athenians. [*Since these things are so*], in order, therefore, that all may know who wish to exert themselves for the city that the people always remembers those conferring benefits on it and returns thanks to each; with good fortune, it has been resolved by the Boule that the *proedroi*, who shall be chosen by lot to preside at the Assembly according to the law, shall deliberate and refer the resolution of the Boule to the People that the Boule resolves to praise Kallias, son of Thymochares, from Sphettos, for his excellence and the good will which he continues to have for the Athenian People, and to crown him with a gold wreath in accordance with the law, and to proclaim the wreath at the contest for new tragedies at the Greater Dionysia.

9.5.2   The Dangerous Life of a Soldier of Fortune[18]

Davus: (*apostrophizing the master who, so far as he knows, is dead*) Cleostratus, at this moment I am living through the saddest day of my life. And my thoughts are far from the hopes I had the day I left. For I pictured you happily safe and sound after the campaign was over,

---

[18]From Menander, *The Shield*, trans. Lionel Casson in *The Plays of Menander* (New York: New York University Press, 1971), pp. 83–85. Used by permission.

and spending the rest of your days in a life of ease with an appointment as commanding officer or trusted counselor to someone. I pictured you returning home to those who missed you so and giving your sister in marriage—after all, it was for her sake that you went off—to a man like yourself. I pictured myself, as I entered old age, finding my devotion rewarded by rest after my never-ending hardships. But now you've gone off, you've been suddenly snatched away from us, and I, your servant since you were a boy, am the one who has come back—with your shield, which time and again you kept safe but which did not keep you safe. (*Sighing*) Ah, you were a man with a great heart, if ever there was one.

(*While Davus is speaking, the door of Smicrines' house opens and Smicrines comes out. He is in his sixties, but looks even older. His clothes are cheap and ill-fitting, his figure is bent and gaunt, his face is a mirror of craftiness and avarice. As he listens intently, his eyes glisten. The minute Davus finishes, he goes over to him.*)

Smicrines: (*rolling his eyes heavenward and speaking in sepulchral tones*) This is an unexpected blow, Davus.

Davus: A terrible one.

Smicrines: How did it happen? How did he die?

Davus: (*shrugging despondently*) What's hard for a soldier to find is the chance to stay alive; chances to die are all around.

Smicrines: (*insistently*) Tell me what happened anyway, Davus.

Davus: There's a river in Lycia called the Xanthus. We fought a good number of battles there, and our side had done well: The enemy had left the plain and fled. (*ruefully*) But I guess not being a great success also has its useful side—the man who slips a bit is put on his guard. A devil-may-care attitude left us in total disorder for what was to come. A lot of the men, you see, left the camp and went off sacking villages, ravaging the fields, selling off booty; everyone came back with quite a haul.

Smicrines: Not bad!

Davus: Cleostratus put together a shipment of some 600 gold pieces, quite a lot of plate, and the batch of prisoners you see over there, and sends me off to Rhodes with instructions to leave it all with some friend and come right back.

Smicrines: Well, what happened?

Davus: I set out at dawn. The day I left, the enemy, managing to sneak past the men we had on watch, was lying in wait, screened by a hill; they had learned from some deserters how disorganized our forces were. When it got dark, the men left the countryside with its rich pickings and all disappeared into the tents. Then, as will happen, most of them got good and drunk.

Smicrines: (*shaking his head*) Bad, very bad.

Davus: Yes, since the enemy, I gather, made a sudden attack . . . [*About three and a half lines are lost here.*] Round about midnight I'm standing guard over the money and the captives, walking up and down in front of my tent, when I hear shouts, groans, wailing, running, men calling out to each other. And from them I heard what had happened. Luckily, where we were there was a small ridge that made a good strongpoint. We all gathered on top of it, and wounded men from the various units kept pouring in.

Smicrines: Lucky thing for you Cleostratus had sent you off when he did.

Davus: At dawn we went about pitching a sort of camp there and stayed put, while the men who had gone off on the forays I told you about kept blaming themselves for our troubles.

On the fourth day we found out that the enemy was off taking their prisoners to the villages inland, so we marched out.

Smicrines: And he had fallen and you saw him among the dead?

Davus: I wasn't able to identify him for sure. After four days of lying there, the faces were all swollen.

Smicrines: Then how do you know?

Davus: (*holding out the shield he has been clutching*) He was lying there with his shield. It was all bashed in—I suppose that's why none of the enemy bothered to take it. (*bitterly*) That fine commanding officer of ours didn't let us gather the bones and hold a funeral for each one, because he saw it would take too much time, but had us collect the corpses and hold a mass cremation. Then he had us carry out a quick burial and break camp right away. We first made it safely to Rhodes and, after staying there a few days, sailed here. (*shrugging despondently*) That's my whole story.

Smicrines: (*being elaborately casual*) You say you have 600 gold pieces?

Davus: That's right.

Smicrines: And plate?

Davus: About forty pounds of it. (*noting Smicrines' face fall*) No more than that, Mr. Legal Heir.

Smicrines: (*in a perish-the-thought tone*) What do you mean? You think that's the reason I'm asking? Good heavens! (*unable to restrain his curiosity*) The enemy get the rest?

Davus: (*nodding gloomily*) Just about the best part of it, except for what I got away with before the trouble started. (*pointing to the bundles some of the captives are carrying*) There are coats and cloaks in there. (*gesturing toward the whole group of captives*) And this bunch you see here is his property.

9.5.3   Recommendation For a Government Job (Egypt, 255 B.C.)[19]

Plato to Zenon, greetings. The father of Demetrius, who will give this letter to you, is living in the Arsinoite nome. The young man, therefore, also wishes to find some work there. On learning of your fairness, some of his friends asked me to write to you on his behalf in the hope that you might find a position for him in your office. Do us a favor, therefore, and see if there is something he can do which you think appropriate, and generally look after him, if, of course, you find him suitable. As a sign (of my feelings in this matter), I have sent to you from Sosus two bushels of chickpeas which I bought for five drachmas, and I will also try to buy an additional twenty bushels for you in Naucratis, if there are any available, and bring them to you. Farewell.

9.5.4   A Woman in Politics: Phyle, Wife of Thessalos (Priene, First Century B.C.)[20]

Phyle, daughter of Apollonios and wife of Thessalos, the son of Polydeukes, after having been the first woman to hold the office of crown bearer, paid for with her own money a cistern for water and the water pipes in the city.

---

[19]*P. Cairo Zen.* 59192.
[20]*Inschriften von Priene* 208.

9.5.5   A Woman Philosopher: The Life of Hipparchia[21]

Hipparchia, the sister of Metrocles, also fell in love with [*Crates'*] teachings. Both Hipparchia and Metrocles were from the city of Maroneia.

She fell in love with the words of Crates and his life and ignored all her suitors and their wealth, noble birth, and beauty. Crates became everything to her. She even went so far as to threaten to her parents that she would kill herself if they did not betrothe her to Crates. Crates, therefore, who had been urged by her parents to discourage their daughter, tried everything. Finally, not having persuaded her, he stood up, stripped off his clothers in front of her, and said, "This is your bridegroom, this is his estate, make your choice from these facts." For she could not be his mate if she would not also share his manner of life.

The girl chose, and assuming the same dress as he, went around with her husband, lived with him in public, and accompanied him to dinners. And when she attended a drinking party hosted by [*King*] Lysimachus, she confounded Theodorus, the man known as the Atheist, by proposing the following sophism: Whatever would not be called wrong if done by Theodorus would also not be called wrong if done by Hipparchia. If Theodorus struck himself, he would not commit a wrong, nor, therefore, if Hipparchia struck Theodorus, would she commit a wrong. He did not reply to what she had said but tried instead to rip off her cloak. Hipparchia, however, was not frightened or upset as a woman would normally be. And when he said to her, "Is this the woman who abandoned the shuttle and the loom?" she replied, "I am that woman, Theodorus; but do I seem to you to have made a mistake if I devoted to education the time I would have spent on the loom?"

9.5.6   A Professional Woman: Phanostrate, Midwife and Doctor (Athens, Fourth Century B.C.)[22]

Phanostrate. . . , the wife of Melitos, midwife and doctor, lies here. In life she caused no one pain, in death she is regretted by all.

9.5.7   A Professional Woman: The Theban Harpist Polygnota, Daughter of Socrates (Delphi, 86 B.C.)[23]

Gods. Good Fortune. The archon being Habromachos (86), month Boukatios, the councillors for the first six-month period being Stratagos, Kleon, Antiphilos, Damon. Resolved by the city of the Delphians. Since Polygnota, daughter of Sokrates, a harpist from Thebes, was staying at Delphi at the time the Pythian games were to be held, but because of the present war, the games were not held, on that same day she performed without charge and contributed her services for the day; and, having been asked by the magistrates and the citizens, she played for three days and earned great distinction in a manner worthy of the god and of the Theban people and of our city, and we rewarded her also with 500 drachmas; with good fortune, the city shall praise Polygnota, daughter of Sokrates, a Theban, for her reverent attitude toward the

---

[21]Diogenes Laertius, *Lives of Eminent Philosophers* 6.7.

[22]*Inscriptiones Graecae* 2.3² 6873.

[23]*Sylloge Inscriptionum Graecarum*³ 738. From Burstein, *The Hellenistic Age from the Battle of Ipsos to the Death of Kleopatra VII*, pp. 105–106. Used by permission.

god and her piety and her conduct with regard to her manner of life and art; and there shall be given by our city to her and to her descendants the status of a proxenos, priority in consulting the oracle, priority of trial, inviolability, exemption from taxes, a front seat at the contests which the city holds, and the right to own land and a house, and all other honors such as belong to the other proxenoi and benefactors of the city, and it shall invite her to the prytaneion to the public table; and it shall provide her with a sacrificial victim to offer to Apollo. God. Good Fortune. Resolved by the city of the Delphians. Since Lykinos, son of Dorotheos, a Theban, visited our city with his cousin Polygnota and behaved during his visit in a manner worthy of his own people and our city, it has been resolved by the city that it praise Lykinos, son of Dorotheos, a Theban, and that he have together with his descendants the status of a proxenos, priority in consulting the oracle, priority of trial, inviolability, exemption from taxes, a front seat at the contests which the city holds and other honors such as belong to the other proxenoi and benefactors of the city; and that it invite him also to the common table of the city. The archon being Habromachos, the son of Athambos, the councillors being Damon, Kleon, Stratagos, Antiphilos.

9.5.8   The Romance of Prince Antiochus and Queen Stratonice[24]

Seleucus, while still living, appointed his son, Antiochus, king of upper Asia in place of himself. If this seems noble and kingly on his part, even nobler and wiser was his behavior in reference to his son's falling in love, and the restraint which that son showed in regard to his passion; for Antiochus was in love with Stratonice, the wife of Seleucus, his own stepmother, who had already borne a child to Seleucus. Recognizing the wickedness of this passion, Antiochus did nothing wrong, nor did he show his feelings, but he fell sick, drooped, and strove his hardest to die. Nor could the celebrated physician, Erasistratus, who was serving Seleucus at a very high salary, form any diagnosis of his malady. At length, observing that his body was free from all the symptoms of disease, he conjectured that this was some condition of the mind, through which the body is often strengthened or weakened by sympathy; and he knew that, while grief, anger, and other passions disclose themselves, love alone is concealed by the modest. As even then Antiochus would confess nothing when the physician asked him earnestly and in confidence, he took a seat by his side and watched the changes of his body to see how he was affected by each person who entered his room. He found that when others came the patient was all the time weakening and wasting away at a uniform pace, but when Stratonice came to visit him his mind was greatly agitated by the struggles of modesty and conscience, and he remained silent. But his body in spite of himself became more vigorous and lively, and when she went away he became weaker again. So the physician told Seleucus that his son had an incurable disease. The king was overwhelmed with grief and cried aloud. Then the physician added, "His disease is love, love for a woman, but a hopeless love."

60. Seleucus was astonished that there could be any woman whom he, king of Asia, could not prevail upon to marry such a son as his, by entreaties, by gold, by gifts, by the whole of that great kingdom, the eventual inheritance of the sick prince, which the father would give to him even now, if he wished it, in order to save him. Desiring to learn only one

---

[24]Appian, *Syriaca*, trans. Horace White. From *The Roman History of Appian of Alexandria*, Vol. 1 (New York: Macmillan Company, 1899), pp. 317–320.

thing more, he asked, "Who is this woman?" Erasistratus replied, "He is in love with my wife." "Well then, my good fellow," rejoined Seleucus, "since you are so bound to us by friendship and favors, and have few equals in goodness and wisdom, will you not save this princely young man for me, the son of your friend and king, unfortunate in love but virtuous, who has concealed his sinful passion and prefers to die rather than confess it? Do you so despise Antiochus? Do you despise his father also?" Erasistratus resisted and said, as though putting forward an unanswerable argument, "Even you would not give Antiochus your wife if he were in love with her, although you are his father." Then Seleucus swore by all the gods of his royal house that he would willingly and cheerfully give her and make himself an illustrious example of the kindness of a good father to a chaste son who controlled his passion and did not deserve such suffering. Much more he added of the same sort and, finally, began to lament that he could not himself be physician to his unhappy boy but must needs depend on Erasistratus in this matter also.

61. When Erasistratus saw by the king's earnestness that he was not pretending, he told the whole truth. He related how he had discovered the nature of the malady and how he had detected the secret passion. Seleucus was overjoyed, but it was a difficult matter to persuade his son and not less so to persuade his wife; but he succeeded finally. Then he assembled his army, which perhaps by now suspected something, and told them of his exploits and of the extent of his empire, showing that it surpassed that of any of the other successors of Alexander, and saying that as he was now growing old it was hard for him to govern it on account of its size. "I wish," he said, "to divide it, in the interests of your future safety, and to give a part of it now to those who are dearest to me. It is fitting that all of you, who have advanced to such greatness of dominion and power under me since the time of Alexander, should cooperate with me in everything. The dearest to me, and well worthy to reign, are my grown-up son and my wife. As they are young, I pray they may soon have children to aid in guarding the empire. I join them in marriage in your presence and send them to be sovereigns of the upper provinces now. The law which I shall impose upon you is not the customs of the Persians and other nations, but the law which is common to all, that what the king ordains is always right." When he had thus spoken, the army shouted that he was the greatest king of all the successors of Alexander and the best father. Seleucus laid the same injunctions on Stratonice and his son, then joined them in marriage and sent them to their kingdom, showing himself even stronger in this famous act than in his deeds of arms.

9.5.9   The Marriage Contract Of Heracleides and Demetria (311 B.C.)[25]

Seventh year of the reign of Alexander, the son of Alexander, fourteenth year of the satrapy of Ptolemy, month of Dius. Marriage contract of Heracleides and Demetria. Heracleides, a freeman, takes as his lawful wife Demetria, a Coan and a freewoman, from her father, Leptines, a Coan, and from her mother, Philotis. Demetria will bring with her clothing and ornaments worth 1,000 drachmas. Heracleides will furnish to Demetria everything that is appropriate for a freewoman. We shall live together in whatever place seems best in the common opinion of Leptines and Heracleides.

---

[25]*P. Elephantine* 1, 2, lines 1–18.

If Demetria shall be detected devising something evil for the purpose of humiliating her husband Heracleides, she shall be deprived of everything she brought to the marriage. Heracleides shall declare whatever charge he brings against Demetria before three men who both approve. Heracleides may not introduce another woman into their home to insult Demetria nor have children from another woman nor devise any evil toward Demetria for any reason. If Heracleides shall be detected doing any of these things and Demetria declares this before three men who both approve, Heracleides shall return to Demetria the dowry of 1,000 drachmas which she brought and he shall pay to her in addition 1,000 silver Alexandrian drachmas. Demetria and those with Demetria shall be able to exact payment, just as though there were a legal judgment, from Heracleides himself and from all of Heracleides' property on both land and sea.

This contract shall be wholly valid in every way wherever Heracleides produces it against Demetria, or Demetria and those with Demetria produce it against Heracleides, in order to exact payment. Heracleides and Demetria each have the right to preserve their contracts and to produce the contracts against each other. Witnesses: Cleon, a Gelan; Anticrates, a Temnian; Lysis, a Temnian; Dionysius, a Temnian; Aristomachus, a Cyrenean; Aristodicus, a Coan.

Chapter 10

Political Culture of the Roman Republic

Monarchy was succeeded by aristocracy in Rome near the end of the sixth century B.C. (the traditional date is 509 B.C.). According to ancient legend, patricians and plebeians (roughly, upper and lower classes) united under the liberator Brutus to depose the tyrannical king Tarquin the Proud and establish a free republic headed by two annually elected consuls.

The challenge facing the new state was to find a governing formula that would guarantee both order and freedom in the midst of a threatening world. Rome's position at a critical crossing point on the Tiber in central Italy made it a vulnerable target. At an early date its inhabitants had to make up their minds whether they were going to control their borders or be trampled on by whoever happened by. Precisely how and when the Romans made that choice we, unfortunately, do not know, but choose they did. It may well have been as early as the period of the kings, but the commitment was not reversed under the Republic.

The constitution that eventually evolved was a version of *polis*-style government. It possessed a council or senate, and a dual-assembly system. One of these assemblies, the Centuriate Assembly (the *comitia centuriata*), was largely, but not completely, dominated by the upper classes; the other, the Tribal or Plebeian Assembly, was considerably more democratic and popular. (For a look at the Roman political process in action, see "The Complexities of War: Foreign and Domistic Issues" in Chapter 11).

This constitution, viewed in its totality as an integrated political, social, and economic system, was ultimately the source of Rome's extraordinary military strength. It had flexibility yet offered surprising stability. It gave all classes a sense of having something in common. The elites dominated the Centuriate Assembly, the major political offices, and all the military commands, yet the remainder of the people were satisfied with the powers that the Plebeian Assembly and its officers, the tribunes, guaranteed them.

The republican constitution served Rome well, allowing it first to survive and then to conquer. Lessons learned during the period of the Republic (509–31 B.C.) formed the basis for Rome's success during the Empire. Roman political culture, combining elements that stimulated and rewarded ambition, while at the same time preserving political freedom and stability, had the ability to bring out the best—and sometimes the worst—in people not just from Rome and Italy, but ultimately from all over the Mediterranean as well as much of Europe and the Middle East.

10.1 Order and Liberty: The Monarchy and the Republic

Five centuries after the founding of the Republic, the historian Livy composed a history of Rome that began with its glorious, legendary founding and reached to "the dark dawning," *as he put it, of his own day. Livy editorialized a lot, and his reflections on Roman history are colored by the events of his own times: the chaotic and bloody collapse of the Republic and the rise of a new, if veiled, monarchy under Augustus Caesar (27 B.C.–A.D. 14). Livy understood full well the difficulty of maintaining the twin ideals of freedom and order. This reading constitutes the preface to Book 2 of his history. Book 1 dealt with the kings and the overthrow of the last of them, Tarquin. Here he mulls over the problems faced by the new state.*[1]

My theme from now on will be the civil and military affairs of the now free Roman people, their annual magistracies, and the sovereignty of their laws, which are superior in their authority over men.

The haughty insolence of the last king, Tarquin the Proud, had caused this liberty to be all the more welcome. The kings before him, by contrast, had ruled in such a manner that they all might well be regarded as successive founders of at least parts of the city, for each had developed new districts to serve as homes for the population they themselves added. Nor is there any doubt that the very same Brutus who had earned so much glory for expelling this haughty monarchy would have done his country great disservice if, through an over-hasty desire for liberty, he had wrested the kingdom from any of Tarquin's predecessors.

For what would have been the consequence if that rabble of shepherds and vagrants, fugitives from their own countries, having under the protection of an inviolable asylum [*the asylum was established at Rome's founding by Romulus to attract migrants to the new city*] found liberty, or at least impunity, uncontrolled by the fear of royal authority? In such circumstances they would no doubt have been distracted by the demagoguery of tribunes and would have engaged in contests with the patrician rulers. This would have happened before the influence of wives and children, and the love of the soil, all of which take time to develop, had united their affections. The nation, not yet matured, would have been destroyed by discord. Luckily, the tranquil moderation of the government of the kings before Tarquin allowed the people, their strength being now developed, to produce wholesome fruits of liberty.

The origin of liberty may be traced to the limitation of the consuls' powers to a single year rather than to any lessening of the regal power of their office. The first consuls had all the kings' privileges and marks of power with only one exception. Instead of two bundles of rods [*the fasces*], one for each consul, with which to strike terror, there was to be only one between them both.

---

[1] Livy, *History of Rome* Book 2, Preface. Translation based on D. Spillan, *The History of Rome by Titus Livius* (New York, 1867). All the readings from Livy in this chapter are based to some extent on Spillan's translation.

Brutus was, with the agreement of his colleague, first attended by the fasces. Yet he had not been a more zealous asserter of liberty than he was afterwards its guardian. First of all he bound the people, still enraptured with their newly acquired liberty, by an oath that they would allow no one to be king in Rome, lest afterwards they might be corrupted by the appeals or bribes of the royal family. Next, in order that a full-strength Senate should enjoy greater authority, he filled its depleted ranks to the amount of 300. Its numbers had been reduced by the murderous activity of Tarquin. To do so he chose men from among the principal ranks of the equestrian order [*the rank immediately below the Senate*]. From now on it is said that the custom was handed down of summoning to the Senate both those who were Fathers (*patres*), and those who were later enrolled (the so-called *conscripti*). This latter term was the designation of those who were elected into the Senate as conscripts. This measure was enormously effective in promoting the concord of the state and in attaching the affection of the plebeians to the patricians.

10.2   The Importance of Concord: Secession and Concession

The importance of concord runs as a theme throughout Livy's history of early Rome. It is emphasized at the end of the previous reading, as we have seen. The great internal social and political problem of the early Republic was the degree to which political power would be divided between the upper-class patricians and the remainder of society. Some kind of equitable solution had to be worked out or the state would not survive. In this reading, Livy tells the traditional story of a major development in this process, the emergence of the plebeian branch of government, the Plebeian Assembly (the Concilium Plebis*), and the office of tribune of the plebs.*[2]

The city was in a state of internal discord. Hatred burned between patricians and plebeians, chiefly on account of those who had been forced into a kind of slavery to their creditors because of debt. These complained noisily that, while fighting abroad for liberty and dominion, they were enslaved and oppressed at home by their fellow citizens. They said that the liberty of the people was more secure in war than in peace, and among their enemies than at home.

This growing resentment was further aggravated by the striking sufferings of one individual. An old man, with all the signs of his misfortunes, flung himself into the Forum. His clothes were squalid and his body still more shocking, being pale and emaciated. His long beard and hair gave the impression of savage wildness to his face. Despite his appearance, he was still recognized as a veteran centurion. People standing around him recalled openly his military awards, and he himself showed the scars on his chest which bore witness to his honorable service in battle.

When he was asked the reason for the squalor of his dress and the condition of his body, the people now having gathered around him like a small assembly, he replied: "During the Sabine War the enemy deprived me of my crops, destroyed my home, and drove off my cattle.

---

[2]Livy 2.23, 31–33. The Centuriate Assembly was presided over by consuls or praetors who had been elected by this assembly. Tribunes of the plebs presided over the Plebeian Assembly, and patricians could not attend. A later modification of the Plebeian Assembly, the Tribal Assembly, differed from the Plebeian Assembly only in so far as it was convened by consuls or praetors and patricians could attend.

Then at this awful moment, taxes became due. I borrowed to pay them and thus fell into debt. This debt, increased by interest, stripped me first of my father's and grandfather's farms, and then of all my other property. Finally, like a disease, ruin spread even to my body. I was taken by my creditor, not to slavery, but to prison and the rack." He then showed them his back disfigured with the marks of recent beatings.

At this a great uproar resulted and spread from the Forum all over the city. Debtors who were already enslaved, and those who were still free, rushed into the streets from all quarters to beg the protection of the people. Everywhere people joined in, running through the streets to the Forum in noisy crowds. The senators who happened to be in the Forum and fell in with the mob were in great danger. Nor would the crowd have refrained from violence had not the consuls, Publius Servilius and Appius Claudius, hurriedly intervened to put down the disturbance. But the mob turned on them and showed them their chains and other marks of misery. These, they said in bitterness, were their rewards for campaigns. Each recounted his individual experiences. They demanded, more with threats than requests, that the consuls convene the Senate. They then surrounded the Senate House itself so that they could both witness and direct the debate.

The Senate assembled, but its debate was interrupted by a series of invasions by neighboring peoples. People and Senate agreed to shelve the debt issue momentarily and fend off the invasion, since, as the consul pointed out, the debt issue concerned only a part of the community whereas the war threatened everyone. Nevertheless discontent continued and the people began to hold secret meetings to plan political actions to free themselves from patrician coercion. The last invasion was so serious, and the Romans so disunited, that the Senate was forced to employ the emergency powers of a dictator. By way of reassurance for the plebs, who felt even more vulnerable to a dictator than to the regular consuls, a popular figure, Manlius Valerius, was appointed to the office. Valerius promised to fix the debt issue when the war was over. The story resumes after the army returned victorious.

Although a triple victory had been won, patricians and plebeians were still uneasy about affairs on the home front. The money-lenders, with great cunning and the assistance of powerful interests, set out to frustrate not only the people, but even the dictator [*Valerius*] himself.

As soon as the consul Vetustius had returned to Rome, Valerius brought up before the Senate as the first item of business the matter of the common people who had been victorious in the recent campaign. He moved that the Senate decide on a policy regarding people who had been bound over for debt. The motion failed. Valerius then addressed the Senate: "You reject me, an advocate of concord. Yet I tell you that you will soon wish that the Roman plebs had patrons like me to deal with. For my part, I will neither further disappoint my fellow citizens, nor will I be a dictator to no purpose. Internal dissensions and foreign wars made the office of dictator a necessity. Peace has been secured abroad but aborted at home. I prefer to play my part as a private citizen when the revolution comes." Then, leaving the Senate House, he abdicated the dictatorship. It was clear to the commons that he had resigned the office because of his indignation at the treatment they had received. Accordingly, as if his commitments to them had been kept, since it was clear it had not been his fault that he had not been able to make good on his promises, the people escorted him home with applause and signs of approval.

Fear seized the patricians, since, if the army was dismissed, secret meetings and conspiracies would once more occur. Accordingly, under the pretext that the Aequi had started hostilities again, they ordered the legions to be led out of the city. The army had been raised by the dictator, but the oath had been sworn to the consuls [*who were still in office*], so presumably the soldiers were still bound by their oath. This maneuver backfired and instead had the effect of accelerating the revolt. At first there was talk, it is said, of killing the consuls and by this means obtaining liberation from the oath, but being told that no religious obligation could be shuffled off by a criminal act, on the suggestion of a man named Sicinius, and without orders from the consuls, the army withdrew to the Sacred Mount across the River Anio, about three miles from the city. . . . There, without any leader, they made a camp with a rampart and trench and remained quietly for several days, taking nothing but what was necessary for their sustenance. They neither received nor gave any provocation.

There was a great panic in the city. All business came to a standstill due to fear. The plebs who were left in the city dreaded the violence of the patricians, and the patricians dreaded the people, uncertain whether they wanted them to stay or leave. The main question was how long the multitude who had left would remain quiet. What were the consequences if, in the meantime, any foreign war should break out? Assuredly, there was no hope left except concord among all the citizens. This had to be restored to the state whether by fair or foul means.

It was resolved, therefore, that Menenius Agrippa, an eloquent man and one who was a favorite with the people because he was himself of plebeian origin, should be sent as ambassador to the people. Being admitted to their camp, he is said to have simply told them the following story in the primitive style of those far-off days:

> There was a time when all the parts of the human body did not as now agree together, but each part had its own scheme and its own ideas. Some of the parts were indignant that everything was procured for the stomach by their care, labor, and service but that the stomach, remaining quiet, did nothing but enjoy the pleasures provided it. They conspired accordingly that the hands would not convey food to the mouth, nor the mouth receive it when presented, nor the teeth chew it. While they sought in their resentment to starve the stomach into submission, the members and the whole body were reduced to the last degree of emaciation. Hence it became apparent that the service of the stomach was not an idle task, that it did not so much receive nourishment as supply it, sending to all parts of the body this blood by which we live and possess vigor, distributed equally to the veins when perfected by the digestion of the food.

By comparing in this way the internal sedition of the body to the resentment of the people against the patricians, he made an impression on the minds of the multitude. Steps were taken toward concord, and a compromise on these terms was brought about:

> That the commons should have their own magistrates [*the tribunes of the plebs*], with inviolable privileges [*the tribunes were to possess* sacrosanctitas, *"inviolability"*], who should have the power of bringing aid against the consuls and that it should not be lawful for any patrician to hold that office.

Two tribunes of the plebs, Gaius Licinius and Lucius Albinus, were accordingly chosen. They in turn appointed three colleagues, one of whom was the Sicinius who had started the revolt. Who the other two were is uncertain. Some authors believe that only two tribunes were elected on the Sacred Mount and that the law of inviolability (the *lex sacrata*) was enacted there.

10.3   Values that Made Rome Great

The public realm—religion, politics, war, law, and administration—was of preeminent importance at Rome. Private affairs were supposed to be subordinate to public. The majesty of the state and its survival were paramount. Basic to the constitution was the principle salus populi suprema lex, "The safety of the people is the supreme law." *In this regard the first safeguard of the state was religion, the* pax deorum, *the friendly relationship between the gods and the people of Rome. Hence the central role of the rituals of the state's public religion; but the private rituals of the individual families were also thought to be vital. Other moral qualities Romans thought significant were the ability to succeed on the battlefield, in politics, and in law—generically termed "virtue" (virtus in Latin). However, until toward the end of the Republic, individual Romans were expected to, and largely did, seek fame and glory, dignity, honor, and wealth for the sake of the state and their families rather than for their own personal benefit. Prized above all were the values of dependability, or trustworthiness, and bravery.*

10.3.1   "All Things Went Well When We Obeyed the Gods, but Badly When We Disobeyed Them": The Speech of Camillus

In 390 B.C. the Roman army was defeated and Rome itself captured and sacked by a marauding band of Celts. The traditional explanation was that the generals had not performed the proper rituals before the battle. The catastrophe was a turning point in the history of the city, psychologically and politically. However, in the aftermath of the disaster there was talk of moving to a new site, the recently captured Etruscan city of Veii. The idea was squelched by the dictator Camillus, who pointed out that Rome was forever tied by its religious connections to the site on which the city had been originally founded "with all due auguries and auspices."[3]

"When you see such striking instances of the effects of honoring or neglecting the divine, do you not see what an act of impiety you are about to perpetrate, and indeed, just at the moment we are emerging from the shipwreck brought about by our former irreligiosity? We have a city founded with all due observance of the auspices and augury. Not a spot in it is without religious rites and gods. Not only are the days for our sacrifices fixed, but also the places where they are to be performed.

"Romans, would you desert all these gods, public as well as private? Contrast this proposal with the action that occurred during the siege and was beheld with no less admiration by the enemy than by yourselves? This was the deed performed by Gaius Fabius, who descended from the citadel, braved Gallic spears, and performed on the Quirinal Hill the solemn rites of the

---

[3]Livy 5.52–54.

Fabian family. Is it your wish that the family religious rites should not be interrupted even during war but that the public rites and the gods of Rome should be deserted in time of peace? Do you want the Pontiffs and Flamens to be more negligent of public ritual than a private individual in the anniversary rite of a particular family?

"Perhaps someone may say that either we will perform these duties at Veii or we will send our priests from there to perform the rituals here—but neither can be done without infringing on the established forms of worship. For not to enumerate all the sacred rites individually and all the gods, is it possible at the banquet of Jupiter for the *lectisternium* [see "Steadiness of the Romans: How They Coped with Defeat" in Chapter 11] to be set up anywhere else other than the Capitol? What shall I say of the eternal fire of Vesta, and of the statue which, as the pledge of empire, is kept under the safeguard of the temple [*the statue of Athena, the Palladium, supposed to have been brought by Aeneas from Troy*]? What, O Mars Gradivus, and you, Father Quirinus—what of your sacred shields? Is it right that these holy things, some as old as the city itself, some of them even more ancient, be abandoned on unconsecrated ground?

"Observe the difference existing between us and our ancestors. They handed down to us certain sacred rites to be performed by us on the Alban Mount and at Lavinium. It was felt to be impious to transfer these rites from enemy towns to Rome—yet you think you can transfer them to Veii, an enemy city, without sin! . . .

"We talk of sacred rituals and temples—but what about priests? Does it not occur to you what a sacrilege you are proposing to commit in respect of them? The Vestals have but one dwelling place, which nothing ever caused them to leave except the capture of the city. Shall your Virgins forsake you, O Vesta? And shall the Flamen by living abroad draw on himself and on his country such a weight of guilt every night [*the Flamen was supposed to never leave Rome*]? What of the other things, all of which we transact under auspices within the Pomerium [*the sacred boundary around Rome*]? To what oblivion, to what neglect do we consign them? The Curiate Assembly, which deals with questions of war; the Centuriate Assembly at which you elect consuls and military tribunes—when can they be held under auspices except where they are accustomed to be held? Shall we transfer them to Veii? Or shall the people, for the sake of the assemblies, come together at great inconvenience in this city, deserted by gods and men? . . .

"Not without good cause did gods and men select this place for the founding of a city. These most healthful hills, a convenient river by means of which the produce of the soil may be conveyed from the inland areas, by which supplies from overseas may be obtained, close enough to the sea for all purposes of convenience, yet not exposed by being too close to the danger of foreign fleets. Situated in the center of Italy, it is singularly adapted by nature for the growth of a city. The very size of so new a city is itself proof. Citizens, it is now in its 365th year. Throughout those years you have been at war with many ancient nations. Not to mention single states, neither the Volscians combined with the Aequi, together with all their powerful towns, not all Etruria, so powerful by land and sea, occupying the breadth of Italy between the Tyrrhenian and Adriatic seas, have been a match for you in war. Since this is so, why in the name of goodness do you want to experiment elsewhere when you had such good fortune here? Though your courage may go with you, the fortune of this place certainly cannot be transferred. Here is the Capitol, where a human head was found which foretold that in that place would be the head of the world, the chief seat of empire [*a play on words; head in Latin is* caput]. Here, when the Capitol was being cleared with augural rites, the gods

Juventas and Terminus, to the great joy of your fathers, refused to be moved. Here is the fire of Vesta, here the sacred shields of Mars which fell from heaven. Here the gods will be propitious to you—if you stay."

10.3.2 The Glory of Rome Before All Else: Mucius Scaevola

A favorite tale that showed the bravery of Roman citizens and their dedication to the state was the story of Mucius Scaevola, "Lefty Mucius." The event is assigned to the period not long after the Romans drove out the kings. Rome is under siege by the Etruscan king Lars Porsena. His aim is to reinstall the deposed Tarquin.[4]

The blockade went on. . . . There was shortage of food, and what was available went for a very high price. Porsena's hopes began to rise that by continuing the siege he could take the city. Then a certain Gaius Mucius, a young Roman nobleman, began to think that it was a disgrace that the Roman people, who, when enslaved under kings, had never been confined within their walls in any war with any enemy, now as a free people were being besieged by these very Etruscans whose armies they had often routed in the past. He made up his mind that such an indignity should be avenged by some great and daring effort.

At first he planned, of his own accord, to make his way into the enemy's camp. However, he was afraid that if he went without the permission of the consuls or the knowledge of anyone, he might be seized by the Roman guards and brought back as a deserter. Indeed, the circumstances of the city at the time would have justified the charge. Accordingly, he went to the Senate and said: "Fathers, I intend to cross the Tiber and enter the enemy's camp if I can, not as a plunderer or as an avenger of their devastations. I have a greater deed in mind if the gods permit."

The Senate approved his plan. He set out with a sword concealed under his clothing, and when he arrived at the enemy's camp, he stood among the thickest of the crowd, near the king's tribunal. There the soldiers were receiving their pay, and the king's secretary sitting by him was dressed nearly in the same style as the king. He was very busy, and the soldiers, for the most part, seemed to talk to him. Being afraid to ask which of the two was Porsena, lest by not knowing the king he should betray himself, as fortune would have it Mucius killed the secretary rather than the king.

As he tried to escape through the frightened crowd, making a way for himself with his bloody sword, he was seized by the king's guards. They dragged him back before the king's tribunal. Though alone and in clearly desperate circumstances, yet he was one more to be feared than fearing. "I am a Roman citizen," he said. "Gaius Mucius is my name. I am your enemy and I came to slay you. I have no less resolution in suffering death than I had in inflicting it. Both to act and endure with courage is the Roman way. Nor have I alone harbored such feelings toward you. There is after me a long line of persons aspiring to the same honor. Therefore, if you choose it, prepare yourself for this peril, to contend for your life every hour, always to have the sword and the enemy in the very entrance of your pavilion. This is the war which we, the Roman youth, declare against you. Fear not an army in array, nor in battle. It will be between you alone with each of us singly."

---

[4]Livy 2.12–13.

Porsena, angry and at the same time frightened, ordered Mucius to be flung into the flames unless he revealed the plot thus obscurely hinted at. Mucius replied, "See how cheaply men hold their bodies when they hope to gain great glory." And with that he thrust his right hand into the fire that was lighted for the sacrifice and let it burn there as though unconscious of the pain. Porsena, astonished at this surprising sight, leaped from the throne and commanded the young man to be removed from the altar. "Go free," he said, "you who have acted more as an enemy to yourself than toward me. I would encourage you to persevere in your courage if that courage were on behalf of my country. I now dismiss you untouched and unhurt, exempted from the penalties of war." Then Mucius, as if making a return for the kindness, said: "Since bravery is honored by you, in gratitude I will give you the information which you could obtain by threats. Three hundred of us, the foremost youths in Rome, have conspired to attack you in this fashion. It was my lot to go first. The rest will follow, each in his turn, as the lot shall send him forward, until Fortune shall have delivered you into our hands."

The release of Mucius, who henceforth was known as Scaevola [*left-handed*] because of the loss of his right hand, was followed by ambassadors from Porsena to Rome. The risk of the first attempt, from which nothing but the mistake of the assailant had saved him, and the prospect of repeated encounters with more conspirators, made so strong an impression on Porsena that of his own accord he made proposals of peace to Rome. . . .

10.3.3 "The Laws of War and Peace": The Schoolmaster of Falerii

The incident recounted here occurred during the siege of Falerii, a town near Rome, sometime before the Gallic invasion of 390 B.C. The story gives Livy an opportunity to preach a sermon on the ideal of a just war, fair dealing, fidelity (fides), honor, and responsibility toward conquered peoples. Despite Livy's idealization, the tale highlights a genuine principle of Roman statecraft. The survival of Rome, as well as its expansion, was as much a function of diplomacy and calculated self-interest as one of successful military campaigns. Rome needed not only to win wars but also to rule justly afterwards.[5]

A regular blockade of Falerii began and the usual siege works were constructed. Occasionally attacks were made by the townsmen on the Roman positions, and small skirmishes took place. Time passed and there did not seem much hope of either side prevailing. The besieged, having collected grain in abundance beforehand, possessed more supplies than did the besiegers. It began to look as though the siege would be as long as that of Veii, when fortune presented to the Roman general at one stroke both a quick victory and an opportunity for displaying the nobility he had already demonstrated in previous wars.

It was the custom among the people of Falerii to employ the same person as teacher and guardian for their children, as in Greece today a number of boys are entrusted to the care of one man. Naturally enough, responsibility for the children of the leading families of the city was given to the most distinguished teacher. This man, during peace, had established the custom of taking the boys out beyond the city for the sake of play and exercise, and he continued this practice after the war began. Sometimes he went a shorter distance from the gate,

---

[5]Livy 5.27.

sometimes a longer, entertaining them with this or that game or story. Being farther away one day than usual, he seized the opportunity to bring the boys through the enemy's outposts, right to the Roman camp and to the headquarters of Camillus. There he compounded his treacherous act with an even more treacherous allegation, claiming that he had in fact delivered Falerii into the hands of the Romans when he put into their power those children whose parents were in control of affairs there.

When he heard this Camillus answered: "Unscrupulous as you are, you come with your vile proposal neither to a people nor to a commander like you. Between us and the Faliscans, it is true, there does not exist a relationship of treaties and contracts, but there does exist, and indeed always will exist, that common humanity which nature has established. There are laws of war as well as of peace, and we have learned to wage them justly not less than bravely. We carry arms not against children, who are spared even when towns are taken, but against men who are themselves armed, and who, having been injured or provoked by us, attacked the Roman camp at Veii. You have succeeded in surpassing these by this unprecedented act of villainy. I shall conquer the Faliscans, as I did the people of Veii, by the Roman arts of bravery, labor, and arms." Then having stripped the schoolmaster and tied his hands behind his back, he gave him to the schoolboys to be brought back to Falerii. He also gave them rods to beat the traitor as they drove him to the city.

To see the sight, a crowd gathered at Falerii, and afterwards the senate of the city was convened by the magistrates to consider the strange affair. So great a change was produced in their sentiments that the entire state earnestly demanded peace from the hands of those who lately, in the fury of their hate and resentment, almost preferred the fate of Veii [*i.e., capture and destruction*] to that of Capena [*a nearby city given federate status by Rome*]. Roman trustworthiness [*fides*] and the justice of the commander were praised in the Forum and the Senate House. By universal agreement, ambassadors set out for the camp of Camillus and from there, by permission of Camillus, to Rome to the Senate to present the submission of Falerii.

When introduced to the Senate, they are said to have spoken in this way: "Conscript Fathers, you and your commander have won a victory over us with which no one, neither god nor man, could find displeasure. We surrender ourselves to you, believing that we will live more happily under your rule than under our own law. Nothing, surely, can be more glorious for a conqueror. As a result of this war, two salutary examples have been exhibited to mankind. You preferred faith in war to an opportunisitic victory. We, challenged by your good faith, have voluntarily given up to you the victory. We are under your sovereignty. Send representatives to receive our arms, our hostages, our city with its open gates. You shall never have to repent of our trustworthiness [*fides*], nor we of your rule [*imperium*]."

10.3.4   Fame, Family, and Self-promotion: The Roman Funeral

Polybius, a prominent Greek soldier and statesman, was brought to Rome in 168 B.C. as a hostage for the good behavior of his native state, the Achaean League. At Rome he was befriended by a young nobleman, Scipio Aemilianus, who later became famous for his capture of Carthage and Numantia. With a ringside seat from which to view the unfolding events of Roman history, Polybius set about explaining to the world Rome's rise to Power. In this excerpt he describes how the Roman upper-class family functioned to promote itself and socialize its younger members. It is found in the section of Book 6 that compares the Roman constitution with others, such as those of Carthage, Sparta, and elsewhere.[6]

Whenever one of their illustrious men dies, in the course of his funeral the body with all of its paraphernalia is carried into the Forum to the Rostra, as the raised platform there is called. Sometimes he is propped upright on it so as to be conspicuous, or, more rarely, he is laid flat on it. Then, with all the people of Rome standing around, his son, if he has one of full age and he happens to be in Rome, or failing him, one of his relatives, mounts the Rostra and delivers a speech about the virtues of the dead man and the successful deeds performed by him in his life.

By these means the people are reminded of what the deceased accomplished and are made to see it with their own eyes—not only those who were involved in the actual deeds, but those also who were not—and their sympathies are so deeply moved that the loss appears not to be confined to the actual mourners but to be a public one affecting the whole people.

After the burial and all the usual ceremonies have been performed, they place the likeness of the deceased in the most conspicuous spot in his house, surmounted by a wooden canopy or shrine. This likeness consists of a mask made to represent the deceased with extraordinary fidelity both in shape and color. These likenesses they display at public sacrifices, and they decorate them with much care.

Also when any notable member of the family dies, they carry these masks to the funeral, putting them on men who seem most like those whose masks they wear in terms of height and other personal characteristics. And these substitutes assume clothes according to the rank of the person represented. If he was a consul or praetor, for example, a toga with purple stripes is worn; if a censor, a wholly purple toga; if he had also celebrated a triumph or performed any exploit of that kind, a toga embroidered with gold. These representatives also ride in chariots, while the fasces and axes and all the other customary insignia of the particular offices lead the way, according to the dignity of the rank in the state enjoyed by the deceased in his lifetime. On arriving at the Rostra, they all take their seats on ivory chairs in a row. There could not easily be a more inspiring spectacle than this for a young man of noble ambitions or virtuous aspirations. For can we conceive anyone to be unmoved at the sight of all the likenesses collected together of the men who have earned glory, all, as it were, living and breathing? Or what could be a more glorious spectacle?

Furthermore, as soon as the speaker who gives the eulogy over the person about to be buried finishes, he then immediately starts upon the others whose representatives are present, beginning with the most ancient, and recounts the successes and achievements of each. By this means the glorious memory of brave men is continually renewed; the fame of those who have performed any noble deed is never allowed to die, and the renown of those who have done good service to their country becomes a matter of common knowledge to the multitude and part of the heritage of posterity.

But the chief benefit of the ceremony is that it inspires young men to shrink from no exertion for the general welfare, in the hope of obtaining the glory which awaits the brave. And what I say is confirmed by this fact. Many Romans have volunteered to decide a whole battle

---

[6]Polybius 6.53–54. Translation based on E. S. Shuckburg, *Polybius: The Histories* (London and New York, 1889).

by single combat. Not a few have deliberately accepted certain death, some in time of war to secure the safety of the rest, some in time of peace to preserve the safety of the commonwealth. There also have been instances of men in office putting their own sons to death, in defiance of every custom and law, because they rated the interests of their country higher than those of natural ties, even with their nearest and dearest. . . .

10.3.5   Money-Making, Religion, Bribery

After the discussion of the function of the Roman funeral, Polybius moves on to compare Roman customs in matters of money, religion, and bribery with those of other states. His discussion of Roman religion, however, is marred by his pedantic application of commonplace Greek rationalization to the subject. Unlike the Hellenistic Greeks of Polybius's day, the Romans still took their gods and rituals seriously.[7]

Again the Roman customs and principles regarding money transactions are better than those of the Carthaginians. In the view of the latter, nothing is disgraceful that makes for gain; with the former nothing is more disgraceful than to receive bribes and to make a profit by improper means, for they disapprove of wealth obtained unlawfully as much as they approve of the art of gaining wealth honorably. A proof of the fact is this. The Carthaginians obtain office by open bribery, but among the Romans the penalty for this is death. With such a radical difference, therefore, between the rewards offered to virtue among the two peoples, it is natural that the ways adopted for obtaining them should be different also.

But the most important difference for the better which the Roman commonwealth seems to me to display is in their religious belief. For I think that what in other nations is looked upon as a reproach, I mean a scrupulous fear of the gods, is the very thing that keeps the Roman commonwealth together. Religious celebrations are accompanied by extraordinary pomp and are pervasive to such an extent in their public and private life that nothing could exceed them. This may surprise many, but in my opinion their object is to use this as a check upon the masses. If it were possible to form a state wholly of philosophers, such a practice would perhaps be unnecessary. But seeing that every crowd is fickle and full of lawless desires, unreasoning anger, and violent passion, the only recourse is to keep them in check by mysterious terrors and the ceremonial pageantry in which the Romans excel. Wherefore to my mind the ancients were not acting without purpose or at random when they introduced to the masses beliefs about the gods and about the punishments of Hades. Much rather do I think that men nowadays are acting rashly and foolishly in rejecting them.

This is the reason why, apart from anything else, Greek statesmen, if entrusted with a single talent, though protected by ten checking clerks, as many seals, and twice as many witnesses, cannot be induced to stay honest, whereas among the Romans, in their magistracies and embassies, men have the handling of a great amount of money and yet, from pure respect for their oath of office, have stayed honest. And again, in other nations it is rare to find a man who keeps his hands out of the public purse and is entirely above reproach in such matters. But among the Romans it is a rare thing to detect a man in the act of committing such a crime.

---

[7]Polybius, 6.56. Translation based on Shuckburg, *Polybius: The Histories.*

10.4   Getting Elected: Techniques for the Candidate

Getting elected to office in Rome was as calculated a procedure as winning an election in modern times. It required visibility, a vast network of friends, money, and a good memory for names and faces. It also required a thorough knowledge of what motivated the electorate and how the electoral system worked. Rome's dual system of government, the Patrician State, and the Plebeian State, was a complicated affair. The Centuriate Assembly, which annually elected consuls and praetors, was structured in favor of the well-to-do on the principle that the rich, having more responsibilities than the poor, deserved more votes. "We weigh votes, not count them," said Cicero. On the other hand, the Plebeian Assembly, which elected tribunes and passed most laws, was more democratic and tended to reflect the needs of the majority of Romans. Its officers, the tribunes, with their powers of veto and intercession, could, potentially at least, provide the masses with protection from rich and powerful interests and from an overly intrusive government. The following reading is in the form of a letter addressed to Marcus Cicero by his brother Quintus. The passage reveals the intensely personal nature of Roman politics; the practical side of Roman-style friendship; how free legal representation in court was repaid by support at the polls; the kind of open house Romans active in the political system were expected to maintain; and the intense networking which was at the core of the political system. Tribes, it should be noted, were geographical areas, not kinship groups.[8]

Networking Relatives and Friends

Canvass for office comes down to activities of two kinds, one of which is securing the loyalty of friends. The other deals with the concerns and feelings of the People. The loyalty of friends must be secured by acts of kindness and attention, by length of time spent with them, and by an easy and pleasant temper. It is a great advantage to be popular among those who are friends on the usual grounds of blood or marriage relationships, membership in the same club or some other close tie. You must make a great effort to see that all who are close to you and your household should love you and desire your highest honor. These would be, for instance, your fellow tribesmen, your neighbors, clients, freedmen and even your slaves, for nearly all the talk which shapes public opinion about you comes from domestic sources [*i.e., if you don't run your household well your reputation is likely to be affected*].

You must secure friends in every class. Some of these will be for show, such as men well known because of their office or name, who, even if they do not give any actual assistance in your electioneering, yet add some dignity to your candidature. Others again are those useful for securing the votes of the centuries, men of high popularity. Take pains to win and secure those who either have gained or hope to gain the vote of a tribe or century or any other advantage through your influence. Do your best to make sure such men are attached to you from the bottom of their hearts and with complete devotion.

In the course of a canvass, you can acquire numerous useful new friendships. For among its annoyances an election has this advantage: you can, without loss of dignity, as you cannot in other affairs of life, admit whomsoever you choose to your friendship. These are the kind of people who you could not at any other time befriend without looking foolish, whereas during a canvass, if you don't befriend and take pains about it, you will be thought to be no use as a candidate at all. Moreover, I can assure you that there is no one, unless he happens to be tied by some special relationship to one of your rivals, whom you could not induce, if you made the

---

[8]*Electioneering Handbook*, 13–55.

effort, to earn your affection by his good services, and to seize the opportunity of putting you under an obligation. Let him fully understand that you value him highly, that you really mean what you say, that he is making a good investment, and that there will result from the relationship not just a brief electioneering kind of friendship, but a firm and lasting one. There will be no one, believe me, if he has anything in him at all, who will let slip this opportunity of making a friendship with you, especially when by good luck you have competitors whose friendship is to be neglected or avoided. . . .

Motivating the Electorate

Men are mainly induced to demonstrate good will and energy in the election process by three considerations: benefits received in the past; hope of benefits to come; and personal affection and good feeling. We should therefore examine these factors to see how we can take advantage of each of them. First, some men are encouraged by very small favors to think they have sufficient reason for supporting you at the ballot-box. Those you have actually saved by your advocacy (and their number is large) cannot fail to understand that if they fail at this critical moment to support you, they will never have anyone's confidence. However, even though this is the case, they still need to be appealed to and must be led to think it possible that whereas they have up until now been under obligation to you, they may now, as it were, put you under obligation to them.

As for your genuine friends, you will have to make them more secure by expressions of gratitude and by making your words coincide with the motives which influenced them to support you in the first place. . . . In all these cases, consider and weigh carefully the amount of influence each possesses in order to estimate the degree of attention needed to be paid to each, and what you can expect in return. For some men are popular in their own neighborhoods and towns and others have energy and wealth, who, even if they have not up to this point sought popularity, yet could easily obtain it for the sake of one to whom they owe, or wish to do a favor, namely, in this instance, yourself. You must make it plain in your attention to these men that you clearly understand what is to be expected from each, that you appreciate what you are receiving, and will remember what you have received.

Identifying the Voters

So see that you have the votes of all the centuries won for you by the number and variety of your friends. The first and most obvious step is to canvass senators and knights [*the second rank of the elite*], and the active and popular men in all the other orders of society. There are many hard-working city men and freedmen engaged in business who are popular and energetic. You will be able by your efforts and through common friends, to win them to your side. See that they are enthusiastic about you. Work hard, seek them out, send friends to them, show them that they are putting you under the greatest obligation. After that review the entire city, all the clubs, districts, neighborhoods. If you can attach their leading men to yourself, you will through these men easily be able to keep a hold on the electorate. Next you must have in your mind a map of all Italy laid out according to the tribe of each town, and learn it by heart, so that you may not allow any municipality, colony, prefecture, or, in a word, any place in Italy, to exist in which you have not an adequate foothold. . . .

The Daily Canvass

You should be very careful to receive every day a large number of every class and order in your home, for from the mere number of these others will be guessing the amount of support you are likely to have among the electorate at large. Such visitors are of three kinds. The first are the morning callers, the second those who escort you to the forum and third those who actually attend you during your canvass. The first are a less select crowd and tend to come in larger numbers. Nevertheless you must contrive to make them think that you value even this slight attention very highly. Let them see that you notice their presence at your house; mention your appreciation to such of their friends as will be likely to repeat it to them; frequently repeat it to the persons themselves. It often happens that people, when they visit a number of candidates, and observe that there is one who above the rest notices them, then it is to this person they devote themselves. They leave off visiting the others and little by little become devoted to you rather than just being neutral.

As for those who escort you to the forum, since this is more important than the morning calls, let them know that this is still more gratifying to you. As far as possible, go down to the forum at fixed times. The daily escort by its numbers produces a great impression and confers great distinction. The third class are those who actually attend you during your electioneering efforts. See that those who do so spontaneously understand that you regard yourself as forever obliged to their kindness. As for those who owe you this attention remind them, as far as their age and business allow, that they should be in constant attendance on you. People who should be there but cannot, should find relatives to take their place. You should always be surrounded by large numbers. To be accompanied by those whom you have defended, preserved and acquitted in the law courts demonstrates the power of your reputation. Persuade this category of people by reminding them that by your efforts and without pay of any kind, some of them have retained their property, others their honor, others their civil existence and entire fortunes. Since there will never be any other time when they can show their gratitude, they should repay you now by this service.

Dangers

Deception, intrigue and treachery are everywhere . . . your high character has made many pretend to be your friends while they are, in reality, jealous of you. So remember the saying of Epicharmus that the key to wisdom is to believe nothing too easily. When you have made sure of your friends, you must next acquaint yourself regarding what your detractors and opponents are saying. They fall into three classes, those whom you have attacked in the courts; those who dislike you for no identifiable reason; and third those who are friends of your competitors. As for those you attacked while pleading a friend's cause against them, frankly excuse yourself; remind them of the ties constraining you; give them reason to hope that you will act with equal zeal and loyalty in their cases if they become friends with you. Do your best to remove the prejudice of those who dislike you without reason by some actual service or holding out hope of such service, or by demonstrating kindly feelings to them. As for those who oppose you because of their association with your competitors, gratify them by the same means as the others, and if you can get them to believe it, show that you are kindly disposed to the very men who are standing against you.

Winning the Ordinary Folk

As for the people at large, to win them over requires a knack for remembering names, good manners, constant attention, liberality and the ability to convey a hopeful feeling about the condition of the state. Make conspicuous use of the faculty you possess of recognizing people and improve it every day; there is nothing so popular or so influential. Next, if nature has denied you some quality, make up your mind to assume it, so as to appear to be acting naturally. For though you are not lacking in the courtesy which good and polite men should have, yet there is a great need to have a flattering manner which, however discreditable it is in other transactions of life, it is essential during electioneering. Certainly were such activities to affect a person for the worse, they would be wrong; but when all they do is to make a person only more friendly, then they do not deserve to be judged so harshly. . . .

Liberality is a trait of wide application. It is shown in the management of your private property, which, even if it does not actually affect the masses of the voters, yet if spoken of with praise by friends, earns their favor. It may also be displayed at banquets which you must take care to attend yourself and cause your friends to attend, whether open ones or those confined to particular tribes. It may again be displayed in giving practical assistance which you should make available far and wide. Be sure to be accessible day and night, and not only by the doors of your house, but by your expression, which is the door of the mind. If your face shows your feelings to be distant and reserved, it is of little good to have your house doors open. . . .

Chapter 11

War and Warfare

"No sane man," wrote Polybius, "goes to war with his neighbors merely for the sake of defeating them, just as no sane man goes to sea simply to get to the other side." Polybius (212–ca. 118 B.C.), soldier, statesman, and historian, was someone who knew: He was a confidant of one of the great aristocratic families in Rome at a time when Roman war-making was in high gear.

War was a normal feature of Roman life. When, in 235 B.C., the doors of the temple of Janus were closed, symbolizing peace, it was so for the first time in 450 years. Why warfare played so large a role in Roman history is partially explained by the vulnerable position of Rome in the middle of the Italian peninsula, and the presence of other warlike peoples on all sides. Travelers, migrants, and would-be conquerers moving up or down the Italian peninsula had no choice but to pass through or near Rome. Italy as a whole was vulnerable to invasion from the north by Celts and Germans, the former regular visitors who sacked Rome in 390 B.C. The Celts remained troublesome neighbors for centuries afterwards, and the Germans eventually brought down the Roman Empire in the west. Initially, however, the main dangers to Rome came from within Italy itself, especially from the powerful Samnite confederation. There were also threats from elsewhere in the Mediterranean. Carthage challenged Rome for supremacy in the western Mediterranean in the third century, though it eventually lost. Two of the Macedonian kingdoms were perceived by the Romans as threats at different times in the second century. Wars with them led to entanglements in Greece, the Balkans, and the whole eastern end of the Mediterranean.

Warfare was a well-integrated aspect of Roman life. It was not just Rome's legions or its leaders or its ordinary soldiers that made Rome so formidable, though all of these factors were important. It was, rather, the special way in which social, political, moral, and religious elements interacted within the framework of the republican constitution as discussed in Chapter 10. The Republic combined a bewildering and contradictory capacity to exact unquestioning obedience from its conscripts as well as nearly total dedication from its upper classes. It possessed a political system that exercised power quickly and efficiently, and an enviable ability to resolve internal conflicts. At moments when outsiders expected the state to collapse, it grew more compact. The Republic knew how to make and remain faithful to treaties. It understood the art of propaganda and the use of intimidation and terror. Centuries later, writing in about A.D. 390 in the late Empire, the Greek soldier Ammianus Marcellinus could say, "Even as Rome declines into old age, … in every quarter of the world it is still looked upon as the mistress and queen of the earth; the name of the Roman people is respected and venerated."

11.1   The Enemy: A Roman View

The cities that fringed the Mediterranean, whether of Greek, Phoenician, or native origin, were often under pressure from the peoples of the less settled regions behind them. In Italy, the peoples of the mountainous central region pushed down into the rich agricultural plains. From northern Europe came Celts (or Gauls) and Germans, driven out by overpopulation, crop failures, climatic changes, or just attracted by the possibility of booty, good land, and warmer, drier climates. The northern menace was intermittently dangerous, and rightly the one most feared by the Romans and their Italian allies. But on a regular, perennial basis the greatest threat came from the Samnites pressing down from their central mountainous homeland. As early as the fourth century they made their presence felt in Campania. Eventually Rome became the principal champion of the lowlanders and city dwellers of Italy against these marauding highlanders of the interior. Both of the following readings derive from hostile sources intent on painting the enemy in as unfavorable a light as possible.[1]

11.1.1   Celtic Ferocity

In their wanderings and in battle the Celts use chariots drawn by two horses which carry the driver and the warrior. When they meet with cavalry in battle, they first throw their javelins at the enemy and then step down from their chariots and fight with their swords. Some of them so despise death that they enter the dangers of battle naked, wearing only a sword-belt. They bring to war with them their freemen attendants, choosing them from among the poor. They use them in battle as chariot drivers and shield bearers.

They have the custom when they have lined up for combat to step in front of the battle line and challenge the bravest of their enemies to single combat, brandishing their weapons in front of them in an attempt to terrify them. When anyone accepts the challenge to single combat, they sing a song in praise of the great deeds of their ancestors and of their own achievements, at the same time mocking and belittling their opponent, trying by such techniques to destroy his spirit before the fight. When their opponents fall, they cut off their heads and tie them around their horses' necks. They hand over to their attendants the blood-covered arms of their enemies and carry them off as booty, singing songs of victory.

Spoils of war they fasten with nails to their houses, just as hunters do the heads of wild animals they have killed. They embalm the heads of the most distinguished opponents in cedar oil and carefully guard them in chests. They show these heads to visitors, claiming that they or their father or some ancestor had refused large sums of money for this or that head. Some of them, it is said, boast that they have not accepted an equal weight of gold for the head they show, demonstrating a kind of barbarous nobility. Not to sell a thing that constitutes the proof of one's bravery is a noble, well-bred kind of thing, but on the other hand, to continue to ill-treat the remains of a fellow human being after he is dead is bestial.

---

[1]Diodorus Siculus, *The Library of History* 5.29; Livy 10.38.

11.1.2   The Samnite Enemy

The Samnites made their preparations for war [*in 293 B.C.*] with the same dedication and effort as on the former occasion and provided their troops with the most magnificent arms money could buy. They likewise called to their aid the power of the gods by initiating their soldiers in accordance with an ancient form of oath. Under this ordinance they levied troops throughout Samnium, announcing that anyone of military age who did not report in response to the general's proclamation, or who departed without orders, would be dedicated to Jupiter [*i.e., they were "sacred" to Jupiter and could be killed with impunity by anyone meeting them*]. Orders were then issued for all to assemble at Aquilonia, and the whole strength of Samnium came together, amounting to 40,000 men.

At Aquilonia a piece of ground in the middle of the camp was enclosed with hurdles and boards and covered overhead with linen cloth. The sides were of equal length, about 200 feet each. In this place sacrifices were performed according to directions read out of an old linen book. The priest performing the rituals was an old man by the name of Ovius Paccius, who claimed that he took these ceremonies from the ancient ritual of the Samnites and that these were the same rituals that their ancestors had used when they formed the secret design of wresting Capua from the Etruscans.

When the sacrifices were finished, the general ordered an attendant to summon all those who were most distinguished by their birth or conduct. These were brought into the enclosure singly. Besides the other ritual objects of a solemnity calculated to impress the mind with religious awe, there were in the middle of the covered enclosure altars around which lay the slain victims. Centurions stood round about with drawn swords. Each individual was led up to the altars—rather like a victim himself than a performer in the ceremony—and was bound by an oath not to divulge what he should see and hear in this place. He was then compelled to swear according to a dreadful formula containing curses of his own person, his family, and his people if he did not go to battle wherever the commander should lead, if he fled from the field, or if he should see any other fleeing and did not immediately strike him down.

At first, some refused to take the oath and were beheaded around the altars. Lying among the carcasses of the victims, they served afterwards as a warning to others not to refuse. When the leading Samnites had been bound under these solemnities, the general nominated ten of them and made each choose a man, and so on until they had brought up the number to 16,000. This body of men was called the Linen Legion, from the covering of the enclosure wherein the nobility had been sworn. They were furnished with splendid armor and plumed helmets to distinguish them from the rest. Somewhat more than 20,000 men made up another army, which neither in personal appearance nor renown in war or in equipment was inferior to the Linen Legion. This was the size of the Samnite army, comprising the main strength of the nation, that encamped at Aquilonia.

11.2   Roman Ferocity: "Decius . . . Summoning and Dragging to Himself the Army Devoted Along with Him"

Although the Romans were the champions of the more urbanized and presumably more civilized areas of Italy, they were not far removed themselves from the barbarous customs of Celts and Samnites. In the desperate battle of Sentinum in 295 B.C. against a combined army of Gauls and Sarnnites, one of the consuls, Decius Mus, "devoted" himself and his enemies to the gods to win victory. The fact that the act of "Devotio" was a formal state ritual, administered by a properly designated pontiff, and not a private vow, says a lot about the way warfare was waged by Rome during the early Republic.[2]

Twice the Romans compelled the Gallic cavalry to give way. At the second charge, when they advanced farther and were briskly engaged in the middle of the enemy's squadrons, they were thrown into confusion by a method of fighting new to them. A number of the enemy, mounted on chariots and wagons, made toward them with such frightening noise from the trampling of the cattle and the thunder of the wheels that the Roman horses were terrified. The victorious cavalry were scattered in panic; in blind flight men and horses fell to the ground. The disorder spread to the legions, and many of the first ranks were trampled underfoot by the horses and wagons which swept through their ranks. As soon as the Gallic infantry saw their enemy in confusion, they pursued their advantage and did not allow them time to recover themselves.

Decius shouted to his men, asking where they were fleeing to or what hope there was in running away. He tried to stop them as they turned their backs, but finding that he could not persuade them to keep their posts because they were so panicked, he called on his father, Publius Decius. "Why do I postpone any longer the fate of our family?" he cried. "It is destined for us to serve as sacrificial victims to avert dangers to our country. I will now offer the legions of the enemy, together with myself, to be immolated to Earth and the Gods of the Underworld."

Having said this, he ordered Marcus Livius, a priest whom he had ordered not to leave his side when they went into battle, to dictate the form of the ritual in which he was to devote himself and the legions of the enemy on behalf of the army of the Roman people. He was accordingly devoted with the same prayers and in the same dress in which his father, Publius Decius, had ordered himself to be devoted at Vestris during the Latin War. Immediately after the solemn ritual prayers he added the following: "I drive away dread and defeat, slaughter and bloodshed, and the wrath of the gods, celestial and infernal; with the contagious influence of the Furies, the Ministers of Death, I will infect the standards, the weapons, and armor of the enemy. The place of my destruction will be that of the Gauls and Samnites also." After uttering these curses on himself and his foes, he spurred forward his horse where he saw the line of the Gauls was thickest, and, rushing on them, met his death.

From then on the battle seemed to be fought with a degree of force that seemed scarcely human. The Romans . . . stopped their flight . . . and were anxious to begin the fight again. Livius the priest, to whom Decius had transferred his lictors[3] with orders to act as propraetor, cried out aloud that the Romans were victorious, having been saved by the death of the consul, and that the Gauls and the Samnites were now the victims of Mother Earth and the Gods of the Underworld; that Decius was summoning and dragging to himself the army devoted along with him. . . .

11.3   Steadiness of the Romans: How They Coped with Defeat

Rome fought two major wars with Carthage—from 264 to 241 B.C. and from 218 to 201 B.C. The second war, known as the Hannibalic War, after the great Carthaginian general Hannibal, stretched Roman society to the breaking point. In the early years one disaster succeeded another. Two legions here

---

[2]Livy 10.28–29.
[3]Attendants of priests, consuls, and some other magistrates.

lost at Trasimene in 217 B.C., and the following year approximately 50,000 perished at Cannae, although not all the casualties were Roman. Yet somehow Rome managed to survive these catastrophes. Writing more than a century and a half later, Livy noted that the first step taken following a disaster was always religious. After Trasimene, the rituals known as the Lectisternium, the "Strewing of the Couches" (described below), and the Sacred Spring were resorted to. In earlier times the latter involved the dedication to the gods of all offspring, human as well as animal, born in the spring of the designated year. Livy does not mention humans in this Sacred Spring. He was, however, shocked at the rituals resorted to after Cannae, in which two Gauls and two Greeks were buried alive in the Cattle Market. But, as he remarks elsewhere of the early Romans, they were a people born "before scepticism was taught about the gods."[4]

This was Fabius's second Dictatorship, and the day he entered office he convened the Senate. Beginning with religious issues, he pointed out that Flaminius's mistake [*at Trasimene*] derived not so much from rashness and inexperience as from his neglect of the proper rituals. He proposed that the gods themselves should be consulted as to the proper form of appeasement, and he prevailed upon the Senate to direct the Board of Ten to consult the Sibylline Books, a step taken only when events of the most awful kind occurred. The sacred books were duly consulted and the Senate informed of the results: First, the vow made to Mars for the successful prosecution of the war at its start had not been properly performed and would have to be repeated on a larger scale. Second, a performance of the Great Games in honor of Jupiter should be vowed, alone, with a shrine to Venus of Eryx and to Mens. Third, a supplication, a day of public prayer, and a *Lectisternium*, a feast of the gods, should be held. Finally, a Sacred Spring should be vowed if the war went well and the state was returned to its previous, pre-war condition. Since Fabius would be preoccupied with military affairs, the Senate ordered the praetor Marcus Antonius to see that these measures were carried out quickly, under the direction of the College of Pontiffs.

After the passage of these resolutions, L. Cornelius Lentulus, the Pontifex Maximus, gave as his opinion, and was supported by the Board of Praetors, that the first step was to consult the people on the matter of the Sacred Spring. That vow could not be made without their approval. The proposal was put as follows: "Do you wish and order that this undertaking be performed? If the Republic of the people and citizens of Rome shall have been preserved in safety from the present wars five years from now, as indeed I wish that it may . . . then the Roman citizens vow as a gift whatever that spring shall have brought forth from its herds of pigs, flocks of sheep, goat, and oxen. . . ."

At the same time a celebration of the Great Games was vowed and 333,333 asses set aside for the expenses. Three hundred oxen were to be offered to Jupiter, along with white oxen and other victims to many other divinities. The vows were properly made in public, and a supplication was proclaimed. The inhabitants of the city, together with their wives and children, participated and also the rural dwelling people who had property and were concerned with the welfare of the state. The *Lectisternium*, the festival of the gods, was held for three days, under the direction of the Board of Ten. Six couches were set out, one for Jupiter and Juno, another for Neptune and Minerva, a third for Mars and Venus, a fourth for Apollo and Diana; Vulcan

---

[4]Livy 22.7–11.

and Vesta got the fifth couch, and the sixth went to Vulcan and Vesta.[5] Then the temples were vowed. Q. Fabius Maximus the Dictator vowed a temple to Venus of Eryx, for the prophetic books said that the ceremony should be performed by the highest officer of the state. The praetor T. Otacilius vowed a shrine to Mens.

Divine things having been thus attended to, the Dictator then put the question of the war and the state, what and how many legions the Fathers thought were necessary to send against the victorious enemy. . . .

11.4   The Complexities of War: Foreign and Domestic Issues

The steadiness of the Senate during the Hannibalic War gave that body practical control of foreign affairs. However, until at least to the middle of the second century, a vote of the Centuriate Assembly was still a requirement for war, or certainly for a major war against an established power. The complexity of waging war had increased as Rome's power extended overseas and brought it into contact with the Greek and Macedonian world. This was Rome's third war with Macedonia (171–167 B.C.). In the first two introductory sections below, Livy copies from Polybius, the Greek historian and statesman, practically word for word—thus the detailed and incisive description of who was on whose side throughout the Greek world. But he then switches sources to a Roman senatorial account for the remainder of the story. The senatorial viewpoint is most noticeable in the account of how the virtuous centurion, Spurius Ligustinus, after a fine speech, inexplicably and anticlimactically betrays his fellow protesters who had been complaining about the conduct of the draft. Otherwise the source provides an interesting and accurate account of the declaration of war and the recruitment of the army. The roll, and especially the number of allies involved, deserves special attention. Rome, emphatically, did not fight alone.[6]

The Diplomatic Situation: The Kings

When Publius Licinius and Gaius Cassius were consuls (171 B.C.), not only Rome and all of Italy but even all the kings and states in Europe and Asia began to be concerned over the possibility of war between Macedonia and Rome. King Eumenes of Pergamum [*in Turkey*] was motivated by his former enmity against Macedonia. Recently he had been further provoked to anger by an assassination attempt [*by Perseus, King of Macedonia*] on him at Delphi. Prusias, King of Bithynia [*northwest Turkey*], had decided to stay out of the quarrel and await the outcome. Prusias thought, on the one hand, that the Romans would not expect him to take up arms against his wife's brother [*i.e., Perseus*], and, on the other, that if Perseus were beaten he could straighten it out with him through his sister. The king of Cappadocia [*eastern Turkey*], Ariarathes, apart from the fact that he had promised help to the Romans, was tied to the policies of Eumenes of Pergamum in both war and peace because of his marriage connection with that monarch.

Antiochus of Syria was threatening the kingdom of Egypt, seeing, an opportunity in the youth of its king and inactivity of its guardians. He expected to have a cause for war by raising disputes in Lebanon and to be able to wage it without the interference of the Romans, who would be busy in Macedonia. However, for this present war he had promised everything to the Senate through his ambassadors to Rome and personally to Rome's own ambassadors. Ptolemy

---

[5]Statues of the gods were laid on the couches, and food of all kinds was piled up in front of them. It was eaten by the priests who prepared it.
[6]Livy 42.29–35.

[*king of Egypt*], on account of his age, was still under guardians: these were preparing for a war with Antiochus in which they hoped to obtain Lebanon. They too promised Rome everything for the coming war with Macedonia.

Masinissa [*king of Tunisia*] was helping Rome with grain and was getting auxiliaries and elephants ready to send under the command of his son Misagenes. Nevertheless, he was ready for any outcome. If the Romans obtained victory, then nothing would change. He could not, for instance, expand at the expense of the Carthaginians, because Rome would not permit it. But if Rome lost against Perseus, then all Africa would be his. . . .

The Diplomatic Situation: The Free Cities

This is what the kings were thinking regarding the coming war. Among free peoples and cities the masses chose, as usual, the least advantageous side, favoring Perseus and the Macedonian cause. Among the elites there was a division of opinion. Some were so enthralled with the Romans as to undermine their own authority by undue partisanship. A few of them were taken by the justice of Roman rule. The majority thought that if they could do some special favor for Rome they would become more powerful in their own states.

A different group was enthusiastic in its support of Perseus. This included some who, because of debt and the desperate state of their own affairs if things remained unchanged, were committed to revolution. Others in this group, because of their flightiness of character, were swept along by popular opinion in favor of Perseus.

Finally there was the group that was also the worthiest and most circumspect. They took the position that if they had to be under someone's dominion, they would rather be under the Romans than under the Macedonians; but if they had a truly free choice, they would prefer that neither side become more powerful by the downfall of the other, but rather that, the strength of both sides being undiminished, an equitable peace should continue. . . .

The Vote for War

On the day they entered their magistracy, the consuls, by the decree of the Senate, offered sacrifices of full-grown victims at all the temples where the *Lectisternium* was accustomed to be held during the greater part of the year. Feeling confident that their prayers had been accepted by the immortal gods, they reported to the Senate that sacrifices and prayers for the war had been properly offered. The entrail inspectors also responded to the Senate, saying that if some new enterprise was going to be undertaken, it should be done right away. Victory, triumph, and the expansion of the empire were predicted.

The senators, with the traditional wish that affairs might be of good omen and fortunate for the Roman people, ordered the consuls to present to the Centuriate Assembly, convened on the first available day, the following resolution:

> That whereas: (1) Perseus, son of Philip, King of Macedonia, has attacked allies of the Roman people and has devastated their lands contrary to the treaty made with Philip his father and renewed with himself, and whereas (2) he has undertaken plans for war against Rome, and gathered arms, soldiers, and a fleet.
>
> Be it resolved: Unless he offers satisfaction for these infringements, a state of war exists between Rome and Macedonia.

The measure passed by vote of the people.

Order of Battle

Next the Senate passed a decree ordering the consuls to arrange with each other the assignment of the provinces—Italy and Macedonia—and if they could not agree, to settle the issue by casting lots. The consul to whom Macedonia should fall was to campaign against King Perseus and his allies unless they rendered suitable satisfaction to the Roman people. Four new legions were voted, two for each consul. A special arrangement was made in the case of Macedonia, namely that whereas the legions of the other consul were set at the traditional 5,200 infantry per legion, in the case of Macedonia a complement of 6,000 infantry per legion was established. For both forces 300 cavalry was allotted. The allied contingent was increased for the one consul: He was to take to Macedonia 16,000 allied infantry and 800 cavalry under the command of Gnaeus Sicinius. Twelve thousand allied infantry and 600 cavalry were judged adequate for Italy.

In connection with the draft for Macedonia, the consul was allowed, as he thought necessary, to enroll former centurions and soldiers up to 50 years of age. Regarding military tribunes, a new practice was started that year because of the Macedonian War. The consuls, following a resolution of the Senate, proposed to the people that the military tribunes should not be chosen by vote that year but that the consuls and praetors be allowed to make the choice.

Commands among the praetors were arranged as follows: The praetor who drew the senatorial lot was to go to the fleet at Brindisi and inspect the naval allies. He was to dismiss the unfit and provide replacements from freedmen. Two-thirds were to be Roman citizens and one-third allies. The praetors who drew Sicily and Sardinia were to provision the fleet from these provinces. They were to impose a second tithe on the Sicilians and Sardinians and this grain was to be transported to the army in Macedonia. . . .

A Problem with the Draft: Tribunes and Centurions

The consuls were conducting the draft with greater care than usual. Licinius was enrolling veteran infantrymen and centurions, but many signed up voluntarily because they saw that those who had fought in the previous Macedonian War and against King Antiochus in Asia had become rich. However, when the military tribunes who had been enlisting the centurions put them down in the order in which they enlisted, twenty-three centurions who had held the rank of chief centurion, upon being treated this way, appealed to the tribunes of the people. Two of the tribunes, M. Fulvius Nobilior and M. Claudius Marcellus, threw the matter back to the consuls. They claimed that the investigation was the responsibility of those to whom the job of conducting the draft and the war had been given in the first place. The other tribunes agreed to investigate the case and, if injury had been done, they would intervene on behalf of the citizens injured.

The procedure took place at the tribunes' benches. Marcus Popilius, a former consul, appeared as counsel for the aggrieved centurions. Also appearing were the centurions themselves and the consul who had been conducting the draft. When Licinius demanded that the investigation take place in a public assembly, the people were duly gathered. Popilius, who had been consul two years earlier, spoke on behalf of the centurions. These experienced soldiers had completed their regular military service, he said. Their bodies were worn down by age and unremitting labor. They had no objection to serving the state, but they requested they not be assigned to a rank lower than they had had during their regular stint.

In response, Licinius the consul ordered the decrees of the Senate to be read, first the one authorizing the war against Perseus, then the decree authorizing the enrollment of as many centurions as he thought necessary and exempting no one under fifty years of age. He went on to request that the people not interfere with the draft being conducted by the military tribunes or prevent the consul from assigning the rank to each as was in the best interest of the state. There was, he reminded them, a new war in progress, near Italy, and against a very powerful king. Should there be any issues in doubt, they should be referred back to the Senate.

Impasse Resolved: Speech of Centurion Ligustinus

When the consul had finished, Spurius Ligustinus, one of the centurions who had appealed to the tribunes of the people, requested permission of the consul and the tribunes of the people that he be allowed to speak. With their permission he began:

"Citizens, I am Spurius Ligustinus of the Crustumina tribe, by origin a Sabine. My father left me an acre of land and a small cottage in which I was born and raised. I live in it to this day. When I came of age, my father found a wife for me, his niece. She brought nothing with her except her free birth and good morals and a fertility that would have been adequate for a rich home. We had six sons and two daughters, both of whom are now married. Four of our sons are grown; two are still boys.

"I began my service in the consulship of Publius Sulpicius and Gaius Aurelius (200 B.C.). I served two years as a private in the army brought to Macedonia for the war against King Philip. In the third year, T. Quinctius Flamininus promoted me to centurion of the tenth maniple of the front rank [*the lowest of the three subdivisions of the legion*] because of my bravery. After the defeat of Philip and the Macedonians, when we had been repatriated to Italy and demobilized, I went to Spain with M. Porcius Cato as a volunteer with the rank of private (195 B.C.). Of all the generals alive, no one is a shrewder observer or judge of bravery. This will be born out by those who, through long service, have served with him as well as other commanders. This general considered me worthy to be assigned centurion of the first century of the front rank. I enlisted a third time as a volunteer and a private in the army sent against the Aetolians and King Antiochus (191 B.C.). Once again I was given the rank of centurion, this time by Manius Acilius. On this occasion, however, I was made a centurion of the first century in the second rank [*a promotion*]. After Antiochus had been driven out and the Aetolians defeated, we returned to Italy. Twice thereafter I served in single, year-long campaigns. Twice I fought in Spain, once with Q. Fulvius Flaccus when he was praetor and once with Ti. Sempronius Gracchus when he held the same office. I was brought home from Spain by Flaccus along with others for his triumph. This was because we had been distinguished for bravery.

"Four Times in a few years I was Chief Centurion. I was decorated for bravery thirty-four times. I won six civic crowns [*given for saving a fellow citizen's life*]. I have served twenty-two years in the army and am over fifty years old. Nevertheless, if I had not completed all my years of service, Publius Licinius, and my age did not give me an exemption, I could still give you four soldiers in my place [*i.e., his own sons*]. I would like you to take what I have said into consideration on my side of the case.

"For my part, as long as I am considered fit for service, I will never refuse to be enrolled. I am willing to accept the rank assigned to me by the military tribunes. This is their responsibility. I will try to make sure that no one in the army exceeds me in bravery. That I have always done so my generals and those who have served with me will attest. Fellow soldiers, even though it is within your right to make this appeal, it is also right that you submit to the authority of the consuls and the Senate. When you were young, you never resisted them. Consider every rank honorable in which you will be defending the state."

When Ligustinus finished his speech, Publius Licinius the consul praised him profusely and conducted him from the meeting to the Senate. There, a motion of thanks was authorized, and the military tribunes made him Chief Centurion in the first legion because of his bravery. The other centurions gave up their appeal and responded obediently to the draft.

11.5   The Sack of Carthage

The most ghastly feature of ancient warfare was the sack of cities. Everyone—men, women, and children, old and young—suffered. Sometimes the entire population was sold into slavery. In particularly bitter wars whole populations were slaughtered. In 146 B.C., Rome destroyed two ancient cities, Corinth and Carthage, and sold their populations into slavery. For some moralists writing in the next century, 146 B.C. was taken as the moment when the Republic began to decay, not because of the awful slaughter or the destruction of two ancient and glorious cities, but because in that year Rome eliminated its last serious competitor in the Mediterranean. With no outside enemy to fear anymore, Rome was without external constraint. The key question then became: Could Rome find the moral strength internally to regulate its now well-developed hunger for conquest? For centuries, Rome had fought for safe frontiers; now it was poised on the brink of empire. No wonder that Scipio, commander of the Roman forces at Carthage, was said to have worried about the fate of his own city, "taking into consideration the mutability of human affairs." This eyewitness account probably ultimately derives from Polybius, who was present with Scipio at the siege. Polybius, having witnessed the downfall of Macedonia, had a special interest in the rise and fall of empires.[7]

The main object of Scipio's attack was Byrsa, the strongest part of the city, where the greater part of the population had taken refuge. There were three streets going up from the Forum to this fortress; on either side along each street there were houses built closely together, six stories high, from which the Romans were attacked with missiles. They captured the first few houses and from them moved against the defenders of the next. When they had gotten control of these, they put timbers over the narrow passageways and crossed as on bridges.

While one war was raging in this way on the rooftops, another was going on in the streets below. Everywhere there was shrieking and shouting and groans and suffering of every kind. Some were stabbed, others hurled alive from the roofs to the pavement, some of them falling on the heads of spears or other pointed weapons or swords. Until Scipio reached Byrsa, no one dared to set fire to the houses on account of the men still on the roofs, but at that point he

---

[7]Appian 8.128–132. Based on translation of Horace White, *Appian's Roman History* (London, 1888).

ordered the three streets burned and the passageways kept clear of burning material so that the advancing detachments of the army could move back and forth freely.

Then came new scenes of horror. The fire spread and brought down everything. The soldiers did not pause to destroy the buildings little by little but pulled them all down together. The crashing grew louder, and many fell with the stones among the dead. Some were seen to be still alive, especially old men, women, and young children who had hidden in the inmost nooks of the houses. Some were wounded, others burned to a greater or lesser degree, and they uttered horrible cries. Still others, pushed out and falling from such a height, along with the stones, timbers, and fire, were torn asunder into all kinds of awful shapes, crushed and mangled. Nor was this the end of their miseries, for those who had been ordered to keep the streets clear and were removing the debris with axes, mattocks, and boat-hooks while making the roads passable tossed with these implements the dead and living together into holes in the ground, sweeping them along like sticks and stones or turning them over with their metal tools. Human beings were used to fill up a ditch. Some were thrown in head first, while their legs, sticking out of the ground, writhed for a long time. Others fell with their feet down while their heads remained above ground. Horses galloped over them, crushing their faces and skulls, not purposely on the part of the riders, but as a result of their headlong haste. Nor did the clearing parties do these things on purpose. The press of war, the glory of the approaching victory, the rush of the troops, the confused noise of heralds and trumpeters all round, the tribunes and centurions changing guard and marching units hither and thither—all combined to make everyone frantic and heedless of what was happening before their eyes.

Six days and nights were taken up in this kind of turmoil, the soldiers being rotated so that they might not be worn out by the toil, slaughter, lack of sleep, and appalling sights. Scipio alone worked without rest, standing over the soldiers or hurrying here and there, not sleeping, eating anyhow as he worked, until, utterly fatigued and worn out, he sat down on a high place from where he could overlook the work. Much remained that could be destroyed, and it seemed likely that the carnage would go on for a very long time, but on the seventh day some suppliants presented themselves to Scipio bearing the sacred garlands of Aesculapius, whose temple was the most famous and richest in the citadel. These, bearing olive branches from the temple, besought Scipio to spare just the lives of all who were willing to depart from Byrsa. He granted this request to all except the deserters. Immediately 50,000 men and women came out together through a narrow gate which had been opened in the wall. They were put under guard.

The 900 Roman deserters, despairing for their life, went to the temple of Aesculapius with Hasdrubal [*the Carthaginians commander*], his wife, and their two sons. Here they easily defended themselves for a long time although they were few in number because of the height and steep nature of the place, which in time of peace was reached by a stairway of sixty steps. Finally, worn down by hunger, want of sleep, fear, weariness, and the approach of doom, they abandoned the enclosures of the temple and fled to the shrine and its roof.

Thereupon Hasdrubal fled secretly to Scipio, bearing an olive branch. Scipio ordered him to sit at his feet and there displayed him to the deserters. When they saw him, they asked silence and, when it was granted, heaped all manner of reproaches on Hasdrubal, then set fire to the temple and were destroyed in it. It is said the fire was lighted by the wife of Hasdrubal. In full view of Scipio she presented herself as best she could in the midst of such a disaster, and setting her children by her side, said so she could be heard by Scipio, "Against you, O Roman, the gods have no cause for indignation, since you exercise the right of war. But upon this

Hasdrubal, betrayer of his country and its temples, of me and his children, may the gods of Carthage take vengeance, and you be their instrument." Then turning to Hasdrubal, she said: "Wretch, traitor, most effeminate of men, this fire will entomb me and my children. But as for you, what Roman triumph will you, the leader of great Carthage, decorate? What punishment will you not receive from him at whose feet you are now sitting?" Having reproached him in this way, she killed her children, threw them into the fire, and plunged in after them. With these words it is said the wife of Hasdrubal died as Hasdrubal himself should have died.

Scipio looked at the city which had flourished for 700 years from its foundation and had ruled over so many lands, islands, and seas, as rich in arms, fleets, elephants, and money as the greatest of empires but far surpassing them in bravery and high spirit, for, when stripped of all its ships and arms, it had sustained famine and a great siege for three years. Now it came to an end in total destruction, and Scipio, beholding this spectacle, is said to have shed tears and publicly mourned for the enemy. After meditating by himself for a long time and reflecting on the inevitable fall of cities, nations, and empires as well as of individuals, and thinking of the fate of Troy, that once proud city, upon the fate of the Assyrian, the Median, and then the great Persian Empire, and most recently of all the splendid empire of Macedonia, either voluntarily or otherwise he spoke the words of Homer:

> The day shall come in which our sacred Troy
> And Priam, and the people over whom Spear-bearing Priam rules, shall perish all.

In a private conversation he was asked by Polybius what he meant (for Polybius had been his tutor); Polybius says that he did not hesitate frankly to name his own country, for whose fate he feared when he considered the mutability of human affairs. And Polybius wrote this down just as he heard it.

11.6   The Triumphal Parade of Aemilius Paullus

A triumph, or its lesser form, an ovation, was awarded on the basis of the significance of the victory and the body count. A minimum of 5,000 was necessary for a triumph. Formally, a triumph was the ritual purification of the army after a campaign, but it also had the effect of driving home the value of war and drawing the whole community together in a grand celebration of the state's success. It was the pinnacle of the triumphing general's career and conferred immortality on his family and on himself. The victor in this triumph was L. Aemillus Paullus, who defeated the Macedonians at the battle of Pydna in 168 B.C. This is the same war whose start we saw in the earlier section, "The Complexities of War: Foreign and Domestic Issues."[8]

The people erected stands in the race tracks (which the Romans call "circuses"), all around the Forum and at every spot in the city from which they could get a view of the show. The spectators were dressed in white garments. All the temples were open and full of garlands and incense. The streets were cleared and kept open by numerous officers, who drove back all who crowded onto or ran across the processional route.

---

[8]Plutarch, *Aemilius Paullus* 32–35.

The triumph lasted three days. The first day was barely long enough for the presentation of the booty in the form of statues, pictures, and colossal images which were conveyed in 250 chariots. The second day the finest and richest armor of the Macedonians, both bronze and steel, all newly polished and glittering, was carried by in many wagons. The pieces were piled up and arranged artfully as though they had been tumbled in heaps carelessly and by chance: Helmets were thrown upon shields, coats of mail on greaves; Cretan light infantry targets [*small shields*] and Thracian wicker bucklers and quivers of arrows lay among horses' bits. Through these there appeared the points of naked swords, intermixed with long Macedonian sarissas [*lances*]. All these arms were attached together just loosely enough that they struck against one another as they were drawn along, making a harsh and frightening noise, so that even as the spoils of a conquered enemy they could not be seen without dread. After the wagons loaded with armor there followed 3,000 men who carried silver coins in 750 baskets, each of which weighed three talents [*roughly 180 pounds*] and was carried by four men. Others brought silver bowls and goblets and cups, all disposed in a way to make the best show, and all unusual as well for their size and the solidity of their embossed work.

On the third day, early in the morning, first came the trumpeters, who played not as they usually did in a procession or solemn entry, but the kind of martial music the Romans used when encouraging their troops to go into action. Next followed 120 oxen with their horns gilded and their heads adorned with ribbons and garlands. These were led by young men with handsomely bordered aprons and boys with basins of silver and gold for the libations. After them was brought the gold coin, which was divided into containers that weighed three talents, like those that contained the silver. There were seventy-seven of these. Next came the bearers of the consecrated bowl which Aemilius had made. It weighed ten talents and was set with precious stones. Then the cups of Kings Antigonus and Seleucus and those of Therikleius were displayed, and all the gold plate that was used at King Perseus' table.

After these came Perseus' own chariot, in which was placed his armor, and on top of that his crown. After a gap, the children of the king were led by as captives, and with them a train of their servants, teachers, and attendants, all shedding tears and reaching out their hands to the spectators. The children themselves were encouraged by their attendants also to beg for compassion. There were two sons and a daughter, whose young age made them only partly aware of their misery, to such an extent that their incomprehension of their condition made them seem the more to be pitied. At any rate, Perseus himself scarcely got as much attention when he passed by. Pity fixed the eyes of the Romans on the infants, and many of them could not stop their tears. Until the children had gone, the viewers were moved by a mixture of pain and pleasure.

After his children and their attendants came Perseus himself, clad in black and wearing the boots of his country, looking shocked and stupefied as a result of his great misfortune. Next came a great crowd of his friends and familiars, whose faces were disfigured with grief and who let the spectators see by their tears and their continued looking at Perseus that it was his fortune they lamented, not their own. Perseus had appealed to Aemilius not to be led in pomp but to be left out of the triumphal procession. But Aemilius rightly refused, reminding Perseus of his cowardice and fondness for life and saying that, as in the past, it was within his power to avoid disgrace, meaning that he could take his own life. But Perseus, relying on who knows what hopes, allowed himself to appear as part of his own spoils.

Four hundred gold crowns in honor of Aemilius' victory, which had been sent to him by the cities, together with their deputations, came next. Then came Aemilius himself, seated on a magnificently adorned chariot. Aemilius, a striking individual even without the trappings of power, was dressed in a robe of purple interwoven with gold and was holding a laurel branch in his right hand. All the army, divided into centuries and cohorts, followed in like manner, with boughs of laurel in their hands. Some sang verses mixed with jokes according to the custom; others sang songs of triumph and praise of Aemilius' deeds. He was indeed admired and regarded as happy by all men, unenvied at least by the good. It seems the responsibility of some god to lessen that kind of happiness, which is too great and disproportionate, and so to mingle the affairs of human life that no one should be entirely free and exempt from disasters. Indeed we read in Homer that those people should think themselves truly happy whom Fortune has given an equal share of good and evil.

At any rate, Aemilius had four sons, of whom Scipio and Fabius were adopted into other families.[9] The other two, whom he had by his second wife and who were still young, he brought up in his own house. One of these died at fourteen years of age, five days before his father's triumph. The other died at twelve, three days after the triumph. There was not a Roman who did not have a deep sense of Aemilius's suffering and who did not shudder at the cruelty of Fortune that had not scrupled to bring so much sorrow into a house resplendid with happiness, rejoicing, and sacrifices, and to intermingle tears and laments with songs of victory and triumph.

Aemilius, however, reasoned rightly that courage and resolution were to resist not merely arms and spears, but all the shocks of ill fortune. He so met and so adapted himself to these mingled and contrasting circumstances as to outbalance the evil with the good, and his private concerns with the public. Thus he did not allow anything either to take away from the grandeur or to sully the dignity of his victory.

11.7   War as Personal Vengeance

Two things are illustrated in the following reading. The first is that in the late Republic, warfare had become personalized in the sense that commanders in the field often campaigned with much more indepen-dence and self-assertion than had their predecessors in the days when the Senate was firmly in control of war-making. The second item illustrated is the emotional state of the Roman commander. We do not often get a sense of what individual Roman soldiers actually felt about war. Much of what we know is presented to us in carefully packaged form. As vivid a scene as the destruction of Carthage (described above) has been carefully worked over for dramatic effect, as has the speech of Spurius Ligustinus't for other reasons. In Julius Caesar's Gallic Wars, however, we have something different. Although they too have been carefully written for maximum propaganda effect, we can occasionally see Caesar's emotions at work behind his cooly rational exterior.

The opportunity to see this results from a disastrous incident during the wars in Gaul, when one of Caesar's legions was wiped out treacherously by Ambiorix, chief of the Eburones. For years, Caesar pursued his enemy, wasting valuable time and resources in the pointless task of trying to devastate his homeland, the difficult Ardennes forest region of modern Belgium. He could never catch up with Ambiorix, though

---

[9]The Scipio referred to here is the Scipio who was the friend of Polybius and the general who sacked Carthage; see the preceeding section.

"again and again prisoners were captured who had just seen Ambiorix in flight and who would turn their heads to see where he was, insisting that he was just out of sight." *Caesar's last chance to get his hands on Ambiorix occurred in 51 B.C.. Once again he set out to settle accounts personally with his hated foe, and once again the elusive Ambiorix slipped away. We never hear of Ambiorix again, nor do we know whether Caesar felt his "honor" was satisfied by the devastation he wrought among the Eburones. Much is crammed into Caesar's terse style.*[10]

Caesar himself set out to plunder and devastate the lands of Ambiorix. The chief was terrified and fled. In the end Caesar was forced to give up hope of being able to get his hands on him. He then thought that the next best thing to do, and indeed that which his honor demanded, was to so thoroughly strip Ambiorix's country of its inhabitants, buildings, and cattle as to make Ambiorix hated by any of his subjects who might survive. [*As a consequence, Caesar hoped*] that Ambiorix would never be able to come back to a state that had suffered so much because of him.

Accordingly, Caesar sent legionary detachments or auxiliaries throughout Ambiorix's territory to kill, burn, and loot. There was total devastation. Large numbers of the inhabitants were either killed or captured.

---

[10]Caesar, *The Gallic Wars* 8.24–25.

Chapter 12

Society and Culture in the Republic

Romans thought of themselves as a family and of Rome as their home. A designated state "family" home and hearth existed in the Forum, and the Vestal Virgins kept the state home fire burning. Just as Roman families were sustained by the rites special to each individual family, so the state was sustained by the observance of rites proper to it. Imported rituals were allowed to be practiced only under very special circumstances, usually state emergencies. Foreign rites performed secretly or without proper authorization were regarded as highly dangerous.

No great divide existed between "society" and the state, or between the Roman people and the Roman government. Society and the state intermingled in intimate and surprising ways. Size had something to do with this situation. It would not be an exaggeration to say everyone knew everyone else (or at least *about* everyone; gossip kept everyone in Rome informed about what was happening in the community—thus the authorities learned of the conspiracy of the Bacchanals through word of mouth). But the formal structure of the state also contributed to this state of affairs. The way the Romans went about their public affairs, passing laws, making decisions, judging, electing, and so forth involved more people directly and intimately *with each other* than any modern democracy does. And this was the case despite the fact that Romans did not think of their constitution as being democratic, or at least not democratic the way, for instance, Athens was democratic.

Modern democracies pride themselves on the simple equality of their citizens. Technically there are no "second-class" citizens: all full citizens in good standing enjoy the same rights and privileges. Romans, by contrast, had very different ideas about citizenship and society. In the Republic, for instance, inhabitants of the state could be full citizens, or citizens without the right to vote, or Latins, who had certain rights in Rome but were not citizens. A person could be freeborn, a slave, a freedman, or freedwoman; each was a separate legal category.

Even full Roman citizens were unequal among themselves in certain ways. Some citizens, for instance, were the hereditary clients of other citizens and had obligations to them as their patrons (and vice versa: patrons had responsibilities toward clients). While some citizens were legally independent (*sui iuris*) and could own and sell property, marry, or divorce as they willed, others, even in adulthood, were still under the legal control of their fathers or guardians.

To make matters more complicated, there were different forms of marriage which had very different legal consequences. In the strict (*manus*) form of marriage, for instance, the wife was inducted fully into the husband's family and escaped her father's control only to come fully under her husband's power. This system had an important impact on the transmission of property. Technically a husband did not owe his wife maintenance; that was the point, among other things, of the dowry. Although a married woman could not own land or property in Italy, she could buy and sell personal goods (such as clothes and jewelry), land, and property as long as they were *outside* Italy.

The Roman family often included not just parents and their unmarried children, but also slaves and freed slaves and *their* children, some of whom would be slave and some free. Slave marriages existed de facto, even if they were not recognized by the law as legal. Adding to these complications was the fact that slaves could purchase other slaves, accumulate property, and purchase their own freedom. Conditions of slaves varied considerably, the worst conditions being found in the countryside or with hardhearted owners such as Cato.

Much more than modern societies, Roman society was a complex jumble of customary and legal relationships. Perhaps the willingness of Romans to accept different gradations of dependency and yet claim to be free can be traced to the character of the Roman family, which was itself a model for the state (and vice versa). The Roman family was a kind of ministate ruled by the father with the assistance of his wife, and senior family members acting as an advisory council (the *consilium*). Although the father, the head of the household (the *paterfamilias*), could act without consulting his little family "senate," he would run into the disapproval of society at large by doing so. Hence, although legally he had enormous powers (he could, for instance, discipline his children by executing those who misbehaved), he could exercise these powers only in consultation with others in the family. The severity of family discipline should be seen, however, in the context of a society that not only had no police force, but actively rejected the idea of one. Policing society was first and foremost a private, family matter.

12.1 "Secret Rites Performed at Night": The Bacchanalian Conspiracy

The separation of church and state is regarded as a characteristic of the modern secular state. For the Romans, however, as for all ancient peoples, such an idea was unthinkable. Indeed, the practice of private rituals not approved by the state or ancient tradition was thought to undermine family tradition, weaken the state, and offend the established gods. The historian Livy provides the following account of a crisis in 186 B.C. over the introduction of the cult of Dionysus. In trying to save his hero Aebutius's reputation while at the same time turning the prostitute Hispala Faecenia into a model Roman, Livy engages in some twisted and unconvincing logic.[1]

---

[1]Livy 39.8–19.

In the next year the consuls Spurius Postumius Albinus and Quintus Marcius Philippus were distracted from their military and administrative duties in the provinces by the need to put down an internal conspiracy. . . . [The movement began with] a lowborn Greek, who first appeared in Etruria. He had none of the culture that the Greek people—that most gifted nation—brought to us for the cultivation of mind and body, but was a mere manipulator of sacrifices and prophecies. Nor was he the kind that fill men's minds with error by publicly announcing their beliefs, but rather an initiator into secret rites, performed at night.

At first the rituals were known only to a few, but then they began to spread widely among both men and women. The pleasures of drinking and partying were added to religion to attract a larger number of people. With the people inflamed by drink and darkness, and the mix of men and women, of young and old, every moral scruple disappeared. All sorts of evils began to be practiced since each had the opportunity to do what he or she was most prone by nature to do. There was not just one kind of vice; free men and women had promiscuous sex; perjured witnesses forged seals and wills and evidence; from the same source came poisonings and secret murders, such that at times not even the bodies were to be found for burial. . . .

This evil spread from Etruria to Rome like a contagious disease. Early on, the size of the city, with its anonymity and tolerance for such evils, hid it, but eventually the consul Postumius caught wind of the evil. It happened this way.

Publius Aebutius, whose father had been a knight, was left in the care of guardians, but when they died he came under the guardianship of his mother, Duronia, and his stepfather, Titus Sempronius Rutilus. His mother was captivated by her husband Titus, Aebutius's stepfather, but Titus so completely mismanaged Publius's estate that he was unable to give a proper account of it to the court, and he decided he had to either get rid of his ward Publius or attach him to himself in some compromising way. He settled on the method of the Bacchanalian rituals.

Duronia claimed to her son that when he was sick she had vowed that if he recovered she would initiate him in the Bacchic rites. Now, since by the kindness of the gods he had recovered, she wished to fulfill her vow. . . .

Duronia's plot, however, is foiled.

There was a well-known prostitute, a freed woman by the name of Hispala Faecenia. She was really much better than a prostitute, but as a slave she had been initiated into the profession and after manumission continued to support herself in this way. She and Aebutius became lovers, since they lived in the same neighborhood. This did no damage to either his reputation or his possessions: He had been loved and sought out, and since his relatives provided so poorly for him he was maintained by the generosity of Hispala. Hispala went further: After the death of her patron, because she was under no one's legal control, she requested a guardian from the tribunes and praetor and, impelled by her love for Aebutius, she made him her sole heir.

Aebutius tells Hispala of his mother's plans to have him initiated into the Bacchic rites. She warns him not to let this happen. When she had been a slave, she explains, she, together with her mistress, had been initiated into the cult and had seen the horrible things the Bacchants did to new members. He agrees with her and refuses to be initiated. The plot thickens. His mother and stepfather become enraged, and in order to protect himself against reprisals, Aebutius seeks help from his aged aunt Aebutia. On her advice he goes to the consul Postumius and tells him everything. The consul is unsure whether he can trust Aebutius's fantastic story.

The consul dismissed Aebutius and told him to return three days later. In the meantime he asked his respected mother-in-law Sulpicia if she knew the elderly lady Aebutia, Aebutius's aunt, who lived on the Aventine. She replied that she did: Aebutia was a good, old-fashioned woman. Postumius then decided he needed to meet with Aebutia and asked Sulpicia to invite her to her home. Aebutia came and then, as if by chance, the consul also came by and inquired casually about Aebutius, her nephew. She broke down in tears and began to bewail the young man's fate. He had been robbed of his inheritance, she said, by those who least of all should have treated him this way. He had then been driven from his home because this upstanding young man—may the gods be forgiving—had refused to be initiated into what were said to be immoral rites.

Postumius, thinking that he could now trust Aebutius's story, has his dependable mother-in-law Sulpicia arrange a meeting with Hispala. After a certain amount of arm-twisting the consul gets the whole story of the Bacchanalia out of Hispala, who, though afraid to reveal the sacred mysteries of Bacchus (another name for the god Dionysus), was (rightly) even more afraid of the consul's power. The consul prudently had Hispala, her slaves, and her household gods moved into Sulpicia's house and had Aebutius move into the house of one of his own clients. With his key witnesses in safety, Postumius was now free to go public with the problem. First the Senate was informed. After debate it decided to investigate the matter and, in the meantime, to end new initiations, to stop celebrations of the rituals, and to keep the priests under surveillance. Next the consuls call an informal meeting of the people (a contio) *to tell them of the affair and to give the official line on the practice of Roman religion. What follows is part of Livy's version of the speech of one of the consuls. The speech follows the usual invocations and prayers.*

"Citizens: Never in any meeting has the solemn prayer to the gods been not only so suitable but also necessary. This prayer reminds us that these are the gods our ancestors appointed to be worshipped, venerated, and prayed to; they are not the kinds of gods who would lead our befuddled minds with their vile and alien rituals, as though stimulated by the furies, to commit every crime and indulge every lust. I do not know how much I should keep secret and how much I should reveal to you. On the one hand, if you are left ignorant of anything, I may be being neglectful. On the other, if I tell you all, I fear I may excite excess terror. Whatever I say, be sure that my words are less than the awfulness and seriousness of the situation. It is our job to take sufficient precautions.

"Both from rumor and from the shouts and howlings you have heard throughout the city, you know that the Bacchanalia has been celebrated all over Italy and even in Rome. Nevertheless, I feel certain you do not know what the Bacchanalia really is. Some regard it as a cult of the gods; others believe that it is an acceptable kind of play and sport, and that in any case, it concerns only a few. As regards this last point, if I were to tell you there were thousands of them, you would be terrified, unless I were to tell you what kind of people they are.

"First, many of them are women, and they are the source of the evil. But there are men who are as bad as the women, debauched and debauchers, fanatical, with their senses dulled by partying and wine, and with the noise and shouts of night. At this point the conspiracy has no strength, but it grows significantly day by day. Your ancestors did not wish that even you should casually assemble unless the emergency signal was displayed on the citadel and the army gathered for a meeting, or the tribunes had called the Council of the Plebs, or some magistrate an informal meeting. Our ancestors thought that wherever there was a crowd gathered, there should also be a legitimate leader present. What kind of meetings do you think these nightly gatherings are? What of the meetings of men and women?"

The speech goes on at length to reveal the supposed evils of the Bacchants and to excite the fears of the people by claiming that the real intent of the practitioners of the new cult was the takeover of the state. However, the main point of the speech was to assert traditional aristocratic ideological claims and convince the people to accept the Senate's decree suppressing and controlling the Bacchanals without debate.

"How often in the time of our fathers and grandfathers was the responsibility given to the magistrates of forbidding foreign cults, keeping manipulators of sacrifices and prophets away from the Forum, searching out and destroying books of prophecies, and suppressing all sacrificial rituals except those performed in the Roman way. Men most skilled in divine and human law judged that nothing was so destructive of religion as sacrifices performed according to alien, not native practice.

"I considered that this warning should be given to you so that you will not be concerned by religious scruples when you see us suppressing the Bacchanalia and breaking up their nightly meetings. All these things, the gods being kind and willing, we will do. It is because the gods are indignant that their majesty was being contaminated by crimes and acts of lust that these matters have been dragged out of darkness into the light of day. . . ."

The "conspiracy" was in due course brutally repressed with out-of-hand executions in Rome and Italy. Regulations were laid down for the future practice of the cult. Special permission for its practice had to be obtained, and it was then allowed only under certain restrictive conditions. The hero and heroine of the event, Publius Aebutius and Hispala Faecenia, were rewarded with large amounts of money and special legal privileges. Livy leaves it to the reader to decide whether Publius and Hispala got married, though he does give a hint by saying that one of the privileges accorded to Hispala was the decree that no disgrace would be incurred by a freeborn man should he marry her.

12.2 Patricians and Plebeians: Patrons and Clients

Dionysius of Halicarnassus, a contemporary of the historian Livy (ca. 30 B.C.), gives the following rosy account of Romulus' creation of the institutions of patricians and plebeians, patrons and clients. The latter institution still functioned in his day as an important aspect of Roman social life.[2]

[Romulus] divided those who were distinguished by birth, virtue, and wealth (at least to the extent it was possible to speak of wealth in those simpler times) . . . from the obscure, the humble, and the poor. Those who belonged to this latter group he called "plebeians" . . . and those of the higher rank "fathers" . . . and their descendants "patricians." After Romulus had divided higher from lower ranks, he established laws specifying the responsibilities of each.

---

[2]Dionysius of Halicarnassus, *Roman Antiquities*, 2.8–10.

The patricians were to be priests, officeholders, and judges and to help him in the running of the state, devoting themselves to the city. The plebeians were freed from these responsibilities, because they were inexperienced in these affairs and because their lack of means did not give them the free time to devote to them. They were to work the land, herd, and engage in useful trades. . . .

He [*Romulus*] gave the plebeians as a trust to the patricians, allowing each plebeian to choose for his patron any patrician he wanted. . . . He promoted the relationship by giving it a proper name, calling the protection of the poor and humble a "patronage." By assigning useful mutual services to each he made the coupling of the two both friendly and political. . . .

It was the duty of patrons to their clients to explain the laws of which they might not have knowledge; to care for them whether they were themselves absent or present, doing everything for them that fathers do for their children in business affairs and contracts; to bring suit on behalf of clients wronged in matters of contracts, and to defend them against those who brought charges against them. In brief, it was the duty of patrons to obtain for their clients in both private and public affairs all that security they most needed. Clients in turn were supposed to help their patrons in providing dowries for their daughters at marriage time if the fathers lacked the means; to pay ransom to an enemy if they or their children were taken prisoner; to pay out of their own resources the losses of their patrons in private as well as public suits, not as loans but as gifts; to share, as though they were family relatives, the costs involved in their public offices and positions and other state-related expenditures.

For patrons and clients alike it was sacrilegious as well as against tradition to accuse each other in lawsuits, to testify or vote against each other, or to be counted with each other's enemies. . . . As a result, the coupling of clients and patrons continued over generations, being no different from the ties of blood relations. The bonds were handed down to their children's children. It was a matter of great renown for the famous families to have as many clients as possible, to preserve the succession of hereditary patronages, and to acquire others by their own merit. It is amazing how great a contest in good will there was between patrons and clients, each striving not to be outdone by the other in kindness. . . .

12.3   *Patria Potestas* and *Materna Auctoritas*: The Power of Fathers and Mothers over Their Children

Dionysius also ascribes the institution of patria potestas *to Romulus. Although considerably softened by the passage of centuries, the power of fathers over their children was still enormous. Dionysius begins by criticizing Greek lawmakers for the* "mild punishments which were not adequate to restrain the foolishness of youth" *and noting by contrast the sternness of Romulus' legislation in this area.*[3]

But the Roman legislator [*Romulus*] gave, so to say, all power to the father over his son, and this power continued throughout the son's life. The *paterfamilias* could imprison his son, whip him, put him to work in chains in the fields, execute him. This was true even when the son was already involved in politics, even if he had held the highest magistracies and was

---

[3]Dionysius, *Roman Antiquities* 2.26.

honored for his services to the state. . . . [*Romulus*] allowed the *paterfamilias* to sell his son. . . . For anyone educated in the loose ways of the Greeks the following would seem harsh and tyrannical: He permitted the father to make a profit by selling his son as often as three times! In this way he gave greater power to a father over his son than to a master over his slaves, for a slave once sold, and then obtaining his freedom, is his own master thereafter. . . .

This law was observed by the kings in the beginning, though whether it was written or unwritten I cannot say. They thought it was the best of laws. And when the kings were overthrown and the Romans first decided to make public in the Forum for the review of the citizens all the ancestral customs and laws . . . they recorded it among the rest. It now appears in the fourth of the so-called Twelve Tables which they set up at that time in the Forum.

In the absence of a father, however, the mother's authority, materna auctoritas, *was an important substitute. An example of this was the role played by Cornelia, after the death of her husband, in the education of her sons, the famous revolutionary tribunes Tiberius and Gaius Gracchus. She was so popular with the people that after her death a bronze statue of her was erected with the inscription "Cornelia, Mother of the Gracchi."* [4]

[*After her husband's death*] Cornelia took charge of the children and the household and showed herself so sound and affectionate a mother and so constant a widow . . . that when King Ptolemy offered to share his crown with her and wanted to marry her, she refused and chose rather to live as a widow. In this state she continued and lost all her children except one daughter, who was married to Scipio the Younger, and two sons, Tiberius and Gaius. . . . Cornelia raised these sons with such care that although they were indisputably first among their peers in terms of natural endowments, they were thought to owe their excellence more to her education than to nature.

It is reported that Cornelia bore the loss of her two sons with a noble and undaunted spirit. She said of the sacred places where her sons had been slain [*Tiberius was assassinated on the Capitol Hill of Rome, and Gaius in the grove of the Furies across the Tiber from the city*] that their dead bodies were worthy of such tombs. She moved afterwards and lived near the place called Misenum but made no change in her usual way of living. She had many friends and hospitably received many strangers at her house; many Greeks and learned men were continually about her. All the kings exchanged gifts with her. Her visitors and those who lived with her were entertained by her stories about her father, Scipio Africanus, and his way of life, but they were moved to admiration when she reminisced with inquirers about her sons without grief or tears and spoke of their deeds and sufferings as though she were narrating the history of some ancient heroes.

12.4   Marriage: Legalities and Realities

The legal complications of marriage forms, especially where they concerned property, are revealed in the following glowing encomium, recorded as an inscription put up by a husband to honor his wife, Turia, after the civil wars at the end of the Republic. The inscription also says much about the relationship of husband and wife among the upper classes at the end of the Republic. [5]

---

[4]Plutarch, *Tiberius Gracchus* 1; *Gaius Gracchus* 19.
[5]*Inscriptiones Latinae Selectae* 8393.

Before the day of our marriage you were suddenly left an orphan when your parents were murdered in an isolated country district. It was, however, principally through your efforts that your parents' deaths did not remain unavenged. Indeed, I had already left for Macedonia and Gaius Cluvius, your brother-in-law, was on his way to Africa. You were so vigorous in pursuing this holy duty . . . that even if we had been present ourselves we could not have done any more. . . .

While you were attending to these affairs, and after the murderers had been punished, you left your father's house to protect your reputation. You went to my mother's house where you waited for me to return. At that time you were pressured to declare that your father's will, in which we were both named as his heirs, was invalid. The alleged grounds were that he had taken his wife in the strict form of marriage (*manus*) by the process of fictious sale (*coemptio*).

This would have necessitated that you and all your father's property revert to the guardianship (*tutela*) of the people who were making this claim (*presumably kin on her father's side*). Nothing would have been inherited by your sister because she had gone from the control of her father to that of her husband, Cluvius. Although I was not there at the time, I heard about the courage with which you listened to their proposals and the circumspect way in which you rejected them.

*The aim of the litigants was to get control of the sizable fortune Turia inherited by forcing her into a guardianship (*tutela*) where she would have been under their thumb. She resisted vigorously, threatening to include her sister in the estate and claiming that, legally, she could not be forced into the proposed guardianship. The claimants backed off. The inscription continues.*

Marriages of such length, broken by death rather than divorce, are truly unusual. Our marriage lasted for forty-one years in true happiness. My only wish is that our union had come to its final end through *my* death. It would have been more just for me, as the older partner, to have yielded to fate.

Do I need to recall your special qualities? You were chaste, deferential, sociable, easy to get on with, faithful to your wool-working. You respected the gods without being too devout. You dressed well, being elegant rather than fussy. . . . By our common household management we kept the whole of the inheritance you got from your parents. You gave it all to me, not being concerned with the care of increasing it. We thus shared the task of administering our property in such a way that I protected your fortune and you guarded mine. . . .

You were generous toward your many relatives. . . . You brought some of your worthy female relatives up in our home. So that they might maintain a social status appropriate to the rank of your family, you gave them dowries. . . .

You helped me to escape by selling your jewelery and giving me all your gold and the pearls you had on your person. . . . I was saved by your advice. You did not allow me to face danger recklessly through overly bold plans, but discreetly provided a safe house for me, choosing as your helpers . . . your sister and her husband, Gaius Cluvius. Were I to go into all these matters, I would go on forever. It is sufficient to say that your plans ensured my safety.

When the world was once again at peace and the Republic restored, we in turn enjoyed peaceful and happy times. We longed for children, which envious Fate had denied us. If Fortune had smiled on us in the ordinary way, what would we have lacked? But age put an end to these hopes. . . .

Despairing of your own fertility and distressed at seeing me without children, you spoke of divorce . . . offering to hand over your house to another, fertile, spouse. . . . You said you would consider the children as shared, and as if they were your own; there would be no division of property, which up until now had been shared in common. . . .

I must admit that I was so angry that I was beside myself, so horrified at your suggestion that I could scarcely control myself. The idea that divorce could have been discussed before Fate had intervened, or that while you were still alive you could think of anything that would have made you cease to be my wife!

But by Fate's decree your course was run before mine. You left me the grief, the longing for you, the sad fate to live alone. . . .

12.5   The Rape of Chiomara

There is little evidence of Roman soldiers raping their female captives, but it is a good guess that it was not an uncommon occurrence. Chiomara was a Galatian woman (the Galatians were the descendants of Celtic tribes who invaded and settled in central Anatolia) who was taken captive by a Roman soldier and raped. The soldier then arranged to ransom her back to her own people. Little did he know what was in store for him at the hands of his apparently docile victim. Whatever the historical truth of this story, Plutarch, unlike many others in his time, believes rape was a shame to be borne by the rapist, not by the victim.[6]

After the Galatians had given the Roman soldier the ransom and had received Chiomara back, she gave a signal to one of them to kill her former captor as he was affectionately taking his leave of her. At her command the Galatian cut off the soldier's head. Chiomara picked it up, and wrapping it in the folds of her dress, went off. When she appeared before her husband she threw the head down before him. In amazement he said: "O wife, marital fidelity is a good thing." "Yes," she said, "but it is even better that only one man be alive who has had relations with me."

12.6   "A Wife Without a Dowry is Under Her Husband's Thumb"

The comedies of the playwrights Plautus and Terence are major sources of information about family life in the Republic. Although the original models were Greek, much of the detail, color, and emphasis are Roman. Dowries had many functions. Marriages were often used to solidify alliances among families, so the giving of a dowry was an important part of political and economic as well as social life. Dowries also helped to ensure that the bride would be properly treated in the new household and, in the event of divorce, would have something to fall back on. But there were other, less obvious effects. Here Euclio overhears the soliloquy of Megadorus (his future son-in-law) on the subject of dowries and their effect on marriage.[7]

Megadorus: I've disclosed my marriage plans to all my friends. They're full of praise for Euclio's daughter. Great idea! Smart move! they say. And they're right. Indeed, if the rest of our well-heeled population would follow my example and marry poor men's dowryless daughters, there would be a lot more peace in the city. For one, we would be less envied by

[6]Plutarch, *Mulierum virtutes* 258f.
[7]Plautus, *Pot of Gold* 375–535.

the poor—and our wives would respect us a bit more! It would be cheaper too. Most people would welcome the idea; the only opposition would come from that greedy handful who are so grasping and insatiable that neither law nor custom can control them. If you ask, however, "Who are the rich women *with* dowries going to marry if the poor are to have this right?" the answer is: "Let them marry whom they please, *provided the dowry doesn't go with them!*" In that case they'll bring better morals than they do now, instead of money. . . .

Euclio: Incredible! How well he speaks of thrift!

Megadorus: Then you'd never hear a wife saying: "I brought you a dowry larger than all your property, so I have a right to fine clothes, jewelery, maidservants, mules, coachmen and footmen, errand boys, and carriages to ride in.

Euclio: Ah, well he knows society wives! I'd like to see him made censor of women's morals.

Megadorus: Nowadays, wherever you go there are more carts in front of town houses than you'd find in a farmyard! And that's nothing compared to what you'll see when the bill collectors show up! Here's the dry cleaner, the embroiderer, the jeweler, the wool merchant; the dealer in flounces, underwear, bridal veils, violet and yellow dyes. There are muff makers and makers of perfumed foot gear; lingerie merchants, shoemakers, slipper makers, sandal makers, and leather stainers, all waiting to be paid. And when you've paid these, another three hundred show up: weavers and lace makers, cabinetmakers and bag makers—all wanting you to settle up. You pay them—is that the lot? What more?

Euclio: I'd interrupt him but I'm afraid he'd stop talking about the ways of women. I'll let him go on.

Megadorus: When all this rubbish has been paid off, in comes the soldier, demanding the army tax. You consult with your banker while the soldier stands by, missing his lunch; unfortunately, you find you owe the banker money—you're overdrawn! . . . These are just some of the problems and expenses that go with large dowries; and there are others. On the other hand, a wife without a dowry is under a husband's thumb; it's the ones with dowries that make their husbands' lives miserable with their squandering.

12.7　"Sell Worn-Out Oxen . . . Old and Sick Slaves"

Like all other ancient societies, Romans accepted slavery as an inevitable aspect of life. People became slaves because the economy was bad, or because they ended up on the wrong side of a war, or just through bad luck. Because it was an accepted part of life, Roman society developed ways of dealing with it on a day-to-day basis that in some ways lessened its most awful features. On manumission, for instance, a slave received citizenship, and within a generation his or her descendants could have become indistinguishable from the rest of Roman society. Race was not a factor. Slaves could make money and purchase their freedom. Rich masters showed their liberality by freeing slaves. Not that these events changed the nature of slavery itself. Slaves in mines or on ranches had little chance of manumission and were often treated brutally. Shepherd slaves, on the other hand, had more freedom (of a sort) than did most other kinds of slaves. Obviously much (if not everything) depended on what kind of masters or mistresses slaves had. A slave who had the bad luck to draw the profit-motivated Cato as a master would not have had much to look forward to.[8]

---

[8]Cato, *On Agriculture* 2.

After the owner (the *paterfamilias*) has arrived at his ranch and prayed to the god of the household, he should make a tour of the farm, if possible that very day; if not, the next. After he has learned how the farm has been worked and knows what has been done and what hasn't, he should call the slave foreman of the farm and ask what jobs are finished and how much remains, and whether they were done on time, and whether it is possible to finish the rest, and what's the situation with the wine, grain, and other products.

When he knows all this he should make a calculation on the amount of labor and time involved. Then, if the amount of work doesn't seem satisfactory, and the manager claims that he tried his best but that the slaves were no good, the weather was bad, the slaves had run away, he had work to do for the state—when he has given all these excuses and many others, produce *your* estimate of the amount of work done and the workers involved. Remind him what kind of work could have been done on rainy days: storage jars could have been washed and tarred, the farm buildings cleaned, grain moved, manure cleared out and a manure pit made, the seed cleaned, the ropes fixed and new ones made. . . . on festivals they might have cleaned out old ditches, worked on the public highway, cut brambles, dug a garden, cleared a meadow. . . .

The owner should check the herd and hold a sale. If the price is right, sell the oil; surplus wine and grain should also be sold. Sell the worn-out oxen, the sub-par cattle and sheep, wool, hides, the old wagon, worn-out tools, the old slave, the sick slave, and anything else that is superfluous. An owner should be a seller, not a buyer.

12.8   Economics of Farming

By the late Republic a sophisticated agricultural economy had developed in Italy. It contrasted sharply with the old system of self-sufficient small farming that preceded it. In this reading, the author, a contemporary of Julius Caesar, offers common-sense advice to well-to-do Romans looking for respectable but profitable investments.[9]

Farms that have suitable means of getting their products to the markets and obtaining in return the things they need are profitable for these reasons. Many landlords, for instance, have farmsteads which, because they do not themselves produce grain and wine, need to import these commodities; on the other hand, some have estates that produce goods that need to be exported. Hence, it is profitable to have large-scale gardens near a city, producing, for instance, violets and roses and many other products for which there is a demand in the city. On the other hand, it makes no sense to grow these items on a distant estate, far from any suitable market.

Likewise, if there are towns and villages nearby, or even well-cultivated lands and estates of rich owners, from which you can buy at reasonable prices whatever you need for your own farm, and to which in turn you can sell your surplus, such as poles or reeds, the farm will be more profitable than if you had to import them from a distance. It may even be cheaper to do this than to produce them yourself. It is for this reason that small farmers

---

[9]Varro, *On Agriculture* 1.16.

like to have in their neighborhood people such as doctors and fullers and other skilled tradesmen with whom they have a yearly contract. This is better than having these skilled people on their own farms, for the death of one such craftsman can wipe out the farms' profitability. . . .

Access to transportation, such as roads suitable for carts or a river navigable by boats, makes a farm more profitable. Goods are brought to and from many estates by both these methods. The way in which your neighbor maintains the land on your common boundary is also important. For example, if he has an oak grove along the boundary, you cannot plant olives alongside it since the two do not get along.

Chapter 13

▼▼▼

The Roman Revolution

Just at the moment when the Romans had eliminated all threats to themselves in the Mediterranean, their own social, cultural, and political system began to disintegrate. Beginning in 133 B.C. with the murder of the tribune Tiberius Gracchus, Rome went through a century of turmoil. Modern historians have called the period the Roman Revolution.

The Romans themselves were well aware of what was happening. Nevertheless, the surviving accounts of that period speak mostly of moral decay among various segments of society beginning at different moments in the past. The politician, soldier, and historian Sallust, a supporter of Julius Caesar, looked back to the fall of Carthage in 146 B.C. as the moment the rot began; Livy saw the collapse starting somewhat earlier—when the army of Manlius Vulso returned from Macedonia in 187 B.C. with an un-Roman appetite for dancing girls, good food, and comfortable living.

While the Roman writers saw the fall of the Republic in moral terms, modern historians see fundamental changes in Roman social, cultural, political, and economic life beginning with the Hannibalic War. In their eyes these changes were so fundamental that the old system was doomed. The result, however, was something less than a thoroughgoing transformation of all aspects of Roman life. Perhaps for that reason the term "Revolution," although commonly used, is not altogether appropriate. Essential aspects of Roman society such as economic relations, social hierarchy, personal patronage, patriarchal gender relations, and so on were not greatly altered—at least not in the long run. What did change was the constitution and the way Romans governed themselves, or, as some of them thought, ceased to govern themselves, for in the end political freedom was abandoned in exchange for personal security and the security of property.

Rome was also transformed culturally as its upper and middle classes became full participants in the common Hellenistic culture of the Mediterranean. But this transition began long before the political, military, and constitutional changes of the Roman Revolution became apparent.

Perhaps the Roman Revolution is most simply understood as the painful, interesting transition of a city-state to a world-state. If this is an accurate description of the event, it is also a measure of the greatness of Rome that even in the depths of its supposed moral collapse it managed to find the necessary resources to make the successful passage from Republic to Empire. It might be said that the most significant aspect of the so-called "Roman Revolution" is that Rome survived its own transformation.

13.1   "Greed, Unlimited and Unrestrained, Corrupted and Destroyed Everything"

Sallust, an ambitious careerist, a gifted writer, and a corrupt provincial governor, was one of the new types of Romans who became prominent in the late Republic. Like Marius and Cicero, he was a "new man" from the Italian municipal aristocracy. Like them, he lacked the "right" family background for a straight-forward political career at Rome and had to struggle to make his way. Although not as able as either Marius or Cicero, he was lucky in that the conditions of the time favored people like him. Just as Sallust's career had reached something of a dead end, the charismatic Julius Caesar began to unite new men from Rome and the Italian cities, some members of the old aristocracy, the people, and the army in a coalition that effectively challenged the control of the senatorial oligarchy. This new coalition spelled the end of the old order of the Senatus Populusque Romanus *(the Senate and the People of Rome).*

Although expressed in traditional moralistic terms, Sallust's brief survey provides a synoptic view of most of the factors that made up the Roman Revolution.[1]

The system of parties and factions, with all their corresponding evils, developed at Rome some years before this war, as a result of peace and the kind of material prosperity that all people prize highly. For prior to the destruction of Carthage, the People and the Senate of Rome ran the government peacefully and with consideration for each other. Citizens did not struggle among themselves for glory or domination. Fear of enemies preserved the good morals of the state. But when this fear was removed, the vices of prosperity, licentiousness, and arrogance arose. Thus the peace the Romans sought in times of adversity, after they had obtained it, turned out to be harder and more bitter than the adversity itself. For the nobles began to abuse their dignity and the people their liberty; each began to look out for its own advantage, to squander and to grab. Accordingly, everything was split between the two. The republic, trapped between the factions, was torn apart.

The nobility had the more powerful faction. The people's power, being divided and scattered among so many, was less effective. Domestic and military issues were decided by a tiny handful of nobles who had control over the treasury, the provinces, the magistracies, all distinctions and triumphs. The people were burdened by military service and poverty. The generals seized the spoils of war and shared them with their friends. Meanwhile, the parents and small children of the soldiers were driven from their homes if they happened to have powerful neighbors.

Thus the possession of power led to the rise of greed; unlimited and unrestrained, it corrupted and destroyed everything. Nothing was respected, nothing held sacred. Eventually this greed brought about its own downfall, for as soon as representatives of the nobility were found who preferred true glory to unjust power, the state began to be shaken, and civil dissension began like an earthquake. For after Tiberius and Gaius Gracchus, whose ancestors had contributed much to Rome during the Carthaginian and other wars, began to assert the freedom of the people and expose the crimes of the oligarchs, the guilty nobles were terrified. They opposed the Gracchi, now through the allies, now through the Knights. These latter

---

[1]Sallust, *Jugurthine War* 41–42.

they won away from the commons by holding out the hope of sharing their special privileges. First Tiberius, then a few years later Gaius, who had followed in his brother's footsteps, were slain, although one was a tribune and the other a member of a commission for the founding of colonies.

13.2   Social and Economic Conditions: The Gracchi

Roman writers such as Sallust (previously) were not interested in the kind of economic and social analysis that is characteristic of modern history. They wrote about people, not about "movements" or "forces." Social and economic explanations have to be pieced together from scattered accounts. Often these accounts are fragments of political tracts or propaganda speeches. Each side, popular or oligarchic, tried to give its own "spin" to its particular account of the issue in question.

Of these issues, none was more inflammatory than the matter of land, poverty, and the army. By the middle of the second century B.C., Rome had become the preeminent military power in the Mediterranean. As a consequence, wealth poured into Italy and undermined the traditional style of family farming, and with it the military basis of the draft. Writing over 200 years later but using earlier sources, the biographer Plutarch gives the following sketchy account of how the problem originated and the efforts of one member of the senatorial class, the tribune Tiberius Gracchus (whose mother, Cornelia, was mentioned in Chapter 12), to address it.[2]

Of the land which the Romans won in war from their neighbors, some they auctioned publicly. The rest they turned into public land and assigned to the poor and needy, for which the latter were to pay a small rent to the state treasury. But when the rich began to offer more by way of rent and drive out the poor, a law was passed that restricted the holding of public land by one person to no more than 500 acres. For a while this law restrained the greed of the rich and helped the poor. They were able to remain on the land they rented, and they continued to occupy the allotment they had from the outset. But then the rich of the neighborhood managed to transfer these rentals to themselves by means of fictitious names. Finally they openly took possession of most of the land in their own names.

The poor who were forced off the land were no longer enthusiastic about military service, or even about raising children. The result was that in a short time there was a distinct manpower shortage of freeborn men all over Italy. In their place gangs of foreign slaves filled the land. The rich used these to cultivate the lands from which they had driven off the free citizens. . . .

On being elected tribune of the plebs, Tiberius took the matter in hand. Most writers say he was encouraged in this plan by Diophanes the rhetorician and Blossius the philosopher . . . but some say that Cornelia, the mother of Tiberius, was partly responsible. She often reproached her sons with the fact that the Romans still called her the daughter of Scipio [*i.e., Scipio Africanus, the conqueror of Hannibal*] rather than the mother of the Gracchi. . . . [However] his brother Gaius claimed in a propaganda tract that when Tiberius was passing through Etruria on his way to Numantia, he saw for himself that the countryside had been stripped bare of its native inhabitants and that the farmers and the tenders of the flocks were imported,

---

[2]Plutarch, *Tiberius Gracchus* 8; 9; *Gaius Gracchus* 3–7 (selections).

barbarian slaves. It was this experience that first led him to develop the policies which were so fatal to the two brothers. Most of all it was the people themselves who excited Tiberius's energy and ambition. By means of messages and appeals written on public porticoes, walls, and monuments, they called on Tiberius to recover the public land for the poor.

And so Tiberius proposed a law for the redistribution of publicly owned land to the landless and thus, he hoped, to restore the traditional basis of the draft. Plutarch preserves a fragment of one of his speeches drumming up support for his program.

The wild animals that wander over Italy have dens and lairs to hide in, but the men who fight and die for Italy have only air and light—and nothing else! Houseless and homeless they wander the land with their wives and children. And when their generals appeal to them before a battle to defend their ancestral tombs and shrines from their enemies, they lie: Not one of them has a family altar; not one of these Romans possesses an ancestral tomb. Instead they fight—and die—for the wealth and luxury of others. They are said to be the masters of the world, but they do not have so much as a single clod of earth they can call their own.

Although the law passed, Tiberius was assassinated by his enemies while still in office. His opponents tried to make a case for the legitimacy of his murder, but the killing of a tribune, protected by sacrosanctitas, *the inviolability and holiness of his office, made a mockery of the traditions of the ancient social pact between rich and poor, patricians and plebeians, that for so long had undergirded the state. More blows to social concord were delivered in the next round of the Gracchan crisis, 123–121 B.C., when Tiberius's brother Gaius took up the cause. Having been elected tribune, he proposed another, much more comprehensive round of reform legislation.*

After Gaius entered office, he instantly became the most prominent of all the tribunes. He was incomparably the best orator, and the passion with which he still lamented his brother's death made him all the more fearless in speaking. He used every occasion to remind the people of what had happened to Tiberius, and he contrasted their cowardly behavior with that of their ancestors. . . . "Before your eyes," he said, "these men beat Tiberius to death with clubs. They dragged his body from the Capitol through the streets and tossed it into the Tiber. Moreover, those of his friends who were caught were put to death without trial. And yet it is the ancient tradition of our fathers that if anyone is accused on a capital charge and does not make an appearance in court, a trumpeter shall go to the door of his house and summon him to appear. Until this is done, the judges may not vote on his case. These were the kinds of safeguards and protections our ancestors believed necessary in capital cases."

After he had stirred up the people with words of this type—and he had a powerful voice and spoke with great conviction—he proposed two laws. One provided that if the people had deprived any magistrate of his office he should be disbarred from holding any future office. The second law made a magistrate who had banished a citizen without trial to be liable himself to prosecution by the people. The first was obviously aimed at disqualifying Marcus Octavius, who had been deposed from the tribunate by Tiberius. The other targeted Popillius, who as praetor had banished the friends of Tiberius. Without waiting for trial, Popillius fled from Italy. The other law, however, was withdrawn by Gaius himself, who said he spared Octavius at the request of his mother Cornelia. This pleased the people and they agreed to its withdrawal, honoring Cornelia no less on account of her sons than of her father. Later on they erected a bronze statue of her with the inscription "Cornelia, Mother of the Gracchi." . . .

He now introduced a number of laws to flatter the People and undermine the power of the Senate. The first regarded public land which was to be divided up among the poor. The next stipulated that soldiers were to be equipped at public cost without any deduction being made from their pay for this, and that nobody under seventeen should be drafted. A third law proposed to extend the franchise to the Italians. A fourth lowered the price of grain for the poor. The fifth had to do with the appointment of jurors.

It was this law that did more than any other to cut down the power of the Senate. They alone served as jurors in criminal cases and this privilege made them feared by the people and the knights alike. Gaius' law added 300 knights to the 300 senators to create a pool of 600 from which the jurors would be drawn. . . . The People not only passed this law but also allowed Gaius to choose the jurors, who were to come from the equestrian order, so that he found himself invested with something like monarchical power. Even the Senate agreed to accept his advice. When he did counsel them, it was always in support of some measure that brought credit to that body. For instance, there was the case of the very equitable and ethical decree concerning the grain which the propraetor Fabius sent to the city from Spain. Gaius persuaded the Senate to sell the grain and to send the proceeds back to the cities of Spain. He had Fabius censured for making the administration of the province intolerably burdensome to the inhabitants. This brought Gaius a great reputation in addition to making him popular in the provinces.

He also introduced legislation for the founding of colonies, the building of roads and public granaries. Although he himself undertook the management and direction of all these projects, he showed no signs of being worn down by these different and demanding tasks. On the contrary, he carried each one out with amazing speed and application as if it were the only one he was doing. Even those who hated and feared him were struck by his efficiency and his ability to get things done. As for the people, they were thrilled to see him surrounded by a mob of contractors, craftsmen, ambassadors, magistrates, soldiers, and scholars. He was on familiar terms with all of these. Yet, while showing kindness and the kind of consideration that was due to each, he was able to preserve his dignity. In this way he was able to demonstrate that those who cast him as intimidating, overbearing, or violent were envious detractors. . . .

His greatest enthusiasm was reserved for the building of roads. These he made beautiful and graceful as well as useful. Made of quarried stone and tamped sand, they were laid out straight across the countryside. Depressions were filled in, watercourses or ravines were bridged. Both sides of the road were leveled or raised to the same height, so that the whole project had everywhere an even and attractive appearance. . . .

Unfortunately for Gracchus, the office of tribune was a weak base on which to try to carry on such an ambitious, independent program. The Senate outbid him in crowd-pleasing legislation and was able to undermine his support. When he ran for a third term as tribune, he was defeated. Then, when the Senate proceeded to take apart his legislative program, Gaius' followers were provoked into a confrontation. In the riot that ensued, violence resulted and the oligarchs in the Senate had the excuse to declare an emergency. Gaius and his followers were slaughtered and their property confiscated. To crown their triumph and rub salt in the wounds, the temple of Concord, which had been built centuries earlier as a monument to the establishment of understanding between plebeians and patricians, was refurbished by Opimius, one of the prime instigators of the emergency decree.

13.3   Politicians and Generals out of Control

In 88 B.C., L. Cornelius Sulla was sent out as commander against the king of Pontus, Mithridates VI, whose generals had invaded the Roman province of Asia Minor and the mainland of Greece. One of the events of the campaign was the siege of Athens. Plutarch, after narrating the barbarous cutting down of the groves of the Academy and Lyceum gymnasia (the locations of Plato's and Aristotle's schools) for lumber for the siege, and detailing Sulla's demands for money, contrasts the behavior of the generals of the past with those of the present. It was precisely the transformation of the generals of Rome from servants of the state to independent dynasts that illustrates the distance between the late Republic and the earlier Republic.[3]

Since he [*Sulla*] needed a great deal of money for the war, he helped himself to the treasures in the sanctuaries of Greece, taking some from Epidaurus and some from Olympia, sending for the most beautiful and valuable objects deposited there. He also wrote to the guardians of Delphi saying that it was better to send the possessions of the god to him: either he would protect them more safely, or, if he used them, he would give back as much. . . .

Accordingly, the treasures were shipped out; most of the Greeks did not know about this. But the great silver wine cask, the last of the royal gifts [*of Croesus, king of Lydia*], was too large and heavy for transportation, and the guardians of Delphi were forced to cut it into pieces. As they did so, they recalled first Titus Flamininus, then Manius Acilius and Aemilius Paulus. Manius had driven Antiochus [*King of Syria*] out of Greece and the others had conquered the Macedonian kings. Not only did these men leave untouched the sanctuaries of Greece but they even made gifts to them and honored them and increased the general veneration felt for them.

These were lawful commanders, they reflected, of well-disciplined men who had learned to serve their leaders without question. The consuls themselves were men of kingly souls and simple in their personal expenses, keeping their costs within the fixed allowances of the state. They thought it more shameful to seek popularity with their men than to fear the enemy. But now the Roman commanders rose to the top by force, not worth, and because they needed armies to fight each other rather than enemies of the state, they were forced to be both demagogues and generals. In order to pay for the gratifications with which they purchased the loyalty of their soldiers, before they knew it, they had sold off the fatherland itself.

Thus, in order to become the masters of those better than themselves they made themselves the slaves of the worst. These kinds of activities drove Marius into exile and again brought him back against Sulla; these made Cinna the murderer of Octavius and Fimbria of Flaccus. And not least, Sulla led the way. For to corrupt and win over those under the command of others, he made lavish expenditures on his own soldiers. As a result of making traitors of the soldiers of other generals and profligates of his own soldiers, he had need of a great deal of money, especially for this siege.

The breakdown of the old system of senatorial control was complete by 60 B.C. Although Roman politics was always characterized by political factions and deal-making, nothing was quite so brazen (at least to that point in time) as the so-called "First Triumvirate" of Pompey, Crassus, and Caesar. The complaints of Cato (the Younger) about the use of women for political purposes does not mean that marriage

---

[3]Plutarch, *Sulla* 12.

was not used for this end in the past, but merely that it had become part of a larger process of "new poli-tics" in which the traditional restraints were gone.[4]

Caesar, shielded by the friendship of Crassus and Pompey, launched his campaign for the consulship and was triumphantly elected with Calpurnius Bibulus. As soon as he entered his office, he immediately began to legislate, but more in the style of a demagogic tribune of the people than a consul. Thus, to please the mob he proposed a variety of laws for the establishment of colonies and the division of land.

In the Senate he was opposed vigorously by the traditional power wielders. But this was just the opportunity he had been looking for a long time, and so, complaining loudly that the Senate's insolence and stubbornness left him no alternative, he took himself off to the Forum. Then, with Crassus on one side of him and Pompey on the other, he asked the people if they approved his laws. When they said they did, he asked them for their help against those who were threatening to oppose him with their swords. They promised him their help, and Pompey added that if it came to swords, he would come with both sword *and* shield. The aristocracy was offended by this crazy and childish talk; they thought it was degrading to Pompey's own dignity and lacked the respect due to the Senate. The people, however, were delighted by it.

Caesar tried to make still greater use of Pompey's power. He had a daughter named Julia, who was engaged to Servilius Caepio. He now engaged her to Pompey, saying that he would give Pompey's daughter to Servilius, although she too was engaged, having been promised to Faustus, the son of Sulla. A little later, Caesar married Calpurnia, the daughter of Piso, and had Piso made consul for the next year. Thereupon Cato violently objected, protesting that it was unbearable that the power of government be bargained away by marriage alliances and that these men should advance each other to the commands of provinces and armies and other positions of power by means of women. Caesar's colleague in the consulship, Bibulus, finding he was unable to obstruct Caesar's legislation and that, along with Cato, he was in danger of being killed in the Forum, shut himself up at home for the rest of his time in office.

Right after his marriage, Pompey filled the Forum with his veterans and helped the people pass Caesar's laws as well as securing for him as his consular province Gaul on both sides of the Alps, along with Illyricum and four legions. The governorship was to last five years. Cato tried to speak against these measures. Caesar, thinking he would appeal to the tribunes, ordered him off to prison. But Cato, without saying a word, went off to jail. Caesar, seeing that both the nobility and the people were displeased, and out of respect for his good character were following him in silence dejectedly, secretly asked a tribune to release him.

13.4   Social and Cultural Changes

13.4.1   "The Beginnings of Foreign Luxury"

By the time Livy set about writing his story of the rise and decline of the Roman Republic, he had plenty of evidence of what looked like moral decay all around him to explain the decline. How much of this was real moral decay and how much was just an aspect of the change from city-state to world-state is a

---

[4]Plutarch, *Caesar* 14.

complicated issue. An additional factor that needs to be emphasized is that Livy was the heir to a long literary tradition of viewing the present in terms of the failure of contemporaries to live up to the glories of their virtuous ancestors. However, if we set aside Livy's complaints about the awful present, we can see some of the changes that really did take place—for instance, the introduction, along with new wealth, of a generally higher standard of living than the puritanical past of the "ancestors" allowed.

The following is a particularly good example of Livy's taking shots at the present in the guise of analysis of the past. Manlius Vulso returned to Rome in 187 B.C. to celebrate his triumph over the Gauls of Anatolia. His enemies spread the rumor that he had relaxed the old-fashioned discipline of Roman commanders and let his troops run riot in his province. Livy uses the opportunity to preach a little sermon.[5]

The origins of foreign luxury were brought to Rome by the returning army [of Manlius]. They were the first to introduce into Rome bronze couches, expensive rugs as covers, curtains and other elaborate woven fabrics, and what *then* were thought to be exotic pieces of furniture—tables with a single leg and marble topped sideboards. To banquets were added women lute and harp players and other pleasures of the feast. The banquets themselves began to be prepared with greater care and expenditure. Then the cook, for our ancestors the lowest of slaves in terms of both actual worth and use, began to have real value. What had been regarded as a mere labor now became an art! Yet these things, which at the time were thought to be remarkable, were merely the seeds of the luxury to come.

13.4.2 "He Mocked all Greek Culture and Learning"

Prolonged contact with the Hellenistic world made the Romans conscious of their cultural backwardness. They also discovered that there were lifestyles other than the rather narrow one that all Romans had been forced to accept up to that time. One of the key aspects of the Roman Revolution was the rapid and self-assured response of the Roman elites to the challenge of Greek culture, though understandably the guardians of traditional values at Rome regarded this response as evidence of moral decadence.

From approximately 200 B.C. onward Romans began first to dabble in, and then become serious practitioners of, many, though not all, aspects of Greek high culture. In due course the Romans would have attractive private alternatives to service to the state, something the shrewd Cato anticipated when an embassy came to Rome in 153 B.C. from Athens to plead against a judicial decision and stayed to "infect" the youth of the city.[6]

Cato was already an old man when a delegation came from Athens to Rome. Carneades the Academic philosopher and Diogenes the Stoic came to beg that the people of Athens be released from a fine of 500 talents that had been imposed on them. The Oropians had brought suit, the Athenians failed to appear, and the Sicyonians had judged against them.

As soon as the philosophers arrived the most intellectual among the younger Romans rushed to see them and listened to them with pleasure and wonder. Most of all they were impressed by the grace and power of Carneades' oratory whose performance did not fall short of his reputation. His speeches attracted a large and sympathetic audience and the city was filled with his praises as if by a great, roaring wind. The word spread all over that a Greek of

[5]Livy 39.6.
[6]Plutarch, *Cato* 22–23.

astonishing ability had come who could overwhelm all opposition by his eloquence. He had so entranced the youth of the city that they had abandoned their pleasures and pursuits and had become enthused with philosophy.

The majority were pleased with this, and were glad to see their youth involved with Greek culture and associating with such distinguished men. But Cato, when passion for words first manifested itself in the city, was much upset, fearing that the younger generation's ambition would be deflected to the glory of mere words rather than military exploits.

Accordingly, when the reputation of the philosophers continued to increase in the city, and no less prominent a man than Gaius Acilius volunteered to act as their interpreter for their first meeting with the Senate, Cato determined to find some plausible excuse to clear all the philosophers out of the city. So, he came to the Senate and proceeded to blame the current magistrates for keeping the embassy in such long suspense although they were men whose powers of persuasion were so great they could obtain anything they wanted. "We ought," he said, "to decide one way or the other on this issue and to vote on what the embassy proposes so that these distinguished men may return to their own schools and lecture the youth of Greece while the young men of Rome may, as in the past, pay attention to their own laws and magistrates."

He did this not as some think because of personal hostility to Carneades, but because he was entirely opposed to philosophy and mocked all Greek culture and learning out of patriotism. . . . In order to discredit Greek culture in the eyes of his son, he spoke too loosely for his years, predicting that the Romans would be destroyed when they became infected by Greek learning. But time has shown how empty this prophecy was, for while the city was at the height of its powers it embraced every form of Greek learning and culture.

13.4.3   In Defense of Public Service

A century later, Cato's presentiments had become reality. By the first century B.C. the Roman upper class discovered pleasures—and ideals—other than service to the state. In 56 B.C., Cicero felt the need to defend the old system in his tract On the Commonwealth (De Re Publica) *and to attack those who proposed the ideal of leisure as an alternative way of life, as it was found in some Greek philosophical systems. Although Cicero cannot avoid giving himself a pat on the back for his service to the state (see especially the closing paragraph), there is a great deal of truth in his eulogy of the old Republican ideal.[7]*

It is not enough to possess virtue as if it were an art of some kind; it must also be applied in real life. While it is true that an art, even if never used, can still be retained in the form of knowledge, virtue on the other hand, depends entirely on use. And its highest use is in the government of the state and the actual performance in deeds, not words, of those principles with which the philosophers make their ivory towers resound.

No principles worked out by philosophers . . . have not also been discovered and put into practice by those who draw up law codes for states. What is the source of our sense of moral obligation and our duty to the gods? What is the source of the law of nations or our own civil code? Whence justice, dependability, fair dealing? From where comes our sense of shame, self-restraint, fear of disgrace, desire for praise and honor? Whence courage in the face of toil and danger? Where else but from those men who have developed these qualities by a system of

---

[7]Cicero, *De Re Publica* 1.2.

education and then either confirmed them by custom or enforced them by laws? Xenocrates, one of the foremost philosophers, was asked, so it is said, what his students learned from him. He replied, "To do of their own free will what the law required them to do." Therefore, the individual who compels *all* men by the authority of the magistrates and the penalties of law to follow a way of life that the philosophers by persuasion can convince *only a few* to follow is to be held superior. . . .

Against these well-founded and sound arguments, those who take the opposite view allege first the amount of work involved in the defense of the state . . . then the grave risks involved in a political career. . . . They say that the most worthless men are attracted to public life. To be compared with them is degrading, to quarrel with them, especially when the mob is worked up, wretched and dangerous. Therefore, it is claimed, the wise man should not get involved in government since he cannot restrain the mindless and untamed furies of the crowd. Nor does a freeman struggle with vile and savage opponents or submit to the scourgings of abuse. . . .

They hold up before the brave man the dishonorable fear of death. Brave men, however, are more likely to regard it a greater disaster to be wasted by the natural processes of aging than to have the opportunity, in preference to all else, of giving up their lives for their country—lives which, in any case, must be surrendered to nature. . . . In truth, our country did not bear us or educate us without expecting some kind of service in return. It has not been only to serve our convenience that it has provided us with a safe refuge for our leisure and a quiet place for our moments of tranquility. Rather, our country has given us these opportunities so that it may take advantage of our most important powers of mind, our talents, and our wisdom, leaving only for our private use what it did not need. . . .

I see that nearly all of whom the Greeks called the Seven Wise Men spent their lives in public service. For there really is no other occupation in which human excellence nearly approaches the divine than the founding of new states or the preservation of those already in existence.

13.4.4   Cicero on the Decadence of the Roman Elite

The previous reading was Cicero in his philosophic mode. As Cicero well knew, however, the kind of leisure activities enjoyed by Romans of the new age did not involve much philosophizing. This is clear in the following brief extract from a letter to his friend and confidant Atticus.[8]

Our leading men think they have transcended the summit of human ambition when the bearded mullets in their fish ponds eat out of their hands while letting everything else go to hell.

13.5   Women of the Late Republic: Standing Up to the Triumvirs

The soldier and senator Velleius Paterculus made the following sardonic comment about family loyalties during the murderous proscriptions of the Triumvirs Antony, Octavian, and Lepidus: "Toward the proscribed [i.e., those who ended up on the death lists] their wives showed the greatest loyalty;

---

[8]Cicero, *To Atticus* 2.1.

their freedmen quite a lot; their slaves some; their sons none." *We have already seen a proof of this in the Turia inscription in Chapter 12. Another example follows, not so much of the loyalty of wives to husbands, but of how women felt that they had the right (and the duty) to protect what was theirs and that they could depend on popular support for their position.*

The background of the story is this. After the murder of Caesar, his avengers needed money to pursue their campaign against the assassins Brutus and Cassius. First the Triumvirs proscribed the property of their enemies, but when they found they were still short, they decided on a different tactic. Note how the women first try to handle the matter privately but, when that does not work, they go public. Aristocratic ideology is heavily emphasized.[9]

The Triumvirs addressed the people on this subject and published an edict requiring 1,400 of the richest women to make a valuation of their property and to furnish for the service of the war an amount the Triumvirs would see fit. It was provided further that if any should conceal their property or make a false valuation, they should be fined, and that rewards would be given to informers, whether free or slave.

The women decided to approach the womenfolk of the Triumvirs. With the sister of Octavian and the mother of Antony they did not fail, but they were repulsed from the doors of Fulvia, the wife of Antony, whose rudeness they could scarcely endure. They then forced their way to the tribunal of the Triumvirs in the Forum, the people and the guards dividing to let them pass. There, through Hortensia, whom they had delegated as their representative, they spoke as follows:

"As befitted women of our rank addressing a petition to you, we had recourse first to the women of your households. But having been treated with discourtesy by Fulvia, we have been driven to come to you in person publicly. You have already deprived us of our fathers, our sons, our husbands, and our brothers, whom you accused of having wronged you. If you take away our property also, you reduce us to a condition unbecoming our status, our manners, and our gender. If we have done you wrong, as you say our husbands have, proscribe us as you do them. But if we women have not voted any of you public enemies, have not torn down your houses, destroyed your army, or led one against you, if we have not hindered you in obtaining offices and honors—why do we share the penalty when we did not share the guilt?

"Why should we pay taxes when we have no part in the honors, the commands, the politics for which you fight against others with such dreadful results? 'Because this is a time of war,' do you say? When have there not been wars, and when have taxes ever been imposed on women, who are exempted by their gender among all humankind?

"Our mothers did once rise above their gender and made contributions when you were in danger of losing the whole empire and the city itself during the Carthaginian Wars. But then they contributed voluntarily, not from their landed property, their fields, their dowries, or their houses, without which life is not possible to free women, but only from their own jewelry, and even these not according to fixed valuation, not under fear of informers or accusers, not by force and violence, but what they themselves were willing to give. What alarm is there now for the empire or the country? Let war with the Gauls or the Parthians come, and we shall not be inferior to our mothers in zeal for the common safety. But for civil wars may we never contribute, nor ever assist you against each other! We did not contribute to Caesar or to Pompey.

---

[9]Appian, *Civil Wars* 4.32–34. Based on the translation of Horace White (London, 1893).

Neither Marius nor Cinna imposed taxes upon us. Nor did Sulla, who held despotic power in the state, do so, whereas you say that you are reestablishing the commonwealth."

While Hortensia was giving her speech, the Triumvirs were angry that women should dare to speak publicly while the men were silent, and that they should demand reasons for their acts from the magistrates. . . . They ordered the lictors to drive them away from the tribunal, which they proceeded to do until cries were raised by the people outside. Then the lictors stopped and the Triumvirs said they would postpone consideration of the matter until the next day.

On the following day they reduced the number of women who were to present a valuation of their property from 1,400 to 400 and decreed that all individuals who possessed more than 100,000 drachmae, both citizens and strangers, freedmen and priests, men of all nationalities without a single exception . . . should lend them at interest a fiftieth part of their property and contribute one year's income to the war expenses.

13.6   The Augustan Settlement

With biting irony the historian Tacitus (d. ca. A.D. 120) describes how the dynast Gaius Octavius (Octavian, later known as Augustus) brought the Roman Revolution to completion. The adopted great-nephew of Julius Caesar, Octavian succeeded on Caesar's assassination in 44 B.C. to the great man's name and fortune. Tacitus gives scant credit to the overwhelming nature of the problems facing Octavian after a century of upheaval, let alone to his adroitness and general success in solving them.[10]

When after the destruction of Brutus and Cassius there was no longer any army of the Republic . . . and when with Lepidus pushed aside and Antony slain . . . then dropping the title of Triumvir and giving out that he was a consul and was satisfied with a tribune's authority for the protection of the people, Augustus won over the soldiers with gifts, the populace with cheap grain, and all men with the attractions of peace. So he grew greater by degrees while he concentrated in himself the functions of the Senate, the magistrates, and the laws. He was wholly unopposed, for the boldest spirits had fallen in battle or in the proscription, while the remaining nobles, the readier they were to be slaves, were raised the higher by wealth and promotion, so that, aggrandized by revolution, they preferred the safety of the present to the dangers of the past. Nor did the provinces dislike that condition of affairs, for they distrusted the government of the Senate and the People, because of the rivalries between the leading men and the rapacity of the officials, while the protection of the laws was unavailing, as they were continually upset by violence, intrigue, and finally by corruption. . . .

At home all was tranquil, and there were magistrates with the same titles; there was a younger generation, sprung up since the victory of Actium [*the battle in 31 B.C. that eliminated Octavian's last rival, Antony*], and even many of the older men had been born during the civil wars. How few were left who had seen the Republic! Thus the state had been revolutionized, and there was not a vestige left of the old-style virtue. Stripped of equality, all looked up to the commands of a sovereign without the least apprehension for the present.

---

[10]Tacitus, *Annals* 2, 3, 4, 9, 10. Based on the translation of A. J. Church and W. J. Brodribb, *The Annals of Tacitus* (London: Macmillan & Co., 1906).

On the death of Augustus, Tacitus reports various opinions about his accomplishments.

Intelligent people . . . spoke variously of his life with praise and blame. Some said that dutiful feeling toward a father [*the duty to avenge his adoptive father, Julius Caesar*], and the necessities of the state in which laws had then no place, drove him into civil war, which can be neither planned nor conducted on any right principles . . . the only remedy for his distracted country was the rule of a single man. Yet Augustus had reorganized the state neither as a monarchy nor as a dictatorship but as a principate [*the rule of the first man in the state, the Princeps*]. The ocean and remote rivers were the boundaries of the Empire; the legions, provinces, fleets—all things were linked together; there was law for the citizens; there was respect shown for the allies. The capital had been beautified on a grand scale; only in a few instances had he resorted to force, simply to secure general tranquility.

It was said, on the other hand, that filial duty and state necessity were merely assumed as a mask. His real motive was lust for power. Driven by that, he had mobilized the veterans by bribery and, when a young man with no official position, had raised an army, tampered with a consul's legions, and pretended attachment to the faction of Sextus Pompey. Then, when by a decree of the Senate he had usurped the high functions and authority of praetor . . . he at once wrested the consulate from a reluctant Senate and turned against the Republic the arms with which he had been entrusted to use against Antony. Citizens were proscribed and lands divided. . . . Even granting that the deaths of Cassius and Brutus were sacrifices to a hereditary enmity (though duty requires us to ignore private feuds for the sake of the public welfare), still Sextus Pompey had been deluded by the phantom of peace, and Lepidus by the mask of friendship. Subsequently, Antony had been lured on by the treaties of Tarentum and Brundisium and by his marriage with the sister of Augustus, and he paid by his death the penalty of a treacherous alliance. No doubt there was peace after all this, but it was a peace stained with blood.

13.7   The Reforms of Augustus

In some respects Augustus' social and cultural reforms were less important than the way in which he handled himself in these areas of Roman life. Rome was still a community where people saw each other—and their rulers—on a day-to-day basis. There was little Augustus could do to reverse the developments of the previous century except perhaps to provide the community with a more secure political environment. The Senate became more inclusive, coming to represent not just the elites of Rome but also the elites of Italy and, to some extent, of the provinces as well. The army was professionalized—a major undertaking with social as well as political implications. The people subsided into a less active, but still important role. They were still aware that they were an imperial people, and they did not hesitate to remind the elites of this fact.

Perhaps Augustus' greatest accomplishment was to create, in low-key fashion, a new consensus, a new social compact among the various components of the state. The biographer Suetonius conveys this in his undramatic, detailed account of the emperor's life. It is a deceptive account. From his matter-of-fact presentation it is as hard to appreciate the significance of Augustus' accomplishments as it is from Tacitus' venomous portrait. Yet Augustus was truly a new Romulus, a second founder of Rome.[11]

---

[11]Suetonius, *Augustus* 24, 28, 29, 30, 31, 34, 35 (selections).

The Army

He made many changes and reforms in the army as well as restoring some of the old traditions. He demanded the severest discipline. He reluctantly allowed his commanders to visit their wives, and then only in the winter months. He sold a Roman knight and his property at public auction because he [*the knight*] had cut off the thumbs of his two young sons to incapacitate them for military service. However, when he saw that some tax collectors were bidding for him, he knocked him down to one of his own freedmen, with the understanding that he should be sent to the countryside and allowed to live there as a free man. He gave the entire Tenth Legion a dishonorable discharge because of its insubordination. Other legions that insolently demanded discharge he disbanded without the usual bounty for service. Cohorts that broke in battle had every tenth man executed; the remainder were fed on barley. Centurions who quit their posts were executed just like the other ranks. He punished other derelictions of duty with various penalties such as having the culprits stand all day in front of the general's tent, sometimes wearing tunics without their sword belts or holding measuring rods or sods of earth [*as though they were common soldiers whose job it was to measure out a marching camp and build its ramparts*]. . . .

He established a fixed scale of pay and allowances for the soldiers everywhere. In order to keep them from revolting after their discharge on the grounds of age or want, he standardized the length of service and discharge bounty according to rank. In order to have funds always in hand for the maintenance of the military and the pensioning off of veterans, he established a military treasury supported by new taxes.

The Senate

He reduced the Senate to its former number and restored its honor by two revisions. It had been swollen by a base and ill-assorted mob and numbered over a thousand. Some were wholly unworthy, having been admitted by favoritism and bribery after Caesar's death. The first revision was left to the senators themselves, each senator naming one other. Then Agrippa and Augustus went through the membership rolls. At that process it was believed that Augustus wore a coat of mail and a sword under his tunic when he presided, while ten of his strongest senatorial friends crowded around his chair. . . . Some senators he shamed into resigning but allowed them to retain their senatorial garb and the right to sit in the orchestra seats at the games and to participate in the order's banquets. . . .

He ordained that privy councils should be chosen by lot every six months. Their job was to discuss in advance matters that were to come before the Senate as a whole. During important debates he called upon senators without warning to give their opinions, not following the old system. The idea was to encourage everyone to give close attention to the debate and participate actively, not just saying "I agree with what's being said."

Religion and Morals

He restored ruined or burned temples. These, along with others, he beautified with the richest gifts. For example, he deposited a single offering of 16,000 pounds of gold together with pearls and other jewels worth 50 million sesterces.

After assuming the office of Pontifex Maximus on the death of Lepidus . . . he collected whatever Greek and Latin books of prophecies were in circulation, under either anonymous names or the names of little-known authors, and burned more than 2,000 of them. He kept only the Sibylline books and purged even these. They were deposited in two gilded cases under the base of the statue of Apollo on the Palatine.

The calendar had been reformed by Julius Caesar but had subsequently, through negligence, fallen into confusion and disorder. Augustus restored it once more. While doing so he renamed the Sixth Month by his own surname, although he was born in September. He did this because he had his first consulship and won his most important victories in this month.

He increased the number and importance of the priests, as well as their privileges; the Vestal Virgins were particularly favored. When the death of one of the Vestals created a vacancy, many families used their influence to keep their daughters from the pool from which the candidate would be chosen by lot. In response, Augustus swore that if any of his granddaughters were of suitable age, he would have proposed her. He revived some of the ancient rites which had gradually fallen into disuse, such as the augury of the Goddess of Safety, the office of Flamen Dialis, the Lupercal Festival, the Secular Games. He forbade beardless youths to run at the Lupercal and would not allow young people of either sex to attend any of the nighttime ceremonies of the Secular Games unless accompanied by an adult relative. He ordained that the Lares of the Crossroads be crowned twice a year with flowers, in the spring and summer.

Next to the immortal gods, he most honored the memory of the leaders who had advanced the dominion of the Roman people from the least to the greatest. Accordingly, he restored the buildings of such men, together with their original inscriptions. In both colonnades of his forum he dedicated statues to all of them in triumphal garb. In a proclamation he declared that he did this to make his fellow citizens demand that he while he lived, along with his successors, should measure up to the example of these great men of the past.

He amended some laws and enacted some new ones, as for example the law against extravagance, on adultery and unchastity, on bribery, and on the encouragement of marriage. Having been more severe in the reform of this last law, he was unable to put it into force because of open refusal to obey it. As a result, he was forced to withdraw it and abolish or mitigate the penalties, increasing the benefits for large families and allowing a three-year interval after the death of a husband or wife. Even then the Knights were not satisfied and agitated for its abolition at a public show. Augustus then sent for the children of Germanicus[12] and showed them off, some sitting in his own lap and some in their father's. By his gestures and looks he made it clear that they would not be overwhelmed if they followed Germanicus' example. When he discovered that the law was being dodged by betrothals with immature girls and frequent changes of wives, he shortened the engagement period and put a limit on divorce.

Building and Administration

Since in appearance the city did not live up to its position as the capital of the Roman Empire and was furthermore exposed to flood and fire, Augustus so beautified it that he could rightly claim that he had found it built of sun-dried bricks but left it made of marble. He built many public works. Among the most important are the following: his forum with the temple of Mars the Avenger; the temple of Apollo on the Palatine; and the sanctuary of Jupiter the Thunderer on the Capitol. He built his forum because of the increase in the population and the corresponding increase in the number of lawsuits, which the existing two forums could not accommodate. . . . He divided the city into districts and wards. The former were under the

---

[12]Germanicus was one of Augustus' potential successors.

control of magistrates chosen each year by lot; the latter, however, were supervised by officers elected by the people in the individual neighborhoods. To guard against fires he organized stations of night watchmen, and to control floods he widened and cleaned up the channel of the Tiber. For some time it had been filled with rubbish and narrowed by overhanging houses.

Rome, Italy, and Demography

After reorganizing Rome and its affairs in this fashion, he increased the population of Italy by personally founding twenty-eight colonies. He provided many municipalities with public buildings and revenues. To some degree he gave them equal rights and dignity with the city of Rome itself by devising a voting system in which the local magistrates and senators voted for candidates in Roman elections. The ballots were sent under seal to Rome to be held there until the day of the elections.

So as not to allow the number of upper-class people to decline, he admitted to the equestrian military career those who were recommended by any town. Similarly, so that the number of commoners might not decrease, he distributed 1,000 sesterces for each legitimate child when he made his round of the city districts.

13.8   Reaction to Augustus' Moral Reforms

Most of Augustus' energies were directed toward solving political and military problems, but he was also confronted with the moral decay of the upper classes, where adultery was common and marriage was infrequent along with childlessness among those who did marry. The marriage laws of Augustus of 18 B.C. and A.D. 9 attempted to do something about this state of affairs. They encouraged marriage and having children, made adultery a crime, and prohibited marriage between freeborn citizens and members of disreputable professions. However, as the following reading demonstrates, Augustus was not exactly a model for others to imitate.[13]

In the meanwhile there was a ruckus in the senate over the disorderly conduct of young men and women. It was alleged that this was the reason for their reluctance to marry. When the senators urged Augustus to do something about this problem, making ironical allusions to his own philandering, he at first replied that the necessary restrictions had already been laid down and that nothing further could be regulated by decree in a similar way. When driven by his questioners into a corner, he said, "You yourselves ought to lay the law down to your wives as you wish; that is what I do." When the senators heard this they questioned him even more, asking to know what admonitions he claimed to give to Livia [*his wife*]. Reluctantly, he made a few remarks about women's dress and their adornment, about their going out and their modest behavior, not a bit concerned that his actions did not conform to his words.

---

[13]Dio Cassius 54.16.3–5.

Chapter 14

The Roman Peace

The Roman Empire was one of the great multicultural, multilingual empires of all time. It was also one of the most successful. Geographically, the empire stretched from Scotland to the Sudan and from Morocco to Ukraine. It embraced most of Western Europe, all of the Mediterranean, and large portions of the Middle East. Before the coming of Rome these regions had never formed a single state. After the collapse of the Roman Empire they were never united again.

Generalizations about the Empire should take these factors into account. For instance, one way of looking at the Roman Empire is to see it simply as the sum total of the myriad peoples, nations, tribes, temple-states, chiefdoms, independent cities, and petty kingdoms that made it up. Over this amalgam presided a handful of Romans who themselves became less and less "Roman" and more and more provincial as the centuries passed.

Yet it would be a mistake to assume that the diverse peoples of the Empire possessed the kind of strong ethnic self-consciousness that is found in modern times and is often associated with the formation of states. Greeks, for instance, while identifying each other as sharers in a common culture spread throughout the Mediterranean and Black Sea areas, never recognized a common "Greek" government or state. Apart from their utopian dreamers, they never demonstrated any great desire or capacity for coming together to form a self-governing nation. On the other hand, among the peoples of the Empire, Jews were exceptional in that they had both a state, Judaea, and a self-conscious culture that extended outside the narrow borders of Judaea. A more common state of affairs was the picture sketched by the Scots chieftain Calgacus, who depicts the Roman army as a rabble of peoples from everywhere in the Empire, even, to his regret, from his own land.

Despite its multi-ethnic character, we have little information about what ordinary people of the Empire thought about it, or even what they knew of it. Did the peasants who constituted perhaps 90 percent or more of the population care much who governed them as long as the government was beneficial to them in some way? We do know, however, a lot about how the Roman upper classes felt about the Empire, and especially what they *thought* was appropriate for their subjects to feel, as can be seen, for instance, in Calgacus' speech mentioned above. We also know how some Romans, such as the poet Juvenal, felt about Greeks and other foreigners and what, at least for public consumption, a provincial such as Josephus had to say about Rome.

That the Empire ultimately fell is no surprise; that it survived for as long as it did is astonishing. What held it together was a complex web of institutions. The army and its great reputation, won primarily in the Republican period, was clearly one, if not the principal, factor, as the survey by Josephus (in the section "Nations by the Thousands…") demonstrates. The emperors were generally hard-working, intelligent men who dealt in person with great as well as very ordinary matters. The system was open enough to allow provincials to make their way in it, as did the forebears of the great African Septimius Severus, as well as Septimius himself. The ancient practice of extending the franchise and involving non-Roman elites in the governing system was practiced to great effect. In general, the case for the Empire is summed up by the clear-sighted historian Tacitus in the blunt speech of Cerialis to the rebellious Gauls: The only alternative to Rome, he said, "was chaos."

14.1   "They Make a Desert and Call it Peace": A View of Rome from the Provinces

Britain was added to the Empire in the first century A.D. *One of the principal architects of the conquest was Agricola, the father-in-law of the great senatorial historian Tacitus. The following reading is found in a eulogy composed by Tacitus in honor of Agricola's accomplishments. The speech is attributed to the Caledonian (Scottish) chieftain Calgacus, who is trying to rally his troops against the Romans. The sentiments are conventional Greco-Roman projection, that is, they express what they thought would or should be the appropriate sentiments of barbarians. Tacitus' intent was not so much to provide historical insight into the mind of a Scot chieftain egging on his reluctant followers to fight, as it was to berate contemporary Romans for their lack of spirit. Although they thought of themselves as masters of the world, Tacitus is saying, they were in reality the slaves of the emperors.*

The picture he paints of the Empire is a bleak one. While it is undoubtedly true that a percentage of Rome's subjects would have shared these sentiments, the opinion that states were nothing but organized robberies was an old one. This speech should not be interpreted as though it were based on a poll of Rome's subjects. Calgacus despairingly suggests that there is some hope in the heterogeneous ethnicity of the Roman army.[1]

"Whenever I review the causes of this war and our present desperate situation, I have great confidence that today our united efforts will be the beginning of Britain's liberty. The reason is that all of us are united. We are free of the effects of enslavement. There is no other land beyond us. Indeed, not even the sea is secure, for Rome's fleet threatens us from that quarter. Thus battle and arms will offer for the brave the most glory, and for the coward the greatest safety.

"Previous battles against the Romans, although fought with varying outcome, have left us the hope of success. We, the best people in Britain, living in the country's inner recesses and never having any contact with the conquered, have, as a result, preserved ourselves unpolluted from the contagion of enslavement. Here at the world's end, we, the last unenslaved people, have preserved our liberty to this day because of our remoteness and our obscurity. Now,

---

[1]Tacitus, *Agricola* 30.

however, the farthest parts of Britain lie open and all the unknown is wondered at. But there are no peoples beyond us, nothing but the waves and the rocks—and the even more cruel Romans. Their arrogance you cannot escape by obedience and submission. Robbers of the world, having exhausted a devastated earth, they now try the oceans! If the enemy is rich they are avaricious; if he is poor they lust for power. Neither East nor West has satisfied them. Alone among humankind they covet with equal rapacity rich and poor. Plunder, slaughter, and robbery they falsely call empire; they make a desert and call it peace.

"Children and kin are by nature our dearest possessions. Yet these are carried off from us by levy to be slaves in other lands. Our wives and sisters, even if they escape the lust of our enemies, are seduced by men pretending to be friends and guests. Our goods and possessions are collected for tribute, our land and harvests for grain requisitions. Our very bodies and hands are ground down by the lash, making roads through marsh and forest. Slaves born into slavery are sold once and for all and are at least fed by their owners; but Britain daily purchases her own enslavement—and to boot, feeds what she has purchased! Just as in the slave-gang the most recent addition is the butt of the jokes of his fellow slaves, so in this worldwide slave-gang we, the most recent and most dispensable, are marked for elimination, for there are no lands or mines or harbors in our land for whose exploitation we might be preserved.

"Bravery and independence of spirit on the part of subject peoples are unpalatable to their masters. Remoteness and isolation, to the degree they provide safety, provoke suspicion. Accordingly, since there is no hope of mercy, even at this late hour take courage, whether it is safety or glory that is most precious to you. The Brigantes under the leadership of a woman were able to burn a colony, storm a camp, and if their success had not made them careless, they might have thrown off the Roman yoke altogether. Therefore, we who are untouched and unconquered, who were bred for freedom not regrets, let us show them at the first battle what kind of men Caledonia has been keeping in reserve.

"Do you imagine that the Romans will be as brave in war as they are lustful in peace? It is our own disputes and feuds that bring them fame; the mistakes of their enemies become the glory of their army. That army, made up of different peoples, is held together by success and will fall apart when things go badly for them. Unless of course you suppose that Gauls and Germans and even, I am ashamed to admit, many Britons, having loaned their support to an alien tyranny of which they have been enemies longer than subjects—unless you think they are attached to Rome by loyalty and affection. Fear and terror are weak ties of attachment; take them away and those who have ceased to fear will begin to hate.

"All the incentives to victory belong to us. The Romans have no wives to inspire them, no parents to reproach them if they run away. The majority have no fatherland at all or at best one very far away. Few in number, uneasy because of their lack of knowledge of the country, looking around at an unknown sky, an unknown sea and forest—they have been delivered by the gods to us like caged prisoners.

"Do not be frightened by their outward show; the flash of gold and silver neither helps nor hurts. We shall find help in the very battle lines of the enemy. The Britons will recognize their own cause, the Gauls will remember their former liberty; the rest of the Germans will desert them just as the Usipi did recently. Behind them there is nothing to fear: empty forts, colonies of old veterans, weak and quarreling towns with their disloyal subjects and unjust rulers. Here in front of you are the general and his army; there on the other side you have taxes and mines and all the other punishments suffered by the enslaved. Whether you endure these forever or avenge them at once rests upon this field. Therefore, as you go into battle, think of your ancestors and your descendants."

14.2   Foreigners in the Roman Army

In the previous reading the Scottish chieftain Calgacus claimed that if the Roman army suffered a defeat it would quickly fall apart because it was made up of foreigners. There was some truth to this. Although the legions were recruited from among citizens, these recruits came from widely scattered parts of the Empire. In addition, the auxiliary units that supported the legions were drawn wholly from the noncitizen population of the Empire. The following are memorial inscriptions put up by legionary and auxiliary soldiers serving in the Roman army in Britain. Avitus' monument, the second below, is elaborate. It shows the deceased in military dress holding his will written on wax tablets in his left hand.[2]

To the spirits of the dead. Marcus Aurelius Alexander, prefect of camp of the Twentieth Legio Valeria Victrix, a Syrian of Osroene. He lived seventy-two years. His heirs set up this monument.

To the spirits of the dead. Caecilius Avitus of Emerita Augusta [*modern Merida in Spain*], centurion's second-in-command, member of the Twentieth Legio Valeria Victrix. He served for fifteen years and lived thirty-four years. This inscription is set up by his heir.

As Calgacus noted to his shame (see previous reading), even Britons served in the Roman army. A degree of Romanization can be inferred from the fact that the father of the dead soldier in the next inscription goes by a Roman name, Vindex.

To the spirits of the departed. Nectovelius, son of Vindex, aged twenty-nine with nine years service. He was a Brigantian [*the Brigantes were a tribe in northern England*] by tribe and served in the Second Cohort of Thracians [*an auxiliary unit made up of volunteers from the Balkans*].

14.3   The Alternative: "If the Romans Are Driven out What Else Can There Be Except Wars Among All These Nations?"

Calgacus' despairing words in the previous reading and his description of the Empire as a "desert" was echoed by later writers, including the great Edward Gibbon, author of the monumental The Decline and Fall of the Roman Empire, *who characterized the Empire as a "dreary prison."*

Realistically, however, what was the alternative? In this reading Tacitus puts the case for Rome. It comes in the form of a blunt speech given by the Roman commander Cerialis to a number of Gallic tribes who had revolted against Rome and had just been reconquered. It is as plain and straightforward as the speech of the barbarian chief Calgacus was florid and bombastic, a supposed characteristic of Celtic rhetoric to which Cerialis refers.[3]

---

[2]R. G. Collingwood and R. P. Wright, *The Roman Inscriptions of Britain* (Oxford, 1965), nos. 490, 492, 2142.
[3]Tacitus, *Histories* 4.73–74.

Cerialis called an assembly of the Treveri and Lingones and spoke as follows:

"I am not one for words; instead, I have always maintained the power of Rome by force of arms. But since words mean a great deal to you people, and you judge things to be good or evil not as they really are but as agitators say they are, I have a few things to say. As the war is over, you may get more benefit from hearing what I have to say than I will get from having to speak.

"Gaul always had its petty kingdoms and wars until you submitted to our power. Although often provoked, we have used the right of conquest to burden you only with the cost of keeping the peace. For peace among nations cannot be maintained without armies; armies cost money, and money can be raised only by taxation.

"We hold everything else in common. You often command our legions; you rule these and other provinces; you are not segregated or excluded by us. You benefit from good emperors though you live far away, while we who live close by suffer from evil ones. Accept the extravagance and avarice of your masters just as you put up with bad harvests and floods and other natural disasters. There will be vices as long as there are men. But they are not eternal, and they are counterbalanced by better times—unless of course you think you will be better off under Tutor and Classicus [*the rebel leaders*], or that the armies to protect you from the Germans and Britons will cost less!

"If the Romans are driven out—Heaven forbid!—what else can there be except wars among all these nations? Eight hundred years of the divine fortune of Rome and its discipline have produced this federal empire and it cannot be pulled apart without the destruction of those attempting to do just this.

"You are in the most dangerous situation. You have gold and wealth—the main causes of war. Therefore, love and care for peace, and also love and care for that city which victors and vanquished alike share on an equal basis. Learn the lessons of fortune for good or evil: Do not choose obstinacy and ruin in preference to submission and safety."

14.4   A Roman View of Foreign Competition

Juvenal (ca. A.D *55–ca. 130) is the author of some of the best vignettes of Roman social life. In sixteen satires he denounces women and men, rich and poor, Romans and foreigners, the corruption of wealth, and the abuse of freedom, with an invective seldom rivaled. He works an old theme that we also encountered in the writings of Livy and Sallust (see Chapter 13).*

In this particular reading, Juvenal is pursuing one of his favorite targets: "Greeks"—that is, just about anyone from the Mediterranean area who spoke Greek (or perhaps just Latin with an accent).[4]

Now let me talk about that race with which our rich is so much enamored but which I cannot abide. Not to put too fine a point upon it, I can't stand a Rome that is Greekized. Yet what fraction of these supposedly Greek dregs actually comes from Greece? Syrian Orontes [*the main river in Syria, a Hellenized province in the Middle East*] has for years deposited its verbal and cultural sewage into our very own Tiber. These Greeks worm their way into our great houses with the aim of becoming their masters. Quick of wit, unrestrained

---

[4]Juvenal, *Satires*, 3.58–107.

in nerve, they have the gift of the blarney in a degree that outstrips even professional word slingers.

What do you think that fellow's profession is? Actually, he has any character you like—schoolmaster, orator, expert in geometry, a painter, an athletic coach, a diviner, a doctor, an astrologer—he's all of these professions in turn if he's hungry enough. If your order him to fly, there, off he goes, airborne. . . . Greece is a nation of actors. If you smile, your Greek friend will explode with laughter; if he sees a friend weep, he weeps—not, of course, that he feels anything; if you say you're cold, he puts on his cloak; if you say you're hot, he sweats. So you see, we don't share a level playing field. The Greek always has the advantage of being ready night or day to borrow his mood from somebody else's.

14.5 "Nations by the Thousands . . . Serve the Masters of the Entire World": What Held the Roman Empire Together

One of the most comprehensive overviews of the geographical extent of the Roman Empire and its military power appears in the form of a speech the Jewish historian Josephus attributes to King Herod Agrippa (A.D. 53–ca.100), who was trying to restrain Josephus' countrymen from revolting. Judaea had suffered at the hands of some particularly poor Roman governors, the last of whom, Gessius Florus, was one of the worst. The country boiled with plots for rebellion. Although Herod does the speaking, the substance of the speech probably reflects the speech Josephus himself gave at the beginning of the war when he found himself in similar circumstances and had to try to dissuade the countrymen of his district from rebelling.

The speech reveals the kind of knowledge of the Romans a provincial upper-class individual such as Josephus possessed at the time of the Jewish Revolt (A.D. 66–70). It also shows the kinds of predicaments people in the provincial upper classes could find themselves in vis-à-vis their hotheaded countrymen. Josephus rather readily went over to the Romans and, as a result, was hated by his countrymen who joined the revolt.

He begins by reminding his hearers that their forebears, although much better organized, had not resisted the Romans effectively in their first encounter with them in 63 B.C. While Josephus/Herod's knowledge of geography and the battle order of the Roman army is impressive, it is hard to believe that people set on revolt would be impressed by this kind of academic approach.[5]

"Your ancestors. . . , the Athenians. . . , the Spartans. . . , the Macedonians—nations by the thousands, who had greater passion for liberty than you, have yielded. Will you alone refuse to serve the masters of the entire world? What troops, what weapons do you rely on? Where is your fleet to sweep the Roman seas? Where are the financial resources for your revolt? You must think you are going to war with Egyptians or Arabs! Are you blind to the magnitude and extent of Roman power? Why do you refuse to weigh your own weakness? Our forces have often been defeated even by our neighbors, while theirs are undefeated throughout the world! Indeed, they want even more. They are not content with the Euphrates as a frontier in the east, the Danube in the north, Libya and the desert beyond to the south, and Cadiz on the west. They have sought a new world beyond the Ocean and fought the previously unknown Britons!

---

[5]Josephus, *Jewish Wars* 2.358–388.

"Face up to it! You are not richer than the Gauls, stronger than the Germans, smarter than the Greeks, more numerous than the people of the inhabited world. What gives you the confidence to tackle the Romans? 'It is cruel to be enslaved,' someone will say. How much more so for the Greeks, who are the most talented of peoples and occupy such a vast territory. Yet they must obey the six fasces *{the bundle of rods symbolizing authority}* of a Roman magistrate! A similar number control the Macedonians, who, more justly than you, are due their liberty. What of the five hundred cities of Asia? Without a garrison they prostrate themselves before a single governor and his consular fasces. Is it necessary to speak of the peoples around the Bosporus, Black Sea, the Sea of Azov. . . ? Previously these peoples did not recognize a ruler even from among themselves, but now they are subject to three thousand legionaries. Forty war ships keep the peace in that formerly unnavigable, dangerous sea. What powerful claims to freedom might be made by the peoples of Anatolia; yet they pay what they owe without the compulsion of arms.

"Then there are the Thracians, a people spread over a country [*Bulgaria and part of Greece*] five days' march in width and seven in length. Their land is more rugged and much more easily defended than yours. Its icy cold repels invaders, but do they not obey two thousand Roman guards? Their neighbors the Illyrians, who live in the land stretching from Dalmatia to the Danube frontier [*i.e., Yugoslavia*], yield to two legions and even cooperate with the Romans to repel the raids of the Dacians [*from Romania*]. . . .

"But if any nation might be excited to revolt by its natural advantages it is surely the Gauls. Nature provides them with the ramparts of the Alps to the east, the river Rhine in the north, the Pyrenees mountains in the south, and the Ocean in the west. Although surrounded by these defenses, with a population of three hundred and five tribes, and prosperity welling as it were from the land and flooding the rest of the world with its products, they nevertheless allow themselves to be treated by the Romans as a source of taxes. They have their own good fortune served back to them by their conquerors. And they accept this, not because of weakness of will or meanness of spirit: They fought for their freedom for eighty years. But they are overawed by the power of the Romans and their good fortune, which wins them more victories than their arms. That is why the Gauls are enslaved to 1,200 soldiers—hardly more than the number of their cities!

"As for Spain—neither the gold from its mines nor the vast stretch of land and sea which separates it from the Romans were sufficient to protect it in its struggle for freedom. Nor for that matter did the Lusitanian and Cantabrian tribes with their passion for war, nor the neighboring Ocean, whose tides terrify even the native, make any difference; the Romans, advancing beyond the Pillars of Hercules and traversing the cloud-capped Pyrenees, enslaved all these peoples. The guard for this remote nation of hard fighters is a single legion!

"Who among you has not heard of the populous German nation? You have seen their huge and powerful figures on many occasions since everywhere the Romans have them as their captives. This people occupies a vast territory. Their spirit surpasses the size of their bodies and disdains death. Enraged they are fiercer than wild beasts. Yet the Rhine stops their expansion. Tamed by eight Roman legions, those captured are enslaved and the whole nation seeks safety in flight.

"You who put your trust in the walls of Jerusalem consider what a wall the Britons had! The Ocean surrounds them; they live in an island as big as our whole Mediterranean world. Yet the Romans crossed the Ocean and enslaved them. Four legions now secure that vast land. But why say any more when the Parthians, the most warlike of peoples, rulers of so many nations and secure by the possession of such great power, send hostages to the Romans? Under the pretext of seeking peace, the elite of the East may be seen in Italy bowing in submission.

"When almost every nation under the sun prostrates themselves before the arms of Rome will you alone make war against them? Consider the fate of the Carthaginians, who boasted of the great Hannibal and the nobility of their Phoenician origins. They fell to the hand of Scipio. . . . This third part of the whole inhabited world [*i.e., North Africa*], whose peoples are hard to enumerate, bounded by the Atlantic Ocean and the Pillars of Hercules and stretching to the Indian Ocean, supporting as it does the countless Ethiopians—they have it all under their thumb. Besides their annual harvest, which feeds the Roman people for eight months, these peoples over and above pay tribute of all kinds. Unlike you, who see outrage in the demands of Rome, they readily contribute to the needs of the Empire, although only a single legion is garrisoned among them.

"Why look so far afield to demonstrate the power of Rome when we can find it in Egypt, our closest neighbor? Egypt stretches as far as Ethiopia and Arabia Felix and is the point of departure for India. It has a population of seven and a half millions, not counting the inhabitants of Alexandria. This is shown by the individual tax returns. Yet this country does not spurn the rule of Rome. What an incentive to revolt it has in Alexandria, with its huge population, its great wealth and size! . . . The tribute Egypt sends to Rome exceeds in one month what you send in a year! The land is protected by impassable deserts, seas without harbors, rivers and swamps. Yet none of these assets were sufficient to resist the Fortune of Rome. Two legions stationed in Alexandria curb the remotest parts of Egypt and the proud Macedonian elite to boot.

"What allies do you hope for in the coming war? You must expect them from the uninhabited wilds, for the inhabited world is all Roman." . . .

14.6   Making It at Rome

14.6.1   The Career of an Emperor: Septimius Severus

Since the first century of the Empire, provincials in increasing numbers entered the Roman Senate. There was nothing unusual about the process itself. For centuries in the Republic there had been a steady, if unspectacular, movement of outsiders into the ranks of the ruling elite. They came first from the immediate areas around Rome, then from farther afield in Italy. Julius Caesar was supposed to have outraged the Senate by the introduction of trousered Gauls. The rise of the great emperor Septimius Severus followed a predictable pattern. His ancestors pioneered the way, though not much is known of their rise to prominence from the out-of-the-way Punic town of Leptis in Libya.

Septimius' own career was as ordinary as the style of the author who relates it. Following a fairly typical career pattern, he moved from one post to another over much of the Empire—from Italy to Spain, to Sardinia, to France, to Hungary, to Sicily. Finally, as luck would have it, he ended up in a major military command in Hungary and was there when its emperor was killed and his own troops took it upon themselves to proclaim him emperor. A bloody civil war followed from which Severus emerged victorious, establishing a dynasty that lasted from A.D. 193 until 238. When the Severan dynasty ended, Rome was plunged into half a century of even more violent civil war.[6]

---

[6]*Septimius Severus* 1–5.

After Didius Julius had been assassinated, Severus, who hailed from Africa, became emperor. His home town was Leptis Magna. His father was Geta, and his ancestors were Roman knights even before the citizenship had been extended to everyone in the Empire. Fulvia Pia was his mother, and his great-uncles were the consulars Aper and Severus. Macer was his father's father, and his mother's father was Fulvius Pius. He himself was born six days before the Ides of April in the second consulship of Erucius Clarus and the first consulship of Severus (A.D. 146).

When still a child, and before he began his Greek and Latin studies (in which he was highly educated), he would engage only in the game of "Judges" with the other children. When he played this game he would have the rods (the *fasces*) and axes carried in front of him and, surrounded by the other children, would sit and pass judgment. At eighteen he gave a speech in public, and after this came to Rome to continue his studies. With the help of his relative [*of the same name*] Septimius Severus, he petitioned and received the broad senatorial purple stripe from the Deified Marcus [*the Emperor Marcus Aurelius*].

On his arrival at Rome he met a man—not someone he knew—who at that very moment was reading the *Life* of the Emperor Hadrian. He took this as an omen of success in his career. . . . He performed the duties of quaestor diligently, having skipped the military tribunate. After the quaestorship he was assigned to the province of Baetica [*southern Spain*] by lot, and from there went back to Africa to settle the affairs of his family, his father having died. But while he was in Africa he was reassigned to Sardinia in place of Spain, which was being ravaged by the Moors. Having served his quaestorship in Sardinia, he was appointed legate to the proconsul of Africa. . . .

He was promoted to tribune of the plebs by the Emperor Marcus Aurelius and executed his responsibilities with great strictness and vigor. It was at this time he married Marciana, although he says nothing of her in the story of his life as a private citizen. When he was emperor, however, he put up statues in her honor. He was designated praetor by Marcus [*Aurelius*]. . . . After he had been sent to Spain he dreamed that he should restore the temple of Augustus at Tarraco, which was in a state of ruin. Then he dreamed that he saw from the top of a very high mountain Rome and the whole world while the provinces sang in harmony to a lyre or flute. Although absent from Rome, he put on the usual games in the city.

He was then put in command of Legio IV Scythica, stationed near Marseilles. After this tour of duty he went to Athens to continue his studies, to perform some religious functions, and to see the public buildings and the ancient monuments. . . .

Next he was appointed legate to the province of Lyons [*in France*]. Meanwhile, since his wife had died and he wished to marry again, he made inquiries into the horoscopes of possible brides, being himself an expert in this field. When he heard there was a certain woman in Syria whose horoscope predicted she would marry a king [*Julia Domna*], he asked her to become his wife and with the aid of friends succeeded. He soon became a father. He was loved by the Gauls as no one else because of his strictness and his sense of honor.

Next he ruled the two provinces of Pannonia [*parts of modern Austria, Hungary, and Yugoslavia*] with proconsular power. After this he was selected by lot to govern the proconsular province of Sicily. Meanwhile another son was born at Rome. While he was in Sicily, he was indicted for consulting soothsayers or Chaldaean astrologers regarding the future of the emperor but was acquitted by the judges because Commodus [*the reigning emperor*] was already hated. His accuser was crucified. He was consul for the first time with Apuleius Rufinus as his colleague [*A.D. 190*] among a very large group appointed by Commodus. After the consulship he spent a year without an official posting. Then on the recommendation of Laetus [*another general*] he was given the command of the army in Germany. . . . In Germany he conducted himself in the legateship in such a way that he was able to increase his reputation, which was already significant.

Thus far he pursued his military career as a subject. But when it was learned that Commodus had been assassinated and that Julianus had taken his place amid universal hatred, he was proclaimed emperor, though against his will, by the German legions at Carnuntum.

14.6.2   A Celt Makes Good

Another example of provincials rising in the Roman administration is the career of Gaius Julius Severus. A descendant of Celts who invaded Anatolia [Turkey] in the third century B.C., Severus began his career in typical fashion by serving in his own homeland, Galatia, and then moving into the Roman federal system.[7]

Gaius Julius Severus, the descendant of kings and tetrarchs [*the old rulers of Galatia*]. Having held all the key offices in his own nation, he was admitted to the rank of tribune of the plebs by the divine emperor Hadrian. He then served as legate of the governor of Asia, and next, by appointment of Hadrian, he was made commander of Legio IV Scythica and administrator of Syria when Publius Marcellus left because of the revolt in Judaea [*the second Judaean revolt, A.D. 132–135; Marcellus took a legion with him*]. He was proconsul of the province Achaea [*in Greece*] with five fasces. Hadrian sent him to the province of Bithynia as curator of accounts. He was prefect of the Treasury of Saturn [*in Rome*], consul, priest, superintendent of Public Works in Rome, and propraetorian legate of Lower Germany. . . . Marcus Julius Euschemon erects this inscription in honor of his benefactor.

14.6.3   Making It in the Ranks

Marcus Vettius Valens rose through the ranks, beginning as a private in the Praetorian Guard at Rome and ending up as procurator, or personal agent and representative of the Emperor Nero in Portugal. He probably got his first appointment as the result of the recommendation of a patron, but thereafter his own abilities and the opportunity to "network" at Rome advanced his career smoothly. The Praetorian Cohorts were elite peace-keeping forces at Rome. The Vigiles served as firemen, and the Urban Cohorts also contributed to maintaining the peace.[8]

This inscription is set up to honor Marcus Vettius Valens, son of Marcus of the Aniensis tribe, patron of the colony of Ariminum [*in Italy*]. He began his career as a private in the 8th Praetorian Cohort [*at Rome*] and was clerk of the Praetorian Prefect. He was recalled for the campaign in Britain [*under Claudius*] and was decorated for bravery. He was then promoted centurion of the 6th Cohort of the Vigiles; next, centurion of the 16th Urban Cohort; next, centurion of the 2nd Praetorian Cohort; enrolled as a member of the Emperor's special escort;

---

[7]*Orientis Graeci Inscriptiones Selectae* 543.
[8]*Inscriptiones Latinae Selectae* 2648.

centurion, Legio XIII Gemina in Pannonia; First Centurion [*with equestrian rank*], Legio VI Victrix in Spain; decorated for successfully waging war against the Asturians; Tribune, 5th Cohort of Vigiles; Tribune, 12th Urban Cohort; Tribune, 3rd Praetorian Cohort; First Centurion for the Second Time, Legio XIV in Pannonia; Procurator Nero Caesar Augustus at the ducenarius level in the Province of Lusitania [*Portugal*].

14.7   Provincial Administration: Hands-On Style

There is a tendency to think of Roman emperors at best in terms of distant autocrats acting through faceless bureaucrats, and at worst as crazed pleasure lovers acting out their fantasies in gaudy palaces. But the reality was much more prosaic, as the following exchange of letters between the Emperor Trajan and his governor in Bithynia {northwestern Turkey}, C. Plinius Secundus, shows. Pliny tended to err on the side of caution, forever sending cases to the emperor that a more resolute (or perhaps unscrupulous) governor might have settled on the spot in consultation with his consilium.

The case reveals a lot about life in the provinces, at least among the upper classes. Flavius Archippus, a philosopher of somewhat dubious reputation, had ingratiated himself with the previous emperor Domitian, but when Domitian was assassinated, his enemies, led by a woman named Furia Prima, got busy and tried to have him condemned to hard labor at the mines. Archippus had kept good records and was able to fight back effectively. Clearly he had been a strong supporter of the previous Flavian regime (as his name suggests) and had cashed in on his position, alienating and victimizing in the process a number of his fellow townsmen. Furia Prima had evidently suffered in some way at his hands. Pliny takes no chances and lets the emperor handle the situation.

The styles of the Emperors Domitian and Trajan contrast with the pomposity of Nerva, who reigned briefly after the death of Domitian. The shrewd reading of the evidence by Trajan and his laconic comment regarding Furia Prima's complaint are of interest. His message to Pliny was: "Tell Furia I've read her letter, and I don't want to hear any more on this subject."[9]

Letter of Pliny to the Emperor Trajan

Sir: When I called the jurors to attend the hearings, Flavius Archippus claimed to be exempted because he was a philosopher. However, some people present said that indeed, not only should he be freed from jury service, but his name should be removed altogether from the jurors' list and that he should be shipped back to the prison from which he had escaped, to complete his sentence. In support of this the judgment of the proconsul Velius Paullus was read. According to this document Archippus had been condemned to the mines for forgery. While Archippus could not prove that the sentence had been reversed, he produced as evidence of his reinstatement a petition he had submitted to the Emperor Domitian along with letters from Domitian honoring him, and a decree in his honor from the people of Prusa. To these he added a letter written by you to him as well as an edict and a letter of our father [*the Emperor Nerva*] confirming the grants made to him by Domitian.

Accordingly, although such charges have been made against him, I thought nothing should be decided until I had first consulted with you. The case seemed to deserve your special attention. I attach to this letter the documents cited by the two parties.

---

[9]*Letters of Pliny* 10.58; 59; 60.

The documents are as follows:

The Letter of the Emperor Domitian to Terentius Maximus {the emperor's agent in Bithynia}

In response to the request of Flavius Archippus the philosopher I have ordered that up to 100,000 sesterces be made available to purchase land for him near Prusa, his native town. The income from this land is for the support of his family. I wish this to be done for him. The full amount is to be written off as an expression of my generosity.

The Letter from the Emperor Domitian to L. Appius Maximus {proconsul of Bithynia under Domitian}

My dear Maximus, I recommend Archippus the philosopher to you as a good person whose character is in harmony with his calling. Please show him every kindness in granting the small requests he may make of you.

The Edict of the Emperor Nerva

Citizens: There are some matters in which in happy times like ours there is no need of an edict, and equally other matters in which the intentions of a good emperor cannot but be clearly understood. I want every one of my citizens to know that I gave up my private life in response to the needs of all. I did so in order to dispense gladly new benefits, and to confirm those of my predecessor.

In order that your public rejoicings may not be spoiled by the misgivings of those who received favors, or because of the memory of the emperor who bestowed them [*the assassination of Domitian had apparently raised fears that Nerva might rescind his acts*], I thought it necessary and agreeable to dispel these doubts by a manifest act of kindness: No one is to think that I will withdraw any of the benefits, either public or private, bestowed by other emperors in order to claim the credit of restoring them for myself. They are fully ratified. Let no one on whom the Good Fortune of the Empire has smiled think his joy needs to apply for a renewal of petitions. On the contrary, give me the opportunity to bestow new favors; let it be known that I need only to be asked for those benefits which have not already been granted.

Letter of Nerva to Tullius Justus {proconsul of Bithynia under Nerva}

The governmental regulations, whether merely initiated or completed under previous regimes, are to be observed. Accordingly, the letters of Domitian remain valid.

Pliny's Covering Letter to the Emperor Trajan

Flavius Archippus has asked me, by your prosperity and immortality, to forward the petition which he has presented to me. I thought I should do this though I should also let his prosecutor [*Furia Prima*] know I was doing this. She has also given me a petition, which I am attaching to this letter. This way, by hearing each side, you might be better able to decide what should be done.

Response of Trajan to Pliny

It is possible that Domitian might not have known the status of Archippus when he wrote all those letters in his favor. However, I think it more reasonable to believe that

Archippus was in reality actually restored to his former status by Domitian's intervention. This is especially likely since the people of Prusa, who could not have been ignorant of the sentence against him by the proconsul Paulus, so often voted him the honor of a statue. But I do not mean to suggest, my dear Pliny, that if any new charges are brought against him, you should be slow to hear them.

I have read the petitions of Furia Prima, his accuser, as well as those of Archippus, which you sent me with your second letter.

14.8   Getting Along Together: The Role of Citizenship

From earliest times the Romans had used the conferral of citizenship as a technique for winning over, or at least neutralizing, the elites of neighboring peoples. In this reading, the historian Tacitus has tidied up a much longer, rambling speech given by the Emperor Claudius urging the Roman Senate to admit Gauls from across the Alps into its ranks. (Claudius' actual speech, in the form of an inscription, is also extant.) In making his case, Claudius responds to arguments that plenty of excellent candidates were to be found in Italy; he indicates that Gauls from the Italian side of the Alps had already been admitted—wasn't that proof enough?—and finally, answers the objection that the admission of rich Gallic provincials would block the careers of the native-born Italians.[10]

These and similar arguments failed to impress the emperor. He immediately refuted them and, after calling the Senate, spoke as follows:

"The earliest of my ancestors, Clausus [*in Latin, Claudius*], a man of Sabine origins, was made both a citizen and a patrician at the same time. This experience encourages me to proceed by the same principle of bringing to this city the best talent from wherever it is found. I am not unaware that the Julii came from Alba Longa, the Coruncanii from Camerium, and the Porcii Catones from Tusculum. But not to spend too much time on antiquity, we are well aware that men from Etruria, Lucania, and all Italy have been admitted to the Senate and that in the end, Italy itself was extended to the Alps, so that not only individuals but whole regions and peoples were joined together with us as Romans. With the enfranchisement of Italy beyond the Po [*i.e., Cisalpine Gaul*] and the enrolling of the best of the provincials in the legions, we revived an exhausted military and had unshaken peace at home and good relations with the rest of the world.

"Are we sorry that the Cornelii Balbi came to us from Spain and other equally distinguished men from southern Gaul? Their descendants are still with us; in their love for Rome they do not yield to us. What proved fatal for Sparta and Athens, no matter what their military strength, was the fact that they treated the people they defeated as aliens. Our founder Romulus, on the other hand, had the wisdom to convert on the same day enemies into Roman citizens. Foreigners have ruled us. The admission of the sons of freedmen to the magistracies is not, as many think, something new. It was a common practice in early times.

"It will be said: We fought against the Senonian Gauls. If that's the case then the Italian Volsci and Aequi never were arrayed against us! 'The Gauls sacked Rome.' Well, yes, but we also gave hostages to Etruscans and went under the Samnite yoke. If you review all our wars,

---

[10]Tacitus, *Annals* 11.24.

you will see that the Gallic War took the shortest time of all. Since then we have had unbroken peace and trust with them. Now that they have assimilated our customs and ways and have intermarried with us, let them bring us their gold and their wealth rather than leaving them keep it to themselves.

"Senators, all our institutions, however ancient they now seem, were once new. Plebeian magistrates followed on patrician, Latin on plebeian, Italian on Latin. This proposal now being considered will in its turn become established practice. What we are today justifying by precedents will itself become a precedent."

The Senate approved the emperor's speech and passed the appropriate decree. The Aedui were the first Gauls to become Roman senators. This was given in recognition of their ancient alliance with Rome and the fact that they alone enjoyed the title of "Brothers of the Roman People."

14.9 The Role of Law

One of the great achievements of Rome was the expansion of what had been the law of a single polis *to a world empire. As we see in the following reading, even when the power of the emperors was indisputably autocratic, the ideal of the rule of law remained intact.* The Institutes of Justinian *were published in* A.D. *533 as an introductory textbook for law students at the same time that Justinian published his monumental codification of Roman law,* The Digest.[11] *For more selections from the* Digest, *see* "Daily Life as Seen through the Law Codes" *in Chapter 16.*

Imperial Majesty should not only be distinguished by arms, but also protected by laws, so that government may be justly administered in time of both war and peace. The Roman Princeps [*i.e., the emperor*] may then not only stand victorious in battle with [*exterior*] enemies but also, by legitimate measures, defeat the evil designs of wicked men [*within the state*]. He can then triumph as much for his administration of justice as for his victories over his foes.

---

[11]From the Preamble of Justinian's *Institutes.*

Chapter 15

Society and Culture in the Roman Empire

It would be misleading to talk about *the* society and culture of the Roman Empire as though the Empire were some kind of modern homogeneous nation-state, a France or a Japan, which possessed a single dominant culture and society. Analogies with multinational empires—Ottoman, Habsburg, or Russian/Soviet—are more helpful, but still misleading because of their huge centralized administrative systems, something Rome completely lacked. Yet the Empire did have a dominant culture and society: a mix of Greek and Latin elements at one level, and local, combined with Latin *or* Greek, at another. Multiple empires coexisted: A developed, urbanized, culturally dominant Greek east was wedded to a more rural, less developed, Latin-dominated west. At the same time, most of the Empire, east as well as west and north, operated at the level of a Third World society: primarily rural, with a small urban population. The hundreds of local and regional cultures were united only to the extent to which they had a connection with one of the dominant cultures.

Rome had no plan, ideological or otherwise, to knit all of these heterogeneous bits and pieces of society into a coordinated whole. Acknowledgment of diversity came naturally, if unavoidably, to the Roman mentality. The only really major issue for Rome was how to maintain order and thereby preserve its privileged position in the chaotic cultural geography Romans called their Empire. This was accomplished by a variety of means. Local elites were tied to the administrative and military system and to each other by patronage and opportunity (as discussed in Chapter 14), but they also found cohesion through religion; common forms of leisure; similar expectations of each other on the part of rich and poor alike; a common high culture including art, literature, and philosophy; and the extension of uniform urban forms of life into areas of the west and north that had never experienced them before. Daily life was altered for millions just by the possibility of easy travel between one part of the Empire and another, as well as by the presence almost everywhere of temples, baths, theaters, aqueducts, amphitheaters, and impressive public buildings of all kinds.

Cultural and social diversity, of course, lay close to the surface, and Greco-Roman culture was always wafer-thin. The frontier with the barbarian world existed not only along the great rivers of Northern Europe and the deserts of Africa and the East, but also within the Empire itself. Nevertheless, despite its apparent brittleness, Greco-Roman culture was remarkably vital and enormously elastic. It had great depth and richness. To the end it managed to attract and hold significant numbers of outsiders. Its ability to cope with diversity has hardly been matched before modern times.

15.1   Obligations of the Rich

While the rich had clearly defined privileges in society, they also had some well-defined obligations. These included, first and foremost, personal service to the local municipality, and then to the imperial government. They were expected to stand for election to local offices, serving in the local senate or council; perform the duties of patron (which included handing out cash); and serve in the legions. For some, service in the imperial administrative system and the Roman Senate was a tradition.

In the first inscription below, Pliny, the Roman senator whom we encountered in Chapter 14 (see "Provincial Administration: Hands-On Style"), and who we will hear from in this chapter (see "Imperial Obligations"), serves as an illustration of a fairly typical career pattern. Among other things, his career reflects the role local aristocrats were expected to play in relationship to their hometowns, in this case the city of Como in northern Italy. The inscription works back and forth chronologically, starting with Pliny's highest offices, then going back to earlier ones, and ending with his benefactions to Como.[1]

Gaius Plinius Caecilius Secundus, son of Lucius, of the Oufentina tribe, consul [A.D. 100]; augur; legate with propraetorian power of the province of Pontus and Bithynia [*parts of modern Turkey*], having been sent there by decree of the Senate with consular power, and by the Emperor Caesar Nerva Trajan Augustus Germanicus Dacicus, Father of the Fatherland. [*He was*] Curator of the Course and Banks of the Tiber and of the Sewers of the City of Rome; Prefect of the Treasury of Saturn; Prefect of the Military Treasury; Praetor; Tribune of the Plebs; Imperial Quaestor; President of a Squadron of Roman knights; Tribune of the Soldiers of Legio III Gallica; member of the Commission of Ten for Decisions on Civil Status.

He ordered by his testament the construction of baths for the municipality [*of Como*] costing . . . [*the amount is lost through a gap in the inscription*], with a further 300,000 sesterces for their decoration . . . [*another gap*] and 200,000 sesterces for their upkeep; likewise he bequeathed 1,866,666 sesterces to his city for the support of his 100 freedmen. The interest on this amount he directed to be afterwards devoted to the feeding of the plebs of Como . . . [*another gap*]; likewise, during his lifetime, he gave 500,000 sesterces for the support of the boys and girls of the urban plebs; he also gave a library and 100,000 sesterces for its upkeep.

Freed slaves were also expected to make contributions to their community and were often glad to do so, as it gave them a certain visibility and respectability. The subject of this inscription, Decimus Eros, had clearly made a success of his life. That his master and patron (of the same name, less the "Eros," a Greek name) belonged to the Roman upper classes and was very wealthy is clear from the fact that he could afford his own private physician. But Decimus Eros himself must have been a good doctor and surgeon so

---

[1]Dessau, *Inscriptiones Latinae Selectae* 2927.

that others in the Roman upper classes appealed to Decimus (the master) for Decimus's (the slave's) services. This work in turn added to the wealth and especially the prestige of the master. In the end, as custom dictated, Decimus Eros obtained his freedom by purchase, and he went on to a career as a municipal patron at Assisi in central Italy.[2]

Publius Decimus Eros Merula, freedman of Publius, clinical doctor, surgeon, ophthalmologist, member of the Board of Six. For his freedom he paid 50,000 sesterces; for the membership of the Board of Six he gave 2,000. He gave 30,000 sesterces for statues in the temple of Hercules. For paving public roads he gave 37,000 sesterces. On the day before he died he left an estate of 100,000 sesterces . . . [*the rest of the inscription is missing*].

15.2   Imperial Obligations

The emperor had his hands full dealing with an interesting collection of problems that came his way on a daily basis. Some problems were generated by the army, a huge force of over twenty-eight legions scattered from Scotland to Egypt. Others originated among the diverse populations of the Empire. Some were unnecessarily passed on to the emperor by nervous governors afraid to make decisions themselves. From the picture provided by the letters of the complacent Pliny, the emperor looks more like a shrewd, although hard-working, bureaucrat than a despot who commanded armies, a terror to those around him.[3]

To Cornelianus:

Lately I had the satisfaction at Centumcellae (as it is now called) of being summoned there by Caesar [*the Emperor Trajan*] to attend a council. Could anything be more pleasing than to see the emperor exhibiting not only his affability but his justice and wisdom, even in private, where those virtues are most observable?

The matters brought before him were a mixed bag. They tested in many instances his abilities as a judge. The affair of Claudius Ariston came up first. Claudius is a nobleman of Ephesus, of great generosity and unambitious popularity. His virtues, however, have made him obnoxious to a kind of people of very different character. These people instigated an informer against him, of the same stamp as themselves. But he was honorably acquitted.

Next the charge against Gallitta, accused of adultery, was heard. Her husband, who is a military tribune, was on the point of standing as a candidate for certain offices in Rome, but she disgraced him and herself by an affair with a centurion. The husband complained to the consul's aide, who in turn wrote to the emperor. Caesar, having examined the evidence, demoted the centurion and banished him. It remained only for some punishment to be inflicted on Gallitta, as it was a crime of which both must necessarily be equally guilty. But her husband's affection for her motivated him to drop this part of the prosecution, though not without some suspicion of connivance. Indeed, he had continued to live with her even after he had started his prosecution, contenting himself, it seemed, with getting rid of his rival. But he was ordered to proceed in the suit. He complied with reluctance. Although her accuser was unwilling, it was necessary that the defendant be convicted, and so she was. She was sentenced under the

---

[2]Dessau, *Inscriptiones Latinae Selectae* 7812.
[3]Pliny, *Letters* 6.31.

Julian Law. In his decree the emperor specified the name and rank of the centurion so that it was clear that this was a matter of military discipline. He did not want all cases of this kind to be referred to him.

The third day was devoted to the examination of Julius Tiro's will, a case that had caused a good deal of speculation. Part of the will was clearly genuine, but part of it, it was alleged, was forged. The persons accused of the fraud were the Roman knight Sempronius Senecio and one of the emperor's freedmen and procurators, Eurythmus. The heirs had jointly petitioned the emperor when he was in Dacia, asking him to conduct the inquiry himself. He agreed to do so, and on his return from the expedition, set a day for the hearing. Then, when some of the heirs, out of consideration for Eurythmus, thought of dropping the case, the emperor insisted, saying: "He is not Polyclitus, and I am not Nero."[4] He had, however, given the petitioners an adjournment, and now that the time had elapsed, he took his seat to hear the case.

Only two of the heirs were present. They petitioned that either all of the heirs should be compelled to appear, as they had all joined in the prosecution, or the case should be dropped. Caesar delivered his opinion with great dignity and restraint, and when the counsel for the defendants Senecio and Eurythmus claimed that unless they were heard their clients would remain under suspicion, the emperor said, "I am not so much concerned with the fact that they are under suspicion but that I am left under suspicion." He then turned to us who made up his council. "Advise me," he said, "how to act in this matter. They complain that I don't let them drop the suit." Finally, on the advice of the council, he ordered that all the heirs were to be called to carry on the case or else each one individually had to justify his withdrawal from the case. Otherwise he would declare them guilty of bringing false charges.

Thus you see the honorable and important way we spent our time at Centumcellae. In the evenings, however, we were able to relax. The emperor invited us to dinner every day, not very grand meals when you consider his position. Then we were entertained by recitations or else passed the night in pleasant conversation. On our last day the emperor, in his usual thoughtful way, sent us presents. As for myself, I was pleased not only with the dignity and wisdom of the judge, the honor of being on his advisory council, the ease and unreserved freedom of the conversation, but also with the attractiveness of the place itself. The delightful villa is surrounded by green meadows and commands a fine view of the sea, where a spacious harbor is being carved out in the shape of an amphitheater.

15.3   Religions and Moralities

The variety of religions in the Roman Empire was staggering. Every city, town, village, and rural community had its own set of deities and cults and a corresponding calendar of holy days and festivals. The celebration of these festivals was considered essential to the communitys' survival and prosperity. This was true even in an age of skepticism and relativism. Rules regarding appropriate rituals, how they were to be performed, and who was to perform them were prominent in municipal law codes. Most of these civic religions, as they are called, were low in doctrinal and ethical content but high in local appeal and personal satisfaction. When there was money available for sacrifices, banquets, games, and other

---

[4]Polyclitus was one of the notorious Emperor Nero's freedmen and a man to be feared.

entertainment, the ritual of the civic religions could be very impressive indeed and served to bring all members of the community together in the worship of the special gods who looked after that particular community. On the other hand there were the simple rituals of the countryside. Mystery religions offered alternatives of a different kind involving initiation into secret rituals and the consolations of such appealing goddesses and gods as Isis and Mithra. Magic and superstition flourished. Holy men performed miracles and exorcised demons.

Syncretism, the process of recognizing one's own gods in the gods of other peoples, helped bring some order to this otherwise chaotic pantheon. Appropriately, Rome itself (or its genius or fortune), along with its rulers, came to be regarded as divine and worthy of worship. Both Rabbinic Judaism and Christianity emerged from a complex background of eschatological expectations and more traditional worship practices. The popular philosophies of Epicureanism, Cynicism, Stoicism, and Skepticism offered, in varying degrees, coherent philosophies of the universe and appropriately related codes of conduct which in turn influenced the moral thought of Jews and Christians alike.

15.3.1   Civic Religion

The Empire was a patchwork of self-governing cities and their attached local villages or, where they existed, tribal communities. It was taken for granted in all of them that the gods, goddesses, heroes, and ancestral spirits would be worshipped at appropriate times of the year and with suitable rituals. During the early Empire the Romans attempted to bring order to this process of honoring the gods if for no other reason than to be sure that the gods always got their due. The pax deorum, *the existence of good relations between gods and humans, had been part of the Roman sense of due order from earliest times. When the Romans came to rule their empire, they continued to promote this simple but vital idea of a tangible, manageable—and therefore legally prescribable—connection between earth and heaven.*

The first reading is from the municipal charter of a Roman colony in southern Spain bearing the name "Colonia Genetiva Julia" (modern Osuna). The texts are from the regulations governing the religious obligations of the colony's annually elected magistrates, the duoviri and aediles. The magistracies of municipalities could be expensive propositions for the individuals concerned. Although they dispensed public funds, they also were expected to make significant contributions themselves to the running of the community. Note the way the ordinance is phrased in regard to public and private disbursements. The magistrates' compensation was the public recognition of their generosity by their fellow citizens (who could also choose to withhold this recognition if they thought the magistrates were being cheap).[5]

LXX. All duoviri, except those first appointed after this law, shall during their magistracy at the discretion of the decuriones celebrate a gladiatorial show or dramatic spectacles to Jupiter, Juno, and Minerva and to the gods and goddesses, or such part of the said shows as shall be possible, during four days, for the greater part of each day, and on the said spectacles and the said shows each of the said persons shall expend of his own money not less than 2,000 sesterces, and out of the public money it shall be lawful for each several duovir to expend a sum not exceeding 2,000 sesterces, and it shall be lawful for the said persons so to do with impunity. Always provided that no person shall expend or make assignment of any portion of the money, which in accordance with this law shall be properly given or assigned for those sacrifices which are publicly performed in the colony or in any other place.

---

[5]*Lex Coloniae Genetivae Juliae* 70–71, trans. E. G. Hardy, *Roman Laws and Charters* (Oxford: Clarendon Press, 1912), pp. 31–32.

LXXI. All aediles during their magistracy shall celebrate a gladiatorial show or dramatic spectacles to Jupiter, Juno, and Minerva, or whatever portion of such shows shall be possible, during three days for the greater part of each day, and during one-day games in the circus or forum to Venus, and on the said spectacles or shows each of the said aediles shall expend out of his own money not less than 2,000 sesterces, and from the public funds it shall be lawful to expend for each several aedile 1,000 sesterces, and a duovir or praefectus shall see that the said money is given and assigned, and it shall be lawful for the aediles to receive the same without prejudice.

15.3.2   The Ideology of Paganism

A statement of the ideology of the civic religion is to be found in the dialogue entitled Octavius, *written by the advocate Minucius Felix sometime in the early third century. The dialogue is presented as a debate between a Christian, Octavius Januarius, and a pagan, Q. Caecilius Natalis. Part of Caecilius' side of the debate is given here. After arguing that the world is not governed by providence, he concludes that it is better to hold on to the traditional forms of religion.[6]*

Since, then, because either chance is blind or nature uncertain, how much more reverent and better it is . . . to accept the teaching of our ancestors. We should cultivate the religions handed down to us and adore the gods whom we were first trained by our parents to fear rather than to know with familiarity. We ought not carry on dogmatically about them, but rather believe our forefathers, who while living in a primitive age, when the world was still young, were able to believe in gods who acted kindly. . . .

So it is that throughout all empires, provinces, and cities, we see that each people has its national rites of worship and adores its own local sets of gods. The Eleusinians [*who lived near Athens*] worship Ceres; the Phrygians [*in modern Turkey*], the Great Mother; the Epidaurians [*in southern Greece*], Aesculapius; the Chaldaeans [*in Iraq*], Bel; the Syrians, Astarte; the Taurians [*in the Crimea*], Diana; the Gauls, Mercury; and the Romans, all divinities. Thus their power and authority has occupied the circuit of the whole world; thus it has advanced the bounds of empire beyond the path of the sun and the frontiers of the Ocean itself. When they fight in the field, they show bravery inspired by religion. At home they fortify their city with sacred rites, with the Vestal Virgins, and with many priestly dignities and titles. When they were besieged [*by the Gauls in 390* B.C.] and all the city except for the Capitol taken, they still worshipped the gods, although other peoples, when their gods were angry, would have neglected them. . . . When, in turn, they capture a city, they venerate the conquered gods, although still full of fury from the struggle. Everywhere they seek the gods of strangers and make them their own. They even build altars to unknown deities and to the spirits of the dead! Thus, while they adopt the rituals of all nations, they have also deservedly won the dominion of all nations. Hence their veneration of the gods has continued without interruption, strengthened rather than impaired by the passage of time. Indeed, antiquity bestows on rituals and temples a holiness proportioned to their age. . . . Therefore, since all nations agree on the existence of the immortal gods, although their

---

[6]Minucius Felix, *Octavius* 6, 8. Based on Alexander Roberts and James Donaldson, *The Ante-Nicene Fathers*, Vol. 4 (Edinburgh: The Christian Literature Company, 1885), pp. 175–177.

nature or their origin may be uncertain, it is intolerable that anyone should have so much audacity or impiety as to strive to undermine or weaken this religion, so ancient, so useful, so wholesome. . . .

15.3.3   The Divine Emperor

For centuries the peoples of the eastern Mediterranean honored their kings as the source of blessings and of protection against enemies. As the maintainers of good relations with the gods, the kings ensured the stability of the state. It was natural that these same peoples should look on their new rulers, the Roman emperors, as divine in this sense also. In the West the provincials were encouraged to worship the goddess Roma, the Genius or Fortune of Rome. With Roma was often associated the cult of the deified emperors, that is, those emperors who had been declared divine by decree of the Senate after their death.

The cult of Roma and the deified emperors was entrusted to the upper classes and served the useful function of involving provincial elites in the Roman governmental system. Significantly, it also brought together some of the disparate elements of the provincial upper classes, such as ex-slaves, who had risen to prominence. But, as was typical with other ancient cults, the community as a whole got something tangible from the festivals. Minimally there was some form of entertainment, but in this instance the reward was meat, wine, and incense.

The following is an inscription on a marble altar set up by the people of Narbo (modern Narbonne) in Southern France.[7]

{Front face of the altar}:

In the consulship of T. Statilius Taurus and L. Cassius Longinus [*A.D. 11*], on the twenty-second day of September, the following perpetual vow to the Divine Spirit (*numen*) of Augustus was made by the people of Narbonese Gaul:

May it be good, favorable, and fortunate for the Imperator Caesar Augustus, son of the divine [*Julius Caesar*], Father of his Country, Chief Priest [*Pontifex Maximus*], holding tribunician power for the 34th time; and also for his wife, children and house [*gens*]; for the Senate and the People of Rome; and for the colonists of Julia Paterna of Narbo Martius who have obligated themselves to worship his spirit forever.

The people of Narbo have set up an altar in the Forum at Narbo. At this altar every year on September 23, the day on which the Good Fortune of the Age produced Augustus as ruler of the world [*i.e., his birthday*], on that day three Roman knights of the plebs and three freedmen shall each sacrifice one animal and at their own expense provide incense and wine for the colonists and residents in order to supplicate his Divine Spirit. Similarly, on September 24, they shall provide incense and wine . . . and on January 1 incense and wine . . . and on January 7, the day on which his command (*imperium*) of the whole world was first initiated, they shall make supplication with incense and wine, and each sacrifice an animal, and provide incense and wine for the colonists and residents of the city. . . .

{On right side of the altar}:

The people of Narbo have dedicated this Altar of the Divine Spirit of Augustus . . . in accordance with the laws written below [*the dedication follows*]:

---

[7]H. Dessau, *Inscriptiones Latinae Selectae* 112 (Berlin, 1892).

"O Divine Spirit of Augustus, Father of his Country! When I give and dedicate this Altar to you today, I shall give and dedicate it in accordance with the laws and regulations which I will proclaim openly here today. . . : 'If anyone wishes to clean, decorate, or repair this Altar as a public service, it shall be right and lawful. If anyone makes a sacrifice of an animal without providing the additional offering, it shall nevertheless be regarded as having been done properly. If anyone wishes to give a gift to this Altar and to further embellish it, it shall be allowed; the same regulation applies to the gift as to the Altar. Other laws for this Altar and inscriptions shall be same as for the altar of Diana on the Aventine [*in Rome*].'

"In accordance with these laws and regulations, just as I have said, I give and dedicate this Altar on behalf of Emperor Caesar Augustus, Father of his Country, Chief Priest, holding the Tribunician Power for the 35th time, and on behalf of his wife, children and house, the Senate and People of Rome, the colonists and inhabitants of the colony of Julia Paterna Narbo Martius, who have bound themselves to worship his Divine Spirit forever. I dedicate this Altar that you may be favorably and propitiously disposed to us."

15.3.4   Rural Religions and Superstitions

The Spanish poet Martial (died ca. A.D. 104), friend of Juvenal and Pliny the Younger, lived in Rome for thirty-five years. He was the author of twelve books of epigrams in which the contemporary life of Rome at every level from high to low is well represented, often salted with mild venom. About to return to Spain toward the end of his life, he commends to his friend Marius the farm at Nomentum, the rural retreat that had made life bearable for him at Rome. Although Martial was no peasant farmer, he refers in this epigram to the gods and goddesses who inhabited the fields and woods of Italy and whose propitiation and honor were the responsibility of the farmer, who acted as a priest to perform these rituals.[8]

Marius, an advocate and sharer of the quiet life, citizen of whom ancient Atina brags, these twin pines, the decoration of this untilled grove, I commend to you, as well as the holm oaks where the Fauns lived, and the altars of Jupiter the Thunderer and shaggy Silvanus, built by the hand of my rough farm manager, often stained by the blood of lambs and goats. I commend to your care the virgin goddess, mistress of her holy shrine, and him whom you see, the guest of his chaste sister, Mars, who is my birthday god, and the laurel grove of sweet Flora, in which she takes refuge when chased by Priapus. Please say to all these gentle deities of my tiny farm, whether you propitiate them with blood or incense: "Wherever your Martial is, behold he, the absent priest, sacrifices with me by this right hand to you. Reckon him present, and grant to each of us whatever we shall pray for."

15.3.5   A Holy Man Stops a Plague at Ephesus

The philosopher-sage Apollonius of Tyana led the life of an ascetic, wandering the Mediterranean world during the first century A.D. According to his biographer Philostratus, he performed miracles, prophesized, and finally ascended bodily into heaven. Despite the legendary aspects of the biography, there is no doubt that Apollonius existed. Nor were the kinds of healings and exorcisms ascribed to him out of character with his lifestyle as a professed holy man, mystic, and magician.

---

[8]Martial, *Epigrams*, 10.92.

Philostratus belonged to the circle of intellectuals around Julia Domna, the wife of the important emperor Septimius Severus (see Chapter 14), and it is possible that it was at her instigation that the Life of Apollonius *was composed. Minimally, the* Life *reveals something of the religious interests of the court. The not always dependable* Augustan History *claimed that Septimius himself had a private chapel where he kept statues of four men: Abraham, Orpheus, Christ, and Apollonius. The parallels in the lives of Apollonius and Christ attracted attention during persecutions of the late Empire, and his biography by Philostratus was used as a source for an anti-Christian tract claiming that Apollonius was the equal of Christ.*[9]

When the plague broke out at Ephesus and there was no stopping it, the Ephesians sent a delegation to Apollonius asking him to heal them. Accordingly, he did not hesitate, but said, "Let's go," and there he was, miraculously, in Ephesus. . . . Calling together the people of Ephesus, he said, "Be brave; today I will stop the plague." Then he led them all to the theater where the statue of the God-Who-Averts-Evil had been set up.

In the theater there was what seemed to be an old man begging, his eyes closed, apparently blind. He had a bag and a piece of bread. His clothes were ragged and his appearance was squalid. Apollonius gathered the Ephesians around him and said, "Collect as many stones as you can and throw them at this enemy of the gods." The Ephesians were amazed at what he said and appalled at the idea of killing a stranger so obviously pitiful, for he was beseeching them to have mercy on him. But Apollonius urged them on to attack him and not to let him escape.

When some of the Ephesians began to pitch stones at him, the beggar who had his eyes closed as if blind suddenly opened them and they were filled with fire. At that point the Ephesians realized that he was a demon and proceeded to stone him so that their missiles became a great pile over him. After a little while Apollonius told them to remove the stones and to see the wild animal they had killed. When they uncovered the man they thought they had thrown their stones at, they found he had disappeared, and in his place was a hound who looked like a hunting dog but was as big as the largest lion. He lay there in front of them, crushed by the stones, foaming at the corners of his mouth as mad dogs do. A statue of the God-Who-Averts-Evil, that is, Heracles, stands at the spot where the apparition was stricken.

15.3.6   Jesus of Nazareth

The exorcisms and miracles of Jesus of Nazareth (died ca. A.D. *30) were of a very different type and purpose from those of Apollonius. In the Gospels, Jesus' language and worldview are those of traditional Jewish apocalyptic eschatology of the Hellenistic period. Among the characteristics of this form of Judaism may be found the following beliefs:*

History is not a meaningless cycle of events but a series of steps directed by God to a final, magnificent conclusion, at which time Israel is to be restored, foreigners driven out, and the scattered people of Israel, both living and dead, reunited in a renewed and glorious Jerusalem; all the nations of the earth are to abandon their idolatry and learn to worship the true God at his new Temple in Jerusalem. The Lord either will himself lead the forces of good or will send his Messiah to do so. For some, including Jesus, this

---

[9]Philostratus, *Life of Apollonius* 4.10.

definitive intervention of the God included salvation from sin, death, illness, and demoniacal possession. The powers of the cosmos who ruled the world since the sin of Adam were to be overthrown and the Kingdom of God inaugurated.

Signs of the nearness of the Kingdom were the miracles and exorcisms Jesus performed. These events were not mere incidents in his life, but proofs that the Last Days of History were at hand. The plans of God, partially revealed in the past by the prophets of Israel and the events of Israel's history, were on the verge of being completed and made fully clear.

Jesus' message was presented not as a code of ethics or a list of commands, but rather in the form of demands for unconditioned acceptance of all that the rule of God involved. The signs of the Coming of the Kingdom were the casting out of devils, the curing of the blind, the lame, and the sick. The expulsion of the money changers from the Temple was both a challenge to the ruling establishment at Jerusalem and a symbol of the closeness of the End of History: The Temple would be destroyed and replaced in the New Age by a glorious Temple "not made by hands" *(Mark 14:58). It may well have been this incident that led to Jesus' final confrontation with the authorities. From among his many disciples, Jesus selected an inner core of twelve (the Twelve Apostles) and among them an even more select group consisting of Peter, James, John, and sometimes Andrew. To the apostles was given the command to baptize and preach to all nations.*

Signs of the Coming Reign of God

When John the Baptist heard in prison about what Jesus was doing he sent his disciples to ask him, "Are you he who is to come [*i.e., the Messiah*] or should we look for another?" Jesus answered them, "Go tell John what you have heard and seen: The blind see, the lame walk, lepers are cleansed, the deaf hear, the dead are raised up and the poor have the good news preached to them." (Matthew 11:2–5)

The Demands of the Kingdom and the Cost of Discipleship

"You have heard that our ancestors were told, 'You shall not murder and anyone who commits murder will be subject to judgment.' But I say to you that anyone who is angry with his brother will be subject to judgment. . . . You have heard it said, 'Do not commit adultery,' but I say to you that anyone who so much as looks at a woman with evil desire has already committed adultery with her in his heart. . . . You have heard that it was said, 'An eye for an eye, and a tooth for a tooth,' but I say to you, 'Do not resist an evil person. If someone strikes you on the right cheek, turn to him the other as well. . . . You have heard it said, 'You shall love your neighbor and hate your enemy,' but I say to you, love your enemies and pray for those who persecute you . . . for if you love only those who love you, what reward do you have? Do not even the tax-collectors do the same? . . . Therefore, whatever you wish that men should do to you, do you also to them, for this is the law and the prophets." (Matthew 5:21–47; 7:12)

"Do not think I came to bring peace to the earth; I came to bring the sword, not peace. I came to set son against father and daughter against mother and daughter-in-law against mother-in-law. The enemies of a man will be his own servants. He who loves father or mother more than me is not worthy of me. Who loves son or daughter above me is not worthy of me. He who does not take up his cross and follow me is not worthy of me. He who saves his life will lose it—and he who loses his life for my sake will find it!" (Matthew 10:34–39)

A scribe came to him and said: "Master, I will follow you wherever you go." Jesus said to him, "The foxes have their holes and the birds of the heaven their nests, but the Son of Man has nowhere to lay his head." One of his disciples said to him, "Master, allow me to go first and bury my father." But Jesus said to him, "Follow me; leave the dead to bury their dead!" (Matthew 8:19–22)

An official asked him, "Good Teacher, what good should I do that I might gain eternal life?" Jesus said to him, "If you wish to enter into life, keep the commandments." He said, "Which do you mean?" Jesus said: "You shall not kill; you shall not commit adultery; you shall not steal; you shall not bear false witness; honor your father and mother, and love your neighbor as yourself." The young man said, "I have kept all these commandments since my youth. What more do I need to do?" Jesus said to him, "There is one thing lacking in you. Go, sell what you have and give it to the poor and you will have treasure in heaven. And come, follow me." When he heard this the young man went away sad because he had many possessions. Jesus said to his disciples, "Truly I say to you, it is difficult for the rich to enter into the Kingdom of Heaven." And again he said, "It is easier for a camel to pass through the eye of a needle than for a rich man to enter heaven!" (Luke 18:18–25)

The Sermon on the Mount and the Golden Rule

"Love your enemies, do good to those who hate you, bless those who curse you, pray for those who mistreat you. If someone strikes you on one cheek, turn to him the other. If someone takes your cloak, let him have your shirt as well. Give to everyone who asks of you. Whoever takes away what is yours, do not ask for it back.

"Do to others as you would have them do to you. For if you love those who love you, what credit is there in that? Even sinners love those who love them. And if you do good to those who do good to you what credit is there for you? Even sinners do the same. And if you lend to those from whom you expect repayment, what credit is there in that? Even sinners lend to sinners in order to receive back the same amount.

"But rather, love your enemies, and do good and lend, expecting nothing in return. Then your reward will be great and you will be the sons of the Most High, for he is kind to the ungrateful and the evil. Be merciful even as your Father is merciful. Judge not and you will not be judged; condemn not and you will not be condemned. Forgive, and you will be forgiven. Give and it will be given to you." (Luke 6:27–38)

Who Is My Neighbor? The Good Samaritan

A certain scholar of the law stood up to test him and asked him, "Teacher, what must I do to inherit eternal life?" Jesus said to him, "What is written in the law? How do you read it?" And he answered, "You shall love the Lord your God with your whole heart and your whole soul and with all your strength, and with all your mind; and your neighbor as yourself." Jesus said, "You have answered right; do this and you will live." But wanting to justify himself he asked Jesus, "And who is my neighbor?" Jesus replied, "A man was going down from Jerusalem to Jericho and fell among robbers who stripped him and beat and went off leaving him half dead. Now by coincidence a priest was likewise going down that road, and when he saw him he passed by on the opposite side. So also a Levite, when he came to the place and saw the man, he also passed by on the other side of the road. But a Samaritan, as he journeyed, came to where the man was and saw him and had compassion for him. He went up to him, poured oil and wine on his wounds and bandaged them up. Then he put him on his own animal and brought him to an inn and took care of him. The next day he took out two denarii [*about two days wages*] and gave them to the innkeeper saying, 'Take care of him and whatever more you have to spend I will repay you when I come back.' Which of these three, do you think, was neighbor to the robber's victim?" He said, "The one who showed mercy to him." And Jesus said to him, "Go and do the same." (Luke 10:25–37)

Who Is in Good Standing with God?

He told this parable to some who were confident in themselves that they were in good standing with God and despised others. "Two men went up to the Temple to pray, one of them a Pharisee, the other a tax collector. The Pharisee stood and prayed in this fashion with himself, 'I thank God I am not like the rest of men, thieves, rogues, adulterers, like this tax collector here. I fast twice a week, I give tithes of all that I have.' But the tax collector, standing afar off, would not so much as lift up his eyes to heaven but beat his breast saying, 'God be merciful to me a sinner!' I tell you this man went down to his house forgiven rather than the other. For everyone who exalts himself shall be humbled and he who humbles himself shall be exalted." (Luke 18:9–14)

True Generosity: The Widow's Mite

And he sat down opposite the temple treasury and watched the crowd making their contributions. Many rich came and gave large sums, but a poor widow came and gave just two copper coins which together make half a cent. He called his disciples together and said to them, "I tell you truly, this poor widow has put in more than all those who are giving gifts to the treasury. For they all gave out of their surplus wealth while she out of her poverty has put in everything she had, even her whole livelihood." (Mark 12:41–44)

The Basis of Judgment at the End of the World

"When the Son of Man comes in his majesty and all the angels with him, then he will sit on the throne of his majesty and all the nations will be gathered in front of him and he will separate them from each other as the shepherd separates sheep and goats. He will set the sheep at his right hand and the goats at his left. Then the king will say to those who are at his right, 'Come, you blessed of my Father, possess the kingdom prepared for you from the foundation of the world. I was hungry and you gave me to eat; thirsty and you gave me to drink; a stranger and you took me in; naked and you clothed me; sick and you visited me; in prison and you came to visit me.' Then the just will respond and say, 'Lord, when did we see you hungry, and we fed you? thirsty and we gave you drink? When did we see you as a stranger and we took you in, or naked and we clothed you and sick or in prison and we visited you?' And the king answering will say, 'Truly I say to you that as long as you did it to the least of my brethren you did it to me.'" (Matthew 25:31–45)

Cleansing the Temple

And when he entered Jerusalem the whole city was disturbed and people asked, "Who is this?" And the crowd responded, "This is Jesus the prophet, from Nazareth in Galilee." And Jesus entered the temple of God and drove out all the sellers and buyers in the temple and the tables of the moneychangers and toppled over the chairs of those selling doves. And he said, "It is written: 'My house will be called a house of prayer'; but you have made it a den of thieves." And the blind and lame came to him in the temple and he cured them. But the leaders of the priests and the scribes saw the wonders he did and heard the young in the temple crying out and saying, "Hosanna to the son of David," and they were enraged and said to him, "Do you not hear what they are saying?" Jesus said to them, "Truly, have you not read: 'Out of the mouths of infants and babes at the breast you have brought perfect praise'?" (Matthew 21:10–16)

The Mission of the Apostles

The eleven disciples went to the mountain in Galilee to which Jesus had told them to come. When they saw him they worshiped him even as some of them doubted. And Jesus came and said to them, "All authority has been given to me in heaven and on earth. Go therefore and make disciples of all nations, baptizing them in the name of the Father, and of the Son, and of the Holy Spirit, teaching them to observe all that I have commanded you. And be assured, I will be with you always, even to the end of the world." (Matthew 28:16–20)

The Keys of the Kingdom: The Role of Peter

It happened that when Jesus was praying by himself and his disciples were with him he asked them, "Who do people say that I am?" They answered: "Some say John the Baptist, others Elijah or Jeremiah or one of the prophets who has come back to life." And he said to them, "But who do you say that I am?" Peter answered, "You are the Christ, the Son of the Living God." Jesus replied, "Blessed are you, Simon Son of Jonah because flesh and blood has not revealed this to you, but my Father in heaven. And I say to you, you are Peter [*"Peter" means rock*] and upon this rock I will build my church and the gates of hell will not prevail against it. I will give you the keys of the kingdom of heaven. Whatever you shall bind on earth shall be bound in heaven, and whatever you loose on earth shall be loosed in heaven." (Matthew 16:13–19)

15.3.7   Paul of Tarsus

Paul of Tarsus (in Asia Minor), a Jew of the diaspora, was educated as a rabbi in Jerusalem and belonged to the sect of the Pharisees. At first opposed to Christianity he experienced a sudden conversion while on a journey to Damascus. Becoming a missionary, he preached Christianity in Asia Minor and Greece, first to Jews and then to gentiles. Paul emphasized that Christianity was not for Jews alone, as many Palestinian Christians believed, but for non-Jews as well. Salvation, he preached, comes through belief in Christ, not from observance of the law (i.e., the Mosiac Law). This was a crucial step in the expansion of the new religion, but one that was at first controversial. Unlike Jesus who left nothing in writing, Paul left his own account of his conversion and the discussion he had with the Christian leadership in Jerusalem regarding the nonobservance of the Law by gentile converts.[10]

For I want you to know, brothers, that the gospel that was proclaimed by me is not of human origin . . . it came to me through a revelation of Jesus Christ. You have heard of my former way of life in Judaism, how violently I persecuted the church of God and tried to

---

[10]Galatians 1:11–15; 2:2–3, 7–9.

destroy it. I advanced in Judaism beyond many among my people of the my age, for I was more zealous than they for the traditions of my ancestors. But when God, who had set me apart before I was born and called me through his grace, was pleased to reveal his Son to me, so that I might proclaim him among the Gentiles, I did not consult with any human being.

Paul began his ministry by traveling in Syria and Asia Minor, but after fourteen years went up to Jerusalem to acquaint the leadership there with his version of the gospel and get their approval. He brought with him two companions, Barnabas and Titus.

I went [*to Jerusalem*] in response to a revelation. Then I laid before them (though only privately with the acknowledged leaders) the gospel that I proclaim among the Gentiles, in order to make sure that I was not running, or had not run, in vain. But not even Titus, who was with me, was compelled to be circumcised, though he was a Greek. . . . [*The leaders in Jerusalem*] imposed no new requirements on me. On the contrary, when they saw that I had been entrusted with the gospel to the uncircumcised, just as Peter had been entrusted with the gospel for the circumcised . . . and when James and Cephas [*i.e., Peter*] and John, who were acknowledge pillars, recognized the grace that had been given to me, they gave to Barnabas and me the right hand of fellowship, and agreed that we should go to the Gentiles and they to the circumcised.

15.4   Christian Practice

The actual practice of early Christianity is described in the Apology *of Justin Martyr. A convert from paganism, Justin (ca.* A.D. *100–165) defends and explains Christian doctrine, ritual, and practice to a hostile readership.*[11] *For a non-Christian account, essentially confirming what Justin says, see the letter in the next section.*

After we have baptized the person who has been convinced and has assented to our teaching, we bring him to the place where those who are called the brethren are assembled to offer prayers in common, both for ourselves and for him who has been illuminated, and for all people everywhere. We do this so that we may be counted worthy, now that we have learned the truth, to be found good citizens and keepers of the commandments, and that we may be saved with an everlasting salvation.

When we have finished these prayers, we salute one another with a kiss. Then the bread and a cup of wine mixed with water are brought to the president of the brethren. He takes them, gives praise and glory to the Father of the universe through the name of the Son and of the Holy Spirit, and offers thanks at considerable length for our being considered worthy to receive these things at his hands. When he has concluded the prayers and thanksgivings, all the people present express their assent by saying *Amen*. This word in Hebrew means "So be it." When the president has given thanks, and all the people have expressed their assent, those who are called by us deacons give to each of those present a portion of the bread and wine mixed with water over which the thanksgiving was pronounced. To those who are absent they carry away a portion.

---

[11]Justin, *Apology* 45–46. Based on Roberts and Donaldson, *The Ante-Nicene Fathers*, Vol. 1, p. 185.

Among us this food is called the Eucharist. Only those who believe the truth of the things we teach, who have been baptized with the washing for the remission of sins and so regenerated and live as Christ directed, are allowed to partake of it. We do not receive the Eucharist as common bread and drink. As Jesus Christ our Savior, having been made flesh by the Word of God, had both flesh and blood for our salvation, so likewise we have been taught that the food which is blessed by the prayer of his word . . . is the flesh and blood of that Jesus who was made flesh. For the apostles, in the memoirs called "Gospels" composed by them, have thus passed down to us what was enjoined on them, namely, that Jesus broke bread, and when he had given thanks, said, "Do this in remembrance of me; this is my body." In the same manner, having taken the cup and given thanks, he said, "This is my blood" and gave it to them alone. . . .

Afterwards we continually remind each other of these things. And the wealthy among us help the needy, and we visit each other continually. At our meals we bless the maker of all things through his Son Jesus Christ and through the Holy Spirit.

On the day called Sunday, all of us who live in cities or in the country gather together in one place. The memoirs of the apostles or the writings of the prophets are read, as long as time permits. Then when the reader has ceased, the president instructs and exhorts us to the imitation of these good things. Next we all rise together and pray, and as we before said, when our prayer is ended, bread and wine and water are brought, and the president in like manner offers prayers and thanksgivings with all his might, and the people assent saying, *Amen*. There is then a distribution to each. . . .

Those who are prosperous and willing give what each thinks fit. What is collected is deposited with the president, who distributes it to orphans and widows and those who, through sickness or any other cause, are in want. This includes those who are in prison, as well as to strangers among us, and indeed any who are in need.

15.5   Pliny's Encounter with Christianity

Pliny, the Roman governor of Bithynia-Pontus (in modern Turkey) about A.D. 111–113, appears to have been a genuinely civilized, humanitarian person (see "Provincial Administration: Hands-On Style" in Chapter 14), yet he casually executed Christians because of their refusal to conform to traditional practice, and he noted with satisfaction the improvement in temple attendance and worship as a result of the executions. The Emperor Trajan, in his response, agrees with Pliny's action but is more sensitive than the complacent Pliny to the role of malice in charges brought against Christians.[12] We begin with Pliny's letter to the emperor.

I am in the habit, My Lord, of referring to you all matters regarding which I am in doubt. For who can be a better guide for my indecision or better enlighten my ignorance?

I have never taken part in trials of Christians: hence I do not know for what offense, nor to what extent it is the practice to punish or to investigate. I have been in a lot of doubt as to whether any distinction should be made for age, or whether the very weakest offenders are to be treated exactly like the stronger; whether pardon is to be granted in the case of repentance,

---

[12]Pliny *Letters* 10.96–7.

or whether a person who was at one time a Christian gains anything by having ceased to be one; whether punishment attaches automatically to the mere name of Christian, even without crimes, or only when the law has been violated.

Meanwhile, this is the course of action I have followed in the case of those denounced to me as Christians. I asked them first whether they were Christians. If they confessed, I asked them a second and third time, along with threats of punishment. If they remained obdurate, I had them executed, for I had no doubt that, whatever it was that they confessed, their stubbornness and their unbending perversity deserve punishment. There were others of similar insanity who, because they were Roman citizens, I have remanded for sending to the City.

Before long, as is often the case, the mere fact that action was taken made the charges commoner, and more cases arose. An anonymous accusation containing many names was circulated. Those who denied that they were or had been Christians, I thought it right to let go since they recited a prayer to the gods at my dictation, made supplication with incense and wine to your image, which I had ordered to be brought for the purpose, together with the statues of the gods, and cursed Christ. Those who are really Christians, it is said, cannot be forced to do any of these things. Others, accused by the informer, said they were Christians but afterwards denied it, explaining that they had been Christians at one time but had ceased to be many years ago, some as much as twenty years before. All these too worshipped your image and the statues of the gods and cursed Christ.

The accused claim that the sum total of their guilt was this: that on a certain fixed day they were accustomed to come together before daylight and to sing by turns a hymn to Christ as to a god, and to bind themselves by oath, not for some criminal purpose, but that they would not commit robbery, theft, or adultery; that they would not betray a trust nor deny a deposit when it was called for. When this was over, their custom was to disperse and to come together again to partake of food of an ordinary and harmless kind. Even this they claimed they had ceased to do after the publication of my edict in which, according to your command, I had forbidden associations. Accordingly, I decided it was all the more necessary to find out the truth by torture from two female servants called deaconesses. I discovered nothing other than a wicked and excessive superstition.

Consequently I have adjourned the case and hastened to consult you. The matter seemed to warrant deliberation, especially on account of the number of those being brought to trial, of every rank and of both sexes. The infection of this superstition has spread not only to the cities but even to the villages and country areas. It seems possible to stop it and bring about reform. It is plain enough that the temples, which had been almost deserted, have begun to be frequented again, that the sacred rites, which had been neglected for a long time, are being resumed, and that from everywhere sacrificial victims are coming for which until now there were scarcely any purchasers. From this it can be easily supposed that a number of people can be reclaimed if repentance is afforded.

Trajan replies to Pliny:

You have followed the correct procedure, my dear Pliny, in conducting the cases of those who were accused before you of being Christians. No general rule can be laid down with a fixed formula. They ought not, however, to be sought out. If they are brought before you and the charge proved, they ought to be punished. But when someone denies that he is a

Christian and proves it by praying to our gods, however much he may have been under suspicion in the past, he should be pardoned as a result of his repentance. Anonymous accusations, however, ought not to be admitted in any charge. They are a very bad example and unworthy of our times.

15.6   Rabbinic Judaism

During the first century A.D. *there were many competing—and interacting—forms of Judaism in Judaea and among Jews outside Palestine (the Diaspora). In Palestine, Sadducees and Pharisees differed over doctrinal issues such as the immortality of the soul and whether there was punishment after death. In interpreting Scripture and the Law, Sadducees took a literal approach, insisting that only the written Scriptures were acceptable sources of revelation. Pharisees were more flexible: They claimed that the Torah (the law), came in two forms, one written and the other oral, each necessary and each God-given. Besides these two main "sects" (which were further divided into subsects), there were numerous other groups of ascetics, revolutionaries, mystics, and believers in apocalyptic restoration. Of these the most important were the Essenes and the Qumran or Dead Sea community (whose library was discovered in caves above the Dead Sea in 1947).*

The communities of the Diaspora possessed yet another variant of Judaism. The destruction of the Temple by the Romans in A.D. *70, and further devastation following the Bar Kochba rebellion of* A.D. *132–135, resulted in a spiritual upheaval comparable to the one that followed the destruction of the Temple of Solomon (the First Temple) by the Babylonians in 587* B.C. *(see "Empire, Exile, and Monotheism" in Chapter 1 and "The Fall of Jerusalem" in Chapter 2) and led directly to the flowering of Rabbinic Judaism. With the destruction of the Second Temple, the influence of the Sadducees faded, the Qumran and Essene sects were destroyed or scattered, and apocalyptic movements were discredited. In the absence of the Temple, the synagogue became the vital focus of Jewish religious life. The rabbi as interpreter and wise man replaced the priest, and prayer became a surrogate for animal sacrifice.*

Of the many traditions of Judaism, Pharisaism proved to be the most vital and capable of responding to the needs of post-revolt Judaism, and it was from this root in particular, though not exclusively, that Rabbinic Judaism developed. In time, the oral tradition of the Pharisees was written down and edited, receiving definitive form around A.D. *200. The resulting document, known as the* Mishnah, *is the basis of Rabbinic Judaism. Although the* Mishnah *contains some material going back to the third century* B.C., *the bulk of it, mostly statements of the law and the original commentaries of the rabbis, derives from the first two centuries* A.D. *In the standard English translation it runs to over 1,000 pages. From about* A.D. *200 to 500, loosely organized groups of scholars in Palestine and Babylonia added further commentaries to the* Mishnah *in a process which ultimately led to the production of two other major documents, the Palestinian and Babylonian* Talmuds.

The Mishnah *is essentially a teaching aid, a curriculum for the study of Jewish law, or a method of instruction in how to think about the law. It is structured around six major thematic areas: (1) agriculture, (2) festivals, (3) marriage and property, (4) civil and criminal law, (5) cult and sacrifice, and (6) cultic purity. Both readings given here come from the third area. Typically, first the law is stated and then the comments of selected rabbis are given. The brevity (and sometimes obscurity) of the written form reflects the original oral nature of the* Mishnah, *one of whose aims was to allow for easy memorization.*

1

In this reading the complex issue of what happens to a widow (or, to be exact, a presumed widow) when her husband reappears is presented for discussion. Various solutions are suggested with the aim, not so much of settling the issues definitively, as of teaching the student how to reason about the subject.[13] *The same problem of disappearing husbands, it will be recalled, was also addressed in the code of Hammurapi (see Chapter 2).*

If a woman's husband has gone overseas and it was told her, "Your husband is dead," and she married again and her husband then returned: (1) her marriage with both of them is annulled; (2) she must receive a bill of divorce from each of them; (3) from neither of them can she lay claim to her Ketubah [*the financial settlement paid at the time of the marriage by the husband to which the wife was entitled if divorced or widowed*]; (4) or to the increase [*of her own property*]; (5) or to alimony; (6) or to indemnity [*for loss suffered to her own property*]. (7) If she has collected anything of (3)–(5) from either one of them, she must restore it. (8) A child conceived by either husband is a bastard. . . .

Rabbi Jose says: "Her Ketubah [*marriage contract*] remains a charge on her first husband's property."

Rabbi Eleazar says: "Her first husband has a claim to anything found by her and to the work of her hands, and the right to set aside her vows. If she was the daughter of an Israelite she becomes ineligible for marriage with a priest. . . .

"But if she had married again without the consent of the court [*since the remarriage was null, in view of the first*], she may return to her first husband. If she had married again with the consent of the court [*and her first husband then returned*], the second marriage is annulled. . . ."

2

This reading discusses occupations and the Torah as the way of life.[14] *It too has echoes of earlier readings (see the Egyptian satire on trades in Chapter 3).*

Rabbi Meir says: "A man should always teach his son a clean and easy trade and let him pray to Him [*i.e., God*] to whom riches and possessions belong, for there is no trade wherein there is not both poverty and wealth; for poverty comes not from a man's trade, nor riches from a man's trade, but all is according to his merit."

Rabbi Simeon ben Eleazar says: "Have you ever seen a wild animal or bird practicing a trade? Yet they sustain themselves without care. And were they not created for nothing else but to serve me? But I was created to serve my Maker—does it not follow that I should sustain myself without trouble? But I have done evil, and so forfeited my right to sustenance without care."

Abba Gorion of Zaidan says in the name of Abba Guria: "A man should not teach his son to be an ass-driver or a camel-driver, or a barber or a sailor, or a herdsman or a shopkeeper, for their craft is the craft of robbers."

Rabbi Judah says in his own name: "Ass-drivers are most of them wicked; camel-drivers are most of them decent; sailors are most of them pious; the best among physicians is destined

---

[13]M. *Yebamot* 10:1, 2. From Herbert Danby, *The Mishnah* (London: Oxford University Press, Geoffrey Cumberlege, 1933), p. 232.
[14]M. *Quiddushin* 4:14. From Danby, *The Mishnah*, p. 329.

for Gehenna [*Hell*], and the best of butchers is a partner of Amelek [*ancient enemy of Israel and a stock term for pagans*]."

Rabbi Nehorai says: "I would set aside all the trades of the world and teach my son nothing but the Torah [*the Law*], for a man enjoys its fruits in this world, and the principal remains for the world to come. But with all other trades it is not so. For when a man gets sick or old or has troubles and cannot engage in his trade, lo, he dies of hunger. But with the Torah it is not so. It guards him from all evil when he is young, and in old age it grants him a future and a hope. Of his youth what does it say? 'They who wait upon the Lord shall renew their strength' [Isaiah 40:31]. Of his old age what does it say? 'They shall still bring forth fruit in old age'" [Psalm 92:14]. . . .

15.7   Judaism of the Diaspora

Jews living in the cities of the Greco-Roman world were presented with great intellectual, moral, and religious challenges to their way of life. A minimum amount of tolerance toward their religion on the part of Greeks enabled them to survive as separate communities, but this tolerance also opened the way for assimilation and absorption. As the use of Hebrew declined among Diaspora Jews, it became necessary to translate the Scriptures into Greek. This translation in turn introduced into the text of Scripture Greek philosophical ideas, as well as Greek terms that often changed the meaning of the original Hebrew and the thought that lay behind it. There was no equivalent in Greek, for instance, for the sacred name of God, Yahweh, so the translators used the common Greek term of address for pagan gods, kurios, which allowed the possible implication that Yahweh was just one of the many gods of polytheism.

The great intellectual challenge of translating one religious idiom into the language of another, and ultimately of synthesizing two cultures, was taken up by a number of great Jewish scholars. The process was especially successful in Alexandria, where it served the dual purpose of strengthening the Jewish community internally as well as of refuting pagan criticisms and presenting Judaism as a reasonable, philosophical religion. The movement reached its height in the writings of Philo Judaeus (ca. 20 B.C.–A.D. 50), but it had a long afterlife. Christians in their confrontation with the subtle intellectual challenges of Hellenism found the way already prepared for them by the activities of these Jewish scholars, and they borrowed heavily from them.

By mid–second century A.D., *however, the vigor of Hellenistic Judaism declined, in part because of assimilation of Jews into the larger pagan population, and also because Christianity was able to press its claims successfully with Gentile proselytes who might otherwise have become Jews. Revolt against Rome among Diaspora Jews in* A.D. *115–117 as well as the rise of Rabbinic Judaism and the consequent Hebraizing of the Greek-speaking synagogues were also major factors in the decline.*

15.7.1   Prologue to the Wisdom of Jesus the Son of Sirach

The difficulty of translating concepts of Hebrew thought into Greek is referred to in this reading, the introduction to the book of Ecclesiasticus or The Wisdom of Sirach.[15] This work, composed in the second century B.C., *is the last example of the genre of wisdom literature, such as Proverbs, found in the Hebrew*

---

[15]Cited by M. Avi-Yonah, *The Jews Under Roman and Byzantine Rule: A Political History of Palestine from the Bar Kokhba War to the Arab Conquest* (Jerusalem: The Magnes Press, 1984), p. 170.

Scriptures. Ecclesiasticus was included in the Greek translation of the Hebrew Bible produced in Alexandria, the so-called "Septuagint." The Septuagint in turn was taken over by Greek-speaking Christians as their version of the Bible.

Since many great teachings have been given to us through the Law and the Prophets and the others who followed after them—for which things' sake we must praise Israel for instruction and wisdom, and since the readers themselves must become adept, and those who love learning must be able to help outsiders [*i.e., non-Jews*] by both speaking and writing, my grandfather Jesus, having given himself much to the reading of the Law and the Prophets and the other books of our fathers, and having acquired considerable familiarity with them, was induced himself to write something pertaining to instruction and wisdom, in order that those who are lovers of learning and instructed in these things might make even more progress by a manner of life lived in accordance with the Law.

You are entreated, therefore, to make your study with good will and attention, and to be indulgent, if in any parts of what we have labored to interpret we may seem to fail in some of the phrases. For what was originally spoken in Hebrew does not have the same meaning when translated into another language. And not only this work, but the Law itself and the Prophecies, and the rest of the books, have no small difference when they are spoken in their original form.

15.7.2   "The *Mishnah* is the Holy One's Mystery"

This reading reflects the gradual disengagement with Hellenism that took place in the Greco-Roman Diaspora from the second century A.D. *onward. The rabbis rejected out of hand the claim of Christians that they alone represented the true Israel, (see Chapter 17.5.1,* "A Different Vision"*), placing emphasis in rebuttal on the doctrine that the oral law found in the* Mishnah *(see previous) was the possession of Jews alone.*[16]

Thus said Rabbi Judah ben Shalom: "Moses asked for the *Mishnah* to be also written down, but the Holy One, blessed be He, foresaw that the nations of the world would translate the Torah and read it in Greek, and that they would say, 'We also are Israel.' So the Holy One said to him, 'I shall write for you most of my Law . . . but the *Mishnah* is the Holy One's mystery, and He does not disclose His mystery but to the just.'"

15.8   Divination, Astrology, Magic

15.8.1   "Will Her Lover Outlive Her?"

As part of his long satire on wives, Juvenal includes the following mocking denunciation of superstitious practices. The picture that emerges is one of widespread use of magic and divination by all classes.[17]

---

[16]Based on R. H. Charles, ed., *The Apocrypha and Pseudepigrapha of the Old Testament* (Oxford: Clarendon Press, 1913), pp. 316–317.
[17]Juvenal, *Satires*, 6.548–597

An Armenian or Commagenian seer will promise you a young lover or a huge bequest from a rich and childless man after inspecting the lungs of a dove or the crop of a chicken or the entrails of a puppy or maybe even a child's. But the Chaldaean seers are more trustworthy. These are the ones your wife goes to consult: When will her mother, who has been ill of the jaundice for a long time, finally die? (She asked about *your* departure long ago.) And when will she bury her sister or her uncles? Will her lover outlive her? What more could she want?

Don't forget to watch out for one of these women clutching a well-worn calendar like a string of worry beads. She's an expert at giving not taking advice, the sort who, if she wants to take even a short ride out of the city will have to consult her almanac to find out what is the right hour. If she has an itch in the corner of her eye, she would never think of applying medicine until the horoscope's been consulted. If she's sick in bed, she will take no food till she calculates what is the right time to eat, as Petosiris the Egyptian directs.

Rich women will consult Phrygian or Indian augurs skilled in the study of the stars and the heavens. Plebeian destinies, however, are determined at the Circus or at Servius Tullius' ancient rampart—should they ditch the barkeeper and marry the old-clothes man? These poor women, however, endure the dangers of childbirth and all the labors of nursing that their poverty inflicts on them. How often, by contrast, does a gilded bed see a woman waiting to give birth, so great are the skills and so strong the drugs for inducting sterility or killing mankind in the womb?

15.8.2   "Thumbs Down Indicates Approval"

"Thumbs down indicates approval." *The elder Pliny, uncle of Pliny the Younger, gives a straightforward, nonmoralizing account of some Roman superstitions.*[18]

Why is it on the first day of the year we wish each other with joyful prayers an auspicious and fortunate New Year? Why on days of purification do we select people with lucky names to lead the sacrificial animals? When the dead are mentioned why do we say, "May they rest in peace"? We believe that odd numbers are more powerful than even as is proved by the attention we give to critical days when someone is sick with a fever. Why do we wish "Good health" to people who sneeze? It is possible, supposedly, for absent people to tell when they're being talked about by ringing in their ears. In Africa nobody decides anything without saying "Africa." To calm themselves some people put saliva behind their ears. A proverb tells us that to turn down our thumbs indicates approval. Everyone agrees that lightning is worshipped by clucking the tongue. It has been noticed that a sudden silence occurs during a meal only when the number of diners is even and that it portends danger to their reputation. Auguries are made from the words or thoughts of diners who drop their food, and the worst omens occur if it is a priest does so at a feast. However, expiation can be achieved by burning the food before the shrine of the Lares [*ghosts of the dead*]. Many people feel bound to cut their nails in silence on market days at Rome, beginning with the forefinger. To cut one's hair on the seventeenth and twenty-ninth prevents hair falling out as well as headaches.

---

[18]Pliny, *Natural History* 28.5.22–28.

15.9 Moral Behavior

At least a percentage of the educated elites of the Roman world took a tolerant, skeptical view of morality and religion. "It is expedient that there be gods" was an old maxim that held true for many among the ruling elites, if for no other purpose than to help keep the masses in line. But for centuries, at least since the time of Socrates, the creation of a coherent ethical code of behavior, universal for all human beings, was one of the major goals of Greek philosophy. Some of the best minds of the centuries between Plato and the great Stoic Emperor, Marcus Aurelius, devoted themselves to this task.

The major Socratic schools—Platonism, Aristotelianism, and Stoicism—offered a variety of approaches to ethics, ranging from the dogmatic claims of the Stoics, who asserted that truth in ethical matters could be attained with certainty, to the cool flexibility of the Skeptics, who denied this possibility. Epicureanism, following the materialism of Democritus and the Atomists, offered yet another view of the moral universe.

The author of the following reading, Sextus Empiricus, lived some time in the second century A.D. *Although his aim is philosophical, much of what he has to say reflects a moral attitude prevalent at least among educated members of the Greco-Roman upper and middle classes.*[19]

15.9.1   Moral Relativism

It might not be out of place here . . . to go specifically though briefly into common assumptions about what is shameful and what is not, what constitutes unlawful or lawful behavior, the nature of law and custom, reverence for the gods, proper behavior toward the dead, and so on. In this way we will discover what a great deal of inconsistency there is regarding moral behavior.

Among Greeks, for instance, homosexual relations are regarded more as shameful than illegal, whereas among some Persians they are not considered shameful, but rather as customary. It is said, too, that long ago the Thebans did not think this practice shameful . . . and some [*for example Plato*] think the intense friendship of Achilles and Patroclus was homosexual in nature. . . . To have sex with a woman in public is thought by Greeks to be shameful but not by some Indians. . . . Again, prostitution is held by Greeks to be shameful and disgraceful, but among many Egyptians it is praiseworthy. . . .

For Greeks tattooing is shameful and degrading, but many Egyptians and Sarmatians tattoo their children. Greeks think it is unacceptable for men to wear earrings, but some barbarians, such as the Syrians, regard earrings as symbols of noble birth. Indeed, some, in order to draw attention even further to their noble birth, pierce the noses of their children and hang rings of silver or gold from them!—something no Greek would do. . . .

Cannibalism is outlawed among Greeks, but among whole tribes of barbarians it is considered indifferent . . . and while most of us think it is wrong to pollute an altar with human blood, the Spartans beat themselves furiously over the altar of Artemis so that blood may flow over it. . . . Greek law commands that children should take care of their fathers, but Scythians slit their throats when they get over sixty years. . . . Roman lawmakers put children under their fathers' thumbs—like slaves. Roman children do not have control of their own property, but rather their fathers until their children are emancipated. Others, however, regard

---

[19]Sextus Empiricus, *Outlines of Pyrrhonism* 3.198–212.

this custom as tyrannical. The law states that murderers should be punished, but when gladiators commit homicide they are often praised. . . .

15.9.2   Moral Dogmatism

A much more dogmatic stance is taken by the famous Stoic philosopher Musonius Rufus, who was active in Rome during the reign of Nero and exiled by him in A.D. 65. Musonius was a major figure in Roman intellectual life and the teacher of one of the best-known philosophers of the early Empire, Epictetus. He was consulted by such important figures as Seneca, at one point tutor of Nero. Unfortunately, his work survives only in the rough-and-ready form of lecture notes made by his students. The following reading is from one of his "diatribes," or popular philosophical lectures. The theory that sexual intercourse was for the purpose of procreation only can be traced to Plato. The idea that to sin is to injure oneself is possibly Musonius' own.[20]

The desire for luxury manifests itself in no small degree in the pleasures of love. This is so because luxury demands a great variety of sexual encounters, not only legitimate, but also illegitimate, not only with women, but also with men. Those addicted to luxury pursue now this kind of lust, now that, and are not content with what is available at hand but seek for unusual experiences, shameful forms of intercourse—the kinds of behavior that are unacceptable for a human being. Those who are not devoted to pleasure-seeking and not morally corrupt regard sexual intercourse as legitimate only within marriage and only for the intent of procreating children. Only these kinds of sexual relations are moral. However, those who seek only pleasure in sexual intercourse, whether within or out of wedlock, are unrighteous and transgressors of the law. Of sexual relations, those in which adultery is involved are the most illicit. But not less immoral are homosexual acts between men because they are shameless acts against nature. Setting aside considerations of adultery, all intercourse with women *not* in conformity with custom is also immoral because it offends against continence or self-restraint. Thus, for example, no temperate individual will go to bed with a prostitute or with a free woman outside of marriage, nor, by Zeus, with his own slave. The immorality and indecency of these acts is a matter of great reproach and shame for those who so eagerly perform them. [*This is demonstrated by the fact that*] no one who is capable of blushing even a little can do any of these acts openly; rather, they hide them and do them secretly, showing thereby that they are not completely dissolute. And indeed, trying to avoid being caught while doing one of these acts is to acknowledge having acted immorally.

A person might well argue that while it is true that an adulterer does an injustice to the husband of the woman he seduces, the man who has sex with a prostitute or with an unmarried woman does injury to nobody. The reason for this is that fornication does not destroy a woman's expectation of having children.[21] I, however, continue to insist that whoever commits this kind of sin automatically does an injustice—if not to his neighbor, then to himself—for the offender shows himself to be thoroughly wicked and dishonorable. The offender, to the degree he offends, is the more evil and despicable.

---

[20]Musonius Rufus, *On Sexual Pleasures* 12.
[21]The meaning is that in the case of adultery the breakup of the marriage results and the wife loses the chance to have children, a family, and a legitimate place in the community.

Setting aside the issue of sins of this type as acts of injustice, we must certainly regard those who allow themselves to be overcome by pleasure as lacking in self-control; happily—like pigs—they wallow in the muck. But this kind of behavior is less grievous than the case of the man who has sex with his own slave woman. Now some think this is not really immoral because, after all, the slave-owner is thought to have full liberty to do what he wants with his slave. But to this I have a simple response: If it seems to someone not immoral or shameful for a master to sleep with his slave, especially if she is without a bed-mate, he should reflect how it would appear to him if the situation involved the *mistress* of a slave, his wife, sleeping with her own slave! Wouldn't the matter seem unacceptable, not only in the case of a mistress who had a legitimate husband sleeping with her slave, but also if she did this without being married? Indeed, shouldn't one think men are perhaps worse than women who act that way? Odd that those who are supposed to be stronger in judgment than "weak women" are less able to discipline their desires—the governors weaker than the governed! To the extent that it is fitting that men be set over women, so much the more should they be self-controlled. The more un-self–controlled they appear, the more immoral they will be. But when a master sleeps with his slave—isn't this a demonstration of incontinence? What more needs to be said? Everyone knows this is true.

Chapter 16

Daily Life in the Roman Empire

Most people in the Roman Empire lived in villages or scattered farmsteads, not cities. Their lives revolved around farming, not trade or industry. The rhythm of everyday activities was dictated by the agricultural cycle of sowing, harvest, orchard maintenance, and food processing. Hard work at particular moments was followed by long periods when there was little or nothing to do. Most people in antiquity were underemployed throughout most of their lives. Unlike today, life was not dominated by unwearying machines that need attention night and day. An exception to this scenario was the work on slave-run estates, which may have had a more agribusiness character than the average farm owned by free citizens.

Mediterranean people's lives were intensely social. Whether in village or town or city there was constant mutual visitation. Much of life was spent outdoors. Women went to the market, the water fountain, shrines, and temples and visited in each other's homes. Men spent a great deal of their leisure time hanging out in the marketplace, the baths, or other public places. Dancing, singing, gossiping, and storytelling were the main forms of entertainment along with the festivals of the year which were coordinated with the events of the agricultural cycle and structured daily life even for urban dwelling peoples.

Food in the Mediterranean revolved around olive oil, wine, wheat or barley, and legumes. By necessity most people were vegetarians, enjoying meat only at festivals. A typical dish was *moretum*, made of crushed garlic, parsley, coriander, and rue, mixed with salt, cheese, oil, and vinegar and kneaded into a ball. Sauces, such as *garum*, a pungent fish sauce, condiments, and herbs were used widely in cooking as they are today. The diet of Atlantic and northern European peoples included much more meat, milk, and milk products. Higher rainfall and the availability of large amounts of pasture allowed the maintenance of large herds of cattle. Northern rivers abounded in salmon and trout. Southerners considered northern use of butter and the drinking of beer—along with the wearing of trousers—as typically barbarian.

In some regions of the Empire, such as Britain and France or western Germany, cities were few and far between. By contrast, cities had existed for thousands of years in Mediterranean coastal areas and peasant life was well integrated with them. Only a few cities reached the size of Rome (about a million); most were in the range of

10,000 to 50,000. Amenities varied considerably. Temples, baths, porticoes, public toilets, basilicas, gymnasia, libraries, aqueducts, fountains, markets, stoas, theatres, and amphitheatres were common. Occasionally, lighted streets were to be found. Even small cities attempted to have some of the public facilities found in the larger cities, and at times found themselves in bankruptcy as a result of overly ambitious expenditures. This was one of Pliny's headaches when he was governor of Bithynia (northwestern Turkey).

16.1 Peasant Life

The Roman poet Ovid provides a romanticized portrayal of peasant life in his story of the couple Baucis and Philemon. The tale begins with Zeus and Hermes in the guise of mortals looking for a place to stay overnight. No one will take them in except the poor peasants Baucis and Philemon. Apart from the picture of agricultural life the story also reveals an important aspect of pagan religion—namely, the awe felt in the presence of unusual natural phenomena, such as the double-trunked tree, which gave rise to the story in the first place.[1]

Once upon a time, long ago, Jupiter and Hermes came looking for a place to stay. They knocked for shelter on a thousand doors and had a thousand doors shut against them. At last one received them, a small cottage roofed with straw and marsh reeds. Within its humble walls lived affectionate Baucis and Philemon. Equal in age, they had married in that cottage in youth and now had grown old there. Owning it helped them make light of their poverty, which they bore contentedly. There were no masters or servants in that house. The two of them were the whole household and together they served and ruled.

So when the heavenly visitors came and bowing entered the low-ceilinged door, Philemon set out a bench and invited them to rest, while Baucis spread a rough rug across it. Then she moved the warm ashes of the dying fire aside, threw leaves and dry bark among the coals and blew them to life. From the rafters she took kindling and twigs and set them under a copper pot that waited near the fire. She trimmed a cabbage that her husband had brought from the well-watered kitchen garden close at hand. Meanwhile, the old man, raising a forked stick, fetched down a side of smoked bacon which was hanging from the black rafters. From the long-hoarded meat he cut off a small piece and tossed it into the steaming water. To pass the time they entertained their guests with small talk. A mattress of soft river grass was smoothed and laid on a couch woven of willow. Over it they draped a cloth which was brought out only on festal days, but even this was poor and old, a good match for the willow couch.

The gods reclined. Then tucking up her skirts and with trembling hands, elderly Baucis set out the table. One of its three legs was too short so she propped it up with a piece of broken pottery. Once it was leveled she spread it with green fresh smelling mint. Then the food was served. First came olives, Minerva's fruit, ripe and brown, and September cherries, pickled in sweet wine, fresh lettuce and radishes, creamed cottage cheese, and eggs lightly baked in the ashes. All these were served on plates of country fashioned earthenware. Next an embossed mixing bowl of the same cheap make was set on the table together with small wooded cups, all lined with amber wax. After a short delay the soup prepared at the hearth was served with

---

[1]Ovid, *Metamorphoses* 8.626–677; 712–724.

not long aged wine. A space was cleared for the next course of nuts, figs, dates, and sweet smelling apples in a flat basket, purple grapes just picked from the vine. In the middle of the table was a comb of clear white honey. . . .

Baucis and Philemon are rewarded for their hospitality. While they watch their modest home is transformed into a temple. Marble columns replace the forked wooden supports, the straw turns yellow and becomes a roof of gold. The gates are richly carved and a marble pavement covers the ground. When asked by the gods what they would like as a reward, they requested that they be made priest and priestess of the temple with a final request that they would die at the same time. Years later they are metamorphosed into two trees side by side in front of the temple.

At last in frail old age as they happened to stand before the temple's doors and speak of years gone by, Baucis saw Philemon sprout green leaves and Philemon saw Baucis do the same. As the tree tops formed around their faces and as bark closed their lips they cried out together, "Farewell, good-bye, dear wife, dear husband." In Bithynia, the natives show the visitors two trees growing from a single trunk. . . . I myself have seen memorial wreaths hanging from those boughs and have refreshed them with new garlands of flowers saying, "Let those whom the gods love be gods, and those who have worshipped the gods be worshipped themselves."

16.2   City Life

16.2.1   How the Urban Lower Classes Coped

Dignity and social ranking had always been preoccupations of Roman society. Where a person stood in the pecking order was all-important. At the highest level was the Senatorial Order; under it came the Equestrian, and below that assorted other rankings. In the Empire there were further gradations and complications as the elites of Roman colonies and municipalities perpetuated and extended these traditions from one end of the Mediterranean to the other, and in turn non-Romans came to imitate them. Even the lower orders were drawn into this upper-class concern with rank and dignity, as can be seen in the following reading, a charter of a burial society that organized itself in A.D. *133 at Lanuvium near Rome.*

The overt purpose of burial societies (collegia, *"colleges," as they were called) was to enable the poor to avoid being buried in the common grave of paupers. In reality these associations, which were open to men and women, slaves and free alike, served a much broader function. Each association, like a miniature municipality, had its own charter, elected officers, and patron deity in whose honor it gathered. Members paid an entrance fee and gathered periodically to eat a meal together or celebrate a festival. Some better-off associations owned their own property, and had shrines, houses, or gardens where they met. It was considered the civic duty of the upper classes to endow these societies. Such benefactors were then honored by being elected patrons—the usual Roman social trade-off.*

The organization of the societies themselves allowed their members to practice a bit of snobbery on each other. Strict precedence was observed at meetings, and donations from patrons were distributed in graded amounts to the members according to their rank in the association. Even the lowliest could be elected to some office or other. In this way the masses of society mimicked their betters and were drawn into the imperial hierarchical system. In Roman society there was a recognized place for everyone.[2]

---

[2]Dessau, *Inscriptiones Latinae Selectae* 7212.

May the Emperor Caesar Trajan Hadrian Augustus, all his household, we ourselves, and our association (*collegium*), enjoy good fortune, happiness, and health. May we well and carefully establish the by-laws of this association that we may suitably discharge our duties regarding the funerals and burials of our dead. Accordingly, having consulted well together we ought to agree unanimously so that our association may endure for a long time.

You who wish to join this association should first read the charter so that, having joined, you do not afterwards complain or cause controversy through your will.

The Laws of the Collegium

Passed unanimously: That whoever wants to join this college should pay an initiation fee of 100 sesterces, an amphora of good wine, and a monthly fee of five asses. Likewise passed: If a member has not paid his/her dues for six months in a row and dies, a funeral will not be provided, even if he/she has made a will stipulating the payment of the arrears. On the other hand, if one of our members dies but is paid up, 300 sesterces are to be set aside for his/her funeral. From this amount fifty sesterces is to be paid to those who attend the funeral; it will be divided up at the funeral pyre. The mourners must, however, walk.

Passed: That if a member of the association should die beyond the 20th milestone from this town, and information regarding said death is duly relayed, then three members of the association should go to that place and make arrangements for the funeral. Afterwards they are to render a true and genuine account to the assembled members of the association. If deliberate fraud is demonstrated, they are to be fined fourfold. These representatives of the association are to be reimbursed for the cost of the funeral and be provided with travel expenses to and from in the amount of twenty sesterces each. However, if one of the members dies beyond the 20th milestone from the town and it was not possible to relay the information to the association, then he who saw to his burial should be a witness to this fact in writing, attested to by the seals of seven Roman citizens. When his account is approved, allowing sufficient time for appeal of the costs and provisions, he should be reimbursed in accordance with the rules of the association. Let there be no willful fraud in our association; let there be no suits against us, neither by patron, patroness, proprietor or proprietresses, or creditor—except where someone was named an heir by testament. If a member dies intestate, he/she will be given due funeral rites by the decision of the president and membership of the association.

Passed: Anyone of this association who is a slave and dies, and his/her master or mistress because of their harsh unreasonableness will not hand over his/her body, or if they have not left a will, then the association will celebrate a funeral in their name.

Passed: If anyone belonging to this association, for whatever reason contrives his/her own death, no funeral arrangements will be made.

Passed: If any member of this association who is a slave is manumitted, he/she should donate an amphora of good wine.

Passed: If any member who, in rotating fashion is Entertainment Director in his/her year, and fails to put on the appointed banquet, he/she will pay thirty sesterces into the treasury and his/her place will be taken by the next person on the list.

Order of Banquets: March 8, the birthday of Caesennius, father of the association's patron; [*a gap in the inscription follows*]; November 27, the birthday of Antinous [*the deified lover of the Emperor Hadrian, in whose temple the association seems to have met on occasion*]; the birthday of the

Goddess Diana and of the association itself, August 13; the birthday of Caesennius Silvanus, brother of the patron, August 20; the 4th of [*blank*], birthday of Cornelia Procula, mother of the patron; December 14, the birthday of L. Caesennius Rufus [*the patron of this association; a local big-wig*].

On Entertainment Directors: Entertainment Directors, chosen four at a time in order from the membership list, shall supply the following: one amphora of good wine each, two asses worth of bread per member, four pickled fish, a tablecloth, hot water, and a waiter.

On Presidents: Passed: The association's president shall, while president, be exempt from [*it is unclear what this privilege was*] and will receive double servings or divisions in all the distributions to the members. Likewise the scribes and summoners of the association will receive, after the terms of office, one and a half times every division to the membership. Likewise, every president who will have discharged his office with distinction shall receive by way of special honor one and a half times all the divisions made to the members, with the purpose of inspiring others to act in a similar fashion. The club president during his/her term of office on festival days shall, while robed in white, make offerings of incense and wine and, similarly garbed, perform his/her other duties. On the birthdays of Diana and Antinous he/she shall provide oil in the public bath building for the members before they dine.

On Troublemakers: Passed: If anyone has a complaint to make or wishes to bring up a business matter, let it be done at the regular meetings and not at banquets, which should be undisturbed and cheery affairs. Likewise, if any member is the cause of trouble and moves around from place at the meetings, he/she shall be fined four sesterces. If any member speaks abusively or causes an uproar, his/her fine will be twelve sesterces. If anyone addresses the president of the association abusively or insultingly during a banquet, his/her fine will be twenty sesterces.

In the late Republic and early Empire, large numbers of slaves, especially urban slaves, were manumitted by their masters and mistresses. Since citizenship was conferred at the time of manumission, it was fairly easy for freedmen to blend with the freeborn population, and even easier for their children to do so. In this inscription, freedmen parents—whose names, in addition to the appellation "freedman" in the title of the father, indicate that they are ex-slaves—put up a memorial to their son, who "made good" in the town of Capena, near Rome. Titus Flavius was aedile, quaestor designate, and a member of the town senate. Unlike his parents, he does not have a giveaway servile name. He possesses the full titulature of a freeborn Roman citizen, a point made with pride by the parents. In the inscription itself, as opposed to the translation given here, Titus's name appears at the very beginning and would be the first item read. The parents, or at least the father, were at one time slaves of the imperial household of the Flavian dynasty (A.D. 69–96) and were clearly well off. Ritual meals were held at burial sites.[3]

T. Flavius Mythus, freedman of Augustus, and Flavia Diogis, parents, have set aside [*this burial area*] for their most devoted son, T. Flavius Flavianus, son of Flavius, of the Quirinal Tribe, aedile and quaestor designate of the federate city of Capena. They do this also for themselves, their freedmen and their freedwomen and their descendants. This property,

---

[3]Dessau, *Inscriptiones Latinae Selectae* 5770.

consisting of about four jugera marked off from the Cutulenian farm, comes with a bath house and adjacent buildings on both sides of the road. An aqueduct supplies water from the Cutulenian farm.

16.2.2   Upper Classes: Technology and the Good Life

In the following sermonette, Seneca, advisor to Nero and a Stoic philosopher, preaches against luxury and praises the simple life. He is arguing against another philosopher by the name of Posidonius, who ascribed the origins of the "arts," that is, technology, to Wise Men or to philosophy itself. Seneca, on the other hand, believes that technology, rather than being the source of progress, is in fact at the root of all modern evils and should not be ascribed to the Wise or to philosophy.

Reading between the lines we can get a pretty good idea of what the life of the well-to-do in Rome was like in terms of creature comforts. We might also note that the debate between primitivists (or naturalists) and those devoted to technology, progress, and development is an old one. Seneca, in fact, was only one of the later contributors to this great debate. The issue of nature versus nurture, civilization versus spontaneity, was a particularly hot issue in the great debates of the Classical Age.[4]

I do not believe that Philosophy invented these cleverly devised buildings of ours, which rise one above the other—where the city's inhabitants are crammed together cheek-and-jowl—any more than Philosophy invented fish ponds for the purpose of sparing gluttons from having to risk storms at sea. No matter how bad the weather, luxury *always* has safe places to raise exotic kinds of fish!

What do you say? Was it Philosophy that taught us to use keys and bolts? No, rather the introduction of these security devices is the consequence of greed. Was it Philosophy that constructed all these dangerous, overhanging tenements? No, it was sufficient for people to provide themselves, happenstance, with any covering, and without art or trouble to provide themselves with some kind of shelter. Believe me! That was a happy age before the age of architects and builders! . . . [*In the good old days*] forked branches at either end propped up their huts. Compact twigs and sloping, thick layers of leaves provided shelter in the heaviest rains. They lived under such dwellings—but they lived in peace! Thatched roofs covered free men, but slavery lives under marble and gold. . . .

I ask you, which of the following is wiser: the person who invents the technique of spraying perfumed saffron to a great height from hidden pipes, who fills and empties canals by sudden gushes of waters and builds a dining room with a ceiling of movable panels that presents one sight after another in coordination with the courses being served? Or is it the one who demonstrates to himself as well as others that nature has not been harsh or difficult when it tells us we can get along *without* the marble cutter or metallurgist; that we can clothe ourselves *without* the silk trade; that we can have everything essential for our needs if we are content with what the earth has placed at hand? If the human race was willing to listen to this kind of advice, it would realize that the chef is as superfluous as the soldier. . . . Essentials are acquired easily enough; it is only luxuries that need effort. If you follow nature, you will not need technology. . . . At birth we're all ready to go! The trouble is we make life difficult for ourselves by disdaining what is easy. Houses, shelter, bodily comforts, food—which

---

[4]Seneca, *Epistle* 90.

are all now a great nuisance—were all available, free and easily acquired. The proper measure of things is always proportionate to the degree they are needed. It is we that have made all these things valuable and desirable and have caused them to be sought after by intense and complicated techniques. Nature is sufficient for essentials, but luxury has departed from nature.

. . . [T]here was a time when everything was offered to the body as to a slave, but now they are offered to it as to a master. Hence, it is that we have textile factories and carpenters' shops, the smells of gourmet cooking, the sexual provocativeness of lascivious teachers of dance and song . . . clothing that conceals nothing—see-through clothing which does not provide protection for the body, let alone protection for modesty!. . . For the natural moderation which limits our desires by what is available has vanished; to want only what is enough is regarded as a sign of backwardness and poverty of imagination. . . .

Seneca continues his attack on the theory that most inventions are the work of Wise Men in the distant past:

We know that certain inventions have come into existence only in our lifetime. For example, of recent origin are windows that admit brilliant light through glass tiles; vaulted baths where pipes for hot air are inserted in the walls to diffuse the heat evenly from top to bottom. Do I need to mention the marble with which our temples and our homes glisten? Or the rounded and polished masses of stone by means of which our porticoes are made big enough for whole masses of people? Or our shorthand by which we write down a whole speech no matter how quickly it is pronounced—speed of hand matching speed of tongue?

The Golden Age before science and technology:

When we have done everything, we will possess much; but there was a time when we had everything! The very land was more fertile when it was not worked and yielded enough for people who did not plunder each other's possessions. People found as much pleasure in sharing discoveries of nature as in making the discoveries in the first place. No one could either surpass or fall short of another in possessions. The stronger had not yet begun to impose on the weaker; the greedy had not yet begun to cut off their neighbors from the necessities of life by squirreling away what they could lay their hands on; each cared for the other as much as for himself. Arms were unused, and the hand, unstained by blood, was turned in all its violence in defense against wild animals. In those days a wood was sufficient to give protection against the sun and the severity of winter rains: under branches men lived and passed peaceful nights without so much as a sigh. We, on the other hand, are vexed in our purple by worries, our sleep is bothered by the sharpest of torments. How soft was the sleep the hard earth gave to the people of ancient times! No fretted and paneled ceilings hung over them as they lay out in the open, and the stars slid quietly above them, and the wonderful pageant of the night passed quickly by, performing in silence its mighty work. By day and by night the vision of this most glorious world lay before them. . . . But you tremble at every creak of your houses; if you hear anything as you sit among your paintings, you flee in terror. They had no homes as huge as cities. The wind blowing free through the open spaces, the gentle shade of rock or tree, pellucid springs and streams unspoiled by man's handiwork, whether pipe or confining channel, but running at will amid fields made beautiful by nature, not by art. In such surroundings they had their rough homes, embellished accordingly. This kind of dwelling was in accordance with nature. There one could live in happiness, fearing neither the home itself nor for its safety. Today our dwellings constitute a large portion of worries.

16.2.3   Leisure: Gymnasia, the Baths, the Circus, the Arena

Urban life in the Empire offered to rich, poor, and middle classes alike a wide variety of leisure activities. Festivals, scattered at intervals throughout the year, provided everyone with a break from the normal routine of life. They were celebrated with processions, games, public meals, competitions of all kinds (including beauty pageants), and even handouts (see "Obligations of the Rich" "The Divine Emperor" in Chapter 15). Most of the larger cities had libraries. No city worthy of the name was without a theater, a proper water supply, public bathing facilities, colonnaded shopping areas, and, in the east, gymnasia.

In the first selection, the orator Dio Chrysostom pokes fun at Greek behavior and love for gymnasia, which formed major focal points of social and educational activity, and not just athletics, throughout the Greek-speaking parts of the Empire.

Baths of every variety from small local dives to huge publicly funded affairs, glorious with marble and heated floors and walls, were also places where people could meet to relax, talk, and, if so inclined, exercise, since most had exercise grounds attached. For the benefit of the culturally inclined some were equipped with libraries, lecture halls, and art galleries.

The circus was perhaps the most popular form of entertainment; whole segments of the population went circus-mad over particular charioteers and teams of horses. By the time of the Empire, the theater had lost the elevated character it had in earlier periods and had become a medium of popular entertainment ranging from the harmless to the truly rank. The bloody arena where criminals were executed, gladiators fought, and hunters stalked and were stalked by wild beasts was popular with a certain segment of the population. Gladiatorial fights, being extremely expensive to stage, were not as widespread as the other activities.

Too much emphasis is often attached to the games. It has been estimated, for example, that on the majority of the days of the games only 1 percent of the population of Rome could have attended the theater. A higher percentage, 20 to 25 percent, might have been able to attend the horse races since the Circus Maximus had a capacity of 200,000. Even fewer could see gladiatorial fights. The Colosseum, for example, the primary venue for such events, held a maximum of only 50,000. Elsewhere in the Empire, for reasons of cost and the lack of facilities, the attendance figures must have been even lower.

Hanging around the Forum, the law courts, and the shopping colonnades; attending the festivals; and visiting the baths and the gymnasia (where they existed) were probably the prime forms of leisure for the urban dwellers of the Empire. For the country people, who must have constituted 90 percent or more of the population, the festivals would have been, as in the past, the primary forms of recreation.

Gymnasia[5]

Anacharsis [*one of the "Seven Wise Men"*] used to say that in each city of the Greeks there is a designated area [*the gymnasium*] where they become mad every day. For when they have gone there and taken off their clothes, they anoint themselves with a drug. This drug, he

---

[5]Dio Chrysostom, *Oration* 32.44. *The Chreia in Ancient Rhetoric*, trans. Ronald F. Hock and Edward N. O'Neil (Atlanta: The Scholars Press, 1986), p. 40. By permission.

said, causes their madness, for immediately some are running, some are throwing one another down, while others put up their hands and fight an imaginary opponent, though others are actually beaten up. When they have done these things, they scrape off this drug [*in reality olive oil*] and at once recover their senses and become immediately friendly with each other. . . .

Baths

The second-century author Lucian speaks with admiration of a bath building designed and erected by Hippias, a contemporary of his.[6]

The entrance is high, with a flight of broad steps of which the tread is greater than the pitch, to make them easy to ascend. On entering, one is received into a public hall of good size, with ample accommodations for servants and attendants. On the left are the lounging rooms, also of just the right sort for a bath, attractive, brightly lighted retreats. Then, beside them, a hall, larger than need be for the purposes of a bath, but necessary for the reception of the rich. Next, large locker rooms to undress in, on each side, with a very high and brilliantly lighted hall between them, in which there are three swimming pools of cold water; it is finished in Laconian marble and has two statues of white marble in the ancient technique, one of Hygieia [*the personification of health*], the other of Asclepius [*the god of healing*].

On leaving this hall, you come into another which is slightly warmed instead of meeting you at once with fierce heat; it is oblong and has an apse at each side. Next to it, on the right, is a very bright hall, nicely fitted up for massage, which has on each side an entrance, decorated with Phrygian marble, that receives those who come in from the exercise floor. Then near this is another hall, the most beautiful in the world, in which one can sit or stand with comfort, kill time without fear of criticism, and stroll about with profit. It also gleams in Phrygian marble clear to the roof. Next comes the hot corridor, faced with Numidian marble. The hall beyond it is very beautiful, full of abundant light and aglow with the purple of porphyry. It has three hot tubs.

When you have bathed, you need not go back through the same rooms but can go directly to the cold room through a slightly warmed apartment. Everywhere there is plenty of sunlight. Furthermore, the height of each room is well proportioned and the width corresponds properly to the length. Everywhere great beauty and loveliness prevail. . . . This is probably due in the main to the light and brightness and the windows.

Hippias, being truly ingenious, built the room for the cold baths to the north, though it does not lack a southern exposure, whereas he faced the rooms that needed the most heat to the south, east, and west. Why should I go on and tell you of the exercise floors and of the cloakrooms which have quick and direct communication with the hall containing the basin. . . . [*Hippias's building*] has all the good points of a bath: usefulness, convenience, light, good proportions, fitness to its site, and the fact that it can be used without risk. Moreover, it is adorned with all other marks of thoughtfulness—with two toilets, many exits, and two devices for telling time; a water-clock that bellows like a bull, and a sundial.

---

[6]Lucian, *Hippias or the Bath* 5–8. *Works of Lucian*, trans. (modified) A. M. Harmon (London: William Heinemann, 1913), pp. 39–43.

Games[7]

Nero put on a huge variety of entertainments: athletic competitions for young men; chariot races; theatrical performances; and gladiatorial shows. . . . Throughout the festival known as the Greatest Games, gifts were distributed to the people: every day a thousand assorted birds and numerous baskets of food, vouchers for grain, clothes, gold, silver, precious stones, pearls, paintings, slaves, horses, mules, and even tame wild animals, and finally vouchers for ships, apartment buildings, and farms. . . . [H]e staged the gladiatorial show in the wooden amphitheater near the Campus Martius . . . but allowed no one to be killed, not even criminals. . . . He put on a naval battle in an artificial salt-water lake which had sea monsters swimming in it.

Tacitus, who disapproved of Nero, also disapproved of his games.

Nero, in his fourth consulship with Cornelius Cossus as his colleague, instituted at Rome games on the Greek model, which were to be held every five years. As is typical with all new things, it received mixed reviews. Some noted that Pompey had been criticized by his older peers for constructing a permanent theater. They said that before its construction, theatrical performances had been given on a temporary stage to an audience on temporary stands, and that even before that the audience stood to watch plays so that people would not learn to spend their time in idleness by sitting in the theater. The old ways ought to be maintained [*so went the criticism; but instead*] our traditional morals have been gradually weakened and finally ruined by imported licentiousness. We thus begin to be able to see in our city everything that can corrupt—or be corrupted. Our youth have been made degenerate by their eagerness for foreign ways, for the gymnasium, for idleness, for perverted sex. . . .

Gladiators: Various Views[8]

You need not imagine that only people of the upper classes have the strength to escape the bonds of human servitude. . . . Men even of the lowest rank have escaped to safety through their own powerful drive. . . . Recently, for example, a German who was slated to be one of the wild animal fighters in the arena was getting ready for the morning show. He withdrew to relieve himself—the only thing he was allowed to do on his own without a guard being present. In the toilet there was a stick with a sponge on the end of it used for wiping away the feces. He rammed the whole thing down his throat, and choked to death. . . . Not a very elegant way to go, it's true, but what is more foolish than to be overly fastidious about our departure? What a brave man!

And in fact, what has Norbanus ever done for us? He produced a show with gladiators worth about a sesterce apiece, so decrepit that one puff and they would have all fallen flat on their faces. The mounted infantry fought like characters on a jug. . . . One, a Thracian, had a bit of spunk in him, but he too fought lackadaisically. At the end of the show they were all flogged while the crowd shouted: Hit them! Hit them! Clearly a bunch of losers. "Still," said Norbanus, "I gave you a show, didn't I?"

---

[7]Suetonius, *Nero* 11; Tacitus, *Annals* 14.20.
[8]Seneca, *Letters* 70; Petronius, *Satyricon* 45; Dessau, *Inscriptiones Latinae Selectae* 5090, 5106, 5142A.

{Inscription at Rome}:

To the shades of M. Antonius Niger, a Thracian-style fighter, who lived to be thirty-eight and fought eighteen times. Put up by his wife, Flavia Diogenis, to her well-deserving husband from her own resources.

{Inscription at Rome}:

To the shades of M. Ulpius Felix, veteran myrmillion [*a gladiator who usually fought against the net-man or the Thracian type of gladiator*], who lived 45 years. By nationality a Tungrian [*modern Belgium*]. . . . His wife, the freedwoman Ulpia Syntyche, and their son Justus erected this inscription to her beloved and well-deserving husband.

{Graffito at Pompeii}:

Heartthrob of the girls, Celadus, Thracian-style fighter; fought three times, won three times.

A Charioteer[9]

{Inscription at Rome}:

To the shades of Diversus Pompeius Musclosus, driver of the Red Faction, born in the Tuscus neighborhood of Rome. He won first place a total of 682 times; three times as charioteer of the Whites, five times with the Greens, twice with the Blues, and 672 with the Reds; put up by his wife Apuleia Verecunda in honor of his memory.

16.3   Daily Life as Seen through the Law Codes

From the Roman law codes we get a somewhat different view of daily life in the Roman world. One of Rome's greatest achievements was the development of a uniform law code for the whole Empire along with the scientific study of law itself. The idea that the same law could be applied everywhere regardless of time, culture, language, religion, or ethnicity was original to the Romans. While the development of Roman law took place over centuries, the process of collecting and updating it occurred late in Roman history. Some legal collections appeared in the third century A.D., *but it was not until the Emperor Justinian published the* Digest of Roman Law *in* A.D. *533 that the definitive codification occurred.*

Roman law has been described as "organized common sense," a characteristic that may be seen in the following selections from the Digest. *The* Lex Aquila, *to which reference is made in the first selection, dates from the period of the Republic; it was the basic law covering claims of negligence. Alfenus was a legal expert of the late Republic; Ulpian, Mela, Proculus, Pomponius, and Marcellus belong to the Empire period.*

16.3.1   "If, While Several Persons Are Playing Ball . . ."[10]

Ulpian, *On the Edict, Book 8:* Mela also says that if, while several persons are playing ball, the ball having been struck too violently should hit the hand of a barber who is shaving a slave at the time, in such a way that the throat of the latter is cut by the razor, the party responsible

---

[9]Dessau, *Inscriptiones Latinae Selectae* 5281.
[10]From S. P. Scott, *The Civil Law in 17 Volumes*, Vol. 3 (Cincinnati, OH: Central Trust Co, 1932), pp. 327, 345.

for negligence is liable under the *Lex Aquila*. Proculus thinks that the barber is to blame, and, indeed, if he had the habit of shaving persons in a place where it is customary to play ball or where there was much activity, he is in a certain degree responsible, although it may not improperly be held that where anyone seats himself in a barber's chair in a dangerous place, he has only himself to blame. . . .

Alfenus, *Digest, Book 2:* Mules were hauling two loaded wagons up the Capitoline Hill [*at Rome*], and the drivers were pushing the first wagon, which was inclined to one side, in order that the mules might haul it more easily. In the meantime the upper wagon began to go back, and as the drivers were caught between the two wagons they jumped out of the way and the last wagon was struck by the first. The second wagon then moved back, crushing a slave boy who belonged to someone.

The owner of the boy asked me against whom ought he to bring an action? I answered that it depended on circumstances, for if the drivers who had hold of the first wagon voluntarily got out of the way, and the result was that the mules could not hold the wagon and were pulled back by its weight, then no action would lie against the owner of the mules, but an action under the *Lex Aquila* could be brought against the men who held the wagon; for if a party, while he was supporting something, by voluntarily releasing his hold enabled it to strike someone, he nevertheless committed damage, as for instance, where anyone was driving an ass and did not restrain it, or where anyone were to discharge a weapon or throw some other object out of his hand.

But if the mules gave way because they were frightened, and the drivers, actuated by fear of being crushed, released their hold on the wagon, then no action can be brought against the men, but one could be brought against the owner of the mules. And if neither the mules nor the men were the cause of the accident, but the mules could not hold the load, or while striving to do so slipped and fell and this caused the wagon to go back, and the men were unable to support the weight when the wagon was inclined to one side, then no action could be brought against the owner of the mules or the men. This, however, is certain; that no matter what the circumstances were, no action would lie against the owner of the mules that were in the rear, as they did not go back voluntarily, but because they were struck. . . .

16.3.2　Bequests[11]

Marcellus, *Opinions:* Seia charged her heir, Publius Maevius, with a bequest as follows: "I give and bequeath to Antonia Tertylla such-and-such a weight of gold, and my large pearls set with hyacinths." She afterwards disposed of the pearls, and at the time of her death did not leave any among her jewels. I ask whether the heir will, under the terms of the trust, be compelled to furnish the value of the property which does not form part of the estate. Marcellus answers that he will not be required to do so. I also ask, if it can be proved that Seia converted her necklace of pearls and hyacinths into some other kind of ornament which afterwards became more valuable through the addition of other jewels and small pearls, whether the legatee can demand the said pearls and hyacinths, and whether the heir will be compelled to remove them from the other jewelry and deliver them. Marcellus answers that the demand cannot be made. For how can a legacy or a trust be held to exist when what is given by a will does not retain

---

[11]From Scott, *The Civil Law*, Vol. 7, p. 240.

its original character? For the bequest is, as it were, extinguished, so that in the meantime it is lost sight of, and hence by this dismemberment and change the intention of the bequestor also appears to have been altered. . . .

16.3.3   "Wolves Carried Away Some Hogs ..." [12]

Ulpian, *On the Edict*, Book 19: Pomponius discusses the following point. Wolves carried away some hogs from my shepherds; the tenant of an adjoining farm, having pursued the wolves with strong and powerful dogs, which he kept for the protection of his flocks, took the hogs away from the wolves, or the dogs compelled them to abandon them. When my shepherd claimed the hogs, the question arose whether they had become the property of him who recovered them or whether they were still mine, for they had been obtained by a certain kind of hunting. The opinion was advanced that, as where animals were captured on sea or land and regained their natural freedom, they ceased to belong to those who took them, so, where marine or terrestrial animals deprive us of property, it ceases to be ours when the said animals have escaped beyond our pursuit. In fact, who can say that anything which a bird flying across my courtyard or my field carries away still belongs to me? If, therefore, it ceases to be mine and is dropped from the mouth of the animal, it will belong to the first occupant; just as when a fish, a wild boar, or a bird escapes from our control and is taken by another it becomes the property of the latter.

Pomponius inclines to the opinion that the property continues to be ours as long as it can be recovered, although what he states with reference to birds, fishes, and wild beasts is true. He also says that if anything is lost by shipwreck, it does not immediately cease to be ours, and that anyone who removes it will be liable for quadruple its value. And, indeed, it is better to hold that anything which is taken away by a wolf will continue to be ours as long as it can be recovered. Therefore, if it still remains ours, I think that an action on the ground of theft will lie. For if the tenant pursued the wolves, not with the intention of stealing the property (although he might have had such an intention), but admitting that he did not pursue them with this object in view, still, as he did not restore the hogs to my shepherd when he demanded them, he is held to have suppressed and concealed them, and therefore I think that he will be liable to an action on the ground of theft, as well as one to produce the property in court; and after this has been done, the hogs can be recovered from him.

16.4   Family Life

16.4.1   An Affectionate Paterfamilias

The poet Horace honors his father, a former slave, whose occupation was that of a tax collector. The family lived in out-of-the-way Apulia in southern Italy, so that the decision to educate Horace in Rome involved considerable sacrifice on the father's part. The reading draws attention to the potential for social mobility in Rome—at least if one had as much talent as Horace and the support of sensible and ambitious parents. [13]

---

[12]From Scott, *The Civil Law*, Vol. 9, p. 171.
[13]Horace, *Satires* 1.6.65–92.

If my character, while generally sound, is only flawed in a minor way—like moles on an otherwise good-looking person—if no one can charge me with avarice or meanness or sexual excess, if (pardon my self-praise) I live a decent life and am a friend to my friends—I owe it all to my father.

Although he was just a poor farmer he would not send me to the local school with the tough sons of tough centurions, their slates and school bags slung over their shoulders, each with his eight cents of tuition due on the Ides. No, he had the courage to send me off to Rome to be taught what sons of senators and knights were taught. If anyone in that bustling city saw my clothes and slave retinue he would have thought my support came from ancestral wealth. But in point of fact my father was my attendant [*i.e., instead of having slaves accompany him as slaves did the rich, Horace's father served in their place*]. He was my incorruptible guardian among my teachers. Need I say more? He kept me chaste, the first grace of virtue, free from shameful deeds as well as their reputation. He wasn't afraid that some day I might end up in some lowly occupations like an auctioneer or a tax collector like himself, and earn a wage. I would not have complained. But as it is I owe him my praise and thanks. Never—at least as long as I am sane—would I be ashamed of such a father, and so I will not defend myself as many like me do, who say it's no fault of theirs that they have not freeborn, famous parents.

16.4.2   A Satirist's View of Marriage

If we were to believe the satirist Juvenal, Roman family values, especially among the upper classes and the well-to-do middle classes, were hopelessly corrupt. (For a different view, see "A Moralist's View of Marriage" in the next section). Spoiled rich women abused their slaves and their weak husbands. But if we set aside the rhetoric and Juvenal's venom, it is possible to get a somewhat different view of the relationship between husband and wife. Juvenal's women are clearly not passive—despite the supposed nearly dictatorial power possessed by the Roman paterfamilias. *Their own resources give them a degree of freedom—at least in their private lives. Many were also educated. The presence of slaves in the household is taken for granted, as is the easy and, from a modern viewpoint, incredibly exploitative sexual power both husband and wife had over them.*[14]

If you are determined to be monogamous then you might as well bow your head and accept the yoke. No wife spares the man who loves her, for though she may be passionate she gets her real pleasure from tormenting and putting down her spouse. The better the husband and the man the less good it will do him. He will never give a present unless she approves. If she objects there will be nothing, I repeat, nothing, that you can buy or sell. She will decide who your friends are going to be. You will find that long-time friends are banished. Pimps and gladiatorial trainers are free to make their wills as they please, even gladiators, but you will find among your heirs more than one of your own rivals.

"Crucify that slave!" orders your wife. "But what capital crime has he committed?" you reply. "Who is the witness? Who is his accuser? Stop and listen. No delay can be too long when a man's life is at stake!" "What, you fool," she says, "you think a slave is a human being? He did nothing? True, but it's my wish, my command—my desire is sufficient reason." . . . If you have turned your back on your wife at night, the woman who cards the wool is done for

---

[14]Juvenal, *Satires* 6.206–223, 475–494, 434–456.

as is the woman in charge of her wardrobe. The man with the litter will be accused of coming late—he'll have to pay for your sin. One will have a rod broken over his shoulders, another will bleed from the strap, the third from the lash. Some wives engage their torturers by the year; it's cheaper. While the flogging is going on, the lady will be making up her face, listening to her friends, or examining a gold-embroidered robe. . . . If she wants to be turned out more nicely than usual, the unfortunate maid, her own hair a mess and her clothes falling off will hear, "Why is this curl standing up?" and down comes the leather thong to inflict punishment for the offending hair. . . .

Worst of all is the woman who has barely sat down to dinner when she starts to praise Virgil, forgives the dying Dido [*the Carthaginian queen whom Aeneas jilts in Virgil's masterwork, the* Aeneid], pits the poets against each other, setting up Virgil on one side of the scales and Homer on the other. The scholars yield, the professors are vanquished, the whole dinner crowd is shut up. No one, not even a lawyer or an auctioneer, can get a word in edgewise—no, not even another woman! She sets down definitions and like a philosopher talks of morals, dying to be both learned and eloquent. How I hate women who are forever consulting Palaemon's grammar! They insist on keeping all the rules and laws of language. Like pedants they quote verses I never heard of and correct their unlettered friends' speech. You would think husbands could at least be allowed to make slips in grammar!

16.4.3   A Moralist's View of Marriage

Just how accurately Juvenal's satire mirrors husband–wife relations in Roman society at large is hard to estimate. Was the kind of behavior described earlier typical of upper-class society as a whole or only of a part of it? What of the middle and lower classes? Was Juvenal's hectic lifestyle common only in Rome? What about Italy and the provinces? Other types of evidence—though it is equally difficult to determine how much they reflect actual practice—are epitaphs found on tombstones (such as Turia's inscription; see "Marriage" in Chapter 12) and the moral codes of the great philosophies of the Empire.

The following reading from Musonius Rufus *(see "Moral Behavior" in Chapter 15) discusses the purpose of marriage.*[15] *The philosophical belief that marriage existed for the sake of a shared life and the procreation of children goes back to Aristotle.*

The main purpose of marriage is twofold: a shared life and the procreation of children. Musonius says that those entering a marriage should be united with each other with the intent of: (1) having a common life together, and (2) begetting and raising children. Indeed, while holding their material goods in common, spouses should consider nothing to be their own, not even their individual bodies. The raising of children is a matter of the greatest importance; indeed, marriage exists for this purpose. While it is possible to achieve the same result outside marriage—just as animals do—this is not fitting. For in marriage there must be full community of life between husband and wife, real love for each other, whether in health or illness, indeed, in all circumstances, since it was for this purpose, as well as for having children, that they married in the first place.

When the love of husband and wife for each other is perfect, and when they share it fully, each spouse seeking to outdo the other, then this is what a marriage ought to be and is indeed

---

[15]Musonius Rufus, *The Purpose of Marriage* 13a.

enviable. Such a union is fine and good. But when each spouse seeks just his or her interest without concern for the other or when, by Zeus, one feels this way and although living in the same house has his or her heart fixed elsewhere, and has no wish to unite his efforts or his sentiments with his yoke-mate, by necessity this union is finished. Spouses who live in a situation like this have a terrible relationship. In the end they separate entirely; their life together is worse than being alone.

16.4.4   An Affectionate Marriage

Pliny, an important Roman senator (see Chapter 15), claims to have had a deeply affectionate relationship with his wife.[16]

You cannot begin to imagine how much I miss you! This is because I love you so much and we are not used to being separated. And so I lay awake most of the night thinking of you. During the day I find that my feet lead me, they really do, to your room at the time I used to visit you. Finding it empty I leave, as sick at heart and sad as a lover locked out by his loved one. The only time I manage to escape these miseries is when I am in court and wearing myself out pleading my friends' lawsuits. You can judge for yourself what a state I'm in when I find relaxation in work, and distraction in troubles and anxieties!

16.4.5   An Epitaph for a Wife

Thousands of grave monuments that were put up by husbands and wives to each other survive. The inscriptions on them are often formulaic and it is difficult to know just how much genuine sentiment is to be inferred from them. They come from all over the Empire. The following was put up in Britain by a Syrian to his freedwoman wife, a native Celt. It is in Latin and Syriac. The monument shows Regina seated wearing a long sleeved robe reaching to her feet. She wears a necklace and bracelets and holds an open jewelry box in her right hand. On her lap are a distaff and spindle. Beside her is a workbasket with balls of wool.[17]

To the spirits of the dead. To Regina, his freedwoman and wife, a Catuvallaunian by tribe. She was aged thirty years. Barates of Palmyra set this up.

In Palmyrene script under the Latin text appears the following:

Regina, the freedwoman of Baratas, alas.

16.4.6   Friendship Among Wives: A Birthday Invitation

During the excavation of the Roman fort at Vindolanda near Hadrian's Wall in England, hundreds of wooden writing tablets, some with the writing still legible, were found. They date from about A.D. 90–120 when the fort was occupied by Cohors I Tungrorum and later by Cohors IX Batavorum, auxiliary units in the Roman army from Germany and the Netherlands, respectively. The officers of the units were Romans (or at least Roman citizens). The wives of several of these officers lived in the fort and the reading

---

[16]Pliny, *Letters* 7.5.

[17]R. G. Collingwood and R. P. Wright, *The Roman Inscriptions of Britain* (Gloucester, U. K.: A Sulton 1990), no. 1065.

that follows is a birthday invitation from Claudia Severa, the wife of an officer, to her friend Lepidina, the wife of Flavius Cerialis, prefect of one of the cohorts at the fort. The words "Sister I shall expect you . . . hail," which are in Claudia's own hand, are the oldest known example of a woman's handwriting in Latin.[18]

Claudia Severa sends greetings to her friend Lepidina. Sister, I happily invite you to be sure to come to our house on my birthday, the third day before the Ides of March, for if you are present you will make the day more enjoyable for me. Say hello to your Cerialis. My Aelius and my little son send their greetings. Sister, I shall expect you. Be well, sister, dearest soul, as I hope to be well, and hail. To Sulpicia Lepidina, wife of Cerialis, from Severa.

16.4.7   Epitaphs for Children

Many, perhaps most, children never survived childhood and were mourned by their grieving parents. The monument to Hateria Superba, who is commemorated in this inscription, depicts her holding in her hands a dove and some fruit, while hovering child angels place a crown on her head. By her side are her pet dog and crow.[19] *The second reading is by the poet Martial (ca. A.D. 40–104), a friend of Juvenal and Pliny. Martial commends the soul of a little girl by the name of Erotion, possibly his slave, to the care of his already deceased parents.*[20]

To the spirits of the departed and to Hateria Superba who lived one year, six months, and twenty five days. Her inconsolable parents, Q. Haterius Ephebus and Julia Sosima, set up this monument for their daughter, for themselves and their household.

To you my father Fronto, and to you my mother Flaccilla, I commend this little girl, my darling sweetheart. In your care may little Erotion not be terrified by the dark shades and the monstrous gaping jaws of Hades' hound. She would have completed six years—less six days—the midwinter day she died. In your protection, now her guardians, may she continue her playful childhood, chattering about me, lisping my name.

Gentle earth weigh lightly on her small bones as she, when living, lightly trod on you.

16.4.8   Christian Marriage: Paul's View

Christians were accused by pagans of sexual crimes such as incest and promiscuity. But there were also allegations that Christianity, along with some other Eastern religions, such as Judaism and the mysteries of Isis, gave greater equality to women. In his Letter to the Galatians, Paul, the great theologian and presenter of Christianity to the non-Jewish Greco-Roman world, makes the following radical proclamation of equality: "You are all sons of God through faith in Christ Jesus. . . . There is neither Jew nor Greek, slave nor free, male nor female, for you are all one in Christ Jesus."[21] *This and similar statements were at odds with at least the ideology of strict patriarchy and the exhortations of pagan moralists that wives, children, and slaves should accept their position in the established hierarchy of subservience. In response, Christians defended themselves in their discussion of*

---

[18]Tab. Vindol. II.291.
[19]H. Dessau, *Inscriptiones Latinae Selectae* (Berlin, 1892), 8005.
[20]Martial, *Epigrams* 5.34.
[21]Paul, Letter to the Galatians 3:26–28.

marriage by adopting the wording of the so-called "Household Codes" of the pagan moralists and giving it a Christian theological interpretation. Whereas the main aim of the pagan household codes was to emphasize the authority of husbands, fathers, and masters over their wives, children, and slaves, respectively, Christian writers, such as Paul in this reading, makes the obligations reciprocal. Lurking behind the reworking of pagan moral values there may also be present an attempt on Paul's part to address a more radical form of Christianity that in fact gave greater freedom to women, especially in religious matters.

The following selection is preceded by a general exhortation to moral behavior. The passage begins with the principle of mutual subordination and then goes on to explain how this is supposed to work in the household—that is, how it applies to wives, husbands, children, and slaves, the traditional family unit.[22]

[*All of us are*] subject to one another out of reverence for Christ. Therefore:

Wives, be subject to your husbands, as to the Lord, because the husband is head of the wife as also Christ is head of the Church. . . . As the Church is subject to Christ, so also let the wives be subject to their husbands in everything.

Husbands, love your wives, even as also Christ loved the Church and gave himself up for it that he might sanctify it. . . . Even so husbands ought to love their own wives as their own bodies. He who loves his wife loves himself, for no one ever hated his own flesh, but nourishes and cherishes it, even as Christ does the Church, for we are members of his body.

Children, obey your parents in the Lord, for this is right. . . .

Fathers, do not provoke your children to anger, but nurture them in the discipline and admonition of the Lord.

Slaves, obey with fear and trembling those who, according to the flesh, are your masters. This is to be done in singleness of heart as to Christ, not by way of eye-service, as pleasing men, but as slaves of Christ, doing the will of God from the soul. Do service with a good attitude as to the Lord, and not to men, knowing that whatsoever good thing each shall have done, this he shall receive again from the Lord, whether he is a slave or free.

Masters, do the same to your slaves and give up threatening, knowing as you do that both their Master and yours is in heaven—and he does not show favors.

16.4.9 Abortion and Infanticide

Abortion and infanticide were practiced throughout the Roman Empire, though to what extent is uncertain. Life expectancy at birth in antiquity was extremely low and parents at all levels of society needed children to carry on the family name and traditions and to look after them in old age. While too many children could be a serious problem for the poor, there were also frivolous reasons for abortion. For the most part, abortion was a resort of the elite since only they could afford the medical costs involved. Exposure was an alternative for the rest of society and for those among the upper class who wished to avoid the dangers and pain of an abortion. Under Roman law the paterfamilias *had extensive rights over his offspring and could choose to raise his infants or not. The Emperor Augustus, for instance, would not allow the child of his granddaughter Julia to be raised after she had been condemned for adultery.*[23] *Fathers of illegitimate children, on the other hand, had no right to expose their children.*

---

[22]Paul, Letter to the Ephesians 5:6.
[23]Suetonis, *Augustus* 65.

Opinion about abortion and infanticide was divided. Aristotle wrote that abortion was legitimate only before the quickening of the fetus, that is before it showed signs of sensation. The well-known Hippocratic Oath forbade doctors to administer abortifacients, and the orator Cicero deplored abortion on the grounds that it reduced the citizen population and made the continuity of families impossible.

Legally abortion was not a crime because in Roman law the fetus was not a person. Until the baby was born it had no legal standing. On the other hand it was not just an inanimate object and could be afforded protections as witnessed by the opinion of the jurist Julian who said, "In practically the whole of civil law the child in the womb is regarded as having real existence."[24] *Accordingly, in Roman law, pregnant women condemned to torture or death could not be executed or tortured until after they had delivered. Exposed children were sometimes brought up as slaves by their finders although if they could later prove they were freeborn, they had to be liberated. The law also protected the rights of birth parents even if they chose not to raise their child. Such parents could later claim the child although there was probably an obligation to reimburse the foster parents for the costs of raising it.*

The family consilium *or council, which included the mother, and advised the father on many issues, probably also advised on this subject. Philo, the great Jewish philosopher from Alexandria, regarded exposure as the equivalent of murder. The* Didache *(The Teachings of the Apostles, ca. A.D. 100), one of the oldest Christian documents outside the New Testament, is the first text to mention abortion explicitly. It condemns the practice. By the later empire, exposure came to be regarded as murder. Infanticide was proscribed in* A.D. *374. In the sixth century the Emperor Justinian enacted that exposed children were to be deemed free. The following readings are from the first-century* A.D. *Roman poet Ovid. The first reading is a fantasy from his work, the* Metamorphoses.[25]

Once upon a time, near the royal city of Knossos in Crete, there lived a man named Ligdus. He was freeborn, but lower class and from a poor family. Nevertheless, although he was poor he was a decent and honorable person. One evening he told his wife, who was pregnant and approaching the time for her baby to be delivered, "I pray for two things. One, that you have an easy labor, and second, that the baby be a boy. A daughter is more trouble and fortune hasn't given us the wherewithal to raise her. I hate to say this, but if it's a girl . . . we'll have to let her die." They both wept. . . . His wife, Telethusa, begged her husband again and again to change his mind, but he wouldn't and stubbornly resisted his wife's appeals.

As her time neared Telethusa had a dream and in her dream she saw the goddess Isis walking toward her bed with a procession of sacred beings. Upon her forehead shone the crescent moon and a wheat yellow garland of glittering gold surrounded her head, a sight of royal beauty. . . . Isis spoke: "O Telethusa, dear child of mine, forget your troubles and do not obey your husband's mistaken command. . . . Protect and nurse your child, boy or girl. I'm the goddess who answers the prayers of those who love me; you have not worshipped a thankless deity." Joyfully Telethusa rose from her bed and raising her innocent hands in prayer to the stars, she begged that her vision might come true.

---

[24]Julian, *Digest* 1.5.26.
[25]Ovid, *Metamorphoses* 9.669–703.

The story goes on to tell how the child—a girl—was born and how Telethusa, pretending it was a boy, raised it. Iphis, as the child was called, grew up healthy and beautiful. Complications arose when it came time for the arrangement of a betrothal. At the intercession of Telethusa, Isis intervened to solve the impasse and metamorphosed Iphis into a male.

In this next reading, Ovid addresses his girlfriend, Corinna, complaining that she is contemplating an abortion just to avoid stretch marks. He uses the metaphor of war and gladiatorial combat to describe the contemplated abortion.[26]

The woman who first tore her tender baby from her womb should have died in the butchery on that battlefield herself. And are you now ready to enter that same sad arena and make a similar slaughter just so that your stomach will be free of wrinkles? If this practice had been engaged in by the mothers of olden times, their crime would have rendered the human race extinct. . . . Had the mother of Romulus and Remus ripped the twins from her swollen womb there would have been no Rome. . . . Had your own mother tried to do what you are now planning, you yourself would have perished, your beauty embryonic! . . . No tigress in Armenia would do a thing like this, no lioness dares to destroy her own cubs. But frail young girls do!

---

[26]Ovid, *Amores* 2.14.5f.

Chapter 17

The Transformed Empire

By the fourth century (A.D. 300–400), the axis of the Roman world had shifted away from the Mediterranean. Italy had become a backwater. Rome itself was rarely visited by the emperors, who now needed bases closer to the danger spots on the frontiers. Trier on the Moselle (in present-day Germany) was the western capital. Milan in northern Italy, Sirmium on the Danube, Byzantium (soon to be renamed Constantinople), Caesarea in Turkey, and Antioch in Syria were all major administrative centers or regional capitals.

But the shift of the axis was more than geographical: There was also a shift in the political, military, social, and especially the cultural life of the Empire. The army was enlarged and rearmed to cope with the threat of Persia in the east and the Germans in the north and west. In turn, a large bureaucracy grew to generate the necessary taxes and round up the recruits needed for the expanded military. The command and administrative structure was revised, and the Empire divided into eastern and western halves. The imperial office itself was surrounded with pageant and ceremony and became more remote and authoritarian.

But the military and administrative reforms were incomplete and inadequate. The army tended to grow on paper while the actual number of available front-line troops declined. Much of the additional revenue that was supposed to go to increasing the size of the army went instead to corrupt officials. Bribery, which had always been an endemic aspect of the Roman system, was now given huge opportunities for growth, on a scale not dreamed of in the past. The traditions of *polis* society, especially in the realm of religion and municipal service, were undermined by the increasing burdens of taxation, administration, and corruption and by the rise of Christianity as an alternative value system.

At the most basic level, the central administration was never able to persuade reluctant municipal elites and even more reluctant peasants in the peaceful parts of the Empire that defending the remote Rhine or Danube frontier or northern England was in their self-interest. The Empire held together only when the external pressures were not too great and the demands on its inhabitants not too heavy. But at some point the demands began to be seen as outweighing the benefits, and then the decay began in earnest.

Oddly, in these years some of the most devoted "Romans" were Germans or other barbarians serving in the army. The key to the future, particularly in the vulnerable western half of the Empire, lay in Rome's relationship with the Germans, and it was in this area that the imperial system ultimately broke down, leading to the rise of multiple, independent German kingdoms in the old western and central European provinces. Paradoxically it was the Church that now became the most vital mediator between the barbarians and the classical, *polis* past.

In the east, the Empire had a much stronger base. More populous and more deeply urbanized, richer, and with a long tradition of submission to autocracy, the east was more receptive to the reforms of Diocletian and Constantine. The Empire survived there to the time of the Arab invasions in the seventh century, and in a more reduced form to the fall of Constantinople to the Turks in A.D. 1453.

17.1   "Now Declining Into Old Age": A Review of Roman History from a Late-Empire Viewpoint

The author of this reading (and a number of others in this chapter) is the Greek army officer Ammianus Marcellinus of Antioch in Syria, who published a history of Rome in the A.D. 390s. A pagan and admirer of the Emperor Julian, who had been the champion of the old religion during his brief reign, Ammianus lived at the time when Christianity consolidated its hold on the Empire. That he chose to retire to Rome and write his great work in Latin rather than his native Greek says something about the continuing power of Rome to attract provincials into its service. He subscribes to conventional moral values and the belief that Providence lay behind Rome's rise to greatness. Within ten to fifteen years of the publication of his history, Rome would be sacked by a Gothic warrior-band under its chief, Alaric, and half a century or so later the last emperor, Romulus Augustulus, would be replaced by a German warlord, but those events should not obscure the general validity of his belief that the reputation of Rome had an extraordinarily high standing among peoples outside as well as within the Empire.[1]

At the time when Rome first rose to world greatness—that Rome which was destined to last as long as the human race—bravery and fortune, though commonly at variance, agreed upon a treaty of eternal peace to assist its rise to glory. If either had been missing, Rome would never have reached its heights of greatness. Its people, from their earliest infancy to the latest moment of their youth, a period which extended over 300 years, carried on a variety of wars with the peoples around its walls. Then, when it arrived at adolescence, after many and various labors in war, it crossed the Alps and the sea, until as youth and adult, it had carried the triumphs of victory into every country in the world.

And now that it is declining into old age, and often owes its victories to its mere reputation, it has come to a more tranquil time of life. Therefore, the venerable city, after having bowed down the haughty necks of fierce nations, and given laws to the world to be the foundations and eternal anchors of liberty, like a thrifty parent, prudent and rich, entrusted to the Caesars as to its own children, the right of governing its ancestral inheritance. And although

---

[1]Ammianus Marcellinus, *Roman History* 14.6. All the selections from Ammianus are adapted from the translation of C. D. Yonge, *The Roman History of Ammianus Marcellinus* (London: Henry G. Bohn, 1862).

the Tribes and Centuries [*i.e., the voting assemblies of Rome*] are no longer active, and the contests for votes have been replaced by a calm recalling of the age of King Numa [*second king of Rome after its founder Romulus*], nevertheless, in every quarter of the world Rome is still looked up to as the mistress and queen of the earth, and the name of the Roman people is respected and venerated.

17.2   New Founders of Rome: Diocletian and Constantine

During the third century A.D. *it seemed as though the Empire was certain to break up, but a vigorous new dynasty of emperors from Illyria (modern Yugoslavia) managed to reestablish the Empire on a new footing. The first of these great emperors was Diocletian. Building on the reforms of previous regimes, Diocletian consolidated them into a coherent new program that enabled Rome to cope with the immediate challenges of civil war and barbarian invasions. His successor, Constantine, took the step of embracing Christianity and building a new capital, Constantinople, on the site of the ancient Greek city of Byzantium.*

The following extremely hostile (and highly rhetorical) account of the reforms of Diocletian was written by Lactantius, a Christian professor of Latin at Nicomedia, the emperor's capital. Understandably prejudiced against the emperor who launched the last bloody persecution of the Church, Lactantius nevertheless distorts the great accomplishments of Diocletian. In order to cope with the problem of the frontiers, the army had to be significantly increased in size. This increase could be accomplished only by major "revenue enhancements" (taxes). Increased taxes required tighter administration—more bureaucrats—and generally more sacrifice all around. Not everyone was pleased, particularly large property owners, on whom the burden was principally supposed to fall. The reading is useful insofar as it accurately describes both Diocletian's reforms and the reaction to them of a segment of the population.[2]

Diocletian was the instigator of crimes and the contriver of evils. He despoiled everything; he could not even keep his hands off God himself! Through greed and anxiety he managed to turn the whole world inside out.

He made three men partners in his rule and divided the Empire into four parts. Correspondingly, he increased the armies since each of the four partners strove to have a much larger number of troops than previous emperors did when the state (*res publica*) was ruled by a single emperor. Naturally, the number of tax recipients began to exceed the number of taxpayers—to such an extent that the farmers' resources were overwhelmed by the enormous size of the state's assessments. Fields were abandoned and cultivated areas were turned into wilderness.

To be sure that everyone was properly terrorized, provinces were chopped up into pieces. Many governors and even more sub-governors were imposed on individual districts, and even on individual cities. Along with them came numerous accountants, administrators, and deputy prefects [*local representatives of the now civilian Praetorian Prefects*]. The actions of these individuals, however, was rarely civil! In fact, they were involved mainly with condemnations and repeated confiscations; to be exact, their demands were not just frequent, but constant, and involved intolerable wrongs.

The methods of raising troops was also intolerable. With insatiable greed, Diocletian would never allow the treasury to be depleted but always piled up surplus resources and funds

---

[2]Lactantius, *The Deaths of the Persecutors* 7.

so as to preserve intact what he had already collected. Likewise, when as a result of his blunders he had generated tremendous shortages, he tried to legislate the prices of goods [*by edict*]. Much blood was then shed over worthless items, and because of fear nothing was offered for sale. Prices rose until, following many deaths, necessity led to the law's repeal.

To all of this was added an unbounded passion for building. This created more pressure on the provinces, more exactions for workers, craftsmen, wagons, and all the other essentials for building. Here basilicas [*large buildings used for public business*], there a circus; here a mint, there an arms factory; here a house for his wife, there one for his daughter. Suddenly a great part of the city would be torn down. Everyone fled, with wives and children, as though the city had been assaulted by an enemy. When the new buildings were all up—and the provinces wiped out in the process—he would say, "No good; they must be done another way." Down they came again, were remodeled and often rebuilt yet again. He was always crazily trying to make Nicomedia [*his capital in Turkey*] the equal of Rome.

17.3   Constantine and Christianity

Constantine took the fateful step of abandoning the ancestral religion of Rome for the new, eastern religion of Christianity. For many pagans of the time this act was the immediate cause of the decline of the Empire, and there is no doubt that it had a dramatic impact on the history of Rome as well as of the Church. Nevertheless, Constantine's decision recognized the need for some kind of accommodation with the upstart religion, and in fact there were some precedents already at hand. Fifty years earlier the Emperor Gallienus had stopped the persecution of the Church that had been initiated by his predecessors, restored confiscated property, and in effect extended recognition to Christianity. Constantine's own involvement was gradual, and in reality the triumph of Christianity was not complete for another half century.

Constantine's first step in recognizing Christianity was the so-called Edict of Milan, published in February A.D. 313. Jointly issued with his co-emperor, Licinius, the decree recognized Christianity as a legitimate religion and extended toleration to all religions (which in Roman eyes meant just about any religion that did not subvert the existing social or political order). As in all matters concerning religion, the first objective of the Roman government was to maintain the goodwill of the gods, or, as the Edict puts it: "That whatever Divinity there may be in the heavens may be appeased and look kindly on us and all under our rule."[3]

I, Constantine Augustus, and I, Licinius Augustus, having met by Fortune at Milan, we thought in the course of our discussions regarding public well-being and security, that our first regulations which would benefit many should concern the respect due to the Divinity: We therefore grant Christians and all others full permission to observe whatever religion they wish, with the intent that whatever Divinity there may be in the heavens may be appeased and look kindly on us and all under our rule.

By this wholesome counsel and just purpose we thought to ensure that no one whosoever should be denied the opportunity to give himself to the observance of the Christian religion—or to whatever religion he should think best for himself. Again, our intent is that the Supreme

---

[3]Lactantius, *The Deaths of the Persecutors*, 48.

Deity, to whose worship we freely yield our minds, may show in everything his usual favor and goodwill.

Therefore, your Excellency should know that we have decided to remove all the conditions whatsoever which were in the previous ordinances handed down to you officially concerning the Christians; regulations that are inappropriate and alien to our clemency are abolished. Henceforth, anyone who wishes to observe the Christian religion may do so freely and openly, without any anxiety or interference. We thought it right to commend these decisions most fully to your care that you may know that we have given to those Christians free and unrestricted opportunity to practice their religion.

When you see that we have granted them this favor, your Excellency will understand that we have also granted to other religions the right of open and free observance of their own cult. We have done this for the sake of peace in our times, that each individual may have the freedom to worship as he pleases and that no cult or religion may be impaired.

17.4   The Majesty of Emperors: Desires and Realities

From the time of the crisis of the third century, the central government tried to cope with the pressures of barbarian invasions by increasing the power of the central government. The pageantry and pomp of the imperial court were designed to impress the people of the Empire with the power of the emperors, thereby encouraging morale while discouraging rebellion. Provinces were divided into more manageable units and taxes were collected with greater efficiency. Nevertheless these reforms, especially in the western half of the Empire, did not produce a proportionate increase in the real power of the emperors.

The pageantry of the court—as manifested, for example, in Constantius's entry into Rome (first reading below)—was coolly received by the blasé inhabitants of the Eternal City; it was the emperor himself who was impressed by Rome's glories. In the second reading we see how even well-intentioned emperors could be frustrated by corrupt officials. The third reading shows what could happen when an Emperor, in this case Valens (A.D. 364–378), made a disastrous policy error.[4]

17.4.1   The Entry of Constantius into Rome: A.D. 357

Constantius [*A.D. 351–361, the son and successor of Constantine*] . . . developed a strong desire to visit Rome and celebrate there his triumph over [*the rebel leader*] Magnentius. . . . Accordingly, after long and expensive preparations . . . the emperor passed through Ocricoli with his army in battle order, attracting the astonished gaze of all who gathered to watch. . . .

Preceded by standards on both sides of the road, he sat alone in a golden chariot brilliant with precious stones which seemed to spread a flickering light all around. His chief officers went before him surrounded by purple banners woven in the form of dragons and attached to the golden or jeweled points of spears. The wind blew through the dragons' gaping mouths and hissed as though inflamed with anger, while the coils of their tails streamed behind them. After these marched a double row of heavy-armed soldiers, with shields and crested helmets glittering and shining, their breast-plates reflecting the sunlight. Among these were scattered heavily armored cavalry protected by cuirasses and belts of steel whom you would think of as

---

[4]*Ammianus Marcellinus,* 16.10.

statues polished by the hand of the sculptor Praxiteles rather than as human beings. The light circular plates of steel that surrounded their bodies and covered their limbs were so well articulated that however they moved the joints of their mail adapted themselves accordingly.

The emperor as he moved along was cheered, and the hills and the shores reechoed the shouts of the people. Despite all the noise, he showed no emotion and kept the same impassive appearance he was accustomed to display when traveling through the provinces. Although he was very short, he stooped when passing through high gates, and he looked straight before him as though his neck was in a vice, statuelike, turning neither to the right nor to the left. When the carriage shook, his head did not nod, nor was he seen to spit or wipe his face or his nose or even move a hand. While this calmness was no doubt an affectation, yet there was other evidence in his personal life of extraordinary patience which one might have thought to have been his alone. . . .

When he entered Rome, that home of empire and all virtues, he mounted the Rostra [*the orators' platform in the Forum*]. From there he gazed with amazed awe on the Forum, the most renowned monument of ancient power. Wherever he turned he was bewildered by the number of wonders on every side. After addressing the nobles in the Senate house and the people from the tribune, he retired with the goodwill of all to the palace, where he enjoyed the pleasures he had anticipated. On a number of occasions, when he celebrated the races in the Circus, he was entertained by the talkativeness of the common people, who maintained their freedom of speech without disrespect. He himself observed a proper moderation. He did not, for example, as was usually done in other cities, allow the length of the gladiatorial games to depend on his caprice but left it to be decided as local customs suggested.

Then he surveyed the summits of the seven hills and the different quarters of the city, whether located on the slopes of the hills or on the level ground. He visited the suburbs as well, and whatever he first saw he thought the most impressive of all. Thus he admired the Temple of Tarpeian Jupiter, which is as much superior to other temples as divine things are superior to human; then it was the baths the size of provinces or the vast mass of the Colosseum, so solidly erected of Tibertine stone, to the top of which human vision can scarcely reach. Or it might have been the Pantheon with its vast extent that caught his eye, its imposing height, and the solid magnificence of its arches and lofty niches rising one above the other like stairs, decorated with the images of former emperors; or the temple of Rome, the Forum of Peace, the theater of Pompey, the Odeum or the race course or any of the other sights of the Eternal City.

But when he came to the Forum of Trajan, the most exquisite structure, in my opinion, under the canopy of heaven, which even the gods admired, he stood transfixed with wonder, casting his mind over the gigantic proportions of the place, beyond the power of mortal to describe, and beyond the reasonable hope of mortals to rival. Therefore, giving up all hope of attempting anything of this kind, he contented himself with saying that he would and could imitate the statue of Trajan's horse which stands in the middle of the hall bearing the emperor on his back.

17.4.2 The Emperor, the Truth, and Corruption

One of the greatest problems faced by the rulers of the late Empire was their inability to control corruption within their own vastly enlarged administrative system. As the following reading shows, they had enormous difficulty just finding out the truth. Pay that was supposed to reach troops in the field was often siphoned off en route. The unpaid soldiers then resorted to barefaced shakedowns of the locals, the worst being refusal to help civilians in moments of real crisis. Then, when complaints were made by the local population to the emperor, there were coverups. The investigators themselves were frequently in collusion and returned to the emperor with false reports.

The story of the unhappy people of Tripoli (modern Libya) was one that appealed to Ammianus, although he had many from which to select. The incident, even though it had a quasihappy ending, reveals the critical inability of the late Empire to provide what every government is supposed to provide: basic security and protection for its citizens from violence. It was ultimately this failure that undermined provincial support for the imperial administration in the west.[5]

From here let us move, as though to another part of the world, to the sorrows of the African province of Tripoli, sorrows over which, in my opinion, Justice herself must have wept. . . .

The Austorians are barbarians who live on the frontiers of this province, always ready for a quick attack and accustomed to live by plunder and bloodshed. Although subdued for a time, they relapsed into their natural state of disorder, claiming the following as the cause of their actions. One of their countrymen, a man named Stachao, while wandering freely in our territories during peacetime, broke the law on a number of occasions. His most serious violation was his effort to subvert the province. . . . Since the evidence against him was undeniable, he was burned to death at the stake.

To avenge his death, the Austorians, claiming that he was their countryman and that he had been unjustly executed, sallied out of their own territory like wild beasts. . . . Fearing to approach close to Leptis, a city with a large population and fortified by strong walls, they occupied the fertile district around it for three days. They massacred the peasants, whom fear at their sudden attack had deprived of all courage or had driven to take refuge in caves. They burned the household goods they could not take with them and returned home with vast plunder, taking with them Silva, the most prominent local magistrate, who happened to be with his family at his country house.

The people of Leptis were terrified at this sudden disaster and, to forestall further incursions by the barbarians, implored the protection of Count Romanus, who had recently been appointed to the command of Africa. When he arrived at the head of his army and received their request to come to their immediate assistance, he said he would not start a campaign without new supplies and 4,000 camels. The unhappy citizens were stupefied by this demand and declared that after the looting and fires it was impossible for them to provide such supplies, even if it were to help them recoup their losses. After fooling them for forty days and attempting nothing militarily, the count marched off with his army.

Disappointed and fearing the worst, the people of Tripoli at their next annual meeting appointed Severus and Flaccianus as ambassadors to the Emperor Valentinian. They were to take some golden images of victory in honor of his accession to the Empire and to set before him fearlessly the miserable situation in the province.

When Romanus heard of this move, he sent a swift messenger to the master of the office, Remigius, his own kinsman and his partner in his shake-downs, warning him to make sure that the affair was referred by imperial decree to himself and his own deputy for investigation. The ambassadors from Tripoli arrived at the court and, having obtained access to the emperor, they

[5]*Ammianus Marcellinus*, 28.6.

laid the matter before him in a set speech and presented him with a decree of their council in which the whole affair was fully described. The emperor read it but trusted neither the report of the master of the offices, who tried to give Romanus's actions a favorable spin, nor the ambassadors' version, which tried to accomplish just the opposite. Instead, a full investigation was promised; typically, however, the investigation was deferred, as frequently happens at high levels of government where the press of more important matters is used [*by collusive officials*] to deceive those in power.

While waiting in suspense and anxiety for some relief from the emperor's military headquarters, the citizens of Tripoli were again attacked by the same barbarians, now elated by their previous success. They ravaged the whole territory of Leptis and Oea, spreading total ruin and desolation everywhere. At last, loaded with enormous quantities of spoil, they withdrew, having killed many of the local magistrates, the most distinguished of whom were Rusticanus, one of the priests, and the aedile Nicasius. . . . A new messenger was sent to Gaul with an account of this fresh disaster and this report roused the emperor to great anger. Palladius, his secretary, who also had the rank of tribune, was sent at once to pay the wages that were due the troops stationed in Africa and to investigate and give a truthful report of what had happened in Tripoli.

This marks the second effort to get to the bottom of the matter, but despite his genuine concern for the province, the emperor is once again frustrated.

When Palladius arrived in Africa, Count Romanus, who knew why the imperial secretary had come and who had been warned to take measures for his own safety, sent orders to his officers through confidential messengers to hand over to Palladius the greater part of the pay he had brought. . . .

This was a blatant attempt to buy the influence of the emperor's confidant. Apparently, however, Palladius was unaware of the source of the money and, although he seems to have had a conscience, found himself trapped, as we shall see, by the wily Romanus.

This was done, and the suddenly enriched Palladius arrived in Tripoli.

In order to get at the facts of the case, he took with him to the districts that had been devastated Erechthius and Aristomenes, two eloquent and distinguished citizens of Tripoli. They freely demonstrated to him the distress that their fellow citizens and the inhabitants of the adjacent districts had suffered. When Palladius got back to the city, he criticized Romanus for his inactivity and threatened to make a true report of the situation to the emperor. Romanus retorted angrily that he too would send a report, pointing out that the man who had been sent as the emperor's incorruptible secretary had diverted to his own use the money that had been intended for the soldiers. Palladius recognized that he had been cornered and proceeded henceforth in concert with Romanus. When he returned to the court, he deceived Valentinian with atrocious lies and declared that the citizens of Tripoli had no grounds for complaint.

The story goes on for several chapters more as the cover-up developed a momentum of its own and the case became more complex. Lies were piled on lies. At one point the emperor, in a rage, thinking he had finally gotten to the bottom of the mess, ordered that tongues of the two whistle-blowers, Erechthius and Aristomenes, should be cut out for supposedly deceiving Palladius. They immediately went into hiding. Gradually, however, the truth emerged. Palladius and Remigius committed suicide and Erechthius and Aristomenes were rehabilitated. The sure-footed Romanus, however, escaped punishment.

17.4.3   The Emperor and the Barbarians

One of the keys to the success of the Roman military throughout its history was its ability to integrate non-Roman auxiliaries into its armies (see for instance, the speech of Calgacus in Chapter 14 in which he claims that the Roman army was a motley collection of peoples from all over the Empire). *In the late fourth century, Rome's ability to do this broke down in the west. In effect, the Empire in that region was overwhelmed by the sheer magnitude of the invasions and the inadequacy of its own resources. In response, whole barbarian war bands and immigrating peoples were given land inside the Empire. Militarily, the effect of this policy was that instead of contributing individual units to fight under Roman officers, the barbarians now fought under their own tribal commanders as federates. In Ammianus's view this was a fatal mistake and led to the end of the Empire.*

The particular incident described here came about when the Germanic Visigoths were driven into the Roman Empire by the advance of the Huns from Central Asia. Ammianus' gloomy forebodings were born out a generation later when this same people sacked Rome in A.D. *410.*[6]

Accordingly, under the command of their leader Alavivus, the Goths occupied the banks of the Danube. They sent envoys to the Emperor Valens and humbly asked to be received by him as subjects, promising to live quietly and to furnish a body of auxiliary troops if any necessity for such a force should arise. . . .

The affair caused more joy than fear. The practiced flatterers around the emperor praised his good fortune. They congratulated him that an embassy had come unexpectedly from the furthest corner of the earth offering him a large body of recruits. By combining these foreign forces with his own resources, he would have an absolutely invincible army. Further, they pointed out that by their substituting cash for recruits from the provinces, a vast amount of money could be accumulated.

Filled with this hope, Valens sent forth officers to bring this ferocious people and their wagons into our territory. And such great pains were taken to gratify this nation which was destined to overthrow the Empire of Rome that not one was left behind, not even of those who were stricken with mortal diseases. Having obtained permission of the emperor to cross the Danube and to cultivate some districts in Thrace, they crossed the river day and night without ceasing, embarking in crowds aboard ships and rafts and canoes made of the hollow trunks of trees. In this endeavor, as the Danube is the most difficult of all rivers to navigate and was at that time swollen with continual rains, a great many were drowned. . . .

Thus, through the misguided zeal of the advisers who pushed the project, the ruin of the Roman world was brought on. . . .

17.5   Christianity, Rome, and Classical Culture

17.5.1   A Different Vision

That there was an intrinsic incompatibility between Christianity and classical values was apparent from the time Romans became aware of the presence of the new religion. Christians were criticized on a variety of grounds, but principally because they had rejected the gods of their ancestors and the civic values of

---

[6]*Ammianus Marcellinus,* 31.4.

Greco-Roman world. Their religion was new; they had turned away from the traditions of their immediate ancestors, the Jews. Because of their refusal to attend the festivals, they were seen as atheists and misanthropists. In popular belief they even practiced incest and cannibalism. In short, they did not fit into the system that had been sanctioned by centuries of classical use.

In some respects the charges were true. Christians, indeed, had other goals than civic life. But in this they were not unlike many in the Empire. The difference was that the Christian viewpoint was articulated as part of an organized religion. The highest honors of civic life, the consulship, the Senate, municipal office, and the command of armies, were not of primary importance for Christians, at least in their ideology. Their kingdom, as they claimed, did indeed seem to lie elsewhere.

In self-defense, Christians attempted to justify their way of life, claiming that they, not the Jews, were the true inheritors of the Hebrew religious tradition; that their values were compatible with traditional Greco-Roman values; that their religion was the true philosophy of life, and because it was revealed by God rather than devised by men it was therefore more certain. Naturally, what was popularly said about them, they claimed, was false. From the second century onward one apology followed another. The anonymous Epistle to Diognetus belongs in this tradition but is presented here because, in a burst of eloquence, its author actually concedes the main charge against Christianity, though he tries to give his admission a favorable spin. In the end, however, it is clear that Christianity did represent a different, and indeed a new, set of values.[7]

Christians are distinguished from other men neither by nationality, language, nor custom. They do not live separately in cities of their own, have their own special language, or lead a life that is peculiar in any way. The way of life they follow has not been devised by human speculation or deliberation. Indeed, Christians do not, like some, proclaim themselves the advocates of any merely human doctrines. Rather, while inhabiting Greek as well as barbarian cities, according as the lot of each of them has determined, and following the customs of the natives in respect to clothing, food, and the rest of their ordinary conduct, they display to us their wonderful and admittedly striking way of life.

They dwell in their own lands—but simply as sojourners. As citizens they share in all things with others, and yet endure all things as if foreigners. Every foreign land is to them as their homeland, and every homeland as a land of strangers. They marry, as do all others; they beget children; but they do not commit infanticide. They share a common table, but not a common bed. They are in the flesh, but they do not live after the flesh. They pass their days on earth, but their citizenship is in the heavens. They obey the prescribed laws and at the same time surpass the laws by their lives. They love all men and are persecuted by all. They are misunderstood and condemned; they are put to death and yet restored to life. They are poor yet make many rich. Lacking all things, they have everything in abundance. They are dishonored but are glorified in their dishonor; slandered, yet vindicated. They are reviled and bless, insulted and yet repay insult with honor. They do good but are punished as evil-doers. When castigated they rejoice like men revived to a new life. . . .

To sum up all in a word—what the soul is to the body, that are Christians to the world. The soul is dispersed through all the members of the body, and Christians are scattered through all the cities of the world. The soul dwells in the body yet is not *of* the body; Christians dwell

---

[7]*Epistle to Diognetus* 5–6. Based on Alexander Roberts and James Donaldson, *The Ante-Nicene Fathers*, (Edinburgh: The Ante-Nicene Christian Library, 1867), pp. 26–27.

in the world yet are not *of* the world. The invisible soul is guarded by the visible body, and Christians are known indeed to be in the world, but their holiness remains invisible.

The flesh hates the soul and wars against it because it is prevented from enjoying its pleasures, though itself suffering no injury. The world similarly hates Christians because they are opposed to its pleasures, though it is in no wise injured by them. Despite this, the soul loves the flesh that hates it, and also its members. Christians, too, love those that hate them. The soul is imprisoned in the body yet preserves that very body. Christians are confined in the world as in a prison, and yet they are the preservers of the world. The immortal soul lives in a moral tabernacle; Christians live as sojourners in corruptible bodies, looking for an incorruptible dwelling in heaven. Finally, Christians, although subjected day by day to punishment, increase in number, just as the soul when poorly provided with food and drink becomes better. God has assigned them this high position, which it is unlawful for them to abandon.

17.5.2   Organization and Ideology

Christians possessed not only a different vision of life and a set of values that was at variance with the traditions of polis *society, they also possessed a new organizational structure and a sophisticated ideology to back it up. In the first reading below, the great church historian and apologist, Bishop Eusebius of Caesarea (in Palestine, ca.* A.D. *260–340) casually describes how the bishops of some of the regions in the western Mediterranean dealt with a disciplinary and doctrinal problem. In the process, he reveals much about how the Church was organized as early as the mid third century. There were problems of ambition and office-seeking within the Church. A great debate raged over Christians who fell away in times of persecution and then wanted to return to the Church. Should they be readmitted? The prestige and authority of the confessors, that is, those who had suffered under the persecution, had the potential to undermine institutional Church authority. Most important of all was the problem of how dissidents within the Church were to be dealt with.*

Eusebius takes for granted that an effective communications network allowed different church communities to coordinate their activities with each other. The citation of official, authoritative documents from key councils and important bishoprics is a characteristic of the process by which Church discipline was established, maintained, and extended.[8]

Novatus, a priest of the church at Rome, was lifted up in arrogance against those who had fallen away during the persecution [*the first empire wide persecution initiated by the Emperor Decius in* A.D. *250*] but had subsequently repented. There was no hope of salvation for them, he held, even if they did everything to prove their conversion was genuine and pure. Novatus became the leader of the heresy of those who, in the pride of their hearts, called themselves "The Pure Ones."

To settle the matter, a very large synod was called at Rome. It consisted of 60 bishops and a much larger number of priests and deacons. In the provinces of the Empire the other bishops and pastors debated privately what ought to be done. The upshot was a decree which unanimously declared that Novatus and those who joined with him and approved of his hatred and inhumanity toward his fellow Christians should be considered to be outside the Church. On

---

[8]Based on translation of A. C. McGiffert and E. C. Richardson in Philip Schaff and Henry Wace, *A Select Library of Nicene and Post-Nicene Fathers of the Christian Church* (New York: Post-Nicene Library of the Christian Fathers, 1890), pp. 286–290.

the other hand, those brothers who had, through misfortune, fallen during the persecutions should be treated and healed with the medicines of repentance.

We have received letters from Cornelius, the bishop of Rome, to Fabius, bishop of Antioch, telling him what had happened at the Synod of Rome and what the local representatives in Italy, Tunisia, and the surrounding areas had decided. There are other letters in Latin from Cyprian [*bishop of Carthage*] and those associated with him which make it clear that they agreed as to the necessity of helping those who had been tempted in the persecutions, and that it was right to cut off from the Catholic Church the leader of the heresy and all who had joined with him. Attached to these was another letter of Cornelius regarding the resolutions of the Synod and others on the conduct of Novatus. It is appropriate that I make selections from these so that any one who reads this work may know the facts about the case. Cornelius tells Fabius what kind of person Novatus was:

"You should know that for a long time this incredible fellow wanted to become a bishop. He kept his ambitions to himself and used as a cloak for his plot those confessors [*i.e., those who had suffered during the persecutions and not fallen away*] who had adhered to him from the beginning. I speak of Maximus, one of our priests, and Urban, who twice gained the highest honor by confessing their faith; along with Sidonius and Celerinus, a man who, by the grace of God, most heroically endured all kinds of torture and by the strength of his faith overcame the weakness of the flesh—these men found him out and detected his unscrupulousness and duplicity, his perjuries and falsehood, his self-preoccupation and false friendship. They returned to the Holy Church and denounced his craftiness and wickedness in the presence of many bishops and priests and laypeople. . . .

"How remarkable, dear brother, the change and transformation which we have since seen take place in this man and in so short a space of time! This most illustrious man, who bound himself with terrible oaths not to seek to become a bishop, suddenly appears a bishop as if dropped into our midst by some machine [*Cornelius means machines like those that were used to make wild animals suddenly pop up in the arena*]. This doctrinal purist, this champion of the Church's discipline, in attempting to grasp and seize the episcopate which had not been given him from above, chose two of his companions who had given up their own salvation. He sent them to an obscure and insignificant corner of Italy to deceive three bishops of the region who were rustic and very simple men. He asserted positively and strongly that it was essential that they come quickly to Rome in order that all the dissension which had arisen there might be worked out through their mediation, along with that of the other bishops. When they came, being, as we have stated, very simple in the craft and artifice of the wicked, they were shut up with certain selected men like himself. By the late afternoon, when they had become drunk and sick, he compelled them by force to consecrate him a bishop through a counterfeit and vain imposition of hands. Because it had not come to him [*as he thought it should*], he avenged himself by craft and treachery. One of these bishops shortly came back to the Church, lamenting and confessing his transgression. We admitted him back as a layman since all the people present interceded for him. We consecrated successors of the other bishops and sent them to the places where they had been.

"This great defender of the Gospel [*i.e., Novatus*] then did not know that there should be only one bishop per Catholic church! Yet he was not ignorant (for how could he be?)

that at Rome there were forty-six priests; seven deacons; seven subdeacons; forty-two acolytes; fifty-two exorcists, readers, and janitors; over 1,500 widows and persons in distress, all of whom the grace and kindness of the Master nourish [*but only one bishop*]. Yet not even this great multitude . . . together with the very many, even innumerable people, could turn him from such desperation and presumption and recall him to the Church. . . .

"You will be glad to know that he has lost support and is abandoned. Every day the brothers leave him and return to the Church. When Moses, the blessed martyr, who late suffered among us a glorious and admirable martyrdom, while yet alive, saw Novatus' insane arrogance, he broke off communion with him and the five priests who along with him had separated themselves from the Church."

At the close of the letter Cornelius gives a list of the bishops who came to Rome and condemned the foolishness of Novatus, together with their names and the sees over which each of them presided. He mentions also those who did not come to Rome but who expressed by letters to these bishops their agreement with the vote, giving their names and the cities from which they individually wrote.

The theory of Church doctrine and how it is to be determined is proclaimed succinctly by Irenaeus, bishop of Lyons in France, writing some time between about A.D. 180 and 200. The way to end doctrinal confusion, he says, is to consult the traditions of the churches founded by the apostles. But since doing this would be a very tedious process, he proposes a simple test: It is sufficient to check the traditions of the Church of Rome; Rome is the guarantor of orthodoxy.[9]

Since, however, it would be very tedious in such a volume as this to reckon up the successions of all the churches, we confound all those who, in whatever manner, whether for evil self-pleasing, or vain glory, or blindness, or perverse opinion, assemble in unauthorized meetings. This we do: (1) by pointing to the faith preached to men, which comes down to our time by means of the succession of the bishops; and (2) by pointing to that tradition derived from the Apostles, of the very great, very ancient, and universally known Church founded and organized at Rome by the two most glorious apostles, Peter and Paul.

For it is a matter of necessity that every church should agree with *this* Church, on account of its preeminent authority . . . for in it the apostolic tradition has been preserved. . . . [*A list of the bishops of Rome from Peter onward is next given, ending with*] Eleutherius, who now holds the see of Rome in the twelfth place from the Apostles. In this order, and by this succession, the ecclesiastical tradition from the Apostles, and the preaching of the truth, have come down to us. And this is the most abundant proof that there is one and the same vivifying faith, which has been preserved in the Church from the Apostles until now and handed down in truth.

17.5.3   The Pagan Response

Logically enough, the official response to Christianity was often repression. The new religion had none of the characteristics that would have given it an approved status. The following, from an apology called The Octavius, *sums up the official view neatly:* "Why do Christians endeavor with such pains to conceal and to cloak whatever they worship, since honorable things always rejoice in publicity while crimes are kept secret? Why have they no altars, no temples, no acknowledged images?

---

[9]Irenaeus, *Against the Heresies* 3.3. Based on Roberts and Donaldson, *The Ante-Nicene Fathers*, Vol. 1, p. 415.

Why do they never speak openly, never congregate freely, unless for the reason that what they adore and conceal is either worthy of punishment, or something to be ashamed of?" [10]

From the Roman viewpoint, Christianity had one of the most dangerous characteristics a religion could possess: It was new; it had no track record on which it could be judged. What they did see, they did not like. Christians not only did not participate in the festivals and rituals of the gods, they also actively refused to do so, and they vilified the civic religion as the worship of demons. Understandably, the authorities regarded this attitude as threatening the stability of the state. The neglect of the all-important duty of honoring the gods might lead to disaster.

Early acts of repression tended to be sporadic and localized, as, for example, in the activities of Pliny (see Chapter 15). Sometimes persecution was the result of simple malice: Neighbors settling grudges against each other. Some persecutions were the result of natural disaster. The second-century Christian apologist Tertullian claimed rhetorically that "if the Tiber rises as high as the city walls; if the Nile does not rise and flood the fields; if the weather is awful; if there is an earthquake, a famine, a plague—immediately we hear the cry: 'Christians to the lions!' " [11]

Repression

Of the many accounts of martyrdom in Christian literature, The Acts of the Scillitan Martyrs *are among the closest to the original Roman court records. The date of the hearing referred to here was July 17, 180 A.D. The martyrs were from Scili in Tunisia (North Africa). Despite the apparent simplicity of the account, it still has a strong rhetorical flavor. Note the reluctance of the judge.* [12]

When Praesens, for the second time, and Claudian, were the consuls, on the seventeenth day of July, at Carthage, there were arraigned in the judgment hall the following: Speratus; Nartzalus; Cittinus; Veturius; Felix; Aquilinus; Laetantius; Januaria; Generosa; Donata; Secunda, and Vestia [*seven men and five women*].

The proconsul Saturninus said: "You can obtain the forgiveness of our Lord the Emperor if you return to your senses."

Speratus: "We have never done ill; we have not lent ourselves to wrong; we have never spoken ill, but when ill-treated we have given thanks, for we pay heed to our Emperor."

Saturninus: "We too are religious, and our religion is simple. We swear by the Genius of our Lord the Emperor, and pray for his welfare, as you also ought to do."

Speratus: "If you will give me a peaceful hearing, I can tell you the real truth of simplicity."

Saturninus: "I will not listen to you when you begin to speak evil of our sacred rites; rather, swear by the Genius of our Lord the Emperor."

Speratus: "I do not recognize the Empire of this world, but rather I serve that God 'whom no man has seen, nor with these eyes can be seen.' I have committed no theft; but if I have bought anything I pay the tax, for I acknowledge my Lord, the King of Kings, and Emperor of all nations."

Saturninus (to all the accused): "Cease to be of this persuasion."

Speratus: "An ill persuasion is to do murder, to speak false witness."

---

[10]Based on Roberts and Donaldson, *The Ante-Nicene Fathers*, Vol 4, p. 178.

[11]Tertullian, *Apology* 40.

[12]*Acts of the Scillitan Martyrs* (whole text).

Saturninus (ignoring Speratus, addresses the others): "Be no partakers in his folly!"

Cittinus: "We have none other to fear, save only our Lord God, who is in heaven."

Donata: "Honor Caesar as Caesar; but it is God we fear."

Vestia: "I am a Christian."

Secunda: "What I am, that I wish to be."

Saturninus (to Speratus): "Do you persist in being a Christian?"

Speratus: "I am a Christian." (*And all agreed with him.*)

Saturninus: "Do you want time to reconsider?"

Speratus: "In a matter so straightforward, there is no need for consideration."

Saturninus: "What are the things in your case?"

Speratus: "Books and letters of Paul, a just man."

Saturninus: "You are granted a reprieve of thirty days to think it over."

Speratus: "I am a Christian." (*And all the others agreed with him.*)

Then Saturninus the proconsul read out his decision from a tablet: Whereas Speratus, Nartzalus, Cittinus, Donata, Vestia, Secunda, and the others have confessed that they live according to the Christian rite; and since after opportunity was offered them of returning to the custom of the Romans, they have obstinately persisted; it is determined that they be put to the sword.

Speratus: "We give thanks to God."

Nartzalus: "Today we are martyrs in heaven; thanks be to God."

Saturninus the proconsul ordered the following to be declared by the herald: Speratus, Nartzalus, Cittinus, Veturius, Felix, Aquilinus, Laetantius, Januaria, Generosa, Vestia, Donata, and Secunda, I have ordered to be executed.

They said: "Thanks be to God." Immediately they were all beheaded for the name of Christ.

Reform

Another approach, reform of paganism, was tried by the Emperor Julian as a way of recovering lost ground. A former Christian, Julian borrowed liberally from Christian ideals and organizational principles and attempted to reform the civic religion of the Empire. He articulated a Christian-sounding value system, a justifying ideology, and an organization that was supposed to match that of the Christians. Julian wrote in the 360s, after Christianity had made great progress toward acceptability, and his efforts tell as much about why Christianity succeeded as about Julian's own mindset. Raised a Christian, he was never quite able to erase the impact of his early training. Julian writes as Pontifex Maximus, *Chief Priest of the State Religion.*[13]

The religion of the Greeks does not yet prosper as I would wish, on account of those who profess it. But the gifts of the gods are great and splendid, better than any prayer or any hope. . . . Indeed, a little while ago no one would have dared even to pray for a such change, and so complete a one in so short a space of time [*i.e., the arrival of Julian himself, a reforming traditionalist, on the throne*]. Why then do we think that this is sufficient and do not observe

---

[13]Julian, *Letter to Arsacius, High Priest of Galatia; Letter to a Priest*. Based in part on the translation of Edward J. Chinnock, *A Few Notes on Julian and a Translation of His Public Letters* (London: David Nutt, 1901), pp. 75–78.

how the kindness of Christians to strangers, their care for the burial of their dead, and the sobriety of their lifestyle has done the most to advance their cause?

Each of these things, I think, ought really to be practiced by us. It is not sufficient for you alone to practice them, but so must all the priests in Galatia [*in modern Turkey*] without exception. Either make these men good by shaming them, persuade them to become so—or fire them. . . . Secondly, exhort the priests neither to approach a theater nor to drink in a tavern, nor to profess any base or infamous trade. Honor those who obey, and expel those who disobey.

Erect many hostels, one in each city, in order that strangers may enjoy my kindness, not only those of our own faith but also of others whosoever is in want of money. I have just been devising a plan by which you will be able to get supplies. For I have ordered that every year throughout all Galatia 30,000 modii of grain and 60,000 pints of wine shall be provided. The fifth part of these I order to be expended on the poor who serve the priests, and the rest must be distributed from me to strangers and beggars. For it is disgraceful when no Jew is a beggar and the impious Galileans [*the name given by Julian to Christians*] support our poor in addition to their own; everyone is able to see that our co-religionists are in want of aid from us. Teach also those who profess the Greek religion to contribute to such services, and the villages of the Greek religion to offer the first-fruits to the gods. Accustom those of the Greek religion to such benevolence, teaching them that this has been our work from ancient times. Homer, at any rate, made Eumaeus say, "O Stranger, it is not lawful for me, even if one poorer than you should come, to dishonor a stranger. For all strangers and beggars are from Zeus. The gift is small, but it is precious." [*Julian is quoting from the Odyssey, 14.53.*] Do not therefore let others outdo us in good deeds while we ourselves are disgraced by laziness; rather, let us not quite abandon our piety toward the gods. . . .

While proper behavior in accordance with the laws of the city will obviously be the concern of the governors of the cities, you for your part [*as a priest*] must take care to encourage people not to violate the laws of the gods since they are holy. . . . Above all you must exercise philanthropy. From it result many other goods, and indeed that which is the greatest blessing of all, the goodwill of the gods. . . .

We ought to share our goods with all men, but most of all with the respectable, the helpless, and the poor, so that they have at least the essentials of life. I claim, even though it may seem paradoxical, that it is a holy deed to share our clothes and food with the wicked: We give, not to their moral character but to their human character. Therefore, I believe that even prisoners deserve the same kind of care. This type of kindness will not interfere with the process of justice, for among the many imprisoned and awaiting trial some will be found guilty, some innocent. It would be cruel indeed if out of consideration for the innocent we should not allow some pity for the guilty, or on account of the guilty we should behave without mercy and humanity to those who have done no wrong. . . . How can the man who, while worshipping Zeus the God of Companions, sees his neighbors in need and does not give them a dime—how can he think he is worshipping Zeus properly? . . .

Priests ought to make a point of not doing impure or shameful deeds or saying words or hearing talk of this type. We must therefore get rid of all offensive jokes and licentious associations. What I mean is this: No priest is to read Archilochus or Hipponax or anyone else who writes poetry as they do. They should stay away from the same kind of stuff in Old Comedy. Philosophy alone is appropriate for us priests. Of the philosophers, however, only those who put the gods before them as guides of their intellectual life are acceptable, like Pythagoras, Plato, Aristotle, and the Stoics . . . only those who make people reverent . . . not the works of Pyrrho and Epicurus. . . . We ought to pray often to the gods in private and in public, about three times a day, but if not that often, at least in the morning and at night.

No priest is anywhere to attend shameful theatrical shows or to have one performed at his own house; it is in no way appropriate. Indeed, if it were possible to get rid of such shows altogether from the theater and restore the theaters, purified, to Dionysus as in the olden days, I would certainly have tried to bring this about. But since I thought that this was out of the question, and even if possible would for other reasons be inexpedient, I did not even try. But I do insist that priests stay away from the licentiousness of the theaters and leave them to the people. No priest is to enter a theater, have an actor or a chariot driver as a friend, or allow a dancer or mime into his house. I allow to attend the sacred games those who want to, that is, they may attend only those games from which women are forbidden to attend not only as participants but even as spectators.

17.5.4   When the Shoe Was on the Other Foot

After Constantine, Christianity gradually secured its hold on almost all aspects of the Empire. Pockets of resistance, however, remained. One of these was the ancient Senate at Rome. In this reading the pagan historian Zosimus describes the dramatic confrontation between the senators and the Emperor Theodosius I (A.D. 375–395). One of the interesting points that emerges is the connection between the poor financial condition of the Empire and the cost of pagan rituals, which could be performed only—so the senators claimed—at public expense. There are echoes here of the speech of Camillus to the Romans urging them not to move from the sacred site of Rome to Veii after the sack of the Gauls in 390 B.C. (see Chapter 10), and of Ammianus Marcellinus' condemnation of Valens' policy of admitting whole peoples into the Empire (see earlier, "The Emperor and the Barbarians"). Theodosius banned paganism in A.D. 391.[14]

Theodosius' success having reached this point, he journeyed to Rome and declared his son Honorius emperor. At the same time he made Stilicho [*an able German*] commander of the legions there and left him in charge as his son's guardian. Then he convened the Senate. The Senators had remained faithful to their long-standing ancestral rites and would not be moved to agree with those who condemned the gods. Theodosius delivered a speech to them in which he exhorted them to recant their "error" (as he called it) and to embrace the Christian faith because it promised forgiveness of every sin and every kind of impiety. None was persuaded by this harangue or was willing to give up the rites which had been passed on from generation to generation since the City's founding, in favor of an absurd belief. For, the Senators said, by preserving the former rites they had inhabited a city unconquered for almost 1,200 years, while they did not know what would happen if they exchanged these rituals for something different.

In turn, Theodosius said that the treasury was burdened by the expense of the rites and the sacrifices; that he wanted to abolish them; that he did not approve of them and, further-more, that military necessities called for additional funds. The Senators replied that the

[14]From *Zosimus: Historia Nova. The Decline of Rome*, trans. James T. Buchanan and Harold T. Davis (San Antonio, TX: Trinity University Press 1967), pp. 191–192. By permission.

ceremonies could not be performed except at public expense. Nevertheless, a law abolishing them was laid down and, as others things which had been handed down from ancestral times lay neglected, the Empire of the Romans was gradually diminished and became a domicile of barbarians. . . .

17.6 The Hellenization and Romanization of Christianity

Christianity had the advantages as well as disadvantages of springing from a highly literate tradition. Its Jewish origins supplied it with sacred writings of great complexity and depth as well as a long apologetic tradition of justification to gentile readers. Greeks and Romans were also highly literate, though their "bible" was much less formalized. Still, there was clearly a canon of classical literature and a developed educational system—so much so that the Emperor Julian felt it necessary to prohibit Christians from teaching the classics. Christian professors were not to be allowed to teach authors such as Hesiod and Homer because in their hearts they felt something else: "I think it absurd that those who expound the works of these writers should dishonor the gods who are honored by them." [15] *In fact, the challenge of Christianity nudged Greeks to the last great intellectual effort of the ancient world, the adaptation of Christianity to Greco-Roman culture. The amalgam produced in the centuries between approximately* A.D. *200 and 450 has not been replaced to the present.*

Of course the amalgam was never entirely satisfactory to all members of the Church. One viewpoint, represented by Tertullian, felt paganism and Christianity were incompatible: "What does Athens have to do with Jerusalem? What is there in common between [Plato's] Academy and the Church? . . . Away with all attempts to produce a "Stoic," a "Platonic," a dialectical Christianity! After possessing Jesus we want no subtle theories, no clever inquiries after the Gospel. With our faith we desire no further belief." [16]

The opposite viewpoint was expressed by Synesius of Cyrene, who agreed to become a bishop only on the condition that while he spoke "myths" in church he was allowed to "think as a philosopher" in private. Perhaps the commonest position was the one stated by Clement of Alexandria: "Philosophy," he said, "is the 'schoolmaster' or teacher to bring the Greeks to Christ, just as the Law brought the Hebrews to him. Thus philosophy is a preparation, paving the way towards perfection in Christ." [17]

17.6.1 Faith and Syllogisms

In the following reading, Eusebius is quoting from a book, The Little Labyrinth, *written against a second-century heretic and still circulating in his time.* [18]

They have treated the Divine Scriptures recklessly and without fear. They have set aside the standard of the ancient faith. They have not known Christ. They do not endeavor to learn what the Divine Scriptures declare but strive laboriously after any form of syllogism [*a form of*

---

[15]*Rescript on Christian Teachers*, in Chinnock, *A Few Notes on Julian*, p. 61.

[16]Tertullion, *Against Heretics* 7.

[17]Clement, *Stromateis* 1.5.28.

[18]Eusebius, *Church History* 5.28. Based on translation of McGiffert and Richardson in Schaff and Wace, *A Select Library of Nicene and Post-Nicene Fathers of the Christian Church*, p. 248.

linguistic argument used in Greek philosophy, especially among the followers of Aristotle] which may be devised to sustain their impiety. And if anyone brings before them a passage of Divine Scripture, they examine it to see whether a conjunctive or disjunctive form of syllogism can be made from it.

Since they are of the earth and speak from the earth, they abandon the holy writings of God and devote themselves to geometry. Some of them laboriously study the geometry of Euclid and admire Aristotle and Theophrastus. Some of them even worship Galen [*famous physician and scientist*]. But those who use the arts of unbelievers for their heretical opinions and adulterate the simple faith of the Divine Scriptures by the craft of the godless, need I say, are far from the faith. . . . Either they do not believe that the Holy Scriptures were spoken by the Holy Spirit, and they are thus unbelievers, or else they think themselves wiser than the Holy Spirit, and in that case what else are they than possessed?

17.6.2   Justin Martyr: "Christianity Is the True Philosophy"

Justin Martyr represents an increasingly common type of second-century convert. Born in Palestine around A.D. 114 to a well-off family, he traveled widely and studied philosophy. The constancy of the Christian martyrs impressed him, and he took up the study of the new religion and was baptized. He moved to Rome, where he set up a Christian school. His teaching and writing apparently generated a pagan backlash, and he was martyred in 165. In his Apologies, *Justin claimed that Christianity was true philosophy, the end and goal of all philosophic endeavor, and that in fact Greek philosophers, insofar as they had discovered the truth, could be said to be "Christians." He attempted to show that contemporary philosophy, especially Platonism, could be harmonized with Christianity.*[19]

Lest some should claim with the intent of turning people from our teaching that we say that Christ was born 150 years ago under Cyrenius, and taught what we say he taught under Pontius Pilate, and then go on to accuse us of saying that everyone who lived *before* him were worthless—let us anticipate and solve this difficulty.

We are taught that Christ is the firstborn of God, and we have demonstrated above that he is the Divine Reason [*or Word*] in whom every race of men are partakers. Thus, those who live according to reason are Christians even though they have been thought to be atheists. Such were Socrates and Heraclitus among the Greeks. . . .

I declare that I prayed and strove with all my strength to be found to be a Christian, not because the teachings of Plato are contrary to those of Christ, but because they are not in all respects like them. The same is true of the doctrines of the Stoics, the poets, and prose writers. For each discoursed rightly, seeing that which was akin to Christianity through a share in the Divine Reason. But those who have uttered contrary opinions seem not to have had the invisible knowledge and irrefutable wisdom. Whatever has been uttered aright by any men in any place belongs to us Christians, for next to God, we worship and love the Reason which is from the unbegotten and ineffable God. . . . All the authors were able to see the truth darkly, through the implanted seed of Reason dwelling in them.

---

[19]Justin, *Apology* 1.46; 2.13.

17.6.3   Monasticism

Christianity introduced a novel form of life, one that in some respects represents the most extreme departure that can be imagined from the old polis *tradition of civic involvement as the fulfillment of the highest goals of human endeavor. This was monasticism. Open to both men and women, monasticism provided a truly radical alternative to contemporary lifestyles. In monasteries, both men and women could find a new kind of autonomy that included spiritual, economic, social, and even, in some sense, political dimensions. In their developed forms, monasteries were self-sufficient economically, and often strong enough to defend themselves against all but the most powerful marauders. They represented attractive alternatives to the growing chaos of society in the west, and the oversophistication of the more urbanized east. For women they offered an opportunity never available before: escape from male domination.*

Jerome, a native of Illyricum, translator of the Bible into Latin, voluminous correspondent, satirist, and irascible polemicist, writes in A.D. *374 to a friend, encouraging him to join him in his monastery in Bethlehem, where the Gospels, in all their literalness, could be practiced. The letter is full of biblical allusions and quotations. Reading between the lines we also get an inside look at life in a comfortable Roman household in the late Empire.*[20] *This letter can be usefully compared with the reading from the Gospels in Chapter 15.*

Pampered soldier, why are you wasting time in your father's house? Where is the rampart, the ditch, the winter campaign under canvas? Behold the trumpet sounds—from heaven! Our General, fully armed, comes amid the clouds to overcome the world. From our King's mouth comes the double-edged sword that cuts down all in its path. Are you going to remain in your chamber and not come out to join in the battle? . . . Listen to your King's proclamation: "He who is not with me is against me, and he who does not gather with me scatters."

Remember when you joined up as a recruit, when buried with Christ in baptism, you took the oath of allegiance to him, declaring that you would spare neither your father nor your mother? But now the adversary in your own heart is trying to kill Christ! Now the enemy's camp has its sights on your loyalty! Though your little nephew twine his arms around your neck; though your mother, with disheveled hair and tearing her robe asunder, point to the breast with which she nourished you; though your father fall down on the threshold before you—trample on his body and go your way! Fly with tearless eyes to the standard of the Cross. In this matter, cruelty is your duty. . . .

I know well the chains which you will say hinder you. Indeed, my breast is not made of iron, nor my heart of stone. I was not born from a rock or raised by Hyrcanian tigers. I have been through this experience too. Your widowed sister may throw her gentle arms around you. The household slaves, in whose company you grew up, will cry, "To what master are you abandoning us?" Your old nurse and her husband, who, after your own natural father, have the next claim to your devotion, say, "Wait awhile until we die so you can bury us!" Perhaps your foster mother, with sagging breasts and wrinkled face, will sing you your old childhood lullaby! . . . But the love of Christ and the fear of Gehenna will easily break such bonds.

---

[20]Jerome, *Letter* 14.

You will claim that the Scriptures command us to obey our parents. On the contrary, whoever loves his parents more than Christ, loses his own soul. If my enemy takes up a sword to kill me, will I be held back by my mother's tears? Should I desert from the army because of my father, to whom in the cause of Christ I owe no burial because in his cause I owe burial to everyone? . . . You may claim that all your fellow citizens are Christians. But your case is not the same as everyone else. Hear what the Lord has to say: "If you would be perfect, go and sell what you have and follow me." You promised to be perfect.

When you resigned from the army and "made yourself a eunuch for the kingdom of Christ," what else had you in mind besides a perfect life? A perfect servant of Christ has nothing besides Christ. Indeed, if he has anything besides Christ, he is not perfect. . . . If you are perfect, why do you pine for your father's property? But if you are not perfect, you have failed the Lord. The Gospel thunders the divine words: "You cannot serve two masters." Does anyone dare to make Christ a liar by serving Mammon *and* the Lord at the same time? Does he not say often, "If anyone will come after me, let him deny himself, take up his cross and follow me"? If I load myself with gold, do I imagine I am following Christ? . . .

O desert, green with the flowers of Christ! O solitude in which the stones of the Great City of the King mentioned in the *Apocalypse* are found! O wilderness rejoicing in the presence of God! Brother, what are you doing in the world when you are so much more important than the world? How long are the shadows of a roof going to hold you back? How long will the smoky dungeon of these cities imprison you? . . . How refreshing to fling off the burdens of the flesh and fly to the sparkling aether? . . . You are spoiled indeed, dear friend, if you wish to rejoice here on earth—and afterwards reign with Christ!

17.7   The Fall of Rome

When Jerome in his monastery in Bethlehem heard of the sack of Rome by Alaric and his band of Goths in A.D. 410, he gave vent to the following lament on the collapse of the Empire in the west. It is inspired as much by Hebrew poetry and the dirges of the prophets over Jerusalem as by Jerome's own classical training. As history it probably does not tell us very much, but it has importance insofar as it helped lodge the impression of a ghastly catastrophe, the Fall of the Roman Empire, in the Western historical tradition.[21] *Six years after the sack of Rome, the poet Rutilius Namatianus writes of the city as though it were still as glorious as ever. The real destruction was to come later.*

Nations innumerable and most savage have invaded all Gaul. The whole region between the Alps and the Pyrenees, the ocean and the Rhine, has been devastated by the Quadi, the Vandals, the Sarmati, the Alani, the Gepidae, the hostile Heruli, the Saxons, the Burgundians, the Alemanni, and the Pannonians. O wretched Empire! Mayence, formerly so noble a city, has been taken and ruined, and in the church many thousands of men have been massacred. Worms has been destroyed after a long siege. Rheims, that powerful city, Amiens, Arras, Speyer, Strasburg—all have seen their citizens led away captive into Germany. Aquitaine and the provinces of Lyons and Narbonne, all save a few towns, have been depopulated; and these

---

[21]Jerome, *Letter to Ageruchia; Commentary on Ezechiel, Preface to Book 3.* Trans. James Harvey Robinson, *Readings in European History*, Vol. 1 (New York: Ginn and Company, 1904), pp. 44–45.

the sword threatens without, while hunger ravages within. I cannot speak without tears of Toulouse, which the merits of the holy Bishop Exuperius have prevailed so far to save from destruction. Spain, even, is in daily terror lest it perish, remembering the invasion of the Cimbri; and whatsoever the other provinces have suffered once, they continue to suffer in their fear.

I will keep silence concerning the rest, lest I seem to despair of the mercy of God. For a long time, from the Black Sea to the Julian Alps, those things which are ours have not been ours; and for thirty years, since the Danube boundary was broken, war has been waged in the very midst of the Roman Empire. Our tears are dried by old age. Except a few old men, all were born in captivity and siege and do not desire the liberty they never knew. Who could believe this? How could the whole tale be worthily told? How Rome has fought within her own bosom not for glory, but for preservation—nay, how she has not even fought, but with gold and all her precious things has ransomed her life. . . .

Who could believe [*Jerome exclaims in another passage*] that Rome, built upon the conquest of the whole world, would fall to the ground? that the mother herself would become the tomb of her peoples? that all the regions of the East, of Africa and Egypt, once ruled by the queenly city, would be filled with troops of slaves and handmaidens? that today holy Bethlehem should shelter men and women of noble birth, who once abounded in wealth and are now beggars?

Chapter 18

Late Antiquity: The World of the Abrahamic Religions

In the period between A.D. 200 and 700, the canon of the New Testament was finalized, and the whole Bible, both its Hebrew and Greek portions, were translated into Latin and transmitted to all of western and central Europe. This translation—the Vulgate—remained the standard text of the Bible in western Christendom for the next millennium. Translations in others languages, such as Gothic and Syriac (closely connected with Arabic), were also available. There was a gigantic outpouring of philosophy, theology, sermons, hymns, liturgical compositions, histories, and religious tracts in Greek and Latin by the "Fathers" of the Christian Church. This period, known as the "Patristic Age," established the basic doctrines of Christianity, which remain to the present the foundation of belief in both eastern and western branches of the Church (i.e., the Orthodox and the Catholic and Protestant churches). During this same period the definitive text of the *Tanakh* (the Hebrew Scriptures) was fixed. Authoritative Jewish oral commentaries on the Scriptures (the "Second Torah"), in the form of the *Mishnah* and the Talmud, were written down, edited, and disseminated among Jewish communities throughout the Mediterranean and Middle East. Normative, or rabbinic Judaism as it is known as today, stems directly from this period. Finally, between approximately A.D. 610 and 623 the Quran, the holy book of Islam, was transmitted by Muhammad to his followers. By A.D. 650, a final written version of the Quran had been produced. It remains unchanged to the present. By about A.D. 700, congregations of one (and sometimes all three) of the Abrahamic religions could be found from Ireland to Bengal, from Sudan to central Asia.

Paralleling and intertwined with these momentous cultural events were social, political and military changes of equally significant proportions. The provinces of the western part of the old Roman empire had now been transformed into Germanic kingdoms where invaders and original Roman inhabitants were in the process of working out a more or less compatible living arrangement. In Italy, the Ostrogothic kingdom fell to the Byzantines (Eastern Romans) and they in turn were succeeded by new invaders, the Lombards. Visigoths established a kingdom in southern Spain, and much of Gaul was divided between Franks, Burgundians, and other Germanic peoples. A Vandal kingdom took the place of the old Roman province of Africa. Angles and Saxons established themselves in England, and in the Celtic fringe of Brittany, Cornwall, Wales, Ireland, and Scotland an indigenous form of Christianity evolved. The absence of a centralized civic authority such as Constantinople provided in the Byzantine east allowed a different and more assertive kind of Christianity to evolve in the west, one in which there was a clear demarcation between spiritual and temporal powers.

By about A.D. 700, the peoples of Europe generally accepted the culture of the Mediterranean and Middle East, and forms of the city and state that they had resisted for centuries. Where Rome failed, a Hellenized and Romanized form of Christianity succeeded. By becoming Christian the peoples of Europe embraced a civilization that was itself a fusion of elements of Middle Eastern, Greek, and Roman cultures.

After the loss of its western provinces, the Roman Empire now consisted of parts of the Balkans, Greece, Anatolia (modern Turkey), Syria-Palestine, Egypt, and Libya. Its center of gravity was the city of Constantinople, which was able to fend off the barbarian invaders who were at work dismembering the western provinces, and at the same time provide a stable administration for the remaining provinces. But this eastern Roman Empire (or, more commonly, Byzantine Empire), was a much altered empire from its predecessor Roman state. Its language and culture were Greek, not Latin, and its geographic orientation was toward the south and east—that is, toward Egypt and Mesopotamia. The core of the imperial state remained the emperor, his court, the army, and the civil service. To these, however, were now joined in close alliance the authority and organizational resources of the Church. Yet, although the Church contributed to the stability and legitimacy of the Byzantine state, it added in some ways to its potential for fragmentation. The challenge of interpreting the complex doctrines of Christianity led in time to whole provinces drifting away culturally from the imperial church. By the time of the Arab invasions in the seventh century A.D., Egypt and Syria were so alienated from Constantinople that they offered little resistance.

In some ways the Arab invasions of the Mediterranean paralleled the Germanic invasions of the west some two centuries earlier. However, while the Germans attacked opportunistically, Arab armies were unified by a vision of the world provided them by one of the world's most important historical personalities, the prophet Muhammad. Before his death in A.D. 632, Muhammad's armies had conquered Arabia and unified its formerly anarchic tribes. After his death, Muslim armies engaged in one of the most rapid and permanent conquests in history. The Byzantines were routed in A.D. 636 and Syria fell the following year. Egypt was absorbed in A.D. 642 and by 711 all of north Africa and Spain had been overcome. The east was conquered with equal rapidity. The Persian Sassanid empire fell in 637 and by the end of the seventh century, Arab armies reached the frontier of China in central Asia. Only the Byzantines held out and in the process prevented Europe from falling under Muslim sway. Constantinople was besieged in 677 and again in 717, but in both cases the attacks were beaten back. The end of the Eastern Roman Empire did not come for another seven hundred years, in 1453, and then only when the walls of Constantinople were battered down by the artillery of the Ottoman Turks.

It is interesting to note that at the very moment Muhammad was transmitting the Quran to his followers and conquering Arabia, the Germanic king of Northumbria in England, along with his followers, were in the process of converting to Christianity.

18.1   The Conversion of a Barbarian King

By the middle of the seventh century A.D. *the British Isles were a mosaic of small and large kingdoms ruled by chiefs who strove to maintain themselves in a highly competitive, violent, and unstable environment. The chiefs in England, Wales, and Southern Scotland had an easier time of it than those in Ireland and northern Scotland since the Romans had already annihilated the native Celtic elites there, thus making it possible for the invading German Angles, Saxons, and Jutes to create larger kingdoms than was possible in other areas of Britain. One of these kingdoms, Northumbria, was ruled by the Germanic king Edwin (*A.D. *616–633). Before becoming king, Edwin had been forced to flee from his enemies, but while in exile he had a vision of a man who promised him he would survive and become king but who demanded that Edwin promise an appropriate act of gratitude—without specifying what—when the time came. As a sign, he laid his hand on Edwin's head.*

An able warrior and administrator, Edwin founded the city of Edinburgh (the city is named after him) on his northern frontier. He was married to Ethelberga, the daughter of another Germanic king, Ethelbert, King of Kent. The influence of his Christian wife and the fact that his powerful father-in-law was already Christian must have been important factors in Edwin's decision to convert, but he had to find a means to convince his followers that it was a good idea that he do so. Our reading comes from the Ecclesiastical History *of Venerable Bede, written by* A.D. *731.*[1]

King Edwin put off responding to the word of God preached to him by Paulinus [*Ethelberga's chaplain*]. He used to sit for hours on end alone, debating with himself what he should do and what religion to follow. Then one day the chaplain came and put his hand on the king's head and asked him if he recognized this sign. The king trembled and would have fallen at Paulinus's feet, but the chaplain raised him up and said in a voice that sounded familiar to Edwin, "With God's help you have escaped the hands of the enemies you feared and have received at His hand the kingdom you desired. Remember the promise you made. Do not delay in receiving the faith and keeping the commandments of Him who saved you from your earthly enemies." . . .

After hearing these words the king answered that he was willing and indeed obliged to receive the faith taught by Paulinus. However, he said he needed to confer with his closest companions and councilors regarding this act. If they agreed with him they would all be consecrated to Christ in the fountain of life [*i.e., baptism*]. Paulinus agreed and the king did as he said he would.

A meeting of the council was held and each of its members was asked in turn what he thought of this previously unknown doctrine and this new worship of the divinity which was being proclaimed. Coifi, the chief of the priests, replied at once. "Pay attention carefully, O king, to the religion now being proposed to us. I freely admit that the religion we have professed up until now has neither good nor utility in it. None of your followers has devoted himself more seriously to the worship of our gods, yet there are many who receive greater gifts and greater honors from you than I do and prosper in all they undertake. If the gods really had any power they would have helped me more readily since I have always served them so faithfully. Therefore it follows that if after examination these new doctrines which have been set out for us are better and more effective, we should without delay accept them."

---

[1]Bede, *Ecclesiastical History* 2.12–13.

Another of the king's companions agreed with this sound advice and then added, "In comparison with the time which is unknown to us, O King, the present life on earth is like this. You are sitting feasting with your councilors and servants in winter time. The fire is burning in the middle of the hall and all inside is comfortable and warm, while outside winter storms of rain and snow are raging.[2] A sparrow comes into the hall and flies swiftly through it. It enters at one door and soon exits by the other. For the few moments it is inside the wintry tempest cannot touch it, but after the briefest moment of serenity it escapes from your sight and returns to the winter storm. So this life of humans appears for but a moment. Of what follows or what came before we have no knowledge at all. Hence, if this new doctrine brings us more certain information, we should rightly accept it." Other elders and councilors of the king continued along the same lines, being divinely guided to do so.

The king, having won the assent of his key followers, accepted the Gospel and renounced idolatry.

18.2 Byzantine Grandeur: The Church of Holy Wisdom, *Hagia Sophia*

The rude wooden palace where King Edwin discussed Christianity with his warrior council contrasts poorly with the magnificence of Hagia Sophia, the Church of Holy Wisdom (the following reading). Hagia Sophia was built in Constantinople between 532 and 537 A.D. by the Byzantine Emperor Justinian. After the conquest of Constantinople in A.D. 1453 Hagia Sophia became a mosque. It is now a museum. The account comes from a contemporary of Justinian.[3]

The emperor, thinking not of cost of any kind, pressed on the work, and collected together workmen from every land. Anthemius of Tralles, the most skilled in the builder's art . . . carried forward the king's zealous intentions, organized the labors of the workmen, and prepared models of the future construction. . . .

[The Church] is distinguished by indescribable beauty, excellent both in its size, and in the harmony of its measures, having no part excessive and none deficient; being more magnificent than ordinary buildings, and much more elegant than those which are not of so just a proportion. The church is singularly full of light and sunshine: You would say that the place is not lighted by the sun from without, but that the rays are produced within itself, such an abundance of light is poured into the church. . . .

Now above the arches is raised a circular building of a curved form though which the light of day shines: For the building, which I imagine overtops the whole country, has small openings left on purpose, so that the places where these intervals occur may serve for the light to come through. . . . As the arches are arranged in a quadrangular figure, the stonework between them takes the shape of a triangle, the lower angle of each triangle, being compressed where the arches unite, is slender, while the upper part becomes wider as it rises in the space

---

[2]The remains of the hall of King Edwin have been discovered at Yeavering near York. The large hall, over 80 × 40 feet, had a raised platform in it with a seating capacity of about 320. We can imagine Edwin addressing and consulting his warriors and councilors on it.

[3]Procopius, *On Buildings* 1.1.23–49, trans. W. Lethaby and H. Swainson, *The Church of St. Sophia, Constantinople* (New York, 1894), pp. 24–28.

between them, and ends against the circle which rests upon them, forming there its remaining angles. A spherical shaped dome standing upon this circle makes it exceedingly beautiful; from the lightness of the building, it does not appear to rest upon a solid foundation, but to cover the place beneath as though it were suspended from heaven by the fabled golden chain. All these parts surprisingly joined on one another in the air, suspended one from another, and resting only on that which is next to them form the work into one admirably harmonious whole, which spectators do not dwell upon for long in the mass, as each individual part attracts the eye to itself.

No one ever became weary of this spectacle, but those who are in the church delight in what they see, and when they leave, magnify it in their talk. Moreover, it is impossible accurately to describe the gold and silver, and gems, presented by the Emperor Justinian, but by the description of one part, I leave the rest to be inferred. That part of the church which is especially sacred, and where the priests alone are allowed to enter, which is called the Sanctuary, contains four thousand pounds' weight of silver.

18.3   The Splendor of the Byzantine Court

The magnificence of Hagia Sophia *was paralleled by that of the palace of the eastern Roman emperors. In this reading the Emperor Justin II (A.D. 565–578) receives an embassy from a barbarous steppe people known as the Avars. The account, which comes from the Byzantine poet Corippus, shows how palace ritual was aimed at impressing and intimidating visitors with the might of the Roman state.*[4]

A lofty hall stands in the huge building, gleaming with a sun of metal, wondrous in its appearance. . . . The imperial throne ennobles the inmost sanctum, girded with four marvelous columns over which in the middle is a canopy shining with liquid gold. . . . Guards stood at the high entrance and kept out the unworthy who wanted to enter, massed together as they were in large numbers and frightening in their disdain and their gestures. When the officials had filled the decorated palace with their groups arranged in order, a glorious light shone from the inner chamber and filled all the meeting place. The emperor came forth surrounded by the great senate. A throng of eunuchs was there to serve him. . . .

When the happy emperor had ascended the lofty throne and settled his limbs high up with his purple robes, the master of offices ordered the Avars to enter and announced that they were before the first doors of the imperial hall begging to see the holy feet of the merciful emperor, and he ordered with gentle voice and sentiment that they be admitted. The barbarian warriors marveled as they crossed the first threshold and the great hall. They saw the tall men standing there, the golden shields, and looked up at their gold javelins as they glittered with their long iron tips and at the gilded helmet tops and red crests. They shuddered at the sign of the lances and cruel axes and saw the other wonders of the noble procession. And they believed that the Roman palace was another heaven. They rejoiced to be stared at and to appear carefree as they entered: as Hyrcanian tigers when New Rome gives spectacles to her people, under the direction of their trainer do not roar with their usual savagery but enter,

---

[4]Corippus, *In Praise of Justin II*, 3.190–270.

go all round the edge, and look up at the circus full of thousands of people, and by their great fear learn gentleness. They lay down their fury and are happy to wear the cruel chains, to come right into the middle, and they love in their pride the very fact that they are stared at. Their eyes range over the benches and the enthusiastic crowds and they lie down in adoration before the throne of the emperor. But when the curtain was drawn aside and the inner part was revealed, and when the hall of the gilded building glittered and Tergazis the Avar looked up at the head of the emperor shining with the holy diadem, he lay down three times in adoration and remained fixed to the ground. The other Avars followed him in similar fear and fell on their faces, and brushed the carpets with their foreheads, and filled the spacious halls with their long hair and the imperial palace with their huge limbs. When the merciful emperor ordered the envoys to rise, the officials raised them up from where they lay. "What do you ask," said the ruler kindly with calm countenance, "tell me, teach us, and bring the message of your king." When the emperor had said this with his tranquil voice, the harsh and cruel Avar began this with sharp words. . . .

18.4   Augustine's Two Cities: The City of God and the City of Man

In the west the relationship between church and state was not as close or as comfortable as it was in the east. Western Roman emperors were almost never in Rome, but on distant frontiers along the Rhine and Danube. As the western Empire crumbled the question arose of the relationship between the dying state and the church. Would the fall of one lead to the fall of the other? In A.D. 426, Augustine, the bishop of Hippo in Africa (and regarded by many scholars as one of the main intellectual forces behind the development of western European culture), attempted to answer this important question by distinguishing between the temporal and passing "City of Man" and the eternal "City of God." While the ultimate destination of the latter was to be found in the next world, it existed meanwhile in the very real and present "City of Man." We have already encountered some of the ideas expressed here in the Epistle to Diognetus *(see "A Different Vision" in Chapter 17), and in some respects Augustine's great tract is simply an elaborate meditation on this theme.*[5]

While the households of unbelievers are focused on the acquisition of temporal peace and comfort from their possessions in this life, the households which live by faith look ahead to the good and imperishable things of heaven. They use material and temporal goods in the spirit of pilgrims, not as traps or obstacles to block their way to God, but as ways to ease, and not increase the weight of this corruptible body which weights down the soul. . . .

So, too, the Earthly City, which does not live by faith, seeks only an earthly peace. It limits its goal to the concord of civic authority and obedience and to the voluntary and collective gathering of things necessary to this life. The Heavenly City, or rather that part of it that is in pilgrimage on earth and lives by faith, uses this peace because it must until our mortality which needs this peace has passed away. Consequently, as long as the Heavenly City lives like a captive and a stranger in the Earthly City (although it has a promise of redemption and the gift of the Spirit as a pledge), it has no hesitation in obeying the laws of the Earthly City

---

[5]Saint Augustine, *City of God* 19.17.

whereby those things necessary for the maintenance of mortal life are looked after. For since mortal life is common to both cities, they ought to be in harmony in regard to what concerns our material and temporal existence.

The City of This World has some philosophers whose doctrines true religion must reject. Either out of their own conjectures or out of demonic deception they came to believe that many gods must be invited to involve themselves in human affairs. They assigned to them different functions in strange arrangements—this one over the body, that over the mind . . . one over flocks, one over wheat, one over wine, one over forests, and so on and on. By contrast, the Heavenly City knew by faith that one god only was to be worshipped. He was to be served with that service the Greeks call *latreia*, which can be given to one god only. Hence it has come to pass that the Celestial City cannot share with the Earthly City common religious legislation. The Heavenly City has been forced to dissent on this score and so to become obnoxious to those who think otherwise and to accept the brunt of their anger, hatred, and violence. . . .

While the Heavenly City sojourns on earth it invites to be its citizens people from all nations and tongues and gathers them together as a single pilgrim band. It does not care about diversities of customs, laws, and institutions by which earthly peace is secured and maintained. Instead of eliminating or tearing down, the Celestial City preserves and appropriates whatever in the diversities of different peoples is aimed at one and the same objective of human peace, so long as there is no hindrance to the worship of the one supreme and true God.

Therefore, while the Heavenly City is wayfaring on earth it not only avails itself of peace on earth but fosters and actively seeks along with others a common agreement regarding the acquisition of the necessities of life so far as it can without damaging its faith and worship. It subordinates this earthly peace to that of heaven, for this alone can be truly called peace for creatures endowed with reason, namely, the perfectly ordered and harmonious communion of those who find their joy in God and in one another in God. When this peace is finally achieved human beings will no longer be subject to death but clearly and perpetually endowed with life. This body, which now wastes away and weighs down the soul will no longer be material but spiritual, in need of nothing, and completely under the control of the will.

18.5   "There are Two Powers by which this World is Ruled"

The pope, as bishop of the city of Rome, claims to be the lineal successor of Saint Peter, to whom Jesus entrusted the "keys of the kingdom of heaven" (Matthew 16:15–19). As a result he asserts his primacy over the whole Church. Just as Peter was the first among the apostles, so the bishop of Rome was the first among other bishops. There were, however, other powerful bishops in other cities, such as Jerusalem, Antioch, Alexandria and Constantinople, who also had claims to authority within the Church. What was their relationship to Rome? What did "primacy" actually mean? Was it just a primacy of honor or did it also involve (as the bishops of Rome claimed) jurisdictional power? In this reading, the bishop of Rome, Gelasius, writes in A.D. 494 to the eastern Roman emperor Anastasius to instruct him on the true nature of authority in the Christian world. Gelasius' distinction between spiritual and temporal powers foreshadowed and inspired the medieval theory of the separation of the two powers, and ultimately the well-known constitutional principle of separation of church and state.[6]

---

[6]Gelasius, *Letter to Anastasius*.

Before the coming of Christ certain figures . . . were both kings and pontiffs (priests), as for example the holy Melchizedech. . . . But when the true king and pontiff came [*namely, Christ*], the emperor no longer took the name of pontiff [*one of the most important titles of the pagan emperors was* "pontifex maximus," *chief priest of the Roman religion*] for himself, nor did the pontiff claim royal dignity. . . . In his desire that His own be saved by salutary humility and not again ruined by human pride, Christ so divided the duties of the two powers that the Christian emperors would need the pontiffs for their eternal salvation and the pontiffs would use the imperial administration for the course of temporal things. As a result, spiritual affairs would be removed from worldly encroachments . . . and secular administrators would not take leadership in divine matters. . . .

Most August Emperor, there are indeed two powers by which this world is mainly ruled. These are the sacred authority of the Popes [*i.e., the bishops of Rome*] and the power of kings. Of these two the priestly power is much more important because it must provide an account of human kings before the tribunal of God. For you know, most devout son, that though you have the first place in dignity over human beings, you must submit yourself with trust to those who are responsible for divine things and look to them for the means of the salvation of your soul. When it comes to the reception and devout administration of the sacraments you know you should submit to the Church's authority rather than try to control it. So, too, in such matters you ought to depend on the Church's judgment rather than trying to make it conform to your will.

18.6   The *Quran*: The Sacred Scriptures of Islam

According to Islamic tradition, the revelations of the Quran *were made over a period of twenty-three years by the angel Gabriel (Jibril) to the Prophet Muhammad. The revelations were made under a variety of different circumstances. Hence the* Quran, *unlike the Bible, is not a chronological narrative but a collection of occasional sayings. Its 114 chapters, or surahs, are believed by Muslims to be the direct revelation of Allah. In receiving them, Muhammad was not a composer or an author but merely the transmitter of God's actual words. Muslim belief is that none of the* Quran *was the creation of the prophet himself.*

For the Prophet's own words the believer must turn to the hadith, *or oral commentaries, remarks, and teachings given by Muhammad over the period of his life. Today they are found in six standard collections each consisting of thousands of the Prophet's sayings. In his life, Muhammad made it clear that the* hadith *should not be confused with God's words, which alone are to be found in the* Quran *itself. Although the* hadith *are not part of the* Quran, *they are considered, along with the life of Muhammad, to make up the example or practice (sunnah) of the Prophet. Reflection on and study of the* Quran, *the* hadith, *and the life of Muhammad along with prayer, fasting, and almsgiving constitute the core of the religious life of the observant Muslim.*

For many Muslims, translations of the Quran *cannot be considered fully authentic. They believe, instead, that the* Quran *should be read in Arabic. As one medieval Spanish Muslim scholar put it: "Non-Arabic is not Arabic, so the* Quran *[in translation] is not the* Quran."

Although Muslims believe that authentic revelations had indeed been made to Jews through Moses and to Christians through Jesus, they feel that those respective communities had misused and corrupted the revelations. Hence the need for a purified—and final—revelation through Muhammad. And since the Quran *repeated the revelations made to Moses and Jesus, Muslims do not find a need to consult either the Hebrew Bible or the New Testament.*

According to tradition, the Quran *was given orally to Muhammad, who first memorized it and then dictated it to others to write down. After the* Quran *was complete, Muhammad recited it twice in its entirety to Gabriel, thus ensuring its completeness and authenticity. Twenty years after Muhammad's death, around* A.D. *650, the Caliph (successor) Uthman made a canonical edition of the* Quran *and ordered all nonconforming recensions to be destroyed. Since the time of Uthman, all copies of the* Quran *have been identical. Scholars think that, in actuality, before Uthman's time a number of scattered collections and individual sayings of the Prophet existed so that Uthman's job was essentially one of compilation. The earliest securely dated complete* Qurans *are from the ninth century.*

By comparison to the evolution of the canon of Jewish and Christian scriptures, the establishment of the canon of the Quran *was an extraordinarily rapid process. The Bible was the work of many hands and took centuries to complete, and Bibles still differ among themselves in the number of books to be included. The* Quran *also stands in contrast to the Bible (as well as to other sacred scriptures such as the Vedas, the sacred text of Hinduism) as a compact, well-defined account of the religion of Islam, extremely useful for the widespread dissemination of the faith to large audiences. The Quran's capacity to be misinterpreted by the selective culling of particular passages to support one view or another is about the same as any of the other sacred scriptures. Like the other Abrahamic religions, Islam has a developed and highly sophisticated tradition for interpreting the meaning of its holy texts.*[7]

18.6.1   The Five Pillars of Islam

The whole point of Islam is to submit one's will and life to the will of Allah. (The word Islam *means "submission.") The simplest mode of expression of this submission is the practice of the "Five Pillars of Islam." The first pillar is bearing witness* (Shahadah)*, which is an affirmation by the individual of the belief that there is no God but Allah and that Muhammad is his prophet, his messenger. The Second Pillar is prayer* (Salah)*, a ritual of words and movement. Five times a day the call to prayer invokes the* Shahadah.

Therefore be patient with what they say, and celebrate constantly the praises of the Lord, before the rising of the sun, and before its setting. Yes, celebrate them for part of the hours of the night, and at the sides [*ends*] of the day that thou mayest have spiritual joy (Q20.130).

So give glory to God when you reach eventide and when you rise in the morning. Yes, to Him be praise, in the heavens and on earth; and in the later afternoon and when the day begins to decline (Q30.17–18).

O you who believe! when the call is proclaimed to prayer on Friday, the Day of Assembly, hasten earnestly to the remembrance of God, and leave off business and traffic. That is best for you if you but knew. And when the Prayer is finished, then may you disperse through the land and seek of the bounty of God and celebrate the praises of God often and without stint that you may prosper (Q62.9–10).

The Third Pillar of Islam is almsgiving, or the religious tax (zakah)*. Zakah is closely connected with prayer. It is a form of sacrificial giving in material things to the less fortunate in the community. Since God alone decides who will be rich and who will be poor, the wealthy have an obligation to give to the poor; it is not a matter of personal choice. And since all things belong to God, when we give back to God what we have, we are merely returning to him what is his in the first place.*

---

[7] All translations from the Quran are from *The Meaning of the Glorious Quran: Text, Translation, and Commentary*, by Abdullah Yusuf Ali (Cairo: Dar Al-Kitab Al-Masri, 1934). By permission.

Alms are for the poor and the needy, and those employed to administer the funds; for those whose hearts have been recently reconciled to the truth; for those in bondage and in debt; for those in the cause of God; and for the wayfarer. Thus is it ordained by God, and God is full of knowledge and wisdom (Q9.60).

As to those who reject faith and die rejecting, never would be accepted from any such as much gold as the earth contains, though they should offer it for ransom. For such is in store a penalty grievous, and they will find no helpers. By no means shall you attain righteousness unless you give freely of that which you love; and whatever you give, of a truth God knows it well (Q3.91–92).

The Fourth Pillar is fasting (Sawm) *during Ramadan, the ninth month of the year. Ramadan is a very special time for Muslims because it was during this month that God began his revelations to Muhammad. Fasting (from food, drink, and sex) is to take place from sun up to sun down. Self-denial was only part of the discipline of Ramadan, whose main aim was the growth of virtue and the development of control over one's evil inclinations. For Muslims, Ramadan has strong social and communal aspects.*

O you who believe! Fasting is prescribed to you as it was prescribed to those before you, that you may learn self-restraint. Fasting is for a fixed number of days; but if any of you is ill, or on a journey, the prescribed number should be made up from days later. For those who can do it with hardship it is a ransom, the feeding of one that is indigent. But he that will give more, of his own free will, it is better for him. And it is better for you that you fast, if you only knew. Ramadan is the month in which was sent down the Quran as a guide to mankind, also clear signs for guidance and judgment between right and wrong. So every one of you who is present at his home during that month should spend it in fasting. . . . God intends every facility for you; he does not want to put you to difficulties. He wants you to complete the prescribed period, and to glorify him in that he has guided you; and perchance you shall be grateful (Q2.183–185).

The Fifth Pillar is the pilgrimage to Mecca (the Hajj), *to be undertaken once in a lifetime by all Muslims who can afford it. The Hajj recalls three events: the forgiveness by God of Adam and Eve; Abraham's sacrifice of his son Ishmael; and the life of the Prophet Muhammad. According to Muslim tradition, Adam and Eve were reconciled to God on Mount Arafat near Mecca, and Adam built the first shrine of the Ka'bah, or Holy House at the site of Mecca. This shrine was later rebuilt by Abraham and Ishmael. All later reconstructions of the Ka'bah have occurred on the same spot.*

Behold! We gave the site [*of Mecca*] to Abraham of the Sacred House, saying: "Associate not anything in worship with Me; and sanctify My House for those who compass it round, to stand up, or bow, or prostrate themselves there in prayer. And proclaim the Pilgrimage among men: They will come to you on foot and mounted on every kind of camel, lean on account of journeys through deep and distant mountain highways; that they may witness the benefits provided for them, and celebrate the name of God through the Days appointed, over the cattle which He has provided for them for sacrifice: then eat you therefore and feed the distressed ones in want. Then let them complete the rites prescribed for them, perform their vows, and again circumambulate the Ancient House. Such is the Pilgrimage: whoever honors the sacred rites of God, for him it is good in the sight of his Lord" (Q22:26–30).

18.6.2   Abraham: The First Muslim

In Islamic belief, Abraham was the first person in history who truly submitted himself to the will of God. Thus he was the first true Muslim. Islam represents a return to the pure faith of Abraham.

And remember Abraham said: "My Lord, make this a City of Peace,[8] and feed its people with fruits, such of them as believe in God and the Last Day. . . . And remember, Abraham and Ishmael raised the foundations of the House with this prayer: "Our Lord! Accept this service from us, for thou are the All-Hearing, the All-Knowing. Our Lord! Make us Muslims, bowing to Thy Will, and of our progeny a people Muslim, bowing to Thy will. . . . And who turns away from the religion of Abraham but such as debase their souls with folly? Him we chose and rendered pure in this world and he will be in the hereafter in the ranks of the righteous." . . . And this was the legacy that Abraham left to his sons and so did Jacob: "Oh my sons! God has chosen the faith for you; then die not except for the faith of Islam. Were you witnesses when death appeared before Jacob? Behold, he said to his sons: What will you worship after me?" They said: "We shall worship your God and the God of your fathers—of Abraham, Ishmael, and Isaac, the One True God, to Him we bow in Islam." . . . They say: "Become Jews or Christians if you would be guided to salvation." Say you, "No! I would rather the religion of Abraham the True, and he joined not gods with God" [*i.e., Jews succumbed to false gods and Christians invented the doctrine of the Trinity*] (Q2:126–135).

18.6.3   The People of the Book

According to Islam, the "People of the Book" are Jews and Christians, to whom revelations were made through Moses and Jesus. Unfortunately, the followers of Moses and Jesus corrupted God's revelations to them, and quarreled among themselves thus necessitating a new and definitive revelation through Muhammad (B). To Muslims, Jesus was an important prophet but he was not the son of God (A).

A

O People of the Book! Commit no excesses in your religion, nor say of God aught but the truth. Christ Jesus the son of Mary was no more than an Apostle of God, and His word, which he bestowed on Mary, and a Spirit proceeding from him: so believe in God and his Apostles. Say not "Trinity"; desist. It will be better for you. For God is one God, glory be to Him. Far exalted is He above having a son. To him belong all things in the heavens and on earth. And enough is God as a disposer of affairs (Q4:171).

B

We gave Moses the Book and followed him up with a succession of Apostles; we gave Jesus the son of Mary clear signs and strengthened him with the holy spirit. Is it that whenever there comes to you an Apostle with what you yourselves do not desire you are puffed up with pride? Some you call impostors and others you slay! . . . Quite a number of the People of the Book wish they could turn you people back to infidelity after you have believed, from

---

[8]That is, Mecca, the City of Islam. The root *salama* in the word *Islam* implies, among other concepts, the idea of peace. Jerusalem also means "city of peace," but when Judaism was superceded by Islam, Mecca became the true "City of Peace," the new Jerusalem for Muslims.

selfish envy, after the Truth had become manifest to them: But forgive and overlook until God accomplish his purpose; for God has power over all things. And be steadfast in prayer and regular in charity, and whatever good you send for your souls before you, you shall find it with God, for God sees well all that you do. And they say, "None shall enter Paradise unless he be a Jew or a Christian." Those are their vain desires. Say, "Produce your proof if you are truthful." Rather, whoever submits his whole self to God and is a doer of good, he will get his reward with his Lord; on such shall be no fear, nor shall they grieve. The Jews say, "The Christians have nothing to stand upon"; and the Christians say, "The Jews have nothing to stand upon." Yet they profess to study the same Book. Like unto their word is what those who know not; but God will judge between them in their quarrel on the Day of Judgment (Q2.87; 109–113).

18.6.4 *Jihad*: The Sixth Pillar of Islam

The theme of "struggling on the path of God" *runs through the* Quran. *The struggle against evil tendencies such as selfishness, ignorance, and lack of compassion is the inner or major* jihad, *or struggle, because all evil arises from the human tendency to put self before God. This is an individual struggle. At other times the struggle was communal in the sense of armed combat against enemies of Islam. In both cases,* jihad *was a fundamental duty of the individual Muslim and is often regarded as the sixth pillar of Islam.*

Fighting is prescribed for you, and you dislike it. But it is possible that you dislike a thing which is good for you, and that you love a thing which is bad for you. But God knows and you know not (Q2.216).

Fight in the cause of God those who fight you, but do not transgress limits; for God loves not transgressors. And slay them wherever you catch them and turn them out from where they have turned you out: for tumult and oppression are worse than slaughter. But fight them not at the Sacred Mosque unless they first fight you there. But if they fight you, slay them. Such is the reward of those who suppress faith. But if they cease, God is oft-forgiving, most merciful. And fight them on until there is no more tumult or oppression and there prevail justice and faith in God. But if they cease, let there be no hostility except to those who practice oppression (Q2.190–193).

18.6.5 Islamic Eschatology: The *Mahdi*, the Antichrist, and the Second Coming of Jesus

Muslims do not believe that Jesus died on the cross but was, rather, rescued by God from death. He will return at the End of Time. The account given in B comes from the great historian-philosopher Ibn Khaldun (d. A.D. 1406).[9]

A

That they said in boast, "We killed Christ Jesus the son of Mary, the Apostle of God," but they killed him not, nor crucified him, but so it was made to appear to them, and those who differ therein are full of doubts with no certain knowledge, but only conjecture to follow, for a surety they killed him not. Rather, God raised him up unto Himself; and God is exalted in power, wise (Q4.157–158).

---

[9]Ibn Khaldun, *The Muqaddima* 3.51, trans. Franz Rosenthal (Princeton, NJ: Princeton University Press, 1967). By permission.

B

It has been well known by all Muslims in every epoch, that at the end of time a man from the family of the Prophet will without fail make his appearance, one who will strengthen the religion and make justice triumph. The Muslims will follow him, and he will gain domination over the Muslim realm. He will be called the *Mahdi* [*the "Guided One"*]. Following him, the Antichrist will appear, together with all the subsequent signs of the Hour [*the Last Judgment*], as established in the sound tradition. After the *Mahdi*, Jesus will descend and kill the Antichrist. Or, Jesus will descend with the *Mahdi*, and help him kill the Antichrist, and have him as the leader in his prayers.